D0622867

HANDBOOK OF
DIGITAL CURRENCY

HANDBOOK OF DIGITAL CURRENCY

Bitcoin, Innovation, Financial Instruments, and Big Data

Edited by

DAVID LEE KUO CHUEN

Sim Kee Boon Institute for Financial Economics, Singapore Management University, Singapore

AMSTERDAM • BOSTON • HEIDELBERG • LONDON
NEW YORK • OXFORD • PARIS • SAN DIEGO
SAN FRANCISCO • SINGAPORE • SYDNEY • TOKYO

Academic Press is an imprint of Elsevier

ELSEVIER

Academic Press is an imprint of Elsevier
125 London Wall, London, EC2Y 5AS, UK
525 B Street, Suite 1800, San Diego, CA 92101-4495, USA
225 Wyman Street, Waltham, MA 02451, USA
The Boulevard, Langford Lane, Kidlington, Oxford OX5 1GB, UK

Notices

Knowledge and best practice in this field are constantly changing. As new research and experience broaden our understanding, changes in research methods, professional practices, or medical treatment may become necessary.

Practitioners and researchers must always rely on their own experience and knowledge in evaluating and using any information, methods, compounds, or experiments described herein. In using such information or methods they should be mindful of their own safety and the safety of others, including parties for whom they have a professional responsibility.

To the fullest extent of the law, neither the Publisher nor the authors, contributors, or editors, assume any liability for any injury and/or damage to persons or property as a matter of products liability, negligence or otherwise, or from any use or operation of any methods, products, instructions, or ideas contained in the material herein.

Library of Congress Cataloging-in-Publication Data
A catalog record for this book is available from the Library of Congress

British Library Cataloguing in Publication Data
A catalogue record for this book is available from the British Library

For information on all Academic Press publications
visit our website at http://store.elsevier.com/

ISBN: 978-0-12-802117-0

Publisher: Nikki Levy
Acquisition Editor: J. Scott Bentley
Editorial Project Manager: Susan Ikeda
Production Project Manager: Nicky Carter
Designer: Matthew Limbert

Typeset by SPi

DEDICATION

This book is dedicated to Noreen and Herman Harrow.

CONTENTS

CONTRIBUTORS

Christian Bach
Swiss Economics, Zurich, Switzerland

Aleksandra Bal
International Bureau for Fiscal Documentation, Amsterdam, The Netherlands

Nirupama Devi Bhaskar
Sim Kee Boon Institute for Financial Economics, Singapore Management University, Singapore

David G.W. Birch
Consult Hyperion, Guildford, Surrey, UK

Aeron Buchanan
Ethereum Foundation, Switzerland

Kim-Kwang Raymond Choo
University of South Australia, Adelaide, South Australia, Australia

Anton Cruysheer
ABN AMRO Bank, Amsterdam, The Netherlands

Primavera De Filippi
CERSA/CNRS/Université Paris II–Berkman Center for Internet & Society at Harvard Law School, Cambridge, Massachusetts, USA

Christian Jaag
Swiss Economics, Zurich, Switzerland

Alyse Killeen
March Capital Partners, Santa Monica, California, USA

Andras Kristof
Tembusu Terminals, Singapore

David LEE Kuo Chuen
Sim Kee Boon Institute for Financial Economics, Singapore Management University, Singapore

Teik Ming Lee
Sim Kee Boon Institute for Financial Economics, Singapore Management University, Singapore

Richard B. Levin
Bryan Cave, LLP, Denver, Colorado, USA

Guo Li
Sim Kee Boon Institute for Financial Economics, Singapore Management University, Singapore

Jonathan W. Lim
National University of Singapore Centre for Banking and Financial Law, Singapore, and Wilmer Cutler Pickering Hale & Dorr (WilmerHale) LLP, London, UK

Ignacio Mas
Saïd Business School, University of Oxford, Oxford, UK

Ralph E. McKinney, Jr.
College of Business at Marshall University in Huntington, West Virginia, USA

Andrew Newman
University of New South Wales, Sydney, New South Wales, Australia

Lam Pak Nian
Sim Kee Boon Institute for Financial Economics, Singapore Management University, Singapore

Pierre Noizat
Co-founder of Paymium, Bitcoin Exchange and provider of e-commerce solutions, Paris, France

Aaron A. O'Brien
Baker & Hostetler, LLP, PNC Center, Cleveland, Ohio, USA

Bobby Ong
Sim Kee Boon Institute for Financial Economics, Singapore Management University, Singapore

Georgios Papadopoulos
Erasmus University Rotterdam, Rotterdam, The Netherlands

Duane C. Rosenlieb, Jr.
Rosenlieb Law Office, St. Albans, West Virginia, USA

Tetsuya Saito
Nihon University, Tokyo, Japan

Gideon Samid
Case Western Reserve University, Cleveland, Ohio, USA

Vrajlal Sapovadia
Shanti Business School, Ahmedabad, India

Dale H. Shao
College of Business at Marshall University in Huntington, West Virginia, USA

Lawrence P. Shao
College of Business at Marshall University in Huntington, West Virginia, USA

Matthias Tarasiewicz
University of Applied Arts Vienna, Vienna, Austria

Ernie G.S. Teo
Sim Kee Boon Institute for Financial Economics, Singapore Management University, Singapore

Nicolas Wesner
Mazars Actuariat, Paris, France

Gavin Wood
Ethereum Foundation, Switzerland

David Yermack
New York University Stern School of Business, New York, New York, and National Bureau of Economic Research, Cambridge, Massachusetts, USA

Madiha M. Zuberi
Baker & Hostetler, LLP, New York, New York, USA

PREFACE AND ACKNOWLEDGMENTS

The year 2008 has left a deep and lasting impression on the Millennials, also known as the Millennial Generation who are born in the early 1980s to early 2000s. It was the year of the financial market crash that started in the United States and soon spilled over to Europe and Asia, thereby triggering the global financial crisis in a time-compressed manner. While governments responded with unprecedented monetary policy expansion and fiscal stimulus, many Millennials have to contend with high unemployment and scarce economic opportunities at a time when they are establishing their careers. But few realize their lives have been shaped not only by happenings in Wall Street and Main Street but also by technology. They will remember 2008 as the beginning of the peer-to-peer decentralized cryptocurrency called the Bitcoin protocol. The white paper by Satoshi Nakamoto first appeared on the Internet via the Cryptography Mailing List in November 2008 (archived in http://www.mail-archive.com/cryptography%40metzdowd.com/msg09959.html) after the global financial crisis as a significant contribution to the world without actually first being published in an academic journal.

Since then, the white paper (https://bitcoin.org/bitcoin.pdf) has generated a lot of interest. First, the timing of the release was a direct response to a crisis of confidence in a reserve currency, and there was no better time than 2008. Faced with an era of disquiet and a gradual loss of trust in the fiat currency system introduced in 1971, as well as the prospect of massive printing of money known as quantitative easing, the white paper offers a set of feasible alternative solutions to those who have little faith in a centralized monetary system. Cryptocurrency was first introduced in the early 1990s by an academic entrepreneur David Chaum in the form of eCash and DigiCash. The National Security Agency released an analytic report of great significance on the same subject over the Internet in 1996. But few in the financial world paid much attention to the development of cryptocurrency until the global financial crisis. It only caught the attention of many financial experts when successive quantitative easings pushed up asset prices. Given that the reversal of quantitative easing has unknown consequences and that China has started its bilateral swap agreements, the BRICS Development Bank and the Asian Infrastructure Investment Bank begin to challenge the conventional international institutions, and interest has begun to center on alternative monetary systems that include the digital currency system. Cryptocurrency, a special class of digital currency, continues to generate interest among those who are uncomfortable with national currency beleaguered by huge liability, rather than backed by assets, of some central governments.

Second, the white paper of Satoshi was the first paper that proposed a distributed monetary system and challenged the central authority that controlled money supply.

The proposed system was designed to address some of the issues that a centralized system could not. In particular, the control was decentralized and the supply of money was predetermined. Given the open-source nature of the Bitcoin protocol, there are too many participants for anyone to effectively monitor and regulate single-handedly. For the first time, governments realize the decentralized nature poses great problems for anyone who intends to regulate a legal entity or small number of entities, let alone to hold them responsible for any wrongdoing.

Third, there are a lot of unanswered questions about the Bitcoin system, thus creating curiosity among those who follow the development. In particular, the identity of the creator or group of creators of Bitcoin remains a mystery. While there have been many attempts to uncover the mystery surrounding Mr. Nakamoto, including at least one hacker who claimed to know the identity of Mr. Nakamoto after gaining access to his e-mail account, Mr. Nakamoto's identity is still unknown to the public. The mysterious nature surrounding Bitcoin has generated even more following. The community remains amazed at the foresight of the creator(s) and respects the reason for remaining under the radar.

Fourth, the Bitcoin invention has put regulators on the spotlight. Any attempt to regulate the cryptocurrency protocol has proved to be extremely difficult. However, regulators have managed to study the issues carefully in regulating the intermediaries and have focused in the areas of consumer protection, antimoney laundering, and counterterrorist financing. The balance between regulation and entrepreneurship has proved to be most challenging to achieve. This has therefore attracted a lot of attention from tax authorities, central bankers, and crime busters. Never before has technology invention attracted so much attention and posed so many challenges as it involves international finance, monetary system, and innovative financial technology with cyber security.

Fifth, the income and wealth inequality of the world has risen rapidly since the quantitative easings. With six times wealth-to-income ratio, the highest since the late 1930s, governments are focusing on financial inclusion. Bitcoin provides a cheap form of payment system and that possibility has brought cryptocurrency into the limelight as an alternative payment system. Organizations such as Bill and Melinda Gates Foundation have made payment systems as one of its priorities, together with the Maya Declaration initiated by the Alliance for Financial Inclusion. We can see that Bitcoin will share the limelight of those serving the 2.5 billion unbanked and attracting the attention of those who are engaged in impact investing as advocated by the Global Impact Investing Network. Both financial inclusion and impact investing are areas of great interest and cryptocurrency is in the right space.

Sixth, cryptocurrency has contributed to innovation and we have seen many interesting developments. It is said that the best brains are in cryptocurrency because it is not only a currency but also a form of programmable money. The developers will be able to program in a way to serve the purpose intended. These innovations include smart accounting, smart contract, crowdsourcing, crowd funding, crypto-equity, and many others that can change the way business is done and managed. Consensus ledger, digital register, Blockchain are a emerging class of technology for the future. It is likely that there will be acceleration in the development of Bitcoin 2.0, blockchain 2.0, and sidechains, with new development only limited by our imagination.

Seventh, the emergence of the digital natives and smart cities has generated even more interest in the development of cryptocurrency. Cities such as Singapore will have its entire country connected to the digital world, with projected growth coming from the digital economy. Its citizens will be natives to the digital world. The technology that is developed in the cyberspace will be of great interest in these countries that spend millions or billions in getting the infrastructure up for a digital economy. Incentives for start-ups will get more interesting and the majority of the investment will certainly be focused on cyber security and connectivity, and that will involve investment in encryption, financial cryptography, decentralized storage, and mobile payments. Cryptocurrency will of course be of great interest given that it leads innovation in securing the payments, decentralized ledger, and encryption.

Given the interest in cryptocurrency, it is not surprising that there was encouragement all-round to start an interesting project on digital currency with special emphasis on cryptocurrency. The foresight of Scott Bentley, who saw the potential of this project, and McKenna Bailey's strong support motivated me to start working on the book in early 2014. I thank Elsevier for their encouragement and support. The title "Handbook of Digital Currency: Bitcoin, Innovation, Financial Instruments, and Big Data" was chosen to convey the idea that the focus is on Bitcoin, Bitcoin 2.0, and associated innovations.

This book would not have been possible without the support of the Sim Kee Boon Institute (SKBI) for Financial Economics, Singapore Management University. In particular, I would like to express my sincere appreciation to Mr. Lim Chee Onn, the chairman, and other advisers of the board, namely, Piyush Gupta, Magnus Bocker, Liew Heng San, Tham Sai Choy, Ronald Ong, Lim Cheng Teck, Aje Saigal, Sunil Sharma, Tan Suee Chieh, Jacqueline Loh, and Leong Sing Chiong, for their valuable counsel. The authors who contributed to the book were mostly guest participants in the Inaugural CAIA-SKBI Cryptocurrency Conference held at Singapore Management University in November 2014 that saw a large turnout. I am grateful to them and all those who had made extraordinary efforts to be at the conference. I would like to especially thank Mikkel Larsen, Tim Swanson, Donald Chambers, Neal Cross, Andrew Koh, Norma Sit, Gunther Sonnenfeld, Chan Hiang Taik, Ong Pang Thye, Jonathan Kok, Reuben Branabahan, Iris Tan, Jason Tyra, Zann Kwan, Peter Peh, Scott Robinson, Anson Zeall, David Moskowitz, and Andras Kristof for their vivacious participation in and substantial contribution to the discussions. The vigor and rigor of the discussions at the conference have spurred me to add new materials to the book. Peter Douglas of the Chartered Alternative Investment Association was instrumental in getting the conference going, and for that, I could not thank him enough.

I am indebted to Professors Arnoud De Meyer, Rajendra Srivastava, and Gerry George, the president, the provost, and the Dean (Lee Kong Chian School of Business) of the Singapore Management University, respectively, who unstintingly supported the research in this exciting area of cryptocurrency. The team at SKBI, especially Philip Foo, Priscilla Cheng, and Elaine Goh was most helpful with their quiet efficiency in various ways, including providing tireless administrative and logistical assistance in many sessions of workshop from the cryptocurrency community. My colleagues Francis Koh, Casiopia Low, Benedict Koh, Chan Soon Huat, Phoon Kok Fai, Phang Sock Yong, Enoch Chng, Robert Deng, and Lim Kian Guan were always around encouraging me during the preparation of this book. My team of researchers Ernie Teo, Lam Pak Nian, Nirupama Devi Bhaskar, and Guo Li worked hard to ensure the chapters were on time. A podcast on some of the materials in this book was recorded with the help of Huang Pei Ling and her team in October 2014.

I would like to thank my family for their encouragement and patience. I am grateful to Koh Kheng Siong for introducing us to Noreen and Herman Harrow. This book is dedicated to the Harrows for taking care of my family and also giving me an opportunity to compile this work in Monterey, thus allowing me to travel to Silicon Valley to harness more ideas from the entrepreneurs and thought leaders in the field. Last but not least, to thank God for revealing and guiding the mission.

I hope the materials in this book will add to the wealth of knowledge and research in this exciting field and benefit those who read and use them.

David LEE Kuo Chuen
February 2015

PART 1

Digital Currency and Bitcoin

Bitcoin and Alternative Cryptocurrencies

CHAPTER 1

Introduction to Bitcoin

Lam Pak Nian, David LEE Kuo Chuen
Sim Kee Boon Institute for Financial Economics, Singapore Management University, Singapore

Contents

1.1 THE NEXT GENERATION OF MONEY AND PAYMENTS

There are various innovative money payment systems in the market today, many of which are built on platforms like the mobile phone, the Internet, and the digital storage card. These alternative payment systems have seen encouraging or even continued growth, from the likes of PayPal, Apple Pay, Google Wallet, Alipay, Tenpay, Venmo, M-Pesa, BitPay, Moven, BitPesa, PayLah!, Dash, FAST, Transferwise, and others.

Beyond payment systems that are based on fiat currency, the growing use of digital currency allows for faster, more flexible, and more innovative payments and ways in financing goods and services. One digital currency, however, stands out among the rest. Bitcoin is one of the most well-known digital currencies today. To be specific, Bitcoin is a *crypto*currency, which is a subset of what is generally known as a *digital* currency. Bitcoin is a unique cryptocurrency that is widely considered to be the first of its kind. Like many created after it, Bitcoin uses the power of the Internet to process its transactions. This chapter introduces the characteristics and features of Bitcoin and sets the stage for further discussion of cryptocurrencies in the rest of this book.

1.2 DIGITAL CURRENCY AS ALTERNATIVE CURRENCY

1.2.1 "Digital" versus "virtual"

Although *digital* and *virtual* are often used interchangeably when describing currencies based on an electronic medium, the term "virtual" has a negative connotation. "Virtual" signals something that is "seemingly real" but not exactly "real" when referring to a currency that is stored in a "digital" or electronic register. Indeed, in languages like Chinese, the word "virtual" is interpreted as "created from nothing" (虚拟的) in the sense that it is not "physical" but computer-generated or computer-simulated. However, the currencies often described as "virtual" are very "real," in the sense that they exist. Thus, the more neutral term *digital currency* is generally preferred over *virtual currency*.

1.2.2 Classifying alternative currencies

Alternative currencies refer to a medium of exchange other than fiat currency. Historically, there are various types of alternative currencies, as classified by Hileman (2014) broadly into two categories: tangible and digital. Tangible currencies, closely associated with "commodity money," derive their value from relative scarcity and nonmonetary utility:

(a) Currencies with intrinsic utility

This class of currency includes metals and cigarettes in post-WWII Berlin and more contemporary examples are prepaid phone cards and, to some extent, cash value smart cards. This class is not dependent upon governance as in the case of monetary instruments, and more importantly, its intrinsic value is not an abstraction and it is not necessarily geographically bound.

(b) Token

Seventeenth- to nineteenth-century British tokens and the Great Depression scrip of the 1930s are historical examples. More contemporary examples are local or community currencies such as Brixton Pound and Bristol Pound that are used in England, BerkShares that is circulated in Berkshire region of Massachusetts, and Salt Spring Dollar in Canada. Token has less intrinsic value as its use is more specific and usually bounded by some social contracts or agreement such as honoring them for exchange for goods or to limit the supply of goods.

(c) Centralized digital currency

Examples are loyalty points from financial, telecom, or retail companies; air miles from airlines; Second Life's Linden Dollar and World of Warcraft Gold, which are closed system with transactions within specific entities; and Flooz and Beenz, which are open market system and can be transacted with other entities. Local currencies such as Brixton Pound, BerkShares, and Salt Spring Dollar also fall under this category besides being classified as tokens. The governance structure is centralized.

(d) Distributed and/or decentralized digital currency

This includes the cryptocurrencies such as Bitcoin, Litecoin, and Dogecoin. They can be transacted with any outside agents and the governance is decentralized mainly but not necessary due to open-source software. There is no legal entity responsible for the activities, and therefore, they fall outside traditional regulation.

1.2.3 Why alternative currencies

There are various socioeconomic forces that drive the demand for alternative currencies:

(a) Localism

By promoting community commerce or "save high street," localism retains consumption within a group of independent retailers or within a geographic area for job creation and improved business conditions.

(b) Technology

It has become much easier to use with improved software and low entry barriers contributing to network effects.

(c) Political economy

There is disillusionment about the high pay of CEOs and bankers and the notion of traditional banks being too big to fail. With high debt and quantitative easing, there is great discomfort with the economic uncertainty.

(d) Environmentalism

There are ecology concerns and the question of whether we have reached the point of maximum extraction of natural resources such as oil.

(e) Inefficiencies

   Financial services are overpriced and whole financial system is too expensive.

(f) Financial freedom

   Some digital currencies such as cryptocurrencies have the advantage of transferring value through the Internet where control is weak. Such digital currencies may allow users to bypass capital controls and may provide safe harbor during a fiat currency crisis.

(g) Speculation

   Buyers of some digital currencies such as cryptocurrencies are anticipating a price appreciation due to subsequent wider acceptance.

It is very easy to create a cryptocurrency as an alternative currency for free today. However, most of these new creations will cease circulation within a relatively short time. With many alternative currencies in competition, only a few will be globally adopted, reach a sufficient scale, or find a suitable market. Unless the idea of national digital currencies takes off, it is likely that many of these alternative currencies will cease circulation because of superseding advancements in technology, tighter regulation, and insufficient demand.

1.3 CRYPTOCURRENCY

1.3.1 The nature of cryptocurrency

Cryptocurrency in its purest form is a peer-to-peer version of electronic cash. It allows online payments to be sent directly from one party to another without going through a financial institution. The network time-stamps transactions using cryptographic proof of work. The proof-of-work Bitcoin protocol is basically a contest for decoding and an incentive to reward those who participate. For Bitcoin, first participant to crack the code will be rewarded with the newly created coins. This contest will form a record of the transactions that cannot be changed without redoing the proof of work.

   Cryptocurrency is a subset of digital currency. Examples of the many digital currencies are air miles issued by airlines, game tokens for computer games and online casinos, Brixton Pound to be spent only in the Brixton local community in the Greater London area, and many other forms that can be exchanged for virtual and physical objects in a closed system and, in the case of an open system, exchanged for fiat currency.

1.3.2 The beginning: eCash

Commercially, it all began with DigiCash, Inc.'s eCash system in 1990, based on two papers by its founder (Chaum, 1983; Chaum et al., 1992). Payments were transferred online and offline using cryptographic protocols to prevent double-spending. The cryptographic protocols also used blind signatures to protect the privacy of its users.

As the first cryptocurrency, the eCash system was available via various banks and smart cards in various countries like the United States and Finland. It slowly evolved into the current form of cryptocurrencies with many refinements by various software developers over the last 20 years.

eCash was a centralized system owned by DigiCash, Inc. and later eCash Technologies. However, after it was acquired by InfoSpace in 1999, eCash and cryptocurrency faded into the background.

1.3.3 Pioneering Internet payments with digital gold

Digital gold currency came into the limelight between 1999 and the early 2000s. Most of these new forms of electronic money based on ounces of gold are stored at the bullion and storage fees are charged. We have seen the growth of e-dinar, Pecunix, iGolder, Liberty Reserve, gBullion, e-gold, and eCache. With a couple of exceptions, most have ended up in the graveyard due to either compliance issues or regulatory breaches.

e-Gold was a pioneer for Internet payments. As the first successful online micropayment system, it pioneered many new techniques and methods for e-commerce, which later became widely used in other online aspects. These techniques and methods include making payments over a Secure Sockets Layer-encrypted connection and offering an application programming interface to enable other websites to build services using e-gold's transaction system. However, its Achilles heel was its failure to fulfill know-your-customer (KYC) and suspicious transaction reporting requirements. With the introduction of the US Patriot Act, compliance has been a major issue for money transmitters. Furthermore, it has to contend with hackers and Internet fraud. Before the motion to seize and liquidate the entire gold reserve of e-gold under asset forfeiture law in 2008, e-gold was processing more than USD2 billion worth of precious metal transactions per year. There are clear lessons to be learned by the cryptocurrency community.

1.3.4 Revival of cryptocurrency

At the onset of the global financial crisis in 2008, interest on cryptocurrency was revived. Cryptocurrency had the potential to counter a few problems associated with the fiat currency system, argued Szabo (2008) in a blog post just at the beginning of the global financial crisis. Given that it is cumbersome to transact using commodities, the concept of bit gold was mooted. As the name suggests, there is gold to be mined and bit recorded on a digital register. The digital record would resolve the issues of a trusted third party, and in his own words,

> Thus, it would be very nice if there were a protocol whereby unforgeably costly bits could be created online with minimal dependence on trusted third parties, and then securely stored, transferred, and assayed with similar minimal trust. Bit gold.

My proposal for bit gold is based on computing a string of bits from a string of challenge bits, using functions called variously "client puzzle function," "proof of work function," or "secure benchmark function." The resulting string of bits is the proof of work. Where a one-way function is prohibitively difficult to compute backwards, a secure benchmark function ideally comes with a specific cost, measured in compute cycles, to compute backwards."

Despite sounding technical, what Szabo described was a simple protocol that requires participants to spend resources to mine the digital gold or bit gold, be rewarded, and in the process validate the public digital register. What differentiated his approach from failed digital currencies of the past were the timing of the financial crisis and the distributed nature of the protocol. The reward to the miners was one innovation and the free access to digital record for the users was another. One of the reasons is that the nature of the Internet makes collecting mandatory fees much harder, while voluntary subsidy is much easier. Therefore, there must be no barrier to access content or digital record, and there must be ease of use and voluntary payments.

Ideas were discussed in the literature, and technology was developed over time by a group of cryptographers, old and new, such as Chaum (1983) on DigiCash, Back (1997) on Hashcash, Dai (1998) on b-money, Szabo (1999, 2002, 2008) on the concept of money, and Shirky (2000) on micropayments. Cypherpunk is an activist group since the early 1980s that advocates the widespread use of strong cryptography as a route to social and political changes. Finney (2004), who ran two anonymous remailers as a cypherpunk member, created the first reusable proof of work (RPOW), which is an economic measure to deter denial-of-service attacks and other service abuses such as spam on a network by requiring some work from the service requester. It means that whoever requests for the information has to incur more processing time on a computer than the provider. Hashcash, used by Bitcoin, is a proof-of-work system designed to limit e-mail spam and denial-of-service attacks (Back, 2002).

At the same time, sociopolitical interest in cryptocurrency grew. Since we abandoned the gold standard in 1971 and adopted the fiat currency system, central banks have used their discretion to print as much as they desired during a crisis. This has created an asset inflation environment and worsened income equality. The supply of cryptocurrency or coins may or may not be limited but the new coins are usually created by a predetermined rule. The loss of trust in the fiat currency system, caused mainly by quantitative easing and huge government debts, has brought attention to cryptocurrency for those who wanted to hedge their positions with a currency that has a finite supply.

Cryptocurrency was thought to possess the characteristics of a currency that can impose fiscal discipline on the government and it is perceived to be a debt-free currency with a constant growth rate with finite supply. For asset managers who were constantly seeking for negative correlation with their core portfolio, cryptocurrency provided a glimpse of hope for a high-risk and complex asset class that enhances the returns of a portfolio with bitcoins acting as a negatively correlated alternative asset class. But the origins of Bitcoin have their roots in cryptoanarchy that started as a movement in 1992:

> Just as the technology of printing altered and reduced the power of medieval guilds and the social power structure, so too will cryptologic methods fundamentally alter the nature of corporations and of government interference in economic transactions. Combined with emerging information markets, crypto anarchy will create a liquid market for any and all material which can be put into words and pictures. And just as a seemingly minor invention like barbed wire made possible the fencing-off of vast ranches and farms, thus altering forever the concepts of land and property rights in the frontier West, so too will the seemingly minor discovery out of an arcane branch of mathematics come to be the wire clippers which dismantle the barbed wire around intellectual property. (May1992)

The use of cryptocurrency as a safe haven and an alternative asset class was demonstrated in the 2013 Cypriot property-related banking crisis where a 6.75% levy was imposed on bank deposits up to EUR100k and 9.9% for larger deposits. With confidence in traditional banking shaken, investors were betting heavily on the most well-known cryptocurrency, bitcoins, to offer a more stable alternative. Many investors converted their fiat money into cryptocurrency, sending the price and volume to spike. The price of bitcoins spiked 57% within a week to USD74. Like gold and other commodities, Bitcoin's price spikes in moments of uncertainty. Both assets are increasingly favored by a small group of managers in alternative investment and critics of contemporary monetary policy. The most common arguments against Bitcoin are (i) the lack of a central issuing authority like that of a central bank, (ii) its fixed supply and deflationary nature by design, (iii) doubts that the price is stable enough to function as a currency, and (iv) the risk associated with it.

1.3.5 The rise of Bitcoin

An example of a cryptocurrency is bitcoins. Satoshi Nakamoto published a paper on the Web in 2008 for a peer-to-peer electronic cash system. Despite many efforts, the identity of Satoshi remains unknown to the public and it is not known whether Satoshi is a group or a person.[1]

The cryptocurrency invented by Satoshi Nakamoto, called bitcoins, is run using open-source software. It can be downloaded by anyone, and the system runs on a decentralized peer-to-peer network. It is not only decentralized but also supposedly fully

---

[1]Satoshi in Japanese means "wise" and someone has suggested that the name might be a portmanteau of four technology companies: SAmsung, TOSHIba, NAKAmichi, and MOTOrola. Others have noted that it could be a team from the National Security Agency (NSA) or an e-commerce firm (Wallace, 2011). Other suggestions are David Chaum, the late Hal Finney, Nick Szabo, Wei Dai, Gavin Andresen, and the Japanese living in the neighborhood of Finney by the same surname Dorian Nakamoto. There are other suggestions such as Vili Lehdonvirta, Michael Clear, Neal King, Vladimir Oksman, Charles Bry, Shinichi Mochizuki, Jed McCaleb, and Dustin Trammell, but most have publicly denied that they are Satoshi.

distributed. That means that every node or computer terminal is connected to each other. Every node can leave and rejoin the network at will and will later accept the longest proof of work known as the blockchain as the authoritative record.

This longest blockchain is proof of what has happened while these nodes were gone. Cryptocurrency is mysterious and misunderstood for a few reasons.

First, no one knows who is really behind some of these cryptocurrency systems. It was designed so that third-party trust is not needed and sometimes there is no legal entity behind it but open-source software.

Second, many have jokingly remarked that Bitcoin sounded more like "big con" especially after the collapse of Mt. Gox. But it is important to note that Mt. Gox was merely a financial intermediary, being just one of many unregulated exchanges that trade in Bitcoins. Mt. Gox was not part the Bitcoin system itself. It is a complex currency system to the men in the street and therein lies the confusion.

Third, cryptocurrency involves mining or proof of work. There are rewards for mining and the reward is given to the first who can solve a cryptography problem. The degree of difficulty of the problem will ensure that the timing to solve the problem is approximately 10 min for Bitcoin. Cryptocurrency cleverly solves the double-spending problem so that every cryptocurrency can be spent only once. It is a financial technology and it involves financial regulation but therein lies the difficulty in execution and understanding even for the professionals. That is why it is an area of great interest to researchers, regulators, investors, and merchants and it is hitting the headlines regularly.

The general arguments for a successful distributed cryptocurrency are as follows:

1. *Open-source software*: A core and trusted group of developers is essential to verify the code and possible changes for adoption by the network.
2. *Decentralized*: Even if it is not fully distributed, it is essential that it is not controlled by a single group of person or entity.
3. *Peer-to-peer*: While the idea is not to have intermediaries, there is a possibility of pools of subnetworks forming.
4. *Global*: The currency is global and this is a very positive point and workable for financial integration with or without smart contracts among the parties.
5. *Fast*: The speed of transaction can be faster and confirmation time can be shortened.
6. *Reliability*: The advantage is that there is no settlement risk and it is nonrepudiable. The savings in cost of a large settlement team for financial activities can be potentially huge.
7. *Secure*: Privacy architecture can be better designed incorporating proof of identity with encryption. If that is done, the issues surrounding Know Your Customer/Client (KYC) and anti-money laundering and terrorist financing (AML/TF) will be resolved.
8. *Sophisticated and flexible*: The system will be able to cater to and support all types of assets, financial instruments, and markets.

9. *Automated*: Algorithm execution for payments and contracts can be easily incorporated.
10. *Scalable*: The system can be used by millions of users.
11. *Platform for integration*: It can be designed to integrate digital finance and digital law with an ecosystem to support smart contracts with financial transactions. Customized agreements can be between multiple parties, containing user-defined scripted clauses, hooks, and variables.

The possible applications will be wide-ranging and include global payment and remittance systems, decentralized exchanges, merchant solutions, online gaming, and digital contracting systems. Each cryptocurrency is a great and an interesting experiment. No one knows where these cryptocurrency experiments are heading but the experiments are interesting because of the technology that is developed along with them.

The technology disrupts the payment system as we know it because it costs almost nothing to transfer payments. Cryptocurrency technology will allow us to reach out to the unbanked and underbanked. It presents the opportunity to function as a conduit for payments and funds. It will transform the way business is being done by diminishing the role of the middleman, whether it is smart accounting or smart contract.

It will also change the way financial world operates especially in fund raising and lending. Basically, it is possible to do an Initial Crowd Offering or crowd lending, all in the peer-to-peer framework, eliminating the middleman.

However, there are downsides or potential risks for cryptocurrency too. Cryptocurrency like Bitcoin depends on mining, and once the incentives for mining disappear, no one knows if the cryptocurrency in question will continue to have consensus on the digital register. They are over 400 cryptocurrencies and the number is increasing on a daily basis. But many of them are in the graveyard.

So, as they say, "let the buyer beware," because what you own may just be worthless once there are doubts about the blockchain. It seems that if the cryptocurrency exhausts most of their coin supply too fast and too early, the probability of the coins dying is higher. For some coins, it is difficult to know who is behind them and whether there could be a backdoor that allows someone to control the system. Cryptocurrency with unknown developers has a higher probability of being buried in the graveyard.

The blockchain may come under attack as well. The blockchain serves as a proof of the sequence of events as well as proof that it came from the largest pool of computing power. As soon as the computing power is controlled by nodes that are cooperating to attack the network, they may produce the longest chain of their choice creating doubts about the validity of the blockchain. This can easily happen once the interest on a particular currency wanes and the number of miners shrinks, which opens up the possibility of having a few blockchains in concurrent existence. Once there is any doubt of the accuracy of the blockchain, even if it was subsequently corrected, the coin will be heading for the graveyard.

When there are no new coins to reward the miners, the system is unlikely to continue. Once no new coins are issued as the mining reward, then the miners are expected to be rewarded purely by transaction fees. This can be a problem. On the other hand, if the fees are increased too quickly or to an unreasonable level, interest on the coins will wane as well. With higher mining cost due to expensive equipment, mining pools will be formed. This is because miners prefer higher probability of success in cracking the code. However, this will lead to an undesirable outcome of mining pools exceeding 30% or even 50% of the network, thus exposing the cryptocurrency to attack. This was indeed the case for Bitcoin when the mining pool accounted for over 50% in the middle of 2014. This is one serious problem that needs to be solved sooner rather than later and consensus ledger or digital register without mining may be one solution.

1.4 GENERAL FEATURES OF BITCOIN

1.4.1 Network and digital currency

Bitcoin is a decentralized network and a digital currency that uses a peer-to-peer system to verify and process transactions. Instead of relying on trusted third parties, like banks and card processors, to process payments, the Bitcoin technology uses cryptographic proof in its computer software to process transactions and to verify the legitimacy of Bitcoins (Nakamoto, 2008) and spreads the processing work among the network. We make a clear distinction between the Bitcoin system where a capital B is used for the word Bitcoin and that of a Bitcoin, which is a unit of the currency or a digital address created by the Bitcoin system.

With the invention of Bitcoin, payments can be made over the Internet without the control and costs of a central authority (Bitcoin Project) for the first time. Prior to the invention, transactions carried out online always required a third party as a trusted intermediary to verify transactions (Brito and Castillo, 2013). For example, when Alice wants to send $10 to Bob, she would have to use a third-party service like a credit card network or PayPal. The function of the third-party service is to provide an assurance that the sender, Alice, has the funds to transfer and that the recipient, Bob, has successfully received the funds. This is possible because these intermediaries help maintain a record, or ledger, of balances for their account holders. Here, when Alice sends Bob the $10, an intermediary like PayPal would deduct the amount from her account and accordingly add it to Bob's account, subject to a transaction fee.

However, the currency unit used in payments on the Bitcoin network is Bitcoins, not a fiat currency. Therefore, bitcoins in itself is also a digital currency, in the sense that it exists "digitally" and, for most intents and purposes, satisfies the economic definition of money: it is a medium of exchange, unit of account, and store of value. Conventionally, the uppercase "Bitcoin" refers to the network and technology, while the lowercase "bitcoin(s)" refers to units of the currency. The currency is also commonly abbreviated to "BTC," although some exchanges use "XBT," a proposed currency code that is compatible with ISO 4217 (Matonis, 2013).

1.4.2 Genesis and decentralized control

The first bitcoin was mined, or created, in 2009, following the online publication of a paper by a Satoshi Nakamoto describing the proof of concept for a currency that uses cryptography, rather than trust in a central authority (Nakamoto, 2008), to manage its creation and transactions. Nakamoto left the project in 2010 and his identity largely remains unknown. However, with the open-source nature of the Bitcoin software protocol, other developers have continued working on it and the Bitcoin community flourishes today.

At the same time, although Nakamoto remains anonymous, users need not be concerned that he, or anyone, secretly has full control of Bitcoin. The open-source nature of Bitcoin means that the source code is fully disclosed. This disclosure allows any software developer to examine the protocol and create their own versions of the software for testing or further development, and so far, no red flag has been raised as to the presence of Nakamoto or any other party with secret control. Furthermore, Bitcoin is designed to operate only with full consensus of all network users. This ensures that software developers who modify the Bitcoin source code in their own versions of the software cannot force a nefarious change in the Bitcoin protocol without breaking compatibility with the rest of the network. The power to change the Bitcoin protocol requires full agreement among Bitcoin users and developers.

1.4.3 How Bitcoin works

To a layperson, bitcoin is a digital currency that is created and held electronically. These bitcoins are sent and received using a mobile app, computer software, or service provider that provides a bitcoin wallet. The wallet generates an address, akin to a bank account number, except that a Bitcoin address is a unique alphanumeric sequence of characters where the user can start to receive payments. Usually, bitcoins may be obtained by buying them at a Bitcoin exchange or vending machine or as payment for goods and services.

However, Bitcoin is revolutionary because the double-spending problem can be solved without needing a third party. In computer science, the double-spending problem refers to the problem that digital money could be easily spent more than once. Consider the situation where digital money is merely a computer file, just like a digital document. Alice could send $10 to Bob by sending a money file to him and can easily do so by e-mail. However, remember that sending a file actually sends a copy of the file and does not delete the original file from the computer. When Alice attaches a money file in an e-mail to Bob, she still retains a copy of the money file even after she has sent and therefore spent it. Without a trusted third-party intermediary to ensure otherwise, Alice could easily send the same $10 to another person, Charlie.

Bitcoin solves the double-spending problem by maintaining a ledger of balances, but instead of relying on a single trusted third party to manage this ledger, Bitcoin decentralizes this responsibility to the entire network. Behind the scenes, the Bitcoin network constantly keeps track of bitcoin balances in a public ledger called the block-chain. The blockchain is a publicly accessible authoritative record of all transactions ever processed, allowing anyone to use Bitcoin software to verify the validity of a transaction. Transfers of bitcoins, or transactions, are broadcast to the entire network and are included onto the blockchain upon successful verification, so that spent bit-coins cannot be spent again. New transactions are checked against the blockchain to make sure that the bitcoins have not been already spent, thus solving the double-spending problem.

Bitcoin extensively uses public-key cryptography to solve the double-spending prob-lem. In public-key cryptography, each transaction has a digital signature and contains a hash that allows for easy tamper detection (see Figures 1.1 and 1.2 for an example of a Bitcoin transaction).

```
{
"hash":"e9a66845e05d5abc0ad04ec80f774a7e585c6e8db975962d069a522137b8
0c1d",
   "ver":1,
   "vin_sz":1,
   "vout_sz":1,
   "lock_time":0,
   "size":225,
   "in":[
      {
         "prev_out":{

"hash":"f4515fed3dc4a19b90a317b9840c243bac26114cf637522373a7d486b372
600b",
            "n":0
         },

"scriptSig":"3046022100bb1ad26df930a51cce110cf44f7a48c3c561fd977500b
1ae5d6b6fd13d0b3f4a022100c5b42951acedff14abba2736fd574bdb465f3e6f8da
12e2c5303954aca7f78f301
04a7135bfe824c97ecc01ec7d7e336185c81e2aa2c41ab175407c09484ce9694b449
53fcb751206564a9c24dd094d42fdbfdd5aad3e063ce6af4cfaaea4ea14fbb"
      }
   ],
   "out":[
      {
         "value":"0.01000000",
         "scriptPubKey":"OP_DUP                         OP_HASH160
39aa3d569e06a1d7926dc4be1193c99bf2eb9ee0 OP_EQUALVERIFY OP_CHECKSIG"
      }
   ]
}
```

Figure 1.1 Example of a raw transaction data.

General information about this transaction		
Hash	e9a66845e05d5abc0ad04ec80f 774a7e585c6e8db975962d069a 522137b80c1d	The hash for this transaction
Block	100000 (2010-12-29 11:57:43)	Obtained from examining the block on the blockchain where this transaction was found
Version	1	Bitcoin software version
Size	225	The filesize in bytes of the transaction is recorded in the transaction data itself
Input from		
Previous output	f4515fed3dc4a19b90a317b984 0c243bac26114cf637522373a7 d486b372600b	The truncated hash of the previous transaction which provides the bitcoins to be sent for this transaction
Previous amount	0.01	The amount in the previous transaction which provides the bitcoins to be sent for this transaction
Public address	1JxDJCyWNakZ5kECKdCU9Zka6m h34mZ7B2	The public address of the sender, obtained from examining the blockchain
Signature	3046022100bb1ad26df930a51c ce110cf44f7a48c3c561fd9775 00b1ae5d6b6fd13d0b3f4a0221 00c5b42951acedff14abba2736 fd574bdb465f3e6f8da12e2c53 03954aca7f78f301 04a7135bfe824c97ecc01ec7d7 e336185c81e2aa2c41ab175407 c09484ce9694b44953fcb75120 6564a9c24dd094d42fdbfdd5aa d3e063ce6af4cfaaea4ea14fbb	The digital signature of the transaction, signed by the sender
Output to		
Index	0	"0" indicates the first recipient in the transaction; here this transaction only has one recipient
Amount	0.01	Amount sent to this user in this transaction
Public address	16FuTPaeRSPVxxCnwQmdyx2PQW xX6HWzhQ	The public address of the recipient, obtained from the scriptPubKey
Bitcoin address (scriptPubKey)	39aa3d569e06a1d7926dc4be11 93c99bf2eb9ee0	A hash160 of the public address
Conditions	OP_DUP OP_HASH160 OP_EQUALVERIFY OP_CHECKSIG	Conditions to be met together with the scriptPubKey for the output bitcoins to be redeemed by the recipient

Figure 1.2 Explanation for the transaction.

1.4.4 Buying and storing bitcoins

Against this technical backdrop, bitcoins are often used simply as payment in exchange for goods and services (Kaplanov, 2012). While the numbers of brick-and-mortar merchants who accept payments in bitcoins remain low, there are many more online merchants who accept bitcoins for both digital and physical goods and services. The price of these goods and services is usually based on the exchange rate between Bitcoin and a real-world currency, which can be found easily online (XE).

Typically, a user who wishes to spend bitcoins obtains it by exchanging real-world currency for bitcoins. This can be achieved by purchasing bitcoins from a vending machine, from an exchange, or simply from another person. Bitcoin vending machines, often called "ATMs," are the most convenient way to buy bitcoins, because one can easily insert cash into a machine to obtain bitcoins instantly (Ulm, 2014). Bitcoin exchanges are also a popular means to obtain bitcoins, but users often face a time delay while waiting for bank transfers to clear (Ulm, 2014). Trading real-world cash for bitcoins is also a possibility but it is inconvenient if bitcoins are needed on the spot. However, marketplace websites like LocalBitcoins have sprouted up to connect people interested in buying and selling bitcoins to enable them to do so privately, whether in person or online (LocalBitcoins). This option is more likely to be used in countries with restricted or no access to Bitcoin vending machines or exchanges.

Bitcoins are typically stored in a wallet, so a user needs to have a wallet available to buy and sell bitcoins. Specifically, it is the private keys that are stored in a wallet (CoinDesk, 2014). These keys are used to access the Bitcoin addresses and sign transactions and therefore must be kept securely. There are various types of Bitcoin wallets, including desktop, mobile, webs, and hardware wallets.

Users who choose to install a desktop wallet on their computer can create and keep wallets on their computer. The original Bitcoin client software, known as Bitcoin Core, which is still in use today, includes the functionality of creating a bitcoin address to send and receive bitcoins and to store the corresponding private key for that address. There are various other wallet software in which users may elect to install on their computer, like the cross-platform MultiBit and the security-conscious Armory (Bitcoin.org). The different wallet software have varying additional features, although the most basic function of a wallet in storing the private keys for corresponding bitcoin addresses remains the same. While the user maintains control of his desktop wallet at all times, such wallets, like any other computer file, are vulnerable to theft by malicious users or software.

Desktop wallets are not the be-all and end-all of wallets, even if they were the first. When transacting at a physical store, a mobile wallet is often the most convenient way to spend some bitcoins. Mobile wallets are simply an application that provides for Bitcoin wallet functionality in a mobile phone. There are apps like Bitcoin Wallet and Mycelium that only exist on the mobile platform, while some desktop wallets like Blockchain.info also have mobile versions (Bitcoin.org). However, in the early 2014, Apple removed Bitcoin Wallet apps like Blockchain.info from its App Store (Southurst, 2014), although unofficial versions and mobile browser-based wallets continue to exist.

Another convenient type of wallet is the online wallet, which is generally accessible from anywhere through a browser with an Internet connection, regardless of the device used (CoinDesk, 2014). The private keys for a user's Bitcoin addresses are kept and stored by the service provider of the online wallet, which may present a risk of the service provider or a third party absconding with the bitcoins, if security was not implemented properly. Blockchain.info also has a popular web-based online wallet and some online wallets offer extra encryption and two-factor authentication for additional security.

Finally, there is small but growing interest in hardware wallets, which are specialized devices that can hold keys electronically and are also able to send and receive bitcoins. An example of a dedicated Bitcoin device is the Trezor, a single-purpose token-sized device for making secure Bitcoin transactions (SatoshiLabs).

1.4.5 Mining to create new bitcoins and process transactions

Bitcoin is designed with a hard limit of 21 million bitcoins, which are expected to be created by 2040 (Figure 1.3). For now, these bitcoins are generated through mining, during which miners, who are Bitcoin users running software on specialized hardware, process transactions and are rewarded with new bitcoins for contributing their computer power to maintain the network. Mining is important not only for new bitcoins to be issued but also because it is a necessary process for transactions to be added onto the blockchain and be subsequently confirmed. The verification process is a computationally intensive process that ensures that only legitimate transactions are verified and recorded onto the blockchain. It is the network that provides the computing power for the transactions to take place and for the transactions to be recorded.

What happens during mining is actually a mathematical process. A real-life analogy to bitcoin mining would be the search for prime numbers: while it was easy to find the small ones, it became increasingly more difficult to find the larger numbers, leading researchers to use special high-performance computers to find them (Tindell, 2013).

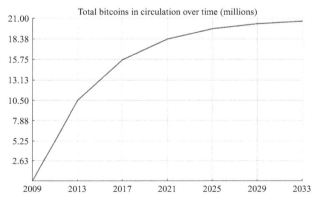

Figure 1.3 Bitcoin supply.

Mining is a computationally intensive task that requires miners to find the solution to a predetermined mathematical problem in order to create a new block. This is the mathematical proof of work. Mining is difficult because besides ensuring that the transactions are valid, miners have to fit the data in a particular manner in order to add it to the blockchain. Miners have to guess and search for a sequence of data that produces a required pattern.

The difficulty of the problem is automatically adjusted so that a new block can only be created every 10 min on average. The Bitcoin protocol is designed to generate new bitcoins progressively, at a predictable but decreasing rate. To ensure a progressive growth in new bitcoins, the reward for solving a block is halved automatically every 4 years, and the difficulty of solving increases over time. These two effects work together to produce an effect that over time, the rate at which bitcoins are produced will be similar to the production rate of a commodity like gold (see Figure 1.3). There will be a point in the future when the hard limit of bitcoins will be reached and the incentive for miners will instead be transaction fees. The arbitrary number chosen to be the limit in number of bitcoins is 21 million. Once the very last bitcoin, or to be specific, the very last satoshi—0.00000001 of a bitcoin—is produced through mining, miners who continue to contribute their computing power to verify transactions will instead be rewarded with transaction fees. This may be a less desirable situation for people and businesses relying on bitcoin payments, which will have to pay a transaction fee, but it ensures that miners will still have an incentive to keep the network up and running even after the last bitcoin is mined.

Every new block that is successfully added onto the blockchain references the previous block, making it exponentially difficult to reverse previous transactions in previous blocks. Because changing a block on the blockchain will require recalculation of the proofs of work of all subsequent blocks (Bitcoin Project), it becomes more and more infeasible for an adversary to manipulate a block after more blocks have been added after it, and the Bitcoin protocol is accordingly designed to prefer longer chains. Miners therefore perform a vital task as they verify transactions and ensure that the blockchain cannot be tampered with.

While bitcoin transfers are broadcast instantaneously over the network, there is, in practice, a 10 min delay for a transaction to be confirmed. This is the result of the 10 min delay for a block to be created and added onto the blockchain. Having a confirmation ensures that the network (of miners) has verified that the bitcoins are valid and have not been already spent. Typically, most users wait for six confirmations, that is, an hour, before considering a transaction to be "confirmed," but each user has the freedom to decide how long they wish to wait before they consider their transaction confirmed.

1.4.6 Security and cryptography

The security of the technology used is supported using secure hash algorithms and has a good track record. The Bitcoin protocol is an open-source and is continuously improved by the developer community subject to consensus among all network users. The hash function mainly used in Bitcoin is SHA-256 (Pacia, 2013), which was incidentally originally designed by the NSA in the United States. There is no need for suspicion against the NSA because the SHA algorithm is part of the public domain and has been extensively analyzed to be secure (Pacia, 2013). SHA-256 is an upgrade from the SHA-1 series and is presently used in Bitcoin for the digital signatures that secure the transactions and blockchain and it forms the basis of the proof-of-work mathematical problem.

Central to Bitcoin technology is public-key cryptography, which with the SHA-256 hash function is used to generate Bitcoin addresses, sign transactions, and verify payments. Public-key cryptography is a technique of reliably determining the authenticity of Bitcoin transactions using digital signatures. It uses an asymmetrical algorithm that generates two separate but asymmetrically linked keys: a public key and a private key. The keys are asymmetrical in the sense that the public key is derived from the private key but it is computationally impossible to obtain a private key from a public key. In such a system, the public key is used to verify digital signatures in transactions while the private key is used to sign transactions to produce those very digital signatures. The public key is publicly accessible; in Bitcoin, it is used as the Bitcoin address to and from which payments are sent. The private key, on the other hand, must be kept secret and safely. The beauty of such a system is that transactions can be easily verified using the public key without sharing the private key used to sign the transactions.

1.4.7 Pseudoanonymity

As seen from Figures 1.1 and 1.2, a Bitcoin address is an alphanumeric sequence of characters. There is no other information that can identify the sender and recipient of the bitcoins. However, it is a common misconception to say that bitcoin is an anonymous currency. This misconception often arises from a lack of understanding of the technology (Brito and Castillo, 2013).

Prior to Bitcoin, online transactions have not been anywhere close to anonymous because they have to go through third-party intermediaries, who have interests in knowing who their customers are, for risk assessment purposes and compliance with the relevant laws and regulations. For example, when Alice makes a transfer of $10 using PayPal to Bob, PayPal will have a record of the transfer. In addition, their PayPal accounts are likely to be linked to their respective credit cards or bank accounts, which will provide information as to their identities. On the other hand, if Alice gives Bob $10 in cash in person, there is neither an intermediary nor a record of the transaction. If the two of them do not know each other, then the transaction can be said to be completely anonymous.

Bitcoin is somewhere in between these two extremes. Bitcoins can be said to be like cash in the sense that when Alice gives bitcoins to Bob, she no longer has them, while Bob does. Since there is no third-party intermediary, nobody knows their identities as well. However, unlike cash, the transaction is recorded on the blockchain. Some of the information recorded includes the public keys of the sender and recipient, the amount, and a time stamp. Every transaction in the history of bitcoin has been recorded and will be recorded on the blockchain and is publicly viewable.

While there is some privacy, the blockchain is a public record of all transactions and it may be possible for anyone to identify the parties behind them, especially if a person's identity is linked to a public key. While bitcoins may be anonymous like cash in the sense that parties can transact without disclosing their identities, it is also unlike cash because transactions to and from any Bitcoin address can be traced. Therefore, Bitcoin is pseudonymous, not anonymous.

It is not particularly difficult for anyone with the right tools and access to join the dots between a pseudonymous Bitcoin address and a real-world identity. Some personally identifiable information is often captured during a transaction on a website, like an IP address. To make it more difficult to connect an identity to a Bitcoin address, one would have to use software methods that obfuscate or shield such personally identifiable information from being tied to Bitcoin addresses.

Early studies have already shown some potential analyses that could erode the pseudonymity of Bitcoin. For those who are persistent in connecting Bitcoin addresses to real-world identities, their work should begin with the blockchain. In a simulated experiment, a study found that up to 40% of Bitcoin users within the experiment could be personally identified using behavior-based clustering methods (Androulaki et al., 2012). The statistical properties of the transaction graph could also, with the relevant analysis, reveal the activity and identity of Bitcoin users (Reid and Harrigan, 2013). Even the use of multiple public keys may not defend against such transaction graph analysis (Ober et al., 2013), as an observer may gradually be able discern patterns in user behavior to link the public keys together, using a process called entity merging (Brito and Castillo, 2013).

Besides the technical aspects of Bitcoin, it is important to also consider the pressures faced by Bitcoin intermediaries from regulators. Bitcoin regulation is evolving, and should Bitcoin intermediaries become regulated, it is expected that anonymity will become less guaranteed (Brito and Castillo, 2013), often with KYC and reporting requirements requiring these intermediaries to collect personally identifiable information from their customers.

1.5 BENEFITS AND RISKS

Bitcoin as a novel technology brings a range of benefits and risks to the table. This section outlines some of the most well-known benefits and risks.

1.5.1 Freedom of payments

Bitcoin was specifically designed for fast transactions at low costs (Nakamoto, 2008). Payments can be processed with little or no fees, with the sender having the option to include a transaction fee for faster confirmations. A low transaction cost is possible because there is no single third-party intermediary. In addition to the lack of restrictions on transactions, users have full control of their bitcoins and the freedom to send and receive bitcoins anytime, anywhere, and to and from anyone.

Users may also choose to use Bitcoin to make fast cross-border transfers easily without paying expensive fees for remittances. There is great potential for remittances because the value of remittances, especially from people in developed countries to those in developing countries, is expected to increase to USD515 billion in 2015 (World Bank Payment Systems Development Group, 2013). The reduced costs of remittances could be substantial if remitted using bitcoins.

1.5.2 Merchant benefits

Bitcoin presents an alternative to the other methods of electronic payments accepted by businesses. Traditional credit card acceptance is expensive for merchants, with customers often having to pay for a merchant account and various fees for transactions, including but not limited to transaction fees, interchange fees, and statement fees. These fees add up and increase the costs of accepting credit cards for payments. Yet, merchants who forgo credit card payments may lose business from customers used to the ease of paying with credit cards. Not having to pay these expensive fees may allow businesses to pass on the cost savings to consumers, benefiting everyone.

Bitcoin transactions are also secure, unlike credit card payments, which may use insecure magnetic stripes and signatures, and are irreversible, unlike credit card payments, which are subject to the possibility of fraudulent charge-backs. The low cost of transactions also allows merchants to accept micropayments, paving the way for Bitcoin to be widely accepted without a minimum transaction level.

1.5.3 User control

Each Bitcoin transaction can only be effected by the user who has the private key, putting the user in full control of his bitcoins. Merchants cannot slip in unwanted charges later, unlike credit cards that offer limited protection against such charges once an unethical merchant has the card details. Transactions also do not contain substantial personal information, which is at risk of leakage and theft.

However, the converse effect of full user control is the point that the private key controls the access to one's bitcoins. Bitcoin, being a digital currency, brings specific security challenges (Kaminsky, 2013). Perhaps the most important risk to end users is that if the private key is lost, access to the bitcoins is irrecoverable. Poor wallet protection may leave users vulnerable to thefts, especially by specially crafted malicious software designed to steal bitcoins (Doherty, 2011). Bitcoin users should therefore be security conscious with Bitcoin, just as they do for other financial activities (Brito and Castillo, 2013).

1.5.4 Platform for further innovation

The Bitcoin protocol may, in its original form, work as a payment network, but it has the potential for further innovation. What actually happens in the Bitcoin network is that data in the form of Bitcoin transactions are broadcasted and verified before being kept on the blockchain. Bitcoin technology may therefore be adapted for the transfer of other types of data, like stocks or bets (Brito, 2013). Feature layers are beginning to be built on top of Bitcoin, which include smart property and assurance contracts (Brito and Castillo, 2013). Being an open-source technology, alternative digital currencies like Litecoin and Dogecoin, among others, have also emerged to suit different objectives.

1.5.5 Internal change and volatility

As a community-driven project, Bitcoin continues to undergo changes as software developers improve and change the software with consensus of network users. At the same time, the price of bitcoins continues to fluctuate as current events affect the price. Some significant price changes are said to resemble a traditional speculative bubble, which may occur when optimistic media coverage attracts investors (Salmon, 2013). This may make it difficult to determine how good bitcoins are as a store of value, and merchants accepting bitcoins therefore often convert them out into fiat currency very quickly. It is also difficult to predict the Bitcoin economy in the future as it is the first widely accessible cryptocurrency, although researchers are already working on models that will attempt to explain behavior in the Bitcoin world. At the same time, it may be possible that the value of bitcoins may become less volatile as familiarity with Bitcoin increases with time.

1.5.6 Facilitation of criminal activity

With the pseudoanonymity and ease of payments offered by Bitcoin, it is no wonder that governments are concerned with the use of Bitcoin in facilitating criminal activity. Indeed, one of the most well-known criminal uses of Bitcoin was on the Silk Road website, a black market often used to trade illicit drugs and counterfeit passports. Silk Road used a combination of Bitcoin payments and the anonymizing network Tor to create a marketplace for such illicit goods and services (Chen, 2011). Another major concern regarding Bitcoin is its use to launder money and finance terrorist activity. These concerns were stoked especially after the Liberty Reserve, a private and centralized digital currency was shut down on money laundering concerns (BBC News, 2013). It is important to remember, however, that bitcoins are like money, and money can be used for both lawful and unlawful purposes. Other methods of transferring money have been used for financing crimes and money laundering even before Bitcoin existed. However, many Bitcoin exchanges are beginning to employ antimoney laundering features that include keeping records of their customers, which will reduce the attractiveness of Bitcoin to criminals.

Bitcoin, however, also offers benefits over traditional money that protect against some forms of financial crime. For example, the mining process of verifying transactions, which solves the double-spending problem, makes it extremely difficult for bitcoins to be double-spent or counterfeited. An adversary needs to amass sufficient computing power to overcome the combined network computing power in order to be able to attempt to modify present and future transactions before the rest of the network catches up.

1.5.7 Legal regulatory attitude

As Bitcoin is novel, its regulation by governments run the gamut of being permissive to outright bans. The regulatory landscape continues to change as governments grapple with the risks and benefits of Bitcoin to their country. For a start, regulators in some jurisdictions are beginning to provide rules and guidance on the treatment of digital currencies in their country, especially in measures relating to antimoney laundering and the countering of terrorist financing, as well as taxes. The challenge for regulators is to encourage beneficial uses and future innovations while minimizing the risks posed and to do so without preventing such innovations from spawning.

1.5.8 Economic risk

Bitcoin is something that is very different from the existing financial system for which country regulators have experience regulating. The innovative use of Bitcoin may be disruptive to the financial and payment markets in that Bitcoin, for example, can scale up to replace money transmission and card payment services, or even stock exchanges, which renders the incumbent service providers obsolete. If these changes occur rapidly, there is a risk that this will destabilize the financial and payment markets and ultimately price stability in a market.

1.6 IMPACT OF THE DIGITAL CURRENCY REVOLUTION

The digital currency revolution will have a lot of impact on the digital and physical world. A lot of devices will be connected to each other via near-field communication (NFC). Devices that are carried by our side or are worn on our body will contain information about our preferences, possibly our current state of health and most likely all our personal records including how much money we have. We may not need to carry physical wallets and identity cards anymore.

These devices will monitor us and improve our experience in every aspect of our life including medical care, education, and financial services. The blockchain technology can play a major role in lowering the cost of financial services via cost sharing through mining, and therefore, financial institutions can reach out to the unbanked and underbanked, as well as those that require lending and fund raising. All these can be done via the peer-to-peer network of cryptocurrency, either decentralized or distributed. Financial services especially banking will likely be disrupted and margin will be affected as what eCash was set out to do in the early 1990s.

A second example is the use of smart contract for a sharing economy. We will be able to share our assets such as cars, hard disks, and computer memory that we do not use and rent them out to others for a fee. Smart contracts via the distributed peer-to-peer network will make all these possible in the future. This will ensure that infrastructure need not increase but excess capacity is used efficiently.

The desire to own entire assets will be less as more peer-to-peer digital assets or digital trusts can be held by the crowd via blockchain technology. There is also the possibility of time banking so that the cryptocurrency is stored in hours of work. One can then trade with the time spent in, say, palliative care when one is young, and then, the same person will be entitled to such care when he or she gets older with the hours that have been deposited. While these can be done with a centralized system, a distributed or decentralized blockchain system has unique advantages especially in terms of distributed computing. Cryptocurrency may not replace the fiat currency, but its blockchain technology will certainly have an impact on the welfare of the people and perhaps even out the inequality.

1.7 CONDITIONS FOR A SUCCESSFUL CRYPTOCURRENCY

1.7.1 Ecosystem

There is always the first-mover advantage and Bitcoin has certainly emerged as the leading cryptocurrency with an estimated 6 million electronic wallets, 70,000 merchants, and a market capitalization of USD5 billion. For the 6 months leading to October 2014, there were 50-80k transactions daily, and approximately USD50 million (equivalent to over 110,000 bitcoins in 2014) are traded daily. The number of wallets is small given that we have more than 7 billion people in the world. Bitcoin has been successful so far and an ecosystem is up to support its existence. Even though the network effect is kicking in, there is still a long way to go.

A successful digital currency must be able to ride on its initial success and leverage on the network effect. The more people use the coin, the more valuable it will become. As it becomes more valuable, the reward for mining will increase, and more miners will join in the competitive accounting exercise. Bitcoin is subject to the same problems we mentioned earlier.

1.7.2 Incentives

As the mining costs go up because equipment becomes more expensive, mining pools will be formed as miners are usually risk averse and want better odds in winning the race. This increases the possibility of an attack or the emergence of a gold finger that determines to cause problems. There are slightly over 13.4 million bitcoins in circulation as of October 2014. Twenty-five bitcoins are created approximately every 10 min from 2013 to 2016 and the number of new coins created will halve every 4 years.

As soon as the full supply of 21 million bitcoins are issued by the year 2040, which is still very distant, the risk of miners dropping out may increase. If the only reward is transaction fees and if fees become too high, the merchants are likely to drop out.

Of course, there are technical solutions to all these and some cryptocurrencies have come up with the idea of proof of stake reducing the probability that any single person can use a quantum computer to overwrite the whole system. There are also attempts to lower the cost of mining so as to reduce the so-called 51% attack or gold finger problem. However, there is still no fool proof solution to the gold finger issue that if anyone with enough financial strength wishes to mess up the record, he or she can theoretically do it.

1.7.3 Identification

There are also cryptocurrencies that are looking into proof of identity to reduce the possibility of using the currency for money laundering or terrorism activities. If that problem can be resolved, cryptocurrency has a very real potential to be very popular.

If a particular cryptocurrency is able to accept that the government is part of the ecosystem and its community engages with the government meaningfully in creating the ecosystem, that cryptocurrency is likely to become more widely accepted. Given that most of the welfare improvement comes from the bottom of the wealth pyramid, emerging markets have the upper hand in harnessing the low-hanging fruits of cryptocurrency via a decentralized but not necessary distributed system. A cryptocurrency that addresses those issues mentioned will have a bright future.

1.8 FUTURE PROSPECTS AND CONCLUSION

Many people see similarities between the growth of the Internet and the growth of cryptocurrency and postulate that cryptocurrency is going to see exponential growth like the Internet. However, from the business perspective, the growth of the Internet has more to do with e-commerce and less to do with finance. On the other hand, with cryptocurrency, for once in the history of mankind, technology is playing a leading role in finance. In future, one should expect a bank to be a digital or technologically savvy bank. The disruptive force has now arrived at the door step of finance and the blockchain technology is one of the solutions.

There are also similarities between hedge funds and cryptocurrency at the industry level. When the hedge fund industry was in its infant stage, it was perceived to be disruptive to the currency system because hedge fund managers were perceived as the bad guys who took big bets. They were seen to be the mavericks who attacked the currency system and caused the stock markets to collapse. Some banks did not want to deal with them as it did not make business sense with the high compliance costs. Start-ups in cryptocurrency today face the same problems.

There is a lot of bad press and misunderstanding in the media regarding cryptocurrency and some banks are unwilling to open accounts with cryptocurrency start-ups because of various reasons. Regulators are also generally uncomfortable at the moment to deal with a financial innovation as complex as Bitcoin or indeed any other cryptocurrency. At the same time, there is a general resistance and reluctance by Main Street to learn about the intricacies of this financial innovation—it is a wait-and-see situation. That is human nature and it is always the universities and those who are interested in the technology who will see the opportunities first.

There are a lot of similarities between cryptocurrency and hedge fund strategies that were inherently quantitative and difficult to understand. It was no surprise to anyone that hedge fund strategies were initially embraced by the university endowment funds that were less constrained than the traditional managers. Again, universities and financial entrepreneurs will be the first to embrace the cryptocurrency technology before it spills over to the main street.

Cryptocurrency is here to stay and will evolve over time. If Bitcoin loses its popularity for whatever reason, a new cryptocurrency will emerge to replace it with better features. Countries with huge debts have the incentive to create their own cryptocurrency and those who wish to promote financial integration may also turn to cryptocurrency, simply because the cost is low in creating a decentralized partially distributed system. There will be welfare improvement in a cryptocurrency world, which is decentralized but not necessary fully distributed, with proof of identity, proof of stake, and the flexibility to incorporate smart contracts for a sharing economy.

Eventually, it is about reduction of business cost, and welfare improvement will follow for those at the bottom of the wealth pyramid. Eventually, all of this will lead to enhanced efficiency in a sharing economy. The outlook on the development of cryptocurrency is much more optimistic because of the blockchain technology. We are likely to see a great leap in its use, with NFC and related mobile technology being the driver behind its boom. At the same time, it is difficult to predict if cryptocurrency is the next big thing as there is still a lot of uncertainty in the cryptocurrency world. But it is a technology that financial institutions cannot ignore.

In conclusion, Bitcoin is a novel invention, which is a breakthrough in terms of the payments and decentralized networks we know today. It brings with it various benefits and risks that users should be cognizant and indeed conversant with should they wish to deal with and in bitcoins. This chapter has mainly discussed the main features of Bitcoin, but other cryptocurrencies are likely to have similar features and a clear understanding of Bitcoin will aid in understanding other cryptocurrencies. It is only with a good foundation in the knowledge of this amazing new technology that we will be able to use it to its fullest potential without fear.

ACKNOWLEDGMENTS

The ideas for this chapter originated from the expertise of David Lee, especially in his introductory lectures on Bitcoin, and from Lam Pak Nian's earlier research on Bitcoin during his undergraduate degree. The authors also wish to thank Nirupamadevi Bhaskar for clarifying some of the basic concepts and for her guidance on interpreting the raw transaction data.

REFERENCES

Androulaki, E., et al., 2012. Evaluating user privacy in bitcoin. IACR Cryptology ePrint Archive 596. Retrieved from http://fc13.ifca.ai/proc/1-3.pdf.

Back, A., 1997. A partial hash collision based postage scheme, s.l.: s.n. Retrieved from http://www.hashcash.org/papers/announce.txt (accessed 25.01.2015).

Back, A., 2002. Hashcash—a denial of service counter-measure, s.l.: s.n. Retrieved from http://www.hashcash.org/papers/hashcash.pdf (accessed 25.01.2015).

BBC News, 2013. Liberty Reserve digital money service forced offline. BBC News. Retrieved from http://www.bbc.co.uk/news/technology-22680297 (accessed 27.05.13).

Bitcoin.org, 2014. Choose your bitcoin wallet. Retrieved from https://bitcoin.org/en/choose-your-wallet.

Bitcoin Project, 2014. Frequently asked questions. Retrieved from Bitcoin.org: https://bitcoin.org/en/faq.

Brito, J., 2013. The top 3 things I learned at the bitcoin conference. Retrieved from Mercatus Center Expert Commentary: http://mercatus.org/expert_commentary/top-3-things-i-learned-bitcoin-conference.

Brito, K., Castillo, A., 2013. Bitcoin: a primer for policymakers. Retrieved from Mercatus Center: http://mercatus.org/publication/bitcoin-primer-policymakers.

Chaum, D., 1983. Blind signatures for untraceable payments. In: Chaum, D., Rivest, R.L., Sherman, A.T. (Eds.), Advances in Cryptology. In: Proceedings of Crypto, vol. 82. Springer, pp. 199–203. Retrieved from http://link.springer.com/chapter/10.1007%2F978-1-4757-0602-4_18.

Chaum, D., Fiat, A., Naor, M., 1990. Untraceable electronic cash. Adv. Cryptol CRYPTO' 88 (403), 319–327.

Chen, A., 2011. The underground website where you can buy any drug imaginable. Gizmodo. Retrieved from http://gawker.com/5805928/the-underground-website-where-you-can-buy-any-drug-imaginable (accessed 01.06.11).

CoinDesk, 2014. How to store your bitcoins. CoinDesk. Retrieved from http://www.coindesk.com/information/how-to-store-your-bitcoins/ (accessed 22.07.14).

Dai, W., 1998. b-money, s.l.: s.n.

Doherty, S., 2011. All your bitcoins are ours... Symantec Blog. Retrieved from http://www.symantec.com/connect/blogs/all-your-bitcoins-are-ours (accessed 16.6.11).

Finney, H., 2004. RPOW—Reusable Proofs of Work, s.l.: s.n. Retrieved from http://cryptome.org/rpow.htm (accessed 25.01.2015).

Hileman, G., 2014. From bitcoin to the Brixton pound: history and prospects for alternative currencies (poster abstract). In: Böhme, R., Brenner, M., Moore, T., Smith, M. (Eds.), Springer, Berlin pp. 163–165.

Kaminsky, D., 2013. I tried hacking bitcoin and I failed. Business Insider. Retrieved from http://www.businessinsider.com/dan-kaminsky-highlights-flaws-bitcoin-2013-4 (accessed 12.04.13).

Kaplanov, N.M., 2012. Nerdy money: bitcoin, the private digital currency, and the case against its regulation. Retrieved from http://ssrn.com/abstract=2115203.

LocalBitcoins, 2014. Buy and sell bitcoins near you. Retrieved from https://localbitcoins.com/.

Matonis, J., 2013. Bitcoin gaining market-based legitimacy as XBT. Retrieved from CoinDesk:http://www.coindesk.com/bitcoin-gaining-market-based-legitimacy-xbt/.

May, T., 1992. The Crypto Anarchist Manifesto. s.l.: s.n. Retrieved from http://www.activism.net/cypherpunk/crypto-anarchy.html (accessed 25.01.15).

Nakamoto, S., 2008. Bitcoin: a peer-to-peer electronic cash system. Retrieved from https://bitcoin.org/bitcoin.pdf.

Ober, M., Katzenbeisser, S., Hamacher, K., 2013. Structure and anonymity of the bitcoin transaction graph. Fut. Int. 5 (2), 237–250. Retrieved from http://www.mdpi.com/1999-5903/5/2/237.

Pacia, C., 2013. Bitcoin mining explained like you're five: part 2—mechanics. Escape Velocity. Retrieved from http://chrispacia.wordpress.com/2013/09/02/bitcoin-mining-explained-like-youre-five-part-2-mechanics/ (accessed 02.09.13).

Reid, F., Harrigan, M., 2013. An analysis of anonymity in the bitcoin system. In: Altshuler, Y. et al., (Eds.), Security and Privacy in Social Networks. Springer, New York. Retrieved from http://arxiv.org/pdf/1107.4524v2.pdf.

Salmon, F., 2013. The bitcoin bubble and the future of currency. Medium. Retrieved from http://medium.com/money-banking/2b5ef79482cb, 3 April, 2013 (accessed 03.04.13).

SatoshiLabs, 2013. What is TREZOR? Retrieved from http://doc.satoshilabs.com/trezor-faq/overview.html.

Shirky, C., 2000. The Case Against Micropayments. O'Reilly Media, Inc. Retrieved from http://www.openp2p.com/pub/a/p2p/2000/12/19/micropayments.html (accessed 25.01.2015).

Southurst, J., 2014. Apple removes blockchain bitcoin wallet apps from its app stores. CoinDesk. Retrieved from http://www.coindesk.com/apple-removes-blockchain-bitcoin-wallet-from-app-stores/ (accessed 06.02.14).

Szabo, N., 1999. The God Protocols. IT Audit, 15 November.

Szabo, N., 2002. Shelling Out—The Origins of Money, s.l.: s.n. Retrieved from http://szabo.best.vwh.net/shell.html (accessed 25.01.2015).

Szabo, N., 2008. Bit gold, s.l.: s.n. Retrieved from http://unenumerated.blogspot.com/2005/12/bit-gold.html (accessed 25.01.2015).

Tindell, K., 2013. Geeks love the bitcoin phenomenon like they loved the internet in 1995. Business Insider. Retrieved from http://www.businessinsider.com/how-bitcoins-are-mined-and-used-2013-4 (accessed 05.04.13).

Ulm, B., 2014. Bitcoin ATMs boom: new locations. CoinTelegraph. Retrieved from http://cointelegraph.com/news/112163/bitcoin-atms-boom-new-locations (accessed 28.07.14).

Wallace, B., 2011. The Rise and Fall of Bitcoin. Wired. (23), November 2011.

World Bank Payment Systems Development Group, 2013. Remittance Prices Worldwide: An Analysis of Trends in the Average Total Cost of Migrant Remittance Services. The World Bank, Washington, DC. Retrieved from http://remittanceprices.worldbank.org/~/media/FPDKM/Remittances/Documents/RemittancePriceWorldwide-Analysis-Mar2013.pdf.

XE, 2014. XBT—bitcoin. Retrieved from http://www.xe.com/currency/xbt-bitcoin.

CHAPTER 2

Is Bitcoin a Real Currency?
An Economic Appraisal

David Yermack[a,b]
[a]New York University Stern School of Business, New York, New York, USA
[b]National Bureau of Economic Research, Cambridge, Massachusetts, USA

Contents

2.1 INTRODUCTION

Bitcoin became a fixture in world financial news in late 2013 and early 2014. The "virtual currency" had been launched 5 years earlier by computer hobbyists, and in late 2013, the US dollar exchange rate for one bitcoin rose more than fivefold in the space of a few weeks. The market value of one bitcoin, which had begun trading at less than five cents in 2010, briefly exceeded $1,200.00. Two days of hearings were held by the US Senate Committee on Homeland Security and Governmental Affairs, and government regulators testified that algorithmic, stateless currencies like bitcoin had the potential to play useful roles in the commercial payment system (US Senate, 2013). Stories appeared in the media about travelers subsisting for lengthy periods by spending only bitcoin, and various businesses, some of them exotic such as Richard Branson's Virgin Galactic space travel, attracted publicity by accepting bitcoin as payment.

The euphoric news surrounding bitcoin at the end of 2013 gave way to catastrophe in February 2014, when the Mt. Gox exchange, once the leader in worldwide bitcoin trading, imploded in a spectacular bankruptcy. Hundreds of millions of dollars worth of bitcoins went missing in connection with the failure of Mt. Gox, yet the value of bitcoins on other exchanges remained surprisingly high at around $600 each at the time of this writing. Figure 2.1 shows the daily closing dollar-bitcoin exchange rate on the Mt. Gox

Handbook of Digital Currency

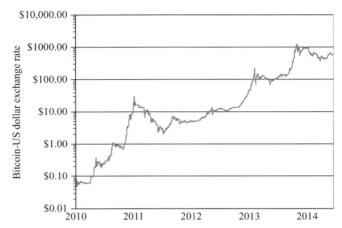

Figure 2.1 *Market value of one bitcoin in US dollars.* The figure shows the value on a logarithmic scale of the bitcoin-dollar exchange rate, recorded daily at midnight on the Mt. Gox exchange in Japan from July 17, 2010 to February 6, 2014, and thereafter until March 21, 2014, on the Bitstamp exchange.

exchange up until February 2014 and thereafter on the Bitstamp exchange, which took over the top spot in trading volume after Mt. Gox folded.

In this paper, I examine whether bitcoin should be considered a currency, an issue that has drawn increasing attention from market regulators concerned about the tax, insurance, and other consequences of how bitcoin is treated legally. I argue that bitcoin does not behave much like a currency according to the criteria widely used by economists. Instead, bitcoin resembles a speculative investment similar to the Internet stocks of the late 1990s.

Money is typically defined by economists as having three attributes: it functions as a medium of exchange, a unit of account, and a store of value. Bitcoin somewhat meets the first of these criteria, because a growing number of merchants, especially in online markets, appear willing to accept it as a form of payment. However, the worldwide commercial use of bitcoin remains minuscule, indicating that few people use it widely as a medium of exchange and those that do can be encumbered by security precautions and long delays needed to verify transactions. I further argue in the sections below that bitcoin performs poorly as a unit of account and as a store of value. Bitcoin requires merchants to quote the prices of common retail goods out to four or five decimal places with leading zeros, a practice rarely seen in consumer marketing and likely to confuse both sellers and buyers in the marketplace. Bitcoin exhibits very high time series volatility and trades for different prices on different exchanges without the possibility of arbitrage. All of these characteristics tend to undermine bitcoin's usefulness as a unit of account. As a store of value, bitcoin faces great challenges due to rampant hacking attacks, thefts, and other security-related problems. Bitcoin's daily exchange rate with the US dollar exhibits virtually zero correlation with the dollar's exchange rates against other prominent currencies such as the euro, yen, Swiss franc, or British pound and also against gold. Therefore, bitcoin's value is almost completely untethered to that of other currencies, which makes its risk nearly impossible to hedge for businesses and customers and renders it more or less useless as a tool for risk management.

Bitcoin lacks additional characteristics that are usually associated with currencies in modern economies. Bitcoin cannot be deposited in a bank, and instead, it must be possessed through a system of "digital wallets" that have proved both costly to maintain and vulnerable to predators. No form of insurance has been developed for owners of bitcoin comparable to the deposit insurance relied on by bank customers in most economies. No lenders use bitcoin as the unit of account for standard consumer finance credit, auto loans, and mortgages, and to date, no credit or debit cards have been denominated in bitcoin. Bitcoin cannot be sold short, and financial derivatives such as forward contracts and swaps that are routine for other currencies do not exist for bitcoin. The absence of these types of market-correcting arbitrage vehicles seems to be the most straightforward explanation for the endurance of bitcoin's value in recent months.

The remainder of this paper is organized as follows. Section 2.2 describes the history and background of bitcoin. Section 2.3 analyzes whether bitcoin fulfills the classical criteria of a currency. Section 2.4 discusses obstacles faced by bitcoin and concludes the paper.

2.2 HISTORY AND BACKGROUND OF BITCOIN

For much of the nineteenth and twentieth centuries, the world's most successful currencies were convertible into fixed amounts of gold or other precious metals, and for thousands of years prior to that, many currencies were minted directly from gold or silver specie. The direct connection between money and gold, secured by sovereign inventories such as the Fort Knox depository in the United States, created public confidence in a currency's value. The gold standard collapsed in most economies between the 1920s and the 1970s, partly due to the pressures of financing two World Wars, but probably even more because worldwide production of gold did not keep pace with economic growth. Since then, nearly every major economy has issued paper fiat currency, the value of which relies on public belief that a nation's government or central bank will not increase the supply of new banknotes too rapidly. Multinational consortia have issued currency like the euro on similar terms. Fiat currencies have circulated for thousands of years, and sooner or later, nearly all of them have been inflated down to worthlessness by governments confronted by strained public finances.

Bitcoin attempts to overcome the weaknesses of both fiat and gold-based money, functioning as an algorithmic currency with a deterministic supply and growth rate tied to the rigor of mathematics. No government or other central authority can manipulate the supply of bitcoins. Instead, the currency is governed by cryptographic rules that are enforced by transparent computer code in a decentralized manner. All of the quantities and growth rates of bitcoins are known with certainty by the public, so its circulation cannot be affected by monetary policy in the way that the Federal Reserve controls the growth rate of the public supply of US dollars. While some enthusiasts have suggested a connection between bitcoin's algorithmic growth rate and the monetary orthodoxy espoused by Milton Friedman, the bitcoin protocol appears to give little or no attention to any optimal rate of monetary growth. Instead, it provides for the rate of seigniorage to slow asymptotically to zero by the year 2140, when the last bitcoin is scheduled to be released and the final total will be fixed at 21 million units.

While the limited supply of bitcoins seems to be a critical aspect of the currency's appeal, whether the supply is truly fixed has become a matter of some disagreement. The case against this view is stated by bitcoin entrepreneur Fred Ehrsam in a recent interview with Goldman Sachs (2014):

> [I]f you needed to create more, you could. That would require 51% of the computing power of the network to switch their software to adopt the change. Changes to the software have occurred a couple of times in the past. There are developer forums where such types of changes are typically discussed and a consensus is ultimately reached across the mining community that maintains the network.

If Ehrsam's interpretation is correct, it implies that the growth of bitcoins could be adapted for reasons of monetary policy, with these macroeconomic decisions emanating from members of an online discussion forum or blog rather than by an expert agency such as the Open Market Committee of the Federal Reserve Board.

Bitcoin originated using a scheme outlined in Nakamoto (2008), a nine-page proposal for a "peer-to-peer electronic cash system." The author or authors of this document have not been identified,[1] but their system was designed in a way that gave them no royalties or residual property rights to benefit from bitcoin's adoption. According to the algorithms proposed by Nakamoto, new bitcoins are created and awarded to computer users who solve prespecified cryptographic problems. These problems become more difficult and less frequent over time. A transparent, decentralized registry tracks the ownership and subsequent transfers of every bitcoin after it is "mined" by its initial owners.

Wallace (2011) reviews the early history of bitcoin and states that Nakamoto mined and introduced the first 50 units into circulation in 2009, essentially to demonstrate the method to a group of online observers. Bitcoin's circulation at first took place among volunteers and enthusiasts from the computer world. Interest grew to the point that bitcoin began to trade in 2010 on a Japanese-based online exchange, Mt. Gox, which had

---

[1] A controversial *Newsweek* story on March 6, 2014, claimed to have located and identified Nakamoto, but the magazine's claim was denied by the subject of the story and has been subject to continuing uncertainty. See http://mag.newsweek.com/2014/03/14/bitcoin-satoshi-nakamoto.html.

originally been created as a platform for exchanging trading cards from the fantasy game Magic: The Gathering. On the first day of trading on Mt. Gox, 20 bitcoins changed hands at a price of 4.951 cents, for a total volume of slightly less than 1 US dollar.

The first purchase of goods and services using bitcoin is said by Wallace (2011) and other sources to have been two pizzas procured at a cost of 10,000 bitcoins in 2009. The pizza parlor did not accept bitcoins directly, and instead, a third-party broker was enlisted who agreed to procure the pizzas using a credit card (based on a real currency) and accept the bitcoins, worth almost $6 million at recent prices, as consideration. Much of the commerce involving bitcoins continues to take place using middlemen who facilitate immediate conversion of bitcoins into conventional currencies on behalf of the participating merchants.

The Silk Road (marketplace), an Internet portal for the sale of illegal narcotics that accepted only bitcoins for payment, was sometimes reported to account for as much as half of the early bitcoin transaction volume, although this estimate is subject to considerable dispute. The Silk Road association helped give bitcoin an early reputation for lawlessness, and this outlaw cachet may not have harmed its appeal at all. Bitcoin usage spread into the bricks-and-mortar economy, and Silk Road was shuttered by US authorities after they arrested its operator in San Francisco in October 2013. Far from hurting bitcoin, this event generated publicity that may have boosted its popularity. Later in the same month, the first bitcoin ATM went into use in a Vancouver coffee shop.

Trading of bitcoin grew rapidly on the Mt. Gox exchange and other platforms. Many online exchanges have now opened to trade bitcoin alongside other virtual currencies that have sprung up as rivals,[2] though some of these platforms are thinly capitalized and trading can appear episodic at best. As bitcoin's value has increased, exchanges have become targets of hackers; Mt. Gox in April 2013 reported three denial-of-service attacks that sharply reduced trading volume on various dates, though in each case, the exchange appeared to recover in a matter of hours. A number of investment funds have opened to cater to bitcoin speculators, including one that has attempted repeatedly to register with the US Securities and Exchange Commission under sponsorship of the Winklevoss twins, who have become famous in the world of digital entrepreneurship due to their legal battles with Mark Zuckerberg over ownership of Facebook.

Bitcoin appeals to two distinct clienteles. One group consists of technology enthusiasts who embrace bitcoin for online commerce. As more and more routine business transactions migrate online, these users believe bitcoin's value should increase due to transaction demand, and they also cite its cost advantages over credit cards and other payment systems for routine bricks-and-mortar retail shopping. A separate group with

[2]See http://coinmarketcap.com/ for a registry of more than 200 alternative digital currencies, which are being created almost by the day. Currently, bitcoin has more than 90% of the world market value of this asset class, according to pricing information on this web site.

pseudo-Libertarian political beliefs finds bitcoin attractive due its lack of connection to any government. Some of these adherents openly distrust the world financial system, and the timing of bitcoin's introduction, coinciding with the very bottom of the global financial crisis in 2008-2009, probably helped swell their ranks.

The technology and libertarian clienteles are united by their enthusiasm for bitcoin but not much else. Discussions about the merits of bitcoin can attract odd mixes of entrepreneurs, academics, and polemicists. An example occurred at a March 2014 panel discussion moderated by a *New York Times* reporter. In response to a conjecture that up to 10% of the bitcoin supply has already been pilfered by computer hackers, bitcoin entrepreneur Andreas Antonopoulos called the 10% theft "a vast improvement over the rest of our economy, where 80% is in the hands of criminals—and that's the banks."[3] As the audience applauded in approval, the famous Stanford economics professor Susan Athey looked on from the other side of the stage with an expression suggesting both exasperation and amusement.

The daily transaction flow of bitcoin trades suggests that the large majority of worldwide demand originates in two countries, the United States and China. While China has taken various steps to ban the use of bitcoin, US regulators have had a more benign attitude. The relative tolerance of bitcoin by American regulators may stem from their recognition that a universal online audit trail exists for bitcoin transactions. Although services such as "tumblers" exist on the Internet that purport to cloak bitcoin transfers in anonymity, confidence in the security of these protocols appears to be naive. The arrest of Silk Road's operator in October 2013, which took place amid widespread publicity of Internet data monitoring by the US National Security Agency, disabused many about the possibility of keeping any bitcoin-related information anonymous. Tax evasion, money laundering, purchases of contraband, and other illicit activities using online transfers become far riskier when the use of a virtual currency like bitcoin can be reconstructed by governments that have sufficient technical skills.

2.3 BITCOIN'S WEAKNESSES AS A CURRENCY

This section presents analyses of ways in which bitcoin fails to conform to the classical properties of a currency. A successful currency typically functions as a medium of exchange, a unit of account, and a store of value. Bitcoin faces challenges in meeting all three of these criteria.

2.3.1 Medium of exchange

Because bitcoin has no intrinsic value, its worth ultimately hinges upon its usefulness as a currency in the consumer economy. Evidence of bitcoin's footprint in daily commerce is

---

[3]See http://www.coindesk.com/despite-challenges-bitcoin-technology-stay.

mostly anecdotal, consisting of newspaper stories about people living only by spending bitcoin or estimates of large numbers of businesses that are willing to accept bitcoin. To date, very few established businesses of any size have begun to take bitcoin, the most prominent being the online retailer Overstock.com.[4] Most of the rankings of the top merchants accepting bitcoins are dominated by computer software and hardware companies selling products narrowly focused on bitcoin applications and by marketplaces or exchanges providing investor services to bitcoin speculators.

Realistic insight into the adoption of bitcoin can be obtained from data drawn from the universal ledger of bitcoin transactions. According to data available at numerous websites, the recent bitcoin transaction count has peaked at daily volumes of approximately 70,000.[5] However, it is widely understood that most of these transactions involve transfers between speculative investors, and only a minority are used for purchases of goods and services. For instance, Fred Ehrsam, cofounder of Coinbase, the leading digital wallet service, estimated in a March 2014 interview that 80% of activity on his site was related to speculation, down from perhaps 95% a year earlier (Goldman Sachs, 2014). If we take this estimate as correct, then about 15,000 bitcoin transactions per day involve the purchase of a product or service from a merchant. In a world with 7,000,000,000 consumers, most of whom make multiple economic transactions each day, bitcoin appears to have an extraordinarily negligible market presence. Ehrsam further states in his interview that 24,000 merchants are registered with Coinbase. If all worldwide bitcoin commerce occurred within this group (almost certainly an exaggeration), these businesses would average well below one transaction per merchant per day. In other words, bitcoin transactions appear to be rarities, even for the small number of merchants that accept them.

One obstacle to bitcoin becoming a widely used medium of exchange arises from the difficulty of procuring new bitcoins. Unless a consumer is successful as a bitcoin miner (an activity now dominated by supercomputers requiring massive capital investments), he or she must source bitcoins from online exchanges or dealers and then find a way to store them securely. These purchases typically cannot be made using a credit card or PayPal, and instead, the buyer must make a bank transfer or link an existing bank account to the exchange.[6] The existing bitcoin exchanges often have low liquidity, significant bid-ask spreads, and a certain amount of execution and custody risk.

One cannot bypass the requirement of possessing bitcoins before procuring goods and services from a merchant. Being able to purchase goods without cash in hand occurs routinely in most retail markets, as customers frequently buy with consumer credit financed by the merchant or a third-party credit card vendor. These options are not available for

[4]A recent article estimated Overstock.com's daily bitcoin revenue at about $30,000. See http://techcrunch. com/2014/03/12/overstocks-bitcoin-purchases-account-for-less-than-1-of-revenue-but-its-growing/.
[5]See, for instance, https://blockchain.info/charts/n-transactions.
[6]See http://howtobuybitcoins.info/us.html.

bitcoins, as no bitcoin-denominated credit cards have yet been issued and consumer loans denominated in bitcoin appear to be unheard-of.

Finally, spending bitcoins requires the merchant and customer to endure a verification process that lasts, on average, 10 min. The delay is necessitated by a connection between transaction validation and mining process for new bitcoins, which is programmed to occur in 10 min cycles. Merchants have the option of trusting the customer and accepting a transaction more quickly, but this would leave them vulnerable to the customer spending the same bitcoins again before the initial transaction becomes embedded into the universal blockchain ledger.

2.3.2 Unit of account

For a currency to function as a unit of account, consumers must treat it as a numéraire when comparing the prices of alternative retail goods. For instance, a cup of coffee that costs $4.00 in one café is quickly understood to be twice as expensive as a cup of coffee selling for $2.00 at another café down the street.

Bitcoin faces a number of obstacles in becoming a useful unit of account. One problem arises from its extreme volatility, an issue discussed in further detail below. Because the value of a bitcoin compared to other currencies changes greatly on a day-to-day basis, retailers that accept the currency have to recalculate prices very frequently, a practice that would be costly to the merchant and confusing to the consumer. In principle, this issue would recede in an economy that used bitcoin as its principal currency, but no such place exists in today's world.

A related problem stems from the diversity of "current market prices" that one can obtain for bitcoin at any given time. For instance, at the moment of writing this paragraph, I consulted a widely used website that posts the prices of bitcoins on markets around the world. For trades reported within the prior minute, prices ranged from $586.00 to $599.20. This disparity of market values represents a clear violation of the classical law of one price, and it would be unthinkable for these conditions to persist in a developed currency market due to the ease of arbitrage. The uncertain market value of one bitcoin presents a conundrum for any third-party vendor or customer seeking to establish a valid reference point for setting consumer prices. As a result, many websites have taken to relying upon unwieldy price aggregations, such as the average bitcoin price over several exchanges over the past 24 h, but these aggregates do not indicate to merchants and consumers the true cost of procuring or selling a bitcoin at the present time.

Perhaps the most serious obstacle to bitcoin becoming a widely used unit of account—and one often overlooked or trivialized by bitcoin enthusiasts—occurs due to the relatively high cost of one bitcoin compared to most ordinary products and services. This requires merchants to quote bitcoin (BTC) prices for most goods in four or more decimal places. Although the mathematics are straightforward, for consumers, these decimal points are likely to be disconcerting. For instance, a visit to one online food retailer yields offers of a jar of salsa for 0.01694 BTC, chocolate bars for 0.00529 BTC, and a tea variety pack for 0.05255 BTC. Alternatively, these prices could be expressed in scientific notation as 1.694×10^{-2} BTC, 5.29×10^{-3} BTC, and 5.255×10^{-2} BTC, respectively. It is hard to find any other currency in the world for which consumer prices are quoted in these units, and indeed, many widely used accounting software products can only accommodate two decimal points in the price of a good.

To the extent that some economies have retail prices that depart from ordinary integers, the pattern usually occurs in the opposite direction as a result of high inflation. Italy prior to the introduction of the euro would be a familiar example for many readers: an ice cream cone from a street vendor in Rome in the 1990s might have cost 5000 lira, for instance, and consumers generally adapted to these prices by ignoring the three zeroes on the end.

A lengthy literature in marketing research has identified heuristics in consumer pricing that include various integer, left-digit, and right-digit reference points. For example, many goods have prices ending in the digit 9 (for a review of this research, see Thomas and Morwitz, 2009). One issue in this literature is the difficulty of computations for consumers in comparing the prices of goods. In the example above, the tea is about 10 times as expensive as the chocolate bars, but even consumers with university degrees would often fail to reach this conclusion with ease due to the length of the decimals and the presence of leading zeros.

Bitcoin proponents tend to dismiss the currency's failure to generate prices that line up with ordinary consumer reference points. Sources tend to agree that existing computational data arrays permit division of bitcoins into eight decimal places, providing the potential for a large enough number of units. For instance, a website on Bitcoin myths (https://en.bitcoin.it/wiki/Myths) opines that "As the value of the unit of 1 BTC grows too large to be useful for day to day transactions, people can start dealing in smaller units, such as milli-bitcoins (mBTC) or micro-bitcoins (μBTC)."

2.3.3 Store of value

When currency functions as a store of value, the owner obtains the currency at a certain time and exchanges it for goods and services at some future time of his choice. When the currency is spent, the owner expects to receive the same economic value that the currency was worth when he acquired it.

Throughout much of history, treating currency as a store of value essentially meant protecting it against theft, either by physically hiding it or by putting it into a bank (which then assumed the security problem). Strategies for hiding bitcoins under mattresses or elsewhere cannot work, because the currency has no physical manifestation. Instead, bitcoins must be held in computer accounts known as "digital wallets," and security for these wallets has become a major difficulty for the bitcoin industry. Some digital wallet companies have contracted with third-party insurers to provide a crude form of deposit insurance. While this strategy might work in principle, it forces the customer to bear the cost of evaluating the security (financial and otherwise) of both the wallet company and the insurance company. Digital wallet companies also offer to transfer bitcoins offline into "cold storage," physically hiding them in remote locations using "virgin" storage devices never previously connected to a computer. These transfers entail delays in obtaining access to one's bitcoins and, of course, additional fees.

If a consumer finds a successful way to hold and secure his bitcoins, he or she faces the further problem of managing the risk arising from bitcoin's volatility. Figure 2.2 shows the volatility of the bitcoin-dollar exchange rate, calculated using daily data from 2013. For comparison purposes, the graph shows the volatilities of the exchange rates of the euro, yen, British pound, and Swiss franc as well as the London price of gold, with all volatilities annualized. Bitcoin's exchange rate volatility in 2013 was 142%, an order of magnitude higher than the exchange rate volatilities of the other currencies, which fall between 7% and 12%. Gold, which is a plausible alternative to these currencies as a store of value, had a volatility of 22% in 2013 based on its dollar-denominated exchange rate. For comparison purposes, most widely traded stocks have volatilities in the range of 20-30%, and even very risky stocks rarely exhibit volatilities as high as 100%. From Figure 2.2, one must conclude that holding bitcoins even for a short period is quite risky,

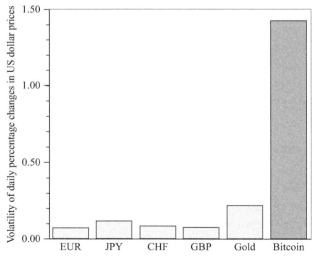

Figure 2.2 *Volatility of bitcoin compared to major currencies and gold.* The figure shows the volatility during the year 2013 of the percentage change in daily exchange rates for four major currencies, gold, and bitcoin, all measured against the US dollar.

Table 2.1 Correlation matrix of daily changes in exchange rates, bitcoin, and gold

	EUR	JPY	CHF	GBP	Gold	Bitcoin
EUR	1.00	0.18	0.61	0.64	0.20	−0.05
JPY		1.00	0.33	0.20	0.07	0.01
CHF			1.00	0.42	0.19	−0.04
GBP				1.00	0.21	−0.02
Gold					1.00	−0.06
Bitcoin						1.00

The table shows simple correlations of the percentage changes in daily exchange rates for pairs of currencies, with all exchange rates measured against the US dollar. In addition, the table shows correlations between each currency and the percentage change in the daily London gold price as measured in US dollars at 3 p.m. Correlations are calculated for the period from July 19, 2010 to March 21, 2014.

which is inconsistent with a currency acting as a store of value and which greatly undermines the ability of a currency to function as a unit of account.

I study the movement of bitcoin compared to the other currencies and to gold in the correlation matrix shown in Table 2.1. The table is based on the daily changes in the London gold price and each currency's exchange rate against the US dollar, using daily data from July 2010 (the inception of trading on the Mt. Gox exchange) up to March 2014. For weekend dates when the exchange markets are closed, I use Friday-to-Monday returns for bitcoins and ignore the intervening price changes on Saturdays and Sundays. As shown in the table, the three European currencies tend to exhibit strong positive correlation, with the euro having 0.61 correlation with the Swiss franc and 0.64 correlation with the British pound and the British pound and Swiss franc having 0.42 correlation. Yen's exchange rate is also positively correlated with those of the other currencies, albeit at a somewhat reduced level. The same is true of the price of gold. In contrast, the bitcoin–dollar exchange rate exhibits almost zero correlation with the exchange rates of any of the four currencies or with the price of gold.

Bitcoin's complete separation from other prominent international currencies and from gold seems telling. Macroeconomic events that impart similar impacts upon the value of various currencies do not seem to affect bitcoin either positively or negatively. The data imply that bitcoin is completely ineffective as a tool of risk management, which is a common use for currencies, and, conversely, that it is very difficult to hedge any risks that might affect bitcoin itself. I examined the trading histories of all US stocks in 2011–2012 to see whether bitcoin could be hedged by selling short individual equities. Using monthly returns from the 2011 to 2012 time period, I found that bitcoin was most closely correlated with Vitamin Shoppe, a retail growth stock with a market capitalization of just under $2 billion (Vitamin Shoppe does not appear to accept bitcoin for transactions on its website). Therefore, to best limit exposure to bitcoin, one would have succeeded up to now by selling short the shares of Vitamin Shoppe.

2.4 CONCLUSION: OBSTACLES FACED BY BITCOIN

For bitcoin to become more than a curiosity and establish itself as a bona fide currency, its daily value will need to become more stable so that it can reliably serve as a store of value and as a unit of account in commercial markets. The excessive volatility shown in Figure 2.2 is more consistent with the behavior of a speculative investment than a currency. As described above, bitcoin also faces difficulties due to its unorthodox decimal pricing of common household goods, the scarcity of merchants who accept it, the delays to verify transactions, and the cumbersome process of procuring bitcoins from a vendor, among other issues. The relatively high level of computer knowledge required for using bitcoins represents a further barrier.

Bitcoin's legitimacy as a currency should also hinge on its integration into the web of international payments and risk management transactions. Even though it is not issued by a sovereign state, bitcoin imparts risk to any business that accepts it for transactions, just like all other currencies. Major companies that deal in more than one currency, such as multinationals, attempt to hedge themselves against risks related to changes in those currencies' values. Data shown in Table 2.1 suggest that no effective way exists to hedge bitcoin against the value of other currencies, and the absence of any swap, forward, or other derivative markets for bitcoin exacerbates this problem. Bitcoin transactions also are risky due to the absence of basic consumer protection, such as the provision of refunds arising from disputes between merchants and customers. While local laws may provide ground rules for resolving such disputes, because a government has no legal way to foreclose and take possession of bitcoins, it ultimately has little ability to step in and enforce its consumer protection laws for bitcoin transactions. Similar problems arise in attempting to secure consumer credit denominated in bitcoin or to pledge bitcoins as collateral for a consumer loan. Again, due to its lack of affiliation to any sovereign, bitcoin is ill-suited for use in credit markets because no government can foreclose and reassign its ownership in the event of a default.

Bitcoin appears to suffer by being disconnected from the banking and payment systems of the United States and other countries. Most currencies are held and transferred through bank accounts, which in turn are protected by layers of regulation, deposit insurance, and international treaties. Without access to this infrastructure, bitcoin has proven vulnerable to fraud, theft, and subversion by skilled computer hackers. However, adherents of bitcoin argue that bitcoin bypasses the well-known flaws in standard financial security systems, which have spawned epidemics of identity theft and related problems for ordinary customers of mainstream businesses.

Finally, bitcoin faces a long-term structural economic problem related to the absolute limit of 21 million units that can ever be issued, with no expansion possible of the bitcoin supply after the year 2140. If bitcoin becomes wildly successful and displaces sovereign fiat currencies, it would exert a deflationary force on the economy since the money supply would not increase in concert with economic growth. This situation would require most workers to accept pay cuts every year, for instance, likely leading to political protests against the currency similar to those experienced in the United States during the Populist movement at the end of the nineteenth century. One can imagine a revival of William Jennings Bryan's 1896 "cross of gold" speech in the next century, updated with futuristic rhetoric about the economic tyranny of an Uber currency with an inflexible supply.

ACKNOWLEDGMENTS

I thank the audience members at the 2013 annual meeting of the Southern Finance Association and my colleagues Geoffrey Miller, Eric Posner, Roy Smith, and Richard Sylla for their for helpful comments. Part of this research was completed while I was a visiting professor at Erasmus University Rotterdam.

REFERENCES

Goldman Sachs Investment Research, 2014. Interview with Fred Ehrsam, Top of Mind 21, 8, March 11.

Nakamoto, S., 2008. Bitcoin: a peer-to-peer electronic cash system. Available from http://pdos.csail.mit.edu/6.824/papers/bitcoin.pdf.

US Senate, 2013. Beyond silk road: potential risks, threats, and promises of virtual currencies. In: Committee on Homeland Security and Governmental Affairs Hearings held November 18–19, 2013. Available from hsgac.senate.gov/hearings/beyond-silk-road-potential-risks-threats-and-promises-of-virtual-currencies.

Thomas, M., Morwitz, V., 2009. Heuristics in numerical cognition: implications for pricing. In: Rao, V.R. (Ed.), Handbook of Pricing Research in Marketing. Edward Elgar Publishing, Northampton, MA.

Wallace, B., 2011. The rise and fall of bitcoin. Wired. Available from http://www.wired.com/magazine/2011/11/mf_bitcoin.

CHAPTER 3

Bitcoin Mining Technology

Nirupama Devi Bhaskar, David LEE Kuo Chuen
Sim Kee Boon Institute for Financial Economics, Singapore Management University, Singapore

Contents

3.1 INTRODUCTION

Bitcoin mining has become a competitive business endeavor. As most of the miners believe in the long-term viability of cryptocurrency, there are also dozens of other online payments called altcoins. Bitcoin is the most popular of these digital currencies. The total value of the Bitcoin system is about $7.6 billion in mid-2014, which is 10 times more than all other cryptocurrencies put together. With the current advanced technology and mining services available, one can earn profits from mining, which is a process of synchronizing transactions in a network of computers. The profit is a function of the cost of mining, which is increasing over time, and cryptocurrency price, which fluctuates.

45

Different methods are followed for mining digital currencies of which Bitcoin uses cryptographic algorithms including elliptic curve digital signature algorithm (ECDSA) and hash functions. Billions of dollars are being spent on custom hardware and software that do nothing but hash computations. The Bitcoin system has gained popularity as numerous opportunities in mining are available owing to the recent technical advancements.

In this chapter, we will outline and discuss the technical aspects of mining and the various schemes for sharing the mined coins for those who are awarded for their efforts in cracking the code and winning the race for the block.

3.1.1 A distributed or decentralized network?

Bitcoin system is supposed to be a distributed network as opposed to a centralized network. However, while a distributed network is totally decentralized, decentralized alone does not mean that the network is fully distributed. One can think of a distributed system as functionality that depends on more than one node performing the function, in the case of miners, many nodes performing the mining of cryptocurrency. A distributed system implies "spread" of functionality. A decentralized system, in this case, is one in which performance of mining does not depend on a single/central node/server. A few pools of miners may be used to achieve the functionality, but it is not necessarily distributed. When the functionality is not fully distributed to the peer-to-peer nodes but via a few pool-to-pool nodes, there is a possibility that collusion by a few concerted parties can dominate the network and end up with an undesired outcome similar to a centralized functionality.

The original thought was that with an increase in the number of miners, it gets harder for anyone to attack the network, thereby securing the Bitcoin network. The security in the system, however, relies on the fact that it would be too difficult and expensive for an attacker to command 51% of the processing power in the network. One of the key elements for Bitcoin network to be secure is that mining, the distributed network process that secures transactions, must be decentralized.

An anonymous mining pool GHash supposedly owned by Russian CEX.io achieved 55% of the total network mining power for about a 24 h span. There was no 51% attack but there has been call to determining pools over 25%. The implication is serious as it casts doubts on the trust of the blockchain, which is central to the Bitcoin system.

3.2 TECHNOLOGY BEHIND BITCOIN

Bitcoin system is a peer-to-peer network. A node in a P2P network is any computer system with software installed in it. A node on receiving data from another node verifies, stores, and propagates the information to every other node connected to it. Information is transferred this way from one node to every other node in the network. A transaction can have any number of inputs and outputs. An input contains the reference to the output from the previous transaction, while the output of a transaction holds the receiving address and the corresponding amount.

Bitcoin is a proof-of-work (PoW) system that requires computation of a piece of data, which is counterintuitive and satisfies certain criteria. It is computationally costly and time-consuming for users to generate this data, but they are rewarded for attempting to do so. PoW computation is a random process and is estimated on trial and error basis. Therefore, a user with higher computational power can influence the network and is not solely based on the number of network identities a user holds. There are many PoW functions, of which Bitcoin uses Hashcash as the mining core (Black, 2002). SHA256 is the most widely used PoW scheme, introduced for Bitcoin system. Few other PoW hashing algorithms include Scrypt, CryptoNight, HEFTY1, Quark, and Blake-256. In addition to PoW system, there are other similar schemes that are used to secure the cryptocurrency network.

Proof of stake is used as an alternative to PoW in cryptocurrencies like Peercoin (Reed, 2014). While the probability of mining a block in PoW scheme depends on the work done by the user, proof of stake requests the user to disclose the amount of his or her stake ownership of that currency. A user holding 5% of the currency has the probability of mining 5% of that currency's proof-of-stake blocks. Proof-of-stake scheme also increases the network security by reducing malicious attacks on the system. This is due to the fact that as an attacker has to own near majority of the network to be successful in his or her attempt, he or she would be affected to a greater extent by his or her very own attack.

Proof of burn is used to destroy (burn) coins. To burn bitcoins means to send those bitcoins to a verifiable yet nonspendable address. This is possible only if the address is not generated from a private key. Chancecoin is a cryptocurrency that uses this scheme.

Proof of solvency is a scheme that allows the users to verify the solvency of the online exchanges that accept Bitcoin deposits. It is based on the proof of assets and liabilities, which can be determined by implementing a code. This scheme can only indicate the insolvency of an exchange and cannot do anything more to prevent it. Bitcoin exchanges like Kraken, Bitfinex, and Bitstamp have proved their proof of solvency. Proof of solvency has been limited to Bitcoin reserves and can be verified from anywhere in the world.

Proof of reserve is similar to proof of solvency and has been designed to prevent bankruptcy of an exchange. Since the demise of Mt. Gox, clients have realized the importance of verifying the reserves held by exchanges. Every exchange selectively discloses information about the funds held while maintaining the privacy of the other clients. Most of the exchanges use Merkle trees for this purpose, where a company can prove the process involved in calculating the total funds held. Bifubao is one good example of exchanges that follows proof-of-reserve scheme to provide extra security to the users (Bifubao, 2014).

3.2.1 Block

The complete history of transactions is stored by everyone, so anyone can verify who the current owner of any particular group of coins is. Transactions are grouped into blocks. The number of transactions in a block is determined by the size. The size limit for a block is 1,000,000 bytes to support quick propagation and reduced anomalies. The size of each transaction is determined by the number of inputs and outputs of that transaction. Figure 3.1 represents a block, which consists of two segments, the header and the body. The transactions are included in the body of a block, while the header consists of seven fields as shown below. A block version number depends on the version of the software used to generate that block. Hash PrevBlock is a 256-bit hash value that serves as the reference to the previous block of the blockchain. The Merkle root is the hash of all the transaction hashes in the block. Transactions of a block are hashed only indirectly through the Merkle root. Therefore, hashing a block with one transaction takes exactly the same amount of effort as hashing a block with 1000 transactions. Time stamp field represents the current time stamp as seconds since 1970-01-01T00:00 UTC (coordinated universal time from January 1, 1970).

The bit field represents the current target value. The SHA256 hash of a block's header must be lower than or equal to the current target for the block to be accepted by the

Version	02000000
Previous block hash (reversed)	17975b97c18ed1f7e255adf297599b553 30edab87803c81701000000000000000000
Merkle root (reversed)	8a97295a2747b4f1a0b3948df3990344 C0e19fa6b2b92b3a19c8e6badc141787
Timestamp	358b0553
Bits	535f0119
Nonce	48750833
Transaction count	63
Transactions	

Figure 3.1 Block structure.

network. This is the mathematical puzzle that has to be solved, in order to validate the block. The target value decreases with increase in the difficulty measure. Difficulty, as its name suggests, is a metric that determines how hard it is to solve transaction blocks, and it varies according to the network hashrate. The target value is inversely proportional to the difficulty of generating a block. A nonce is an 8-byte field in the block header.

The value of nonce is altered so that the hash is below the target. It starts with "0" and is incremented for every hash. The value is guessed until the hash containing the required number of leading zeros is found. The number of transactions included in the block is displayed in the last field of the header.

3.2.2 Blockchain

Blockchain is a sequence of blocks, which holds the complete record of transactions like a public ledger. This indicates the order in which the transactions occurred. Figure 3.2 represents a blockchain where the most recently validated block points to the immediately prior block generated.

Each block in the chain confirms the integrity of the previous one, all the way back to the first block called the genesis block. No party can overwrite previous records by forking the chain.

3.2.3 Block-hashing mechanism

Bitcoin uses Hashcash functions like SHA256 (double-SHA256 function to avoid partial attacks). SHA256 transforms the input message into a 256-bit message digest. Hashrate is the measure of the number of calculations (hashes) per second that the hardware can perform, as it tries to crack the mathematical problem. The higher the hashrate when compared with the current average hashrate of the network, the more likely it is to solve a transaction block.

A node after verifying the entire blockchain collects the newly generated (unconfirmed) transactions and suggests to the network what the next block should be. There

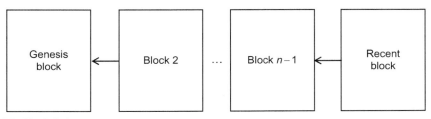

Figure 3.2 Blockchain.

is a possibility for multiple nodes to create such blocks at the same time; therefore, in order to validate a block, the node must contain a solution to a very special math problem.

Computers use a cryptographic hash to estimate an output until it is below the target value (given by the "bits" header field), and the only way to predict the output is by random guesses. The first node to solve the block broadcasts it to the network and gets accepted as the next block in the chain.

Let H be a fixed hash function of the network that is built into the protocol. If x represents the pending transactions and n represents the nonce, then n is appended to x and the combination is hashed. The output hash begins with zeroes and has to be lesser than the target (bits header field) to validate the block. The puzzle here is to determine the value of the nonce for which the hash output is lesser than the target. The number of zeroes at the start of the output value indicates the difficulty of solving a block. A complex PoW puzzle will have a longer run of zeroes and this increases with more mining activity. The difficulty in solving a puzzle is because of the fact that the cryptographic hash function produces a random number. A change in the input by one bit would generate an entirely different output, thereby making it hard to predict. The block header represented by the hash output is therefore lesser than the target on the validation of the block. Once solved, the hash output is like a fingerprint that uniquely identifies that block. This hash output is also used as the previous block reference. The target value is automatically adjusted by the network to ensure that a validation process takes about 10 min on average. On determining the appropriate nonce value, the node transmits the block of transactions along with the nonce value to the other nodes in the network. The other nodes verify the validity of the solution and update their blockchain with the new block received. For instance, consider a nonce value of 0 that is appended to a string value. The hash output generated may not be lesser than the target. Nonce ($x = 9270$) is incremented for every trial until the output determined is less than the target.

H("Hello!0") =
1312af181c275f94028d480a6adc1e125b1caa44c749ec81976192e2ec934c64

H("Hello!9270") =
0000000002fc32107f1fdc0241fa747ff97342a4714df7cc52ea464e12dcd4e9

The validation process of a block is called mining. A bitcoin miner receives an incentive for expending their computation power for validation, which strongly supports the PoW system. A miner receives bitcoins for every block of transactions validated. Initially, 50 bitcoins were awarded for every successful validation. However, approximately, for every 210,000 validations ($\sim$4 years), the number of bitcoins rewarded halves. Currently, the reward is 25 bitcoins. In addition to this, a miner also earns transaction fee that has increased slightly from 0 with the recent popularity of Bitcoin system. The reward system has made Bitcoin mining extremely competitive. The most important factor that determines a miner's probability of being successful is the amount of computing power held, as it is more likely to earn more bitcoins with larger computing resources.

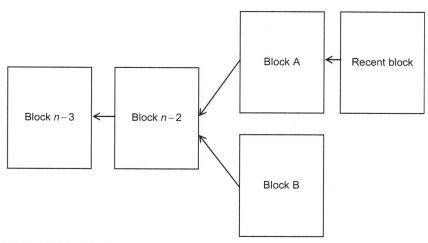

Figure 3.3 Fork in blockchain.

It is also possible for multiple nodes to validate a block at the same instant. This creates a fork in the blockchain. Figure 3.3 represents such a case, where the other subsequent nodes keep track of both the forks. Miners work to extend the fork that is the longest in the blockchain. Consider two forks created by simultaneously validated blocks A and B. Miners work on both the forks and add the newly generated block to one of them. When a new block is added to block A, the miners working on fork B will switch to A and block B is abandoned. Block B now becomes an orphan block.

3.2.4 Bitcoin address

To make a bitcoin transaction, a user generates the public and the private key pair using the "wallet" program installed in the computer. A new key pair can be created for every transaction made and each one is entirely independent of the prior. The wallet data file holds the Bitcoin addresses and the corresponding private keys. A Bitcoin address is a 160-bit hash value of the public key. The key pair created is based on ECDSA. Figure 3.4 shows the flow of the process of generating a Bitcoin address.

The public key is hashed using SHA256. The result is again hashed using RIPEMD-160, which is a cryptographic hash function that generates a 160-bit value. The version (1 byte, 0×00) is appended to the start of the 160-bit hash. Double-SHA256 iteration is performed on this value.

Checksum is the leftmost 4 byte of the double hash. This checksum is added at the end of the RIPEMD-160 result, after which it is converted to a base58 string using Base58Check encoding. This format of Bitcoin address is referred to as Base58Checked address. Bitcoin wallets check the validity of the address before every transaction. The addresses contain built-in check code, thereby making it resistant to typological errors.

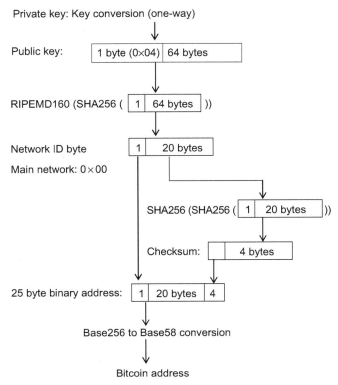

Figure 3.4 Bitcoin address generation process.

The PubKeyHash is Base58Check encoded to get the Bitcoin address with a version number and checksum. The probability of the checksum resulting in an incorrect but a valid PubKeyHash on decoding is approximately 1 in 4.3 billion. To lose bitcoins in such a case, in addition to an invalid address, there has to be a valid one that decodes to a different PubKeyHash that generates the exact same checksum. For a transaction of the sort, it will be spendable only by the person who knows the private key for the incorrect address (public key).

These addresses are randomly generated numbers and it is unlikely for two or more users to have the same address at a given time. If there is a collision, then both the owners can spend the money sent to that address. However, neither of them can spend the entire amount in that particular colliding address. It is more likely for a user to earn profits from mining bitcoins and transaction fees rather than creating a collision intentionally, because it would approximately take 2^{107} times longer to collide with an address than to solve a block. Bitcoins can also be sent to IP addresses, but the current implementation does not provide authentication for the same. So a middleman can intercept the transaction, pretend to be the destination address, and receive the bitcoins. Nowadays, advanced computers are being used in the competitive Bitcoin mining environment and efforts are being taken to also develop a quantum computer for the same. The implications of quantum computing in Bitcoin world are further discussed in the article (http://www.bitcoinnotbombs.com/bitcoin-vs-the-nsas-quantum-computer/; Chris, 2014).

3.3 MINING PROCESS

Bitcoins are created by mining. Mining is the process of maintaining the blockchain by adding newly validated blocks to it. As a reward for dedicating the computing power to the network, the miners are rewarded with newly mined bitcoins and transaction fees. The miners with high computing power are most likely to solve a block first; however, the difficulty of mining increases as more blocks are solved. The first transaction transferred 50 bitcoins to all the nodes in the network. Per the Bitcoin protocol, the reward halves once in every 4 years. Currently, 25 bitcoins are awarded to a node validating a block. However, once the limit of 21 million bitcoins is reached, there will be no more rewards and miners would only earn the transaction fees. A special transaction called coinbase, which is a claim for the reward, is included along with the other transactions. Mining has become a competitive business recently, with specialized technology used for the purpose. Billions of dollars are invested in mining to reap profits sooner.

3.4 MINING POSSIBILITIES

The three ways to mine bitcoins are solo mining, mining contracts, and mining pools.

3.4.1 Solo mining

In solo mining, miners compute hashes individually and the reward on solving a block will be paid entirely to the owner of the hashing computer. The odds of earning new bitcoins are very low and the variance is substantial. A well-equipped solo miner would take an average of 3 months to earn any reward. Mining process is random and memoryless. So if the miner does not solve a block by the end of 3 months, then he or she is not any close to solving a block than he or she was at the beginning of the period. Moreover, the efficiency of a single hardware of certain hashing power reduces with the consistent increase in difficulty. Currently, the difficulty is high, and even with a mining equipment of, say, 1 GH/s, it would take more than 70 years on an average to solve a block. The average time taken to solve a block can be calculated approximately using

$$\text{Time} = \frac{\text{Difficulty} \times (2^{32})}{\text{Hashrate}}$$

For a hashrate of 1 GH/s and a current difficulty level of 16,818,461,371, the time taken to solve a block is

$$\text{Time} = 16,818,461,371 \times \left(2^{32}\right) / \left(10^9\right) / 60 / 60 / 24 / 365 = 2290.55$$

A solo miner with an equipment of 1 GH/s hashrate would approximately take an average of 2290 years to solve a block. The setup of a bitcoin miner is, however, easy and a user would be in need of hardware mining equipment and software.

3.4.2 Hardware

Miners have experimented with different kinds of hardware with the only motive to increase computation power. Table 3.1 shows the statistics of the mining performance of some of the hardware products used in a Bitcoin mining rig.

There are four main categories of hardware used by bitcoin miners:

- Central processing unit (CPU) mining

    The CPU, a part of computer, was the earliest device used for mining bitcoins. The cost of operating CPU exceeded the profits from mining new bitcoins. This has been the least powerful and slowest method of mining when compared to today's standards. The computing power of CPUs is <10 MH/s.

- Graphics processing unit (GPU) mining

    Graphics hardware was used to enhance the performance of a CPU. GPU is the 3-D graphics and visual effects rendering system of computer that can also make

Table 3.1 Hardware products

Product	Advertised MH/s	MH/J	MH/s/$	Watts	Price (USD)	Communication ports
Bi Fury	5000	1176	24	4.25	209	USB
BFL SC	50,000	166	50	300	984	USB
Avalon2	300,000	–	–	–	3075	USB/ethernet
BFL Monarch BPU 600 C	600,000	1714	273	350	2196	PCIe, USB
Bitcoin Ultra Enigma 1	750,000	1000	320	860	3200	USB, ethernet
AntMiner S2	1,000,000	900	442	1100	2259	Ethernet
CoinTerra TerraMiner IV	1,600,000	–	500.2	2100	3199	Ethernet
HashFast Sierra Evo 3	2,000,000	1492	294	2200	6800	USB
KnC Neptune	3,000,000	1429	231	2100	12,995	Ethernet
HashCoins Zeus	3,500,000	1436	–	2400	10,999	USB
Extolabs EX1	3,600,000	1895	379	1900	9499	USB, ethernet
Minerscube 15	15,000,000	–	1666	2475	9225	Ethernet

Mining Hardware comparison, n.d.; https://en.bitcoin.it/wiki/Mining_hardware_comparison.

complex calculations in high-end video games and is efficient at solving transaction blocks by SHA mathematics. GPUs are faster and more efficient than CPUs. Mining rigs are specifically built for the purpose of mining bitcoins. Rigs built using graphic cards cost about a few hundreds of dollars; however, they are not profitable anymore. High-end Intel- or AMD-based rigs have a computing power in the range of 200 MH/s to 2 GH/s. ATI and NVIDIA are some of the main vendors of GPU.

- Field-programmable gate array (FPGA) mining

    FPGA is an integrated circuit that can be customized per users' needs after manufacturing. Bitcoin miners utilized these chips to support mining, as they can operate at high hashrates with low-power consumption. The range of computing speed is much higher than GPUs at around 100 MH/s to 25 GH/s. Mining using FPGAs was once dominant in the industry for its ease of implementation and is still prevalent on a much smaller scale. Sklavos and Koufopavlou (2005) had illustrated the implementation of the SHA2 hash function using FPGAs. However, it is necessary to combine a few chips together to match the performance standards of application-specific integrated circuit (ASICs).

- Application-specific integrated circuit (ASIC) mining

    ASIC has been pivotal in the growth of semiconductor industry over the last few decades. With the increasing popularity of Bitcoin, the need for more computation speed led to the development of ASICs that are designed especially for bitcoin mining since 2013. The most efficient bitcoin mining equipment utilizes custom-designed ASICs. They are expensive because of the specialized and time-consuming fabrication. A single chip can compute at the rate of 5-500 GH/s. Bitcoin ASICs of 28 nm LP (low-power) specification, currently used, are highly efficient in comparison to other mining equipment. ASICs with computing power of 2 TH/s and much higher are being designed.

3.4.3 Software

Special software is necessary to connect the miners to the blockchain and mining pool. As an interface, it is responsible for delivering the work to the miners, receiving the completed work from the miners, and transmitting this information back to the blockchain and mining pool. Mining software can operate on operating systems including Windows, Linux, and Mac OS X. It has also been designed to work on Raspberry Pi, with a few modifications for drivers depending on the mining setup. The software mainly supports the display and monitoring of the general statistics such as the equipment temperature, hashrate, fan speed, average speed of the miner, and overlock periods.

Some of the most commonly used mining software includes the following:

- CGMiner

    This is currently the most popular mining software as it is based on the original code Cpu Miner. The coding language is C and works on all platforms including

Windows, Linux, and Mac OS X. Its framework is OpenCL (Open Computing Language); therefore, it can operate on different mining platforms like CPU, GPU, FPGA, and ASIC. Its features include overclocking, monitoring, fan speed control, remote interface capabilities, self-detection of new blocks with a minidatabase, and multi-GPU support and CPU mining support.

- BFGMiner

  BFGMiner is a modular ASIC/FPGA miner. It is written in C language and has OpenCL framework. It is a derivative of CGMiner with a few improvements in its features like dynamic clocking, monitoring, vector support, integrated overclocking, fan control, and remote interface capabilities.

- EasyMiner

  A GUI-based miner for Windows, Linux, and Android. It also includes support and binaries for RPi, OpenWrt routers, and others as well. EasyMiner acts as a convenient wrapper for the built-in CGMiner and BFGMiner software.

- Bitminter

  This software is like a mining pool that pays the user with the share of coins it creates and the income from transaction fees. Its framework is OpenCL and allows the user to mine on GPUs or ASICs/FPGAs. It is coded in Java. Bitminter assures a good mining speed and long polling in order to reduce stale work.

Other commonly used software are BTCMiner, Poclbm, and DiabloMiner. There are many software available that differ in the coding language and other features, to support the diverse needs of the miners. It is highly important for a miner to choose the appropriate software.

3.4.4 Factors to consider

Some of the factors to consider while selecting the suitable hardware and software for mining include the following:

- Cost of mining equipment

  The cost of the mining equipment depends on the hashrate and the lead time (amount of time that it would take to receive the product from the order time). The cost is usually measured per GH and the average consumer price ranges between $5 and $10 per GH. Difficulty increases consistently with increase in hashrate by 10–20% in a fortnight. So the average useful life of the mining equipment is about 3-6 months approximately. Successful miners in the industry need to reinvest the profits earned consistently in updating the mining hardware and software several times. Before purchasing the equipment, it is possible to calculate the projected profitability and estimate how long it would take to pay back the investment. As the market price of bitcoin increases and advanced ASIC devices hit the market, many new miners are drawn into the system. The capital expenditure of the miners and operating expenses increase over time, owing to the increased hashrate of the network and difficulty. However, the value of bitcoin would also grow proportionately.

- Electricity cost

    Hardware with less power consumption is preferred as they are more efficient and emit relatively less heat. An average of 1-1.2 W/GH is the standard. For the entire Bitcoin network currently, at $100 per MWh, the electricity cost incurred would be $70,712,000 per year.

- Difficulty

    Difficulty is the measure of how difficult it is to find a hash below a given target. It is an arbitrary value and has no unit. It is recalculated every 2016 blocks based on the assumption that the 2016 blocks would be solved in exactly 2 weeks if everyone had been mining at that difficulty level. Intuitively, increased difficulty indicates the decrease in the probability of generating a block at a given computation power. The current expected probability is a reduction of about 10-15% for every 2 weeks.

3.4.5 Mining contracts

Mining contracts are for those who would like to invest in bitcoin mining without the hassle of either managing the hardware or operating the software. These contracts provide mining services, with specified performance for a certain period. Mining shares are also available, that is, shares of hardware of large-scale mining centers. Cloud mining actually means using shared processing power run from remote data centers. A user only needs a home computer for communication purposes, optional local bitcoin wallets, and the like.

There are three types of mining contract options:

- Hosted mining

    A user leases a mining machine that is hosted by the provider. It contributes some systematic risk to the network. For this type of mining, when a substantial amount of computing power is consolidated in large hosting providers, there is a possibility for the provider to control the network to a certain extent.

- Virtual hosted mining

    In virtual hosted mining, a user can create a virtual private server to mine bitcoins and also install his or her own mining software.

- Leased hashing power

    A user can lease an amount of hashing power without having a dedicated physical or virtual computer from a data center that is formed by a group of bitcoin miners. The data center then takes a share from any newly mined bitcoins.

Some of the leading mining contractors include E-Pickaxe, Antminer, KnC, Cloud Hashing, CoinTerra, NimbusMining, and CloudHashers. Joining a mining pool has advantages including no added electricity costs, equipment and concerned problems (i.e., ventilation and hardware failures), system building, and software configuration. The setup is practically instant. Some of the disadvantages are lower profits (as the operator bears the incurred costs), lack of control, and flexibility. With the consistent increase in the difficulty metric, the value of the hashrate that a user buys in a contract decreases over time. In certain cases, such contracts turn out to be profitable, but for the majority, it ends up as a costly lesson.

3.5 MINING POOLS

Mining pools are groups formed by many miners that collectively use all their resources and mine together with the motive to generate combined higher hashing power. Being a part of a mining pool increases the probability of quickly mining a block, as the probability of solving a block is in direct proportion to the computational resources. Bitcoin mining is made less risky by such pools. The reward is split among the participants based on their level of contribution. The income earned per miner is steady but lesser, because the transaction fee is not cashed out and additional fee is charged by the pool operator to compensate for the incurred expenses.

It is also possible to switch mining pools to one that has more hash power. Figure 3.5 represents the distribution of hashrate among the existing mining pools as of July 2014, from Blockchain.info. GHash.IO and BTC Guild are the two largest existing mining pools. Every pool is characterized by distinct features like its size and payout reward type. Bigger pools provide consistent earnings with smaller variance from the expected profit. Though small pools are characterized by larger variance and less frequent larger payments, they help avoid potentially harmful concentration of hashing power.

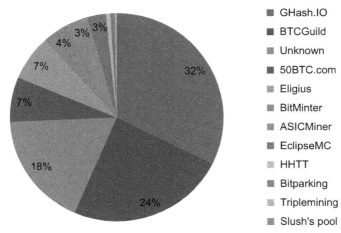

Figure 3.5 Hashrate distribution among mining pools.

Table 3.2 Mining pools

Name	Found blocks	Average hashrate
GHash.IO	29,742	No data
BTC Guild	22,177	641,826.56 GH
Unknown	16,409	No data
50BTC.com	6406	32,342.24 GH
Eligius	6401	299,667.54 GH
Bitminter	3580	195,870.72 GH
ASICMiner	3127	55,711.50 GH
EclipseMC	2566	150,432.12 GH
HHTT	601	9621.96 GH
Bitparking	583	12,546.32 GH
Triplemining	111	2308.09 GH
Slush's pool	56	389,577.18 GH
CoinLab	47	No data
MegaBigPower	37	No data
Discus fish	34	No data

Table 3.2 provides the list of mining pools that have solved the highest number of transaction blocks. Miners are determined to maximize their rewards. New miners prefer to join pools with higher hashrate hoping to increase their chances of solving a block. Some of them use strategies like hopping to pools that are more attractive at a given time, while a few follow selfish mining.

Selfish miners direct the honest miners to waste their computational time on a branch that is to be orphaned. This is made possible by selective disclosure of the miners' blocks to an honest miner. Selfish mining pools secretively work on their validated private branch, while the honest miners expend their resources on adding blocks to the shorter public fork of blockchain. As the selfish miners do not form the majority of the computing power in the network, the private chain held by them would not stay longer than the public chain indefinitely. The selfish mining pool reveals its private branch when the honest miners are too close. This makes the honest miners to abandon the shorter public chain per the protocol, to work on the recently added blocks of the selfish miners' chain. Selfish miners look forward to form the majority of the network, to control the blockchain. When they form the majority, they would no longer need to follow the strategy as other miners can not be any faster than their pool.

3.5.1 Reward types

When a pool solves a block, the 25 bitcoins earned is distributed among the pool clients based on the type of reward provided by that mining pool. There are multiple approaches to pooled mining. It is important to consider the reward type before joining a mining pool, as every pool has its own benefits. Rosenfeld (2011) in his research work in

2011 had analyzed the mining reward systems in detail. A share, with respect to a pool, refers to a proof of work at the expected difficulty. The payout from a mining pool can be any of the following types:

- Proportional (Prop)

    This is the simplest of pooled mining reward systems. The reward received by the pool on solving a block is distributed among all miners in direct proportion to how many shares each of them submitted in that round. The operator holds back a certain amount as fee. This system is vulnerable to pool hopping. Mining later in a round leads to less than normal reward, while mining early in the round gives higher than normal reward. The threshold point where the expected payout is approximately equal to average payout is when the number of shares submitted is 43% of the difficulty. Miners prefer to mine only when the round is earlier to the point, after which they hope to other pools and return back when a new round begins. Those who stick to one particular pool, hoping to earn their due reward, would receive lesser than what they expected. This reduction in the reward received will, however, depend on the number of hoppers and the hopping techniques applied.

- Pay per share (PPS)

    Each submitted share is worth a certain amount of bitcoins. When a client submits a share, a payment is paid to him or her irrespective of how many blocks were solved. This payment is net of the fees and depends on the contribution of the share. The payout is a deterministic value and so easily predictable. The difference between the actual earnings and the PPS earnings paid is called extra credit. The pool keeps count of the unpaid PPS credits and pays them off when a new block is solved. When new bitcoins are earned, the payments to the miners depend on the funds available. If there are pending funds to be settled, they are accumulated as future payouts. The operator absorbs the variance faced by a miner with respect to the reward per share. A pool operator takes a lot of risk in this case (if a block is not solved in the expected time, the operator bears the risk without any compensation in return) and so it has the highest percentage fees. The operator should balance the fees charged and the financial reserve held to make payments, in order to reduce the probability of bankruptcy. However, pools like btcserv.net and abcpool.co charge no fees. They only hold back the transaction fees.

- Shared maximum pay per share (SMPPS)

    The pool keeps a record of a participant's due reward. When a participant submits a share, the corresponding due reward increases in the pool. If extra credit of certain bitcoins is earned in the first round, some proportion of it will be paid every round, until it is paid off entirely. This means that the shares could also be underpaid. SMPPS is not hopping proof. Though expected reward is constant, the time (maturity) it takes to receive the reward is not. When the maturity time is less, SMPPS proves to be very attractive compared to the other alternatives. Whereas when maturity time is high, the hoppers leave the pool as the rewards are delayed.

- Equalized SMPPS

  It is similar to SMPPS but equalizes payments fairly among all those who owe rewards. The pool keeps track of the shares submitted, the payment made for each, and the payments due. The payments are made with the available funds. Those that are due are paid with the next reward earned, in a manner so as to maximize the minimum percentage paid among all shares. For instance, if a share receives 90% of PPS, then it will not be paid again until every other share in the pool is paid the same percent of PPS. One major drawback is when a share receives a relatively high payment, then it is less probable for it to receive any additional payment until every other share, including the newly added shares, receives the same amount of payment. This reward system also supports hopping and so pools that follow it are mostly used as backup pools by miners when no other pool satisfies their criteria.

- Recent shared maximum pay per share (RSMPPS)

  This system focuses on the recent miners. The extra credits issued are remembered in order. On earning new bitcoins, the reward is distributed to the recent shares first in the current round, only after which the unpaid rewards from the previous rounds are settled. This is continued to the previous rounds until all the pending payments are made.

- Capped pay per share with recent backpay (CPPSRB)

  It is a variant of MPPS reward system. This type of pool does not go bankrupt mostly because of the high variance; however, the miners have an overall lower variance than the other types of reward systems like double geometric method (DGM). CPPSRB pays the newest shares first (last-in-first-out order) and no shares are underpaid in this system unlike SMPPS.

- Score-based system (score)

  Score-based reward system was modeled with the main intention to resist pool hopping. There are three main types of score-based systems that include the following:

  Slush's method

  Each share submitted contributes to a metric called score maintained by the system. At the end of a round, the reward is distributed to the participants in proportion to their respective score. To counter the effect of hoppers who leave a pool at the later stage of a round as in proportional reward system, in score-based system, the score credited increases with time. For each share, the score is updated by

  $$s = \exp\left(\frac{t}{c}\right)$$

  where t represents the time and c is a constant. So a miner who submits a share later earns a higher reward in this system.

  Geometric method

  This method is also a hopping proof method and is the improvisation of Slush's method. It has two types of fees: fixed fee and variable fee. Fixed fee is the constant amount from the reward obtained from every block and the variable fee is based on a score. This score value decreases as time passes from the beginning of the round. Therefore, shorter rounds have higher fees and vice versa. This method has been developed based on a solid mathematical model, in a way so that there is no disadvantage between mining earlier and mining in the later stage of a round.

Pay per last N shares (PPLNS)

This system is similar to proportional, but instead of looking at the number of shares in a round, it considers the last N shares regardless of round boundaries. To solve the problem of hopping, it distributes the reward based on which miners submitted the last N shares regardless of any blocks found in the last period. N represents twice the number of shares per round. This way, it eliminates the concept of earning rewards for mining early in a round.

- DGM

   The DGM is a hybrid between PPLNS and geometric reward types that combines the advantages of both and so is resilient to hopping pools. Round boundaries are crossed, but not ignored as in PPLNS, and every block found reduces the reward to be given for future blocks. The share-based variance (due to discontinuities in share submission) is reduced in addition to the pool-based variance (due to smaller pools).

- Pay per last N groups/shifts (PPLNSG)

   Bitminter is a pool that pays by PPLNSG. When a block is found, a client is paid proportionally to his or her number of shares submitted against those of others in the pool for the last "N" rounds. The number of rounds differs from pool to pool.

- Pay on target (POT)

   POT is a high variance PPS that pays on the difficulty of work returned to pool. The payout increases for shares of higher difficulty and is the maximum for the miner who solves the block.

3.6 THREATS TO MINING

The Bitcoin network gets stronger in terms of security as more miners join the network. The complexity of hacking the system increases with the hashrate of the network. In order to cause damage to the Bitcoin network, the attacker must possess a mining power that forms the majority in the network. This could most probably be initiated only by a mining pool that holds the major computing part of the network. When a pool covers 51% or more of the network, it can easily cause mayhem by building its own chain faster than the network and broadcast whenever it likes.

Eyal and Sirer (2014) had outlined certain selfish mining strategies that one can adopt. According to them, if the hash power is 0-25%, selfish mining will yield profits above fair share unless Bitcoin's block propagation protocol is patched. Between 25% and 33%, it will yield profits above fair share even if Bitcoin is patched. Between 33% and 50%, no fix is possible and a selfish miner need not be well connected to the network to win. Double spends against five confirmed transactions are possible. When it is greater than 50%, there is a loss of decentralized trust as double spends against six confirmed transactions are certain to succeed. Furthermore, pool can reject any selected block found by any competing miner, reject any selected transaction, deprioritize certain transactions, and extort high fees from particular address for transaction to be included in the blockchain. The most damaging of all is the complete denial of service in the sense that pool can ignore and orphan every single block found by competitors, thus stopping all bitcoin transactions. While there are no incentives for anyone to do that as yet, those mentioned above are possible and can be damaging to any cryptocurrencies that subject themselves to such possible threats. It is not entirely true that Bitcoin requires no trust as all participants have to trust the good intention of the miners that gathered more than 51% computing power. Eyal and Sirer (2014) went further to state that

> If users were okay with trusting the good intentions of a single entity, we'd do away with the entire protocol, save all the electricity that goes into mining, and keep all the account balances on a database administered by GHash. We'd make sure to use something like HyperDex so it can handle the high transaction rate and is consistent and fault-tolerant. The resulting system would be cheaper, faster and more convenient for everyone, but all of Bitcoin's unique features would have been lost.

In such a situation, the attacker can reverse transactions that he or she sends while in control (double-spend transaction), prevent transactions from receiving confirmation (invalid), or even prevent other miners from solving blocks for a short period. However, the attacker cannot reverse other's transactions, prevent transactions from being sent at all, and create or steal coins. In case when such an attack could successfully take place, it is likely that the confidence in the currency would be lost and its value as a currency would decline rapidly.

3.7 RECENT ADVANCEMENTS

Bitcoin industry has seen technological advancement that is all focused to improve the computing power to facilitate mining in lesser time. The product of Spondoolies-Tech, which is still under development, is claimed to be the masterpiece of the system. This Bitcoin SHA256 miner would have a mining power of 6 TH/s, the highest by far, and the software would be incorporated in the equipment itself, thereby supporting many advanced features.

Mining pools are investing millions of dollars in technology. CoinTerra has built a giant mining plant, which includes more than 2500 rigs (hardware equipment). Each rig is capable of computing at the rate of more than 1.6 TH/s (1.6 trillion of the special numbers). However, this consumes an enormous amount of energy at approximately

20 kW per stack of 10 rigs. The total hashing power of this plant is about 4 PH/s (4000 trillion).

The total hashing power of the Bitcoin network is currently 79 PH/s, which is 564 times higher than the 140 TH/s it handled just a year ago. The computing power required to achieve this is now 6000 times more powerful than the top 500 supercomputers of the world combined. NSA also attempts to build a quantum computer that could crack most types of encryption. This could have a major impact on the Bitcoin system as it could mine at mind-crushing speeds and it also has the capacity to determine the public and the private keys of a user.

3.8 CONCLUSION

Bitcoin is the most widely used digital currency, driven by the ease of transaction and the incentives to mine. This chapter details the fundamentals of technology behind Bitcoin network. It also explains the basic process, opportunities, and rewards of mining activity. Miners seek to maximize their rewards by following strategies like selfish mining and pool hopping based on their needs and the pool reward system. Bitcoin system is also prone to potential takeover by a miner who forms the majority share of the network. Bitcoin industry has witnessed major technological advancements in the recent years, and there is still more room for better innovations.

REFERENCES

Bifubao, 2014. Proof of reserves. http://blog.bifubao.com/en/2014/03/16/proof-of-reserves/.
Black, A., 2002. Hashcash—a denial of service counter-measure.
Blockchain, 2014. https://blockchain.info/pools (accessed July 2014).
Chris, 2014. Bitcoin vs. the NSA's quantum computer. http://www.bitcoinnotbombs.com/bitcoin-vs-the-nsas-quantum-computer/.
Eyal, I., Sirer, E.G., 2014. How a mining monopoly can attack Bitcoin. http://hackingdistributed.com/2014/06/16/how-a-mining-monopoly-can-attack-bitcoin/.
Mining Hardware comparison. https://en.bitcoin.it/wiki/Mining_hardware_comparison.
Reed, S.L., 2014. Bitcoin cooperative proof-of-stake. arXiv preprint arXiv:1405.5741.
Rosenfeld, M., 2011. Analysis of bitcoin mining reward systems. arXiv 1112.4980.
Sklavos, N., Koufopavlou, O., 2005. Implementation of the SHA-2 hash family standard using FPGAs. J. Supercomput. 31 (3), 227–248.

FURTHER READING

Bogliolo, A., Polidori, P., Aldini, A., Moreira, W., Mendes, P., Yildiz, M., Ballester, C., Seigneur, J.M., 2012. Virtual currency and reputation-based cooperation incentives in user-centric networks. In: Proceedings of the IEEE Wireless Networking Symposium (IWCMC2012-Wireless Nets), Limassol, Cyprus, pp. 895–900.
Courtois, N.T., Grajek, M., Naik, R., 2014. The Unreasonable Fundamental Incertitudes Behind Bitcoin Mining. University College London, UK.
Decker, C., Wattenhofer, R., 2013. Information propagation in the bitcoin network. IEEE P2P.

Eyal, I., Sirer, E.G., 2013. Majority Is Not Enough: Bitcoin Mining Is Vulnerable. Cornell University, NY.

Karame, G.O., Androulaki, E., Capkun, S., 2011. Two Bitcoins at the Price of One? Double Spending Attacks on Fast Payments in Bitcoin. IACR Cryptology ePrint Archive, p. 248.

Kondor, D., et al., 2014. Do the rich get richer? An empirical analysis of the Bitcoin transaction network. PLoS ONE 9 (2), e86197.

Kroll, J.A., Davey, I.C., Felten, E.W., 2013. The Economics of Bitcoin Mining, or Bitcoin in the Presence of Adversaries. In: Proceedings of WEIS, vol. 2013.

Martins, S., Yang, Y., 2011. Introduction to bitcoins: a pseudo-anonymous electronic currency system. In: Proceedings of the 2011 Conference of Center for Advanced Studies on Collaborative Research, IBM Corp.

McEvoy, R.P., Crowe, F.M., Murphy, C.C., Marnane, W.P., 2006. Optimisation of SHA-2 family of hash functions on FPGAs. In: IEEE Computer Society Annual Symposium on Emerging VLSI Technologies and Architectures (ISVLSI'06). IEEE Computer Society, Washington, DC, pp. 317–322.

Nakamoto, S., 2009. Bitcoin: A Peer-to-Peer Electronic Cash System. http://bitcoin.org/bitcoin.pdf.

Pouwelse, J., et al., 2014. Operational distributed regulation for bitcoin. arXiv preprint arXiv:1406.5440.

Reid, F., Harrigan, M., 2012. An Analysis of Anonymity in the Bitcoin System. Security and Privacy in Social Networks. Springer Verlag, Berlin, Germany.

Satoh, A., Inoue, T., 2005. ASIC-hardware-focused comparison for hash functions MD5, RIPEMD-160, and SHS. Integration VLSI J. (1), 3–10.

Wallace, B., 2011. The rise and fall of bitcoin. Wired Magazine. http://www.wired.com/2011/11/mf_bitcoin/all.

Why 20 Bitcoin Companies Are Backing a New Deal for Digital Identity. http://www.ahametals.com/20-bitcoin-companies-backing-new-deal-digital-identity/.

CHAPTER 4

National Cryptocurrencies

Andras Kristof
Tembusu Terminals, Singapore

Contents

4.1 THE FIRST WAVE

As bitcoin gained prominence in the public domain, better understanding of the technology behind it made it easy for people to create alternative cryptocurrencies (altcoins), and there would be special coins created and tailored. These include coins created for specific purposes or specific demographic groups, such as Permacredits, a type of cryptocurrency that is aimed to be the established trade currency for sustainable agriculture companies, or possibly altcoins for children, senior citizens, etc.

The most common category of specific purpose coins was the "national cryptocurrencies," as nations across different continents sought to introduce and accelerate the adoption of their own digital currencies to fulfill their various goals and objectives. These coins, in addition to the usual benefits claimed by altcoins, try to build momentum by appealing to people of certain nationality. Some common themes used include patriotism, sovereignty, nationalism, and even nostalgia.

Interestingly, many of these coins are coming from the Eurozone. The Eurozone altcoins can be divided into two main categories.

The economies of Spain, Ireland, and Greece have all suffered since the crisis of 2008, and unsurprisingly, all have their own national coins. The aim of these coins is to "fix" the economy and promise to provide a viable alternative to invigorate the economy. In some cases, a single country has more than one altcoin, and the coins are competing with each other.

The other Eurozone category is the "nostalgia coins"—Deutsche eMark, Ekrona, and eGulden—all seem to be named after pre-euro currencies, the Deutsche Mark of Germany; the krona of Sweden, Norway, and Denmark; and the gulden (or guilder) of the Netherlands, respectively. In most of these countries, the economy has been functioning reasonably well, and these coins seem to be playing on nostalgic sentiments of their respective citizens and are introduced as alternatives to their current financial systems.

Regardless of whether they were prompted into existence due to a bad economy or nostalgia, most of these coins share a common pattern: they do not have any comprehensive economic design or planning behind them. They are mostly simple clones of Litecoin, with a dash of nationalism, and not much planning and forethought was put into them. This unfortunately seriously limits their usefulness and potential for growth. In some cases, they may actually do more harm than good. In order for any form of money to work, it has to be seen as viable enough as a medium of exchange, a unit of account, and a store of value,[1] and in many cases, the implementation of these currencies failed to perform any of the aforementioned successfully. Noticeable failures that some of these currencies have in common were disruptions in payments that were seen as precipitating wider economic crises, and the payment method became seen as posing substantial systemic risk[2] both domestically and internationally.[3]

Fortunately, there are also some exceptions that have enjoyed some degree of success.

4.1.1 AuroraCoin

Home page   http://auroracoin.com/
Market cap $180,451
Market cap source   http://coinmarketcap.com/currencies/auroracoin/
Current value $0.111164
Creation date   February 27, 2014

---

[1]Williamson, S.D., 2011. Macroeconomics, fourth ed. Pearson Education, Boston, MA, p. 397.
[2]Schooner, H.M., Taylor, M.W., 2010. Global Bank Regulation: Principles and Policies. Academic Press, London, p. 224.
[3]Ibid., p. xvi.

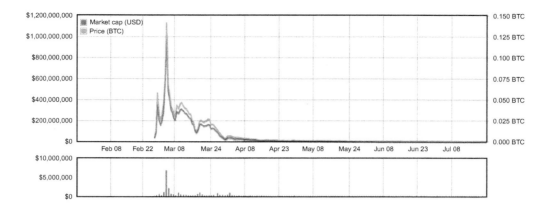

AuroraCoin is possibly the most well-known national altcoin to date. It was mooted to offer Icelandic citizens the option to consolidate their wealth, as the state has strict capital controls regarding wealth conversion to prevent excessive outflows. It was essentially designed to rebuild economic bridges between Iceland and the rest of the world, using the technology of cryptocurrencies.

After the initial peak in prices shortly after its release, where at one stage, it was the cryptocurrency with the third largest market capitalization, the value of AuroraCoin has fallen drastically. This can be attributed to a variety of factors, and a lack of knowledge and awareness among citizens has been commonly cited as well.

One of the major factors contributing to the failure was the airdrop, a process by which AuroraCoin was distributed to the country's citizens on the week beginning March 25, 2014.[4] While the idea itself was great, execution was less than optimal. For example, there were no merchants signed up to accept the coins, and instead, large "whale investors" bought large amounts of AuroraCoin before dumping it and lowering the price in a classic "pump and dump."[5] The only thing the citizens of Iceland could do with the coins was to turn around and sell it for bitcoins. And this is exactly what happened. These actions combined caused the price to drop dramatically.

Furthermore, partially because of the large amount of premine (the act of mining a coin before it is officially launched), miners did not have enough incentive to stay on the network.

Since the miners were leaving, the transactions were processing really slow. Twelve-hour confirmation times were not unusual further helping to crash the price and contributing to the downward spiral.

The continuing departure of miners has dealt the final blow to the coin. With the mining hash rate reaching dangerously low levels, a 51% attack became easy to execute.

[4]http://www.wickedfire.com/shooting-the-shit/179500-lesson-learned-auroracoins-death.html.
[5]http://www.usacryptocoins.com/thecryptocurrencytimes/uncategorized/auroracoin-one-of-the-biggest-pump-and-dumps-in-cryptocurrency-history/.

And indeed, an attack was launched splitting the block chain. And then, it was split again. With three splits, the currency lost its validity.

4.1.1.1 SpainCoin

Home page   http://spaincoin.org/
Market cap $25,558
Market cap source   http://coinmarketcap.com/currencies/spaincoin/
Current value $0.000803
Creation date   March 15, 2014

SpainCoin exhibits all the signs and symptoms of a noble and failed attempt in designing a national cryptocurrency and exhibiting the signs of a typical pump and dump scheme, as after the airdrop was implemented, there was little action done to ensure the coin remained in circulation and to maintain usage levels. The coin was released with 50% being allocated to "people who don't have access to or don't even know anything about cryptocurrencies"[6] in order to encourage them to use it. Initial price shot up incredibly, then crashed quickly, and started a long, flat price curve approaching zero. However, it may be too early to classify SpainCoin as an outright failure, as its developers intended for this to be adopted only in the long run when there is sufficient public awareness.

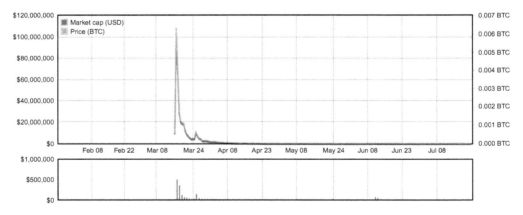

True to its name, it plays to the nationalist sentiments of the Spanish people. Its tagline is "SpainCoin is the perfect cryptocurrency for the Spanish people to break free from their shackles." One interesting feature, their home page, besides Spanish and English, is also available in a third language: Chinese.

4.1.1.2 PesetaCoin

Home page   http://pesetacoin.info/
Market cap $31,980
Market cap source   http://coinmarketcap.com/currencies/pesetacoin/

[6]http://blog.spaincoin.org/spaincoin-distribution/.

Current value $0.000706
Creation date   February 22, 2014

The PesetaCoin was the first cryptocurrency created for Spain, before SpainCoin. It was released with a plan for its adoption to be gradual and arise organically, so there was no planned airdrop to Spanish citizens. The market price graph pattern more resembles that of a cryptocurrency growing in adoption, with peaks and troughs at different time intervals. Unnecessary competition with SpainCoin, though, has hampered its progress.

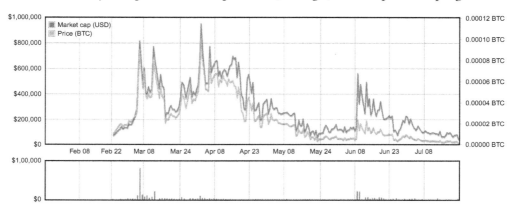

4.1.1.3 GreeceCoin

Home page   http://www.greececoin.net/
Market cap $30,718
Market cap source   http://www.cryptocoinrank.com/Greececoin
Current value $0.0018
Creation date   March 22, 2014

GreeceCoin[7] was created in highly similar circumstances to that of SpainCoin against the backdrop of a country recovering from the financial crisis. The airdrop composed of 50% of the currency that was premined and was distributed to a combination of citizens and business merchants, in a multistaged format. Throughout the entire process, there were issues with the coin servers, and GreeceCoin experienced periods of inactivity with zero transactions due to these technical faults.

4.1.1.4 ScotCoin

Home page   http://scotcoin.org/
Market cap $ 206,041
Market cap source   http://coinmarketcap.com/currencies/scotcoin/
Current value $0.000268
Creation date   May 26, 2014

[7]No market cap graph is available for GreeceCoin.

ScotCoin was released by Derek Nisbet, a professional with many years of experience in the financial industry. A national cryptocurrency was put forth as a viable alternative in the national dialogue about the country's future mode of money, as they were unsure as to persist with the existing currencies or switch to something else entirely. The entire implementation process also involved a larger number of stakeholders, as a variety of organizations were part of the planning and execution process.

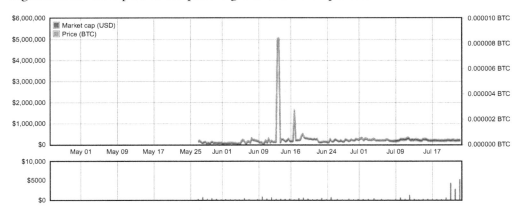

Another key feature of ScotCoin was that it was almost fully premined before release.[8] This was meant to minimize the level of competition in mining and volatility in price of the coin, so that adoption of it would merely be a switch in the mode of money, without all the uncertainty in market conditions that are part of cryptocurrencies.

4.1.2 AphroditeCoin

Home page   http://www.aphroditecoin.org/
Market cap $3687
Market cap source http://www.cryptocoinrank.com/Aphroditecoin
Current value $0.00016
Creation date   March 30, 2014

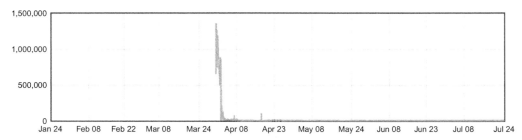

[8]http://www.coindesk.com/coindesk-guide-worlds-national-altcoins/.

In the aftermath of the financial crisis, many Cypriots sought to buy bitcoins as a means of hedging their own savings against the instability of their own currency. AphroditeCoin was released under a pseudonym "Costa Themistocleus," without further details provided. At present, the coin's main web page server is down, leaving holders of the coin in the dark over the status of the currency. Many observers have questioned the legitimacy of AphroditeCoin from the beginning and its market price graph also follows the pattern of a pump and dump scheme.

4.1.3 GaelCoin

Home page   http://www.gaelcoin.org/
Market cap $2709
Market cap source   http://coinmarketcap.com/currencies/gaelcoin/
Current value $0.000291
Creation date   March 20, 2014

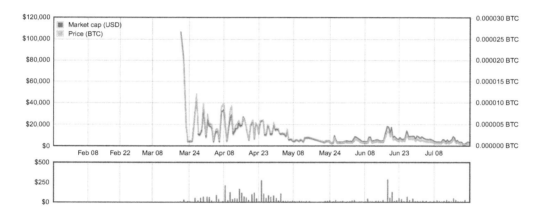

GaelCoin is the first of two Irish cryptocurrencies and was also marketed as a measure to spark the economy back into life. Its web portal is among the most updated and informative, with news and technical details readily available for any currency holders or miners. It differs from the regular national cryptocurrency models because of its 1% only premine condition, as it aims to be accessible to as many people as possible.

4.1.4 IrishCoin

Home page   http://irishcoin.org/
Market cap
Market cap source
Current value
Creation date   May 17, 2014

There are no data available for IrishCoin because it is not obtained via traditional methods of mining or an airdrop; instead, it was designed as a tool to help promote the tourism sector in Ireland. Hence, the coin is introduced through merchants, acting as either a discount voucher or payment remittance. Even after creation, circulation of the coin has been minimal, and there are no statistics regarding the coin.

4.1.5 CryptoEscudo

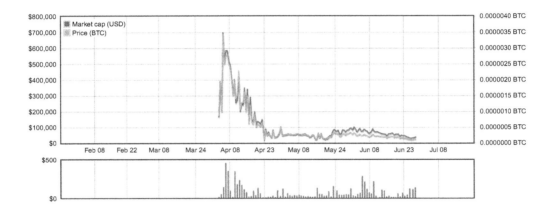

The Portuguese cryptocurrency, CryptoEscudo, was also introduced with lofty ambitions of becoming a currency across borders. However, uptake has been slow, and the developers have taken a long-term view to the survival of the currency, stating that they expect proper adoption to take 5-25 years.

4.1.6 Deutsche eMark

Home page	http://www.deutsche-emark.org/
Market cap	$40,848
Market cap source	http://coinmarketcap.com/currencies/deutsche-emark/
Current value	$0.004029
Creation date	December 15, 2013

The Deutsche eMark was the earliest "nostalgia" coin released, as it did not have a specific purpose to fulfill but was introduced based on elements of nationalism to become a viable alternative currency. Despite its early entry, its dissemination plan was more comprehensive than many of the other countries' coins, and the eMark is already accepted at a number of German retail merchants.

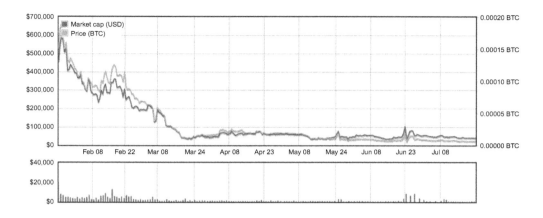

4.1.7 Ekrona

Home page	http://ekrona.org/
Market cap	$522
Market cap source	http://www.cryptocoinrank.com/Ekrona
Current value	$0.00043
Creation date	March 30, 2014

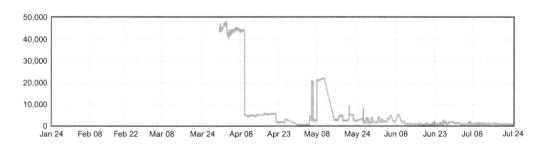

Ekrona is the virtual currency to be used in Scandinavian countries of Norway, Sweden, and Denmark. Despite the initial optimism surrounding its launch, poor technological support has hampered the coin's growth, and many improvements are needed from the developers.

4.1.8 eGulden

eGulden is the Netherlands' attempt at creating an electronic version of a previously successful currency. Despite being half premined, the currency has been circulated with a certain degree of freedom and is experiencing gradual adoption.

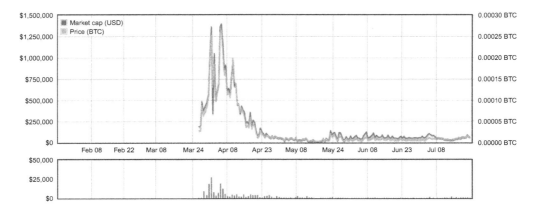

4.1.9 MazaCoin

Home page	http://www.mazacoin.org/
Market cap	$64,112
Market cap source	http://coinmarketcap.com/currencies/mazacoin/
Current value	$0.000126
Creation date	February 27, 2014

MazaCoin is one of the most intriguing examples of how a cryptocurrency can be successfully introduced and adopted. Founder Payu Harris wanted the coin to demonstrate greater fiscal autonomy for the Native American communities. There was no deliberate airdrop of the currency, and the amounts were regulated and released at fixed intervals, under the stewardship of Kimitsu Asset Management. Additional premined coins are either withheld or placed in a trust fund to maintain stability of the MazaCoin. The way in which it was publicized was also very organized, with good supply of information, regular news updates, and constant redevelopment of tools such as wallets and hardware receivers.

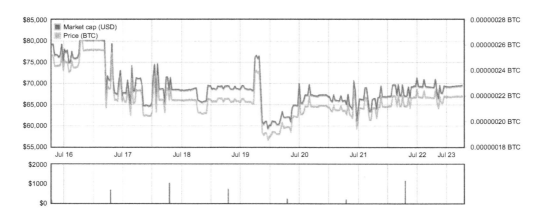

One of the possible reasons why MazaCoin has been more successful than most other national coins is that it belongs to a sovereign state and not a legislated nation with its own fiat currency. This means that it appeals to a specific demographic that does not have to compete with an established common currency, and the coin appears to fulfill a previously unmet need.

4.1.10 MapleCoin

Home page   http://www.maplecoin.eu.pn/index.html
Market cap
Market cap source
Current value
Creation date   March 22, 2014

MapleCoin is the national cryptocurrency of Canada and was meant to be a safe of sorts for the nation's finances, to preserve the wealth of Canada. This means that it was projected as a virtual commodity similar to gold, rather than a currency for exchange. Users were encouraged to collect and hold them and to use them to hedge against the external conditions for fiat currencies. However, this means that with little or no MapleCoin in circulation, there is no way to ascertain what the fair value of the coin is. Currently, there are no data available for the current value and market capitalization of MapleCoin.

4.1.11 IsraCoin

Home page   http://www.isracoin.org/
Market cap $76,626
Market cap source http://coinmarketcap.com/currencies/isracoin/
Current value $0.006985
Creation date   April 8, 2014

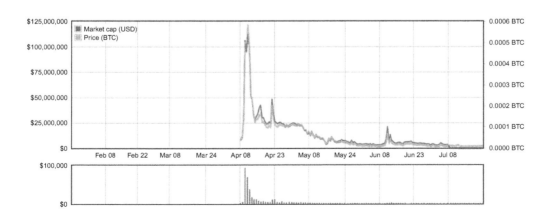

The developers of IsraCoin hoped that it would disrupt the established banking system so that the wealth would be decentralized, creating a more level playing field for all. At first glance, Israel looks to be an ideal candidate for quick introduction of a national cryptocurrency with its high technological penetration and small size. However, the reception of coin among the nation has been lukewarm at best, and more time is needed before it is properly assimilated into the Israeli economy.

4.2 THE FUTURE OF NATIONAL CRYPTOCURRENCY

The first wave of national cryptocurrencies was all grassroot efforts. They were initiated by individuals. Recently, however, there are more and more mentions and even actions from governments. All attempts thus far were trying to address real or imagined issues. Nevertheless, they prove that the cryptocurrency phenomenon now raised the attention of governments.

On July 17, 2014, the New York Department of Financial Services published its proposal for a "BitLicense." The community had high hopes for the proposal; it was expected to clear the grounds for licensed, well-organized bitcoin businesses.

In Ecuador, on July 2014, the government banned all digital currencies before announcing that they would be implementing their own digital currency by October 2014. The digital currency will be state-controlled and inflationary. At this point, there is not much known about the currency, neither from the technical nor from the monetary implementation details.

In Mexico, an ambitious plan was introduced to create a digital version of the country's currency, the peso. If executed, it can help with taxation and with the fight against corruption. This would not be a separate currency like bitcoin, but simply the digital version of the country's existing fiat currency.

In August 2014, the Managing Director of the Monetary Authority of Singapore, Ravi Menon commented on digital currencies in an interview. He was quoted:

It is hard to divine how technology and practices will evolve, 20 or 30 years from now. I would say virtual currencies have a role to play, but I doubt they will replace the fiat money that central banks issue – but I could be wrong.

His words show a very open-minded approach that is encouraging for the community.

4.2.1 More than currency

Mr. Menon's words also highlight a very important point—for a national cryptocurrency to have any impact, much more is required than enthusiasm and technology. The support of governments or friendly legislative environments is of paramount importance. Prudent financial regulation looks at maintaining market confidence as fundamental to the successful operation of the market.[9] Governments should avoid the impulsive desire[10] to clamp down on perceived "disruptive" technology like cryptocurrencies as a knee-jerk reaction to illicit activity, and like any other currency, its uses both illicit and legitimate should be considered.

Certain commentators have also suggested that despite cryptocurrency's lack of management by a central bank that has thus contributed so far to its appeal and volatility, bodies such as the IMF (International Monetary Fund) that is a forum for monetary and foreign exchange cooperation can be given "indirect control" by purchasing pools of cryptocurrency as "separate currency," as imperfect a workaround as it may be.[11] Properly designed monetary features, merchant support, POS integration, ATM integration, marketing, and business relations all need to be the part of the plan.

When all of the above are executed properly, then the full potential of a national cryptocurrency can be realized. By implementing the necessary KYC (know your customer) features, the currency can be made accepted by the banking industry, can make taxation simple (or even automatic), and can become a platform for a host of other application.

With KYC in place, then national cryptocurrencies can be used to write smart contracts and found autonomous companies. It can then also be used to store proof of ownership—everything from ownership of digital books to cars and properties and more. If implemented properly, it can be a tool to integrate the nation's unbanked into the existing financial system.

4.3 CONCLUSION

Zero-maintenance, distributed, resilient, block chain-based digital currencies can help make national trade and international trade frictionless. But the technology, given governmental, industry, and possibly even IMF support, can become much more than a transaction processing system.

It can help to simplify or automate taxation and help the fight against corruption, provide a platform to check ownership rights, integrate low-income people, and generate value and jobs. Used right, national cryptocurrencies may just be the new wave of the future.

---

[9]Foot, M., 2003. What is financial stability and how do we get it? ACI (UK), The Roy Bridge Memorial Lecture, April 3, 2003, online: Financial Services Authority, http://fsa.gov.uk/Pages/Library/Communication/Speeches/2003/sp122.shtml (paragraph 51).

[10]Brito, K., Castillo, A. Bitcoin: a primer for policymakers, online: Mercatus Center, http://mercatus.org/sites/default/files/Brito_BitcoinPrimer_embargoed.pdf, p. 34.

[11]Plassaras, N.A., 2013. Regulating digital currencies: bringing bitcoin within the reach of the IMF. Chicago J. Int. Law, 14 (Forthcoming), preliminary draft online: SSRN, http://papers.ssrn.com/sol3/papers.cfm?abstract_id=2248419, p. 3.

SOURCES

Brito, K., Castillo, A. Bitcoin: a primer for policymakers, online: Mercatus Center, http://mercatus.org/sites/default/files/Brito_BitcoinPrimer_embargoed.pdf.

Foot, M. What is financial stability and how do we get it? ACI (UK), The Roy Bridge Memorial Lecture, April 3, 2003, online: Financial Services Authority, http://fsa.gov.uk/Pages/Library/Communication/Speeches/2003/sp122.shtml (paragraph 51).

http://www.wickedfire.com/shooting-the-shit/179500-lesson-learned-auroracoins-death.html.

http://www.usacryptocoins.com/thecryptocurrencytimes/uncategorized/auroracoin-one-of-the-biggest-pump-and-dumps-in-cryptocurrency-history/.

http://blog.spaincoin.org/spaincoin-distribution/.

http://coinmarketcap.com.

http://www.coindesk.com/coindesk-guide-worlds-national-altcoins/.

http://spaincoin.org.

http://www.forbes.com/sites/ericmack/2014/03/24/national-bitcoin-alternative-auroracoin-launches-to-save-icelands-economy/.

http://www.coindesk.com/auroracoin-forcing-digital-currency-discussion-iceland/.

http://www.coindesk.com/price-iceland-auroracoin-fall-50-bitcoin-airdrop/.

http://www.coindesk.com/auroracoin-airdrop-iceland-embrace-national-digital-currency/.

http://www.coindesk.com/ecuador-bans-bitcoin-legislative-vote/.

http://www.newsmax.com/Finance/Ecuador-dollar-digital-currency/2014/08/15/id/588937/.

http://www.coindesk.com/singapore-head-regulator-digital-currencies-role-play-despite-risks/.

Plassaras, N.A., 2013. Regulating digital currencies: bringing bitcoin within the reach of the IMF. Chicago J. Int. Law, 14 (Forthcoming), preliminary draft online: SSRN, http://papers.ssrn.com/sol3/papers.cfm?abstract_id=2248419.

Schooner, H.M., Taylor, M.W., 2010. Global Bank Regulation: Principles and Policies. Academic Press, London.

Williamson, S.D., 2011. Macroeconomics, fourth ed. Pearson Education, Boston, MA.

CHAPTER 5

Evaluating the Potential of Alternative Cryptocurrencies

Bobby Ong, Teik Ming Lee, Guo Li, David LEE Kuo Chuen
Sim Kee Boon Institute for Financial Economics, Singapore Management University, Singapore

Contents

5.1 INTRODUCTION

Bitcoin is the first open-source, decentralized cryptocurrency ever created. With no central issuing authority, Nakamoto (2008), the anonymous founder of Bitcoin introduced the idea of a distributed blockchain[1] to prevent counterfeiting of Bitcoin. The blockchain, also known as the public ledger is a technical innovation that solves a 20-year-old computer science problem known as the General Byzantine problem (Lamport et al., 1982). This distributed public ledger solves a problem that all distributed systems face, i.e., how to reach consensus in a system without any central authority giving instructions.

The Bitcoin system was carefully designed with many details and features that addressed problems of the existing monetary system. In Nakamoto's (2009) own words and quoted below, it was clear that he has created Bitcoin not only as a form of peer-to-peer currency, but a low or no cost system for micropayments:

> The root problem with conventional currency is all the trust that's required to make it work. The central bank must be trusted not to debase the currency, but the history of fiat currencies is full of breaches of that trust. Banks must be trusted to hold our money and transfer it electronically, but they lend it out in waves of credit bubbles with barely a fraction in reserve. We have to trust them with our privacy, trust them not to let identity thieves drain our accounts. Their massive overhead costs make micropayments impossible.

Bitcoin's source code is open-source and publicly available from its Github repository.[2]

The code is free for anyone to view and programmers worldwide are free to contribute to the code or copy the code to launch their own alternative cryptocurrencies (altcoins). The modification of the original Bitcoin system is for reasons that we will discussed below. One of the main benefits is that some of the developers further enhance the original features and that usually leads to further innovations in the cryptocurrency technology.

There are well over hundreds of cryptocurrencies already in the market. At the time of writing, there are over 440 *active* altcoins according to Coinmarketcap.com and the number of altcoins is increasing each day. This figure does not include altcoins that have

---

[1]A blockchain is a database containing all the transactions happening in a currency and is shared by all the nodes participating in the digital currency protocol. See https://en.bitcoin.it/wiki/Block_chain.
[2]Bitcoin's Github repository is accessible at https://github.com/bitcoin/bitcoin.

not lasted the test of time[3] or coins that have not been listed by the administrators of Coinmarketcap.com. The list of altcoins in the graveyard is included as a supplementary figure in the online version (reproduced from the Web site with permission from the author; supplementary data associated with this chapter can be found, in the online version, at http://dx.doi.org/10.1016/B978-0-12-802117-0.00005-9).

5.2 DIFFERENT TYPES OF ALTCOINS

Altcoins come in various denominations but they are all essentially built upon the fundamental innovation of Bitcoin, which is the decentralized public ledger. This public ledger is a database of all the transactions in the *coin* economy that has been agreed upon by all the miners who are responsible in maintaining the integrity of the system. There are several altcoin categories as noted in Table 5.1.

Most altcoins are direct copies of Bitcoin's C++ source code where programmers make minor modifications to the coin's parameters such as total coin supply or confirmation time. An example of a coin where the developers made only minor changes to parameters is Terracoin. The Terracoin developers changed Bitcoin's parameters such as total coin supply from 21 to 42 million and block time from 10 to 2 min.

Due to the large market capitalization of Bitcoin, it is not suitable to be a test bed for new innovative ideas. As a result of that, new ideas are developed and implemented as part of a new altcoin, completely isolated from Bitcoin. Examples of new ideas include changing Bitcoin's SHA-256 hashing algorithm to scrypt (Litecoin) to make mining more decentralized, changing Bitcoin's Proof-of-Work system to a Proof-of-Stake

Table 5.1 Different categories of altcoins

No.	Category of altcoin	Example
1.	Coins with minor changes of parameter	IxCoin, Terracoin
2.	Coins with technical innovation	Litecoin (hashing algorithm), Namecoin (distributed DNS), Peercoin (Proof-of-Stake)
3.	Coins that are coded in different programming language	NXT (Java)
4.	Coins with new ideas	Counterparty, Ethereum (Turing-complete coin), Mastercoin
5.	Appcoins	Storjcoin X, SWARM Coin, MaidSafeCoin

---

[3]"Necronomicon thread: Altcoins which are dead." A Bitcointalk forum thread maintained by user Cryddit containing a list of altcoins that are no longer active. Available at https://bitcointalk.org/index.php?topic=588413.0.

system (Peercoin) to make the process of maintaining the integrity of the network more energy-efficient, or introducing a new feature such as anonymous transactions (Darkcoin).

Coins like NXT draw inspiration from Bitcoin and have their entire source code rewritten from scratch in a different programming language, in this case Java.

The creation of altcoins is where we see innovation in programming ideas. New ideas such as implementing Turing-complete programming in the protocol level and smart contracts, introduces a paradigm shift on the way we think about decentralization and digital money. However, implementing these features on top of Bitcoin can prove to be very challenging as these features are not what Bitcoin was created for. Hence, a new category called "Bitcoin 2.0" has been coined for coins such as Ethereum.

There is another category of coins known as Appcoins, which are essentially cryptoequity. Appcoins can be looked upon as "shares" in a Decentralized Autonomous Organization (DAO)[4] and are sold in crowdfunding manner like Kickstarter.com. These are coins that are issued on top of Bitcoin 2.0 coins and are known as assets.

The above categories are neither exhaustive nor mutually exclusive. Some coins actually belong to a few of the suggested categories. Two main contributions of Nakamoto (2009) are that the Bitcoin system promotes innovation in the way currency is created and the way payment is made. Altcoins that are created continue to have new features and likely to speed up mainstream adoption of digital currencies and lower the cost of payments. We shall see that altcoins, in whatever future form it will take, will be the driving force behind digital and social banking, leading to social welfare improvement in the area of micropayments and in reaching out to the unbanked and underbanked via categories 4 and 5.

5.3 LAUNCHING AN ALTCOIN

Altcoins are usually launched on the Bitcointalk forum under the Alternative Cryptocurrencies board.[5] To launch an altcoin, one will need a developer to tweak the source code

---

[4]A DAO is an "entity" with a certain agenda, business plan, or protocol but without any central point of control. It is argued that Bitcoin is the first DAO. There are several variations to this, with the original idea known as Decentralized Autonomous Corporation. Several articles have been published and are available here: http://coinwiki.info/en/Decentralized_autonomous_corporation. https://github.com/DavidJohnstonCEO/DecentralizedApplications/blob/master/README.md. https://github.com/jkandah/Decentralized-Application-Business-Model/blob/master/README.md.
[5]The Bitcointalk Alternative Cryptocurrencies board is available at https://bitcointalk.org/index.php?board=67.0. Look for threads beginning for [ANN] for the announcement of new altcoin launches.

and compile executable binaries of it so that the official coin client, usually known as the QT or Core client can be installed on Windows, Mac, and Linux.

There are also services publicly available on the Internet allowing anybody to launch an altcoin without any programming knowledge. Coingen.io and Coincreator.net are two such services where with a fee paid in Bitcoin, one can launch one's own altcoin with some specific parameters. With such low barriers to entry in creating a new altcoin, it is not surprising that the market has been flooded with many altcoins.

5.4 DATA COLLECTION AND ALTCOIN EVALUATION STRATEGY

With over 440 *active* altcoins already in the market, evaluating altcoins can be really tough and time consuming. Coinmarketcap.com, one of the most popular cryptocurrency ranking Web site, ranks coins by market capitalization,[6] which they define as Price multiplied by Available Coin Supply.

Using market capitalization as the sole metric of evaluating altcoin is reasonable as a higher market capitalization will mean that there are more people willing to hold onto the altcoin. However, market capitalization is easily manipulated when there is a small float or a high pre-mine. Market capitalization also does not give any indicator of all the other activity surrounding the altcoin.

To get a more holistic evaluation of a coin to evaluate its mid-term potential, one can look at all other metrics involving a coin and benchmark them against other coins. The first two authors did exactly that and created a Web site called CoinGecko.com to collect various data on coin community support, developer activity, trading volume, price, market capitalization, and network hashrate.

The two leading authors Ong and Lee grouped most of the data collected into three distinct groups, namely, community support, developer activity, and liquidity. The motivation behind this is to get a gauge of the activeness of the developer team, the support that is received from the community, and the trading volume behind each coin. The three distinct groups are given roughly equal weightage and the coins are then benchmarked against each other into an index to create a Complete Metrics Score.

---

[6]Strictly speaking, altcoins do not have market capitalization as market capitalization is the total value of issued shares of a publicly traded company. Altcoins do not issue shares the same way fiat currencies do not issue shares and thus do not have a market capitalization. The market capitalization term is widely used in the cryptocurrency circle because of the Coinmarketcap.com Web site.

Collecting data for all these altcoins is not an easy task as the data need to be aggregated from various sources. Using a combination of API[7] integrations and Web scraping,[8] the authors built a Web application capable of collecting data on a continuous basis at an interval decided by the authors. Since the first day of data collection in March 2014 until the time of writing, over 1 GB of data has been collected and this number is increasing exponentially.

For community data, the official API from Reddit, Facebook, and Twitter is used. For developer data, the official API from Github and Bitbucket is used. For price and volume data, a third-party price service API is used. Market capitalization data are obtained from Coinmarketcap.com, while altcoin network hashing rate is obtained from Coinwarz.com.

5.5 ALTCOIN EVALUATION RESULTS

5.5.1 Community support

A currency without users will not have any value and a strong indicator of a coin's strength is reflected in its community support. To measure community support, there are several metrics that can be used as a proxy such as Twitter followers, Facebook Likes, Reddit[9] activity, Bitcointalk official announcement thread, activity on coin's individual forum, Google searches, meet-ups worldwide, Wikipedia views, and so on.

CoinGecko takes into account community activity on Reddit, Facebook, and Twitter. Table 5.2 contains a brief explanation of the community metrics used.

Coins with a more active community base will usually have more people clicking on the Facebook Like button and following the official Twitter handle for updates. The coin will also usually have a larger Reddit subscriber base.

A huge caveat would be that some of these numbers are easily manipulated by community managers buying fake followers, Likes, and subscribers. This will require a deeper level of analysis by looking at actual activity surrounding these social media sites. For example, Twitter activity can be gauged by also looking at the number of hashtag mentions[10] of a coin. By using activity-based metrics, it would make it harder for community managers to manipulate their metrics scores.

---

[7]API stands for Application Programming Interface which specifies how software components should interact with each other.

[8]Web scraping is a computer software technique of extracting information available from Web sites. This method is normally used to extract information whenever an API is not available.

[9]Reddit is a type of news board or pseudo-forum where users can share new links and comments. Users can "upvote" or "downvote" the links and comments that they like or dislike. See http://www.reddit.com/about.

[10]A hashtag mention is a tweet containing the symbol "#" followed by the cryptocurrency name. Examples include #bitcoin, #litecoin, and #peercoin.

Table 5.2 Explanation of CoinGecko community support metrics

No.	Metric	Explanation
1	Reddit subscribers	Number of users subscribed to the coin's subreddit[a]
2	Average online Reddit users	Average count of online users at the coin's subreddit over the last 48-h period. This is a good indicator to note if any of the subscribers above are fake
3	Average new Reddit "Hot" posts per hour	This is the average number of new submissions to the coin's subreddit over the last 48-h period that makes it to the front page of the subreddit, known as the hot posts
4	Average new comments on Reddit "Hot" posts per hour	This is the number of new comments over the last 48-h period that appeared in posts that are on the front page of the subreddit
5	Twitter followers	This is the number of followers of the coin's official Twitter account
6	Facebook Likes	This is the number of Likes of the coin's official Facebook page

[a]All popular cryptocurrencies have a discussion board on Reddit, known as a subreddit, to encourage discussions among the community members. The popularity of each subreddit differs widely and is used as a measurement tool.

CoinGecko attempted to look at these activity-based metrics by evaluating Reddit activity. This helps to make the ranking more robust and less subject to manipulation. A coin with a high Reddit subscriber count but low figures for average Reddit online users, average new "Hot" posts or comments per hour will usually be indicative of a coin that have bought their high subscriber count.

Coins with many new "Hot" posts and comments indicate that there are many people interested in the coin and are actively discussing the prospect, development, and progress of the coin.

However, one should be aware that these metrics may not fully reflect all user behavior. Not all Internet users worldwide are active on Reddit because Reddit primarily caters to English-speaking males. Coins that have a high concentration of users from non-English-speaking countries may not be fully represented. Also, some coin communities do not undertake many discussions on Reddit but have their discussions on their own individual forums and these data have not been factored into the ranking due the difficulty of data collection.

With that in mind, the data collected is still a reasonable proxy of the community support that each coin receives and Table 5.3 is a snapshot of the top 10 cryptocurrencies measured in terms of community support on July 23, 2014.

5.5.2 Developer activity

Cryptocurrencies require developers to maintain the source code to ensure that it is bug free. Developers worldwide also collaborate to add features onto the coin protocol.

Table 5.3 Top 10 coins measured in terms of community support (July 23, 2014)

No.	Cryptocurrencies	Reddit subscribers	Reddit online users	Reddit new posts	Reddit new comments	Facebook Likes	Twitter followers
1	Bitcoin	130,131	771	2.22	165	22,758	58,991
2	Dogecoin	87,670	300	2.08	190	63,764	163,673
3	Reddcoin	22,179	45	1.71	53.9	17,034	38,117
4	Litecoin	20,906	36	0.6	14.0	5466	15,711
5	Vertcoin	5276	30	0.4	10.5	2748	28,973
6	Blackcoin	3261	21	0.6	9.57	3520	6092
7	Darkcoin	2460	12	0.6	4.51	2465	3320
8	Potcoin	1727	7	0.3	3.12	7233	3063
9	Peercoin	3361	5	0.2	2.67	1188	2000
10	NXT	878	6	0.5	2.10	13,024	1855

Because cryptocurrencies are mostly open-source[11] and hosted on Github or Bitbucket, it is possible to track the development of the coin's source codes.

Using the Github and Bitbucket API, Table 5.4 contains several metrics available that can be used to benchmark and evaluate cryptocurrencies. Image 5.1 is a brief explanation of the metrics available on Github using a screenshot of Bitcoin's Github page on June 30, 2014.

A certain amount of data normalization had to be done on data obtained from Github. This is because coins that are forked from Bitcoin's source code repository continue to take into account values that are obtained from Bitcoin.

An example of this would be contributor count. For example, if the Bitcoin repository is forked, the new forked code will already read 216 contributors. After changing some code and committing the new changes, the repository will now read 217 contributors. The figure has to be normalized to reflect one contributor for a new coin.

CoinGecko also considers commits from every branch[12] in the Github repository. This is used as a pulse check as the measurement takes into account the total number of commits in all branches in the last 4 weeks.

CoinGecko also measures Merged Pull Requests, i.e., the number of Pull Requests that had been accepted to be part of the main source code repository.

---

[11]Some cryptocurrencies were closed-source at time of launch such as NXT and Ripple. Both of these coins have since released their source code to the public for other developers to scrutinize.

[12]Git is an open-source distributed version control system that tracks code changes in an easier manner. A Git branch is a movable pointer to one of the code snapshots also known as the "commit."

Table 5.4 Explanation of Github metrics using Bitcoin as an example

No.	Metric	Explanation
1	Watch	There are 750 people watching the Bitcoin code repository. These are developers who want to keep track of the development of the Bitcoin code repository and this metric indicates developer interest.
2	Star	There are 5524 people who clicked Star on this code repository. This can be roughly translated as the Github version of the Facebook Like button.
3	Fork	There are 3931 people who have "cloned" this code repository to work on the source code. A higher fork count indicates that there are more developers who are interested in copying or contributing to this source code which is a proxy for developer interest due to a potential technical innovation.
4	Commits	There are 6092 commits to the Bitcoin source code repository. This is the number of times the source code has been updated. A higher commit count indicates that there is more development activity going in the repository.
5	Contributors	There are currently 216 contributors who have contributed code to the Bitcoin source code repository.
6	Issues	The 405 figure written here is the number of Open issues that are raised by developers with regards to the code. Coins that have the attention of developers will see a large number of Issue requests. This means that there are developers who are scrutinizing the code and found bugs which need to be fixed by the core team.
7	Pull Request[a]	A Pull Request is a way for contributors to tell the core developers that they have improved the source code and would like the core developer to "Merge" their changes into the source code.

[a]Further explanation of a Pull Request is available at http://oss-watch.ac.uk/resources/pullrequest.

Image 5.1 Screenshot of Bitcoin's Github page (June 30, 2014).

A higher Merged Pull Request figure indicates that more development is happening in the repository.

One of the challenges with the Developer section is that there is an altcoin (NXT) that is not hosted on Github but on Bitbucket. The authors had to write custom code to obtain data from Bitbucket and roughly map these data into Github's equivalent metrics. As such NXT comparison is not perfectly comparable and there is a possibility that NXT developer interest is underestimated (NXT is ranked 21 in terms of Developer Activity).

Table 5.5 is a snapshot of the top 10 cryptocurrencies measured in terms of developer activity on July 23, 2014.

5.5.3 Liquidity

CoinGecko collects trading volume data for each cryptocurrency that is tracked from all major centralized exchanges such as Cryptsy, Mintpal, Poloniex, and Bter. Trading volume data from distributed exchanges[13] are currently not taken into account. Trading volume differs widely from day to day as the attention of traders switch to whichever coin that shows some form of activity or price swings. As a result, the liquidity rank may change very significantly each day. Chart 5.1 is a snapshot of the top 10 cryptocurrencies measured in terms of trading volume taken on July 23, 2014.

5.5.4 Market capitalization

The market capitalization of the top 10 cryptocurrencies on July 23, 2014 is reflected in Chart 5.2.

An interesting point to note is that Bitcoin takes up over ¾ of the trading volume of the top 10 cryptocurrencies but in terms of market capitalization, Bitcoin represents nearly 95% of the market capitalization of the top 10 cryptocurrencies.

5.5.5 Overall rank

CoinGecko takes the liquidity, developer activity, and community support sections to benchmark into an Overall Rank index. Each of these groups represents roughly ⅓ of the Overall Rank calculated on CoinGecko as shown in Table 5.6 and Chart 5.3.

5.6 EMPIRICAL RESEARCH USING SOCIAL NETWORK DATA

The scope of research is currently limited to the data that are easily available from simple API integration or Web scraping. There are various other cryptocurrency metrics that are available that would require running a full node of each altcoin and traversing every single transaction in the altcoin economy.

---

[13]A distributed exchange is an exchange with no central clearing house.

Table 5.5 Top 10 coins measured in terms of developer activity (July 23, 2014)

No.	Cryptocurrencies	Stars	Watchers	Forks	Total issues	Closed issues	Merged Pull Requests	Contributors	Total commits in last 4 weeks
1	Bitcoin	5625	768	4032	4566	4172	2068	213	278
2	Dogecoin	959	171	416	577	529	202	53	80
3	Ripple	838	234	201	0	0	64	13	47
4	Namecoin	286	49	58	140	110	55	11	15
5	Litecoin	941	237	685	167	153	24	14	0
6	Monero	23	20	28	64	48	29	11	39
7	Counterparty	67	29	44	200	133	39	9	66
8	Maidsafecoin	260	88	48	122	118	5	4	85
9	Mastercoin	99	53	39	229	153	63	17	8
10	Reddcoin	121	119	43	15	12	9	6	49

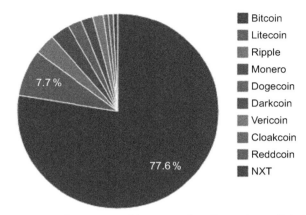

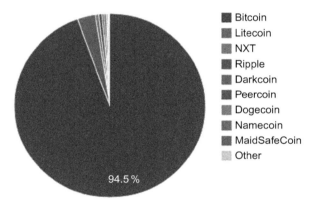

Chart 5.1 Top 10 cryptocurrencies measured in terms of trading volume (July 23, 2014).

Chart 5.2 Top 10 cryptocurrencies measured in terms of market capitalization (July 23, 2014).

Table 5.6 Top 10 coins measured in terms of overall rank (July 23, 2014)

No.	Cryptocurrency	Total score	Liquidity	Developer activity	Community support
1	Bitcoin	98	97	99	97
2	Dogecoin	76	55	86	85
3	Litecoin	68	84	70	53
4	Reddcoin	62	57	64	63
5	Ripple	59	63	78	36
6	Darkcoin	55	63	62	42
7	Monero	54	63	69	30
8	Namecoin	50	41	71	37
9	Blackcoin	49	46	57	45
10	NXT	46	53	47	39

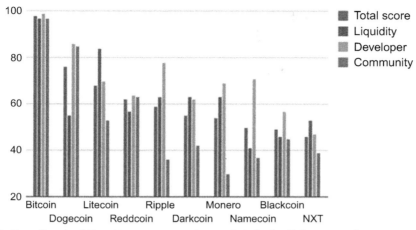

Chart 5.3 Overall rank of Top 10 cryptocurrencies on CoinGecko (July 23, 2014).

Examples of metrics that will be made available by running a full node include the number of wallet addresses, growth of wallet addresses, number of transactions per day, growth of transaction count, percentage of top 100 richest addresses (a measure of income equality), and average transaction size.

There are also other metrics that would require a significant amount of effort to procure the data as it is a very manual process. Examples of these would be aggregating the number of merchants who accept the altcoin in purchases. Only Bitcoin and Litecoin currently have a service aggregating this metric at Coinmap.org.

Since many altcoin discussions also happen in forums, it is important that forum activity measurement is included in the future. One method that the authors have tried evaluating is to use the number of page count in the [ANN] threads of altcoins in the Bitcointalk forum. However, this method runs into several problems because it is common for altcoins to move discussions into their own dedicated forums once a significant discussion mass on the initial Bitcointalk [ANN] thread is achieved. This limits a like-for-like [ANN] page count comparison between all coins.

A fair comparison would be to evaluate the number of users, number of threads, and number of posts in each altcoin's individual forum. Obtaining this figure however is very challenging as this will require Web scraping every single altcoin forum for this information. It would also be good to measure Twitter hashtag mentions of the altcoin, Wikipedia views, number of meet-ups globally on Meetup.com, and number of Google searches for the altcoin. Another measure that would be interesting is to create an index evaluating and ranking the technical innovation of each coin. However, this is challenging because technical innovation evaluation becomes a rather subjective exercise.

The result of the above ranking exercise has been very interesting in evaluating which coin shows the most mid-term potential. Bitcoin is still the clear market leader with a very strong network effect. Its market capitalization is nearly 95% of the top 10 cryptocurrencies by market capitalization, while its trading volume takes up over ¾ of the top 10 cryptocurrencies by trading volume.

Whether or not altcoins will continue taking up a larger share of the top 10 market capitalization or trading volume will be very interesting to note in the next 6 months. As Jackson Palmer, the founder of Dogecoin once said, "6 Months is an Eternity in Crypto."[14] The composition of coins in the rank will change very rapidly in the next few months as events unfold. Some new coins may break in the top 10 rank, while some others may disappear.

That being said, it should be noted that the cryptocurrency industry is still not regulated and is subject to intense price volatility due to insider trading and market manipulation. There is also no consumer protection and it is common to hear of cases of outright cheating, robbery, network attack, and hacking. Any of these incidences can result in the demise of even a large coin and it will be interesting to note the composition of the rank as it changes with each passing week.

5.7 EMPIRICAL ANALYSIS USING TIME SERIES AND CROSS-SECTION DATA

Using the data from CoinGecko, we set out to investigate what variables drive the growth of market capitalization. The first part of the empirical study tries to identify the factors that cause the increase in market capitalization of Bitcoin using time series data while the second part of the study attempts to find the factors that will make altcoins successful. The technical details of this empirical study are contained in Appendix.

The results of the first study using time series data seem to suggest that it is likely that the growth in the market capitalization is the factor that is driving the trading volume rather than the other way. Given that the daily data collected are merely 2 months

---

[14]CoinTelegraph Interview with Jackson Palmer. Available at http://cointelegraph.com/news/112136/6-months-is-an-eternity-in-crypto-jackson-palmer-interview.

and that Bitcoin is not a matured product, we advise readers to interpret the results with great care.

On the cross-sectional study on altcoins, it appears that there are a set of key factors that influence the market capitalization. These key factors are

(i) Repository Merged Pull Requests
(ii) Repository Contributors Count
(iii) Average Online Reddit Users
(iv) Average New Comments on Reddit "Hot" Posts per Hour

Our results suggest that (i) and (iii) show positive effect on market capitalization, while (ii) and (iv) show negative effect. However, given these are mostly discrete variables and that their correlations among them are high, the results need to be interpreted with great care.

5.8 CONCLUSION

Bitcoin was created in 2009 by a person or group of developers which until today, the identity is unknown. That remains the biggest risk to a large-scale adoption because a big unknown of who is behind remains and despite the claim that no trust is needed between two parties in transactions, users need to trust the Bitcoin system. Users, particularly those who hold Bitcoin, need the comfort that during a crisis of a 51% attack or an intended disruption of the digital register, their entitlement or holding of their Bitcoin remain accurately reflected. They need the comfort that the digital addresses that entitle them to their Bitcoin are reliable and reflect their true holding. Many alternative cryptocurrencies (altcoins) have been created but few can claim to give the comfort that is needed by the users or investors.

There are now over 440 active altcoins in the market and new ones are being created each day. An altcoin may emerge with the right attributes to address the main concern of reliability of the system. Before that happens, with every altcoin claiming to offer distinctive features, it is becoming increasingly difficult for investors to evaluate the potential of each altcoin. This chapter explores the various types of altcoins in the market and methods to evaluate their mid-term potential using social network data. The chapter also discussed a practical approach to rank altcoins based on social network. It is a simple and yet useful approach. The results from traditional econometric techniques are at best exploratory and hardly useful to those investing a large amount in altcoins. Until better estimation, crowd sourcing, and crowd forecasting techniques are available, the simple approach will remain relevant in evaluating the potential of a new altcoin. One should never bet anything that one cannot lose on altcoins until the issue of crisis management is addressed as that remains the biggest risk of this Bitcoin and altcoins experiment.

APPENDIX: EMPIRICAL ANALYSIS OF BITCOIN AND ALTCOINS

5A.1 TIME SERIES DATA ANALYSIS OF BITCOIN: COINTEGRATION ANALYSIS THROUGH VECM AND GRANGER CAUSALITY TEST

5A.1.1 Data

Given the abundance of data, there are few reasons to conduct fixed interval time series and cross-section data analysis. However, it takes tremendous resources to collect the data and while our efforts of big data collection are ongoing, it would be interesting to employ traditional econometric techniques purely for exploratory purposes using a smaller sample. Eventually, crowd data and crowd sourcing may yield more meaningful results. Our exploratory results using a subset of the network data (mainly from social network) here may shield some light on the behavior of some new altcoins.

We use time series and cross-section data published by CoinGecko from May 13, 2014 to July 19, 2014. The overall sample consists of 16 variables and 68 daily observations. Table 5A.1 summarizes the definitions of the dependent and explanatory variables used in our empirical analysis. Table 5A.2 lists the descriptive statistics of the differenced

Table 5A.1 Data specification

Variable	Definition
market_cap_usd	Total market capitalization in US dollar
Liquidity	
total_volume_btc	Total trading volume in Bitcoin
Developer activity	
stargazers_count	Total stars on Github/Bitbucket
watchers	Total watchers on Github/Bitbucket
forks_count	Total number of forks (developer copying the codebase)
open_issues_count	Total number of issues raised by community (bugs and feature proposal)
closed_issues_count	Total number of issues closed by core dev (bugs solved, postpone, etc.)
merged_count	Total number of proposals being merged into the core codebase
user_merged_count	Total number of unique collaborators who have ever contributed some code
Community strength	
subscribers	Total number of Reddit subscribers for the coin thread
average_account_active_48_hours	Average Reddit users online in the last 48 h
average_posts_delta_48_hours	Average new Reddit posts on the front page in the last 48 h
average_comments_delta_48_hours	Average new Reddit comments on the front page in the last 48 h
likes	Number of Facebook page Likes
followers_count	Number of Twitter followers

Table 5A.2 Summary statistics

Variables		n	Mean	SD	Median	Trimmed	MAD
market_cap_usd	1	67	0.006	0.028	0	0.003	0.015
price_usd	2	67	2.779	16.376	-0.399	1.226	9.681
total_volume_btc	3	67	0.003	1.062	0.001	-0.016	0.417
stargazers_count	4	67	3.418	2.251	4	3.473	2.965
watchers	5	67	0.075	1.778	0	0.109	1.483
forks_count	6	67	3.97	3.321	4	3.818	2.965
open_issues_count	7	67	0.224	3.696	1	0.545	2.965
closed_issues_count	8	67	5.403	4.469	4	4.927	4.448
merged_count	9	67	2.761	2.791	2	2.327	1.483
user_merged_count	10	67	0.269	0.51	0	0.182	0
subscribers	11	67	0.001	0.003	0.001	0.001	0
average_accounts_active_48_hours	12	67	0.045	107.766	-6	1.109	63.752
average_posts_delta_48_hours	13	67	-0.006	0.254	0.015	0.012	0.163
average_comments_delta_48_hours	14	67	-0.411	32.144	2.561	2.422	25.546
likes	15	67	6.776	4.641	7	6.745	2.965
followers_count	16	67	0.002	0	0.002	0.002	0

	Min.	Max.	Range	Skew	Kurtosis	SE
market_cap_usd	-0.066	0.088	0.155	1.051	1.833	0.003
price_usd	-38.037	50.803	88.84	0.978	1.716	2.001
total_volume_btc	-5.274	5.457	10.731	0.247	16.712	0.13
stargazers_count	-3	7	10	-0.299	-0.325	0.275
watchers	-5	5	10	-0.318	1.209	0.217
forks_count	-2	14	16	0.608	0.571	0.406
open_issues_count	-11	8	19	-0.9	1.082	0.452
closed_issues_count	0	19	19	1.024	0.756	0.546
merged_count	0	13	13	1.449	1.903	0.341
user_merged_count	0	2	2	1.673	1.908	0.062
subscribers	0	0.021	0.021	6.324	42.424	0
average_accounts_active_48_hours	-350	281	631	-0.329	2.622	13.166
average_posts_delta_48_hours	-0.939	0.63	1.568	-0.895	2.368	0.031
average_comments_delta_48_hours	-105.388	61.327	166.714	-1.023	1.584	3.927
likes	-3	19	22	0.054	0.023	0.567
followers_count	0.001	0.003	0.002	0.441	-0.343	0

variables. As with most discrete variables, the median and standard deviation are relative small (e.g., user_merged_count and subscribers_count). It is reasonable to assume popular and standard techniques may not yield meaningful results. Given that the correlation between prices and market capitalizations are almost 1 (shown in Table 5A.3) we will focus on using market capitalization as common dependent variable in the analysis.

5A.1.2 Methodology

5A.1.2.1 Unit root test

Since macroeconomic time series data are usually nonstationary and thus conducive to spurious regression, we test for stationarity of a time series at the outset of cointegration analysis. For this purpose, an augmented Dickey-Fuller (ADF) test is conducted, based on the t-ratio of the parameter in the following regression.

$$\Delta y_t = \alpha + \beta t + \gamma y_{t-1} + \delta_1 \Delta y_{t-1} + \ldots + \delta_{p-1} \Delta y_{t-p+1} + \varepsilon_t$$

Δ is the first difference operator, t captures any time trend, ε_t is the random error, and p is the maximum lag length. The optimal lag length is identified so as to ensure that the error term is white noise, while the rest of parameters are the ones to be estimated. If the null hypothesis gamma = 0 cannot be rejected, it is safe to conclude that the series under consideration has a unit root and is therefore nonstationary.

5A.1.2.2 Cointegration test

The econometric frame work used for analysis in the study is the Johansen (1998) and Johansen and Juselius' (1990) Maximum-Likelihood cointegration technique, which tests both the existence and the number of cointegration vectors. This multivariate cointegration test can be expressed as:

$$Z_t = K_0 + K_1 \Delta Z_{t-1} + K_2 \Delta Z_{t-2} + \ldots + K_{p-1} \Delta Z_{t-p} + \Pi Z_{t-p} + \mu_t$$

where $Z_t = (Y, X)$, $Z_t = $ a 2×1 vector of variables that are integrated of order one [i.e., I(1)], Y and X consist the cointegration system under test, $K = $ a 2×2 matrix of parameters, and $\mu_t = $ a vector of normally and independently distributed error term. The presence of r cointegrating vectors between the elements of Z implies that Π is of the rank r ($0 < r < 2$).

To determine the number of cointegrating vectors, Johansen developed two likelihood ratio tests: Trace test and maximum eigenvalue test. If there is any divergence of results between these two tests, it is advisable to rely on the evidence based on the maximum eigenvalue test because it is more reliable in small samples (see Dutta and Ahmed, 1997; Odhiambo, 2005).

Table 5A.3 Correlation matrix

	market_cap_usd	price_usd	total_volume_btc	stargazers_count	watchers	forks_count	open_issues_count	closed_issues_count
market_cap_usd	1	1	0.004	−0.031	0.06	0.005	−0.023	0.107
price_usd	1	1	0.004	−0.032	0.06	0.005	−0.024	0.108
total_volume_btc	0.004	0.004	1	0.231	0.05	0.11	−0.003	−0.019
stargazers_count	−0.031	−0.032	0.231	1	0.079	0.113	−0.015	−0.023
watchers	0.06	0.06	0.05	0.079	1	0.362	−0.019	−0.071
forks_count	0.005	0.005	0.11	0.113	0.362	1	−0.288	0.106
open_issues_count	−0.023	−0.024	−0.003	−0.015	−0.019	−0.288	1	−0.68
closed_issues_count	0.107	0.108	−0.019	−0.023	−0.071	0.106	−0.68	1
merged_count	−0.005	−0.003	0.032	−0.126	0.095	0.153	−0.531	0.69
user_merged_count	0.027	0.028	0.175	0.02	0.161	0.166	−0.177	0.331
subscribers	−0.021	−0.021	0.002	0.003	0.189	0.158	0.075	0.095
average_accounts_active_48_hours	−0.028	−0.03	0.007	0.194	−0.008	−0.007	0.126	−0.043
average_posts_delta_48_hours	0.054	0.055	0.065	0.071	0.139	0.03	0.057	−0.066
average_comments_delta_48_hours	−0.074	−0.078	0.008	0.113	0.159	0.11	0.013	0.176
likes	−0.036	−0.038	0.272	0.05	−0.071	0.101	0.033	−0.07
followers_count	−0.141	−0.141	−0.267	0.111	0.13	0.337	−0.112	0.005

Table 5A.3 Correlation matrix—cont'd

	merged_count	user_merged_count	subscribers	average_accounts_active_48_hours	average_posts_delta_48_hours	average_comments_delta_48_hours	likes	followers_count
market_cap_usd	−0.005	0.027	−0.021	−0.028	0.054	−0.074	−0.036	−0.141
price_usd	−0.003	0.028	−0.021	−0.03	0.055	−0.078	−0.038	−0.141
total_volume_btc	0.032	0.175	0.002	0.007	0.065	0.008	0.272	−0.267
stargazers_count	−0.126	0.02	0.003	0.194	0.071	0.113	0.05	0.111
watchers	0.095	0.161	0.189	−0.008	0.139	0.159	−0.071	0.13
forks_count	0.153	0.166	0.158	−0.007	0.03	0.11	0.101	0.337
open_issues_count	−0.531	−0.177	0.075	0.126	0.057	0.013	0.033	−0.112
closed_issues_count	0.69	0.331	0.095	−0.043	−0.066	0.176	−0.07	0.005
merged_count	1	0.28	0.039	−0.174	0.091	0.072	−0.067	0.053
user_merged_count	0.28	1	0.125	0.036	0.008	0.236	0.032	−0.011
subscribers	0.039	0.125	1	0.019	−0.059	0.078	0.026	0.034
average_accounts_active_48_hours	−0.174	0.036	0.019	1	−0.042	0.429	−0.132	0.237
average_posts_delta_48_hours	0.091	0.008	−0.059	−0.042	1	0.393	−0.037	0.153
average_committents_delta_48_hours	0.072	0.236	0.078	0.429	0.393	1	−0.173	0.284
likes	−0.067	0.032	0.026	−0.132	−0.037	−0.173	1	−0.159
followers_count	0.053	−0.011	0.034	0.237	0.153	0.284	−0.159	1

5A.1.2.3 Vector error-correction model

VECM can be used if there is evidence of cointegration among two or more series. The model fits the first difference of the nonstationary variables, but a lagged error-correction term is added to the relationship.

In the case of two variables, this term is the lagged residual from the cointegrating regression, of one of the series on the other in levels. It expresses the prior disequilibrium from the long-run relationship, in which that residual would be zero.

In the case of multiple variables, there is a vector of error-correction terms, of length equal to the number of cointegrating relationships, or cointegrating vectors, among the series.

Consider two series, y_t and x_t, that obey the following equations:

$$y_t + \beta x_t = \varepsilon_t, \; \varepsilon_t = \varepsilon_{t-1} + \omega_t$$
$$y_t + \alpha x_t = \nu_t, \; \nu_t = \rho\nu_{t-1} + \zeta_t, \; |\rho| < 1$$

Assume that ω_t and ζ_t are i.i.d. disturbances, correlated with each other. The random-walk nature of ε_t implies that both y_t and x_t are also $I(1)$, or nonstationary, as each side of the equation must have the same order of integration.

By the same token, the stationary nature of the ν_t process implies that the linear combination $(y_t + \alpha x_t)$ must also be stationary, or $I(0)$. Thus y_t and x_t cointegrate, with a cointegrating vector $(1; \alpha)$.

We can rewrite the system as

$$\Delta y_t = \beta\delta z_{t-1} + \eta_{1t}$$
$$\Delta x_t = -\delta z_{t-1} + \eta_{2t}$$

where $\delta = \frac{1-\rho}{\alpha-\beta}$, $z_t = y_t + \alpha x_t$, and the errors (η_{1t}, η_{2t}) are stationary linear combinations of (ω_t, ζ_t).

When y_t and x_t are in equilibrium, $z_t = 0$. The coefficients on z_t indicate how the system responds to disequilibrium. A stable dynamic system must exhibit negative to rise to clear the market.feedback: for instance, in a functioning market, excess demand must cause the price.

5A.1.3 Empirical results

To show how the three groups of variables affect the market cap, we use Bitcoin dataset as an example to construct the VECMs on the following three systems to do the cointegration analysis (as indicated by Johansen test, only the VECM on the liquidity system is constructed; for the other two systems, we conducted the Granger causality test on differenced data). Cointegration analysis helps us understand the long-term and short-term causality among the variables included in the cointegration system. To some extent, although there exists a long-run equilibrium in the system, it is difficult to know how the transformation system looks like. Through VECM, these causality transmission mechanisms can be studied.

1. Cointegration analysis between market capitalization and liquidity
   Endogenous variables: market_cap_usd, total_volume_btc
   Note: To regard all the rest of the variables as exogenous variables.
2. Cointegration analysis between market capitalization and developer activity
   Endogenous variables: market_cap_usd, open_issues_count, closed_issues_count, forks_count, merged_count, stargazers, user_merged_count, subscribers_count
   Note: To regard all the rest of the variables as exogenous variables.
3. Cointegration analysis between market capitalization and community strength
   Endogenous variables: market_cap_usd, average_accounts_active_48_hours, average_comments_delta_48_hours, followers_count, likes, average_posts_delta_48_hours, subscribers
   Note: To regard all the rest of the variables as exogenous variables.

5A.1.3.1 Unit root test results

First, unit root test is applied to all 16 variables. The results show that only Trading volume and Accounts_active_48 are stationary. For the rest of the variables, all of them are not stationary in $I(0)$, but become stationary in $I(1)$. The results are presented in Table 5A.4.

After that, Johansen test is adopted to check whether there exists any cointegration relationship among the three systems.

There are two types of Johansen test, either with trace or with eigenvalue, and the inferences might be a little different. The null hypothesis for the trace test is that the number of cointegration vectors $r \leq n$ and the null hypothesis for the eigenvalue test is that $r = n$, where r stands for the rank of matrix under test and n stands for the number of cointegration equations (Table 5A.5).

As suggested in Table 5A.5, of the three systems considered, cointegration only exists in the first system. However, no cointegration relationship exists in either second or third system. Thus, the VECM is constructed for the liquidity system. In all cases, the lag length is selected using AIC, BIC, and LR criteria under nonrestricted VAR model. That is, the best number of lags for Johansen test should be $\max\{(k-1), 1\}$, where k stands for the optimal lag for VAR model.

In the meantime, since there are no cointegration relationships in Developer system and Community system, we may not want to take those variables as key factors to analyze the market capitalization of cryptocurrency especially for forecasting. In addition, the potential reason for no cointegration relationship detected under these two systems is that some variables exist only for several months. By contrast, for market cap, data of nearly 5 years are available. For those variables, it is likely that data range is too short to reveal any stable relationship, resulting in a biased estimation. Therefore, follow-up research is required to get a better understanding in the real effect of those variables when more data are available.

Table 5A.4 ADF unit root test

Original data series	Level (5%)	First-order differenced data	Level (5%)
market_cap_usd(lags = 1)	−0.927(−3.131)	market_cap_usd(lags = 1)	−4.334(−3.136)***
price_usd(lags = 1)	−0.916(−3.131)	price_usd(lags = 1)	−4.345(−3.136)***
total_volume_btc(lags = 1)	−5.657(−3.131)***	total_volume_btc(lags = 3)	−6.476(−3.067)***
average_accounts_active_48_hours (lags = 9)	−3.253(−2.791)***	average_accounts_active_48_hours (lags = 1)	−9.645(−3.136)***
average_comments_delta_48_hours (lags = 2)	−2.425(−3.100)	average_comments_delta_48_hours (lags = 1)	−6.065(−3.136)***
followers_count (lags = 3)	−2.037(−3.064)	followers_count (lags = 2)	−5.280(−3.104)***
likes(lags = 1)	−0.869(−3.131)	likes(lags = 1)	−5.193(−3.136)***
average_posts_delta_48_hours (lags=10)	−1.075(−2.743)	average_posts_delta_48_hours (lags=10)	−6.518(−3.136)***
subscribers_count (lags = 1)	−1.692(−3.131)	subscribers_count (lags = 1)	−4.952(−3.136)***
open_issues_count (lags = 1)	−1.279(−3.131)	open_issues_count (lags = 1)	−5.978(−3.136)***
closed_issues_count (lags = 1)	−0.642(−3.131)	closed_issues_count (lags = 1)	−4.981(−3.136)***
forks_count (lags = 1)	−1.673(−3.131)	forks_count (lags = 1)	−3.797(−3.136)***
merged_count(lags = 1)	−0.658(−3.131)	merged_count(lags = 1)	−5.295(−3.136)***
stargazers_count (lags = 1)	−0.594(−3.100)	stargazers_count (lags = 1)	−4.965(−3.136)***
user_merged_count(lags = 1)	−2.465(−3.131)	user_merged_count(lags = 1)	−5.784(−3.136)***
watchers(lags = 1)	−2.740(−3.131)	watchers(lags = 1)	−4.968(−3.136)***

Table 5A.5 Johansen test for cointegration

System	Trace		Maximum eigenvalue	
	R = 0	R = 1	R = 0	R = 1
Market capitalization and liquidity (k = 1)	54.14(15.41) ***	5.84(3.76) ***	48.29(14.07) ***	5.84(3.76) ***
Market capitalization and developer activity (k = 1)	142.62(156.00)	93.81 (124.24)	48.81(51.42)	31.82(45.28)
Market capitalization and community strength (k = 1)	77.0134(94.15)	48.66(68.52)	28.35(39.37)	20.75(33.46)

5A.1.3.2 Granger causality test on developer activity and community strength system

Despite the results above, it doesn't mean that variables in developer activity and community strength system are meaningless. Since all the variables are stationary after taking first-order difference, Granger causality test can be adopted on the differenced data. And the result has been shown in Tables 5A.6 and 5A.7.

The results for Granger causality test are sensitive to the length of lags. Seen from the above tables, majority of the variables in these two systems do not show significant Granger causality to market cap, verifying the Johansen test that no cointegration relationship exists in the two systems.

Meanwhile, there are weak signals of causality between market capitalization and some variables, such as open_issue_count, forks_count, merged_count, user_merged_count, likes, and average_posts_delta_48_hours. For example, by including the first lag, open_issue_count Granger cause market capitalization at 95% confidence level.

5A.1.3.3 VECM for liquidity system

(a) VECM estimation: When the VECM is constructed, all coefficients of exogenous variables are insignificant. As a result, only the trading volume and market capitalization in the liquidity system are taken into account. The estimation results have been shown in Table 5A.8.

Based on the cointegrating equation, coefficient of total volume is significant. Long-term equilibrium relationship is as follows:

$$market\_cap\_usd = -4.00e + 10 + 41,184.45 \times total\_volume\_btc$$

As for short-term equilibrium relationship, if market capitalization goes up in the long run, it's supposed to revert to its previous level in the short run. That is to say, it will fall and trading volume will increase. Therefore, the coefficient for cointegration term in the equation, where D.total_volume_btc (first-order difference of total_volume_btc) is the dependent variable, should be positive and it should be negative in the equation whose dependent variable is D.market_cap_usd, both with absolute value between 0 and 1.

Table 5A.6 Developer system

	Lag = 1	Lag = 2	Lag = 3	Lag = 4	Lag = 5
(a) Market capitalization and open_issues_count					
H0: D.open_issues_count does not Granger cause D.market_cap_usd	Prob > chi2 = 0.0405 (**)	Prob > chi2 = 0.1482	Prob > chi2 = 0.2763	Prob > chi2 = 0.2184	Prob > chi2 = 0.1982
H0: D.market_cap_usd does not Granger cause D.open_issues_count	Prob > chi2 = 0.5620	Prob > chi2 = 0.6640	Prob > chi2 = 0.6777	Prob > chi2 = 0.2767	Prob > chi2 = 0.0921 (*)
(b) Market capitalization and closed_issues_count					
H0: D.market_cap_usd does not Granger cause D.closed_issues_count	Prob > chi2 = 0.1311	Prob > chi2 = 0.2135	Prob > chi2 = 0.3027	Prob > chi2 = 0.2309	Prob > chi2 = 0.1477
H0: D.closed_issues_count does not Granger cause D.market_cap_usd	Prob > chi2 = 0.4201	Prob > chi2 = 0.8307	Prob > chi2 = 0.8873	Prob > chi2 = 0.7658	Prob > chi2 = 0.5862
(c) Market capitalization and forks_count					
H0: D.forks_count does not Granger cause D.market_cap_usd	Prob > chi2 = 0.0400 (**)	Prob > chi2 = 0.1557	Prob > chi2 = 0.2370	Prob > chi2 = 0.3127	Prob > chi2 = 0.2348
H0: D.market_cap_usd does not Granger cause D.forks_count	Prob > chi2 = 0.3286	Prob > chi2 = 0.5062	Prob > chi2 = 0.5379	Prob > chi2 = 0.3372	Prob > chi2 = 0.0615 (*)
(d) Market capitalization and merged_count					
H0: D.merged_count does not Granger cause D.market_cap_usd	Prob > chi2 = 0.2974	Prob > chi2 = 0.5871	Prob > chi2 = 0.3343	Prob > chi2 = 0.0325 (**)	Prob > chi2 = 0.0159 (**)

Continued

Table 5A.6 Developer system—cont'd

	Lag = 1	Lag = 2	Lag = 3	Lag = 4	Lag = 5
H0: D.market_cap_usd does not Granger cause D.merged_count	Prob > chi2 = 0.7779	Prob > chi2 = 0.9155	Prob > chi2 = 0.6480	Prob > chi2 = 0.8068	Prob > chi2 = 0.7065
(e) Market capitalization and stargazers_count					
H0: D.stargazers_count does not Granger cause D.market_cap_usd	Prob > chi2 = 0.2169	Prob > chi2 = 0.2587	Prob > chi2 = 0.2754	Prob > chi2 = 0.3499	Prob > chi2 = 0.2713
H0: D.market_cap_usd does not Granger cause D.stargazers_count	Prob > chi2 = 0.2614	Prob > chi2 = 0.3642	Prob > chi2 = 0.4835	Prob > chi2 = 0.6246	Prob > chi2 = 0.7359
(f) Market capitalization and user_merged_count					
H0: D.user_merged_count does not Granger cause D.market_cap_usd	Prob > chi2 = 0.3348	Prob > chi2 = 0.2670	Prob > chi2 = 0.4833	Prob > chi2 = 0.3807	Prob > chi2 = 0.5445
H0: D.market_cap_usd does not Granger cause D.user_merged_count	Prob > chi2 = 0.5150	Prob > chi2 = 0.1546	Prob > chi2 = 0.0160 (**)	Prob > chi2 = 0.0092 (***)	Prob > chi2 = 0.0076 (***)
(g) Market capitalization and watchers					
H0: D.watchers does not Granger cause D.market_cap_usd	Prob > chi2 = 0.1626	Prob > chi2 = 0.2509	Prob > chi2 = 0.4036	Prob > chi2 = 0.3550	Prob > chi2 = 0.2118
H0: D.market_cap_usd does not Granger cause D.merged_count	Prob > chi2 = 0.7779	Prob > chi2 = 0.9155	Prob > chi2 = 0.6480	Prob > chi2 = 0.8068	Prob > chi2 = 0.7065

Table 5A.7 Market and community

	Lag = 1	Lag = 2	Lag = 3	Lag = 4	Lag = 5
(a) Market capitalization and average_accounts_active_48_hours					
H0: D.average_accounts_active_48_hours does not Granger cause D.market_cap_usd	Prob > chi2 = 0.3355	Prob > chi2 = 0.3143	Prob > chi2 = 0.1304	Prob > chi2 = 0.0884 (*)	Prob > chi2 = 0.2140
H0: D.market_cap_usd does not Granger cause D.average_accounts_active_48_hours	Prob > chi2 = 0.1318	Prob > chi2 = 0.2187	Prob > chi2 = 0.2142	Prob > chi2 = 0.0605 (*)	Prob > chi2 = 0.0958 (*)
(b) Market capitalization and average_comments_delta_48_hours					
H0: D.average_comments_delta_48_hours does not Granger cause D.market_cap_usd	Prob > chi2 = 0.1707	Prob > chi2 = 0.1416	Prob > chi2 = 0.2374	Prob > chi2 = 0.1815	Prob > chi2 = 0.3164
H0: D.market_cap_usd does not Granger cause D.average_comments_delta_48_hours	Prob > chi2 = 0.1179	Prob > chi2 = 0.4736	Prob > chi2 = 0.6894	Prob > chi2 = 0.6587	Prob > chi2 = 0.5552
(c) Market capitalization and followers_count					
H0: D.followers_count does not Granger cause D.market_cap_usd	Prob > chi2 = 0.1065	Prob > chi2 = 0.1930	Prob > chi2 = 0.2788	Prob > chi2 = 0.2481	Prob > chi2 = 0.2026
H0: D.market_cap_usd does not Granger cause D.followers_count	Prob > chi2 = 0.4645	Prob > chi2 = 0.5377	Prob > chi2 = 0.3237	Prob > chi2 = 0.2974	Prob > chi2 = 0.4940
(d) Market capitalization and likes					
H0: D.likes does not Granger cause D.market_cap_usd	Prob > chi2 = 0.7428	Prob > chi2 = 0.3788	Prob > chi2 = 0.1494	Prob > chi2 = 0.0707 (*)	Prob > chi2 = 0.0755 (*)
H0: D.market_cap_usd does not Granger cause D.likes	Prob > chi2 = 0.1892	Prob > chi2 = 0.0151 (**)	Prob > chi2 = 0.0362 (**)	Prob > chi2 = 0.0581 (*)	Prob > chi2 = 0.0123 (**)

Continued

Table 5A.7 Market and community—cont'd

	Lag = 1	Lag = 2	Lag = 3	Lag = 4	Lag = 5
(e) Market capitalization and average_posts_delta_48_hours					
H0: D.average_posts_delta_48_hours does not Granger cause D.market_cap_usd	Prob > chi2 = 0.3912	Prob > chi2 = 0.0211 (**)	Prob > chi2 = 0.0449 (**)	Prob > chi2 = 0.0771 (*)	Prob > chi2 = 0.1231
H0: D.market_cap_usd does not Granger cause D.average_posts_delta_48_hours	Prob > chi2 = 0.0544	Prob > chi2 = 0.1538	Prob > chi2 = 0.4075	Prob > chi2 = 0.4963	Prob > chi2 = 0.1922
(f) Market capitalization and subscribers					
H0: D.subscribers does not Granger cause D.market_cap_usd	Prob > chi2 = 0.8925	Prob > chi2 = 0.9993	Prob > chi2 = 0.9990	Prob > chi2 = 0.9891	Prob > chi2 = 0.9830
H0: D.market_cap_usd does not Granger cause D.subscribers	Prob > chi2 = 0.6798	Prob > chi2 = 0.7600	Prob > chi2 = 0.9080	Prob > chi2 = 0.8097	Prob > chi2 = 0.9019

Table 5A.8 Estimation results of vector error-correction model

```
Vector error-correction model

Sample:  3 - 68                              No. of obs   =        66
                                             AIC          =  70.56354
Log likelihood = -2319.597                   HQIC         =  70.68152
Det(Sigma_ml)  =  1.15e+28                   SBIC         =  70.86213
```

Equation	Parms	RMSE	R-sq	chi2	P>chi2
D_market_cap_usd	4	2.2e+08	0.0373	2.40253	0.6622
D_total_volume~c	4	527342	0.5141	65.60776	0.0000

	Coef.	SE	z	P>|z|	[95% Conf. Interval]	
D_market_c~d						
_ce1						
L1.	.0009065	.0018153	0.50	0.618	-.0026514	.0044643
market_cap~d						
LD.	-.0475373	.1268897	-0.37	0.708	-.2962366	.201162
total_volu~c						
LD.	24.07258	52.18154	0.46	0.645	-78.20136	126.3465
_cons	31552.17	8.35e+07	0.00	1.000	-1.64e+08	1.64e+08
D_total_vo~c						
_ce1						
L1.	.0000256	4.41e-06	5.81	0.000	.000017	.0000343
market_cap~d						
LD.	-.0001142	.0003085	-0.37	0.711	-.000719	.0004905
total_volu~c						
LD.	.0287368	.1268801	0.23	0.821	-.2199436	.2774172
_cons	-1115149	203052.4	-5.49	0.000	-1513124	-717173.1

```
Cointegrating equations
```

Equation	Parms	chi2	P>chi2
_ce1	1	34.4655	0.0000

```
Identification:  beta is exactly identified

                  Johansen normalization restriction imposed
```

beta	Coef.	SE	z	P>|z|	[95% Conf. Interval]	
_ce1						
market_cap~d	1	.	.	.	.	.
total_volu~c	-41184.45	7015.215	-5.87	0.000	-54934.02	-27434.88
_cons	4.00e+10	.	.	.	.	.

According to the integration equation of the liquidity system, the coefficient for error-correction term is positive, which is not consistent with our expectation. What's more, *t*-test indicates that the coefficient is insignificant, implying no short-term equilibrium relationship. Therefore, in the long run, trading volume does not Granger cause market capitalization.

On the other hand, based on integration equation of trading volume, with significant *t*-statistics, the coefficient is positive and lies between 0 and 1. Consequently, market capitalization is Granger causality for trading volume in the long run.

In the short run, there is no causality effect between market capitalization and trading volume since all the coefficients of the lag term are insignificant. We can also reach this conclusion from IRF plots shown in the following figures. Graph about Response of total_volume_btc to market_cap_usd shows that one standard deviation shock in the market capitalization has few effects on the total_volume_btc—no significant shock was observed in the IFM.

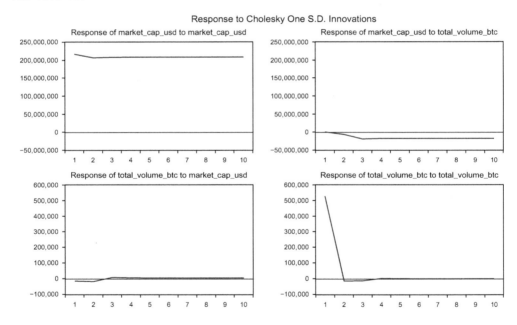

(b) *Diagnostic test*: By doing residual test, we find that the residual series follows white noise process, seen in the following table. Hence, the long-run effect from market capitalization to trading volume has some merits.

```
Portmanteau test for white noise

Portmanteau (Q) statistic =      29.4953
Prob > chi2(31)            =       0.5435
```

So far, the cointegration for the liquidity system has been well identified—First, Johansen tests indicate that there exists a cointegration relationship in the liquidity system. After that, we find this unique cointegration system by constructing VECM based on optimal lags. Finally, the white noise test on residual series suggests that the model is well established.

However, constructing VECM on 2 months' data may fall into data mining issue. We can only say that the result is shown as above by using current dataset. Under such circumstances, we also provide VECM stability test as supplementary information in the following figures.

Eigenvalue stability condition

Eigenvalue	Modulus
1	1
-.05818182 + .1716413i	.181234
-.05818182 - .1716413i	.181234
.04213935	.042139

The VECM specification imposes a unit modulus.

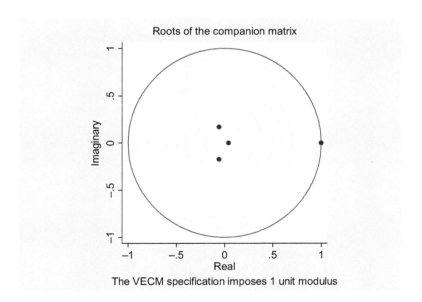

Roots of the companion matrix

The VECM specification imposes 1 unit modulus

The table shows that the eigenvalues of the companion matrix and their associated moduli. One of the roots is 1. The table footer suggests that the specified VECM imposes 1 unit modulus on the companion matrix, indicating that there is a real root at about 0.95.

Although there is no distribution theory to measure how close this root is to one, per other discussions in the literature (for example, Johansen, 1995; 137-138), we conclude that the root of 0.95 may indicate that predicted cointegrating equation is probably not stationary.

What's more, the graph plots the eigenvalues of the companion matrix with the real component on the x-axis and the imaginary component on the y-axis. Although the information is the same as in the table, the graph shows visually how close the root with modulus 0.95 is to the unit circle.

Both stability testing results indicate that the model is not stable, which is consistent with our expectation that the model may suffer from data mining issue. So we have to take other information into account to avoid any erroneous conclusion rather than taking the cointegration relationship for granted. More follow-up research is recommended.

5A.2 CROSS-SECTIONAL DATA ANALYSIS ON ALTCOINS: LINEAR AND QUANTILE REGRESSION

5A.2.1 Data

A cross-section sample of cryptocurrency from CoinGecko database collected on July 14, 2014 is used in this study. Face_book_likes data is excluded due to multiple missing values. The overall sample consists of a total of 61 cryptocurrencies and a total of 793 observations.

The variables used here are exactly the same as those in time series analysis except for the average_commits, which means the number of times the source code has been updated. A higher commit count indicates that there is more development activity going in the repository. In addition, we have excluded the closed_issues_count due to multiple missing values (Tables 5A.9 and 5A.10).

The summary statistics suggest that the correlation between market capitalization and market price is approximately 1. Almost all independent variables have positive correlation to both market capitalization and market price. The open_issues_count is usually regarded as a negative signal to market capitalization or market price since it reflects the potential risk of investing in cryptocurrency. However, in the initial period after the coin creation, this variable may reflect the participants' passion (i.e., the more popular the cryptocurrency is, the higher the issues that will be found at developing period) as other variables do.

5A.2.2 Methodology

5A.2.2.1 Linear regression

In statistics, linear regression is an approach for modeling the relationship between a scalar-dependent variable y and one or more explanatory variables denoted as X. The case of one explanatory variable is called simple linear regression. For more than one

Table 5A.9 Summary statistics

Variables		n	Mean	SD	Median	Trimmed	MAD
market_cap_usd	1	61	1,407,52292.947	1,032,608,541.849	623,897.49	2,618,082.218	888,262.045
price_usd	2	61	11.064	79.435	0.02	0.237	0.03
total_volume_btc	3	61	455.303	2480.148	3.933	26.05	5.721
stargazers_count	4	61	170.033	733.604	13	30.755	16.309
watchers	5	61	41.033	105.871	9	17.898	8.896
forks_count	6	61	105.656	517.023	14	19.49	16.309
open_issues_count	7	61	14.902	51.969	2	4	2.965
merged_pull_requests	8	61	45.459	262.352	4	6.265	5.93
user_merge_count	9	61	8.443	27.329	3	3.878	2.965
average_commits	10	61	4.656	12.599	0	1.531	0
subscribers	11	61	4889.885	19,994.383	272	597.878	308.381
average_account_active_48_hours	12	61	19.18	85.655	2	3.224	0
average_posts_delta_48_hours	13	61	0.16	0.46	0	0.045	0
average_comments_delta_48_hours	14	61	8.725	38.482	0.021	0.548	0.031
followers_count	15	61	7410.918	23,158.258	1630	2021.51	1742.055

	Min.	Max.	Range	Skew	Kurtosis	SE
market_cap_usd	1.379	8,069,228,567	8,069,228,565.621	7.418	53.976	132,211,975.89
price_usd	0	620.867	620.867	7.414	53.936	10.171
total_volume_btc	0.004	18,305.641	18,305.637	6.379	41.683	317.55
stargazers_count	0	5591	5591	6.658	45.934	93.928
watchers	1	764	763	5.443	33.079	13.555
forks_count	0	3999	3999	7.022	49.742	66.198
open_issues_count	0	383	383	6	38.626	6.654
merged_pull_requests	0	2049	2049	7.301	52.763	33.591
user_merge_count	1	211	210	6.738	46.59	3.499
average_commits	0	74	74	3.966	16.652	1.613
subscribers	14	129,319	129,305	5.131	26.466	2560.018
average_account_active_48_hours	2	628	626	6.21	39.737	10.967
average_posts_delta_48_hours	0	2.479	2.479	4.064	16.646	0.059
average_comments_delta_48_hours	0	265.521	265.521	5.511	31.62	4.927
followers_count	0	164,208	164,208	5.383	32.045	2965.111

Table 5A.10 Correlation matrix

	market_cap_usd	price_usd	total_volume_btc	stargazers_count	watchers	forks_count	open_issues_count
market_cap_usd	1	0.999	0.948	0.967	0.898	0.985	0.924
price_usd	0.999	1	0.941	0.963	0.893	0.982	0.927
total_volume_btc	0.948	0.941	1	0.958	0.929	0.976	0.874
stargazers_count	0.967	0.963	0.958	1	0.973	0.992	0.953
watchers	0.898	0.893	0.929	0.973	1	0.947	0.932
forks_count	0.985	0.982	0.976	0.992	0.947	1	0.933
open_issues_count	0.924	0.927	0.874	0.953	0.932	0.933	1
merged_pull_requests	0.994	0.994	0.934	0.977	0.912	0.986	0.941
user_merge_count	0.967	0.967	0.921	0.981	0.933	0.979	0.942
average_commits	0.716	0.715	0.664	0.747	0.782	0.726	0.705
subscribers	0.815	0.81	0.804	0.889	0.871	0.869	0.8
average_account_active_48_hours	0.927	0.925	0.887	0.957	0.909	0.952	0.886
average_posts_delta_48_hours	0.634	0.627	0.655	0.74	0.764	0.711	0.633
average_comments_delta_48_hours	0.439	0.435	0.425	0.565	0.575	0.519	0.478
followers_count	0.288	0.284	0.29	0.428	0.457	0.376	0.343

	merged_pull_requests	user_merge_count	average_commits	subscribers	average_account_active_48_hours	average_posts_delta_48_hours	average_comments_delta_48_hours	followers_count
market_cap_usd	0.994	0.967	0.716	0.815	0.927	0.634	0.439	0.288
price_usd	0.994	0.967	0.715	0.81	0.925	0.627	0.435	0.284
total_volume_btc	0.934	0.921	0.664	0.804	0.887	0.655	0.425	0.29
stargazers_count	0.977	0.981	0.747	0.889	0.957	0.74	0.565	0.428
watchers	0.912	0.933	0.782	0.871	0.909	0.764	0.575	0.457
forks_count	0.986	0.979	0.726	0.869	0.952	0.711	0.519	0.376
open_issues_count	0.941	0.942	0.705	0.8	0.886	0.633	0.478	0.343
merged_pull_requests	1	0.987	0.734	0.859	0.955	0.686	0.516	0.366
user_merge_count	0.987	1	0.746	0.917	0.981	0.771	0.625	0.482
average_commits	0.734	0.746	1	0.747	0.751	0.728	0.563	0.448
subscribers	0.859	0.917	0.747	1	0.969	0.947	0.872	0.761
average_account_active_48_hours	0.955	0.981	0.751	0.969	1	0.859	0.741	0.608
average_posts_delta_48_hours	0.686	0.771	0.728	0.947	0.859	1	0.932	0.854
average_comments_delta_48_hours	0.516	0.625	0.563	0.872	0.741	0.932	1	0.946
followers_count	0.366	0.482	0.448	0.761	0.608	0.854	0.946	1

explanatory variable, the process is called multiple linear regression. The model takes the form

$$y_i = \beta_1 x_{i1} + \ldots + \beta_p x_{ip} + \varepsilon_i = X_i^T \beta + \varepsilon_i, \ i = 1, \ldots, n$$

where y_i is called the endogenous variable, $x_{i1}, x_{i2}, \ldots, x_{ip}$ are called exogenous variables and β is a p-dimensional parameter vector. Its elements are also called regression coefficients, which stand for the partial derivatives of the dependent variable with respect to the various independent variables. ε is called the error term. This variable captures all other factors that influence the dependent variable y_i other than the regressors x_i.

5A.2.2.2 Quantile regression

As we know, quantile regression is a type of regression analysis used in statistics and econometrics. Whereas the method of least squares results in estimates that approximate the conditional mean of the response variable given certain values of the predictor variables, quantile regression aims at estimating either the conditional median or other quantiles of the response variable. Consider the τth conditional quantile function

$$Q_{(Y|X)}(\tau) = X\beta_\tau$$

where Y is a $N \times 1$, X is $N \times k$ matrix, and β_τ is $k \times 1$ vector.

Given the distribution function of Y, β_τ can be obtained by solving

$$\beta_\tau = \arg \min_\beta E(\rho_\tau(Y - X\beta))$$

Solving the sample analogue gives the estimator of β.

$$\hat{\beta}_\tau = \arg \min_\beta \sum_{i=1}^{N} (\rho_\tau(y_i - x_i\beta))$$

where y_i is the ith element of Y, x_i is the ith row of X, $\rho_\tau(u) = u(\tau - I(u < 0))$, I is the indicator function, and τ is between 0 and 1.

5A.2.3 Linear regression estimation

Due to high correlation among the variables, subsets are chosen from these variables by running a regression of y (dependent variable) on a constant and all independent variables listed above. Regressors are retained if they have a t-statistic greater than 2.575. Results are given in Table 5A.11.

Results in the table show that merged_pull_requests, subscribers, and average_account_active_48_hours have a positive effect on the market capitalization. Moreover, user_merge_count and average_comments_delta_48_hours have a negative effect on the market capitalization.

Table 5A.11 Estimation results of linear regression model

	Estimate	SE	t-value	Pr(> |t|)
Model 1: Dependent variable: market_cap_usd				
merged_pull_requests	3,170,035.06	196,414.01	16.14	0
user_merge_count	−11,678,119.14	982,009.27	−11.89	0
subscribers	12,929.31	2182.26	5.92	0
average_account_active_48_hours	5,892,077.58	844,230.02	6.98	0
average_comments_delta_48_hours	−9,736,504.61	584,760.76	−16.65	0
Model 2: Dependent variable: price_usd				
stargazers_count	−0.04	0.01	−5.38	0
watchers	0.08	0.02	3.46	0
merged_pull_requests	0.32	0.02	16.26	0
user_merge_count	−0.73	0.12	−5.89	0
subscribers	0	0	3.66	0
average_account_active_48_hours	0.34	0.09	4.01	0
average_comments_delta_48_hours	−0.67	0.06	−10.27	0

Table 5A.12 Diagnostic tests

Diagnostic tests	Model 1 log(TNT)	Model 2 log(TNL)
Misspecification test: Ramsey RESET	$F(1,55) = 254.57[0.00]^{**}$	$F(1,53) = 17.37[.00]$
Normality test: Jarque-Bera test	Jarque-Bera $= 85.86$ $[.00]^{**}$	Jarque_Bera $= 128.56$ $[0.00]^{**}$
Heteroskedasticity test: Breusch-Pagan-Godfrey test	$CHSQ(5) = 15.15[0.01]^{*}$	$CHSQ(7) = 23.67[0.00]^{**}$
Normality test: Jarque-Bera test	$F(5,55) = 3.64[0.01]^{*}$	$F(7,53) = 4.80[0.00]^{**}$

For price_usd, it is negatively affected by stargazers_count, user_merge_count, and average_comments_delta_48_hours. watchers, merged_pull_requests, subscribers, and average_account_active_48_hours have a positive impact on it.

Among them, merged_pull_requests, user_merge_count, average_account_active_48_hours, and average_comments_delta_48_hours are usually statistically significant. As a result, these variables play an important role in determining the price and market capitalization for the Bitcoin (Table 5A.12).

The null hypothesis of Ramsey RESET test is rejected, so the model suffers from misspecification. JB test shows that the residual series is not normally distributed. Also, the heteroskedasticity test tells us that estimated variance of the residuals is dependent on the values of the independent variables.

5A.2.4 Quantile regression estimation

In order to know more about the potential relationship among the variables, a quantile regression is constructed to look at the different quantiles of the estimated results. The following graphs show the estimates of the 13 control variables in each of the 19 quantiles from 0.05 to 0.95 with an increment of 0.05 per quantile. Corresponding estimation results have been reported below.

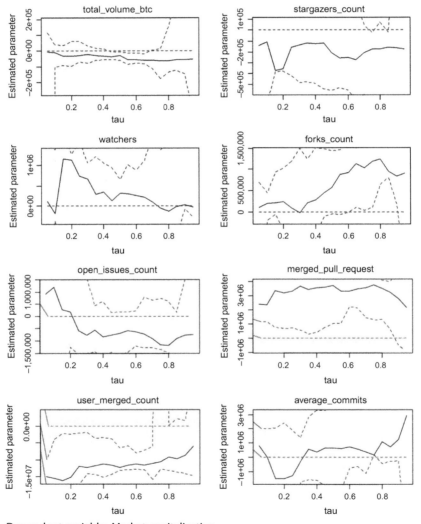

Model 1 Dependent variable: Market capitalization

Continued

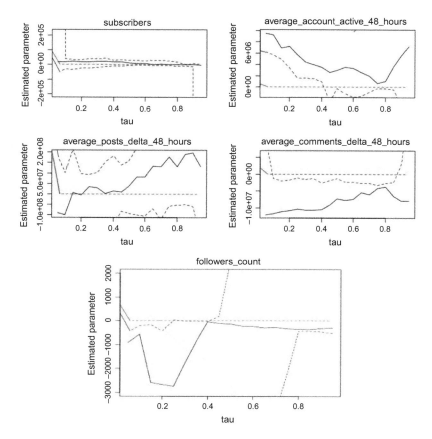

Model 1—Cont'd

Before looking into the graphs, we define the key factors as variables whose coefficients are significant in more than 50% of total quantiles. We also define the weak factors as variables whose coefficients are significant in more than 20% but less than 50% of total quantiles. Those variables, whose coefficients are significant in less than 20% but more than 5%, are defined as semi-weak variables. The rest variables are simply treated as noise information.

As a result, we can summarize the graphs in Table 5A.13.

First, the quantile-varying estimates of the coefficient of watchers, open_issues_count, subscribers, and average_posts_delta_48_hours are insignificant for all the 19 quantiles in Model 1 (i.e., from 0.05 to 0.95). This indicates that no systematic pattern exists for the quantile-varying estimates of these variables. For those key factors, the coefficients remain relatively consistent across the quantiles, for instance, merged_pull_requests has a significant positive effect on the market capitalization across the quantiles and user_merged_count has a negative effect below 0.65 quantiles.

As for the second model, exactly the same key factors as Model 1 are selected. However, weak factors and noise information in the two models differ. For example, weak

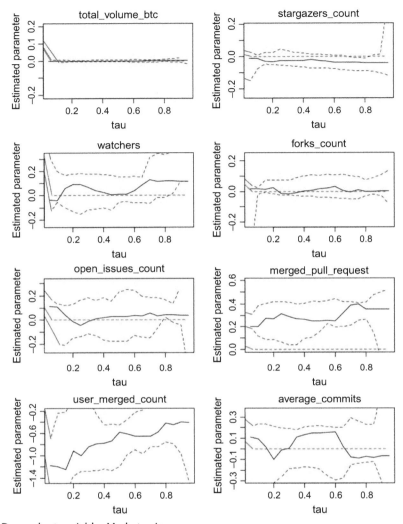

Model 2 Dependent variable: Market price

Continued

factors, such as total_volume_btc, followers_count and forks_counts, in market capitalization become noise information in market price. Furthermore, watchers is the only semi-weak factor in market price.

KEY FACTORS' ANALYSIS

Here, by constructing the quantile regression on the key factors, we get the estimation results as follows:

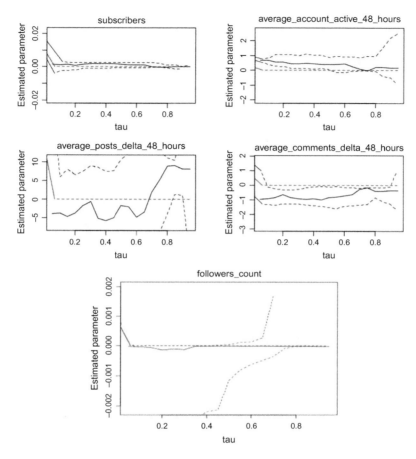

Model 2—Cont'd

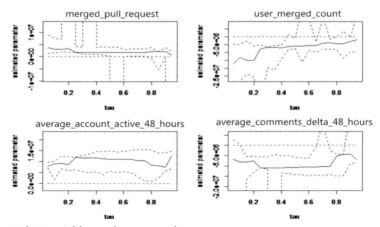

Model 1 Dependent variable: market_cap_usd

Table 5A.13 Classification of variables

Model 1	Model 2
Dependent variable	
market_cap_usd	price_usd
Key factors	
merged_pull_requests	merged_pull_requests
user_merge_count	user_merge_count
average_account_active_48_hours	average_account_active_48_hours
average_comments_delta_48_hours	average_comments_delta_48_hours
Weak factors	
total_volume_btc	watchers
forks_count	
followers_count	
Semi-weak factors	
stargazers_count	stargazers_count
average_commits	open_issues_count
	average_posts_delta_48_hours
Noise information	
watchers	trading volume
open_issues_count	forks_count
subscribers	average_commits
average_posts_delta_48_hours	subscribers
	followers_count

The figures plot the estimates of the four control variables in each of the 19 quantiles from 0.05 to 0.95 with an increment of 0.05 per quantile.

To some extent, the estimates of the coefficients of merged_pull_requests from the QR model show that the merged request has a significantly positive effect on the market capitalization in the lower quantiles (0.05-0.50). This relation becomes insignificant in higher quantiles (0.50-0.95). In addition, the coefficient is relatively consistent across the quantiles and the curve is flatter than that of other variables in model 1.

As for the user_merge_count, it has an overall upward trend in model 1. Similar to that of merged_pull_requests, the estimates of user_merge_count is significant in lower quantiles but becomes insignificant at higher quantiles. And this variable has a negative effect on the market capitalization.

In comparison to other variables, estimates for average_account_active_48_hours are much better since it is quite significant across the quantiles and have a positive effect on the market capitalization. This is a unique variable which is significant at any quantile.

For the average_comments_delta_48_hours, the estimate is not significant at 0.05 but becomes significant at the middle range quantiles (i.e., the 0.10-0.65 quantiles) in model 1. It shows a negative relationship between average_comments_delta_48_hours and market capitalization.

Compared to that of Model 1, the plot for the estimates of merged_pull_requests shows that this variable has a significant effect across the quantiles except for the upper 20% quantiles (0.80-0.95) in model 2.

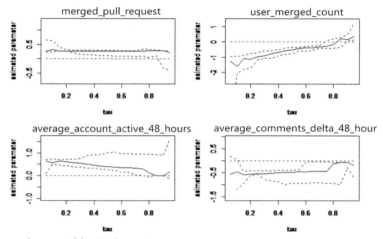

Model 2 Dependent variable: Market price

In model 2, in terms of the user_merge_count, it needs extra explanation. The estimate has an overall upward trend. And we find that the user_merge_count has a significant negative effect on market price from 0.05 to the 0.70 quantiles. However, the effect becomes significantly positive at the 0.90 and 0.95 quantiles. Such a trend indicates that this variable has more distinct effects on the higher market price quantiles than other market price quantiles.

Similar to merged_pull_requests, the estimates for average_account_active_48_hours are significantly positive from 0.05 to the 0.75 quantiles in model 2. However, it falls into insignificant level in the high quantiles, meaning that cryptocurrency with higher market capitalization quantiles will be less influenced by users online.

For average_comments_delta_48_hours, the estimates are significant across the quantiles except for the lower quantiles (i.e., 0.05 and 0.10 quantiles) in model 2. Overall, this variable has a negative effect on market price. And the effect decreases when approaching to higher quantiles (i.e., almost 0 in 0.90 and 0.95 quantiles).

To sum up, all the four key factors have significant effects on both market_cap_usd and price_usd, confirming the previous quantile regression analyses.

5A.3 CONCLUSION AND ISSUES

To show the evaluation process, two samples are taken. For the time series data, all data are of the same order of integration, $I(1)$. Then the Johansen test is applied to find the cointegration relationship among the three systems (liquidity, developer activity, and community strength).

Results show that there is a long-run equilibrium between market capitalization and total trading volume. Later, the VECM is constructed for the liquidity system and the model indicates that market capitalization is the Granger causality to the trading volume in the long run, but not vice versa. However, there doesn't exit short-run effect between these two variables. For the remaining two systems (developer activity system and community strength system), Johansen tests show that there are no cointegration equations. However, since variables in these two systems are all stationary at $I(1)$, we did Granger causality test on the differenced data one by one. The result suggests that some of them, such as open_issues_count, forks_count, merged_count, user_merged_count, likes, and average_posts_delta_48_hours, send weak signals of causality to market capitalization. All the other variables have no significant effects.

For the cross-sectional data, by constructing linear and quantile regression based on the threshold criteria, four key factors are found, merged_pull_requests, user_merge_count, average_account_active_48_hours, and average_comments_delta_48_hours, whose estimation results are quite significant and relatively consistent across the quantiles under both two models.

To some extent, merged_pull_requests and average_account_active_48_hours have significant positive effect on both market capitalization and market price. Besides, user_ merge_count and average_comments_delta_48_hours have a negative effect on market_cap_usd and price_usd.

What's more, we noted that the signs of the estimated coefficient were not always consistent with those of correlations. The probable explanation is that the high correlation among the control variables will result in multicollinearity. Under such circumstances, the real effect of a certain variable will be assimilated by other variables in a way.

Also, there are some potential issues with our analyses.

To begin with, the data used for the time series analysis is not mature enough. Especially for average_accounts_active_48_hours, average_posts_delta_48_hours, average_ comments_delta_48_hours, and user_merged_count, comparing to market capitalization and price, they may be too immature to be included in the model. Some of them can only date back to this May. There is a doubt that the real pattern hasn't been well established yet, meaning that these variables cannot reflect the real trend well and are sensitive to the time period we selected at the moment. In addition, the whole period collected for time series analyses is only 2 months, too short to ensure the reliability of the results.

Meanwhile, cross-sectional data suffers from a similar issue as a majority of cryptocurrencies don't possess such information yet. We have to set those variables to 0, such as average_ posts_delta_48_hours, average_comments_delta_48_hours, and average_commits.

However, it doesn't mean that these variables are meaningless. These variables reflect the passion of investors. Up till now, the investors' attention has been focused on certain cryptocurrencies, such as Bitcoin, and Dogecoin. That's why majority of the cryptocurrencies have the values of 0. Nevertheless, this situation will change in the future. As we know, decentralizing is the trend for cryptocurrency market. Accompanied by development of the market, more and more investors will be attracted to those emerging cryptocurrencies. As a result, it is likely that those variables will become increasingly vibrant and more and more important in analyzing the cryptocurrency market.

To sum up, follow-up research is required to get a better understanding of the real effect of those variables.

APPENDIX

Model 1 Dependent variable: market_cap_usd

	total_volume_btc	Lower Bd	Upper Bd	stargazers_count	Lower Bd	Upper Bd	watchers	Lower Bd	Upper Bd	forks_count
0.05	−8080.961	−1.797693134862232e+308	113,725.294	−142,968.955	−3,561,554.69	493,657.995	119,126.624	−1,972,959.277	1,630,208.156	106,168.557
0.1	−10,556.059	−100,762.314	40,578.252	−107,272.907	−674,078.608	235,135.941	−18,2782.314	−359,633.934	1,394,585.918	205,063.395
0.15	−31,628.614	−94,995.269	36,620.612	−369,247.123	−380,382.934	343,532.983	1,162,101.96	−1,598,128.925	1,826,587.451	219,666.811
0.2	−32,045.399	−95,679.802	61,947.579	−354159.676	−377,524.962	398,756.628	1,132,961.07	−1,644,545.559	1,275,905.512	249,635.433
0.25	−30,600.301	−71,691.358	62,881.964	−156,651.203	−418,491.512	469,503.764	741,514.185	−1,908,288.484	1,605,861.808	91,524.526
0.3	−22,012.761	−76,526.551	30,287.302	−132,313.506	−482,487.836	454,962.065	673,852.611	−1,998,871.838	1,054,592.824	−16,685.968
0.35	−29,673.013	−61,130.141	18,226.733	−117,436.123	−474,000.577	348,559.219	292,415.1	−1,910,972.865	1,225,410.654	213,476.371
0.4	−34,094.349	−55,482.374	14,069.144	−125,197.668	−490,624.932	392,612.395	350,389.854	−1,892,321.513	1,063,448.299	282,038.633
0.45	−36,478.394	−54,661.439	−7486.579	−118,685.181	−542,707.74	362,520.37	137,362.508	−1,831,736.269	940,081.925	452,128.679
0.5	−29,557.987	−61,044.074	−7302.198	−203,879.516	−551,769.512	415,530.483	322,348.294	−1,741,715.124	659,922.441	573,470.68
0.55	−54,708.433	−87,023.223	−14,190.01	−256,041.347	−531,912.311	384,964.088	301,032.448	−1,810,473.372	1,018,109.227	884,390.26
0.6	−55,150.017	−78,538.49	−13,367.133	−249,365.214	−551,851.465	403,089.647	257,512.5	−1,600,014.507	884,873.415	921,788.103
0.65	−58,104.087	−83,756.276	−17,851.781	−273,686.911	−652,162.049	306,873.948	213,469.819	−1,001,791.756	1,114,116.187	1,122,925.388
0.7	−59,410.668	−113,655.785	5970.19	−205,596.823	−592,559.912	46,134.719	102,566.255	−680,134.138	1,776,515.423	1,028,005.292
0.75	−63,486.968	−178,212.746	11,747.789	−17,3009.178	−1,019,221.131	−25,577.337	−57,992.321	−649,141.324	1,399,403.551	1,180,284.287
0.8	−61,258.996	−133,819.188	157,638.57	−175,536.982	−885,189.328	76,204.037	−130,748.682	−633,149.35	1,620,984.807	1,240,785.264
0.85	−56,520.385	−122,585.291	363,749.817	−158,287.127	−785,628.424	−20,657.309	−15,649.93	−797,556.607	1,965,564.294	946,625.862
0.9	−53,932.065	−146,324.636	441,968.595	−159,997.995	−1.797693134862232e+308	110,7073.002	31,523.837	−73,653.829	3,607,653.41	838,875.425
0.95	−50,879.67	−391,551.946	1.797693134862232e+308	−173,507.882	−1,052,994.535	3,294,147.865	−29,200.922	−281,144.89	10,756,078.034	899,143.528

Continued

Model 1 Dependent variable: market_cap_usd—cont'd

	Lower Bd	Upper Bd	open_issues_count Upper Bd	open_issues_count Lower Bd	Upper Bd	Lower Bd	merged_pull_requests Upper Bd	merged_pull_requests Lower Bd	user_merge_count Upper Bd	user_merge_count Lower Bd
0.05	−1,668,410.242	698,574.036	936,417.768	−1.79769313486232e+308	2,534,297.526	1,163,222.597	1.79769313486232e+308	2,415,796.335	−15,041,555.403	−57,886,808.782
0.1	−191,222.524	455,308.907	1,196,742.904	−2,715,397.99	1,639,301.491	1,153,550.757	4,772,945.943	2,377,666.976	−15,626,963.492	−27,518,798.273
0.15	−51,995.132	938,391.456	282,735.961	−2,593,349.266	1,550,771.289	776,618.532	4,721,113.669	3,361,747.8	−16,274,477.021	−28,434,347.043
0.2	−404,112.454	1,020,413.433	181,704.725	−1,261,860.899	1,527,925.398	681,972.87	4,421,403.587	3,202,222.896	−15,195,341.403	−18,385,177.525
0.25	−404,631.848	1,182,163.223	−573,131.877	−1,553,427.293	3,785,012.44	715,201.865	4,177,458.602	3,311,724.718	−11,902,336.826	−17,455,200.052
0.3	−484,267.753	1,501,311.441	−772,556.333	−1,504,556.661	1,586,690.308	578,343.041	4,313,320.565	3,675,652.063	−12,246,733.402	−14,092,062.59
0.35	−612,409.732	1,231,623.889	−561,658.148	−1,429,227.912	443,565.202	265,990.113	4,266,241.88	3,442,508.358	−11,812,212.039	−14,293,314.173
0.4	−505,959.932	1,512,468.883	−832,614.103	−1,675,027.986	623,514.645	407,374.169	4,302,928.11	3,553,786.746	−11,263,287.453	−15,184,739.849
0.45	−94,391.681	1,490,004.822	−766,252.308	−1,472,511.128	149,622.219	766,970.677	4,559,507.841	3,610,036.101	−11,543,972.471	−14,291,900.295
0.5	−41,622.925	1,448,409.273	−688,527.435	−1,567,297.497	183,549.818	1,025,503.087	4,336,036.02	3,724,790.394	−12,342,701.286	−13,064,097.267
0.55	−57,440.253	1,453,900.38	−584,393.003	−1,467,055.3	184,149.915	1,036,810.922	4,396,834.659	3,323,589.686	−11,631,832.066	−12,913,645.085
0.6	−7638.693	1,590,913.918	−639,692.26	−1,201,404.235	229,369.97	2,255,127.585	4,661,709.763	3,324,070.45	−11,336,432.402	−12,877,256.673
0.65	112,663.044	1,497,474.2	−715,089.674	−1,267,467.092	794,984.042	2,128,816.609	4,443,598.24	3,483,561.242	−11,523,139.231	−13,059,777.227
0.7	35,691.219	2,120,156.781	−911,075.447	−1,273,031.715	663,841.059	1,434,805.576	4,500,461.182	3,571,781.467	−11,021,012.096	−15,936,530.461
0.75	109,507.149	2,099,423.02	−1,172,592.37	−1,356,936.089	739,927.78	1,304,920.85	4,940,928.421	3,782,967.428	−10,559,993.608	−12,843,681.137
0.8	645,980.582	2,323,171.673	−1,191,275.06	−1,481,448.709	613,465.386	1,306,146.865	4,085,639.727	3,524,216.226	−9,287,627.061	−13,232,927.425
0.85	812,368.48	2,416,432.553	−912,410.418	−1,751,272.093	157,185.533	601,718.832	3,997,207.959	3,238,080.604	−9,698,271.668	−13,630,681.662
0.9	170,352.73	2,461,797.785	−771,696.688	−1,524,608.011	1,464,186.812	−457,811.82	5,007,184.462	2,818,460.392	−8,649,347.026	−14,229,165.528
0.95	−1,268,108.35	7,437,946.062	−741,910.533	−1,868,050.605	1.79769313486232e+308	−950,837.321	6,053,376.841	2,165,839.09	−5,875,308.633	−14,896,537.204

	Upper Bd	average_commits Lower Bd	average_commits Upper Bd	Upper Bd	subscribers Upper Bd	subscribers Lower Bd	Upper Bd	Lower Bd	average_account_active_48_hours Lower Bd	average_account_active_48_hours Upper Bd
0.05	−10,649,976.315	−1.79769313486232e+308	824,975.09	2,028,149.506	17,615.151	−59,772.004	1.79769313486232e+308	9,512,170.736	6,233,805.88	10,308,454.441
0.1	−3,906,263.504	−14,404,297.915	19,636.916	2,016,735.658	17,355.381	−31,396.754	39,769.374	9,252,150.121	5,774,348.348	10,524,247.376
0.15	−2,201,909.144	−6,054,576.139	−1,464,195.215	2,050,829.82	21,983.34	−34,063.912	33,067.687	6,884,278.233	4,947,032.385	13,642,593.182
0.2	−2,285,582.109	−5,754,257.926	−1,490,857.694	2,427,826.865	19,886.196	−23,370.105	32,875.015	7,236,610.383	3,407,727.856	13,881,482.227
0.25	−2,021,471.043	−3,856,223.348	−1,257,852.002	1,910,520.216	19,515.519	−22,198.752	41,321.605	5,733,737.075	1,569,357.794	15,299,999.356
0.3	−1,858,172.748	−1,717,281.649	−249,815.222	1,381,448.44	22,097.501	−19,106.936	40,041.254	4,431,684.346	1,563,963.385	14,381,497.59
0.35	−3,543,397.255	−1,566,258.469	577,974.933	2,811,806.479	21,513.705	−13,073.122	42,286.308	4,023,813.06	1,540,042.781	16,239,807.538
0.4	−3,309,439.478	−1,583,295.043	367,605.355	3,305,321.524	19,990.719	−9306.489	30,963.792	3,525,869.726	1,003,513.943	15,890,719.746
0.45	−3,706,296.416	−2,012,859.203	642,363.847	3,288,503.501	18,306.12	−8706.507	31,974.158	2,629,142.571	−2,505,172.409	14,352,174.299
0.5	−6,495,883.744	−2,045,005.195	670,908.857	3,514,411.66	11,033.693	−6224.545	29,225.491	3,023,240.503	−244,212.018	11,985,173.588
0.55	−5,802,934.461	−2,228,833.457	617,562.586	3,604,698.192	9285.098	−3298.318	28,557.667	3,574,962.046	−1,160,077.989	11,663,577.517
0.6	−7,925,078.224	−740,003.882	722,829.332	3,471,187.836	8262.356	−3304.589	27,458.813	3,380,839.775	−1,713,878.736	9,682,325.365
0.65	−7,075,209.522	−635,858.188	559,407.287	4,174,580.568	2413.402	−6471.859	28,155.62	2,659,390.493	−1,568,022.422	11,340,865.512
0.7	−5,883,156.474	−1,120,626.179	360,546.349	5,147,999.997	5518.651	−6452.251	29,373.684	1,997,314.373	−852,476.561	10,629,260.726
0.75	291,816,260.976	157,752.881	164,003.204	5,964,457.056	1398.08	−6780.937	26,608.416	675,769.504	−232,131.883	10,487,513.024
0.8	230,101,367	−434,866.911	1,082,896.554	6,457,668.203	−350.225	−7900.774	19,025.902	1,094,821.064	−198,624.216	14,145,770.742
0.85	2,272,596.064	−249,170.517	742,851.147	8,462,147.021	838.601	−9859.77	2958.656	3,605,624.135	−410,937.762	17,294,975.877
0.9	1,808,643.935	−215,682.984	1,250,655.082	9,393,720.595	−188.973	−12,764.64	7469.247	5,538,255.818	−3,222,534.068	17,596,771.243
0.95	15,370,600.889	−6,024,974.863	2,937,895.438	1.79769313486232e+308	−3762.842	−1.79769313486232e+308	5732.411	7,234,935.67	−8,463,817.182	19,103,748.302

	average_posts_delta_48_hours	Lower Bd	Upper Bd	average_comments_delta_48_hours	Lower Bd	Upper Bd	followers_count	Lower Bd	Upper Bd
0.05	−89,733,464.342	−1.7976931348623232e+308	185,931,775	−12,069,138.262	−17,738,087.493	10,146,563	−916.618	−1.7976931348623232e+308	−471.32
0.1	−99,726,312.053	−530,200,492.606	100,093,084	−11,819,831.885	−17,487,489.924	−1,290,106.919	−556.54	−1.7976931348623232e+308	−207.707
0.15	8,164,274.7	−275,015,560.975	214,535,051	−11,147,240.831	−17,147,066.221	−2,072,749.526	−2593.34	−1.7976931348623232e+308	−160.431
0.2	−5,000,285.999	−277,717,030.569	96,126,347	−10,763,557.174	−22,079,368.941	−1,732,375.797	−2682.721	−1.7976931348623232e+308	−435.026
0.25	34,844,457	−318,369,294.241	93,738,253	−10,395,870.275	−19,394,083.905	−1,130,124.017	−2758.121	−1.7976931348623232e+308	37.951
0.3	29,146,652	−196,896,048.178	101,119,201	−10,706,464.342	−17,669,551.313	−1,517,377.018	−1780.516	−26,289.231	−8.529
0.35	3,436,832.2	−166,723,479.339	152,772,278	−10,645,579.97	−18,341,126.964	−1,276,404.789	−840.593	−25,590.675	−22.549
0.4	14,861,993	−148,714,288.633	183,984,466	−10,521,939.756	−17,780,809.151	−2,721,859.435	−31.354	−19,377.193	−19.444
0.45	9,169,620.1	−81,786,019.105	137,630,400	−9,200,251.995	−17,935,163.76	−1,871,353.449	−109.002	−17,619.932	183.815
0.5	36,589,490	−91,888,303.419	159,072,104	−7,354,055.236	−17,963,491.685	−1,293,613.162	−140.629	−15,967.806	2574.693
0.55	81,186,162	−97,936,271.617	222,628,540	−7,779,743.184	−16,685,518	−2,320,322.485	−224.77	−5650.06	3336.181
0.6	82,522,507	−102,867,211.386	234,690,410	−7,376,602.857	−16,645,860.506	−2,418,106.805	−237.243	−8395.547	2694.215
0.65	132,252,534	−69,522,007.279	276,162,578	−5,456,758.023	−17,148,999.815	−2,686,185.847	−284.749	−4840.478	6952.44
0.7	130,828,691	−117,445,600.586	312,578,443	−5,996,359.363	−18,029,993.501	−2,655,771.882	−280.788	−3847.444	15,533.623
0.75	176,998,734	−56,969,024.227	308,961,528	−4,237,076.198	−15,522,925.13	−3,281,599.501	−333.373	−2220.505	1.7976931348623232e+308
0.8	129,877,309	−50,837,565.409	422,660,684	−3,765,651.111	−15,448,930.193	−2,605,430.696	−349.171	−428.921	1.7976931348623232e+308
0.85	191,139,301	−50,455,824.615	279,219,735	−6,504,188.081	−17,409,963.659	−2,458,300.433	−356.809	−436.327	1.7976931348623232e+308
0.9	197,133,063	−59,622,139.395	455,164,387	−7,865,314.4	−20,927,567.78	2,875,805	−323.94	−454.723	1.7976931348623232e+308
0.95	131,373,402	−205,878,521.732	1.7976931348623232e+308	−7,871,928.344	−25,328,735.507	18,044,426	−289.558	−514.014	1.7976931348623232e+308

Model 2 Dependent variable: price_usd

	total_volume_btc	Lower Bd	Upper Bd	stargazers_count	Lower Bd
0.05	−0.0019491657830628	−1.79769313486232e+308	0.00950811025460308	−0.0104952029030628	−0.164498474639694
0.1	−0.00195224855740925	−0.00940664404393606	0.00654534167241554	−0.00810789353207367	−0.0794052041403241
0.15	−0.00176934753855862	−0.00941026599108347	0.00429565870604853	−0.0287707409181833	−0.0447518026495186
0.2	−0.00225293684198252	−0.00576398179384041	0.00307763646444779	−0.0326490495710629	−0.0503999930019677
0.25	−0.00143219547936419	−0.00556884159917421	0.00311753852520797	−0.0252649458620277	−0.0517485375911264
0.3	−0.00148440414596353	−0.00547024486800492	0.00312347200549705	−0.0229239936020977	−0.0572007268310073
0.35	−0.00106909293260844	−0.0062567692301192	0.00421631724959194	−0.023596438735975	−0.0581717685485032
0.4	−0.00155239692018484	−0.00554776309757412	0.0048892776488036	−0.0226642914912111	−0.0638894650042118
0.45	−0.00206841281050434	−0.00465949131125865	0.00386932727239409	−0.0186506537879847	−0.0689692346074021
0.5	−0.00174327334995135	−0.00465742294825378	0.00379654801073291	−0.0250283009922594	−0.0697993784174599
0.55	−0.00178693004378279	−0.00488815351989276	0.0039478137397048354	−0.0262147525962305	−0.0717747854722296
0.6	−0.00178085705908153	−0.00669247700426951	0.00901695398294149	−0.0365211484152781	−0.0732270359399409
0.65	−0.00079346681547802	−0.00631862700735706	0.00447771745827014	−0.033940984688658	−0.0819946430574651
0.7	0.00120127410292167	−0.00754868890520555	0.00401770843370999	−0.0346008030281951	−0.0847164151029946
0.75	0.000737730699953789	−0.00800617415016068	0.00420738728586069	−0.0336263184455655	−0.0901141848901426
0.8	0.000644950933556177	−0.00541596437328858	0.0102494148401692	−0.0380416213547803	−0.0874606831235478
0.85	0.000754660608324124	−0.00711207622117575	0.0126004974600184	−0.0370319394150468	−0.0909341544232276
0.9	0.000700944419447445	−0.00814916524287455	0.0144979374357331	−0.0384556982486681	−0.102051799688851
0.95	0.000713622343091814	−0.0168150897995971	1.79769313486232e+308	−0.0384053635059573	−0.117464431536421

	Lower Bd	Upper Bd	open_issues_count	Lower Bd	Upper Bd
0.05	−0.460936426496365	0.0449462769295775	0.11583750271645	−1.79769313486232e+308	0.181427264502027
0.1	−0.0192434881912296	0.0242302333526595	0.108678471817386	−0.200329961268617	0.131927483325868
0.15	−0.00413428504416904	0.0730800503134875	0.0425988775299205	−0.205669994310082	0.122775253787142
0.2	−0.0153466686110095	0.0747064897364437	−0.0124763359944874	−0.147054865878091	0.129643347274624
0.25	−0.0250185609038718	0.072783392375001	−0.0443758057492867	−0.139045101769545	0.165952102869933
0.3	−0.0256904931092751	0.0728718595199049	−0.0126194880375624	−0.113428160656162	0.181798082603987
0.35	−0.0296568117139753	0.0877573598357553	0.0120954362679897	−0.126245760200594	0.158392515114426
0.4	−0.0310829255154883	0.0976195566896723	0.0190809540877289	−0.164783545678674	0.184126637268177
0.45	−0.0325804215214492	0.107571896785236	0.0292732007788385	−0.17707597850648	0.155914454451478
0.5	−0.0406481189683905	0.104919014524723	0.0308316813554139	−0.17654525727899	0.229741146847901
0.55	−0.0398886412158	0.109130689660122	0.0303100292295102	−0.172791907943319	0.247111456273012
0.6	−0.0418380252664408	0.107982145241575	0.039574819304171	−0.126751525715848	0.242845632010979
0.65	−0.0451715461388322	0.108891468873231	0.0337386607180719	−0.143223810487943	0.19264188992794
0.7	−0.0507749129982168	0.0991876229661464	0.0594005725832387	−0.145464483399768	0.183352029436311
0.75	−0.0489568018629727	0.0970597606901095	0.0368517617650740052	−0.0698854460061428	0.182762535696354
0.8	−0.0302318427075238	0.0729565668556126	0.0425611048133314	0.0231926073752554	0.165126063025826
0.85	−0.0204036346659533	0.0896677195541705	0.0458914142134612	−0.0195743967639207	0.139311492395915
0.9	−0.0287716732655701	0.107537044131093	0.0394829637810964	−0.0389836279004668	0.267287311250186
0.95	−0.0797148807868188	0.136968742269536	0.0396296413503117	−0.437493896683152	1.79769313486232e+30

	Upper Bd	average_commits	Lower Bd	Upper Bd	subscribers
0.05	−0.74016660162511	0.109699532943964	−1.79769313486232e+308	0.204392566458202	0.00140345794810117
0.1	−0.232256141448826	0.090760686315128	−1.6882149269884	0.233615343435537	0.00128397566224966
0.15	−0.222914532475486	0.0146301880046609	−0.437955499728861	0.231836043497083	0.00141363011664357
0.2	0.0351846776042897	−0.0975335960596828	−0.325084161259799	0.210046631404434	0.000784205350750992
0.25	0.0679146782847105	−0.0114382841821153	−0.261399340290391	0.196063583570237	0.00161311870581379
0.3	0.0353669043587447	0.00605044032701746	−0.184101144579615	0.189499857528876	0.00189784671638917
0.35	−0.252579861369699	0.108917755992488	−0.181023117264584	0.182013290055379	0.0018204470395177
0.4	−0.445980401039044	0.131416675298799	−0.168158672318922	0.209010990740471	0.00177015845945392
0.45	−0.436697849962489	0.145720061636941	−0.1753221242728	0.213919334635115	0.00194606852441578
0.5	−0.444577014303555	0.149033621310185	−0.193688762579	0.216083617583375	0.0014122566159887
0.55	−0.352763885317036	0.151138077005074	−0.257326040207643	0.208347537179248	0.00132161990876579
0.6	−0.220097752257977	0.158638936475582	−0.295901928083344	0.201066240467404	0.00112627957868048
0.65	−0.172974450282491	0.0221532025977023	−0.278586382632514	0.203767707345508	0.00106963818460194
0.7	0.0716700976404524	−0.0790896253181446	−0.150590875232434	0.294454423589626	0.000251801218333335
0.75	0.0674738216173077	−0.0866589034024507	−0.137520866045673	0.262354563488729	−7.89598011969582e−(
0.8	0.263021776374456	−0.0738740800728634	−0.126670127413972	0.229733070027037	−2.40140747974111e−●
0.85	0.259868570840627	−0.0799157610199232	−0.120599767322796	0.23001918447761	−1.06729801956965e−(
0.9	0.27312709859962	−0.0665258221596999	−0.312887501958584	0.556049880897595	5.17838703182995e−06
0.95	2.86716042443629	−0.0667719880628487	−0.614927532388862	1.79769313486232e+308	6.23507944831587e−06

Upper Bd	watchers	Lower Bd	Upper Bd	forks_count
0.032835745156469	−0.0378461544395639	−0.146037729579003	0.320747489378632	0.0176230673411184
0.00834283029889731	−0.0417164321123637	−0.0561202849585929	0.200849704093362	0.0183578015781428
0.027686633167090	0.0603196200667194	−0.100568824324003	0.169156368329319	0.0118478043174966
0.025348008982804	0.0901799077110676	−0.131134636436459	0.178210372523587	0.0227127249047456
0.04760804609145	0.0921474151776205	−0.154220566662528	0.18070515961296	−0.0123093048796752
0.0358511218408012	0.0679328917319776	−0.114856254449465	0.179793528267085	−0.0169435125994735
0.025080786300512	0.0404649911137282	−0.11147368907189	0.178394205759241	−0.00954097296619512
0.021774561445854	0.0268322729195359	−0.101537699066368	0.172732944330961	0.00361652757809029
0.015517026055029	0.00539006125419453	−0.119510783697763	0.17009669465083	0.00578395862821262
0.0154696861850837	0.0115305906677346	−0.0567464930578569	0.155061163706535	0.0171731417708632
0.0118793003585078	0.0121803315869059	−0.0521113663968878	0.15427076220589	0.0222771653542112
0.007742698913316	0.037732436596845	−0.0588491076079969	0.157550133594578	0.0337906787072671
0.00876529476524201	0.0892715406619746	−0.0614669401155722	0.150449837166105	0.0692635033474629
−0.00331258191014644	0.128692948704256	−0.0656786020073945	0.314880355182557	−0.00572985212557716
−0.00628505851743287	0.11767172762177	−0.0166431750825592	0.349149558797075	0.00934219602498525
−0.00825872497380581	0.12247474957801	−0.0167493550037927	0.34047075613655	−0.000559619552663564
0.00652755376089859	0.122913335181108	0.0150216645950985	0.360966032381187	−0.00362041384162953
0.0159173282987567	0.118275571151035	0.118275571151035	0.35074509910904	0.000852072087267312
0.374873881151413	0.118252027652083	0.114621214210444	0.765320895385417	0.000701252510317818

merged_pull_requests	Lower Bd	Upper Bd	user_merge_count	Lower Bd
0.19950484453542	0.19893093890761	0.288900097822444	−1.1805391895211	−3.75049730620122
0.19989425683813	0.114306149428488	0.380517916502589	−1.19708738463629	−1.94768099181431
0.273211780082165	0.0856742311390283	0.404826115774938	−1.2505367080812	−1.66946742323242
0.266751968609325	0.0839114439983773	0.419661229305163	−0.914085159751427	−1.36692785203417
0.314712411503264	0.0647971119082213	0.419306233390937	−0.99786542919386	−1.28493849672654
0.290053226016057	0.036723431023342	0.412487099511003	−0.847901921073568	−1.27949542271345
0.266208076708963	0.0368747553007041	0.397895549354375	−0.794563628630124	−1.26974552826427
0.260664719486427	0.0947332212817168	0.403058271532279	−0.781212106755544	−1.23753816479305
0.246261506630929	0.104238869115347	0.420455750334664	−0.735101192990929	−1.27014629142572
0.246848077886924	0.153663868339049	0.416848418404585	−0.586323096005461	−1.19554701827915
0.250715037022325	0.221883796784512	0.429798262254477	−0.611253402576147	−0.979853005760432
0.249450166302684	0.194866781559314	0.444145536517543	−0.657606760475948	−0.889915061989131
0.315749572124407	0.197261114534255	0.418540391884931	−0.655582931735286	−0.96717917589034
0.387741984279273	0.207809398115047	0.417078747503172	−0.656408501168313	−0.841969523860661
0.398682660828661	0.255628294343971	0.40916427436435	−0.58136859925474	−0.840335208585515
0.351856694623728	0.261551524263317	0.410250171434088	−0.414355222817898	−0.75951485894884
0.354880716433725	0.13156775532116	0.477474316726638	−0.447287077904982	−0.791864873375201
0.351887614559203	−0.0996352132248076	0.502208478652926	−0.399824639063497	−0.97883740757786
0.352052728386135	−0.319071588483523	0.521221948620317	−0.401454780334742	−1.46187206915408

Lower Bd	Upper Bd	average_account_active_48_hours	Lower Bd	Upper Bd
−0.00466764802630336	1.79769313486232e+308	0.674676155965933	0.611366369468505	0.698907044421535
−0.00222895183336232	0.00332573831543143	0.681356441737735	0.402432051992114	0.840980073312835
−0.00214446432008331	0.00258359145748934	0.566561793336151	0.290161496352387	1.05511968863329
−0.00201218816205889	0.0024714653943881	0.555562234740199	0.259197239992274	1.04819771641215
−0.000796257413498264	0.00248218538859595	0.426536052266908	0.141089693164787	1.04688691069699
−0.00058581835077751795	0.00248948436283677	0.436725269392089	0.13759846964942	0.981938945196477
−0.000916040681958565	0.00255746166294886	0.468625764407543	0.111456810172274	1.09443937292176
−0.000825813789797041	0.00255796856487139	0.426865438030009	0.10249232376187	1.03022250243114
−0.000624662807396753	0.0025481983154906	0.415994320190936	0.117104240229621	1.01983990514056
−0.000476525482946253	0.00252306656684522	0.398614528130943	0.048526946348403	0.871777114801693
−0.000401780307039306	0.00252332838341627	0.382374489877638	−0.165059211784554	0.935810377558371
−0.000485561542813781	0.00250335747016861	0.418888985626568	−0.146399344908671	0.922165256104618
−0.000440145197209698	0.00249325892159411	0.256535554762922	−0.0857515455075726	0.920146961745941
−0.000312602811390398	0.00250791552557011	0.0736710940244314	−0.0375637209253646	0.880601082674292
−0.00025250946873359	0.0022697714102611	−0.0238627047452354	−0.0238627047452354	0.934023583280318
−0.000374389037943531	0.00113763247908612	0.192662689814611	−0.0774128017811634	0.943174016848289
−0.0010772313200445	0.00116902122727702	0.196747841617547	−0.435195227990546	1.51983926982977
−0.00107661931797287	5.17838703182995e−06	0.18177914855863	−0.502957780221658	2.20396189373486
−1.79769313486232e+308	0.00131344189203665	0.181878772898092	−1.02857121862709	2.49336975483368

Continued

Model 2 Dependent variable: price_usd—cont'd

	average_posts_delta_48_hours	Lower Bd	Upper Bd	average_comments_delta_48_hours
0.05	−3.89589698052491	−1.79769313486232e+308	26.0572540257519	−0.959931712167953
0.1	−3.80798769797526	−26.9867748325056	5.84984393344175	−0.924214039903002
0.15	−4.76828692727262	−25.0958171379162	8.10912174531902	−0.844638130177792
0.2	−3.80721939550938	−19.1214658017572	6.61955224535746	−0.647194412821327
0.25	−1.74414970327773	−22.6620687369959	7.49980310348364	−0.836935286819877
0.3	−0.631119996291099	−24.3490600747415	9.05217119466274	−0.938668331363416
0.35	−5.22575652444708	−23.297467918247	8.55456488927788	−0.972720622753388
0.4	−5.80357867634918	−19.7147454350063	7.41731166870859	−0.929829692856092
0.45	−5.11733947711753	−20.4278554284546	7.62684262211389	−0.987983225623305
0.5	−1.8386096185565	−22.7489437796229	10.6791068750505	−0.854579988289259
0.55	−2.07448209137477	−22.3923543381944	12.2778451491943	−0.808052882549383
0.6	−4.95973477576318	−21.6229625773236	26.7144044344705	−0.737328221818789
0.65	−3.57295867455519	−19.5947419731385	21.9214354096878	−0.618636920139815
0.7	1.85241439374477	−15.7157439639584	16.5300985858081	−0.281468144882153
0.75	5.10602381617309	−9.15357012508841	13.036407941036	−0.148236370991796
0.8	8.83246679953654	−4.1486342440933	11.1056489109775	−0.377895426929077
0.85	9.06844152371177	1.15131222134698	10.5099788178725	−0.38301800196519
0.9	8.05521453301198	1.10519829651424	19.1446505779304	−0.369469740962432
0.95	8.05929071416945	−15.5720253724294	1.79769313486232e+308	−0.369653657001879

Lower Bd	Upper Bd	followers_count	Lower Bd	Upper Bd
−1.26712099418189	1.15985199051755	−1.91395007843992e−05	−1.79769313486232e+308	1.07019927728858e−05
−1.33562045274353	−0.111322367816204	−2.85484684206416e−05	−1.79769313486232e+308	6.46498985993105e−06
−1.35163556270665	−0.224938301682384	−5.29932888483979e−05	−1.79769313486232e+308	3.04506935559308e−07
−1.26231187404799	−0.322643060749259	−0.000139071021517024	−1.79769313486232e+308	4.99199403009835e−07
−1.27110419761924	−0.299620817756877	−0.000101912320858325	−1.79769313486232e+308	7.1564305516994e−07
−1.29068232715572	−0.260123315472381	−0.00012745463572787	−0.00462420025581989	2.46558042100102e−06
−1.36492730398206	−0.168749524469927	−1.19305030492579e−05	−0.00243643226128038	2.03035880585325e−06
−1.38339650923457	−0.120173332351706	−1.39314919077669e−06	−0.0022062950536909	8.43008132645868e−07
−1.43057833228422	−0.0872563505027224	−3.73464064274381e−06	−0.00214290141458758	2.79511643961141e−05
−1.53452368003279	−0.102089689837728	−3.51591393823859e−06	−0.00114534720087732	3.99309322804955e−05
−1.62118745307083	−0.0875151712570646	−5.94881926322803e−06	−0.000812418441751332	0.0001250028892801
−1.45196003095018	−0.17320349589439	−1.07160770819008e−05	−0.000622376848078198	0.000134123998494673
−1.39450152973737	−0.170028325157254	−1.1193127912019e−05	−0.000486095280104454	0.000269233129614997
−1.35483735017096	−0.182208461895455	−1.12973551258661e−05	−0.000354871846630295	0.00175069846554486
−1.33372277776184	−0.148236370991796	−1.24337589850393e−05	−7.61646349286554e−05	1.79769313486232e+308
−0.834030340031735	−0.170115859122543	−9.38689044832352e−06	−1.67930239138945e−05	1.79769313486232e+308
−1.1006569767156	−0.15738737024026	−1.06242180068721e−05	−1.06242180068721e−05	1.79769313486232e+308
−1.2960683412598	−0.107588466190714	−1.30974902057408e−05	−1.30974902057408e−05	1.79769313486232e+308
−1.76893257061519	1.18126817591103	−1.32068265271682e−05	−1.32068265271682e−05	1.79769313486232e+308

KEY FACTORS' ANALYSIS

Model 1 Dependent variable: market_cap_usd

	merged_pull_requests	Lower Bd	Upper Bd	user_merge_count	Lower Bd	Upper Bd
0.05	3,732,664.01	1,425,264.23	8,966,935.44	−16,950,077.44	−111,610,005.88	−4,694,548.45
0.1	3,088,206.25	1,540,505.06	7,547,711.71	−13,289,015.33	−28,164,968.46	−4,935,058.57
0.15	3,226,411.8	2,006,030.16	7,281,767.21	−14,869,829.16	−23,756,590.54	−2,994,098.21
0.2	3,341,347.34	1,812,631.61	1.79769313486232e+308	−14,845,342.41	−25,771,226.51	−5,819,897.94
0.25	1,828,570.65	1,745,746.84	4,212,562.97	−7,756,162.92	−40,920,087.02	−5,269,888.72
0.3	1,836,321.18	1,054,955.76	4,121,679.79	−6,910,681.18	−19,572,015.52	−6,522,322.82
0.35	1,836,672.9	970,611.45	1.79769313486232e+308	−6,914,258.87	−21,155,986.34	−5,526,694.15
0.4	1,841,188.67	955,054.93	3,961,680.85	−6,960,193.18	−13,779,902.72	−5,256,420.41
0.45	1,844,687.04	633,068.37	4,051,387.94	−6,165,974.52	−8,277,498.66	1,321,637.98
0.5	1,852,110.09	366,304.15	3,813,132.79	−5,838,545.06	−7,393,132.85	−1,095,644.96
0.55	1,860,449.98	−1.79769313486232e+308	4,062,938.69	−5,773,884.61	−16,067,194.23	19,898,686.38
0.6	1,861,084.92	157,436.04	3,082,041.09	−5,542,552.1	−8,697,374.81	11,066,066.06
0.65	1,864,545.74	305,882.27	3,330,680.32	−5,592,586.16	−10,048,540.73	−3,261,200.87
0.7	1,867,854.71	262,050.65	3,242,556.75	−4,257,166.06	−7,771,377.84	12,205,440.1
0.75	1,868,698.51	247,249.14	3,320,665.48	−3,916,628.36	−7,912,497.65	−1,544,299.05
0.8	2,197,635.42	−733,162.95	3,964,354.95	−4,419,776.68	−8,280,957.51	−56,649.65
0.85	2,235,903.76	−5,311,549.97	2,239,419.59	−4,445,206.83	−13,705,760.03	3,345,862.15
0.9	2,215,205.68	−582,682.22	3,750,061.84	−2,968,989.37	−9,548,094.97	−447,932.11
0.95	718,433.55	−1.79769313486232e+308	2,183,156.74	−1,732,778.45	−10,263,362.32	15,232,306.04

	average_account_active_48_hours	Lower Bd	Upper Bd	average_comments_delta_48_hours	Lower Bd	Upper Bd
0.05	7,884,934.65	6,983,692.05	9,802,568.95	−6,741,812.28	−1.79769313486232e+308	2,656,855.1
0.1	9,047,665.18	1,758,610.43	9,986,248.57	−8,113,759.64	−1.79769313486232e+308	630,732.23
0.15	9,079,032.74	6,703,709.85	12,499,412.63	−7,977,369.96	−16,958,632.35	−5,469,426.35
0.2	8,617,521.78	5,784,017.95	12,071,218.7	−7,642,906.28	−12,629,240.75	−5,430,686.55
0.25	11,929,764.78	6,285,812.95	12,041,136.58	−11,008,678.07	−11,032,651.12	−5,758,132.48
0.3	11,587,091.41	5,592,307.39	12,798,434.24	−10,859,498.63	−11,380,562.67	−5,649,045.05
0.35	11,586,997.84	4,973,077.68	13,325,104.32	−10,859,111.08	−1.79769313486232e+308	−4,628,722.55
0.4	11,585,796.58	5,502,001.96	14,693,577.3	−10,854,135.34	−13,458,848.56	−5,277,245.8
0.45	11,279,083.41	3,943,288.97	14,559,689.8	−10,724,022.19	−13,887,754.82	−5,028,463.02
0.5	11,128,626.79	5,555,556.99	14,770,342.5	−10,654,534.43	−14,380,064.99	−5,782,848.47
0.55	11,071,319.9	4,959,763.14	14,473,925.66	−10,622,598.91	−14,289,938.06	−6,210,450.39
0.6	10,983,525.05	5,431,872.73	14,511,838.57	−10,585,718.31	−14,865,114.58	−6,243,915.18
0.65	10,988,069.53	4,989,429.09	15,173,927.23	−10,584,161.54	−14,383,190.46	−1,104,491.79
0.7	10,482,684.08	3,159,709.84	15,338,971.36	−10,372,203.95	−14,725,942.07	11,211,878.44
0.75	10,353,808.69	1,330,132.5	15,638,795.53	−10,318,153.88	−14,382,649.61	−2,604,687.98
0.8	8,300,158.68	1,107,738.23	15,305,392.33	−5,120,749.15	−15,012,549.21	−4,409,723.02
0.85	8,064,242.33	2,187,764.12	13,991,097.75	−4,583,914.15	−14,620,274.17	−4,381,515.66
0.9	7,601,208.79	5,659,538.63	13,983,508.14	−4,403,896.55	−8,924,915.95	17,810,077.75
0.95	12,706,200.24	6,592,503.64	14,878,217.11	−7,260,941.96	−8,350,129.65	1.79769313486232e+308

Model 2 Dependent variable: price_usd

	merged_pull_ requests	Lower Bd	Upper Bd	user_merge_ count	Lower Bd	Upper Bd
0.05	0.27	0.24	0.66	−1.26	−6.69	−0.98
0.1	0.32	0.26	0.64	−1.59	−2.06	−0.94
0.15	0.26	0.26	0.39	−1.12	−1.79	−0.87
0.2	0.27	0.26	0.32	−1.13	−1.74	−0.77
0.25	0.26	0.21	0.31	−0.97	−1.19	−0.72
0.3	0.26	0.14	0.31	−0.89	−1.06	−0.59
0.35	0.26	0.14	0.31	−0.78	−1.07	−0.57
0.4	0.27	0.13	0.31	−0.66	−0.9	−0.5
0.45	0.27	0.12	0.3	−0.58	−0.79	−0.42
0.5	0.27	0.1	0.3	−0.51	−0.78	−0.36
0.55	0.27	0.1	0.3	−0.42	−0.59	−0.35
0.6	0.27	0.09	0.29	−0.38	−0.61	−0.28
0.65	0.27	0.09	0.29	−0.37	−0.53	−0.26
0.7	0.27	0.08	0.29	−0.32	−0.41	−0.23
0.75	0.27	0.09	0.33	−0.3	−0.4	0.09
0.8	0.28	0.05	0.33	−0.14	−0.42	0.22
0.85	0.29	0.12	0.31	0.2	−0.34	0.28
0.9	0.29	−0.33	0.29	0.17	0.07	0.5
0.95	0.22	−0.4	0.29	0.38	0.13	1.28

	average_ account_ active_ 48_hours	Lower Bd	Upper Bd	average_ comments_ delta_ 48_hours	Lower Bd	Upper Bd
0.05	0.65	0.08	0.72	−0.56	−1.79769313486232e +308	0.19
0.1	0.58	0.5	0.72	−0.47	−1.22	0.07
0.15	0.64	0.46	0.71	−0.58	−0.93	−0.44
0.2	0.61	0.44	0.74	−0.56	−0.61	−0.43
0.25	0.57	0.38	0.72	−0.55	−0.57	−0.42
0.3	0.54	0.38	0.75	−0.54	−0.81	−0.41
0.35	0.5	0.33	0.88	−0.52	−0.85	−0.42
0.4	0.46	0.32	0.92	−0.5	−0.89	−0.4
0.45	0.42	0.28	0.92	−0.49	−1.01	−0.4
0.5	0.4	0.27	1.01	−0.48	−0.95	−0.4
0.55	0.37	0.22	1.03	−0.46	−0.95	−0.39
0.6	0.35	0.16	0.97	−0.45	−0.94	−0.05
0.65	0.34	0.16	0.96	−0.45	−0.93	−0.05
0.7	0.32	0.05	0.96	−0.44	−0.93	−0.05
0.75	0.31	0.03	0.94	−0.44	−0.95	−0.05
0.8	0.14	−0.06	0.95	−0.13	−0.95	−0.06
0.85	0	0	0.92	−0.07	−1.01	−0.07
0.9	0	0	0.9	−0.07	−0.28	−0.07
0.95	0.18	−0.15	1.62	−0.19	−0.72	1.79769313486232e +308

REFERENCES

Dutta, D., Ahmed, N., 1997. An aggregate import demand function for Bangladesh: a cointegration approach. Appl. Econ. 31 (1999), 465–472.

Johansen, S., 1988. Statistical analysis of cointegrating vectors. J. Econ. Dyn. Control 12, 213–254.

Johansen, S., 1995. Likelihood-based inference in cointegrated vector autoregressive models, OUP Catalogue, Oxford University Press, number 9780198774501, March.

Johansen, S., Juselius, K., 1990. Maximum likelihood estimation and inference on cointegration—with applications to the demand for money. Oxf. Bull. Econ. Stat. 52 (2), 169–210.

Lamport, L., Shostak, R., Pease, M., 1982. The Byzantine generals problem. http://dl.acm.org/citation.cfm?id=357176.

Nakamoto, S., 2008. Bitcoin: a peer-to-peer electronic cash system. https://bitcoin.org/bitcoin.pdf.

Nakamoto, S., 2009. Bitocin open source implementation of P2P currency. http://p2pfoundation.ning.com/forum/topics/bitcoin-open-source.

Odhiambo, N., 2005. Financial development and economic growth in Tanzania: a dynamic casualty test. Afr. Financ. J. 7 (1), 1–17.

SECTION TWO

E-Payment and Security

CHAPTER 6

The Effect of Payment Reversibility on E-commerce and Postal Quality

Christian Jaag[a] and Christian Bach[a]
[a]Swiss Economics, Zurich, Switzerland

Contents

6.1 INTRODUCTION

In contrast to the most prevalent traditional payment systems, transactions in virtual currencies are irreversible, which shifts the risk of a transaction from the receiver of the payment to its sender. This chapter explores the effect of virtual currencies on competition between online and offline merchants.

Traditionally, commerce has been conducted in physical shops, where merchant and customer interact directly. The purchase of the good is carried out over the counter: the customer chooses a good and the merchant proceeds the payment. Good and payment are thus exchanged simultaneously. In contrast, electronic commerce (e-commerce) takes place only indirectly between the customer and the merchant via an online platform. The crucial difference between traditional commerce and e-commerce consists in the dissolution of temporal and spatial unity of the purchasing process, the merchant and the customer. On behalf of the merchant this separation necessitates software enabling virtual goods display, shopping basket, and secure payment systems as well as a delivery channel. For the customer, e-commerce merely requires access to the Internet. By eliminating the physical interaction component of traditional commerce, e-commerce also enables producers to act as merchants directly linked to customers without retail merchants as intermediaries.

Research on e-commerce has recently been reviewed and classified by Wang and Chen (2010). With 5% scientific enquiries on e-commerce in the category of economics, the topic is still comparably small. Salient economic e-commerce themes that have recently been studied include pricing, reputation, and comparison with retail commerce. For instance, Stahl (2000) developed a game-theoretic model in which pricing and advertising levels of online merchants are studied. Staatsamoinen (2009) found empirical evidence that very large and small merchants in e-commerce may benefit most form reputation in competition. Lee and Tan (2003) proposed a model of consumer choice between online and physical purchase, in which their choice depends on the service and product risks of the respective good. In particular and not surprisingly, they concluded that consumers tend to buy less from less known online merchants. Fahy (2006) considered a dupoloy between an online and physical firms, and inferred that the advantage of one commerce format over the other depends on the degree of differentiation between the firms' products as well as on the extent of customer search.

In recent years, e-commerce has become a blooming and fast-growing field of business activity and it has significantly challenged traditional commerce. In the year 2011, global B2C e-commerce sales added up to approximately 961 billion US dollars (Interactive Media in Retail Group, 2012). Still, the e-commerce market continues to expand in 2013 with 18% yearly growth rates in Europe and 16% in the United States (International Post Corporation, 2014). In terms of welfare, total gains for EU consumers from lower online prices and increased online choice are estimated to amount to 204.5 billion Euros, which is roughly equivalent to 1.7% of the EU's gross domestic product (Civic Consulting, 2011). From the point of view of postal operators, the rise of e-commerce provides attractive growth opportunities via parcel delivery services. It constitutes a relief in times of declining letter mail demand due to e-substitution from email and other electronic means of communication. Indeed, the parcel sector of postal operators has done strikingly well in the last few years. For instance, the corresponding revenue as well as parcel volume of USPS increased by 14% from the year 2010-2012 (United States Postal Service, 2013). In the EU, the share of e-commerce shipments in B2C volumes amounts to 60% in 2012 (Copenhagen Economics, 2013). The increase in parcel volumes and the decline in letter mail delivery are illustrated in Figure 6.1.

Yet, there still exists some obstacles for e-commerce. In particular, FTI Consulting (2011) found that cross-border e-commerce is still rather weak. Delivery quality and payment issues can be considered to be the two most significant obstacles for e-commerce. According to Copenhagen Economics (2013), problems related to delivery services are a key reason for not buying online. For example, in their survey, delivery-related problems are responsible for 68% of the situations where e-shoppers have added items to their shopping cart, but abandoned it before sending off the order. Postal quality thus plays an important role for the success and further growth of e-commerce. Moreover, the security and reliability of the payment channel is essential for e-commerce. Credit card payment as one of the main payment channel in e-commerce, exhibit several weaknesses: online merchants are confronted with the risk that payment be reversed after they have delivered. Empirically, this risk is significant. According to CyberSource (2013), the estimated loss

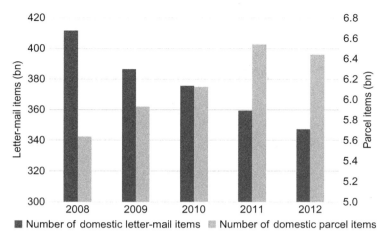

Figure 6.1 Global delivery volumes 2008-2012. *(Source: UPU, 2013).*

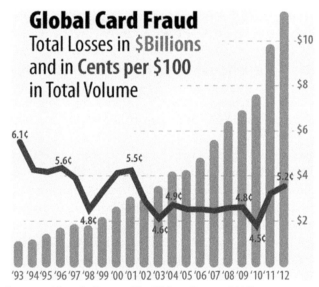

Figure 6.2 Losses from card fraud. *(Source: The Nielsen Report, 2013).*

to online payment fraud amounted to 3.5 billion US dollars in 2012 for North America (USA and Canada), where charge-backs accounted for 43% of all fraud claims. See Figure 6.2 for the development of losses due to card fraud over the past years. The issues of merchants associated with credit cards have been addressed from a theoretical point of view by, for instance, Hayashi (2006), Chakravorti and To (2007), as well as Wright (2012). The losses due to card fraud result from the reversibility of online payments and the risk of theft of data related to the payment system (e.g., credit card data theft).

Only recently, a novel payment system has been put forward: virtual currencies, especially their most prominent offshoot Bitcoin. It was developed by Nakamoto (2008) and set up in 2009 as an open-source software which is entirely decentralized, being based on a peer-to-peer network. It is a payment system with its own currency. In contrast to conventional currencies, Bitcoin is not issued or guaranteed by a central bank and does not enjoy a status as legal tender. Instead, the monetary base grows algorithmically; newly created Bitcoins (seigniorage) are awarded to those users who contribute to secure the network by performing cryptographic functions. By halving the number of newly rewarded Bitcoins at regular intervals, the money supply is capped at 21 million units. As a currency, Bitcoin is freely exchangeable for traditional currencies at a floating (and currently very volatile) exchange rate.

Bitcoin as a payment system does not rely on centralized institutions either. Each user is able to send and receive Bitcoins on his own without financial intermediaries. As a result, payments in Bitcoin are irreversible and cannot be revoked. With regards to e-commerce, Bitcoin as a payment system provide several advantages. Due to its peer-to-peer nature and independence of financial intermediaries, the Bitcoin technology generally facilitate trade. In particular, e-commerce involving cross-border transactions benefits from Bitcoin not being bound to specific countries. Besides, virtual currencies also enable consumers without access traditional payment systems, e.g., credit cards or banking services, to participate in e-commerce. With Bitcoin, there is no credit card number that a malicious actor can collect in order to impersonate someone. In fact, it is even possible to send a payment without revealing one's identity, almost like with physical money.

Arguably, the most immediate effect virtual currencies like Bitcoin can exert on e-commerce is linked to their property of payment irreversibility. Transactions in virtual currencies cannot be reversed, but only refunded by the receiving party. Being as quick and private as cash, virtual currencies are capable of bringing these advantages form traditional commerce to e-commerce and to resolve the problem of payment reversibility of card payments faced by online merchants. Payment irreversibility of virtual currencies reallocates risk from merchants to the consumers, since they may not receive the purchased goods. However, the extent of this risk is lessened by a reputation incentive for online merchants (and involved posts) to correctly dispatch and deliver, respectively. Indeed, compared to consumers, merchants have a much stronger incentive to maintain a reputation of trust.

Another type of risk is the highly volatile exchange rate of virtual currencies when traded for traditional currencies. However, there are liquid exchanges and payment providers that exchange between currencies instantaneously. Hence, in order to trade in virtual currencies, no exposure to their exchange rate risk is necessary.

In this chapter, we study the effects of the shift of risk from merchants to consumers in a model of competition between an online merchant and a bricks-and-mortar (offline) merchant. The chapter proceeds as follows: in Section 6.2 our basic model of horizontally differentiated offline and online merchants is laid out. Two scenarios are then considered in turn. Section 6.3 studies the welfare effects of online payment irreversibility without the presence of postal operators. Section 6.4 extends the model by assuming a postal operator to deliver online merchandise and studies the effects of delivery quality on the demand for the online merchant. Section 6.5 concludes.

6.2 THE MODEL

The model represents the competitive situation of retail merchants offering their goods to consumers (B2C commerce). Suppose a duopoly between two horizontally differentiated firms, an offline merchant, formally denoted as *off*, and an online merchant, formally denoted as *on*. The two merchants are differentiated by the delivery method (direct or via mail) and its consequences discussed further below. A representative consumer's utility function is assumed to be as follows:

$$u(q_{\text{off}}, q_{\text{on}}, m) = m + q_{\text{off}} - \frac{\beta}{2}q_{\text{off}}^2 + \varphi q_{\text{on}} - \frac{\beta}{2}\varphi^2 q_{\text{on}}^2 - \alpha\beta\varphi q_{\text{off}} q_{\text{on}},$$

where *m* denotes the amount of money spent on other goods; $\beta > 0$ is a parameter affecting the slope of the derivable demand curve; and $\varphi \in [0,1]$ is a quality measuring whether and how the goods are received by the consumer thus taking into account the possibility of failed dispatch or delivery (either by the merchant or a postal operator) to the consumer. The parameter φ therefore formally represents the differentiation characteristics of the two goods. As the offline merchant trades directly over the counter, uncertainty about delivery only affects goods purchased from the online merchant. The last term denotes the perceived degree of differentiation, i.e., it reflects the fact that the two products are not perfect substitutes but differentiated, with the parameter $\alpha \in [0,1]$ being closer to zero, the higher the extent of differentiation, and with $\alpha = 1$ representing the case of the two goods being perfect substitutes.

As only the relative prices matter, the good *m* representing the amount of money spent on all other goods is fixed as numéraire good with price index $p_m = 1$. The consumer's budget constraint is then given by

$$p_{\text{off}} q_{\text{off}} + p_{\text{on}} q_{\text{on}} + m = I,$$

where *I* denotes his income.

Constrained utility maximization yields the demand functions for the two differentiated products:

$$q_{\text{off}}(p_{\text{off}}, p_{\text{on}}) = \frac{1}{\beta\varphi(1 - \alpha^2)}(\varphi - \alpha\varphi - \varphi p_{\text{off}} + \alpha p_{\text{on}});$$

$$q_{\text{on}}(p_{\text{off}}, p_{\text{on}}) = \frac{1}{\beta \varphi^2 (1 - \alpha^2)} (\varphi - \alpha \varphi + \alpha \varphi p_{\text{off}} - p_{\text{on}}).$$

The two firms have the following profit functions:

$$\pi_{\text{off}} = (p_{\text{off}} - c_{\text{off}}) q_{\text{off}}(p_{\text{off}}, p_{\text{on}}),$$

$$\pi_{\text{on}} = (\psi p_{\text{on}} - c_{\text{on}}) q_{\text{on}}(p_{\text{off}}, p_{\text{on}}),$$

where c_{off} and c_{on} are the two firm's unit costs, respectively, and the parameter $\psi \in [0,1]$ is a probability measure representing payment reversibility. It denotes the probability that the online merchant obtains the payment and customers do not reverse their payments after having received their order. Payment irreversibility simply sets $\psi = 1$. Profit maximization induces the following price reaction functions for the two firms:

$$p_{\text{off}}(p_{\text{on}}) = \frac{1}{2\varphi} (\varphi - \alpha \varphi + \alpha p_{\text{on}} + \varphi c_{\text{off}}),$$

$$p_{\text{on}}(p_{\text{off}}) = \frac{1}{2\psi} (\varphi \psi - \alpha \varphi \psi + \alpha \varphi \psi p_{\text{off}} + c_{\text{on}}).$$

The resulting optimal prices for the two firms are

$$p_{\text{off}}^* = \frac{1}{\varphi \psi (4 - \alpha^2)} (2\varphi \psi - \alpha \varphi \psi - \alpha^2 \varphi \psi + \alpha c_{\text{on}} + 2\varphi \psi c_{\text{off}});$$

$$p_{\text{on}}^* = \frac{1}{\psi (4 - \alpha^2)} (2\varphi \psi - \alpha \varphi \psi - \alpha^2 \varphi \psi + \alpha \varphi \psi c_{\text{off}} + 2c_{\text{on}}).$$

In our analysis, we make the following assumptions:
1. Offline transactions are irreversible; delivery is immediate.
2. Online transactions are possibly reversible. If payment is reversible, consumers will reverse their payment if they do not receive the purchased good or only in faulty condition. Hence, with reversible payment there is no risk on the buyer's side.
3. With online transactions there is a possibility of nondelivery. If payment is irreversible, there is no risk on the seller's (merchant's) side.

6.3 BASIC CASE

In the basic case, we abstract from postal quality. We compare the two situations in which payments for online commerce are reversible and irreversible, respectively. Table 6.1 gives an overview of these two situations.

If payments are reversible, the online merchant has to commit to dispatch and delivery (or equivalent consumer compensation), since consumers would otherwise reverse their payments. Also, there is no postal operator who may delay delivery or damage the good,

Table 6.1 Basic case without postal quality

	Payment reversibility	Payment irreversibility
Online merchant	$\varphi = 1 \; \psi \leq 1$	$\varphi \leq 1 \; \psi = 1$

hence $\varphi = 1$. However, consumers may defraud merchants, i.e., not pay even though they receive their purchased goods, therefore $\psi \leq 1$. With irreversibility, consumers cannot revoke their payments. Hence, it is the consumer who may be defrauded by the merchant who does not deliver after payment.

Under payment reversibility, the optimal prices of the two firms are as follows:

$$p_{\text{off}}^{\text{rev}} = \frac{\psi(\alpha^2 + \alpha - 2c_{\text{off}} - 2) - \alpha c_{\text{on}}}{(\alpha^2 - 4)\psi},$$

$$p_{\text{on}}^{\text{rev}} = \frac{\psi(\alpha^2 + \alpha - \alpha c_{\text{off}} - 2) - 2c_{\text{on}}}{(\alpha^2 - 4)\psi}.$$

Quantities are

$$q_{\text{off}}^{\text{rev}} = \frac{\alpha c_{\text{on}} + \psi(-\alpha^2 - \alpha + (\alpha^2 - 2)c_{\text{off}} + 2)}{(\alpha^2 - 4)(\alpha^2 - 1)\beta\psi},$$

$$q_{\text{on}}^{\text{rev}} = \frac{(\alpha^2 - 2)c_{\text{on}} - \psi(\alpha^2 + \alpha - \alpha c_{\text{off}} - 2)}{(\alpha^2 - 4)(\alpha^2 - 1)\beta\psi}.$$

Comparing the prices and the quantities of the two firms in the reversibility situation yields

$$p_{\text{off}}^{\text{rev}} - p_{\text{on}}^{\text{rev}} = \frac{c_{\text{on}} - \psi c_{\text{off}}}{\alpha\psi + 2\psi},$$

$$q_{\text{off}}^{\text{rev}} - q_{\text{on}}^{\text{rev}} = \frac{\psi c_{\text{off}} - c_{\text{on}}}{(\alpha^2 + \alpha - 2)\beta\psi}.$$

As a result, $p_{\text{on}}^{\text{rev}} > p_{\text{off}}^{\text{rev}}$ iff $c_{\text{on}} < \psi c_{\text{off}}$. Hence, if online payments are reversible and if costs are approximately symmetric ($c_{\text{on}} \approx c_{\text{off}}$), then the online merchant will generally charge a higher price than the offline merchant to compensate for the risk of nonpayment by the customer. Consequently, the online merchant's quantity is lower than the offline merchant's quantity.

With irreversibility, the optimal prices of the two firms are as follows:

$$p_{\text{off}}^{\text{irrev}} = \frac{\varphi(\alpha^2 + \alpha - 2c_{\text{off}} - 2) - \alpha c_{\text{on}}}{(\alpha^2 - 4)\varphi},$$

$$p_{\text{on}}^{\text{irrev}} = \frac{\varphi(\alpha^2 + \alpha - \alpha c_{\text{off}} - 2) - 2c_{\text{on}}}{\alpha^2 - 4}.$$

Quantities are

$$q_{off}^{irrev} = \frac{\alpha c_{on} + \varphi(-\alpha^2 - \alpha + (\alpha^2 - 2)c_{off} + 2)}{(\alpha^2 - 4)(\alpha^2 - 1)\beta\varphi},$$

$$q_{on}^{irrev} = \frac{(\alpha^2 - 2)c_{on} - \varphi(\alpha^2 + \alpha - \alpha c_{off} - 2)}{(\alpha^2 - 4)(\alpha^2 - 1)\beta\varphi^2}.$$

Comparing the prices and the quantities of the two firms in the irreversibility situation yields

$$p_{off}^{irrev} - p_{on}^{irrev} = \frac{\varphi(c_{off}(\alpha\varphi - 2) - (\alpha^2 + \alpha - 2)(\varphi - 1)) - c_{on}(\alpha - 2\varphi)}{(\alpha^2 - 4)\varphi},$$

$$q_{off}^{irrev} - q_{on}^{irrev} = \frac{\varphi(\alpha^2((c_{off} - 1)\varphi + 1) - \alpha(c_{off} + \varphi - 1) - 2\varphi c_{off} + 2\varphi - 2) + c_{on}(-\alpha^2 + \alpha\varphi + 2)}{(\alpha^2 - 4)(\alpha^2 - 1)\beta\varphi^2}.$$

A direct comparison in general terms is not instructive. Assuming that $c = c_{off} = c_{on}$ the comparisons simplify to

$$p_{off}^{irrev} - p_{on}^{irrev} = \frac{(\varphi - 1)(\alpha(\varphi + 1)c - (\alpha^2 + \alpha - 2)\varphi)}{(\alpha^2 - 4)\varphi} > 0,$$

$$q_{off}^{irrev} - q_{on}^{irrev} = \frac{(\varphi - 1)((\alpha^2 - 2)(\varphi + 1)c - (\alpha^2 + \alpha - 2)\varphi)}{(\alpha^2 - 4)(\alpha^2 - 1)\beta\varphi^2} > 0, \quad \text{if} \quad c > \frac{(\alpha^2 + \alpha - 2)\varphi}{(\alpha^2 - 2)(1 + \varphi)}.$$

Hence, if online payments are irreversible and with symmetric cost, the online merchant's price is lower than the offline merchant's in order to compensate consumers for their risk of nondelivery. Yet, consumers demand a higher quantity from the offline merchant due to imperfect online delivery if costs are sufficiently high, i.e., if $c > \frac{(\alpha^2 + \alpha - 2)\varphi}{(\alpha^2 - 2)(1 + \varphi)}$.

Comparing the two situations in e-commerce with payment reversibility and irreversibility respectively in terms of prices and quantities yields the following results:

$$p_{off}^{irrev} - p_{off}^{rev} = \frac{\alpha c_{on}(\varphi - \psi)}{(\alpha^2 - 4)\varphi\psi},$$

$$p_{on}^{irrev} - p_{on}^{rev} = \frac{(\varphi - 1)\psi(\alpha^2 + \alpha - \alpha c_{off} - 2) - 2c_{on}(\psi - 1)}{(\alpha^2 - 4)\psi},$$

$$q_{off}^{irrev} - q_{off}^{rev} = \frac{\alpha c_{on}(\psi - \varphi)}{(\alpha^2 - 4)(\alpha^2 - 1)\beta\varphi\psi},$$

$$q_{on}^{irrev} - q_{on}^{rev} = \frac{(\varphi - 1)\varphi\psi(\alpha^2 + \alpha - \alpha c_{off} - 2) - (\alpha^2 - 2)c_{on}(\varphi^2 - \psi)}{(\alpha^2 - 4)(\alpha^2 - 1)\beta\varphi^2\psi}.$$

Hence, in market equilibrium, not only the online merchant's price is affected by the (irr–) reversibility of its payments, but also the offline merchant's price. It can be reasonably assumed that $\psi \leq \varphi$, i.e., the payment moral in the situation with payment reversibility does not exceed delivery quality in the case with irreversible payments. Intuitively, the online merchant risks losing his reputation and future business if he defrauds customers, while postal operators have an incentive to provide a high quality due to competitive pressure. In contrast, consumers may illegitimately reverse payments without any significant consequences. Under this assumption, the offline merchant's price is lower under a payment irreversibility online scheme compared to a system with payment reversibility. Moreover, the quantity of the offline merchant will be lower, too. Payment irreversibility in e-commerce thus has an adverse effect on the offline merchant.

If $c_{\text{off}} > \alpha + 1 - \frac{2}{\alpha}$, then the online merchant charges a lower price with payment irreversibility than with reversibility. This is the case if the offline merchant has a high cost, i.e., whenever the online merchant is comparatively competitive. If the offline merchant's cost is not too low, then the online merchant's price is lower with payment irreversibility than with reversibility since there is no longer a risk associated with reversed payment. Moreover, suppose $\psi \leq \varphi^2$ ensuring that $(\varphi - 1)\varphi\psi(\alpha^2 + \alpha - \alpha c_{\text{off}} - 2) - (\alpha^2 - 2)c_{\text{on}}(\varphi^2 - \psi) > 0$. Hence, if the online merchant's quality is sufficiently high, then consumers' online demand is higher under payment irreversibility.

6.4 RESULTS WITH POSTAL QUALITY

In the above considerations, we have assumed that it is only the online merchant's behavior which affects whether his products are correctly delivered. In reality, delivery quality also depends on the postal operator who conveys the parcel and may delay delivery or damage the parcel. In this section, such effects are taken into account by allowing $\varphi \leq 1$ also in the situation with reversible payment (see Table 6.2). This implies that the goods purchased online may not arrive on time or in good order due to the postal operator's fault which in turn degrades perceived quality. The probability of correct delivery in the case of payment irreversibility, which is denoted by σ, becomes even lower, since then also the online merchant may not be reliable, i.e., not dispatch correctly. Hence, delivery quality $\sigma < \varphi$ represents the possibilities of both the online merchant's and the postal operator's failure.

Table 6.2 Model with postal quality

	Payment reversibility	Payment irreversibility
Online merchant	$\varphi \leq 1 \; \psi \leq 1$	$\sigma \leq 1 \; \psi = 1$

With payment reversibility, the optimal prices and quantities of the two merchants are

$$p_{\text{off}}^{\text{rev}} = \frac{1}{\varphi\psi(4-\alpha^2)}(2\varphi\psi - \alpha\varphi\psi - \alpha^2\varphi\psi + \alpha c_{\text{on}} + 2\varphi\psi c_{\text{off}}),$$

$$p_{\text{on}}^{\text{rev}} = \frac{1}{\psi(4-\alpha^2)}(2\varphi\psi - \alpha\varphi\psi - \alpha^2\varphi\psi + \alpha\varphi\psi c_{\text{off}} + 2c_{\text{on}}),$$

$$q_{\text{off}}^{\text{rev}} = \frac{\alpha c_{\text{on}} + \varphi\psi(-\alpha^2 - \alpha + (\alpha^2 - 2)c_{\text{off}} + 2)}{(\alpha^2 - 4)(\alpha^2 - 1)\beta\varphi\psi},$$

$$q_{\text{on}}^{\text{rev}} = \frac{(\alpha^2 - 2)c_{\text{on}} - \varphi\psi(\alpha^2 + \alpha - \alpha c_{\text{off}} - 2)}{(\alpha^2 - 4)(\alpha^2 - 1)\beta\varphi^2\psi}.$$

Comparing the prices and the quantities of the two firms in the reversibility situation yields

$$p_{\text{off}}^{\text{rev}} - p_{\text{on}}^{\text{rev}} = \frac{\varphi\psi((\alpha\varphi - 2)c_{\text{off}} - (\alpha^2 + \alpha - 2)(\varphi - 1)) - (\alpha - 2\varphi)c_{\text{on}}}{(\alpha^2 - 4)\varphi\psi},$$

$$q_{\text{off}}^{\text{rev}} - q_{\text{on}}^{\text{rev}} = \frac{\varphi\psi(\alpha^2((c_{\text{off}} - 1)\varphi + 1) - \alpha(c_{\text{off}} + \varphi - 1) - 2c_{\text{off}}\varphi + 2\varphi - 2) + c_{\text{on}}(-\alpha^2 + \alpha\varphi + 2)}{(\alpha^2 - 4)(\alpha^2 - 1)\beta\varphi^2\psi}.$$

Again assuming that $c = c_{\text{off}} = c_{\text{on}}$ the comparisons simplify to

$$p_{\text{off}}^{\text{rev}} - p_{\text{on}}^{\text{rev}} = \frac{(\alpha(\varphi^2\psi - 1) - 2\varphi(\psi - 1))c - (\alpha^2 + \alpha - 2)(\varphi - 1)\varphi\psi}{(\alpha^2 - 4)\varphi\psi},$$

$$q_{\text{off}}^{\text{rev}} - q_{\text{on}}^{\text{rev}} = \frac{(\alpha^2(\varphi^2\psi - 1) + \alpha(\varphi - \varphi\psi) - 2\varphi^2\psi + 2)c - (\alpha^2 + \alpha - 2)(\varphi - 1)\varphi\psi}{(\alpha^2 - 4)(\alpha^2 - 1)\beta\varphi^2\psi}.$$

Hence, if $\alpha(\varphi^2\psi - 1) < 2\varphi(\psi - 1)$, then $p_{\text{off}}^{\text{rev}} > p_{\text{on}}^{\text{rev}}$. Moreover, if $\alpha^2(\varphi^2\psi - 1) + \alpha(\varphi - \varphi\psi) - 2\varphi^2\psi + 2 < 0$, then $q_{\text{off}}^{\text{rev}} < q_{\text{on}}^{\text{rev}}$.

With payment irreversibility the optimal prices and quantities of the two firms are

$$p_{\text{off}}^{\text{irrev}} = \frac{\sigma(\alpha^2 + \alpha - 2c_{\text{off}} - 2) - \alpha c_{\text{on}}}{(\alpha^2 - 4)\sigma},$$

$$p_{\text{on}}^{\text{irrev}} = \frac{\sigma(\alpha^2 + \alpha - \alpha c_{\text{off}} - 2) - 2c_{\text{on}}}{\alpha^2 - 4},$$

$$q_{\text{off}}^{\text{irrev}} = \frac{\alpha c_{\text{on}} + \sigma(-\alpha^2 - \alpha + (\alpha^2 - 2)c_{\text{off}} + 2)}{(\alpha^2 - 4)(\alpha^2 - 1)\beta\sigma},$$

$$q_{\text{on}}^{\text{irrev}} = \frac{(\alpha^2 - 2)c_{\text{on}} - \sigma(\alpha^2 + \alpha - \alpha c_{\text{off}} - 2)}{(\alpha^2 - 4)(\alpha^2 - 1)\beta\sigma^2}.$$

Comparing the prices and the quantities of the two firms for the situation with irreversible payment yields the following expressions:

$$p_{\text{off}}^{\text{irrev}} - p_{\text{on}}^{\text{irrev}} = \frac{\sigma(c_{\text{off}}(\alpha\sigma - 2) - (\alpha^2 + \alpha - 2)(\sigma - 1)) - c_{\text{on}}(\alpha - 2\sigma)}{(\alpha^2 - 4)\sigma},$$

$$q_{\text{off}}^{\text{irrev}} - q_{\text{on}}^{\text{irrev}} = \frac{\sigma(\alpha^2((c_{\text{off}} - 1)\sigma + 1) - \alpha(c_{\text{off}} + \sigma - 1) - 2\sigma c_{\text{off}} + 2\sigma - 2) + c_{\text{on}}(-\alpha^2 + \alpha\sigma + 2)}{(\alpha^2 - 4)(\alpha^2 - 1)\beta\sigma^2}.$$

In the case that $c = c_{\text{off}} = c_{\text{on}}$, the comparisons simplify to

$$p_{\text{off}}^{\text{irrev}} - p_{\text{on}}^{\text{irrev}} = \frac{(\sigma - 1)(\alpha(\sigma + 1)c - (\alpha^2 + \alpha - 2)\sigma)}{(\alpha^2 - 4)\sigma} > 0,$$

$$q_{\text{off}}^{\text{irrev}} - q_{\text{on}}^{\text{irrev}} = \frac{(\sigma - 1)((\alpha^2 - 2)(\sigma + 1)c - (\alpha^2 + \alpha - 2)\sigma)}{(\alpha^2 - 4)(\alpha^2 - 1)\beta\sigma^2} > 0, \quad \text{if} \quad c > \frac{(\alpha^2 + \alpha - 2)\sigma}{(\alpha^2 - 2)(1 + \sigma)}.$$

Hence, if online payments are irreversible and with symmetric cost, the online merchant's price is lower than the offline merchant's price in order to compensate consumers for their risk of nondelivery. Yet, consumers demand a higher quantity from the offline merchant due to imperfect online delivery if costs are sufficiently high, i.e., if $c > \frac{(\alpha^2 + \alpha - 2)\sigma}{(\alpha^2 - 2)(1 + \sigma)}$.

The difference between the situations with reversible and irreversible payments in e-commerce in terms of price and quantity are

$$p_{\text{off}}^{\text{irrev}} - p_{\text{off}}^{\text{rev}} = \frac{\alpha c_{\text{on}}(\sigma - \varphi\psi)}{(\alpha^2 - 4)\sigma\varphi\psi},$$

$$p_{\text{on}}^{\text{irrev}} - p_{\text{on}}^{\text{rev}} = \frac{\psi(\alpha^2 + \alpha - \alpha c_{\text{off}} - 2)(\sigma - \varphi) - 2c_{\text{on}}(\psi - 1)}{(\alpha^2 - 4)\psi},$$

$$q_{\text{off}}^{\text{irrev}} - q_{\text{off}}^{\text{rev}} = \frac{\alpha c_{\text{on}}(\varphi\psi - \sigma)}{(\alpha^2 - 4)(\alpha^2 - 1)\beta\sigma\varphi\psi},$$

$$q_{\text{on}}^{\text{irrev}} - q_{\text{on}}^{\text{rev}} = \frac{\sigma\varphi\psi(\alpha^2 + \alpha - \alpha c_{\text{off}} - 2)(\sigma - \varphi) - (\alpha^2 - 2)c_{\text{on}}(\sigma^2 - \varphi^2\psi)}{(\alpha^2 - 4)(\alpha^2 - 1)\beta\sigma^2\varphi^2\psi}.$$

The offline merchant's price will be higher under e-commerce payment irreversibility iff $\sigma < \varphi\psi$, yet its quantity will then still be higher compared to the offline merchant's quantity if payment in e-commerce is reversible. The price of the online merchant will be lower under payment irreversibility, if c_{off} is not too small or definitely if $c_{\text{off}} \geq 1$. If $\psi \leq \left(\frac{\sigma}{\varphi}\right)^2$, then the e-commerce quantity is higher with payment irreversibility. Hence, payment irreversibility has a positive effect on e-commerce if payment moral under reversibility is low—a condition that seems to be in line with the empirical facts about credit card fraud.

As shown above, postal quality affects the outcome of competition between offline and online merchants. The stronger the effect of postal quality on the online merchant's volume, the stronger is the incentive for the post to invest in quality. The marginal effect of delivery quality on e-commerce quantity is evaluated for the two situations with payment reversibility and payment irreversibility. Note that σ represents the online merchant's and the post's combined quality, while φ represents only the post's delivery quality (since dispatch by the online merchant is guaranteed by payment reversibility).

$$\frac{\partial q_{on}^{rev}}{\partial \varphi} = \frac{\varphi \psi (\alpha^2 + \alpha - \alpha c_{off} - 2) - 2(\alpha^2 - 2)c_{on}}{(\alpha^2 - 4)(\alpha^2 - 1)\beta \varphi^3 \psi}$$

$$\frac{\partial q_{on}^{irrev}}{\partial \sigma} = \frac{\sigma (\alpha^2 + \alpha - \alpha c_{off} - 2) - 2(\alpha^2 - 2)c_{on}}{(\alpha^2 - 4)(\alpha^2 - 1)\beta \sigma^3}$$

Hence, if $\psi \leq \left(\frac{\sigma}{\varphi}\right)^3$, then $\frac{\partial q_{on}^{rev}}{\partial \varphi} \geq \frac{\partial q_{on}^{irrev}}{\partial \sigma}$ due to $\sigma < \varphi$: The marginal effect of delivery quality on the consumers' demand for the online good is stronger if they can reverse their payment. However, loosely speaking, if consumers' payment moral is rather high and/or the merchant's reliability is rather low, then the effect of delivery quality on demand can be higher in the case of payment irreversibility compared to payment reversibility. Intuitively, with irreversible payment, it is the perceived risk of incorrect delivery that deters customers from ordering online. Since the marginal effect of increased delivery quality on online volume is decreasing, an increase in postal quality strongly affects volume if merchant reliability is low.

6.5 CONCLUSION

In this chapter, we developed a stylized model of competition between brick-and-mortar merchants and online retailers with which we explore the effect of virtual currencies on prices and quantity as well as the importance of postal delivery quality for e-commerce. An offline transaction, matching payment with delivery, is without risk for both the seller and the buyer. In an online transaction the seller faces the potential risk of nonpayment while the buyer risks failed delivery. The effects of these two risks depend on the reversibility of payment.

While traditional payment systems for e-commerce are reversible, transactions in virtual currencies like Bitcoin are irreversible. This shifts the risk from the receiver of the payment to its sender. Hence, with reversible payment, the online merchant includes a surcharge to compensate for his risk of nonpayment. With irreversible payment, the online merchant has to grant a discount compared to the offline merchant in order to compensate customers for their risk of failed delivery. Overall, under reasonable conditions, payment irreversibility strengthens e-commerce compared to reversible payment due to reduced overall risk.

With postal delivery of goods purchased online, quality of delivery is not fully controlled by the merchant, but also by the postal operator. The model suggests that postal quality is more important if payment is irreversible than with reversible payment under the condition that consumers' payment moral is high and/or the merchant's reliability is low. Moreover, with payment irreversibility postal operators may have stronger incentives for quality since it affects volumes more strongly than if payment is reversible.

REFERENCES

Chakravorti, S., To, T., 2007. A theory of credit cards. Int. J. Ind. Org. 25, 583–595.

Civic Consulting, 2011. Consumer market study on the functioning of e-commerce and internet marketing and selling techniques in the retail of goods, Final Report, Civic Consulting.

Copenhagen Economics, 2013. E-commerce and delivery: A Study of the State of Play of EU Parcel Markets with Particular Emphasis on E-Commerce. European Commission, DG Internal Markets and Services.

CyberSource, 2013. 2013 Online Fraud Report. CyberSource Corporation.

Fahy, C., 2006. Internet versus traditional retailing: an address model approach. J. Econ. Business 58, 240–255.

FTI Consulting, 2011. Intra-community cross-border parcel delivery. Study for the European Commission.

Hayashi, F., 2006. A puzzle of credit card payment pricing: why are merchants still accepting card payments? Rev. Netw. Econ. 5 (1), 144–174.

Interactive Media in Retail Group, 2012. B2C Global E-Commerce Overview 2012. Research and Markets.

International Post Corporation, 2014. Market Flash: E-Commerce Special. Issue 480.

Lee, K., Tan, S., 2003. E-retailing versus physical retailing: a theoretical model and empirical test of consumer choice. J. Business Res. 56 (11), 877–885.

Nakamoto, S., 2008. Bitcoin: A Peer-to-Peer Electronic Cash System. Mimeo.

Staatsamoinen, J., 2009. Returns on reputation in retail e-commerce. J. Electron. Comm. Res. 10 (4), 196–219.

Stahl, D., 2000. Strategic advertising and pricing in e-commerce. In: Baye, M. (Ed.), Industrial Organization, Advances in Applied Microeconomics, vol. 9. Emerald Group Publishing Limited, pp. 69–100.

The Nielsen Report, 2013. Chart of the month, August 2013. http://www.nilsonreport.com.

United States Postal Service, 2013. Readiness for package growth-delivery operations. Report Number DR-MA-14-001.

UPU, 2013. Postal statistics. http://pls.upu.int/pls/ap/ssp_report.main.

Wang, C., Chen, C., 2010. Electronic commerce research in latest decade: a literature review. Int. J. Electron. Comm. Stud. 1 (1), 1–14.

Wright, J., 2012. Why payment card fees are biased against retailers. RAND J. Econ. 43 (4), 761–780.

CHAPTER 7

Blockchain and Digital Payments: An Institutionalist Analysis of Cryptocurrencies

Georgios Papadopoulos
Erasmus University Rotterdam, Rotterdam, The Netherlands

Contents

7.1 INTRODUCTION

This chapter discusses the contribution of Internet-based payment platforms employing the blockchain technology known as "cryptocurrencies" or "altcoins" and describes the reasons, the principles, and the conditions of their integration in the official payment system. There are a variety of different cryptocurrencies with bitcoin being the first and by far the most popular. Following David Evans, I argue that "their use of a decentralized public ledger, or blockchain, is their key distinguishing characteristic and the[ir] fundamental innovation" (Evans, 2014, p. 1). There also other shared characteristics, the most important of which are their peer-to-peer structure and their double-key cryptography and the fact that they employ or benefit from[1] free open-source software. All these characteristics allow altcoins to be treated as a group. The analysis will use a framework

---

[1] Not all cryptocurrencies use open-source or free software. For example, Darkcoin does not disclose its source code. Nevertheless, all cryptocurrencies have benefited from the open source code of bitcoin, which they replicated or partly used for their own platforms.

153

coming from original institutional economics that can explain how the financial innovation[2] of payment vehicles that were developed employing the blockchain, the digital public ledger that supports the operation of all cryptocurrencies, could be integrated in the official, that is, regulated, system of digital payments. The establishment of cryptocurrencies presupposes the development of the management structures internally and regulation of their operations externally. The interests of the stakeholders, including the programmers, the miners, the official financial intermediaries, and of course the central banks and the intergovernmental regulatory institutions define the whole process. This chapter will be structured as follows:

Section 7.1 describes the distinguishing characteristics of cryptocurrencies explaining why they should be defined as public ledger currency platforms instead of money or currency. The distinguishing and defining innovation of all these payment platforms is the blockchain, and the analysis is going to focus on the significance of this innovation and of the other characteristics that make cryptocurrencies unique.

Section 7.2 investigates the economic conditions of the supply and the demand of cryptocurrencies and the interests of the agents involved. In an attempt to motivate the discussion, some comparisons will be drawn in relation both to other open-source projects and to the payment industry.

Section 7.3 describes the theoretical framework for analyzing financial innovation and institutional adjustment using original institutional economics to offer a set of principles that define the regulation of the blockchain and its integration in the financial architecture.

Section 7.4 considers the recent developments in the regulation of cryptocurrencies in the United States, describing how they get "ceremonial encapsulated" in the established framework of the digital payments industry.

Section 7.5 reflects on the challenges that cryptocurrencies are going to face in the next few months and speculates on possible scenarios for future regulation.

Section 7.6 summarizes the argument.

7.2 DEFINITION

In order to discuss the place of cryptographic, peer-to-peer coins in the financial architecture, it is important to have clear understanding of their identity and their functions.

---

[2]Frame and White (2004, p. 118) define a financial innovation as "something new that reduces costs, reduces risks or provides an improved product/service/instrument that better satisfies participants demands. Financial innovations can be grouped as new products (e.g., adjustable rate mortgages, exchange traded index funds); new services (e.g., online securities trading, internet banking); new 'production' processes (e.g., electronic record-keeping for securities, credit scoring); or new organizational forms (e.g., a new type of electronic exchange for securities, internet only banks)".

Defining altcoins is a necessary first step[3] before considering their possible contribution in the payment system and the challenges posed for issuers, users, and regulators. Analytic scrutiny serves a further important role to establish the defining characteristics of cryptocurrencies (more than 400 at the time of writing) that allows for a uniform study. The terms "cryptocurrencies" and "altcoins" are going to be used interchangeably in the chapter to describe platforms that rely on the blockchain and on double-key cryptography and employ a peer-to-peer structure, to "issue digital cash," usually called "coin," with the aim of transmitting economic value across the Internet. The analysis of cryptocurrencies is going to fall back on the study of the bitcoin, which at the time of writing is by far the most visible, popular, and larger in terms of market capitalization.[4] Bitcoin is also where the innovative technology of the blockchain was first introduced, and this cryptocurrency developed the source code the other altcoins adopted through a process of replication and variation. This chapter is also going to take into consideration other accepted altcoins, but because of their variation and their number, not all them can be accurately represented and described by the basic characteristics listed earlier.

Before describing and defining cryptocurrencies, it is important to note that none of them, including bitcoin, is money proper. Cryptocurrencies are legally defined as "convertible digital currencies" (according to the US Financial Crimes Enforcement Network directive issued early in 2013) or as a "digital equivalent of cash" (according to the European legislation EC/2009/110 on electronic money). The legal definition applies to the cryptocurrencies that are directly convertible to official currencies employing digital marketplaces and exchange sites. Despite its convertibility, digital cash cannot be considered money (Evans, 2014; Hanley, 2013; Yermack, 2014). Money in economics is defined by its functions, primarily as a means of exchange according to the reigning commodity theory of money (Menger, 1892) or as a standard of abstract value for the state theory of money (Knapp, 1924). The two functions are interrelated, since the dominant means of exchange tends also to be the main unit of account and vice versa. In order for an asset or a payment vehicle to be money, it has to be the universal means of exchange and standard of value at least in the geographic area of a state or the economic area of a market; neither is the case for any of the altcoins in circulation. On the contrary, the operation of bitcoin and of other digital cash relies heavily on official currencies that serve the function

---

[3]"Proponents can't easily explain what a cryptocurrency is. If you can't explain what you are and how you fit into the current legal and regulatory scheme, you are at the mercy of the ignorant. The 'what this is' answer needs to address not just things like 'is it money transmission?' but more mundane yet important questions like 'where is a bitcoin located?' and 'where and when does a transaction take place?' Cryptocurrency supporters should address whether crypto-currency is a currency/store of value or a payment system or a hybrid of both" (Middlebrookt and Hughestt, 2014, p. 839).

[4]Bitcoin market capitalization was around 7.6 billion USD, more than 10 times the capitalization of all the other cryptocurrencies aggregated together. Data according to https://coinmarketcap.com/ quote for the 26th of July 2014.

of the standard of value and of means of final settlement of payment (Evans, 2014, p. 9; Yermack, 2014, p. 10). Even if there is nothing that prevents altcoins from replacing the state currencies and their "moneyness" or not is an empirical question, it is important to keep in mind that bitcoin and other cryptocurrencies are designed as protocols that transmit economic value across the Internet and not as money. As Satoshi Nakamoto claimed in the inaugural Bitcoin design paper, "What is needed is an electronic payment system based on cryptographic proof instead of trust, allowing any two willing parties to transact directly with each other without the need for a trusted third party" (Nakamoto, 2009, p. 1).

David Evans argued that the important innovation of Nakamoto was the blockchain, an encoded, distributed, digital ledger of transactions. Evans (2014, p. 2) described the bitcoin and the other "virtual currencies" like it as "decentralized public ledger platforms" capturing the distinguishing characteristic of these payment systems. Anyone who holds altcoins also has the exact copy of the blockchain, making all transactions visible to the users of the system, eliminating the information asymmetries that characterize the traditional hierarchical system of financial intermediation, and enhancing the security of the public ledger of the transactions. More importantly, the existence of the blockchain makes intermediation from third parties like commercial banks or credit card companies obsolete by delegating the verification of transactions to a distributed peer-to-peer network and rewarding the nodes that are successful in verifying transactions. The verification process and the consequent reward of the effort and the infrastructure involved in solving the mathematical equations related with the processing of transactions and the verification of the blockchain are described as "mining."[5] Mining is also the way that new digital cash comes to existence, providing an automatic mechanism for the supply of the cryptocurrencies.

Cryptocurrencies combine a high degree of identity protection with a decentralized system of verifying transactions that does not rely to a third party, making the use of altcoins for digital transactions equivalent to cash payments. Most of the altcoins employ a double-key cryptography, which is based on a hashing algorithm (the most popular is the SHA 256) that protects the privacy of the payers and the payees (DuPont, 2014); while altcoin transactions are recorded in public ledgers and are accessible by everybody, the privacy of the participants of the system is safeguarded and only their alias is recorded in the blockchain.[6] The relative anonymity of transactions represents a comparative

---

[5] "The node that succeeds in solving the cryptographic puzzle starts a new block by submitting its 'proof of work' to the network. Solving the puzzle is a computationally demanding process, and it becomes more demanding each time, requiring increasing amounts of computing power to decipher. The node in the network that 'wins' the race to decode the next block receives as its reward the ability to create a fixed quantity of new bitcoins for itself. Via this incentive, the algorithm effectively harnesses the computing power of all the Bitcoin holders to the process of verifying all the Bitcoin transactions in the world" (Maurer et al., 2013, pp. 264–265).

[6] "Bitcoin is frequently described as anonymous, because while every transaction is recorded in the public 'block chain,' parties are identified only by a Bitcoin address.' It is possible to trace transactions although it may be difficult to associate a transaction with a particular individual" (Middlebrookt and Hughestt, 2014, p. 819).

advantage to other digital payment platforms. Especially after the NSA affair and the increased awareness that Internet activity is monitored by governments and corporations, privacy protection has assumed more importance for Internet users. Nevertheless, privacy is always a matter of degree and not a binary concept.[7] The importance is how much privacy is provided by the system, and here, cryptocurrencies offer different methods and different degrees of protection. The main questions concerning privacy that also are resolved differently by different altcoins are as follows: Who controls the process and the technology of encryption? Is this process reversible by the administrators of the system? and What is the cost for a third party to uncover the identity of a user or a transaction? All these issues are extremely important for regulation, since money laundering, financing of illegal activities, and tax evasions are top priorities of the oversight institutions in the payment industry.

The innovative technology of cryptocurrencies and its resilience are supposed to explain the appeal of such platforms and account for their economic value. Technology, it is argued, can replace the state or the commodity as the guarantee for the future value and the acceptability of cryptocurrencies.[8] Nonconvertible fiat money is enacted by law as legal tender and is the only acceptable means of paying taxes. Cryptocurrencies are not able to offer a comparable guarantee for their future acceptance, so technology is advertised as their ultimate source of reliability and trust. Again, a leap of faith is necessary for accepting the value of cash, be it digital or material. Technology should function not only as an agent of cryptographic verification of transactions but also as the foundation of a system of values that can carry the expectations of suppliers and users of cryptocurrencies. Expectations are of the essence since present value "depends on expectations concerning demand and supply of the asset over time [and] like any asset we would expect that market participants would engage in speculation over the future value of the asset" (Evans, 2014, p. 6). The cryptocurrencies are not an exception, and the volatility of their price is both an indication of the high uncertainty concerning the future performance of technology and a symptom of their novelty. The fact that the emission of new coins is automatic, hardwired in the protocol as a reward

---

[7]Even if the use of cryptocurrencies provide complete identity protection for its users, privacy can be compromised in other points of the transaction, for example, when an amount in cryptocurrencies has to be converted. Third-party intermediaries can function as identity "check points," when one has to rely on third parties to convert cryptocurrencies to official currencies, then government regulation can be implemented on and through these intermediaries. If you have to have an account with a third party like bitcoin.de that you need to follow their payment instructions.

[8]"The monetary value of Bitcoin rests as much in the future potential that its users imagine for it as on its current, relatively limited capacity to act as a medium of exchange. Similarly, its semiotic value grows out of the aspirations of Bitcoin adherents. The point is not whether Bitcoin 'works' as a currency, but what it promises: solidity, materiality, stability, anonymity, and, strangely, community" (Maurer et al., 2013, p. 263).

mechanism to the miners, contributes further to their volatility, by making any intervention to fine-tune supply and demand impossible.[9]

Cryptocurrencies offer an alternative to the established digital payment instruments, like *PayPal* or the digital applications of credit card companies and commercial banks. Their decentralized architecture and the privacy safeguards make them attractive to users that look for a payment method similar to cash for their digital payments. Still, cryptocurrencies can only exist in virtue of a network of programmers and miners that offer their services and resources in order to run the system, fix possible bugs in the code, and propose improvements. In the next section, we will look closer how the networks that support altcoins operate, their incentives, and the rewards for the producers and the consumers of the services that altcoins provide, and we will compare them with other organizations in the digital payment industry and other open-source projects.

7.3 THE STRUCTURE AND THE INCENTIVES BEHIND THE SUPPLY AND DEMAND OF CRYPTOCURRENCIES

Bitcoin provides the model and the source code for the other cryptocurrencies, while it remains the most popular among them, so it can provide also prototype for the management, the organization, and the business model for the other altcoins. Of course, not all of the altcoins share Bitcoin's governance model,[10] but this is because most of them do not have the resources or the need of a more elaborate management structure, so they rely to a small team of developers or to an individual programmer.

Bitcoin is supported by a core development group, who is responsible for the official code repository and has the ultimate control over the direction of the project. A special place among the core development team is held by the "chief scientist" of the project, a place initially held by Satoshi Nakamoto, who invented the blockchain and introduced the Bitcoin. In 2010, Nakamoto "disappeared" leaving Gavin Andresen as his successor, a

---

[9]"Market could provide solutions to volatility. For example, some Bitcoin wallet providers such as Coinbase insure merchants against the volatility. Consumers buy coins for the wallets. When they pay a merchant that accepts Bitcoins the wallet provider pays the merchant with a traditional currency. The logical extension would be to extend provide this same benefit to the consumer so they would not bear any currency risk either. Consider the second case where the consumer and the merchant are both insured. In that case the transaction makes no sense. The consumer uses dollars to buy coins from the wallet provider for a transaction, the wallet provider buys coins from an exchange, then the wallet provider sells the coins back to the exchange since it needs to pay the merchant in dollars, then wallet provider pays the merchant in dollars, and the consumer gets their purchase. Of course the wallet provider could dispense with coins entirely and simply take dollars from the consumer and pay the merchant" (Evans, 2014, pp. 9–10).

[10]"Ripple has taken a different approach. The public ledger platform software was developed by a for-profit company, which has secured private investment. It made the software open source, which enables it to benefit from open source development by volunteers but also makes the software available freely to everyone who has opens up the possibility of forking and fragmentation" (Evans, 2014, p. 16).

position that Andersen keeps until today. In the spirit of open-source projects, changes to the Bitcoin code can be proposed by anyone. When proposals address simple and non-controversial improvements, it is up to the core developers to approve them and incorporate them in the code (Evans, 2014, p. 16). Important changes need to be approved by the community of users, following a decision rule of "economic majority," where the interest of users and especially of the merchants has a weight to the decision-making process according to their economic gravity. The whole project and the group of the core developers are supported by the Bitcoin foundation that acts as a representative and also is responsible for the financial support of the development of the code. The foundation was established in 2012 and is "dedicated to the development, safety, and promotion of Bitcoin" (https://bitcoinfoundation.org/). A further important function of the foundation is to lobby for favorable legislation (Neal, 2014), an important precondition for the development of the Bitcoin project and for other cryptocurrencies.

The structure of the Bitcoin is not uncommon in open-source projects and many of them, most notably Mozilla, Linux, and Wikipedia, feature nonprofit foundations and a core developers' team as their main governance bodies. They also try to appeal to the wider community an effort to enhance the legitimacy of the decision and keep their audience involved. Open-source projects are inspired by a democratic and participatory ethos, which is necessary in order to maintain the support of their communities. The distinguishing characteristic of cryptocurrencies to other open-source projects is that they not only rely to the labor and the skill of their programmers but also require a substantial investment in resources by individual users for their continued operation. Cryptocurrencies rely on a protocol of cryptographic rules and techniques for processing transactions. Running the protocol requires the effort of programmers employing substantial computer power to determine whether a posted set of encrypted transactions, commonly known as "blocks," are valid and, if this is the case, they are integrated in the blockchain. The programmers are called "miners," as a reference to gold and silver currencies and also because of the new bitcoins that are paid as a reward for their effort and the employment of their resources (processing power and energy). Mining is a zero sum game; many miners are occupied with the computation of a block, but only the one who is first to verify a block and integrate it in the blockchain is the one who gets rewarded with newly emitted bitcoins. The structure of the mining game leads to a waste of resources and energy, since the process of verification is made simultaneously by many miners that compete for the reward. With the computation of new blocks becoming more difficult and the number of miners increasing, competition is intensifying and mining is becoming an increasingly sophisticated and expensive business. Cryptocurrencies need to employ the necessary resources for the operation and for that they have to put in place the appropriate system of rewards: "There is no reason laborers would provide these critical services for free or to the extent needed for the platform. Recognizing this, public ledger currency platforms have implemented 'incentive schemes' that are designed to elicit the supply of labor and other necessary resources. The Bitcoin white paper proposed to do this by giving bitcoins to laborers as rewards for their services in addition to possible Bitcoin-based transaction fees. This incentive system served a dual purpose. It injected new bitcoins into the system as it grew in addition to providing compensation for the effort expended" (Evans, 2014, p. 12). It is questionable if this incentive structure is the most efficient way to run cryptocurrencies or even if it will suffice to support the operation of Bitcoin or other similar projects in the future, especially as the computational complexity of the blocks increases and with it the resources that are required. Nevertheless, cryptocurrencies need to provide different kinds of rewards than the other open source project in order to secure the resource of their operation, at the same time as they are not able to fall back on the proprietary model of traditional financial intermediaries.

The economic interests that condition the supply of cryptocurrencies, namely, the incentives of the code developers, the miners, and the foundation, can only be fulfilled if there is a demand for such services that create the revenue that covers the costs for the supply of such services and that can create a profit. The market of payments is particular. It has a double-sided structure, and it is necessary for two groups of users to be active for a new payment service to be operational. Merchants and clients, payers, and payees are both necessary for the system. The double-sided structure of the market raises two fundamental challenges that need to be addressed: how is it possible to attract both parties simultaneously for a payment service to be operational and how are the costs going to be divided between the two parties. Again, we will have to rely on the Bitcoin in order to get an insight how these challenges could be addressed by cryptocurrencies.

Bitcoin initially relied to a community of volunteers and enthusiasts, who were inspired by its innovative technology and the promise of an anarchic system for the processing of payments. The utopian aspirations of the Bitcoin design for a more transparent and equitable payment system resonated the legitimacy deficit of the financial architecture after its collapse in 2008. With countries like Greece and Spain in the brink of default, an appropriation of bank accounts in Cyprus and the public debt of the United States reaching its ceiling and leading to a short-term suspension of payments, some users saw in Bitcoin an attractive alternative to the defunct system of official currencies. The crisis created a window of opportunity and publicity that allowed the Bitcoin to reach a critical mass of users and eventually gave rise to a speculative bubble with the price of the Bitcoin well above €800 toward the end of 2013 from less than 100 earlier that year.

The Bitcoin popularity broke the deadlock of the double-sided payment market attracting enough speculators to make it also interesting for merchants. Internet giants like Amazon, Google, and recently Expedia started accepting Bitcoin both as publicity stunt and as a genuine effort to cater for new community of customers. Still, the decision for somebody to use cryptocurrencies for payments or money transfers, ideology or hype factors aside, can also be rationalized in economic terms, using a cost and benefit analysis. Benefits are associated with the number of other agents using the same payment technology, increasing the number of potential transacting parties. There are also network effects involved where an inflow of new users creates a feedback loop that encourages more agents to adopt a new payment technology (Luther, 2013, p. 5). Such network effects lead to a very centralized market in payment service, where *Visa*, *MasterCard*, and *PayPal* dominate the landscape of digital payments. Merchants are especially interested in adopting popular payment technologies in order to increase their customer base. Next to the benefits are also the costs in adopting a new payment technology. Such costs can be divided into the sunk-in costs associated with the investment in the appropriate infrastructure for accepting a new type of transaction and the possible fees involved with the processing of this transaction if a financial intermediary is involved in the process. In the case of cryptocurrencies, no special equipment is required, since they rely on the Internet, so a personal computer is enough for the purpose at hand and the software is usually free and open source. Transaction fees, when they exist, are set much lower than its competitors. Usually, merchants need to use the services of a third party to facilitate the payment and also to convert their proceeds in the official currency, since the use of Bitcoin can be cumbersome to the technological novice and there are still many bottlenecks in exchanging bitcoins for official currencies. Third-party services can be offered for a fee, or the intermediary creates a revenue through the conversion of cryptocurrencies into official currency. There is no uniform pricing system of fees and services by third parties, but in end effect, bitcoin and other altcoins are considerably cheaper than traditional digital payment services like *PayPal*, *MasterCard*, and *Visa* where the usual fee is around 2.5% of the value of the transaction. Still and despite their advantage in pricing, the volume of purchases in bitcoins remains negligible, and the same applies for the number of merchants that are accepting bitcoins at the moment (Yermack, 2014, p. 10). The penetration of other cryptocurrencies is much smaller, but the use of Bitcoin in e-commerce gave incentives for developing applications that can be in principle used also by other altcoins. An important first step has been made with the success of Bitcoin, which has made altcoins visible and exciting.

Cryptocurrencies represent an innovation that may challenge the traditional business model of digital payments in the future. The peer-to-peer architecture of systems like Bitcoin and the fact that they do not rely on transaction fees for their operation but rather on a distributed network of nodes that contribute their resources in exchange of virtual cash payments make it difficult for them to be integrated in the traditional banking system that relies on the creation of credit, on interest rates, and on fees. Still, cryptocurrencies have to find a niche in an environment dominated by financial intermediaries that have much more resources, technical know-how, and infrastructure. As long as the uncertainty about the resilience of their technology, their future economic value, and their function remains, it is very difficult to imagine that it would be possible for them to compete with the established platforms in e-payments. More importantly, as long as cryptocurrencies remain unregulated and thus confined in a gray area of legal limbo, it would be unlikely that the general public, both on the side of merchants and on the side of consumers, will prefer cryptocurrencies to credit cards or other official e-payment services for their day-to-day transactions.

7.4 UNDERSTANDING INSTITUTIONAL CHANGE

Technology is one of the motors of social development, with technological innovation being the cause that disrupts the institutional equilibrium leading to change and to progress. We can simply define technology as the fulfillment of human purpose (Arthur, 2007, p. 276), and in the case of money, this purpose is the fulfillment of its functions—as a standard of abstract value, means of payment, store of value, and abode of purchasing power. The invention and employment of the blockchain in digital public ledger payment systems, like Bitcoin, are a cause of progress in the monetary system, facilitating the more efficient processing of payment at the same time as it is a force of disruption of the institutional equilibrium, challenging the established practices in payments and the business models of the industry that facilitates them. The proposed analysis of the institutional change of the payment system is combining original institutional economics (Bush, 1987; Bush and Tool, 2003; Foster, 1981a,b; Veblen, 1964, 1996) with social ontology (Searle, 1995, 2005, 2010). The key in understanding the evolution of money is in the relation between the regulation, particularly normative rules, dictating the admissible courses of action for the fulfillment of the functions of money, especially as a means of payment, and the technological possibilities to facilitate such action. Social constitution is the prerequisite of social significance and action (Searle, 1995, 2010), but technological capabilities (in similar fashion to natural necessities) provide the set of alternative courses of action and, consequently, the institutional arrangements available to fulfill the functions of money.[11] Technological innovation can expand these possibilities, providing alternative configurations for the constitutive and the normative rules that give rise to payment or transfer of monetary value, which, when adopted, can alter the payment system. The state, through its institutions, is in the center of this process controlling regulation and enacting the necessary regulation for the integration of technological innovation in the monetary system and enforcing acceptance.

Technological devices that are used in the context of the institution of money, or of any institution for that matter, need to be socially constituted and regulated in order to acquire social significance and efficacy.[12] A credit card, if we are to examine a specific case of technological innovation in payments, can only be used as a payment device in virtue of its legal and social status as a credit card, in the same fashion as a banknote is valuable

---

[11]According to Hodgson (2006, p. 4), "the set of possible rules can be enlarged by technological and other institutional developments," one example being the way that "the technology of writing makes feasible the rule that a valid contract on paper must be signed".

[12]"While it is entirely possible for human behaviour to exhibit random characteristics, institutionalists argue that all behavior within a community is ultimately subject to social prescriptions or proscriptions. This especially true of all problem-solving (purposive) behavior. The community at large has a stake in the manner in which is tools and its intelligence are brought to bear on its life processes."

because it is collectively accepted as representing money. The technical characteristics of this (or any) device suggest the possible uses, but they do not automatically carry any social meaning. The admissible use of bitcoins is defined by regulation, and its social significance depends on collective acceptance that ascribes it with its social status as a means of payment or carrier of value. Any regulation that is put in place needs to be supported by the group of users to have any real impact in social interaction. At the same time, regulation can only dictate a course of use that is consistent with the technical characteristics of any payment device: for the encryption technology, the protocol of use in payment, and the system for the verification of transfers. Still, regulation cannot sanction courses of action that supersede the technical standards of such payment media; for example, these rules cannot require that altcoins that are Internet-based by designed would be used for POS transactions, when the available technology cannot support this possibility. Regulation indicates exactly which of the technically possible types of action are admissible and socially significant and can socially useful. The introduction of credit cards is suggestive of the multifaceted character of financial innovation. Cryptocurrencies rely to a complex institutional structure in order to acquire social and consequently economic efficiency. At the same time, they represent an innovation in the market for payment services, competing with other means of payment including cash. As a result, the market for payments transforms and the variety and consequently the pricing of the services offered change, altering the overall structure of the payments industry, including the regulatory framework of its operation.

Thorstein Veblen was the one of the first economists to analyze systematically the interplay between institutions and the transformative power of technological innovation. In his effort to construct a theoretical framework for the analysis of institutional change, Veblen introduced a dichotomy between "instrumental" and "ceremonial" values against which a possible technological adjustment can be appraised (Waller, 1988, p. 757). The two systems of valuation are antagonistic but at the same time, they coexist, embedded in the institutional structure. Ceremonial values mirror the power relations, the distribution of status, and the invidious interests that define the institutional structure. Ceremonial considerations give rise to a system of "sufficient reason" (Tool, 2000, p. 55) for the acceptance of the institutional rules and are connected with invidious consumption and the dominance of the leisure class (Veblen, 1964). Instrumental values are directed toward the application of knowledge for the solution of specific social problems. If ceremonial values are the bastion of the status quo and the social hierarchy, instrumental thinking is the voice of progress and "instrumental efficiency" (Tool, 2000, p. 60). In the monetary system, the ceremonial values defend the privileges and the rents of the banks and the state, while the instrumental values express the concerns about the efficient operations of the monetary system.

The definition of technology as the fulfillment of human purpose (Arthur, 2007) should inform the meaning of technological change as an expression of "instrumental" values in action and as the cause for their further growth.[13] Technological development contributes to the growth of human knowledge, which in turn has a cumulative effect on social attitudes, individual and collective behavior, technological tools, and social institutions. Original institutional economics claims that technological progress produces also knowledge that has an effect on institutional adjustment by influencing the attitudes toward the established institutional structures and consequently on the collective beliefs of the community.[14] Technology gets integrated in everyday experience and encourages a practical awareness of scientific knowledge that can challenge the conceived ideas about social organization, which often mirror ceremonial concerns. Technology not only does provide new devices but also alters, sometimes radically, the narratives that inform our social interaction including our relationship to our institutions. The available technological knowledge and the attitudes toward social organization shape one another; technological change influences the expectations and the beliefs toward the institutional structure raising the social standards about efficiency that are used in the evaluation of the established institutional arrangements.[15] The increased efficacy from the application of novel technologies in one area enhances the optimism that is connected with technological progress and creates further expectations for institutional progress in other fields. Technology brings with it a new "material culture,"[16] inspired by new technological

---

[13]"In his discussion of the dynamics of institutional change, Veblen speaks of the impact of technology on the institutional structure. Technological processes, he argued, required a matter of fact preoccupation with cause and effect at the exclusion of any consideration of status or power relations. Problem solving in the technological continuum of human experience is inherently dynamic as the solution to one problem (or set of problems) opens up new areas of possibilities of consideration. This has a dislocating effect on the *status quo* of the existing institutional structure" (Bush and Tool, 2003, p. 19).

[14]"Veblen's conception of 'cumulative causation' explains the dynamics of the process that produces 'progressive' institutional change. Technological innovation changes the objective circumstances of the community; the new set of circumstances alters the habits of thought and behavior; these new habits of thought and behavior are projected into other areas of the community experience, giving rise to further innovations in the arts and sciences, which in turn, produce new technological innovations in the community's efforts 'to turn material things to account.' Veblen believed that the change in the material circumstances of culture brought about through the introduction of machine technology during the Industrial Revolution conditioned working people to think in terms of cause and effect" (Bush, 1987, p. 1101).

[15]"The principle of technological determination is simply that social problems can only solved by adjusting the institutional structures involved in the problem so as to bring them into instrumentally efficient correlation with the technological aspects of the problems. What is meant by 'instrumentally efficient correlation' is that instrumental functions of the institution in question be carried on at a level of efficiency tolerable to the members of the institution in view of the possibilities indicated by those same technological factors" (Foster, 1981a, p. 932). Reference in Tool (2000, p. 92).

[16]Technology should be thought of in broad terms, including applied science. A different description of this broad understanding of technology is given by the term "material culture," which suggests both the use of technology and the knowledge that is accompanying this use. See, for example, Castells (1996) or Williams (1977).

applications in the social domain and the consequent popularization of science and technology.

Innovation has to be integrated in the institutional structure in order to become socially significant, but only up to the point that it does not create friction with the established system of rules and privileges.[17] New technology is both enabled and constrained by social rules that ascribe to it social significance and defines its domain of application. Veblen described the inherent conservatism of the social structures against the integration of technological innovation as "ceremonial encapsulation" (Bush, 1988, pp. 142–149). Ceremonial encapsulation describes the constraints in the adaptation of technology into already existing institutional structures. A tension characterizes the adaptation of the ceremonial to the instrumental system of values. Ceremonial values remain inert, even backward looking, despite the pull from novel technology toward progress and efficiency. The emphasis on the conservatism of institutional structures and of the values that inspire them provides an important insight in the mechanism of institutional adjustment and of the socialization of technological innovation. The resilience of institutions as opposed to the progressive influence of technology points to the importance of stability and continuity that the social institutions serve.

7.5 THE CEREMONIAL ENCAPSULATION OF CRYPTOCURRENCIES IN THE ESTABLISHED MODEL OF REGULATION FOR DIGITAL PAYMENTS

The invention of the blockchain, the success of the Bitcoin, its subsequent replication in a wide variety of other cryptocurrencies, and the proliferation of services to support them have attracted the interest of regulators,[18] especially in the developed countries, where the oversight of the digital payment systems is much more progressed and sophisticated. Following the analysis of the previous sections, we see how the cryptocurrencies' innovative processing of payment technology gets ceremonially encapsulated in the already

---

[17]"The technological innovation is encapsulated within ceremonial patterns of behavior in such a manner as not to change the existing value structure of the community" (Bush and Tool, 2003, p. 27).

[18]"Cryptocurrencies have the potential to challenge government supervision of monetary policy by the disruption of current payment systems and the avoidance of existing regulatory schemes. In particular, they offer, or at least are perceived as providing, the ability to cloak transactions with a level of anonymity that is currently found only with certain cash transactions. . . . Additionally, cryptocurrencies are theoretically open to use to transfer funds to persons who themselves are Specially Designated Nationals or to nations that are covered by one of many economic sanctions programs under the supervision of the Treasury Department's Office of Foreign Asset Controls. No wonder that they are attracting much attention from the United States government" (Middlebrookt and Hughestt, 2014, pp. 816–817).

established regulation of the payment industry and how the interests of the state, the commercial banks, the payment intermediaries, and the public play out in the process.[19]

Regulation has three different aims or it is related with three different sets of interests. The main issue is the interest of the state, expressed in the regulation against money laundering, financing crime, and tax evasion. In addition, there is a legal protection in place that secures the monopoly of the state in issuing currency. There are the interests of the commercial banks and the companies that are involved in the payments industry. Payment intermediaries are concerned with competition of incumbents and try to defend their business and their position in the market, by seeking government intervention and regulation of their competitors. Finally, there are the interests of the consumers, the protection of which provides a further reason for state regulation.[20] Since consumers only indirectly and marginally can influence the process of regulation and oversight of the payment industry, their only power, and a very substantial power in that, is to decide to use a service or not, that is, to "vote with their feet" adopting or not a novel payment instrument. In all three cases, it is the state, through its institutions and especially through regulation and oversight, that can decide on and enforce the condition of the adoption of a financial innovation, like the digital public ledger payment systems.

Many states seem to adopt an attitude of nonintervention in relation to Bitcoin, which is the most visible and therefore the more liable to governmental scrutiny. Among the states that are considering or actually pursue the regulation of altcoins, we could distinguish between two distinct policies, which are related with the definition of what these altcoins are and do. The more strict line argues that altcoins are money proper, and in that sense, they are not legal as far as they can compromise the monopoly of the state in issuing legal tender. This hard line is adopted by countries like Russia or China, which have rendered Bitcoin illegal. Such policies are problematic because they start from the false premise that Bitcoin, and possibly other altcoins that may suffer under the same prohibition, is money and also because they hamper financial innovation in the very important area of digital payment services and consequently in the area of e-commerce.

A different, more promising policy, and also one that is more consistent with the identity and the functions of cryptocurrencies, treats them as payment systems that are used to transmit economic value. Such a solution may not be tailor-made for

---

[19]"Since virtual currencies first came into the marketplace in the 1990s, those responsible for monetary policy, federal anti-money laundering and economic sanctions programs, along with federal and state consumer protection regulators, payment systems operators, businesses, and consumers have grappled with understanding how these 'currencies' work, whether they should be deemed 'lawful' payment methods in the United States, and, if so, the manner and extent to which they should be regulated" (Middlebrookt and Hughestt, 2014, p. 814).

[20]"Ordinary, law-abiding individuals eventually will expect the same kinds of protections from unauthorized or fraudulent transactions they receive on credit and debit cards" (Middlebrookt and Hughestt, 2014, p. 842).

cryptocurrencies, but rather seems to encapsulate them in the model of the already established payment business, dominated by companies like *MasterCard, PayPal, or VISA*. The ceremonial encapsulation of cryptocurrencies may seem as conservative reaction, which serves the interests of the payment industry by enforcing their standards and their business model on cryptocurrencies but, at the same time, provides a context for the development of cryptocurrencies in the official payment system, an attitude that seems more progressive than the outright prohibition of altcoins and their exile into the fringes of Internet payments.

The United States offers a representative example for the regulation of cryptocurrencies as payment instruments. The United States is also important because it is one of the biggest markets for e-commerce and digital payments, the domicile of some of the most important IT companies, and financial intermediaries with an Internet presence. A critical development in the regulation of cryptocurrencies is the directive issued by the US Department of the Treasury's Financial Crimes Enforcement Network (FinCEN) spelling out the compliance obligations of virtual currencies under the Federal Bank Secrecy Act (BSA).[21] According to the directive, virtual currencies are considered to be vehicles of money transmission so long as they can be readily converted to dollars (or in other official currencies or recognized financial assets, including precious metals), and all those entities have to obtain the appropriate state license and comply with federal and state money transmitter requirements. The directive builds upon the case brought by the Federal Government of the United States against e-gold, a digital payment provider, which offered anonymous value transmission and payment services, denominated in precious metals. The use of precious metals was intended to bypass the regulation concerning money transmissions, which was enacted in the United States. The indictment charged e-gold with transmitting funds from illegal activity or with the intent of promoting illegal activity or knowingly concealing the source of the proceeds of the illegal activity. According to the government, e-gold failed to obtain a money transmitter's license as is required by law and ignored federal requirements to implement an anti-money laundering program and to file suspicious activity reports (SAR) with the treasury (Middlebrookt and Hughestt, 2014, pp. 823–824). The court rejected e-gold's argument that it was not required to comply with the money transmitters license directive, because it did not deal with cash or coin, an argument that could also be applied to cryptocurrencies. The court provided an expansive definition of the Section 1960 on money transmission, arguing that "a business can clearly engage in money transmitting without limiting its transactions to cash or currency and would commit a crime if it did so without being licensed. . . . Section 1960 defines 'money transmitting' broadly to including

---

[21]Bank Secrecy Act, tit. I–II, Pub. L. No. 91-508, 84 Stat. 1114, 1114-24 (codified as amended at 12 U.S.C. §§ 1829b, 1951-1959; 31 U.S.C. §§ 5311-5314, 5316-5332 (2012)). Reference in Middlebrookt and Hughestt (2014, p. 815).

transferring 'funds,' not just currency, by 'any and all means;' it is not limited to cash transactions" (Middlebrookt and Hughestt, 2014, pp. 825–826).

The directive issued by the US Department of the Treasury's Financial Crimes Enforcement Network (FinCEN) builds on the decision against e-gold. FinCEN starts by distinguishing "real" currency from "virtual" currency, with virtual currency not having a legal tender status and thus not considered and legally treated as currency. Nevertheless, some virtual currency, like bitcoin, has an equivalent value in and can be readily converted to currency, and so, it can be used as a "substitute" for real currency, and FinCEN deems this "convertible virtual currency" (Middlebrookt and Hughestt, 2014, p. 827). In cases of "convertible virtual currency," a money transmitter's license is required and all the legal requirements and safeguards are active. Following FinCEN, the Department of Financial Services in New York (NYDFS) opened an investigation into virtual currencies and subpoenaed 22 companies providing Bitcoin-related services and a number of venture capital firms that have invested in Bitcoin business. In California, the State Department of Financial Institutions "issued a cease and desist letter to the Bitcoin Foundation charging the foundation with engaging in the business of money transmission without obtaining a license or other authorization required by California's Money Transmission Act" (Middlebrookt and Hughestt, 2014, pp. 815–816).

Cryptocurrencies need to be regulated in order to be fully integrated to the financial system. In many jurisdictions, regulation is nonexistent and in others absolutely prohibitive, denying cryptocurrencies their place in the financial system. In case of the United States and the FinCEN, we see a different, even though imperfect, solution to the problem of the institutionalization of cryptocurrencies. US regulation ceremonially encapsulates them, defining them as services of monetary transmission and enforcing them in the model of the payments industry. The European Union has adopted a similar stance treating cryptocurrencies under the Electronic Money Directive 2009/110/EC. In the subsequent section, we will speculate on different scenarios of the evolution of cryptocurrencies, considering the challenges they are facing or they are going to face in the near future.

7.6 CRYPTOCURRENCIES AS MATURE PAYMENT TECHNOLOGIES: CHALLENGES IN THE NEAR FUTURE

Cryptocurrencies raise expectations for the future, representing a promise for an efficient, transparent, privacy enhancing, and reliable medium of payment in the Internet. Still, there is a set of challenges to be met, if cryptocurrencies are to break out and offer a trustworthy payment service for the general public. This final section will address these challenges, starting from the question of regulation and touching upon the questions of privacy, volatility, internal organization, and infrastructure.

Regulation is important in order to ascribe cryptocurrencies with a clear and stable legal status, which is going to underlie their economic significance and integrate them into financial system.[22] The position that cryptocurrencies should not or need not be regulated is both unrealistic and unproductive. It is unrealistic because regulation agencies, due to security concerns, due to lobbying, and in an effort to maintain their control over the payment systems, will intervene and try to enforce a legal framework upon cryptocurrencies (Middlebrookt and Hughestt, 2014, p. 840). Even if one could argue that Internet payments are not easily controllable, because of problems of location, flexibility, and technology, the state could still control the links between cryptocurrencies and official money by enforcing regulation to exchange markets (Stokes, 2012, p. 231). If altcoins are prevented from being converted to currency, then their economic value and their functionality are compromised rendering them unusable for the general public. Their path to the markets and the general public passes through regulation, and until a clear, consistent, and comprehensive framework is in place, it will be very difficult for them to achieve substantial levels of use.

If regulation is necessary, the optimal solution would be to design a unique cryptocurrency regulatory scheme. Both in the United States and in the EU, cryptocurrencies seem to be forced in the established legal framework of payment technologies. Regulation usually treats new products and technologies by ceremonial encapsulating them to the existing regulatory framework rather than devising a new, tailor-made framework (Middlebrookt and Hughestt, 2014, p. 840). This is the case with the FinCEN directive, which treats cryptocurrencies as money-transmitting vehicles, and the same applies for the EU, where cryptocurrencies are defined as electronic cash regulated by the Electronic Money Directive 2009/110/EC. Nevertheless, it still possible, even though improbable to enact a regulatory framework specially developed to accommodate them. To that effect, cryptocurrencies need to acquire a critical mass in transactions beyond speculation. Only then could be possible to lobby for a more favorable regulation countering the mistrust of government and the efforts of competitors to push cryptocurrencies to the established business model of electronic payments.

Price volatility poses an equally serious barrier as inappropriate legislation (Evans, 2014, p. 6). Most merchants do not keep any of their revenue in cryptocurrencies, but convert them daily in the official currency.[23] During the early stages, some volatility

---

[22]"Bitcoin appears to suffer by being disconnected from the banking and payment systems of the U.S. and other countries. Most currencies are held and transferred through bank accounts, which in turn are protected by layers of regulation, deposit insurance, and international treaties. Without access to this infrastructure, Bitcoin has proven vulnerable to fraud, theft, and subversion by skilled computer hackers" (Yermack, 2014, p. 17).

[23]"Expedia the big online travel site, announced on Wednesday [the 9th of June 2014] it will begin accepting Bitcoin for hotel bookings through its website, becoming the first major travel-agency to take the digital currency. . . . Expedia, which is using Coinbase for bitcoin processing, won't hold the digital currency it receives, but that's not 'a statement on bitcoin, pro or con,' Mr. Gulmann explained. Rather, Coinbase's default setting is for a daily settlement back into U.S. dollars." *The Wall Street Journal*, June 11, 2014. Web. http://blogs.wsj.com/digits/2014/06/11/expedia-starts-accepting-bitcoin-for-hotel-bookings/?mod=ST1 (accessed July 28, 2014).

is to be expected, but eventually, much of the uncertainty should be resolved if cryptocurrencies are to be used as independent media of exchange. The price instability may be a further reason why there is no widespread acceptability of cryptocurrencies by merchants, despite their comparably low transaction fees. In the few cases that merchants accept altcoins, they convert their revenues to the official currency immediately or rely to third parties for helping them to manage their operations and their volatility risk (Evans, 2014, p. 10). The requirement of this kind of intermediation adds to the cost of processing transactions but more importantly compromises the business model of altcoins and makes them dependent to third parties, which take over their operation and their revenues. Volatility creates yet another, potentially, more serious problem. The erratic movement of cryptocurrencies has made them a vehicle of speculation, where individuals bet on the future value in order to achieve short-term profits. The tendency of speculation is further encouraged by the fact that some of the cryptocurrencies, most prominently bitcoin, constrain their supply up to a given number, creating a deflationary effect. Speculation causes ever more price volatility, which prevents cryptocurrencies from serving efficiently and independently their function as media of payment.

Privacy is one of the main issues for regulators at the same time as it is one of the distinguishing characteristics of cryptocurrencies. Their ability to conceal the identity of the transacting parties and to protect them from data mining, surveillance, and exclusion gives them an important comparative advantage. At the same time, governments are concerned about money laundering, finance of criminal activities and terrorism, and the use of cryptocurrencies to that effect (Stokes, 2013, p. 2). A delicate balance needs to be kept between ensuring the privacy of transactions and preventing criminal use by placing safeguards in the system. Two recent events make the issue of privacy in economic transactions even more contested. The NSA affair proved that mass surveillance is a reality and raised the awareness and the desire of the public for privacy protection. At the same time, the Silk Road marketplace, where bitcoins were used to purchase illegal goods and services, including narcotics and stolen credit card numbers, pointed to the dangers from the illegitimate use of privacy enhancing payment technologies.[24] It seems difficult to find a balance between privacy protection and crime prevention, but this is essential not only for the development but also for the survival of cryptocurrencies.

A final challenge relates to the supporting infrastructure of cryptocurrencies, and here, we refer both to the internal management structure of cryptocurrencies, including the decision makers, the programmers, and the miners, and to the providers of external services,

---

[24]"The Silk Road marketplace, an Internet portal for the sale of illegal narcotics which accepted only bitcoins for payment, was sometimes reported to account for as much as half of the early Bitcoin transaction volume although this estimate is subject to considerable dispute. The Silk Road association helped give bitcoins an early reputation for lawlessness, and this outlaw cachet may not have harmed its appeal at all" (Yermack, 2014, p. 6).

especially the markets and the supporting software providers. The recent collapse of Mt. Gox, the biggest Bitcoin exchange, proves with the most vivid and immediate fashion that the payment industry needs reliable and professional solutions (Yermack, 2014, pp. 1–2). It is imperative that the organization of cryptocurrencies is improved to ensure consumer protection concerning both the operation of cryptocurrencies themselves and the associated services, be it software or exchange support. The question of regulation reemerges with renewed force here and also the role that established companies and business models in the development of cryptocurrencies after the collapse of Mt. Gox.

7.7 CONCLUSIONS

Much of the discussion around cryptocurrencies and the motivation of some of these projects is inspired by a utopian vision for a new monetary system without intermediation, where banks and states will have no role or power. The "new money" is going to be developed upon the invention of the blockchain and will be equitable, independent, and transparent harnessing the power of the Internet and using distributed network of users who will contribute computer power in exchange of newly minted altcoins. Still, despite the waves of enthusiasm around Bitcoin and the speculative bubble that they created, cryptocurrencies still lag behind the utopian vision of an anarchic monetary system. Ironically, the solution to their problems could be regulation and integration in the official monetary system, even adopting the existing business models of the payment industry and the commercial banks, which cryptocurrencies were designed to challenge. Only when the appropriate regulation is in place could these new payment technologies integrate and achieve their full potential. The current situation is discouraging; cryptocurrencies are trapped between the Scylla of ceremonial encapsulation in the established but inappropriate models of regulation for digital payments and the Charybdis of an unregulated existence where uncertainty, fraud, and criminality are pervasive. It remains to be seen if new regulation will be enacted to allow them to operate safely and efficiently. This may be doubtful but promising since the blockchain has a lot more to offer to digital payments and beyond.

ACKNOWLEDGMENTS

I am grateful to Matthias Tarasiewicz from the University of Applied Arts Vienna, for reading an early version of this chapter, checking the facts on Bitcoin, and providing me invaluable information. Many of my ideas on the subject of cryptocurrencies were developed in our conversations.

REFERENCES

Arthur, B.W., 2007. The structure of invention. Res. Policy 36, 274–287.
Bush, P.D., 1987. The theory of institutional change. J. Econ. Issues 21 (3), 1075–1116.

Bush, P.D., 1988. The theory of institutional change. In: Tool, M.R. (Ed.), Evolutionary Economics I: Foundations of Institutional Thought. M.E. Sharpe, Armonk, NY, pp. 125–166.

Bush, P.D., Tool, M.R., 2003. Foundational concepts for institutionalist policy making. In: Bush, D., Tool, M.R. (Eds.), Institutional Analysis and Economic Policy. Kluwer Academic Publishers, Dordrecht, pp. 1–46.

Castells, M., 1996. The Rise of the Network Society. Blackwell, London.

DuPont, Q., 2014. The politics of cryptography: bitcoin and the ordering machines. J. Peer Prod. 4, 1–10.

Evans, D.S., 2014. Economic aspects of bitcoin and other decentralized public-ledger currency platforms. Coase-Sandor Instituted for Law and Economics Working Paper No. 685, pp. 1–21.

Foster, J.F., 1981a. John Dewey and economic value. J. Econ. Issues 15 (4), 871–879.

Foster, J.F., 1981b. The relation between theory of value and economic analysis. J. Econ. Issues 15 (4), 899–905.

Frame, W.S., White, L.J., 2004. Empirical studies of financial innovation: lots of talk, little action? J. Econ. Lit. 42 (1), 116–144.

Hanley, B.P., 2013. The false premises and promises of bitcoin. Discussion Paper, pp. 1–30.

Hodgson, G., 2006. What are institutions? J. Econ. Issues 40 (1), 1–24.

Knapp, G.F., 1924. The State Theory of Money. Macmillan, London.

Luther, W.J., 2013. Cryptocurrencies, network effects, and switching costs. Working Paper 13-17, pp. 1–37.

Maurer, B., Nelms, T.C., Swartz, L., 2013. When perhaps the real problem is money itself: the practical materiality of bitcoin! Soc. Semiot. 23 (2), 261–277.

Menger, K., 1892. On the origin of money. Econ. J. 2 (6), 239–255.

Middlebrookt, S.T., Hughestt, S.J., 2014. Regulating cryptocurrencies in the United States: current issues and future directions. William Mitchell Law Rev. 40 (2), 813–848.

Nakamoto, S., 2009. Bitcoin: A Peer-to-Peer Electronic Cash System.

Neal, M., 2014. Bitcoin is hiring lobbyists. Motherboard, May 12, 2014.

Searle, J., 1995. The Construction of Social Reality. The Free Press, New York.

Searle, J., 2005. What is an institution? J. Inst. Econ. 1 (1), 1–22.

Searle, J., 2010. Making the Social World. Oxford University Press, Oxford.

Stokes, R., 2012. Virtual money laundering: the case of bitcoin and the Linden dollar. Inform. Commun. Tech. Law 21 (3), 221–236.

Stokes, R., 2013. Anti-money laundering regulation and emerging payment technologies. Bank. Fin. Services Po. Rep. 32 (5), 1–10.

Tool, M., 2000. Value Theory and Economic Progress: The Institutional Economics of J. F. Foster. Kluwer Academic Publishers, Boston.

Veblen, T., 1964. The Instinct of Workmanship and the State of the Industrial Arts. Augustus M. Kelley, New York, NY.

Veblen, T., 1996. The Theory of the Leisure Clash. Dover, London.

Waller, W.T., 1988. The concept of habit in economic analysis. J. Econ. Issues 22 (1), 757–771.

Williams, R., 1977. Marxism and Literature. Oxford University Press, Oxford.

Yermack, D., 2014. Is Bitcoin a real currency? An economic appraisal. Unpublished paper, pp. 1–22.

CHAPTER 8

Counterfeiting in Cryptocurrency: An Emerging Problem

Ralph E. McKinney, Jr.[a], Lawrence P. Shao[a], Duane C. Rosenlieb, Jr.[b], Dale H. Shao[a]
[a]College of Business at Marshall University in Huntington, West Virginia, USA
[b]Rosenlieb Law Office, St. Albans, West Virginia, USA

Contents

8.1 CHAPTER OVERVIEW

In this chapter, we will explore counterfeiting and counterfeiting deterrents (e.g., legal, countermeasures, and security features) as it relates to cryptocurrency. To accomplish this, we first address the functionality of currency: ownership and transferability, the ability to store value, and security. As cryptocurrency is not widespread (i.e., accepted in most transactions) and relatively evolving, the comparison between the "hard" currency of coin and paper and that of cryptocurrency of virtual and digital environments is illustrated. This is essential in understanding why counterfeiting occurs and the impact that counterfeiting can have on a currency. Ultimately, a currency can be destabilized and decimated through counterfeiting actions.

At the conclusion of this chapter, you should
- understand the difference between hard currencies and cryptocurrencies;
- understand the functionality of currency with respect to ownership, transferability, and security;
- define counterfeiting and the importance in deterring counterfeiting;

- identify key security features used to deter counterfeiting; and
- identify major events and global initiatives to protect currency and how those apply to cryptocurrencies.

8.2 INTRODUCTION: CRYPTOCURRENCY HAS VIRTUALLY EVOLVED FROM HARD CURRENCY

Advances in technology and the advent of Internet protocols have provided a means for reality to be simulated in a *digital* or *virtual* environment (McKinney et al., 2011). This has given rise to new methods of conducting financial transactions from credit and debit cards to e-purchases, e-money, e-cash, and digital value units (McKinney et al., 2015; Tavakol, 1999; Schreft, 2002; Sorokin, 2013). Although there are many different distinct classifications of currency, only two primary classifications exist: *tangible* and *intangible* (McKinney et al., 2015). Intangible currency distinctly requires that technology facilitates the exchange in ownership. Examples of such are MintChip (Jackson, 2012), Bitcoin, Litecoin, Namecoin, and Peercoin (Grinberg, 2011; Rogojanu and Badea, 2014; Sprankel, 2013). For tangible currency, ownership is facilitated merely by the exchange of coin, paper, scrip, token, or other physical representations of the conceptual idea of money (Champ, 2008; Hart, 2007; Shao et al., 2013a,b; Western Union, 2014).

Currency, at its central core of definitions, is by all accounts a conceptual idea (Guinchard, 2010; Hubbard and O'Brien, 2013; Shao et al., 2013b). Ideas, as we well know, can be stolen, pirated, and reproduced (Shelley, 2012) and that reproduction or *simulation* of the real idea is, at the heart of it, counterfeiting (Shao et al., 2013a). Before we fully explore counterfeiting, we must consider the idea of currency and how this "idea" of currency has historically been recognized and developed. While it is important to note that local communities have "created" their own currencies for trade, these currencies have traditionally been geographically limited and do not have significance beyond the community as the national currencies (Timberlake, 1987). As such, this chapter primarily considers national currencies.

Chinese accounting ledgers (Aiken and Lu, 1998) known as *jingtian* or "well-field" (Yang and Zhang, 2003) of the Western Zhou dynasty were used from 1100 to 771 BCE (Mundell, 2002) as a necessity to account for taxes, land ownership, and agricultural production (Yang and Zhang, 2003). Although other civilizations such as the Egyptians, India, and Scythia had paper currency (Mundell, 2002), the earliest paper medium of exchange has been attributed to the Chinese as an invention reaching back to the Tang dynasty from 617 to 907 BCE (Horesh, 2012). Individuals would deposit or exchange valuables for paper scrip known as *feigian*, flying cash, in the *guifang*, counting houses, much like the modern banking system of today, only without the aid of computers (Horesh, 2012). It is certainly possible that paper currency existed before the Tang dynasty, but the penal codes of the *Tanglü shuyi* of 737 BCE cannot be fully understood due to the incompleteness of the surviving records (Wilkinson, 1973).

In addition to paper currency, coins have been found in Asia Minor and the Lydian civilization dating back to 700 BCE (Mundell, 2002). The longevity of early metal coins is contingent on peace as during war times, the metal may be converted for other purposes. For example, conflicts in China caused the Northern Song dynasty (960–1127 ACE) to utilize copper for war preparations, thus causing a scarcity of metal coins (Horesh, 2012). This made it necessary for the Northern Song to fully support the widespread use of paper currency or potentially destabilize the economy without a reliable medium of exchange. The conversion problems of metal coins are not limited to China. In 1787, England declared that the pound sterling was not convertible into precious metal coins (Besomi, 2010). Conversion issues will be further discussed under the Basic Function of Currency.

Factors affecting the evolution of currency discussed in the preceding sections include
• Organization and consistency of businesses enterprise
• Technology
• Politics
• Government regulations
• Availability of various metals

The combinations of factors affecting the evolution of currency are sometimes random and sometimes predictable (such as constantly improving technological innovations).

Figure 8.1 brings together the unique factors and events that have shaped the development of currency in a timeline form.

Cryptocurrency is having a relatively significant effect on society and the global economy. At present, cryptocurrency is not a major player in the global economy. It is a concept whose time has come and will continue to grow in its importance. Hard currency is quickly being replaced by the use of credit and debit cards. Credit and debit cards will eventually be replaced by cryptocurrency. Moreover, the legal status and use of cryptocurrencies is being debated. The figure below illustrates this debate. The first panel represents the hard currency, the second panel the current discussion of how transactions will be recognized and conducted, and the third panel represents the acceptance of

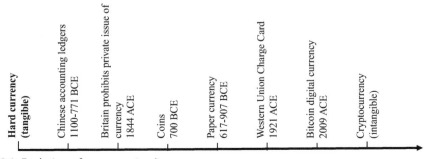

Figure 8.1 Evolution of currency timeline.

Figure 8.2 Hard currency versus virtual currency debate.

cryptocurrencies in financial transactions. Some of the events and requirements that will have to occur are discussed in the next few sections (Figure 8.2).

Much as the horseless carriage replaced the steam engine, virtual currency is in the process of replacing the hard currency and the currently popular charge card. Eventually, the capabilities of the charge card, such as short-term credit, will be absorbed into the cryptocurrency medium:

> *In contrast to real currency, 'virtual' currency is a medium of exchange that operates like a currency in some environments, but does not have all the attributes of real currency. In particular, virtual currency does not have legal tender status in any jurisdiction. This guidance addresses 'convertible' virtual currency. This type of virtual currency either has an equivalent value in real currency, or acts as a substitute for real currency.*
>
> *FinCEN (2013)*

In essence, cryptocurrency is a virtual currency, and virtual currencies, in this definition, do not include any currencies confined or limited by the issuer such as online games (McKinney et al., 2011). Although many online games have economies that can be influenced through the purchase of resources and of "digital" currencies by "real" currencies, the "digital" currencies are not convertible to "real" currencies nor can they be used for "real" goods and services (Kennedy, 2008). Moreover, transactions using "brokered monetary value" such as PayPal and Dwolla are not virtual currencies only facilitators of transactions (Champ, 2007). It is the utility of the currency that drives the definition of virtual currency and also the users' rights to that property (Smith, 2012). Furthermore, as technology and new innovations are discovered, the conceptual definitions must be adapted to include the new permutations of *things*; and by default, this would include the development and execution of cryptocurrencies. According to Dostov and Shust (2013), virtual currencies may be limited to function, whereas cryptocurrencies are higher functioning and more secure than virtual currencies, which can be further defined into centralized and decentralized units.

McKinney et al. (2015) state, "*How currency is represented is not the primary issue, but its ability to be **an instrument of purchasing** power, economic mobility, and social mobility.*"

Cryptocurrencies meet that definition if the issuer is a centralized government or a decentralized entity. Although a formal definition has not been accepted universally for either cryptocurrencies or virtual currencies (Dostov and Shust, 2013), it is the conceptual idea that is represented electronically and operates as a medium of exchange with the basic functions of currency (McKinney et al., 2013). The next sections describe the basics of how cryptocurrency has and will continue to grow.

8.3 THE BASIC FUNCTION OF CURRENCY: A MEDIUM OF EXCHANGE

Cryptocurrency must operate as a medium of exchange in similar ways as the currency of coins and paper; primarily, cryptocurrency must be able to facilitate merchant transactions between sellers and buyers (Gladstone, 1997). In order to do this, it must offer users common characteristics such as

- ownership and transferability,
- the ability to store value, and
- the security of the currency.

In fact, these three must intersect in order for any medium of exchange to endure as common currency. If these characteristics falter, so will the users' faith in that currency to the extent that he or she may seek a substitution for that medium of exchange.

In the United States in 1931, a local bank failed in a city (Preston, 1933). This was not unusual during this time in American history as the Great Depression had caused widespread bank failures and financial disarray in every part of the country. What was unique was how the citizens of Tenino dealt with this dilemma: a substitutive wooden currency would temporarily replace the US dollars until such time that the bank's assets could be liquidated. Although wooden currency had existed in other civilizations and cultures, this was the first occurrence in the United States. Moreover, this solution was so intriguing that it was a subject for discussion according to the April 7, 1932 Congressional Record. Eventually, the bank's assets were liquidated, and the Tenino wooden currency was redeemed or kept with the return of the US dollar.

In the case of the Tenino wooden currency, the inability of owners to access their assets (i.e., US dollars) resulted in the interruption of financial transactions (Preston, 1933). The simple action of transferring ownership of dollars between buyers and sellers failed on a massive scale. This failure was further strengthened by the scarcity of the dollars stemming from the same inability to obtain those dollars. In fact, the core characteristics of currency were questionable, and the dollars were substituted in Tenino as a result of the failure to transfer dollars, the inability to get dollars, and the stored value associated with the dollars. In essence, the dollar lost its utility and therefore its value was diminished.

The challenge for any cryptocurrency is its ability to meet these basic functions of ownership and transferability and the ability to store value, and the security in property rights of the currency is indispensable (McKinney et al., 2015). As these concepts are being discussed sequentially in the next sections, consider how cryptocurrency should operate.

8.3.1 Ownership and transferability

As Price (1893, citing Dr. Benjamin Franklin) noted, fiat money is nothing more than paper promises. Devoid of conversion of currency to precious metal, is currency nothing more than an *I Owe You* (IOU) or *You Owe I* (UOI) (McKinney, 2009)? In fact, during the 1800s and possibly from the shortage of coins during the 1700s, coins of precious metals without regard to country of origin were kept by wealthy Americans (Price, 1893). A person's social status could be advanced simply by hoarding such currency. In essence, ownership of currency can provide opportunities (cf. Aaronson and Mazumder, 2007; Banks, 2007; Björkland and Jäntti, 1997; Mazumder, 2007; Shao et al., 2012).

With the ownership or control of assets that include currency, an individual can leverage his or her purchasing power to increase wealth (economic mobility) and support a political position while increasing social attractiveness (social mobility) (Shao et al., 2012). The key to ownership is not only holding or controlling the asset but also the ability to transfer the asset and its value to another. The attractiveness and utility of currency are partially rooted in not only the ownership and transferability of the said currency but also its ability to store value.

8.3.2 The ability to store value

With any medium of exchange, currency must operate with users having a common understanding of the units of exchange, and these units of exchange must hold their value (Hart, 2007; Williamson, 2002). The conversion of a medium of exchange is a critical function directly related to a currency's ability to store value. Historically, this conversion has been from paper to metal coins and back again as noted in the previous section. Moreover, the problems of converting metal coins are not limited to China (Horesh, 2012) and England (Besomi, 2010), and the value of such financial instruments is not just hinged on conversion.

Political corruption can considerably subvert a currency on a global scale. In 1764, the Currency Act was passed that required selected colonists of the British Empire to purchase goods and silver by precious coins (Ernst, 1965). The British Parliament did make exceptions to the Currency Act of 1764, notably to New York and Pennsylvania, and subsequently amended it though acts made in 1773 (Perkins, 1991). Although the primary goal of the Currency Acts was the stabilization of colonial currency exchanges (Perkins, 1991), the colonists protested and a revolution was fought in 1776 (Greene and Jellison, 1961). Although the Currency Act of 1764 was a means to protect financial transactions as a whole between Virginia and British merchants (Ernst, 1965), it could not completely protect against political corruption.

From 1755 to 1763, the Virginia treasurer Mr. Robinson stole approximately £100,000 in Virginia notes earmarked for destruction as required of notes that have been retired. Subsequently, he used these funds for personal and political gains. Mr. Robinson's failure to retire those notes artificially increased the supply of currency that ultimately eroded its value and led to a substitutive form of currency: precious metal coins. The corruption of one individual resulted in a substantial loss on a global scale. Before Mr. Robinson, there had been other cases of financial losses on a global scale (Perkins, 1991). In 1672, England defaulted on up to £2.25 million when the Exchequer ordered the stoppage of all payments. In France, the Scotsman John Law advised King Louis XV about fiat money that in 1720 completely failed due to overissuance causing the national economy to collapse. The overissuance of currency can systematically cause inflation in the currency's value (Besomi, 2010), thus reducing its store of value:

> Money has been introduced by convention as a kind of substitute for a need or demand, and. . .its value is derived not from nature but law and can be altered or abolished at will.
>
> **Aristotle (cited by Tavakol, 1999, p. 1203)**

Does cryptocurrency represent an opportunity to correct corruption, overissuance of units, artificial inflation, and deflation? This is subject to debate and the limitations imposed by the creators and issuers of cryptocurrency. Consider Bitcoin—a cryptocurrency that has gained international popularity as an alternative to government-backed currencies (Grinberg, 2011). Notably, Bitcoins have been used in the facilitation of criminal activities and not a large base of legitimate enterprises (Grinberg, 2011; McKinney et al., 2015). Grinberg (2011) speculated that successful cryptocurrency markets are not necessarily in the "real" goods but in "virtual" goods and services and microtransactions are too small or too expensive for traditional forms of payment such as credit cards. In fact, this means that the store of value of the cryptocurrency would be upheld and not eroded by third-party intermediaries acting to facilitate transactions. However, the legal status of ownership and the ability to seek recourse in disputes of ownership are risks that impact the store of value (Grinberg, 2011; McKinney et al., 2015).

The ability to store value can wane when individuals have little or no security in their property rights over the currency in which they own and may transfer. In the next section, the security in property rights will be examined.

8.3.3 Security in property rights

To protect ownership including the right to transfer ownership and the value of currency, the property rights surrounding currencies, including that of cryptocurrencies, must be codified in some form to ensure security of the financial instrument (McKinney et al., 2015). Consider this example. In England, efforts to stop the private issuance of currency had begun around 1411 ACE (Tan, 2011). These efforts would not begin to be realized until after 400 years had passed. The Truck Act of 1831 halted the practice of compensating workers with nonlegal tender (i.e., scrip and credit vouchers). Subsequently, the Bank Acts of 1844 and 1845 fully prohibited the private issuance of money. These acts represent the steps to promote the pound as a national currency and ensured its security through the elimination of competition and the exchange of intranational currencies.

England was not the only government to outlaw issuances of private currency. Within the United States during the late 1800s, several states outlawed denominations of less than $5 of private issuances (Grinberg, 2011). Further national debate led to the passage of *The Stamp Payments Act of 1862* where postage stamps could be used as currency as well as metal coins. As with the early Asian currency (see Horesh, 2012), the metal in the coins became a greater utility than the value assigned to the coin by the issuer (Grinberg, 2011). With cryptocurrency, the value is established and cannot be changed by the material construction as cryptocurrency has not been physically constructed.

With cryptocurrency, the security in property rights must be codified by agreement either by the government or by a usage agreement (McKinney et al., 2015). Cryptocurrency is unique as it is a circulating currency and it is also similar to intellectual property as a whole. However, classification of intellectual property especially of copyrights may be erroneous and seems to always be applied to instances where uncertainty in legal standing exists (Balganesh, 2009). In fact, McKinney et al. (2015) suggest that *"virtual currency must be considered intangible personal property **similar** to trademarks, copyrights, patents, intellectual property, and virtual property."* Thus, perhaps it is time for a separate but related category for cryptocurrency must be established to foster property rights.

As cryptocurrencies become more accepted as financial instruments, they will be a greater target for criminal profiteering such as counterfeiting.

8.4 COUNTERFEITING: METHODS, MOTIVATION, AND OPPORTUNITIES

This section defines counterfeiting and presents the common methods counterfeiters undertake, the motivations behind counterfeiting, and the opportunities in which counterfeiting was successful.

McKinney et al. (2015) present this overview of counterfeiting:

Counterfeiting may also be described as the replication or manufacture of a financial instrument (e.g., currency, stamps, bank notes, scrip, and tokens) with the intent to defraud an individual, entity, or government. However, there are similar definitions without the intent to defraud. We believe that the intent is [to defraud] critical to the definition of counterfeiting. Furthermore, the primary motive behind counterfeiting is to increase one's financial position either through the use of fraudulent currencies in the acquisition of goods and services or [to damage a country's economy such as causing] by the destabilization of a currency in the case of war.

Breaking down this definition to the critical elements, counterfeiting is *making a financial instrument to defraud someone*. Thus, an artist may replicate a coin or depict currency without the intent to defraud, and a banker may present photographs of currency to educate employees about the changes in appearance and security measures. So the *replication of currency* is not counterfeiting unless the criminal intent is behind it. Moreover, a victim is needed to fully facilitate and recognize the criminal act of counterfeiting. Of course, different jurisdictions may place limitations and enact penal laws that may differ from the definition above, but the definition presented includes the core requirements that should be included when discussing coin and paper currencies as well as cryptocurrencies.

With the ability to destabilize economic faith in currency, the development and implementations of counterfeiting countermeasures help deter criminal activities. These countermeasures are a direct response to the methods employed in counterfeiting. Sometimes, countermeasures are enough, but even the best countermeasures can be circumvented (Grandi, 2004). Table 8.1 presents the primary countermeasures of *real*, that is, coin and paper, and *virtual* currencies.

With respect to coins and notes, any anticounterfeiting measures are limited to physical modifications upon the financial instruments. This means when new anticounterfeiting features are added, preexisting hard currency must be replaced through willful exchanges and redemptions by the users. Consequently, legitimate changes to virtual currencies can be carried out by means of updating digital wallets and software. Essentially, a mass redemption translates to a uniformity of a financial instrument. This "crypto-uniformity" is a significant advantage over hard currencies as deviations within currencies can sometimes be chaotic and exploited. It is this exploitation that is pivotal in orchestrating successful instances of counterfeiting.

Although countermeasures and criminal laws help reduce instances of counterfeiting (Grandi, 2004), individuals are still motivated to engage in the practice of counterfeiting. With hard currency, mass counterfeiting requires resources to create but it is also limited by geography (Tavakol, 1999). Once counter currency is created, it must be transported

Table 8.1 Traditional currency versus virtual currency debate
Counterfeiting deterrents

Coins and notes	Cryptocurrency
Micro-microprinting	Improved security against hackers
Security threads	Cryptographic capabilities in software
Watermarks	Virtual wallet apps
Tricky images	Erase smartphone's memory remotely
Color changing inks	
Enlarged off-center portraits	
Changes in the design of currency	
Special high-grade paper	

and delivered. Contrariwise, counterfeiting cryptocurrency needs fewer resources and is designed, by its very nature of being virtual, to be transferred electronically. Thus, there may be greater motivations to create counterfeits of cryptocurrency than hard currencies simply as the cost to create such is greatly reduced and the perceived rewards are grander.

On a large scale, a motivating factor for counterfeiting could be war and conflict (Newman, 1958). During the American Colonial Revolution against England, the British were able to inject counterfeit currency on such a large scale from 1776 to 1781 that the currency of $40 million was replaced. But sometimes, mass counterfeiting fails. Telzrow (2008) recounted that in 1945, the German *Operation Bernhard* had amassed approximately £132 million, roughly 15% of circulating currency, which was to be introduced into Britain's economy. To counter Operation Bernhard, no British currency was allowed to enter the country.

In war, counterfeiting is used as an economic and strategic tactic to weaken a currency by targeting the faith of its users in the currency's ability to store value (Newman, 1958). When a currency's value is questioned on a mass scale, users seek alternative financial mediums to conduct business. Other currencies, precious metals, and bartering are most likely to result. In fact, this is the primary goal of the counterfeiters—the disruption of a currency to the point that users abandon it—to which the counterfeiter attains a stronger economic position by default. Terrorism and organized attacks against groups of people fall into this category of war whether or not sanctioned or supported by a government (Kohlman and Bijou, 2013).

Newman (1958) notes that "*. . .counterfeiting for personal gain has a record as old as currency itself. . . .*" The motivation for self-enrichment is driven by the access to resources, technology, and even social identity, which can be provided through increased purchasing power (Shao et al., 2012). Criminal behaviors may be enabled through the suppression and deprivation of a social group's *rights* in achieving fair access to the fruits that purchasing power can provide (Banks, 2007; Shao et al., 2012). According to Wells (2005), an unsharable problem (e.g., financial pressures, social pressures, and family stressors) can lead players to committee actions that otherwise would never be considered. In either event, the motivation is similar in every instance: personal gain.

Some (Machaj, 2007) argue that counterfeiting cannot occur if currency is not legitimately authorized by a government. Others (Block, 2010) contend that any replication of a medium of exchange, whether legitimate or illegitimate, with malicious intent is counterfeiting. Ultimately, criminal behaviors that orchestrate the redistribution of wealth, including self-enriching, should not be tolerated. Furthermore, criminal behaviors and actions are not just confined to "real"-world situations, but have trespassed in virtual worlds (Gorrindo and Groves, 2010). In the next section, the global anticounterfeiting initiative exemplifies what actions have been undertaken to deter these criminal behaviors.

8.5 THE GLOBAL ANTICOUNTERFEITING INITIATIVE

Although the counterfeiting of money has been traditionally associated with the use of fraudulent currencies in the acquisition of goods and services (Newman, 1958), counterfeiting globally *includes* goods and services on a massive scale; but not all governments recognize every "currency" including cryptocurrencies. Moreover, the term *cryptocurrency* may not be used to identify the conceptual framework surrounding the idealism of this financial instrument. For example, the United States predominately uses the term *virtual currency* to describe a convertible security that is digital and has the properties of a financial medium (FinCEN, 2013). In some cases, *digital currency* and *e-cash* are used for similar concepts (McKinney et al., 2015). Definitions are critically important when considering the globalization of commercial and private transactions. As such, it is important to understand the meanings behind the terminology so that *common ground* (a foundation that is familiar among all parties) is established (Keysar et al., 2000). This is more important when users of cryptocurrencies assert rights of ownership or claim legal protections from criminal activities such as counterfeiting.

In an effort to protect currencies from counterfeiting, the League of Nations established the *Protocol to the International Convention for the Suppression of Counterfeiting Currency* on April 20, 1929 (Grandi, 2004). Essentially, this protocol promotes uniformity in counterfeiting laws and includes provisions for alleged counterfeiters to be extradited to face judicial proceedings within the charging country. Consequently, not all countries have ratified this agreement and some countries have ratified only selected portions of the protocol. After the League of Nations dissolved, this protocol was adopted by the United Nations and its overall application to cryptocurrency cannot be assured.

The United Nations Office on Drugs and Crime (2014) has expressed a number of concerns about virtual currencies: anonymous transactions, the ability for law enforcement to identify that a transaction has occurred, and the ability to transfer large amounts of stored value without government oversight. These concerns revolve around criminal behaviors associated with money laundering activities, and not necessarily in counterfeiting, which are part of the greater goals of the United Nations in promoting a standard in electronic commerce. Part of this standard is the solution in recognizing that it will take international cooperative efforts to identify the property rights that cryptocurrencies should and will have.

Even though currency counterfeiting does degrade a currency's use as a medium of exchange (McKinney et al., 2015), the sheer volume of counterfeit products and goods being produced is so great that it has caused a shift from enforcing of counterfeit currency to reducing instances of counterfeit goods and pirated products (OECD, 2008). Counterfeit and pirated products—a rather extensive list from luxury items, such as designer clothing and jewelry, to items affecting health and safety such as food, protective sporting gear, and pharmaceutical products—are being produced and consumed in virtually every country. In 2005, the cost of counterfeited and pirated products in international trade is estimated to exceed $200 billion USD (OECD, 2008, p. 13). If all counterfeit and pirated products produced and consumed were included, this global total is estimated to exceed $650 billion USD (€477 billion) (INTA, 2014). As a result, several global initiatives have targeted counterfeiting from the perspective of international laws and agreements and the employment of technology.

The International Criminal Police Organization (INTERPOL) is perhaps one of the most well-known global networks employed to combat crime, including currency counterfeiting (INTERPOL, 2014). The INTERPOL is composed of 190 member countries working together on cross-border investigations and providing forensic support, operational assistance, and technical databases to combat currency counterfeiting worldwide. Each member country maintains a National Central Bureau (NCB) staffed by law enforcement officers. The INTERPOL coordinates efforts among official law enforcement agencies, such as the US Secret Service and Europol, with international organizations and central banks, such as the European Anti-Fraud Office (OLAF), European Central Bank (ECB), the US Federal Reserve Bank (FRB), and the Central Bank Counterfeit Deterrence Group (CBCDG), and with private industries.

In recognition that counterfeiting has advanced with technology into the digital arena as evidence of the emergence of cryptocurrencies, the INTERPOL will cohost the 2nd Annual INTERPOL-Europol Cybercrime Conference in October 2014 (Europol, 2014). One of Europol's primary duties is enforcing anticounterfeiting laws against the euro. With the theme *Cybercrime Investigations: The Full Cycle*, this conference focuses on enhancing global cooperation on cybercrime prevention and detection, investigation techniques, search and seizure, forensics, and prosecution and trial. In fact, Europol held discussions in June 2014 on the *criminal exploitation of virtual currencies* (Europol, 2014), which is in line with Kohlman and Bijou's (2013) assertion that more resources need to be dedicated to cyberspace and the deterrence of illicit activities in that realm.

As a member of the INTERPOL, the United States has a vested interest in protecting its dollar against counterfeiting acts. While the national framework does not directly outlaw the counterfeiting of virtual currencies, it does outlaw *securities and current coin* (McKinney et al., 2015). Consequently, the legal standing of virtual currencies has not been yet fully defined. Guidance has been given to the executive branch of government by FinCEN about the treatment of virtual currencies, but the judiciary and the Congress are deliberating these issues separately. Moreover, this debate may be settled one cryptocurrency at a time. Meanwhile, the void in federal actions shifts the responsibility to each state and only about 16% have such regulatory authority over virtual currency.

The act of crypto-counterfeiting has not been fully addressed by governments and legislation. In fact, much of the efforts focus on the transmission and transference in ownership between parties and the prevention of clandestine financial transactions (Lisina and

Sorokin, 2013). Thus, the prevention of crypto-counterfeiting relies on the issues of the financial instrument itself.

8.6 DETERRING COUNTERFEITING IN THE FUTURE

The issuance of hard currency will not discontinue in the very near future, but the increased importance of cryptocurrency will quickly rise in the world economy. It offers many advantages over hard currency. However, many governments have started to discuss how virtual currency and cryptocurrencies will function within their jurisdiction. Much of the crypto-counterfeiting deterrence is placed on the issue with laws being considered on how best to regulate it. Is cryptocurrency in fact a currency similar to the US dollars, the euro, and the yen? Or is it similar to a brokered monetary unit? Moreover, each jurisdiction may choose to define cryptocurrency differently. By default, this could impact its ability to function in international transactions as a medium of exchange.

8.7 SUMMARY

In this chapter, we have presented an overview with case examples of how counterfeiting has impacted currencies. Moreover, the methods, motivation, and opportunities of counterfeiting have been presented. Finally, the global initiative to protect users against counterfeiting and how this relates to virtual currencies has been discussed. Counterfeiting currency, financial instruments, and mediums of exchanges are nothing new. Although cryptocurrencies are growing beyond individual concepts into shared and virtual realities, the success of cryptocurrencies will be based on its utility and much more on the consumer faith and security of its ability to store value and of how its ownership is defined and protected. Thus, anticounterfeiting measures for cryptocurrency are essential to its ability in becoming a greater functioning financial instrument and away from a technological curiosity.

REFERENCES

Aaronson, D., Mazumder, B., 2007. Intergenerational economic mobility in the United States, 1940 to 2000. J. Hum. Resour. XLIII (1), 139–172.

Aiken, M., Lu, W., 1998. The evolution of bookkeeping in China: integrating historical trends with western influences. ABACUS 34 (1), 140–162.

Balganesh, S., 2009. Foreseeability and copyright incentives. Harv. Law Rev. 122 (6), 1569–1633.

Banks, C.B., 2007. The sociology of inequality. Race Gender Class 14 (3-4), 175–188.

Besomi, D., 2010. Paper money and national distress: William Huskisson and the early theories of credit speculation and crises. Eur. J. Hist. Econ. Thought 17 (1), 49–85.

Björkland, A., Jäntti, M., 1997. Intergenerational income mobility in Sweden compared to the United States. Am. Econ. Rev. 87 (5), 1009–1018.

Block, W.E., 2010. In defense of counterfeiting illegitimate money: rejoinder to Murphy and Machaj. Am. J. Econ. Sociol. 66 (2), 867–880.

Champ, B., 2007. Private money in our past, present, and future. Econ. Comment. 1, 1–4.

Champ, B., 2008. Stamp scrip: money people pay to use. Federal Reserve Bank of Cleveland. Econ. Comment. April. 1–4.

Dostov, V.L., Shust, P.M., 2013. Virtual currencies and cryptocurrencies: new possibilities or new risks. Finan. Secur. 2013 (3), 61–64.

Ernst, J.A., 1965. Genesis of the currency act of 1764: Virginia paper money and the protection of British investments. William Mary Q. 22 (1965), 33–74.

Europol, July 17, 2014. Website. Accessed on July 17, 2014 from https://www.europol.europa.eu/content/page/about-europol-17.

Financial Crimes Enforcement Network, U.S. Department of the Treasury, March 18, 2013. Application of FinCEN's Regulation to Persons Administering Exchanging, or Using Virtual Currencies [FIN-2013-G001].

Gladstone, J.A., 1997. Exploring the role of digital currency in the retail payment system. N. Engl. Rev. 31, 1193–1321.

Gorrindo, T., Groves, J.E., 2010. Crime and hate in virtual worlds: a new playground for the Id? Harv. Rev. Psychiatry 18 (2), 113–118.

Grandi, C., 2004. The protection of the euro against counterfeiting. Eur. J. Crime Crim. Law Justice 12 (2), 89–131.

Greene, J.P., Jellison, R.M., 1961. The currency act of 1764 in imperial-colonial relations, 1764-1776. William Mary Q. 18 (3), 485–518.

Grinberg, R., 2011. Bitcoin: an innovative alternative digital currency. Hast. Sci. Technol. Law J. 4 (8), 160–209.

Guinchard, A., 2010. Crime in virtual worlds: the limits of criminal law. Int. Rev. Law Comput. Technol. 24 (2), 175–182.

Hart, K., 2007. Money is always personal and impersonal. Anthropol. Today 23 (5), 12–16.

Horesh, N., 2012. From Chengdu to Stockholm: a comparative study of the emergence of paper money in east and west. Provincial China 4 (1), 68–99.

Hubbard, R.G., O'Brien, A.P., 2013. Macroeconomics, fourth ed. Pearson, New York, NY.

International Trademark Association, July 14, 2014. Press Release. Accessed on July 17, 2014 from http://www.inta.org/Press/Pages/WCO_MOU.aspx.

Jackson, E., 2012, April 11. Royal Canadian mint to create digital currency. Toronto Star.

Kennedy, R., 2008. Virtual rights? Property in online game objects and characters. Inf. Commun. Technol. Law 17 (2), 95–106.

Keysar, B., Barr, D.J., Balin, J.A., Brauner, J.S., 2000. Taking perspective in conversation: the role of mutual knowledge in comprehension. Psychol. Sci. 11 (1), 32–38.

Kohlman, E.F., Bijou, R., 2013. Planning responses and defining attacks in cyberspace. Harv. Law Rev. 126, 173–175.

Lisina, I.A., Sorokin, K.G., 2013. BitCoin—new virtual currency in real economy. Finan. Secur. 2013 (3), 68–70.

Machaj, M., 2007. Against both private and public counterfeiting. Am. J. Econ. Sociol. 66 (5), 977–984.

Mazumder, B., 2007. Trends in intergenerational mobility. Ind. Relat. 46 (1), 1–6.

McKinney Jr., R.E., May 7-9, 2009. Purchasing power or indentured service?: A look at how credit affects social and economic mobility. Debt and Slavery: The History of a Process of Enslavement. Indian Ocean World Centre, McGill University, Montreal, PQ.

McKinney Jr., R.E., Shao, L.P., Shao, D.H., 2011. Can digital worlds simulate reality? Using virtual reality as an education tool. Int. J. Bus. Res. 11, 157–165.

McKinney Jr., R.E., Shao, L.P., Shao, D.H., Rosenlieb Jr., D.C., 2013. The reality of digital currency as a financial medium of exchange. J. Int. Fin. Stud. 13 (3), 45–50.

McKinney Jr., R.E., Shao, L.P., Shao, D.H., Rosenlieb Jr., D.C., 2015. The evolution of financial instruments and the legal protection against counterfeiting: a look at coin, paper, and virtual currencies. J. Law Technol. Policy. 2.

Mundell, R.A., 2002. The Birth of Coinage. Working Paper (#0102-08). Columbia University, New York, NY.

Newman, E.P., 1958. The successful British counterfeiting of American paper money during the American revolution. Br. Numis. J. 29 (1958), 174–187.

Organisation for Economic Co-Operation and Development, 2008. The Economic Impact of Counterfeiting and Piracy. OECD Publishing, Paris, France.

Perkins, E.J., 1991. Counterfeiting views on fiat currency: Britain and its North American colonies in the eighteenth century. Banks Money 33 (3), 8–30.

Preston, H.H., 1933. The wooden money of Tenino. Q. J. Econ. 47 (2), 343–348.

Price, H., 1893. The state bank of Iowa. Annu. Iowa 1893, 266–293.

Rogojanu, A., Badea, L., 2014. The issue of competing currencies. Case study—bitcoin. Theor. Appl. Econ. 21 (1), 103–114.

Schreft, S.L. (2002). Clicking with dollars: how consumers can pay for purchases from E-tailers. Federal Reserve Bank of Kansas City, Economic Review, First Quarter, pp. 37-64.

Shao, L.P., McKinney Jr., R.E., Shao, D.H., 2012. Purchasing power of credit, social mobility, and economic mobility. Eur. J. Bus. Res. 12 (4), 73–78.

Shao, L.P., Shao, D.H., McKinney Jr., R.E., Rosenlieb Jr., D.C., 2013a. Counterfeiting: examining the states' ability to regulate federal, foreign and digital financial instruments used as currency. Eur. J. Bus. Res. 13 (3), 5–12.

Shao, L.P., Shao, D.H., McKinney Jr., R.E., Rosenlieb Jr., D.C., 2013b. The reality of digital currency as a financial medium of exchange. J. Int. Finan. Stud. 13 (3), 45–50.

Shelley, L.I., 2012. The diverse facilitators of counterfeiting: a regional perspective. J. Int. Aff. 66 (1), 19–37.

Smith, H.E., 2012. Property as the law of things. Harv. Law Rev. 125, 1691–1726.

Sorokin, K.G., 2013. Discussion of E-money, cards and payments 2013. Finan. Secur. 2013 (3), 65–67.

Sprankel, S., 2013. Technical Basis of Digital Currencies. Working Paper, Technische Universität Darmstadt, Darmstadt, Germany.

The International Criminal Police Organization (INTERPOL), July 17, 2014. Website. Accessed on July 17, 2014 from http://www.interpol.int/.

Tan, E., 2011. Scrip as private money, monetary monopoly, and the rent-seeking state in Britain. Econ. Hist. Rev. 64 (1), 237–255.

Tavakol, S., 1999. Digital value units, electronic commerce and international trade: an obituary for state sovereignty over national markets. John Marshall J. Inf. Technol. Priv. Law 17 (4), 1197–1234.

Telzrow, M.E., 2008. Nazi counterfeiters. New Am. 24 (17), 33.

Timberlake, R.H., 1987. Private production of scrip-money in the isolated community. J. Money Credit Bank. 19 (4), 437–447.

United Nations Office on Drugs and Crime (UNODC), 2014. Basic Manual on the Detection and Investigation of the Laundering of Crime Proceeds Using Virtual Currencies. UNODC, Washington, DC.

Wells, J.T., 2005. Principles of Fraud Examination. John Wiley & Sons Inc., Hoboken, NJ.

Western Union Charge Card, 2014. Accessed on July 19, 2014 from http://en.wikipedia.org/wiki/Credit_card.

Wilkinson, E.P., 1973. The History of Imperial China: A Research Guide. Harvard University Press, Cambridge, MA.

Williamson, S.D., 2002. Private money and counterfeiting. Fed. Reserv. Bank Richmond Econ. Q. 88 (3), 37–57.

Yang, H., Zhang, X., 2003. Economy and trade. In: Ji, X.-B. (Ed.), Facts About China. The H.W. Wilson Co., New York, NY.

Big Data and Network Effect

CHAPTER 9

Emergence, Growth, and Sustainability of Bitcoin: The Network Economics Perspective

Ernie G.S. Teo
Sim Kee Boon Institute for Financial Economics, Singapore Management University, Singapore

Contents

9.1 NETWORK ECONOMICS AND CRYPTOCURRENCIES

Network externalities exist when the value of a good or service is affected by the number of buyers or users. Cryptocurrencies exhibit strong positive network externalities; the study of network economics is a key factor in understanding the interactions between various parties in the cryptocurrency network. A large and well-connected set of users is essential for the survival of Bitcoin or any other peer-to-peer cryptocurrency. These interactions affect the evolution of the network, incentives of miners, and demand and supply of coins.

> *"The essential relationship between the components of a network is complementarity."*
> **Economides, 1993**

Complementary products for cryptocurrencies play an important part in creating value to the network. As the Bitcoin market matures, Bitcoin-related companies (such as financial exchanges, payment systems firms, software makers, automated teller machine manufacturers, and other hardware manufacturers) have also increased in numbers. These companies provide complementary services to Bitcoin and create indirect positive externalities in the market, giving people more incentive to use Bitcoins.

Such networks are self-reinforcing, and more users create more incentives for more users to join. This usually means that a critical mass exists in these networks. In the next section, we look at the idea of critical mass in more detail.

9.1.1 Gaining critical mass

Many network businesses fail to become viable as they are unable to attain critical mass. A small network can grow explosively from a small base as long as the critical mass constraint is satisfied. In this section, we look at the dynamics of such systems using the framework described in Evans and Schmalensee (2010).[1]

9.1.1.1 Direct externalities

The utility a participant derives from the participation of other similar participants is known as direct externalities. When more of a person's network of acquaintances uses the same cryptocurrency, his or her utility of using it increases as he can now send and receive coins to more people. We start with a model of direct externalities in this subsection. Let $N(t)$ be the number of participants of a network at time t and N be the total population of possible participants. An individual would participate in the network at time t if and only if (from Evans and Schmalensee, 2010)

$$V_i[N(t)|\alpha_i] - \theta_i - P \geq 0 \text{ or } \Omega_i \equiv V_i^{-1}(\theta_i + P|\alpha_i) \leq N(t), \tag{9.1}$$

where V_i is the individual's direct utility from participating in the network, α_i is his or her preference for network size, θ_i is his or her cost of participation, and P is the price charged. α_i and θ_i are particular to individual i and differ among individuals. Ω_i is the inverse utility function, which represents the minimum number of other participants needed to entice individual i to participate in the network. Summing up Ω_i for the whole population, the number of individuals (given full information) who will want to participate at time t is given by $F[N(t)|P]N$. When $N(t)$ equals this quantity, expectations are fulfilled. Figure 9.1 illustrates this given fixed values of α and P. If $F[N(t)|P]N$ is above the 45° line, N is increasing. Thus, if $N(t)$ is below the point C (as shown in Figure 9.1), N will converge to the origin. However, if critical mass is attained, $N > C$, the equilibrium point E will be reached.

For Bitcoin, critical mass was obtained via the mining/coin generation process in the first year. As more individuals got involved in mining, they become part of the network. Different from the above diagram, miners who obtained coins have no incentive to leave the network even if critical mass was not reached. These individuals have high incentives to keep the network going as they are supportive of a decentralized currency and/or cryptography. They also have a vested interest as they now own coins. Only when a

---

[1]Evans and Schmalensee (2010) was written in reference to Internet social network platforms such as Facebook. However, the analysis applies similarly to cryptocurrencies.

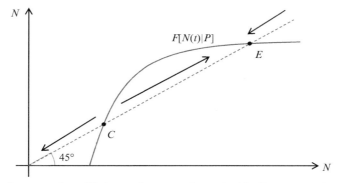

Figure 9.1 Critical mass and equilibriums of a network good with direct network externalities.

substantial critical mass was established did we see more transactions. In fact, the first real transaction took place on May 22, 2010, nearly 17 months after the genesis block was established.

9.1.1.2 Indirect externalities

Indirect externalities refer to the utility a participant derives from complementary goods in the network. In cryptocurrencies, this would refer to merchants such as trading firms, payment processors, crowd-funding platforms, wallet application makers, and other software developers. With indirect externalities, the critical mass problem becomes two-dimensional. Evans and Schmalensee (2010) demonstrated the dynamics of such systems in the context of a two-sided platform. Applying similar analysis (in Figure 9.2), we can obtain a graph similar to Figure 9.1 but in two dimensions, where N_a is the number of participants and N_b is the number of complementary products.

Critical mass is a combination of both the number of participants and the number of complementary goods. A minimum number of each is required for momentum to pick

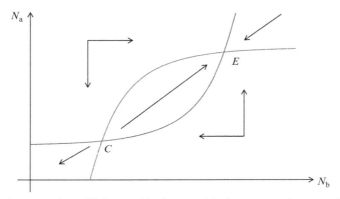

Figure 9.2 Critical mass and equilibriums with direct and indirect network externalities.

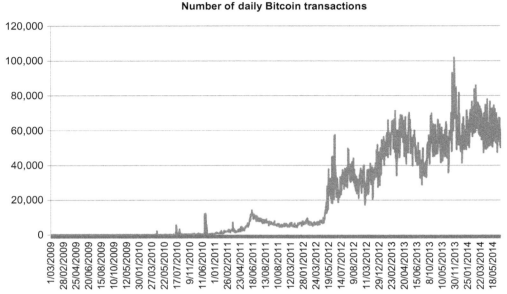

Figure 9.3 The number of daily Bitcoin transactions. *Data obtained from https://blockchain.info/charts.*

up; we observe this phenomenon in Bitcoin. Although the first exchanges were introduced in 2010, the numbers started to grow in 2011. This was about the time where the number of Bitcoin transactions per day started to increase exponentially; see Figure 9.3.

9.1.1.3 Other implications of network externalities

Since the value of the good increases with network size, participants will also become more willing to pay for charges. Therefore, gaining a large network is important for a cryptocurrency as transaction costs are needed to ensure the long-run sustainability of the network. Another important factor for network goods is switching cost. If it is easy for a participant to switch to a rival cryptocurrency, the ability to charge transaction costs will be greatly diminished. However, with the network effect, individual switching will be costly as the participant will not be able to transact with the previous network. This means that unless a large part of the network can coordinate to switch, it is likely that one or a few cryptocurrencies will dominate the market for transactions.

Another issue in cryptocurrencies is that not all parties enjoy direct network externalities. Miners' utility will diminish and become negative when the total number of miners goes above a threshold. However, a good amount of miners are needed for the network to be efficient. Thus, it is important to provide the right incentives/rewards for miners to participate. The current protocol for Bitcoin dictates a finite currency supply; the rewards for mining will diminish over time. To ensure sustainability of the network, it is important to come up with ways to entice participation of miners or nodes in the network. In the next section, we present a simple model of miners' incentives and how this changes with the rewards. We also look at an incentive scheme proposed by Babaioff et al. in their 2012 paper "On Bitcoin and Red Balloons."

9.2 SUSTAINABILITY OF A CRYPTOCURRENCY NETWORK

In this section, we examine the sustainability of a cryptocurrency network. Given the current reward system, we are interested in how miner's incentives will change over time. This will give us an idea how the composition of miners will change over time.

9.2.1 Incentives of mining

We first start by defining the incentives of a miner. A potential miner has to weigh the costs and benefits before making the decision to mine. Kroll et al. (2013) presented a similar model of mining, assuming a fixed expected reward. In our model, we endogenize the probability of getting the reward by making it dependent on the amount of effort put in by the miner compared to the total amount of effort put in by the entire population. This is given by the probability function $p(\varepsilon_i, \varepsilon_{-i})$, where ε_i is the effort put in by miner i and ε_{-i} is the total effort put in by all other miners. Potential miners are assumed to be heterogeneous in their risk attitudes[2]; this is represented by the utility function $v_i(R)$, where R represents the reward. If an individual decides to mine, we assume that they face different costs from each other. Some miners may have access to better technologies or have superior intrinsic skills; this is represented by γ_i. If the following condition is satisfied, the potential miner prefers to mine (individually) instead of not mining:

$$p(\varepsilon_i, \varepsilon_{-i})v_i(R) - \gamma_i \geq O_i. \tag{9.2}$$

O_i is the individual opportunity costs or outside option. Next, we introduce an option to join a mining pool. In this case, the probability of mining the block is given by $p(\varepsilon_P, \varepsilon_{-i})$, where ε_P is the total effort put in by the pool. The share of the reward becomes $v_i(\varepsilon_i R/\varepsilon_P)$. An individual prefers to join a mining pool over not mining if the following is satisfied:

$$p(\varepsilon_P, \varepsilon_{-i})v_i(\varepsilon_i R/\varepsilon_P) - \gamma_i \geq O_i. \tag{9.3}$$

Whether the potential miner prefers to mine individually or join a pool depends in his or her risk attitude (given fixed levels of effort, reward, and cost). Figure 9.4 gives an example of this.

The line with the gentler slope represents utility from joining the mining pool and the line with a steeper slope represents utility form individual mining. If we assume that O_i is normalized at zero for all individuals, then those with risk attitude below 0.4 will not

---

[2]For example, a risk-averse individual may have the utility function $v_i = R^{1/2}$ and a risk-loving one may have the function $v_i = R^2$.

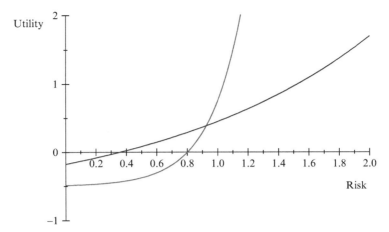

Figure 9.4 Miners' utility given different risk attitudes.

mine. Individuals with risks between 0.4 and 0.9 will join the mining pool where those with risk attitude greater than 0.9 will mine individually. The figure above has not considered the dimension of heterogeneous costs. In order to observe the behavior of agents with two dimensions of heterogeneity, we run an agent-based computer simulation, which will allow us to examine how the composition of miners changes over time as the reward changes.

9.2.2 An agent-based simulation of miners' incentive over time

We present an agent-based simulation in this section to look at miner's incentives. In this simulation, there are 500 heterogeneous agents with randomly assigned α_i (risk attitude, ranging from 0 to 1.5) and γ_i (cost of participation, ranging from 0 to 1). Figure 9.5 represents the agents' position in the two-dimensional space.

We assume that each agent can only put in one unit of effort to mine. If the agent decides to mine individually, his or her utility is given by

$$u_a = (1/(1+N))R^{ai} - \gamma_i \tag{9.4}$$

$p(\varepsilon_i, \varepsilon_{-i}) = (1/(1+N))$, where N is the total number of miners. This is similar to contest success functions used in the auction literature such as those described in Münster (2009). Next, we assume that the agents can choose to join a mining pool.[3] If the agent decides to join the mining pool, his or her utility will be (where MP is the mining pool's total effort)

---

[3] We assume that there is only one mining pool, and in period 1, agents expect that there will be 40% of the population in the pool.

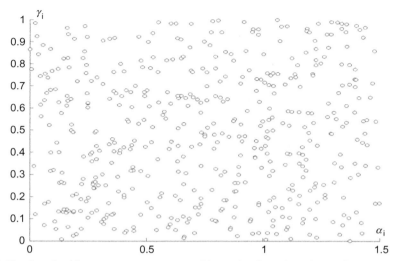

Figure 9.5 Five hundred heterogeneous agents with randomly assigned α_i and γ_i.

$$u_b = (MP/(1+N))(R/MP)^{ai} - \gamma_i. \tag{9.5}$$

We assume that the utility from nonparticipation is normalized to zero or $u_c = 0$. In each period, agents can choose to switch between three states, "Mine Individually," "Mining Pool," and "Nonparticipation." We run the simulation for 100 periods, dropping the reward by half every 20 periods. As the rewards fall, the utility of miners falls. Since the outside option remains constant, we expect to see more miners dropping out over time. Will individuals or the mining pool be more resilient to the fall in reward? Figures 9.6 and 9.7 demonstrate the results. As expected, the number of miners in total will drop as the reward decreases. We also notice that the numbers of mining pool participants are more resilient to the drop in rewards. Individual miners on the other hand decrease by a larger amount when reward falls.

One of the assumptions we have made in the model is that the external value (or exchange rate) of the coins remains constant over time. This is not true in reality; there are two effects to this. Firstly, in the initial stages, value should increase as uptake increases. This will retain miners and we should see fewer drops in miners when the rewards decrease. Secondly, when the number of miners starts to decrease over time, the value of the coin may drop as transactions may now take longer to be verified. This will cause a chain reaction, which may incite a large exodus of miners. The model also did not consider the effect of transaction fees. Future research could fit historical coin prices to the model to extract or endogenize pricing mechanism. Other than the variations described above, there could be many possible extensions to the model one can look at; we leave this for future research.

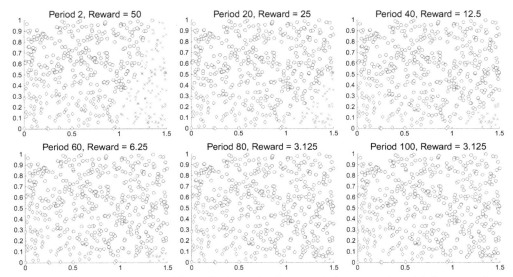

Figure 9.6 Changes to composition of miners in the population over time (circle, non-miners; diamond, mining pool; cross, individual miners).

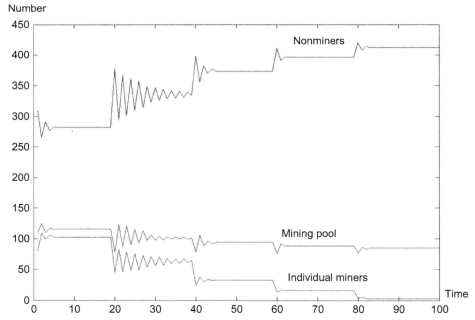

Figure 9.7 Number of types (of miners) over time.

When the number of miners decreases, there is an increased likelihood of a 51% attack as the cost of mounting such an attack is lower with fewer miners. This can potentially cause the coin to fail; thus, it is quite important to ensure that there is continual interest to mine or to act as nodes. Miners and nodes need sufficient incentives to participate in the network. Some types of individuals would have sufficient incentives on their own; they may own a large amount of coins or have personal agendas. Merchants, stakeholders such as exchanges, and other coin-related businesses also have incentives to act as nodes to ensure the survival of their own businesses.

Another way to provide incentives is to pay transaction fees. The current Bitcoin protocol awards all transaction fees within a block to the miner. This may not adequately provide incentive for nodes. When mining rewards become small, mining nodes will have little incentive to broadcast transactions they receive and try to keep fees for themselves. This will slow down the verification process. In the next subsection, we look at an incentive design proposed by Babaioff et al. (2012), which attempts to address this issue.

9.2.3 On Bitcoins and red balloons

In Babaioff et al.'s (2012) paper, they looked at scenarios where the goal is to ensure that some information will propagate through a large network of nodes. Their goal is to design that "incentivize information propagation and counter dis-incentive that arises from the competition from other nodes." The scheme also aims to have low overheads (or rewards) proofed from identity forging. Without going into technical details,[4] a "hybrid scheme" of the following form was proposed:

1. The sender of the transaction specifies a constant fee he or she is willing to pay and sends it to a fixed number of nodes (termed seeds).
2. Each "seed" sends along the information to other nodes (termed child). The public addresses of these "children" are encrypted into the transaction passed on.
3. One of the nodes in any of the chains could successfully mine the block. All nodes between the "seed" and the miner will get a share of the transaction fees.
4. The share of transaction fees received depends on "height" (the distance from the miner).
5. The scheme also incentivizes efficiency by awarding more to the miner if the total chain required is lower than a specified number.

The authors provided a theoretical framework for such types of incentive schemes, and it may well prove to be the solution to the incentive problems when mining rewards become insignificant. Future research can focus on the analysis of the implementation process and empirical experimentation.

---

[4]Readers may refer to the original article for the mathematics.

9.3 DISCUSSION/CONCLUSION

In this article, we looked at the insights provided by network economics and how it affects cryptocurrency systems. An important implication for new cryptocurrencies is the need to attain critical mass. This depends on not only how much benefits participants derive from each other's participation but also the amount of complementary products available in the network. It is also important to maintain the network of miners and nodes as the value of the cryptocurrency depends on the network's ability to validate transactions quickly.

To examine the sustainability of a cryptocurrency network, we presented a simple model of miners' incentives and looked at how miner and node participation will be affected by the current reward system over time. Given the absence of transaction fees, we expect that as the reward falls over time, the number of miners will fall. There will also be relatively less individual miners compared to participants joining the mining pool.

One solution is to make tweaks to the protocol such as those proposed by Babaioff et al. (2012). The cryptocurrency industry is constantly changing and protocols being updated or modified. As the industry evolves, stakeholders should keep in mind the sustainability of the system and think of ways such as those suggested in this article to ensure the system's longevity. Network effects should be considered and efforts be made to ensure that incentives to participate (for all types of participants) are in place.

REFERENCES

Babaioff, M., Dobzinski, S., Oren, S., Zohar, A., 2012. On bitcoin and red balloons. In: Proceedings of the 13th ACM Conference on Electronic Commerce. ACM, pp. 56–73.

Economides, N., 1993. Network economics with application to finance. Finan. Markets, Inst. Instruments 2 (5), 89–97.

Evans, D.S., Schmalensee, R., 2010. Failure to launch: critical mass in platform businesses. Rev. Netw. Econ. 9 (4), 1–28.

Kroll, J.A., Davey, I.C., Felten, E.W., 2013. The economics of bitcoin mining, or bitcoin in the presence of adversaries. In: Proceedings of WEIS (vol. 2013).

Münster, J., 2009. Group contest success functions. Econ. Theory 41 (2), 345–357.

CHAPTER 10

Cryptocurrencies as Distributed Community Experiments

Matthias Tarasiewicz[a], Andrew Newman[b]
[a]University of Applied Arts Vienna, Vienna, Austria
[b]University of New South Wales, Sydney, New South Wales, Australia

Contents

10.1 INTRODUCTION

The design of secure "digital cash" systems was first postulated by Chaum (1983) and the discourse continued (Chaum et al., 1990; Tanaka, 1996; Szabo, 1997; Dai, 1998; Hove, 2000) until 2008, when Satoshi Nakamoto introduced Bitcoin with a self-published paper (Nakamoto, 2008), describing the blockchain ledger and inventing the first "cryptocurrency." The idea of using cryptography (rather than a central authority) to control the creation and transactions of such a "digital money" created the basis for the cryptocurrency ecosystem of today. Yet despite its widespread adoption, Bitcoin's underlying structure and technology have faced major criticism: its economic system of a deflationary currency, the inefficiency of mining (in terms of electricity), the long transaction verification time, and the inability to implement real anonymity into the protocol. Additional problems arose because Bitcoin as "experimental currency" has been in existence for only 5 years. In its current implementation, the blockchain does not scale, the attribute of being "anonymous" has been challenged, and Bitcoin could lose its decentralized nature because of a mining-pool monopoly.

Handbook of Digital Currency

This chapter outlines the major criticism cryptocurrencies faced since Bitcoin's introduction in 2009 that resulted in the iterative development of various "altcoins." These alternative cryptocurrencies, which can be seen as "distributed community experiments," introduced new algorithms while also tackling social and other evolving problems that emerged throughout the various phases of adaptation and collective learning processes. Often introduced through self-published white papers or online announcements, these alternative coins represent hypotheses by the respective creators until they can show a significant user base and ultimately are accepted in online cryptocurrency exchanges. We examine the important experiments and alternative approaches to specific issues of the Bitcoin design and describe differences in coins that have been launched. We not only discuss successful experiments but also show attempts that failed in the relatively short but eventful past 5 years of cryptocurrencies. We demonstrate how the initial design of Bitcoin has been extended and improved by the so-called next-generation cryptocurrencies, while the two main aspects—the blockchain ledger and strong cryptography—remain key elements to all of these new systems. Finally, we outline possible future problems and developments around the blockchain, which not only is the invention that started cryptocurrencies but also remains the most experimental and challenging part with no long-term strategy yet.

10.2 FROM BITCOIN AS SINGLE CRYPTOCURRENCY TO AN ECOSYSTEM OF CRYPTOCURRENCIES

In 2011, the community of Bitcoin grew significantly.[1] The year also saw the introduction of the first altcoins, with *Namecoin* becoming the first alternative cryptocurrency based on the Bitcoin source code. By the end of 2011, there were 10 cryptocurrencies in existence (all based on Bitcoin), producing a total of 215 coins by the end of 2013 (5 not based on Bitcoin). Bitcoin's code repository on github.com currently shows 4.069 existing forks (8/2014), not including forks of forks. Each of these forks has the possibility of developing into an alternative coin although only few show technical improvements. As of August 2014, there are 440 coins listed on coinmarketcap.com (14 of which are not based on Bitcoin); cryptocoincharts.com currently lists 825 altcoins—but there is strong evidence that many more exist, with new coins appearing on an almost daily basis. Traditionally, new cryptocurrencies are announced on the Bitcointalk forum—our research found over 1500 coins that have been discussed before August 2014. More than 50% have been introduced; a vast amount represented the

---

[1]The growth of the Bitcoin community is most clearly evident within the statistics of the bitcointalk.org forum, which demonstrate an increase of members from 656 in July 2010 to 36,713 in July 2011. At the time of writing (August 1, 2014), there are 361,236 members of the bitcointalk.org forum, although not necessarily all are active. This is only an example of one of many forums, although arguably the most significant, where the cryptocurrency community congregates.

so-called scamcoins, which have been premined or were designed to only benefit the creators. Others vanished quickly or could not actually gather a significant user base, before they could even show a "market."

Cryptocurrency exchanges will often only choose to have a new coin included in their marketplace after it has reached a certain "significance" and has been subject to extensive review. The criteria for inclusion usually involve the availability of a "block explorer" (public availability of the ledger), a website for the coin, a unique "genesis block" (the initial block on the blockchain), and a compiled "wallet" (the client and software for transactions). Furthermore, reviews of the source code, interest of the community, and innovation are aspects for coin exchanges to review the quality and market potential of altcoins.

Altcoins recently had to face a lot of criticism, since often they are used for "insider trading." These "pump and dump scams" involve buying cheap coins, creating a buzz, and ultimately selling quickly once the price rises. The "buzz phase" is particularly interesting, since forums and chats of the cryptocurrency exchanges as well as the "Bitcointalk" forum are abused, including fake user accounts and social media to create a maximum hype. But not all altcoins represent "get rich quick" schemes or are intended for speculation. The whole cryptocurrencies' ecosystem represents a vivid distributed culture of experimentation (experimental culture), which is tackling the different arising technical, social, and theoretical problems of "electronic cash" in creative and novel ways.

10.3 ALTCOINS AS EVOLUTIONARY PROBLEM SOLVING AND "PROOF OF CONCEPTS"

Since the public availability of the Bitcoin source code in 2009 (announced January 2009 on the Cryptography Mailing list by Satoshi Nakamoto) and especially after the discussion forum moved from sourceforge.com to bitcointalk.com, the "Bitcointalk" forum has become the center of discussion, announcements, and critique for the community of cryptocurrencies. We are arguing that although most of the critiques about Bitcoin's technology are posted and discussed in this forum, as well as described in academic papers (Barber et al., 2012), only very few of the proposed innovations are actually included into Bitcoin's source code. This often leads to the creation of a new cryptocurrency as a proof of concept that focuses on specific changes or adaptations of the system, especially targeting possible attacks or vulnerabilities. Altcoins play an important role even if they do not gain widespread use or develop "exchange value," since their proof of concepts and possible solutions are nourishing the global discourse about the future of decentralized cryptocurrencies.

The development of alternative cryptocurrencies is motivated by a diversity of aspects; we are, however, primarily focusing on altcoins that have been developed to address the technical and social limitations of Bitcoin. Altcoins are developed for a variety of other reasons though; there are altcoins that target niche online communities (such as in gaming). These coins are often not particularly innovative and are usually clones of currently existing open-source coins. Similarly, there are a variety of altcoins that are primarily developed for financial gain, often dubbed "scam coins" within the cryptocurrency community; these coins also often do not offer technical innovations, or if they do, they are compromised by having a significant premine (a premine retains a volume of currency for the original developer or development team). There is also a significant array of altcoins that are developed for what could be described as playful or experimental reasons. *Shitcoin*, for example, was developed to combine all the worst features of failed altcoins; it generates an extraordinarily large amount of coins per a block (500 million) and the block reward is halved almost every day (it took almost 4 years for the block reward to halve for Bitcoin). *OneCoin* is another unusual altcoin launched, with its total cap of possible coins generated limited to only one coin. *JackpotCoin* is another playful coin that has a randomized superblock payout that rewards "winners" jackpots. *Pizza-Coin* was also announced although it is still under development as the problem of proof of pizza still needs to be solved.

This rich ecosystem does, however, offer up various altcoins that provide experimental proving grounds for the future of cryptocurrency.

10.4 OVERVIEW OF THE MAIN CRITIQUE AND DISCOURSE ON CRYPTOCURRENCIES

10.4.1 From a distributed system to possible centralization: The mining arms race

Mining is needed to secure the network and provide integrity by creating checksums (cryptographic hashes) of individual transactions bundled in blocks. To make mining attractive, the miners are earning small rewards for finding new blocks (block reward) as well as transaction fees from the network. For a new block to be valid in the blockchain ledger (the chain of digital transactions), it needs to contain only valid nonconflicting transactions as well as a sequence number (block version number), a hash of the previous block, the "Merkle root" (a hash of all the transactions in this block), a time stamp, and a "difficulty" statement (nonce). Finding a new block in the Bitcoin blockchain is based on "proof of work," which describes a cryptographic "puzzle" generating a piece of data that is easy to verify but takes a long time to produce (hashing). The SHA-256 hash of a block's header must be lower or equal than the current "difficulty," called "target." A lower target makes the generation of new blocks more difficult. Every 2016 blocks (roughly every 2 weeks), Bitcoin clients compare the time it took to generate the blocks and modify the target, which is called "retargeting." Bitcoin's protocol

List of cryptocurrencies mentioned in this chapter

Name	Sym	Announce	Block time	Max coins	Hashing		Fork of	Specifics
Bitcoin	BTC	January 2009	10 min	21m	SHA–256d	PoW	–	The first "cryptocurrency"
Namecoin	NMC	April 2011	10 min	21m	SHA–256d	PoW	BTC	Key-value store, introduced merged mining (with BTC)
SolidCoin	SC	August 2011	3 min	18.9m	SHA–256d	PoW	BTC	Faster block generation, fixed fees
Geist Geld	GG	September 2011	15 s	No limit	SHA–256d	PoW	BTC	Experimental, high transaction rates, no limits to supply
Tenebrix	TBX	September 2011	5 min	No limit	Scrypt	PoW	GG	CPU-friendly, GPU-hostile mining. Introduced Scrypt
Fairbrix	FBX	October 2011	5 min	No limit	Scrypt	PoW	TBX	Nonpremined Tenebrix
Litecoin	LTC	October 2011	150 s	84m	Scrypt	PoW	TBX	Faster block generation and transaction time. Second-most forked coin after Bitcoin
BlackCoin	BC	February 2014	60 s	No limit	Scrypt	PoS	NVC	Pure proof-of-stake coin
Darkcoin	DRK	January 2014	150 s	~22m	X11	PoW/PoS	QRK	Proof of service
Peercoin	PPC	August 2012	10 min	No limit	Scrypt	PoW/PoS	PPC	Also known under the name PPCoin, Peercoin was the first coin utilizing proof-of-stake and proof-of-work system
Dogecoin	DOGE	December 2013	60 s	100bn	Scrypt	PoW	LKY	Merge-mined with LTC

Continued

List of cryptocurrencies mentioned in this chapter—cont'd

Name	Sym	Announce	Block time	Max coins	Hashing	PoW/PoS	Fork of	Specifics
CloakCoin	CLOAK	June 2014	60 s	4.5m	X13	PoW/PoSA	–	Proof-of-stake anonymity. Introduced *One Ledger*, a p2p decentralized marketplace
Monero	XMR	April 2014	60 s	~18.4m	CryptoNight	Egalitarian PoW	Crypto Note	Popular coin based on CryptoNote
Primecoin	XPM	July 2013	60 s	2 bn	Primechain	rPOW	BTC	Cryptocurrency, which is proof of work based and searching for prime numbers
Zetacoin	ZET	August 2013	30 s	160m	SHA-256d	PoW	BTC	Quick transactions and quick difficulty adjustment
Vertcoin	VTC	January 2014	150 s	84m	Scrypt-N	PoW	YAC	Introduced Scrypt with "Adaptive *N*-Factor" to stay one step ahead of any possible ASIC development
Coiledcoin	CLC	October 2011	120 s	No limit	SHA-256d	PoW	BTC	Merged mining, killed in 51% attack
Liquidcoin	LQC	January 2012	300 s	No limit	Scrypt	PoW	TBX	Fixed difficulty
Freicoin Talkcoin	FRC TAC	June 2012 May 2014	10 min 20 s	100m No limit	SHA-256d NIST5	PoW PoW	BTC	Demurrage fee Democratic block reward. Voting coin
Anoncoin	ANC	October 2013	180 s	4.2m	Scrypt	PoW	LTC	Anonymous currency with support for I2P and Tor, with Zerocoin planned
Reddcoin	RDD	January 2014	60 s	109,000m	Scrypt (128k,1,1)	PoW/ PoSV	LTC	Proof-of-stake velocity, tipping, social

QuarkCoin	QRK	July 2013	30 s	247m	Quark	PoW	SIC	Extremely fast block generation (30 s). Using multiple algorithms for hashing
Florincoin	FLO	June 2013	40 s	160m	Scrypt	PoW	LTC	Fast block generation, transaction comment stored in blockchain
CryptoNote coin	n/a	July 2014	—	—	CryptoNight	Egalitarian PoW	—	Reference implementation and the technology showcase of CryptoNote
duckNote	XDN	June 2014	4 min	~8590m	CryptoNight	Egalitarian PoW	Crypto Note	Popular coin based on CryptoNote
Boolberry	BBR	April 2014	2 min	~18.45m	Wild Keccak	Wild Keccak PoW	Crypto Note	Extended CryptoNote and reduces "blockchain bloat." Wild Keccak PoW algorithm
Bytecoin	BCN	March 2014	2 min	184.46bn	CryptoNight	PoW	CryptoNote	Popular coin based on CryptoNote
Feathercoin	FTC	April 2013	150 s	336m	Scrypt	PoW	LTC	Uses "advanced checkpointing" to make the blockchain more secure
iXcoin	IXC	August 2011	10 min	21m	SHA-256d	PoW	BTC	Fork of Bitcoin with twice the inflation rate of 96 iXcoins
iocoin	IOC	August 2011	10 min	21m	SHA-256d	PoW	BTC	iocoin is a not premined clone of iXcoin
Novacoin	NVC	February 2013	10 min	No limit	Scrypt	PoW/PoS	PPC	The first PPC (Peercoin) fork and was forked very often itself
Mastercoin	MST	June 2013	35 s	~18.2m	Scrypt	PoS	—	Coin that exists entirely inside the Bitcoin blockchain

defined that the target cannot be changed more than by a factor of 4 to prevent large changes in the next difficulty.

The initial design of Bitcoin, and especially through the implementation of mining, forced an arms race, since the acceptance of new blocks would favor the miner with more computational power (see Kroll et al., 2013). In the beginning of mining, the so-called mining pools emerged, which are joint efforts to offer higher chances of getting block rewards and splitting them according to hashing power contributed over time. As the race continued, the computations have been extended from being CPU only to making use of graphics processing units (GPUs) and later dedicated hardware to speed up the hashing. Field-programmable gate arrays (FPGAs) were first introduced in 2011, and in late 2012, application-specific integrated circuits (ASICs) were developed, which as of today can already produce various terahashes per second (TH/s).

Our data researching the Bitcoin blockchain as of August 2014 show a total network hash rate of over 133,492,059 GH/s. The estimated total rewards of mining are at least 2 million USD (3600 BTC) per day, with the current block reward of 25 BTC, the Bitcoin price at approx. $580, and a new block being found at least every 10 min.

As stated by Muller (2014) in the white paper of *Vertcoin*, the developers of Bitcoin could not know which potential threats would arise in the future when originally designing the first cryptocurrency. Muller (2014) argued that "millions of dollars were spent by various companies to build ASIC computers in an attempt to monopolize mining"—this specific hardware changed the game and effectively also transformed Bitcoin from a decentralized and distributed "currency" to become a much more centralized and vulnerable system than originally intended.

10.4.2 The "Goldfinger Attack" and the "Tragedy of the Commons"

There are basically two main ways the blockchain ledger could be corrupted: by fraudulently adding to or modifying it, both of which the Bitcoin system is allegedly secured against. Since Bitcoin is a distributed system, fake additions to the blockchain would not populate throughout the network. The digital signatures (public-key cryptography) have to be signed with the private keys, and only signed transfers are added to the ledger. Modification attacks (e.g., changing only the values of a transaction) are secured by the structure of the blockchain itself. To change a single transaction, it would also be mandatory to recompute the hash of the block that this transaction is in, as well as all the following blocks. While this is theoretically possible, it requires more than 50% of the network's hashing power. Such an attack has been heavily discussed in the past (Casey and Vigna, 2014). Kroll et al. (2013) considered attacks to the system, aiming "to destabilize the consensus about the rules or state of Bitcoin", and outlined the "51% attack" as well as the "Goldfinger attack." Since mining pools had not originally been thought of during the initial design of Bitcoin, a cartel of miners controlling more than half of the network hashing power could effectively also control the transactions. So "double spending" as well as censorship of transactions could possibly happen. Kroll et al. (2013) believed that "it is very unlikely that a cartel could double-spend enough to recover the cost of an attack" since it "must outmine [...] and thus outspend [...] the entire Bitcoin network for as long as it would remain a cartel." While not being feasible, the "51% attack" could have other aims, described as the "Goldfinger attack," which could be intended "to block Bitcoin transactions, to enforce the law, deter money laundering, or achieve some other institutional goal" (Kroll et al., 2013). A single entity (GHash.io) has already contributed more than 51% of Bitcoin's total cryptographic hashing output for spans as long as 12 h in 2014 (cf. Eyal and Sirer, 2014), which cannot be considered an actual threat, since their actions would be visible. Ghash.io as an economically rational mining pool would risk losing miners and possible customers if it undertook such an attack. Gavin Andresen (chief scientist of the Bitcoin Foundation) had knowledge of this potential attack since at least 2012, describing possible countermeasures (Andresen, 2012), which shows that Bitcoin's development team was aware of future issues and challenges and is considering code adaptations and changes. Bitcoin after all represents an ongoing experimental process rather than a finished product.[2]

Altcoins in the past have faced various "51% attacks"; these have included *Feathercoin*, *Coiledcoin*, *Powercoin*, and *TerraCoin*. *Feathercoin* survived its attack, introducing an advanced "checkpointing" mechanism. Checkpoints are hard-coded blocks in the clients of cryptocurrencies, ensuring that the history of the blockchain cannot be entirely rewritten. As described by Barber et al. (2012), the "history-revision attack" (another way of describing the "51% attack") "in the extreme case [...] would cause the entire coin base ever created to be replaced with a figment of its forgery." Checkpoints often get introduced with new versions of the clients in cryptocurrencies, the oldest example being Bitcoin's "genesis block" (the first block of a blockchain), which initially had been hard-coded in the source code. Although *Feathercoin's* advanced checkpointing mechanism provided more security against attacks, it has also been criticized by purists for compromising the coin's decentralized nature because the checkpoint master node is deployed and maintained by the lead developer. *Feathercoin's* approach, however, provides an experimental space for future altcoins to analyze and learn from and is an example of how the ecosystem of altcoins functions as distributed community experiments.

The "tragedy of the commons" (Hardin, 1968) could be a possible scenario of "market failure," which could happen with Bitcoin if the block reward from mining drops near zero and the only fees miners earn at this time are transaction fees. Miners would compete on these fees, so their price would drop significantly (since miners would accept decreasing fees). Since mining is not profitable anymore at this point, miners are leaving

---

[2]The Bitcoin website states that "Bitcoin is still experimental" and "Bitcoin is an experimental new currency that is in active development."

and there would not be enough total hashing power to effectively secure the system. The difficulty would be lower than what the public desires, resulting in higher possibilities of 51% attacks to appear. An important issue to counter the "tragedy of the commons" was the introduction of "merged mining" in *Namecoin*, which offers the possibility of mining for multiple blockchains at once. Auxiliary proof of work in this context allows the creation of an NMC block even while mining BTC. Merged mining has been implemented as well with *iXcoin* and *iocoin* (both introduced in 2011)—which are still in circulation today—and most recently in August 2014, it was introduced into *Dogecoin* (merged mining with *Litecoin*) as a countermeasure since it had been facing various 51% attacks.

10.4.3 Block generation time and transaction speed

Bitcoin by design takes up to 10 min to find a block (6-7 min on average); transactions need six blocks to be fully confirmed in the blockchain, effectively making full approvals last a maximum of 1 h. This block generation time was deliberately selected by Satoshi Nakamoto in order to minimize the amount of wasted computation by the miners: during the time of populating the information generated by the introduction of a new block, all mining is wasted because only one new block can be accepted and miners are competing against the new block instead of adding to it.

Dubbed an "experimental cryptocurrency," *Geist Geld* was introduced in September 2011 as a fork of the experimental Bitcoin client *Multicoin*. Its purpose was to undertake experiments by introducing a stable block generation rate and no upper limit or alteration to the supply of units. The experiments of *Geist Geld* continued with *Tenebrix*, which not only tested the limits of block generation but also additionally investigated the outcomes of restricting mining to CPU hashing, by specifically resisting the creation of efficient GPU, FPGA, and even ASIC implementations[3] by introducing a new hashing algorithm (Scrypt). One of the stated aims of this currency was to create a more diverse adoption base not requiring the use of the specific custom-built hardware that was currently dominating Bitcoin mining. The creators of *Tenebrix* acknowledged that mining pools could use their underutilized CPU power, as they were mining Bitcoin with GPU rigs at this time. The development of *Fairbrix* followed soon, and the experiments with these coins led to the development of *Litecoin* (LTC), currently the second-most forked cryptocurrency.

The problems caused by the long confirmation time were targeted during the very early stages of cryptocurrencies. Early 2011, most of the newly introduced coins were offering a faster block generation rate, starting with 3 min in *SolidCoin 1.0*. However, the faster blockchain generation alongside the sharp growth of these new currencies made them more vulnerable to attacks. *SolidCoin 1.03* was eventually abolished after one of these attacks and was followed by a bitter community dispute over the actions of the

---

[3]Scrypt had at a later stage been made possible to mine with GPU; ASICs are available since January 2014.

original developer. An increase in the blockchain generation rate without compromising security was later more successful with the introduction of *Litecoin*, which generates blocks every 2.5 min on average, making confirmations last a maximum of 15 min. *QuarkCoin* as an extreme example generates a new block every 30 s; the average "confirmation time" for a *Quark* transaction is less than 40 s.

10.4.4 Energy usage

Since Bitcoin's creation, proof of work has been the foundation of minting new coins while also concurrently securing the network transactions and validity. Proof of work is a computation, which is known to be hard to compute but easy to verify. One of its applications has been "Hashcash," an SHA-256-based proof of work intended to throttle systematic abuse of unmetered Internet resources such as e-mail, introduced by Adam Back (1997). Bitcoin with its implementation of SHA-256d (Hashcash with double-iterated SHA-256) faced a large amount of criticism for its energy inefficiency, since the hash rate of the complete Bitcoin network was counted at 162,993,873 billions of hashes per second at the end of July 2014 (source: blockchain.info). By December 2013, the whole Bitcoin network had been estimated to purportedly use between 109.2 and 130 GWh/day[4]; in April 2013, the generation of Bitcoins was estimated to cost 150,000 USD per day in power consumption costs.[5]

This problem has been targeted by multiple altcoins in different ways: either changing to another system of minting (such as proof of stake or proof of burn), making the hashing useful (such as implemented in *Primecoin*), or changing the cryptographic hashing algorithm.

King and Nadal (2012) outlined the concept of "coin age" and facilitated an alternative design to the minting process—proof of stake (PoS). Coin age is defined as "currency amount times holding period" (Nadal and King, 2009) and already available in Bitcoin since its beginning, but only used for prioritization of transactions. Nadal and King proposed to use the already existing coin age to create PoS, which had already been discussed in the Bitcoin community since 2011.[6] PoS requires the prover to show ownership over a certain amount of money; blocks are separated in two different types: proof-of-stake and proof-of-work blocks. The PoS in these new types of blocks is a special transaction (coinstake), where the owner pays an amount to himself, consuming the coin age and at the same time generating a new block and minting with PoS. Additionally, *Peercoin* chose a

---

[4]See https://medium.com/@interdome/how-much-electricity-does-bitcoin-use-c350bd84c64e.
[5]See http://techcrunch.com/2013/04/13/the-cost-of-a-bitcoin.
[6]There have been different proposals for proof of stake, but only King and Nadal's version has been implemented, since Sunny King is also the author of PPCoin (Peercoin). See https://en.bitcoin.it/wiki/Proof_of_Stake and also Bentov et al. 2014 for more information.

mint rate of 1 cent per coin-year consumed to give rise to a low future inflation rate. There are, however, significant drawbacks to PoS, especially pure proof-of-stake systems (such as in *BlackCoin*, *VeriCoin*, and *Peercoin*) as they are more susceptible to "bribe attacks" than pure proof-of-work systems. Attackers could "double spend"—sending a transaction, receiving goods for exchange, and after that reverting the last six blocks by bribing stakeholders to sign the blocks in the attacker's branch (see Bentov et al., 2014).

In 2013, Sunny King published another white paper to describe *Primecoin*, a cryptocurrency introducing a new type of proof of work based on searching for prime numbers (King, 2013). As Buterin noted, in the current Bitcoin mining, most of the research costs go into developing more effective hardware (ASICs, optimized circuits, etc.), while *Primecoin* is a good example and prototype of how the research is focusing on more efficient ways of doing arithmetic and number theory computation, which have additional applications beyond cryptocurrencies (Buterin, 2013).

Another example of countering the problem of energy use is the changing of the hashing algorithm, which could also be a security measure to prevent 51% attacks. While Bitcoin and most of the coins use SHA-256d, Scrypt is the second-most used hashing algorithm that already showed significant improvements. Most recently launched cryptocurrencies use multiple hashing algorithms (Quark, X11, NIST5, etc.) to also provide long-term security in case one of the algorithms gets compromised in the future. The lesser known algorithms are "Momentum," a proprietary algorithm used by *BitShares PTS* (formerly *ProtoShares*) that uses a 512-bit SHA-1 or "Cuckoo Cycle," a graph-theoretic proof-of-work system (cf. Tromp, 2014), which has no implementation in a cryptocurrency yet.

As long as developers of custom mining hardware continue developing ASIC devices, the race with new hashing methods will continue, as can be seen on the recent introduction of Scrypt ASIC miners, which led to a huge amount of new algorithms to counter the mining arms race. The following table provides an overview of the hashing algorithms implemented in cryptocurrencies.

Name	Description	Used in coins
SHA-256d	A double hashing with Secure Hash Algorithm (256 bits) using Merkle trees. Introduced with Bitcoin (BTC)	Bitcoin (BTC), Namecoin (NMC), Devcoin (DVC), and many others
SHA-3 (Keccak)	SHA-3 is a standard that had been developed to replace SHA-2, if it would be compromised. The implementation in cryptocurrencies had been to make the use of ASIC impossible	Introduced first in MaxCoin (MAX) 29.1.2014. Also in Slothcoin (SLOTH), Cryptometh (METH), Sifcoin (SIF), JackpotCoin (JPC), Diamond (DMD)

Wild Keccak	Keccak hybrid using blockchain data as a "scratchpad." ASIC-resistant, but GPU miner existing already	Introduced in Boolberry (BBR), 17.5.2014
Scrypt	Scrypt, as described by Percival (2009), is "sequentially memory-hard," storing a lot of data in RAM during hashing. The high RAM requirements made it unfeasible for ASIC mining. Since January 2014, Scrypt ASICs are available	Introduced with Tenebrix (TBX) 26.09.2011 Also in Litecoin (LTC), Dogecoin (DOGE), Feathercoin (FTC), WorldCoin (WDC), Reddcoin (RDD), Catcoin (CAT), Infinitecoin (IFC), Bitmark (BTM), Novacoin (NVC), etc.
Scrypt-N	Scrypt-N extends Scrypt with an "Adaptive N-Factor." This N-factor determines how much memory is required to compute the hashing functions and increases with time to stay one step ahead of any possible ASIC development	Introduced by YACoin (YAC) in May 2013. Also in Vertcoin (VTC), Execoin (EXE), GPUcoin (GPUC), ParallaxCoin (PLX), SiliconValleyCoin (XSV), SineCoin (SIN), etc.
Scrypt-Jane (Scrypt-Chacha)	Scrypt-Jane is Scrypt-N with a different hashing function	Introduced with YACoin (YAC) in May 2013 Also in Ultracoin (UTC), Velocitycoin (VEL)
Quark	Quark has nine rounds of hashing from six unique hashing functions (*blake*, *grøstl*, *blue midnight wish*, *jh*, *keccak*, and *skein*), and three rounds deliver a random hashing function. This offers additional security in case one of the algorithms get compromised in the future	Introduced with Quark (QRK) 21.7.2013 Also in Animecoin (ANI), BitQuark (BTQ), Cthulhu (OFF), Diamondcoin (DMC), FairQuark (FRQ), Frozen (FZ), MinCoin (MINI), Wikicoin (WIKI), Particle (PRT), etc.
X11–X17	Chained proof-of-work (PoW) algorithms inspired by the chained-hashing approach of Quark by increasing the number of hashes. X11 includes *blake*, *bmw*, *grøstl*, *jh*, *keccak*, *skein*, *luffa*, *cubehash*, *shavite*, *simd*, and *echo* X13: X11, adding *hamsi* and *fugue* X14: X13 + *shabal* X15: X14 + *whirlpool* X17: X15 + *loselose* and *djb2*	Introduced with Darkcoin (DRK) 18.1.2014 Also in Hirocoin (HIRO), X11coin (XC), DarkCash (DRKC). X13 was introduced in MaruCoin (MARU), 14.4.2014 and is also in BoostCoin (BOST), Britcoin (BRIT), X13Coin (X13C). X15 was introduced June 2014 in X15Coin (X15C), MaiaCoin (MAIA), Soundbit (SND), Firecoin (FRC), etc.
Blake-256	The Blake-256(optimized) algorithm was originally written to be a	Introduced with Blakecoin (BLC) in October 2013. Also in Dirac

Continued

Name	Description	Used in coins
	candidate for SHA-3. For cryptocurrencies, the hash rate is two to three times faster in comparison to Bitcoin	(XDQ), Electron (ELT), Photon (PHO), Landcoin (LND), and Universal Molecule (UMO)
HEFTY1	Hashing method that has no proof of security yet. For this reason, Heavycoin uses HEFTY1 as a secondary hash, while the original input is still hashed by SHA-256, *keccak*, *grøstl*, and *blake*. Intended to be CPU only	Introduced by Heavycoin (HVC) on 17.2.2014. Also in Mjollnircoin (MNR)
CryptoNight	CryptoNight can only be CPU-mined for the time being. "It relies on random access to a slow memory and emphasizes latency dependence" (Saberhagen, 2013)	Introduced with the CryptoNoteCoin 10.7.2014. Also in Aeon (AEON), Bytecoin (BCN), duckNote (XDN), and Monero (MRO)
NIST5	Chain of the five final round candidates for SHA-3 of the National Institute of Science and Technology: *blake*, *grøstl*, *jh*, *keccak*, *and skein* (Chang et al., 2012). Promises better power efficiency and security than other algorithms	Introduced by Talkcoin (TAC) on 21.5.2014 Also in IcebergCoin (ICB), eUtopium (UPM), EthanCoin (ETHAN), Ntcoin (N5), and ChatCoin (CHAT)

10.4.5 Velocity of circulation and the deflationary spiral

One of the major critiques of Bitcoin is that it is beginning to function more as a digital property asset than a currency (Ren, 2014). Quantitative analysis of the full bitcoin transaction graph by Ron and Shamir (2013) has demonstrated that at least 55% of Bitcoins are dormant and were not used in transactions between 2010 and 2013. This tendency to save Bitcoins rather than to spend them is caused by the appreciation potential of the Bitcoin due to its capped supply. There have been arguments in the media and on forums that this hoarding of Bitcoin could cause a "demand crisis" or "deflationary spiral" (Seward, 2013; Barber et al., 2012) although according to Russ Roberts, there will "likely be a slow and steady deflation" in Bitcoin because deflation is anticipated due to the capped supply (Simonite, 2011). Additionally, "zombie coins" (Barber et al., 2012), coins whose private key has been lost or destroyed, contribute to deflation. *Quark-Coin*, for example, introduced an inflation rate of 0.5% per year to counteract the additional deflation caused by these "zombie coins," also capping the first year of supply to 27 million coins mined, and every subsequent year to a limit of 1 million coins, but introduced no overall total cap unlike Bitcoin.

The deflationary aspects of cryptocurrencies have been addressed in different aspects. *Freicoin* (announced June 2012) emerged from the Occupy movement and introduced a demurrage fee (4.89%) ensuring its circulation and bearers of the currency pay this fee automatically. The parameters used in *Freicoin* were selected to eliminate the liquidity premium and encourage sustainable investments with a currency that maintains a stable value with neither price inflation nor deflation. *Freicoin* was inspired by the economic theory of Silvio Gesell and in particular his concept of "Freigeld" that was introduced in his work "Natural Economic Order" (Gesell, 1916/1958). It was believed that this separation of money's roles as store of value and medium of exchange would bring an end to boom and bust cycles. *Freicoin* has appeared relatively stable in terms of price in comparison to other altcoins, but one of its creators (Mark Friedenbach) has acknowledged that it will be some time before it can prove its hypothesis, as the coin's value remains speculative despite its intentions to function otherwise (Bradbury, 2013).

Bitcoin is based on a deflationary model that has a limit of 21 million units that can ever be produced. Alternatively, some coins are based on an inflationary model: *Peercoin* (Nadal and King, 2012) does not have a limit on the number of possible coins and is designed to eventually attain an annual inflation rate of 1%. *Peercoin*'s fork *Novacoin* (as well as most of *Novacoin* forks) and *Dogecoin, Coiledcoin*, and *Tenebrix* (and forks *Fairbrix* and *Liquidcoin*) also do not limit the amount of their possible units. *Fluttercoin* is another inflationary coin with no cap of total supply that also uses proof of transaction: rewards were distributed for being involved in a transaction, including both sending and receiving coins. This method encourages the circulation of currency, although it is arguably more a form of psychological encouragement, as the reward for transactions is almost entirely random. *Fluttercoin* still maintains proof of work and PoS, but the introduction of proof of transaction was one of the first attempts in an altcoin to address the problem of velocity of circulation. With *Fluttercoin*, people were rewarded for mining (proof of work), saving (PoS), and also spending (proof of transaction).

A similar approach is proof-of-stake velocity (PoSV) that was introduced in *Reddcoin* to "encourage both ownership (stake) and activity (velocity)" (Ren, 2014). It is based on the assumption that a higher velocity of money "indicates a more flourishing economy, richer members and a healthier financial system" (Ren, 2014), which, while it could be working for the specifics of *Reddcoin*, is not initially intended to be implemented in other cryptocurrencies.

Proof of burn is another alternative method that was introduced by Stewart (2012) and provides an example of an even more deflationary system: it proposes that an alternative expense to computer power (work) for miners could be the destruction (burn) of coins. Stewart suggested that this public reduction in the number of coins of a known-total-stock-issued currency would function as a "remurrage" (a term he invented to describe the opposite of demurrage). Proof of burn is mainly beneficial to the establishment of new cryptocurrencies by providing a form of distribution that can be considered more fair and proportional. The *Counterparty* native cryptocurrency XCP was one of the first altcoins to make use of this method. The amount of XCP coins created was limited to the amount of Bitcoins that were willingly offered to be destroyed. This immediately ensured that the newly minted XCP coins had a form of value that did not require proof of work while at the same time contributing to the further deflation of Bitcoin by burning Bitcoins and creating even more "zombie coins."

10.4.6 Anonymity and privacy in cryptocurrencies

Bitcoin is considered to support strong anonymity, but in its current implementation is not particularly anonymous (Reid and Hamilton, 2011; Barber et al., 2012; Bonneau et al., 2014), since all the transactions are visible in the blockchain. There have been a series of altcoins developed and launched that attempt to provide more anonymity; the innovations that are implemented in each of these distributed experiments demonstrate examples of evolutionary problem solving. Anonymity is a feature that is in high demand with all current altcoins supporting high anonymity showing a high acceptance on cryptocurrency exchanges. True anonymity seems to be also a driving force of public acceptance throughout the community.

Zerocoin by Miers, Garman, Green, and Rubin (Miers et al., 2013) describes "coin mixing" without the use of a trusted third party. "Laundry services" had been used before alternative; more secure coins were existing but had severe limitations: "operators can steal funds, track coins, or simply go out of business" (Miers et al., 2013). *Zerocoin* had been proposed as an extension to Bitcoin as an own currency that gets stored in the BTC blockchain, which in difference to the other "coin-mixing" services would be secured on a protocol level. The concept of *Zerocoin* had not been implemented in Bitcoin but is currently extended to be included in *Anoncoin* in late 2014. *Anoncoin* is also the first cryptocurrency to support the I2P darknet ("The Invisible Internet Project").

CoinJoin, an idea originally posted on Bitcointalk,[7] particularly received attention as it has been implemented into the very popular website blockchain.info, branded as "Shared Coin," and was later also implemented into *Darkcoin*. *CoinJoin* is based around the idea to collate the inputs to the transactions of multiple users so that a single "master transaction" can be built. This approach is not entirely anonymous, but enhances anonymity by the amount of users participating in the joint effort. *Darkcoin* (Duffield and Hagan, 2014) is originally launched under the name "Xcoin" and uses a decentralized mixing service called "DarkSend," which is in beta state and will according to the developers be "open-sourced when complete." DarkSend is based on *CoinJoin* but additionally reroutes the money flows by breaking it up into smaller pieces and sending them through random "master nodes" (called Master Nodes in the original paper), which are based on the Tor

---

[7]See https://bitcointalk.org/index.php?topic=279249.0.

protocol. *Darkcoin* implements a hybrid type of PoS: operators of "master nodes" get 20% of mined blocks as reward for their service.

CloakCoin introduced PoSA (proof-of-stake anonymity), which is not based on *CoinJoin* (Z, 2014), and extends proof-of-stake mining to perform anonymization processing in exchange for processing fees. CloakCoin added "OneMarket," a peer-to-peer marketplace that is decentralized.

CryptoNote introduced an own technology to offer "untraceability" as well as "unlinkability," which is achieved through "group signatures." The *CryptoNoteCoin* reference implementation had been designed to ensure the "relationship between the user and his purchases must be untraceable" (Z, 2014). Other coins based on the CryptoNote protocol are *duckNote*, *Monero*, *Boolberry*, and *Bytecoin*, all of which show significant acceptance on altcoin exchanges.

Stablecoin had been introduced with a large amount of coins premined, supposedly used to be for an integrated coin-mixing service. After the main developer vanished for over 5 months, the community had lost trust in the cryptocurrency and was shrinking. *Stablecoin* still gets traded and implements "mixed transactions," which use "mixing nodes" and "broadcast nodes," both operating behind the Tor network.

10.4.7 Social currencies

There have also been efforts to extend the adoption of altcoins beyond its currently fairly technocratic community into the broader social net. *Reddcoin* is probably the most significant example of this yet, with its introduction of the social wallet that allows transactions to easily occur over social media platforms such as Twitter, Youtube, and reddit. *Reddcoin* was especially designed to encourage online tipping culture, allowing users to tip one another with micropayments to demonstrate appreciation for content produced, be it in the form of a tweet, a blog post, or a reddit comment. This tipping culture was predominantly established with the introduction of *Dogecoin*, another altcoin that was developed to target a user base that extended beyond the traditional specialized cryptocurrency community. *Dogecoin* was originally developed as a fun cryptocurrency in response to a popular internet meme, despite (or perhaps because of) being considered a joke it garnered widespread adoption and popularity. The high velocity of *Dogecoin* due to its nature as a tipping currency also led the altcoin to becoming the second-most transacted cryptocurrency after *Bitcoin*; between December 2013 and February 2014, *Dogecoin* actually had the most transactions of all cryptocurrencies, even topping Bitcoin.[8] Bitcoin itself has proven too expensive in terms of transaction price to be adopted as a "tipping currency" (minimum transaction fee of the client is 0.0001 BTC for smaller transactions than 0.01 BTC). This is why these altcoins have been adopted so rapidly.

---

[8]This can be seen by comparing the blockchains of the two clients. See http://bitinfocharts.com/comparison/transactions-btc-ltc-drk-ppc-doge.html.

Dogecoin was also utilized in various community fundraising events, for example, more than 26 million *Dogecoin* were raised to send the Jamaican bobsleigh team to the 2014 Winter Olympics in Sochi, Russia.

There have been other experiments with cryptocurrencies within the social sphere, such as *Talkcoin*, which uses the *Bitcoin* protocol to create a decentralized chat program that does not store messages on any server, allowing secure and anonymous communications. *Florincoin* introduced its blockchain as a publishing and freedom-of-speech platform, allowing the possibility of uncensorable and unchangeable messages to be placed into the blockchain. It also introduced the idea of proof of love by allowing users to publish "eternal" declarations of love in the blockchain in a similar vein to carved etchings in park benches or tree branches.

Each of these coins demonstrates experiments in the social uses of cryptocurrencies. *Reddcoin* itself is a clear example of how an altcoin can develop and innovate from the often unexpected consequences and outcomes of the experiments of previous altcoins, in this case particularly *Dogecoin*.

10.5 THE FUTURE OF THE BLOCKCHAIN

Antonopoulos (2013) created an interesting taxonomy of innovation in the cryptocurrency ecosystem, with dividing in "alt-coins, meta-coins, and para-chains". He described "alt-coins" as Bitcoin forks, which show different implementation fundamentals. "Meta-coins" are technologies, which do not have their own blockchain, but use Bitcoin's ledger to store their data (he mentioned *Zerocoin* and *Bitnotar* as examples). "Para-chains" are described as implementations having a blockchain, but encoding "noncurrency, nonpayment data" (Antonopoulos, 2013).

Alternative uses of the blockchain have been introduced with *Namecoin* in 2011, which had been existing as idea under the name "BitDNS" originally posted by Satoshi Nakamoto already in November 2010.[9] This post led to speculation about the possibility of creating a decentralized DNS system based on the technology of Bitcoin. A possible implementation had been discussed in December 2012 (called "domainchain"), but was not considered to be implemented in the Bitcoin source code. Instead, on April 18, *Namecoin* had been announced on the Bitcointalk forum, with a new blockchain separate from the main Bitcoin chain, extending the concept of the blockchain to a distributed data-value storage.

Multicoin (introduced in June 2011), an experimental altcoin and fork of the Bitcoin client, allowed multiple blockchains and the creation of new chains within the framework. It also introduced new methods of linked chains and advanced methods of transactions including escrow and multisign transactions. The absence of escrow in Bitcoin has

[9]See https://bitcointalk.org/index.php?topic=1790.0.

been an ongoing subject of discussion, since the original design was built around "transaction irreversibility." Although the possibility "to embed scripts in their Bitcoin transactions" is possible within the Bitcoin system design (Barber et al., 2012), these features have not yet been implemented in its client as of today. Through scripts, "rich transactional semantics and contracts" would be possible, for example, "deposits, escrow and dispute mediation, and assurance contracts, including the use of external states" (Barber et al., 2012).

"Next-generation cryptocurrencies" (sometimes also referred to as "cryptocurrencies 2.0" or "Bitcoin 2.0") already extended the usage of the blockchain and the technologies introduced. *Mastercoin* (Willet, 2012) exists entirely inside the Bitcoin blockchain and also makes user-defined currencies possible that could be traded within the Mastercoin network. With Colored Coins, Bitcoins can be extended with specific attributes, which turns them into tokens that could be used "[. . .] for alternative currencies, commodity certificates, smart property, and other financial instruments such as stocks and bonds." (Rosenfeld, 2012). *Colored Coins* can "virtually [represent] any kind of asset or contract" but, as Rosenfeld also states, also create "blockchain bloat." A lot of services are using the Blockchain as data storage. Especially gambling services such as "SatoshiDice" have been described to be responsible for "spamming" the network (Bruce, 2014).

10.5.1 The Bitcoin blockchain does not scale (yet)

In May 2014, the blockchain was identified to contain a signature of the virus "Stoned" (created in 1987) and had the blockchain automatically deleted by antivirus software all over the world, producing additional bandwidth waste, since a lot of users had to redownload the whole blockchain history. The actual virus had not been in the blockchain, but a similar hex signature seems to have been the cause of the false alarm. This incident shows that potential threats and attacks on the blockchain will evolve in the future.

The initial design of the blockchain as a public ledger poses problems for long-term use, since its size already reached the 20 GB mark in early August 2014. This not only poses a problem of increasing network traffic but also destroys the usability of the software clients (the "Wallets"), since new users have to download the entire blockchain. This issue had been tackled by the so-called light wallets, which do not download the whole blockchain. Another alternative is "web-based wallets," most prominently via blockchain.info for Bitcoin; these are, however, not available for all the alternative cryptocurrencies in existence and again support centralization. Also, web wallets are single points of failure, since if the service becomes compromised, all the hosted wallets could be compromised as well.

There have been vivid discussions on how to solve the problem of the ever-growing blockchain, Bruce (2014) suggested a much slimmer variant of the public ledger called "mini blockchain scheme" and described other efforts and issues, such as "ultimate blockchain compression," which remains an ongoing discussion.

A very recent project, *Ethereum* (Buterin, 2014), extends the blockchain concept with a programming language, making distributed applications possible and improving "upon the concepts of scripting, altcoins and on-chain meta-protocols" (Buterin, 2014). Although showing huge potential, *Ethereum* also has no solution for the issue of scalability yet. "Like Bitcoin, Ethereum suffers from the flaw that every transaction needs to be processed by every node in the network" but at least outlines additional strategies to cope with the increasing of data. Buterin also stated that if Bitcoin's network was to process the same amount of the transactions such as VISA (2000 transactions/s vs. 7 transactions/s in Bitcoin), the blockchain would grow by 8 TB a year. Such sizes of the public ledger pose additional risks of centralization and might block the further adoption of Bitcoin.

10.6 CONCLUSION

Problems and issues that arose with Bitcoin as a community experiment have been tackled to a large extent by altcoins. Innovation is introduced with newly appearing cryptocurrencies at first, since some changes are drastic and involve a transition of the blockchain ledger or alterations to other parts of the system, which are in the case of Bitcoin not easy to undertake because it is already used and traded heavily. Even small changes to the storage of the ledger (i.e., compression) could render useless these services that use the blockchain for other purposes. Next-generation cryptocurrencies are introducing additional uses for the public ledger, although there are severe issues of scalability of the blockchain that are not yet solved.

Alternative cryptocurrencies will continue to be important for the development of truly decentralized currencies; Bitcoin as the most used cryptocurrency still shows severe issues if we consider that "privacy and anonymity are the most important aspects of electronic cash" (Saberhagen, 2013). Saberhagen (2013) had also noted that "[. . .] critical flaws that cannot be fixed rapidly deter Bitcoin's widespread propagation. In such inflexible models, it is more efficient to roll-out a new project rather than perpetually fix the original project", which is supporting our theory of the importance of altcoins as experimental culture. Especially in context with highly discussed topics such as anonymity and privacy, future altcoins will introduce solutions to problems that are not on the radar yet.

It is evident through our analysis of the various altcoins that have developed in response to the various limitations and critiques of Bitcoin that the ecosystem provides an experimental model to test and extend the development of cryptocurrencies. Although many of the coins we have described already function in effect and have reasonable sized markets to ensure that they continue to exist, much like Bitcoin, they behave as experimental systems.

Satoshi Nakamoto's idea for a cryptocurrency that is based on "one-CPU-one-vote" (Nakamoto, 2008) as method for decision making has been undermined with the development of specific hardware (ASICs). A cryptocurrency as intended by Nakamoto "must not enable a network participant to have a significant advantage over another participant" (Saberhagen, 2013). The current situation of mining monopolies produces an inequality, which does not compromise the network's security, but proves problematic to think of Bitcoin as a decentralized and democratic currency. With the discourse and experiments that emerged through the last years in cryptocurrencies, the financial and cryptographic literacy of the community also evolved, making it possible to create a truly distributed "digital currency" in the future. Until this time, the cryptocurrencies represent a vivid ecosystem to discuss, test, and experiment new theories.

REFERENCES

Andresen, G., 2012. Neutralizing a 51% attack. GavinTech. May 1. Retrieved from: http://gavintech. blogspot.co.at/2012/05/neutralizing-51-attack.html.

Antonopoulos, A., 2013. The crypto-currency ecosystem. Radar. Retrieved from: http://radar.oreilly. com/2013/06/the-crypto-currency-ecosystem.html.

Back, A., 1997. Hashcash. Online announcement. Retrieved from: http://www.hashcash.org/papers/ announce.txt.

Barber, S., Boyen, X., Shi, E., Uzun, E., 2012. Bitter to better—how to make bitcoin a better currency. In: Keromytis, A.D. (Ed.), Lecture Notes in Computer Science: Financial Cryptography and Data Security, vol. 7397. Springer, Berlin, pp. 399–414.

Bentov, I., Gabizon, A., Mizrahi, A., 2014. Cryptocurrencies without proof of work. ArXiv Preprint ArXiv: 1406.5694. Retrieved from: http://arxiv.org/abs/1406.5694.

Bonneau, J., Narayanan, A., Miller, A., Clark, J., Kroll, J.A., Felten, E.W., 2014. Mixcoin: anonymity for Bitcoin with accountable mixes. In: The 18th International Conference on Financial Cryptography. Retrieved from: http://www.jbonneau.com/doc/BNMCKF14-FC-mixcoin_full.pdf.

Bradbury, D., 2013. Freicoin's attempt to free the economy. Coindesk. Retrieved from: http://www. coindesk.com/freicoins-attempt-to-free-the-economy/.

Bruce, J.D., 2014. The mini-blockchain scheme. Self-published white paper. Retrieved from: http:// cryptonite.info/files/mbc-scheme-rev2.pdf.

Buterin, V., 2013. Primecoin: the cryptocurrency whose mining is actually useful. Bitcoin Magazine. Retrieved from: http://bitcoinmagazine.com/primecoin-the-cryptocurrency-whose-mining-is-actually-useful/.

Buterin, V., 2014. Ethereum: a next-generation smart contract and decentralized application platform. Self-published white paper.

Casey, M.J., Vigna, P., 2014. BitBeat: mining pool rejects short-term fixes to avert "51% attack". Wall St. J. Retrieved from: http://blogs.wsj.com/moneybeat/2014/06/16/bitbeat-a-51-attack-what-is-it-and-could-it-happen/.

Chang, S., Perlner, R., Turan, M.S., Kelsey, J.M., Paul, S., Bassham, L.E., 2012. Third-Round Report of the SHA-3 Hash Algorithm Competition. NISTIR 7896. National Institute of Standards and Technology. Retrieved from: http://dx.doi.org/10.6028/NIST.IR.7896.

Chaum, D., 1983. Blind signatures for untraceable payments. In: Chaum, D., Rivest, R.L., Sherman, A. T. (Eds.), Advances in Cryptology: Proceedings of Crypto 82. Plenum Press, New York, pp. 199–203.

Chaum, D., Fiat, A., Naor, M., 1990. Untraceable electronic cash. In: Proceedings on Advances in Cryptology—CRYPTO '88. Lecture Notes in Computer Science, vol. 403. Springer, London, pp. 319–327.

Dai, W., 1998. B-Money. Self-published white paper. Retrieved from: http://www.weidai.com/bmoney.txt.

Duffield, E., Hagan, K., 2014. Darkcoin: peer-to-peer crypto-currency with anonymous blockchain transactions and an improved proof-of-work system. Self-published white paper. Retrieved from: https://www.darkcoin.io/wp-content/uploads/2014/09/DarkcoinWhitepaper.pdf.

Eyal, I., Sirer, E.G., 2014. It's time for a hard Bitcoin fork. Hacking, distributed. Retrieved from: http://hackingdistributed.com/p/2014/06/13/in-ghash-bitcoin-trusts/.

Gesell, S., 1958. The Natural Economic Order. Peter Owen Ltd, London (Original work published in 1916).

Hardin, G., 1968. The tragedy of the commons. Science 162 (3859), 1243–1248.

Hove, L.V., 2000. Electronic purses: which way to go? First Monday, 5(7).

King, S., 2013. Primecoin: cryptocurrency with prime number proof-of-work. Self-published white paper. Retrieved from: http://primecoin.io/bin/primecoin-paper.pdf.

King, S., Nadal, S., 2012. PPCoin: peer-to-peer crypto-currency with proof-of-stake. Self-published white paper. Retrieved from: http://peercoin.net/assets/paper/peercoin-paper.pdf.

Kroll, J.A., Davey, I.C., Felten, E.W., 2013. The economics of bitcoin mining, or bitcoin in the presence of adversaries. In: Proceedings of WEIS (vol. 2013).

Miers, I., Garman, G., Green, M., Rubin, A.D., 2013. Zerocoin: anonymous distributed e-cash from Bitcoin. In: IEEE Symposium on Security and Privacy (Oakland). Retrieved from: http://zerocoin.org/media/pdf/ZerocoinOakland.pdf.

Muller, D., 2014. Vertcoin. Self-published white paper. Retrieved from: https://vertcoin.org/Vertcoin-DavidMuller.pdf.

Nakamoto, S., 2008. Bitcoin: a peer-to-peer electronic cash system. Self-published white paper.

Percival, C., 2009. Stronger key derivation via sequential memory-hard functions. Conference presentation at BSDCan '09. Retrieved from: http://www.bsdcan.org/2009/schedule/attachments/87_scrypt.pdf.

Reid, F., Hamilton, M., 2011. An analysis of anonymity in the Bitcoin system. arXiv:1107.4524 [physics.soc-ph]. Retrieved from: http://arxiv.org/abs/1107.4524.

Ren, L., 2014. Proof of stake velocity: building the social currency of the digital age. Self-published white paper.

Ron, D., Shamir, A., 2013. Quantitative analysis of the full bitcoin transaction graph. In: Sadeghi, A.R. (Ed.), Lecture Notes in Computer Science: Financial Cryptography and Data Security, vol. 7859. Springer, Berlin, pp. 6–24.

Rosenfeld, M., 2012. Overview of colored coins. Self-published white paper. Retrieved from: https://bitcoil.co.il/BitcoinX.pdf.

Saberhagen, N., 2013. CryptoNote v 2.0. Self-published white paper. Retrieved from: https://cryptonote.org/whitepaper.pdf.

Seward, Z.M., 2013. Yes, people are hoarding bitcoins. Quartz. Retrieved from: http://qz.com/72118/yes-people-are-hoarding-bitcoins/.

Simonite, T., 2011. What bitcoin is, and why it matters. MIT Technol. Rev. May 25. Retrieved from: http://www.technologyreview.com/news/424091/what-bitcoin-is-and-why-it-matters/.

Stewart, I., 2012. Proof of burn. Bitcoin wiki. Retrieved from: https://en.bitcoin.it/wiki/Proof_of_burn.

Szabo, N., 1997. Formalizing and securing relationships on public networks. First Monday, 2(9).

Tanaka, T., 1996. Possible economic consequences of digital cash. First Monday, 1(2).

Tromp, J., 2014. Cuckoo cycle: a graph-theoretic proof-of-work system. Self-published white paper. Retrieved from: https://eprint.iacr.org/2014/059.pdf.

Willet, J., 2012. The second bitcoin white paper. Self-published white paper. Retrieved from: https://sites.google.com/site/2ndbtcwpaper/2ndBitcoinWhitepaper.pdf.

Z. Cloak Technical Services Division, 2014. Decentralized P2P crypto currency transaction anonymity via proof of stake protocol extension. Self-published white paper. Retrieved from: https://mega.co.nz/#!1c9UnKBI!BdEaoBuYDAr5F4nwltpYjYNOrZt7Jretk07eGc-oPDc.

CHAPTER 11

Extracting Market-Implied Bitcoin's Risk-Free Interest Rate

Nicolas Wesner
Mazars Actuariat, Paris, France

Contents

11.1 INTRODUCTION

Through his famous essay, *The Denationalization of Money*, Hayek (1976) advocated the establishment of competitively issued private moneys. According to Hayek, the main benefit of a decentralized money supply in addition to the increase of consumer choice and hence economic welfare would be price stability.

The emergence of Bitcoin among other digital currencies seems to echo Hayek writings, even more so that Satoshi (2008) peer-to-peer payment system is totally decentralized, operating through open-source software, and that the money supply growth is set to a publicly available and predetermined schedule. Meanwhile, price stability of the system, if measured by volatility of exchange rates, is far from being achieved.

Price instability and lack of liquidity are currently the main obstacles to the development of Bitcoin protocol as a universal payment system. Nevertheless, the protocol is constantly evolving, and many specifications are continuously discussed and can be modified though an open process of validation. In parallel, compatible technologies like Colored Coins[1] are under construction and could procure the material for building complex financial vehicles

---

[1]Colored Coins is an exchange protocol that makes use of the existing Bitcoin infrastructure. Colored Coins can be stored and transferred without the need for a third party; they can then have special properties supported by either an issuing agent or public agreement and have value independent of the face value of the underlying Bitcoins.

denominated in Bitcoin. As a potential use cited by Rosenfeld (2012), bonds denominated in Bitcoins can be issued with a particular face value and repayment schedule.

This chapter focuses on the time value of Bitcoin. Since risk-free interest rates[2] on digital currencies like Bitcoin are not observable, for now, due to the fact that no organized, deep and liquid market exists for low-credit-risk Bitcoin-denominated bonds, the following deal with the expected properties of Bitcoin interest rate.

Given the exogenous and predictable nature of monetary supply, which cannot be manipulated by a central authority, one should expect credit risk-free interest rates on Bitcoin to perfectly reflect collective preferences, namely, time preferences. Nevertheless, as will be further explored herein, many factors indicate that it could not be the case.

Without entering the sterile debate about whether Bitcoin is a currency or not, one can easily argue that Bitcoin is currently essentially a speculative asset since no goods or service is primarily priced in Bitcoin. Investors hold Bitcoin as an asset and its appreciation relies on the expectation that it will become an established medium of exchange. For this reason, Bitcoin's value as a currency is necessarily defined with reference to a major currency and so does its time value.

The first part of this chapter uses simple open economy macroeconomic model in order to extract estimates of Bitcoin interest rates from market data. Second part concludes on risk factors that should be considered in the determination of Bitcoin interest rates.

11.2 A MODEL FOR THE DETERMINATION OF BITCOIN'S RISK-FREE INTEREST RATE

11.2.1 Uncovered interest rate parity

Uncovered interest rate parity was introduced by Keynes (1923) and is nowadays the cornerstone of many macroeconomic models. If uncovered interest rate parity holds, such that an investor is indifferent between any of two money cash deposits (say, euro and US$), then any excess return on euro deposits must be offset by some expected loss from depreciation of the euro against the dollar. Conversely, some shortfall in return on euro deposits must be offset by some expected gain from appreciation of the euro against the dollar.

The strictest version of uncovered interest parity supposes risk neutrality so that risk premiums should be identically zero, implying that a currency's expected appreciation should equal the current interest differential:

$$_t s^e_{t+k} - s_t = i_t - i^*_t \tag{11.1}$$

---

[2]Numerous peer-to-peer lending sites exist, but those rates are by definition polluted with credit risk and no significant historical data are available.

Here, s_t represents the (log) spot exchange rate at time t, measured as domestic currency units per foreign currency unit, and i_t and i_t^* represent foreign and domestic nominal interest rates, respectively.

Thus, under risk neutrality and rational expectations, "a" should be zero and "b" should be unity in Equation (11.2):

$$_ts_{t+k}^e - s_t = a + b\left(i_t - i_t^*\right) \tag{11.2}$$

Empirical studies find otherwise: risk premiums appear to be highly variable and strongly related to interest differentials. The statistical rejection of this linear model does of course not invalidate the rational expectation hypothesis since it can mean simply that the model specification is wrong or that other important variables are omitted. According to Fama (1984), empirical results are coherent with the existence of a time–varying risk premium.

11.2.2 Monetary economic theory

According to Fisher (1930), nominal interest rates can be decomposed into real rate and inflation expectation: $i = r + \pi^a$. Using this relation, uncovered interest rate parity can be written:

$$_ts_{t+k}^e - s_t = \left(r_t - r_t^*\right) + \left(\pi^a - \pi^{*a}\right) \tag{11.3}$$

Since a virtual currency as Bitcoin is decentralized, it cannot be associated with a foreign country, so that $r = r^*$ can be assumed (in the same way, equality between home and foreign national outcome $y = y^*$ can be assumed). This leads to relative purchasing power parity:

$$_ts_{t+k}^e - s_t = \pi^a - \pi^{*a} \tag{11.4}$$

We consider then some assumptions that form the basis of the monetary approach. Some of those assumptions fit well with the current framework of a virtual currency like Bitcoin where almost all goods are priced primarily in a domestic currency like US$ and where no deep, liquid, organized bond market exists. First demand for money is stable and supply exogenous. Moreover, we consider that the money market is in continuous equilibrium and it is cleared by price movements, not interest rates.

According to this basic monetarist model, a change in the relative money supply affects the exchange rate because it affects the relative price level. A higher relative money supply implies a higher relative price level, and by relative purchasing power parity, the exchange rate changes with the relative price level. Therefore, in this framework, the movement in the spot rate is proportional to the movement in the relative money supply:

$$_ts_{t+k} - s_t = m_{t+k} - m_t - \left(m_{t+k}^* - m_t^*\right) \tag{11.5}$$

Here, m_t^* and m_t represent (log) foreign money supply and domestic money supply, respectively.

11.2.3 A time-varying premium model

Risk neutrality is not assumed since the existence of a risk premium is considered, but rational expectation and no arbitrage condition are the core of the approach.

In the following, we suppose that the parameter a in Equation (11.2) is time-varying and reflects all important variables other than interest rates that determine exchange rate dynamics. We note $* = $ Bitcoin, so that Bitcoin is the "foreign" currency.

In order to derive an empirical interest rate, deviations from Equation (11.5) are measured directly from historical data and are used to characterize a "crude" exchange rate premium Rp_t:

$$Rp_t = {}_t s_{t+k} - s_t - \left[m_{t+k} - m_t - \left(m^*_{t+k} - m^*_t \right) \right] \tag{11.6}$$

This crude premium contains all factors not included in Equation (11.5) that affect Bitcoin exchange rates and is isolated in order to derive a risk-free Bitcoin interest rate. Those can be unanticipated shocks to macroeconomic or financial variables as well as factors related to liquidity and risk aversion.

Interest rate on Bitcoin exchange rates is then derived from Equations (11.2) and (11.6), with $b = 1$ and $a = Rp_t$:

$$_t s^e_{t+k} - s_t = Rp_t + i_t - i^*_t \tag{11.7}$$

Assuming rational expectations $({}_t s^e_{t+k} = {}_t s_{t+k}, \; {}_t m^e_{t+k} = {}_t m_{t+k})$, this permits to derive the theoretical Bitcoin interests rate from observed data:

$$i^*_t = i_t + \left[m^*_{t+k} - m^*_t - \left(m_{t+k} - m_t \right) \right] \tag{11.8}$$

In this model, Bitcoin interest rates are driven by reference currency, interest rates, and money growth differential.

Since growth of the Bitcoin supply is predefined by the Bitcoin protocol and total supply is capped, this equation implies that Bitcoin interest rate dynamics contain a determinist trend that will progressively disappear. Moreover, a more expansive monetary policy for reference currency will lead to lower Bitcoin interest rates.

11.3 APPLICATION TO US$ AND EURO DATA

$The following presents an application of Equations (11.6) and (11.8) to euro and US$ data. Data used for this application are daily Libor and Euribor 1-month interest rates, monthly euro M3 and US M2 aggregate data, and Mt. Gox daily exchange rates for the period July 19, 2010 to February 23, 2014, the end of the period corresponding to the collapse of the exchange. For euro data, the observation period range from August 29, 2011 to February 23, 2014. For comparison purposes, the observation period was extended to June 2014 with use of euro data from btcde exchange.

Results on the graph below show that the "crude premium" defined by Equation (11.6) is time-varying with high volatility.

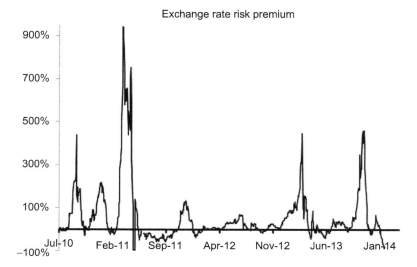

Daily average premium amounts 55.6% on the period of observation (measured with US data), and estimates from euro and US$ data are highly correlated (the correlation coefficient is 97%). One can note that premium dynamics display peaks that correspond, considering 1-month lag, to events that marked Bitcoin history and, for the end of the period, to the history of the leading financial provider related to Bitcoin networks, Mt. Gox. For recent history on year 2013, two peaks are striking. On and around April 10, Bitcoincharts, another major exchange, had issues keeping its site up, while Mt. Gox also announced a cease to trading. Later, in the year on December 5, the Chinese Government announced that they are not going to support the validity of the currency, and it turned out that Bitcoin price dropped to 600 USD. Finally, during the few days before the collapse of the exchange in February 2014, price fell slowly to 100 USD.

Graph below displays the 1-month Bitcoin interest rate dynamics extracted from US$ and euro data over the period July 2010 to January 2014.

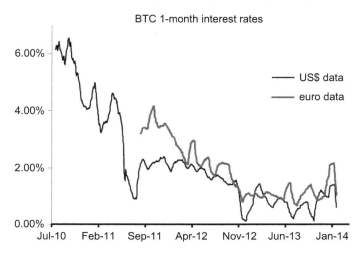

Graph below displays the 1-month Bitcoin interest rate dynamics extracted from euro data and exchange rates from Mt. Gox and btcde over the period February 2011 to May 2014.

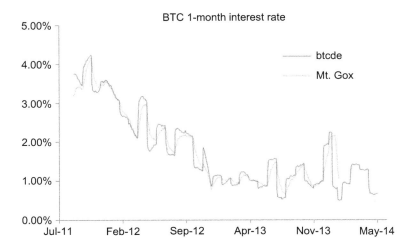

The negative trend observed in Bitcoin interest rates is not surprising given the model specification and Equation (11.8): the mechanical decline in Bitcoin's money supply growth rate combined with the decrease of US$ and euro interest rates over the period explains this dynamic. Within this framework, it suggests also that the development of Bitcoin as a means of payment could naturally lead to negative risk-free interest rates. Indeed, Bitcoin's money supply growth being bounded to zero, low, or negative domestic rates associated with negative differential of monetary supply growth could lead to this extreme case.

11.4 PERSPECTIVE ON BITCOIN INTEREST RATE

Basic economic theory links interest rates to the time value of money, the idea that money available at the present time is worth more than the same amount in the future due to its potential earning capacity. For Austrian economist like von Mises, a natural psychological bias explains why interest rates cannot be negative:

> Time preference is a categorical requisite of human action. No mode of action can be thought of in which satisfaction within a nearer period of the future is not—other things being equal—preferred to that in the later period.
>
> **Ludwig von Mises (1949)**

Nowadays, negative interest rates on deposits or bonds can be observed for major currency and are either the result of a unilateral decision from Central Bank or flight to security. The decentralized nature of the Bitcoin protocol prevents this type of discretionary policy, and for obvious reasons explained hereafter, flight to security cannot be considered for Bitcoin at this time. Nevertheless, other barriers to negative interest rates on the Bitcoin currency exist. Even without credit risk,[3] different risk premiums could affect yields on Bitcoin-denominated bonds.

First and most obvious is currency risk: high volatility of Bitcoin exchange rates should eventually reflect in Bitcoin-denominated bond prices. Interest rates and exchange rate risk premium estimates previously obtained illustrate this contagion effect. This uncertainty should naturally affect yields on Bitcoin-denominated bonds through a risk premium.

The illiquidity of Bitcoin currency exchange market is the main source of price instability and should also naturally be reflected in Bitcoin-denominated bond prices. In the current state of the Bitcoin foreign exchange market, it is impossible for large investor or financial institution to enter with the purpose of making large transaction without significantly affecting exchange rates. The illiquidity of the currency market should necessarily limit the size of any secondary market for Bitcoin-denominated bonds, and the lower liquidity of those bonds may eventually translate into higher yields.

Other risk factors that should be considered by investors are somewhat linked to the concept of country risk but are specific to the Bitcoin protocol. Indeed, investor holding a Bitcoin-denominated bond would face technological risks. Large oversea transactions are often targeted by hackers, and many platforms of exchange were subject to cyberattack, fraud, or malfunction causing important losses for Bitcoin holder, the collapse of Mt. Gox being a prime example. The absence of a political central authority that can guarantee the convertibility of Bitcoin and the recoverability of any Bitcoin-denominated debt is certainly the main obstacle to the viability of the digital currency. Without a credible backstop buyer, Bitcoin should simply disappear should perceptions of its usefulness decline. Political risk in the sense of adverse regulation effect, mainly in terms of taxes on transaction, should also be considered when assessing its efficiency as a means of exchange.

11.5 CONCLUSION

Figures obtained through this application are the results of many strict assumptions, and time will tell if Bitcoin would establish a viable currency, but if a deep and organized market for high-quality Bitcoin-denominated bonds emerges, it would offer a brand new perspective to the study of price discovery process.

---

[3]Credit risk is traditionally supposed to affect yields through a spread that lower bond prices: rational investors accept to bear the risk of default of their debtor in exchange of an additional reward (through higher interest rate).

Many factors like liquidity, political, and even technological risks could influence interest rates on Bitcoin deposit or yields on Bitcoin-denominated bonds, even in the context of exchange rate stability. Ultimately, it seems that credibility is the most important challenge that Bitcoin should achieve in order to develop a viable bond market.

REFERENCES

Fama, E.F., 1984. Forward and spot exchange rates. J. Monetary Econ. 14, 319–338.
Fisher, I., 1930. The Theory of Interest. Porcupine Press, Philadelphia.
Hayek, F., 1976. The Denationalization of Money. Institute of Economic Affairs, London.
Keynes, J.M., 1923. A Tract on Monetary Reform. MacMillan, London.
Mises, L., 1949. Human Action: A Treatise on Economics. Yale University Press, New Haven.
Rosenfeld, M., 2012. Overview of colored coins. White paper.
Satoshi, N., 2008. Bitcoin: a peer-to-peer electronic cash system. White paper.

CHAPTER 12

A Microeconomic Analysis of Bitcoin and Illegal Activities

Tetsuya Saito
Nihon University, Tokyo, Japan

Contents

12.1 INTRODUCTION

Recent theoretical study (Saito, 2015a) extended the second-generation money-search model (Trejos and Wright, 1995) in a dual-currency environment, *á la* Craig and Waller (2000). The results clarify that a sufficiently lower storage cost (or larger benefit) must be maintained compared to traditional currencies in order to keep virtual currency in circulation. The crash of Mt. Gox impacted the credibility of the bitcoin system and raised the potential cost of holding bitcoins. According to Saito (op. cit.), bitcoin should start shrinking in terms of circulation after the Mt. Gox incident in February 2014. However, the exchange rate suggests that bitcoin seems not to be case. According to the CoinDesk BPI, as depicted in Figure 12.1, the exchange rate went down to $360.84 in May 2014. However, it started rising again to reach $620 in the middle of July 2014.

There are several reasons for the revival of bitcoin. Big players such as China and entry of major vendors such as eBay held up the value of bitcoins. However, the existence of demand for bitcoins in black markets may not be ignored. Silk Road (discontinued in October 2013) was the largest anonymous online black market. Christin (2012) estimated that Silk Road dealt more than 23,000 illegal items, over 1.22 million USD monthly in

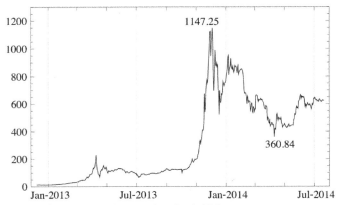

Figure 12.1 USD-BTC exchange rate. *(Source:* CoinDesk BPI*)*

2012. Currently, Silk Road 2.0 is the successor of Silk Road, and several other online black markets are Black Market Reloaded, DarkMarket, Sheep Marketplace, and Agora Marketplace. Due to anonymity of bitcoins, these transactions use bitcoins as a medium of exchange and create demand for bitcoins. In addition to these "public" black markets, online casinos accept bitcoins, while some countries prohibit gambling.[1] The exact value of illegal deals is unknown. The demand for bitcoins by those dealing with illegal items affects the currency exchange market and compliant bitcoiners. If there are illegal items in the market, law enforcement authorities will try to penalize transactions of these items. With these notions, this study focuses on the demand for illegal items and the bitcoin exchange market in terms of law enforcements using a monopolistic competition model with free entry, similar to a new trade theory (NTT) framework of Krugman (1979, 1980).

Illegal activities are not only transactions of illegal items. A recent problem in bitcoin is theft. Bitcoins are encrypted, but it does not mean that bitcoins cannot be confiscated or stolen, and actually the price did collapse (Mt. Gox in February 2014). A post at the BitcoinTalk forums[2] reports more than 40 known theft cases, as illustrated in Table 12.1. Severity is measured by current USD. The number for the 2014 Mt. Gox Collapse is taken from *Wall Street Journal*; 41.6 million USD is from theft. In all cases, 517.9 million USD is confiscated or stolen since 2010. Interestingly, many major cases are observed in major black markets. Even if we exclude the 2014 Mt. Gox Collapse, more than 10 million USD is annually stolen. Theft that could account for nearly 70% of illegal items traded in Silk Road in 2012 (15 million USD). In addition to black markets for illegal

---

[1] The problem of online access to such casinos was also discussed in the WTO as a court case for GATS before bitcoins between the United States and Antigua and Barbuda (DS285).

[2] List of Major Bitcoin Heists, Thefts, Hacks, Scams, and Losses (https://bitcointalk.org/index.php?topic=576337).

Table 12.1 List of known bitcoin theft cases

No.	Case	Severity in USD
1.	Silk Road seizure	26,867,560
2.	Sheep Marketplace incident	4,070,923
3.	Silk Road 2.0 incident	3,624,866
4.	Bitcoin Savings and Trust	2,983,473
5.	PicoStocks hack	3,009,397
6.	MyBitcoin theft	1,072,570
Subtotal		*41,628,789*
7.	$10k-$100k (19 cases)	5,776,430
8.	Less than $10k (18 cases)	539,470
9.	2014 Mt. Gox collapse	470,000,000
Grand total		*517,944,689*

items, bitcoin theft is also one illegal activity that should be monitored carefully. This study provides a theoretical analysis of bitcoin theft to see how it affects the exchange rate, as an extension of baseline model.

The discussion is developed as follows. The baseline model is introduced in Section 12.2. In the model, there are varieties of legal and illegal items. Legal and illegal items are classified by law enforcement penalties: no penalty on legal items while fines on illegal ones. Demands for these items create demands for traditional money and bitcoins, which also determine the exchange rate as described in Section 12.4. Noncompliant consumers believe that paying with bitcoins reduces the chance of apprehension. In the baseline model, fines are independent of the volume of consumption of illegal items. We extend the model by introducing fines dependent on the volume of consumption of illegal varieties and bitcoin theft in Section 12.5. Most of these arguments are based on numerical simulations. The conclusion is in Section 12.6.

12.2 THE BASELINE MODEL

We consider a *new trade theory* framework *á la* Krugman (1979, 1980). In the NTT, consumers are distributed in more than two countries. In our model, however, consumers are distributed in two groups, compliant and noncompliant, that are active in a digital economy. There are $n \geq 0$ compliant consumers and $m \geq 0$ noncompliant consumers; hence, the total population N is provided by

$$N = n + m. \tag{12.1}$$

For simplicity, these consumers are supposed to be risk-neutral. Each consumer is endowed with $h > 0$ labor hours to be active in the digital economy; hence, the labor endowment is Nh. Compliant consumers consume only legal items and engage only in legal productions. Noncompliant consumers consume both legal and illegal items and engage in both legal and illegal productions.

We assume that each individual has one's own variety. Thus, there are n legal and m illegal varieties. However, there are no demand and supply of legal variety if $n=0$ and similarly no demand and supply of illegal variety if $m=0$; hence, n and m as indexes of varieties start from $n=1$ and $m=1$ instead of $n=0$ and $m=0$, respectively. Each item is monopolistically competitive, but free entry is allowed. For simplicity, producers are supposed to have long-run perspectives, so that, there is no economic gains in equilibrium. In this case, N remains open, while n/N and m/N (or m/n) are going to be endogenously determined.

In addition to these $n+m$ varieties, there is a numéraire good (legal). Varieties of legal and illegal items are paid both with bitcoins and traditional money, but the numéraire is only paid with traditional money. Consumers then derive utility from consuming these goods in accordance with a Dixit-Stiglitz utility function (Dixit and Stiglitz, 1977), as discussed in Sections 12.2.1 and 12.2.2.

12.2.1 Compliant consumers

Compliant consumers consume only legal items indexed by $i=1, \ldots, n$. Letting z and u be the quantity of consumption of the numéraire good and the utility from legal varieties, respectively, the utility function of a representative compliant consumer is provided in a Cobb-Douglas form:

$$U(z, u) = z^\alpha u^{1-\alpha}, \tag{12.2}$$

where $\alpha \in (0, 1)$ is the expenditure share of the numéraire; hence, $1 - \alpha \in (0, 1)$ is the expenditure share of the differentiated goods. The utility from varieties of legal items is provided in a CES (constant elasticity of substitution) form:

$$u(x) = \left(\sum_{i=1}^{n} x_i^\theta \right)^{1/\theta}, \tag{12.3}$$

where x_i is the volume of consumption of ith legal variety, $x = (x_i)_{i=1}^n$ the vector representing a consumption bundle of legal items, and θ the preference parameter associated with elasticity of substitution σ as $\theta = (\sigma - 1)/\sigma$. In this model, all items are substitutes of each other and $\sigma > 1$ is bounded; hence, $\theta \in (0, 1)$. This compliant consumer maximizes $U(z,u)$ subject to the budget constraint:

$$z + \sum_{i=1}^{n} p_i x_i = wh, \tag{12.4}$$

where $w > 0$ is the average wage rate and $p_i > 0$ the price of ith legal variety. The average wage rate is computed as a convex combination of wage rates engaging in productions of the numéraire good and a legal variety (two wage rates coincide with each other at the equilibrium).

12.2.2 Noncompliant consumers

Noncompliant consumers consume both legal and illegal items indexed by $i = 1, \ldots, n$ and $j = 1, \ldots, m$, respectively. Similarly to the legal consumers, letting v be the utility from legal and illegal varieties, the utility function of a representative noncompliant consumer is represented by

$$U(z, v) = z^\alpha v^{1-\alpha}. \tag{12.5}$$

The utility from varieties of legal and illegal items is represented by a CES form:

$$v(x, y) = \left(\sum_{i=1}^{n} x_i^\theta + \sum_{j=1}^{m} y_j^\theta \right)^{1/\theta}, \tag{12.6}$$

where y_j is the volume of consumption of jth illegal variety and $y = \left(y_j \right)_{j=1}^{m}$ the vector representing a consumption bundle of illegal items.

The noncompliant consumer receives w by engaging in legal item production and $w' > 0$ in illegal item production. Letting $\varepsilon \in (0, 1)$ be the share of working hours engaging in the legal item production, the average wage income is provided as

$$\omega h = \varepsilon w h + (1 - \varepsilon) w' h. \tag{12.7}$$

At the labor market equilibrium, however, no worker has an incentive to work for the illegal item production if the expected wage rate is less than the market wage rate w. Therefore, $w' = w$ in Equation (12.7), and wage income of noncompliant consumer is provided by

$$\omega = w. \tag{12.8}$$

This noncompliant consumer maximizes the utility function subject to the budget constraint provided by

$$z + \sum_{i=1}^{n} p_i x_i + \sum_{j=1}^{m} \pi_j y_j = wh - \gamma, \tag{12.9}$$

where $\omega > 0$ is the average wage rate, $\gamma \geq 0$ the fine against illegal consumption, and $\pi_j > 0$ the price of illegal variety j. The collected fines compensate for the cost of investigations.

12.2.3 Production technologies

A unit of numéraire good uses a constant return to scale technology with unit marginal cost. Letting L_0 be the labor input and Z^S be the quantity of supply for production of the numéraire good, the production function is represented by

$$L_0 = Z^S \tag{12.10}$$

Letting L_i be the labor input and X_i^S be the quantity of supply for production of a legal item i, the production technology of this item is represented by

$$L_i = f + aX_i^S, \tag{12.11}$$

where $f > 0$ and $a > 0$ are a common fixed input and a common input coefficient across varieties, respectively.

The production technologies of illegal items are identical to legal items. Letting L_j' be the labor input and Y_j^S be the quantity of supply for production of illegal item j, the production technology of this item is represented by

$$L_j' = f + aY_j^S. \tag{12.12}$$

In our framework, legal and illegal items are distinguished by fines, so that there is no difference between them if $\gamma = 0$. In addition, there is no noncompliant consumer if $\gamma = h$. If noncompliant consumers are fined, they expand varieties of illegal items in consumption to compensate for the loss in their income. The volume of consumption of illegal items is then either increased or decreased depending on the scale effect in production. Hence, it is expected that fines suppress the production of illegal items if fines are sufficiently large, but an increase in fines increases the production of illegal items if fines are insufficient. Such a mechanism seems similar to the argument about the existence of the worst configuration of trading blocs, as shown in Krugman (1991) and Bond and Syropoulos (1996): complete separation and unification are identical to each other (free trade).

12.3 MARKET EQUILIBRIUM

In the labor market, the wage rate w^* is determined competitively so as to equalize wage rates in all productions including the numéraire good. Since the production technology of the numéraire is classical, the *zero-profit condition* is applied to obtain

$$wL_0 = Z^S \Rightarrow w^* = 1. \tag{12.13}$$

Preference and production structures are symmetric. At the equilibrium, consumptions of numéraire good and legal items by compliant consumers are provided by $z = z^*$ and $x_i = x^*$ for all legal items for all compliant consumers, respectively. Similarly, consumptions of the numéraire and legal and illegal items by noncompliant consumers are provided as $z = z^\star$, $x_i = x^\star$, and $y_j = y^\star$ for all legal and illegal items for all noncompliant consumers. Let Z^D, X^D, and Y^D be aggregated demands for the numéraire, a legal item, and an illegal item, respectively. At the symmetrical equilibrium, respective aggregate demands are provided by

$$Z^D = nz^* + mz^\star, \tag{12.14}$$

$$X^D = nx^* + mx^\star, \tag{12.15}$$

$$Y^D = my^\star. \tag{12.16}$$

At the equilibrium, the budget constraint of the compliant consumer is provided by

$$z^* + pnx^* = w^*h \Rightarrow \begin{cases} z^* = \alpha w^*h, \\ pnx^* = (1-\alpha)w^*h, \end{cases} \tag{12.17}$$

where the last equation follows from the two-stage budgeting procedure based on the Cobb-Douglas utility function (Equation 12.2) whose expenditure share of the numéraire is α. Similarly, the budget constraint of the noncompliant consumer is provided by

$$z^\star + pnx^\star + \pi my^\star = w^*h - \gamma \Rightarrow \begin{cases} z^\star = \alpha(w^*h - \gamma), \\ pnx^\star + \pi my^\star = (1-\alpha)(w^*h - \gamma). \end{cases} \tag{12.18}$$

From Equations (12.17) and (12.13), x^* is computed as

$$z^* = \alpha h \text{ and } x^* = \frac{(1-\alpha)h}{np}, \tag{12.19}$$

and the corresponding indirect utility function as

$$u^* = \frac{(1-\alpha)hn^{1/(\sigma-1)}}{p}. \tag{12.20}$$

In the equilibrium, the first-order conditions of the noncompliant consumer provide

$$\frac{p}{\pi} = \left(\frac{x^\star}{y^\star}\right)^{-1/\sigma} \Rightarrow y^\star = \left(\frac{p}{\pi}\right)^\sigma x^\star, \tag{12.21}$$

which is substituted into Equation (12.18) with Equation (12.13) to obtain

$$z^\star = \alpha(h - \gamma) \text{ and } x^\star = \frac{(1-\alpha)(h-\gamma)}{np + m\pi(p/\pi)^\sigma}. \tag{12.22}$$

From Equations (12.21) and (12.22), the indirect utility function is computed as

$$v^\star = \frac{(1-\alpha)(h-\gamma)}{p}\left(n + m\left(\frac{p}{\pi}\right)^{\sigma-1}\right)^{1/(\sigma-1)}. \tag{12.23}$$

Comparing $U(z^*, u^*)$ and $U(z^\star, v^*)$, noncompliant consumers can dispose illegal items if $\zeta u^* > v^*$, where ζ is

$$\zeta \equiv \left(\frac{z^*}{z^\star}\right)^{\alpha/(1-\alpha)}. \tag{12.24}$$

Similarly, potentially noncompliant consumers purchase illegal items if $\zeta u^* < v^*$. Thus, equilibrium utility levels of compliant and noncompliant consumers must be indifferent:

$$z^{*\alpha} u^{*1-\alpha} = z^{\star\alpha} v^{\star 1-\alpha} \Rightarrow \zeta u^* = v^*. \tag{12.25}$$

Substituting Equations (12.19) and (12.22) into Equation (12.25), $\mu = m/n$ (varieties of illegal items relative to legal ones) are computed as

$$\mu = \frac{1}{(p/\pi)^{\sigma-1}} \left[\left(\frac{\zeta h}{h-\gamma} \right)^{\sigma-1} - 1 \right]. \tag{12.26}$$

At the equilibrium, by symmetry, $L_i = L^*$ and $L_j' = L'^*$ are held for all i and j. From the zero-profit condition for each item, $pX^S = w^* L^*$ and $\pi Y^S = w^* L'^*$, the value of supply of a legal item and that of an illegal item are provided as

$$pX^S = \frac{fp}{p-a} \text{ and } \pi Y^S = \frac{\pi f}{\pi - a}. \tag{12.27}$$

It should then be noted that the supply of the numéraire Z^S is computed from the resource constraint:

$$L_0 + \sum_{i=1}^{n} L_i + \sum_{j=1}^{m} L_j' = Nh. \tag{12.28}$$

By zero-profit conditions, Equation (12.28) is arranged to obtain Z^S:

$$Z^S = Nh - Nf - anX_i^S - amY_j^S. \tag{12.29}$$

The aggregate demand for the numéraire is provided by Equation (12.14); whence, the demand for numéraire for each consumer is computed as

$$z^* = \frac{hZ^S}{Nh - m\gamma} \text{ and } z^\star = \frac{(h-\gamma)Z^S}{Nh - m\gamma}. \tag{12.30}$$

From Equations (12.15), (12.16), (12.19), (12.21), and (12.22), the value of aggregate demand for a legal item and that of an illegal item are computed as

$$pX^D = (1-\alpha)\left(h + \frac{h-\gamma}{\mu^{-1} + (p/\pi)^{\sigma-1}} \right), \tag{12.31}$$

and

$$\pi Y^D = \frac{(1-\alpha)(h-\gamma)(p/\pi)^{\sigma-1}}{\mu^{-1} + (p/\pi)^{\sigma-1}}, \tag{12.32}$$

respectively. Using Equation (12.26), expression $\mu^{-1} + (p/\pi)^{\sigma-1}$ in Equations (12.31) and (12.32) is arranged into two alternative forms, such as

$$\frac{1}{\mu} + \left(\frac{p}{\pi}\right)^{\sigma-1} = \frac{1}{\mu}\left(\frac{\zeta h}{h-\gamma}\right)^{\sigma-1}, \tag{12.33}$$

$$\frac{1}{\mu} + \left(\frac{p}{\pi}\right)^{\sigma-1} = \left(\frac{p}{\pi}\right)^{\sigma-1}\left[1 - \left(\frac{h-\gamma}{\zeta h}\right)^{\sigma-1}\right]^{-1}. \tag{12.34}$$

Substituting Equation (12.33) into Equation (12.31) provides

$$pX^{\mathrm{D}} = F(\mu) \equiv (1-\alpha)h\left[1 + \zeta\mu\left(\frac{h-\gamma}{\zeta h}\right)^{\sigma}\right]. \tag{12.35}$$

Similarly, substituting Equation (12.34) into Equation (12.32) provides

$$\pi Y^{\mathrm{D}} = W \equiv (1-\alpha)(h-\gamma)\left[1 - \left(\frac{h-\gamma}{\zeta h}\right)^{\sigma-1}\right]. \tag{12.36}$$

The equilibrium price of each variety is determined by equalizing respective values of demand and supply:

$$pX^{\mathrm{D}} = pX^{\mathrm{S}} \Rightarrow p^* = \frac{aF(\mu)}{F(\mu)-f}, \tag{12.37}$$

$$\pi Y^{\mathrm{D}} = \pi Y^{\mathrm{S}} \Rightarrow \pi^* = \frac{aW}{W-f}. \tag{12.38}$$

From Equations (12.37) and (12.38), conditions to obtain feasible p^* and π^* are provided by

$$F(\mu) > f \text{ and } W > f, \tag{12.39}$$

respectively. In addition, Equations (12.35) and (12.36) provide $F(\mu) > W$; hence, illegal varieties vanish before legal ones do.

From Equations (12.37) and (12.38), the equilibrium relative price of legal item in terms of illegal one is provided by

$$\frac{p^*}{\pi^*} = \frac{F(\mu)}{F(\mu)-f}\frac{W-f}{W}. \tag{12.40}$$

The obtained relative price Equation (12.40) is substituted into Equation (12.25) to obtain the fixed point problem to determine the ratio of varieties of illegal and legal items:

$$\mu = G(\mu) \equiv \left[\left(\frac{\zeta h}{h-\gamma}\right)^{\sigma-1} - 1\right]\left(\frac{F(\mu)-f}{F(\mu)}\frac{W}{W-f}\right)^{\sigma-1}. \tag{12.41}$$

Using the next remark, we obtain Figure 12.2 to graphically show the existence of the solution for the above fixed point problem.

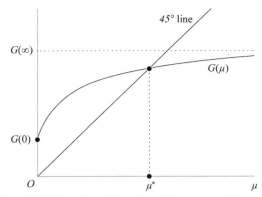

Figure 12.2 Determination of relative size of illegal varieties ($\mu = m/n$).

Remark 12.1 For a constant γ, if legal and illegal varieties are produced, $G(\mu)$ satisfies $G'(\mu) > 0$ and $G''(\mu) < 0$ for all $\mu > 0$, and $G(0) > 0$ and $\lim\limits_{\mu \to +\infty} G(\mu) < +\infty$.

Proof. $F(\mu)$ is a linear function and W is independent of μ. In addition, $\{F(\mu) - f\}/F(\mu)$ is increasing and concave in μ; hence, $G'(\mu) > 0$ and $G''(\mu) < 0$. For $F(\mu) > f$ and $W > f$, $G(0)$ and $\lim\limits_{\mu \to +\infty} G(\mu)$ are directly computed to complete the proof:

$$G(0) = \left[\left(\frac{\zeta h}{h - \gamma} \right)^{\sigma - 1} - 1 \right] \left(\frac{(1 - \alpha)h - f}{(1 - \alpha)h} \frac{W}{W - f} \right)^{\sigma - 1} > 0, \qquad (12.42)$$

$$\lim\limits_{\mu \to +\infty} G(\mu) = \left[\left(\frac{\zeta h}{h - \gamma} \right)^{\sigma - 1} - 1 \right] \left(\frac{W}{W - f} \right)^{\sigma - 1} < +\infty. \qquad (12.43)$$

□

The model is simulated using parameters provided in Table 12.2. Figure 12.3 shows the results for share of illegal varieties, m/N, and relative demand for illegal varieties, $mY^{\mathrm{D}}/(nX^{\mathrm{D}} + mY^{\mathrm{D}})$ with respect to fines in total income, γ/h. In this simulation, as Equation (12.39), illegal varieties are supplied if γ/h is in $0.1211 < \gamma/h < 0.7909$.

This simulation suggests that an increase in fines initially expands varieties of illegal items, as the reduced income level of noncompliant consumer by fines must be compensated by an increase in varieties in consumption. If fines are not sufficiently large, the

Table 12.2 Parameters

Parameter	Value
h	10,000
f	1000
α	0.5
σ	2

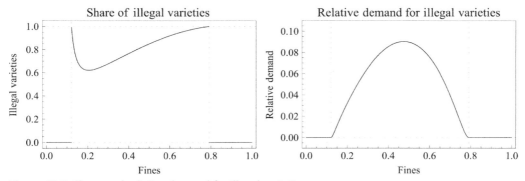

Figure 12.3 Share and relative demand for illegal varieties.

increasing–return effect increases both varieties of illegal items and illegal varieties in consumption. However, sufficiently large fines that dominate the increasing–return effect reduce illegal varieties in consumption to vanish illegal varieties eventually.

In a context of *economics of crime*, as Ehrlich (1996) summarized,[3] an increase in fines unambiguously decreases the crime rate if there is only one type of crime. However, fines in our model may not reduce the consumption of illegal items, because there are alternative illegal items. If there are alternative illegitimate activities, as Ehrlich (1973, 1974) analyzed, an increase in fines reduces some types of offenses, while other offenses may increase; hence, results of this study do not contradict existing results in economics of crime. Smith (1976) and Becker and Murphy (2006) also suggest analogous results when there are several alternatives. In addition, Qui and Yu (2014) find similar theoretical and empirical results in an international trade context: tariffs expand scope of varieties. Further explorations in the base model are provided in Saito (2015b).

12.4 DEMAND FOR BITCOINS

There are two payment methods for legal and illegal varieties: traditional money and bitcoins. Traditional money and bitcoins are distinguished by the likelihood of apprehension. In particular, due to relatively higher level of anonymity in using bitcoins, purchasing illegal items with bitcoins reduces the chance of apprehension for noncompliant consumers; hence, there is no incentive for them to trade illegal items using traditional money insomuch as bitcoins are not excessively overvalued.

Let M and B be the demands for traditional money and bitcoins by transactions. If bitcoins are not excessively overvalued, illegal items are traded only by bitcoins. Letting $\phi > 0$ be the exchange rate from bitcoins to traditional money, the market clearing conditions for the two moneys are provided as

[3]See also Ehrlich and Saito (2010) for further expositions.

$$M = Z + (1 - b)npX \text{ and } \phi B = bnpX + m\pi Y, \tag{12.44}$$

where $b \in [0, 1]$ represents the share of bitcoins in the payment for legal items. With this specification, b is the average of bitcoin payment among compliant and noncompliant consumers for legal items. In order to determine the exchange rate, the ratio of bitcoin to traditional money is β, so that

$$\frac{B}{M} = \beta. \tag{12.45}$$

For each β and b, the exchange rate is determined by

$$\phi = \frac{\beta\{Z + (1 - b)npX\}}{bnpX + m\pi Y}. \tag{12.46}$$

A unit of a legal item is traded at p if it is paid with traditional money or $\phi^{-1}p$ with bitcoins. In other words, the purchasing power of traditional money is $1/p$ and that of bitcoins is $1/(\phi^{-1}p)$. Thus, there is no incentive for compliant consumers to use bitcoins if $1/p > 1/(\phi^{-1}p)$ or equivalently $\phi^{-1}p > p$. Similarly, there is no incentive for compliant consumers to use traditional money if $\phi^{-1}p < p$. Compliant consumers are indifferent between bitcoins and traditional money if and only if $\phi p = p$. The share of bitcoins in the payment for legal items at the equilibrium b^* is thus determined by

$$\begin{cases} b^* = 0 & \text{if } \phi < 1, \\ b^* = 1 & \text{if } \phi > 1, \\ 0 \leq b^* \leq 1 & \text{if } \phi = 1. \end{cases} \tag{12.47}$$

We suppose that fines are discounted by δ if a noncompliant consumers makes a bitcoin payment. When a consumption level of an illegal variety is given by y, δ is defined to discount the payment πy as $\phi \pi y/(1 - \delta)$ with bitcoin. In this case, the exchange rate is determined by

$$\begin{cases} b'^* = 0 & \text{if } \phi < 1 - \delta, \\ b'^* = 1 & \text{if } \phi > 1 - \delta, \\ 0 \leq b'^* \leq 1 & \text{if } \phi = 1 - \delta, \end{cases} \tag{12.48}$$

where b' is the share of bitcoin payments for illegal items and b'^* the equilibrium value for b'. Since $1 - \delta < 1$, $b^* = 0$ is held if $b'^* < 1$, as Equation (12.47). The demands for moneys are then provided by

$$M = Z + npX + (1 - b'^*)m\pi Y \text{ and } \phi B = b'^* m\pi Y \tag{12.49}$$

The relative money supply is provided by Equation (12.45), so that the exchange rate is computed as

$$\phi = \frac{\beta\{Z + npX + (1 - b'^*)m\pi Y\}}{b'^* m\pi Y}. \tag{12.50}$$

Figure 12.4 exhibits a numerical result for parameters provided in the previous section (Table 12.2) and additional ones provided in Table 12.3. In the figure, CC and NC denote the shares of bitcoin payments by compliant and noncompliant consumers, respectively.[4]

In a static microeconomic framework, exchange rate is fixed for interior solutions for b^* and b'^*, as Equations (12.47) and (12.48), respectively. In order to put such a framework into work, pressures of devaluation and appreciation are considered. For $\phi = 1$, for instance, an increase in b^* indicates the existence of devaluation pressures and a decrease in b^* the existence of appreciation pressures. Similarly, for $\phi = 1 - \delta$, a decrease in b'^* indicates the existence of appreciation pressures. With such notions, Figure 12.5 shows an anticipated exchange rate movement in terms of fines:

1. Bitcoin is stable insomuch as there is no supply of illegal items, as indicated by intervals 0-a and e-1 in Figure 12.5 (the same applies hereafter).
2. Bitcoin jumps up when the first transaction of an illegal item is started (point a).

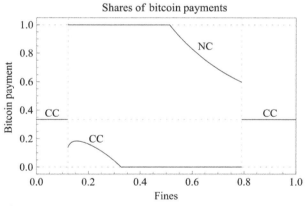

Figure 12.4 Shares of bitcoin payments (Equation 12.1).

Table 12.3 Parameters

Parameter	Value
β	0.2
δ	0.5

---

[4] As we have already seen, illegal varieties are supplied while γ is in a certain range ($0.1211 < \gamma/h < 0.7909$). If illegal varieties are not supplied, according to the simulation, $b^* = 1/3$ is realized.

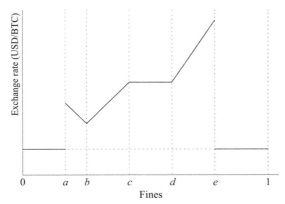

Figure 12.5 Anticipated actual bitcoin exchange rate.

3. Bitcoin declines as fines increase while fines are small (intervals *a–b*).
4. Bitcoin rises as fines increase while fines are not small (intervals *b–c*).
5. Bitcoin is stable while compliant consumers do not use bitcoins for payment and noncompliant consumers pay all the amount by bitcoins (intervals *c–d*).
6. Bitcoin rises again as fines increase while fines are large enough (intervals *d–e*).
7. Bitcoin drops down when transactions of illegal varieties vanish (point *e*).

12.5 EXTENSIONS
12.5.1 Variable fines

In the previous discussions, fines γ are fixed and independent of illegal varieties. As an extension, we consider variable fines g depending on varieties of illegal items as

$$g = \frac{m\gamma}{n+m} \Rightarrow g = \frac{\gamma}{1+\mu^{-1}}. \tag{12.51}$$

In this case, illegal items are effectively penalized than in case of fixed fines. Using parameters provided in Table 12.2, results are shown in Figure 12.6, where the horizontal axis measures fines by g/h instead of γ/h. In this figure, CC and NC denote shares of bitcoin payments for compliant and noncompliant consumers, respectively, and the dashed curve depicts the case for the baseline model. Results for the share and relative demand for illegal varieties in the extended model are identical to the baseline model.

The result suggests that the exchange rate of Bitcoin declines if variable fines are employed when noncompliant consumers purchase illegal items with traditional money; whence, introducing variable fines reduces the value of bitcoins, as fines more effectively penalize consumption of illegal items than fixed fines.

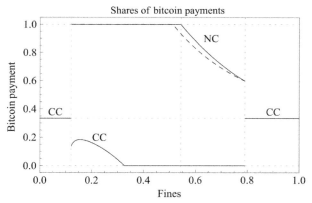

Figure 12.6 Shares of bitcoin payments (Equation 12.2).

12.5.2 Bitcoin theft

As an extension, we consider a case in which bitcoins are stolen from both compliant and noncompliant consumers. For simplicity, all stolen bitcoins are supposed to be distributed among noncompliant consumers.[5] In addition, shares of bitcoin payments by compliant and noncompliant consumers for legal items are uniformly given by b. If the probability of confiscation is s, $sb(1-\alpha)h$ is confiscated from each compliant consumer and $s\tilde{b}'(1-\alpha)(h-\gamma)$ from each noncompliant consumer, where $\tilde{b}'$ represents the share of bitcoin payments made by a noncompliant consumer inclusive of payments for legal and illegal items. There is no law enforcement against the theft. The total of stolen bitcoins is then computed as

$$nsb(1-\alpha)h + ms\tilde{b}'(1-\alpha)(h-\gamma),\qquad(12.52)$$

and it is distributed among m noncompliant consumers, so that the dividend for each noncompliant consumer is computed as

$$\frac{sb(1-\alpha)h}{\mu} + s\tilde{b}'(1-\alpha)(h-\gamma) - s\tilde{b}'(1-\alpha)(h-\gamma) = \frac{sb(1-\alpha)h}{\mu},\qquad(12.53)$$

and subsequently, the net income disposable for varieties of legal and illegal items becomes

$$(1-\alpha)\left\{\left(1+\frac{sb}{\mu}\right)h - \gamma\right\}.\qquad(12.54)$$

Using parameters provided in Tables 12.2 and 12.3, the simulated result for $s=0.5$ with fixed fines is depicted in Figure 12.7. In this figure, the share of bitcoin payment of

[5]In practice, not all stolen bitcoins go back to circulation, as some of them are destroyed.

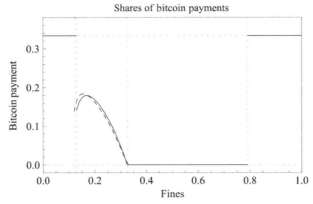

Figure 12.7 Shares of bitcoin payments (Equation 12.3).

noncompliant consumer is omitted as it is identical to the base model (Figure 12.4). In this figure, the dashed curve again depicts the case for the baseline model.

The simulation suggests that Bitcoin will be more valued by the theft when there are devaluating pressures. On the other hand, bitcoin will be undervalued by the theft when there are appreciating pressures. Currently, bitcoin seems in a rising phase, and that implies that, in accordance with the simulation, bitcoin is likely undervalued by possible bitcoin theft. If this is the case, appropriate law enforcement reducing the theft will improve the value of bitcoins.

12.6 CONCLUDING REMARKS

With a notion that illegal activities are one of important factors to watch, this study has investigated a monopolistic competition model. In the model, illegal items are fined, but legal items are not. Since the model is not a dynamic model, however, the exchange rate of bitcoins is predicted from shares of bitcoin payments by compliant and noncompliant consumers. Within an effective range, where both legal and illegal items are produced, an increase in fines reduces the value of bitcoins only when fines are small. If fines are not small, a further increase in fines does not reduce the value of bitcoins, as an increase in fines must be covered by an increase in illegal varieties in consumption and that increases the demand for bitcoins.

The model has extended in two ways. One uses variable penalty scheme depending on the varieties of illegal items. Others consider bitcoin theft. Variable fines provide almost identical results as the baseline model. The bitcoin theft also provides similar results, but it suggests the theft reduces the value of bitcoins when bitcoin is in a rising phase while it raises the value of bitcoins when bitcoin is in a declining phase.

In the future, bitcoin theft may increase its severity, as the stock of bitcoin expands and that improves hacking techniques, as rewards increase. In this case, technological competitions among offenders and defenders will be the key to protect Bitcoin from offensive activities. For a further study, a study in gun-control policy by Ehrlich and Saito (2010) can be extended to study this problem by introducing penalties against Bitcoin theft. In the competition, as usual, the winner is unknown. However, law enforcement against Bitcoin theft should unambiguously reduce the offensive activities and probably the severity as well. In order to suppress the theft, Bitcoin needs to have an effective enforcement scheme or accept interventions of public law enforcement authorities that Bitcoin society may not prefer to do so.

ACKNOWLEDGMENTS

The author is truly grateful to Isaac Ehrlich, David LEE Kuo Chuen, Yasuhiko Nakamura, Ernie Teo, Miaojie Yu, and all participants of Cryptocurrency Conference 2014 at Singapore Management University for many helpful comments and suggestions on underlying works. All remaining possible errors and shortcomings are mine.

REFERENCES

Becker, G.S., Murphy, K.M., 2006. The market for illegal goods: the case of drugs. J. Polit. Econ. 114 (1), 38–60.

Bond, E., Syropoulos, C., 1996. The size of trading blocs: market power and world welfare effects. J. Int. Econ. 40 (3–4), 411–437.

Christin, N., 2012. Traveling the Silk Road: a measurement analysis of a large anonymous, online marketplace, arXiv:1207.7139v2.

Craig, B.R., Waller, C.J., 2000. Dual-currency economies as multiple-payment systems. Fed. Reserve Bank Cleveland Econ. Rev. Q1, 2–13.

Dixit, A.K., Stiglitz, J.E., 1977. Monopolistic competition and optimum product diversity. Am. Econ. Rev. 67 (3), 297–308.

Ehrlich, I., 1973. Participation in illegitimate activities: theoretical and empirical investigation. J. Polit. Econ. 81 (3), 521–565.

Ehrlich, I., 1974. Participation in illegitimate activities: an economic analysis. In: Becker, G.S., Landes, W.M. (Eds.), Essays in the Economics of Crime and Punishment. Columbia University Press, New York, NY.

Ehrlich, I., 1996. Crime, punishment, and the market for offenses. J. Econ. Perspect. 10 (1), 43–67.

Ehrlich, I., Saito, T., 2010. Taxing guns vs. taxing crime: an application of the market for offenses model. J. Policy Model 32 (5), 670–689.

Krugman, P.A., 1979. Increasing returns, monopolistic competition, and international trade. J. Int. Econ. 9 (4), 469–479.

Krugman, P.A., 1980. Scale economies, product differentiation, and the pattern of trade. Am. Econ. Rev. 70 (5), 950–959.

Krugman, P.R., 1991. Is bilateralism bad? In: Helpman, E., Razin, A. (Eds.), International Trade and Trade Policy. MIT Press, Cambridge, MA.

Qui, L., Yu, M., 2014. Multiproduct firms, export product scope, and trade liberalization: the role of managerial efficiency. Working Paper No. 02-2014, Hong Kong Institute for Monetary Research, Hong Kong SAR, China.

Saito, T., 2015a. Bitcoin: a search-theoretic approach. Int. J. Innovat. Digit. Econ. 6 (2), 52–71.

Saito, T., 2015b. Regulating illegal items under variety effect. Working Paper No. 15-01. Research Institute for Economic Science, Nihon University, Tokyo, Japan.

Smith, R.T., 1976. The legal and illegal markets for taxed goods: pure theory and an application to state government taxation of distilled spirits. J. Law Econ. 19 (2), 393–429.

Trejos, A., Wright, R., 1995. Search, bargaining, money, and prices. J. Polit. Econ. 103 (1), 118–141.

PART 2

Finance Markets and Bitcoin

Regulation and Taxation

CHAPTER 13

Legal Issues in Cryptocurrency

Vrajlal Sapovadia
Shanti Business School, Ahmedabad, India

Contents

13.1 INTRODUCTION

Plenty of basic information on cryptocurrency have been said in the previous chapters, and we deliberately repeat some issues in this chapter to set the tone of the chapter titled as "Legal Issues in Cryptocurrency." Cryptocurrency (like Bitcoin, Dogecoin, Litecoin, or Peercoin) is a digital virtual, e-commerce currency or electronic currency. The nomenclature is borne out of use of cryptography for embedding security in computer programs. To date, cryptocurrency is promoted by nongovernment organizations. Cryptocurrency is more convenient to generate as it requires no physical resources like metal, paper, plastic, and printing ink. It is easy to store, transact, and operate cryptocurrency. It is cheaper and faster to transact. Cryptocurrency is one of the widely known species of currency that is promoted by non-governmental organizations. The cryptocurrency is not issued by any government or central banks, rendering in principle immune to government interference or manipulation. But you may not be protected by the government in case of a dispute or a fraud involving cryptocurrency. The promoters of cryptocurrency claim that it is difficult to counterfeit because of special and complex security features. But computer programs and the Internet are facing constant security threats; the cryptocurrency is in bedrock of computer and the Internet. Another security lies in the value of any currency. Official currencies are backed by the government and are minted after securing assets like gold, coupled with sovereign guarantee. Cryptocurrency market operates without such formal procedure and backing.

The cryptocurrency is a decentralized, virtually anonymous, substantially unregulated digital currency that has become exponentially popular in the recent years. The cryptocurrency is promoted by nongovernment persons or entities using peer private network, operating on the basis of decentralized autonomy. The anonymous nature of cryptocurrency transactions makes them well suited for a multitude of despicable activities such as unauthorized transactions to save identity of the transactors, illegal transactions, money laundering, and tax evasion. The governments are becoming alarmed and concentrating more over such transactions.

One of the cryptocurrencies "Bitcoin" is open-source and their transactions require no third-party intermediary. The buyer and seller interact directly (peer to peer) but their identities are encrypted and no personal information is transferred from one to the other. However, unlike a fully anonymous transaction, there is a transaction record. A full transaction record of every Bitcoin and every Bitcoin user's encrypted identity is maintained on the public ledger. For this reason, Bitcoin transactions are thought to be pseudonymous, not anonymous.

Cryptocurrencies are legal in few countries but not in many countries. It remains uncertain when the government will take over any perceived legal shield. We categorically used the word perceived shield, because in many countries, cryptocurrency is not expressly declared illegal, but it does not mean cryptocurrency becomes legal thereby. With this context, cryptocurrency has raised several new complicated legal, social, economic, and administrative issues.

Many private decentralized trust or corporate networks support alternative currencies like cryptocurrency; branded currencies, for example, "obligation-based" stores of value like quasi-regulated Bartercard; loyalty points (credit cards and airlines) or game credits (MMO games) that are based on reputation of commercial products; and highly regulated asset-backed "alternative currencies" such as mobile-money schemes like MPesa (called e-money issuance) by a telecom company in India. These all are alternative of currencies.

The rising popularity of cryptocurrencies is due to the convenience to generate or manufacture, store, handle, manage, and account cryptocurrencies and transact them; get shield from discovery by government authorities for taxation or, otherwise, to carry illegal transactions; and so forth. The promoters require no material resources to produce cryptocurrency, as it is generated through computer programs, stored on computers, and transacted through the Internet. Promoters require no license or gold in their treasury to generate cryptocurrency unlike governments and central banks that require certain security, assets, and procedure to follow when uncertain how much currency the government can print. Cryptocurrency is designed to operate without any sovereign regulation.

The above-described characteristics of cryptocurrency become the core cause of legal problem that one can face. The legal problem may range from being sued by the government for involvement in the transaction that has no legal validity as currency to availing justice in case one becomes a victim of fraud by other participating peers or promoters. The transactions of cryptocurrency occur in the absence of government, bank, authorized dealer, payment network, or regulator. As all transactions are on the Internet, users interact with each other directly, without any license, anonymously, and without third-party interventions. In the absence of legal evidences, the victim may not be supported by court.

The cryptocurrency transaction occurs only on the basis of trust on the promoters, peers, and system. If the trust imposed is materialized into reality, any dispute may not arise. But if the reality becomes far from the perception, dispute may arise, which will not be honored by court of justice. Official currencies are denominated by specific number under promise and undertaking of the national government or central agencies. Official currencies have back up of law and court of justice. Cryptocurrency is in a unit of accounts that have no physical verifiable counterpart with legal tender. The transactions are carried by peers without any legal backing. The interaction between any official currency and cryptocurrency is not regulated by law in many countries. The value of cryptocurrency is determined by perception of demand and supply link. As there is no security, undertaking, or promise of any national government, the perceived value of cryptocurrency is merely on the basis of speculation. Few governments in advanced countries have started to work on regularizing cryptocurrency markets. As this is emerging market, there will be flood of rules in several other countries. We have discussed some of the real-life experiences that are legally relevant to cryptocurrency stakeholders.

Several instances of dispute or fraud have surfaced in recent past. Few hackers mounted a massive series of distributed denial-of-service attacks against the most popular Bitcoin exchange. A trader was arrested who subsequently became bankrupt. In August 2012, an operation titled Bitcoin Savings and Trust was shut down by the owner, allegedly leaving around 5.6 million USD in Bitcoin-based debts.

In September 2012, Bitfloor, a Bitcoin exchange, was reported to be hacked, with 24,000 Bitcoins stolen. As a result, Bitfloor temporarily suspended operations. In April 2013, Instawallet, a web-based wallet provider, was hacked, resulting in the theft of over 35,000 Bitcoins. With a price of 129.90 USD per Bitcoin at the time, or nearly 4.6 million USD in total, Instawallet suspended operations. In August 2013, the Bitcoin Foundation announced that a bug in the software within the Android operating system had been exploited to steal from users' wallets. In October 2013, a Bitcoin bank, operated from Australia but stored on servers in the United States, was hacked, with a loss of 4100 Bitcoins.

The largest obstacle for regulators is that Bitcoin was built not to be regulated. Unlike the centralized US dollar system, where the government has a monopoly control on the production of money and doles it out to licensed banks, the Bitcoin universe is decentralized by design. They're produced by random players around the world. They're transferred seamlessly via nameless digital wallets.

13.2 LEGALITY VERSUS ILLEGAL

The modern constitutions of various nations grant authority to coin money, regulate the value thereto, and oversight and control any kind of currency. In any country, if there is no express ban on using cryptocurrency, it does not make automatically the cryptocurrency or any transaction a legal one. Similarly, if any tax is levied on cryptocurrency as an asset, as a transaction, or as an income, it does not render cryptocurrency as legal. Cryptocurrency by its nature becomes *sub judice* under laws related to central bank, domestic currency, foreign currencies, contract, property (wealth), income, sales, intellectual property, and civil and criminal suites.

Regulators in China banned the handling of Bitcoins by financial institutions. In Russia, it is difficult to judge legality as cryptocurrencies are not expressly said illegal; it is illegal to actually purchase goods with any currency other than the Russian ruble. This principle applies in almost many countries. This is equally true in India as well.

Some cryptocurrencies have legal issues such as Coinye, an altcoin that used, without permission, rapper Kanye West as its logo. This altcoin has been compared to the popular Dogecoin. Upon hearing of the release of Coinye, originally called Coinye West, attorneys for Kanye West sent a cease and desist letter to the e-mail operator of Coinye, whose name remains unknown. The letter stated that Coinye was willful trademark infringement, unfair competition, cyberpiracy, and dilution and instructed Coinye to stop using the likeness and name of Kanye West. Kanye West filed a trademark lawsuit against the creators of the cryptocurrency "Coinye." The US federal government announced arrests and seizures of Liberty Reserve, a company that provided transfer and exchange service of virtual currencies, including Bitcoin. News agencies describe Liberty Reserve as a favorite of cybercriminals due to lax anti-money laundering recordkeeping for customers.

Legal issues that become relevant to cryptocurrency can be broadly classified into six categories:

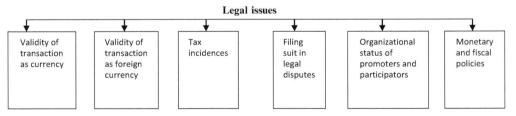

13.2.1 Validity of transaction as a currency

The national government has sole authority to manage currencies, beginning from the concept to commissioning, printing, circulation, withdrawal, or disposal. The national government may delegate this power to central bank or any other authority under its control and supervision (Doughlas et al., 2010).

The official currency is transacted within legal framework. Cryptocurrency lacks regulatory framework and public over sight. Therefore, cryptocurrency poses serious legal threat pertaining to liquidity, operational risk, fraud, credit and solvency. The transactions are carried out on the Internet, which itself poses risk of security, access, hacking, virus, malware, corrupt program, identity of operator, and data storage.

Currency is a system of money in common use within country, for example, Indian rupee, British pounds, US dollars, Chinese renminbi, and European euros are valid legal currency in India, the United Kingdom, the United States, China, and Europe, respectively. These currencies are physical objects in the form of paper, metal, or plastic; it stores value that is subject to trading within the nation and between nations in foreign exchange markets. Currencies in the sense used by foreign exchange markets are well defined by governments, and each currency type has limited boundaries of acceptance. Foreign currency is acceptable subject to rule of both transacting countries. These rules may vary on the basis of citizenship, residence, the assets or liabilities involved, type and purpose of transaction (current or noncurrent or present or future), sectors, and the amount involved.

National government, central bank, or any authority empowered by the government manages domestic currencies. For example, the Reserve Bank of India (RBI) manages currency in India. The government, on the advice of the RBI, decides on the various denominations. The RBI consults with the government for the designing of banknotes and security features in the currency. This kind of consultation in cryptocurrency is not evident. The RBI estimates the quantity of notes that are likely to be needed denomination-wise and places the indent with the various presses through the government of India. The notes received from the presses are issued and a reserve stock is maintained. Notes received from banks and currency chests are examined. Notes fit for circulation are reissued and the others (soiled and mutilated) are destroyed so as to maintain the quality of notes in circulation (http://www.rbi.org.in/). Cryptocurrencies are unregulated and have digital form, so no question arises to soil or mutilation. But no evidences are available about cryptocurrency's accounting, stock, or inventory.

The Federal Reserve Act authorizes the Board of Governors of the Federal Reserve System to issue Federal Reserve notes (known as lawful money or legal tender) in the United States. The act states that Federal Reserve notes shall be obligations of the United States and shall be receivable by all national and member banks and Federal Reserve Banks and for all taxes, customs, and other public dues. They shall be redeemed in lawful money on demand at the US Department of the Treasury, in the city of Washington, District of Columbia, or at any Federal Reserve Bank. US money is a valid and legal offer of payment for debts when tendered to a creditor. United States defines money as coins and currency (including Federal Reserve notes and circulating notes of Federal Reserve Banks and national banks) that are legal tender for all debts, public charges, taxes, and dues. There is, however, no Federal statute mandating that a private business, a person, or an organization must accept currency or coins as payment for goods or services. Private businesses are free to develop their own policies on whether to accept cash unless there is a state law that says otherwise (http://www.federalreserve.gov/).

The Board of Governors of the Federal Reserve System is the issuing authority for Federal Reserve notes, the primary form of currency in circulation in the United States. The board has a wide range of responsibilities related to Federal Reserve notes, from ensuring an adequate supply to protecting and maintaining confidence in US currency. The board's role in coin operations is more limited than its role in cash operations, as the US Mint is the issuing authority for coins. Reserve banks distribute new and circulated coin to depository institutions to meet the public's demand and take as deposits coin that exceeds the public's needs. Federal Reserve notes are not redeemable in gold, silver, or any other commodity. The notes shall be redeemed in lawful money on demand at the US Department of the Treasury, in the city of Washington, District of Columbia, or at any Federal Reserve Bank.

Euro is floated by the national central banks (NCBs) and the European Central Banks (ECBs) have issued euro banknotes on a joint basis. Euro is managed and administered by the Frankfurt-based ECB and the Eurosystem (composed of the central banks of the eurozone countries). As an independent central bank, the ECB has sole authority to set monetary policy. The Eurosystem participates in the printing, minting, and distribution of notes and coins in all member states and the operation of the Eurozone payment systems. The ECB issues 8% of the total value of banknotes issued by the Eurosystem (http://www.ecb.europa.eu/home/html/index.en.html). 92% of the Euro banknotes are issued by the NCBs in proportion to their respective shares in the capital key of the ECB calculated using national share of European Union (EU) population and national share of EU GDP, equally weighted (http://www.ecb.europa.eu/).

The ECB is the central bank for Europe's single currency, euro. The ECB's main task is to maintain the euro's purchasing power and thus price stability in the euro area (http://www.ecb.europa.eu/).

In India, the reserve bank derives its role in currency management on the basis of the Reserve Bank of India Act, 1934, enacted through parliament's legislative power. One rupee note is issued by the central government. All other higher denomination currency notes are promissory notes issued by the governor, RBI. "I Promise to pay the bearer a sum of rupees" is written in all higher denomination currency notes. No person other than the bank or, as expressly authorized by this act, the central government can draw, accept, make, or issue any bill of exchange, hundi,[1] and promissory note. No such promise or undertaking is issued in cryptocurrency. The domestic currency is legally valid within the national boundary. Domestic currency has implied power as legal tender, for example, the bank cannot refuse to accept the currency in any denomination.

---

[1]Indianized form of bill of exchange, used by local traders among and within limited scope.

This legislative power is lacking in cryptocurrency. One cannot compel the payee to accept the cryptocurrency.

The renminbi (composed of yuan) is the official currency of China. The renminbi is the official tender in China; the currency production is carried out after prescribed procedure by the state-owned China Banknote Printing and Minting Corporation (http://www.cbpm.cn/English/).

In most of the cases, a central bank has a monopoly right to issue the coins and banknotes for circulation; it regulates the production of currency through monetary policy. An exchange rate is the price at which two currencies can be exchanged against each other. This is used for trade between the two currency zones. Exchange rates can be classified as either floating or fixed. In the former, day-to-day movements in exchange rates are determined by the market; in the latter, governments intervene in the market to buy or sell their currency to balance supply and demand at a fixed exchange rate. No such widespread public institutional arrangement exists in cryptocurrency market.

The national government of a country has control of its currency; the control is exercised either by a central bank or by a Ministry of Finance. Monetary authorities have varying degrees of autonomy from the governments that create them. In the United States, the Federal Reserve System operates without direct oversight by the legislative or executive branches. A monetary authority is created and supported by its sponsoring government, so independence can be reduced by the legislative or executive authority that creates it.

Uncertainty looms over cryptocurrency transactions. The government is authorized to declare any other mode of currency as invalid or the transaction as illegal, or the government can initiate civil/criminal suit against those who are involved at any stage of the transaction of cryptocurrency. This can also attract many other penal provisions like impersonation, cheating, and forgery, destabilizing sovereign government and running parallel government.

13.2.2 Validity of transaction as a foreign currency

In modern business and society, currency transactions are not limited within a country. During transaction across the border, it is pertinent to understand several legal issues involved, at both domestic and international levels. Neither at domestic level nor at international level has any significant attention been drawn of the concerned authorities.

A citizen or resident person can deal in or transfer any foreign exchange or foreign security to any person through an authorized person per the rule of the country. A citizen or resident person cannot make any payment to or for the credit of any person resident outside India in any manner other than the rule of the country. A citizen or resident person can only receive per the law of the country through an authorized person any payment by order or on behalf of any person resident outside India in any manner.

There is no uniform law across the globe on foreign currency, foreign assets, foreign liabilities, and related transactions. Generally, a person resident in a country cannot acquire, hold, own, possess, or transfer any foreign exchange, foreign security, or any immovable property situated outside the country. Those acts are subject to the law. So one can acquire the property outside the country after due procedure or within prescribed limitations. Any person may sell or draw foreign exchange to or from an authorized person if such sale or drawl is a current account transaction. The government can impose restriction on amount and that may change depending upon the purpose. An authorized person is the license holder, who deals and reports subject to the foreign exchange rules.

Now, consumers of many countries can use cryptocurrency to buy goods and services within and across borders including making donations to political parties. The governments are beginning to explore how to regulate this emerging industry. Advocates of virtual currencies also say that because personal information is not tied to transactions, digital currencies are less prone to identity theft. The question arises whether transactions carried by currency that is not legal tender (like cryptocurrency) are valid and legal. In the absence of any express provision that declares such transaction as illegal, it may not be considered as illegal transaction, but the transaction cannot become legal too.

The International Monetary Fund (IMF) is accepted as an apex organization by member countries to assist in regularizing international foreign currency transactions. IMF's currency SDR (special drawing rights) is based on a basket of currencies. Member countries are represented by respective national government. IMF rules apply only to the member countries (Nicholas, 2013). Promoters of cryptocurrency are member of neither the IMF nor national government. Neither can the IMF transact with any person other than national government, nor can it transact in any other currency unless it is promoted by any member country through its national government. Few governments are looking at digital currencies as payment systems which could fall under money transmission laws that typically cover money transfer services. Prominent money transfer agencies are Pay-Pal, Western Union, SafetyPay, Xoom, MoneyGram, MPesa, etc. The governments have started to work on preventing such digital transactions or bringing regulation to protect the public interest.

13.2.3 Tax incidences and stamp duty

Cryptocurrency is a currency and hence it is an asset. Therefore, cryptocurrency transactions are subject to tax like any other asset or currency. Cryptocurrency transaction may attract capital gain tax, income tax, transaction tax, and wealth tax. Even if cryptocurrency transaction is void and illegal, the tax law is empowered to charge taxes on such transactions. In March 2014, the Internal Revenue Service in the United States ruled that Bitcoin will be treated as property for tax purposes as opposed to currency. This means

Bitcoin will be subject to capital gains tax. It makes the income generated through transaction using cryptocurrency taxable but it does not make income or transaction legal. Any illegal income equally attracts tax. Indian income tax and wealth tax definitions are wide and liberal when an income or asset is to be taxed, but the tax incidence does not give legality to that income or asset. The deal of cryptocurrency may be charged with transaction tax.

Cryptocurrency may be considered as medium of exchange, negotiable instrument, property, and subject of the contract. Depending upon the transaction and power of legislation to tax such transaction, tax incidences are pertinent for cryptocurrency. Some of the taxes that can be charged include income tax, gift tax, wealth tax, value-added tax, service tax, inheritance tax, transaction tax, capital gain tax, property tax, and many more.

13.2.4 Filing suit in cases of legal disputes

The transaction cryptocurrency is based on trust on peers, promoters, and the system. In case of any breach, the victim may not be able to produce acceptable legal evidences for recovery of the damages. Many of the headlines generated by Bitcoin and other digital currencies to date have focused on problems with the system. In January, for example, federal prosecutors charged the chief executive officer of BitInstant, a major Bitcoin exchange company, with laundering digital currency through Silk Road, an online drug marketplace. Mt. Gox, based in Tokyo and once the largest Bitcoin exchange in the world, stopped trading in February and filed for bankruptcy protection, saying it had lost half a billion dollars in virtual money (http://time.com/money).

The cryptocurrency used information technology and hence the possible disputes encompass rule on information technology, for example, hacking and digital licenses. Other legislations that may be relevant are law on banking, money laundering, negotiable instrument, and contract, property law including intellectual property, and consumer protection law.

13.2.5 Organizational status of promoters and participators

The normal currency is governed by the national government or central bank. The governing entity is a public institute and always accountable. The cryptocurrency is governed by nongovernment entities, anonymous promoters in the form of trust or society or some hybrid form or through any unknown status. The jurisdiction within which such entity operates and the form of the organization is not publicly known. The framework of organization is highly decentralized working on the Internet through peers. The court may not be able to consider such entity as juristic or artificial person, and people behind the organization may not be traceable. In case of any dispute, establishing accountability and applying principle of lifting of corporate veil will be virtually difficult.

13.2.6 Monetary and fiscal policies

In order to stabilize economy, boost growth, control inflation, and maintain fiscal balances, the government agencies control money supply through several measures like liquidity, interest rate, and security deposits. Cryptocurrency is not within purview of the government, but those who hold investment in cryptocurrency cannot use this virtual currency as liquidity for banking and other official purposes. The gold standard is a monetary system in which the standard economic unit of account is a fixed weight of gold and all currency issuance is to one degree or another regulated by the gold supply. To protect the public and guarantee the nation against any bankruptcy, the RBI keeps a certain percentage of gold in the government's treasury, in proportion to the additional currency minted and directed into the circulation.

Currently, cryptocurrency market is small and has negligible impact on monetary system. But if the volume of transaction increases, it could have an impact on the conduct of monetary policy to the extent that it would substantially affect the quantity of money and influence the velocity of money through the economy by reducing the demand for other currencies.

13.3 GLOBAL REGULATORY MOVEMENT

The cryptocurrency can be obtained against (1) sales of goods and service and (2) any other official currencies and (3) by self-generation or developing and cracking the computer program. If the transaction is across the border involving sales of goods and services, the World Trade Organization may also have its role to play so as to regularize international trade among treaty countries. Although digital currencies are far from widespread in their acceptance, their growing popularity and potential for misuse have prompted states to weigh in on what was previously uncharted territory. "As far as we know, most state laws are completely silent on this topic," said David J. Cotney, chairman of the Conference of State Bank Supervisors' Emerging Payments Task Force, which in March began exploring virtual currency. Among the questions the task force will consider, Cotney said, is whether Bitcoins should be classified as currencies, investment securities, or commodities, which could determine which regulators should apply. In April 2014, the task force presented a model consumer guidance to help states provide consumers with information about digital currencies. A number of states, including California, Massachusetts, and Texas, have issued warnings to consumers that virtual currencies are not subject to "traditional regulation or monetary policy," including insurance, bonding, and other security measures, and that values can fluctuate dramatically. At the federal level, the Department of the Treasury's Financial Crimes Enforcement Network (FinCEN) issued a guidance in March clarifying that digital currencies are subject to rules targeting money laundering and that virtual currency exchanges are required to register with FinCEN (http://www.pewtrusts.org).

Cryptocurrency transaction volume has triggered various governments. New York became the first state to propose regulations for the digital currency industry when it unveiled in July 2014 (http://www.pewtrusts.org/en/research-and-analysis/blogs/stateline/2014/07/28/states-debate-regulating-digital-currency), a broad-ranging proposal that aims to address consumer protection, money laundering, and cybersecurity.

"We have sought to strike an appropriate balance that helps protect consumers and root out illegal activity without stifling beneficial innovation," said Benjamin M. Lawsky, the New York Superintendent of Financial Services. "Setting up common sense rules of the road is vital to the long-term future of the virtual currency industry, as well as the safety and soundness of customer assets." The proposed rules, which could be finalized by the end of the year, would require Bitcoin exchanges and companies that receive, store, transmit, or issue virtual currencies to obtain "BitLicenses." Customers and merchants that simply accept Bitcoin as payment would not have to obtain licenses. The rules would also require virtual currency firms to hold as much virtual currency as they owe to customers, hold a bond or trust account in US dollars, provide receipts with every transaction, and comply with anti-money laundering provisions, among other requirements.

Benjamin Lawsky, superintendent for New York's Department of Financial Services, proposed new rules for virtual currency businesses. The "BitLicense" plan, if approved, would apply to all companies that store, control, buy, sell, transfer, or exchange Bitcoins (or other cryptocurrency). "In developing this regulatory framework, we have sought to strike an appropriate balance that helps protect consumers and root out illegal activity without stifling beneficial innovation. These regulations include provisions to help safeguard customer assets, protect against cyber hacking, and prevent the abuse of virtual currencies for illegal activity, such as money laundering."[2]

Some in the industry argue the proposed regulations are so tough they will inhibit innovation in the industry. David Landsman, executive director of the National Money Transmitter Association, a trade association, said the proposed rules were as strict as those for traditional money transmitters, but with added cybersecurity provisions. Landsman said it appeared New York "really does not care about encouraging small entrepreneurs. They care mostly about enforcing consumer protection standards and anti-money laundering standards."

The failure of Mt. Gox, one of Bitcoin's largest exchanges, following the theft of more than $450 million in virtual currency, also drew attention to Bitcoin's lack of consumer protections. In his Reddit post, Lawsky specifically referenced Mt. Gox as a reason why "setting up common sense rules of the road is vital to the long-term future of the virtual currency industry, as well as the safety and soundness of customer assets."

New York's proposed regulations require digital currency companies operating within the state to record the identity of their customers, including their name and

---

[2]Lawsky in a post on Reddit.com's Bitcoin discussion board, July 2014.

physical address. All Bitcoin transactions must be recorded, and companies would be required to inform regulators if they observe any activity involving Bitcoins worth $10,000 or more.

The proposal also places a strong emphasis on protecting legitimate users of virtual currency. New York is seeking to require that Bitcoin businesses explain "all material risks" associated with Bitcoin use to their customers, as well as provide strong cybersecurity to shield their virtual vaults from hackers. In order to ensure companies remain solvent, Bitcoin licensees would have to hold as much Bitcoin as they owe in some combination of virtual currency and actual dollars.

The traders have welcomed the legislation and have felt positive momentum. Cameron and Tyler Winklevoss, two of Bitcoin's largest investors, endorsed the new proposal. "We are pleased that Superintendent Lawsky and the Department of Financial Services have embraced Bitcoin and digital assets and created a regulatory framework that protects consumers. We look forward to New York State becoming the hub of this exciting new technology."

Gil Luria, an analyst at Wedbush Securities, also saw the regulations as beneficial for companies built around virtual currency. "Bitcoin businesses in the U.S. have been looking forward to being regulated."[3] "This is a very big important first step, but it's not the ultimate step." One particularly controversial aspect of the law appears to ban the creation of any new cryptocurrency by an unlicensed entity. This would not only put a stop to virtual currency innovation (other Bitcoin-like monies include Litecoin, Peercoin, and the mostly satirical Dogecoin) but also could theoretically put Bitcoin's anonymous creator, known by the name Satoshi Nakamoto, in danger of prosecution if he failed to apply for a BitLicense.

One major issue not yet settled is whether other states, or the federal government, will use this proposal as a model for their own regulations. Until some form of regulation is widely adopted, New York's effort will have a limited effect on Bitcoin business. "I think ultimately, these rules are going to be good for the industry," Lawsky told the Times. "The question is if this will spread further." Bitcoin exchanges might also be forced to adopt "know-your-customer" requirements, which force financial institutions to keep an eye on customer behavior and report suspicious activity to law enforcement. And Lawsky is even considering rules for those who use their computers to "mine" and create Bitcoins in the first place. Know-your-customer requirement may drive back the pressure of governments on money laundering activities (http://time.com/money/3004751/new-york-bitcoin-regulations-benjamin-lawsky/).

Until recently, California prohibited the use of alternative currencies. Last month, Democratic Gov. Jerry Brown signed legislation to allow the use of alternative currencies, including digital currencies. "Here in California, we're interested in being

---

[3]The New York Times, July 2014.

innovative and cutting-edge," said Democratic Assemblyman Roger Dickinson, who sponsored the legislation, although he acknowledged that the measure was largely a formality since he was not aware of anyone who had been prosecuted under the previous statute. "It didn't seem to make much sense to have this anachronistic statute on the books."

California's Department of Business Oversight, which oversees financial services, has been studying virtual currencies and trying to figure out how to proceed. Spokesman Mark Leyes said some virtual currency businesses have been working with the department to determine whether they would be required to apply for a money-transmitting license under state law.

The Texas Department of Banking said in April that Texas will not treat Bitcoin and other digital currencies as money. "What it means, from our perspective, is just simply that it's not money for the purposes of money transmission or currency exchange," said Daniel Wood, an assistant general counsel in the department. "A Bitcoin is basically property." However, most Bitcoin exchanges would be considered money transmitters, and exchanging digital currency for sovereign currency would in most cases be considered money transmission.

In July 2014, the Kansas Office of the State Bank Commissioner issued guidance like Texas that digital currencies are not considered money under the Kansas Money Transmitter Act, but a property, the transaction of which may attract applicable tax to any other property.

EU financial services chief Michel Barnier believes it is "imperative" to look at possible EU regulation for virtual currencies like Bitcoin. "We will now look into what can be done to possibly introduce regulation in this sector, particularly to address the risks of financial crime that arise from the anonymity that characterises many virtual currencies, it is imperative to move quickly on this issue. The potential for money laundering and terrorist financing is too serious to ignore. He emphasized that lenders should steer clear of virtual currencies until rules are in place." From the footsteps of New York, California, Kansas, and Texas, many governments are realizing the importance of regulating cryptocurrency market. It is expected that the moves will protect consumers and open doors for more species in cryptocurrency.

The IMF, the institution responsible for coordinating the stability of foreign exchange rates, is ill-equipped to handle the widespread use of Bitcoins into the foreign exchange market. It is imperative to intervene in the interest of public and global stability (Aart, 2003).

13.4 CONCLUSION

The short history of cryptocurrency and its rising popularity are moving toward matured and systematic markets. The promoters, players, and consumers of cryptocurrency have experience and learned complex issues including the legal challenges while transacting in cryptocurrency. The stakeholders like the governments, financial authorities, researchers, and consultants are on the job to harvest benefit of using technology and innovative idea for governance of currency. The governments and international bodies have to establish legal framework to make the cryptocurrency transaction secure and consumer safe and a stable and transparent market, immunizing the world from economic instability due to eruption of huge cryptocurrency and its volatility. The regulations are expected to take care of cryptocurrency market in terms of domestic and foreign currency, valuation, exchange, taxation, organizational status of the players, internal disputes, frauds, consumer protection, and monetary and fiscal policies.

REFERENCES

Aart, K., 2003. Do high interest rates defined against currencies during speculative attacks? J. Int. Econ. 59, 297–298.

Doughlas, W., et al., 2010. Central Banks & Central Bank Corporation in the global financial system. Pac. McGeorge Global Bus. & Dev. L. J. 1, 12–15.

Nicholas, A.P., 2013. Regulating digital currencies; bringing BITCON within the reach of the IMF, SSRN. 14 Chi J Intl L. http://papers.ssrn.com/sol3/papers.cfm?abstract_id=2248419, forthcoming.

CHAPTER 14

How to Tax Bitcoin?

Aleksandra Bal*

International Bureau for Fiscal Documentation, Amsterdam, The Netherlands

Contents

14.1 INTRODUCTION

Bitcoin, a decentralized cryptocurrency with no government or central bank, grabbed the public attention as its value skyrocketed in 2013. Interestingly, the rise in the Bitcoin value coincided with the economic collapse of Cyprus. People who lost faith in financial institutions started putting more trust in independent peer-to-peer payment systems. Between August and December 2013, Bitcoin usage increased by over 75% and the market value of bitcoins in circulation increased more than tenfold (from about USD 1 billion to USD 12 billion). Due to its global and decentralized nature, digital currency raises a number of difficult legal questions. The one especially interesting for tax practitioners and tax scholars is what the tax consequences of mining and trading in digital currencies are.

---

*This chapter is based on the PhD thesis of the author: Bal, A. Taxation of Virtual Currency (Leiden University 2014) and was completed in July 2014. See Bal, A., 2013. *Stateless Virtual Money in the Tax System*, European Taxation (53)7 and Bal, A., 2014. Should Virtual Currency be subject to Tax. Available at http://papers.ssrn.com/sol3/papers.cfm?abstract_id=2438451.

The purposes of this chapter are to explain the most common taxation problems related to the use of digital currency and to examine how tax authorities of various countries are struggling to solve them. Section 14.2 briefly describes the characteristics and nature of Bitcoin. Sections 14.3 and 14.4 describe the basic features of individual income tax and consumption tax systems and examine how digital currency could fit within the existing legal framework. Since tax laws vary from country to country, the taxation of digital currency cannot be addressed in a one-fits-all manner. The section on income tax looks at the income tax rules in some exemplary countries, whereas consumption tax challenges are shown on the basis of the EU VAT system. Corporate income tax aspects are outside the scope of this chapter. This chapter is focused on individuals since it is individuals who began trading in digital currencies. Section 14.4 discusses approaches to taxation of digital currency taken by various countries, for example, the Netherlands, Singapore, the United Kingdom, and the United States. Section 14.5 summarizes the main challenges adding some conclusions.

14.2 CHARACTERISTIC AND NATURE OF BITCOIN

In 2009, a person (or persons) operating under the pseudonym Satoshi Nakamoto created Bitcoin—a digital currency traded online via a peer-to-peer network, allowing its users to interact with one another anonymously and without a third-party intervention (Nakamoto, 2009). Nakamoto's decentralized currency was a response to the financial crisis and governments' reactions to it and to the role of banks and other payment intermediaries in mediating financial transactions. Bitcoin is not the first example of decentralized digital money but undoubtedly the most prominent so far.

In simple terms, bitcoins are transferred from computer to computer via a system of cryptographic hashes and kept secure through public-private key cryptography. Users can store their currency in a "wallet," which takes the form of either software installed on their computer or a web-based account. Each payment transaction is broadcast to the network and included in the block chain, so that the used Bitcoins cannot be spent twice. New Bitcoins are generated in a distributed fashion at a predictable rate. Computers called "bitcoin miners" solve complicated algorithms to generate new Bitcoins. The mathematics of the Bitcoin system was set up so that it becomes progressively more difficult to "mine." The upper limit of Bitcoins cannot exceed 21 million.

Digital decentralized money offers some substantial advantages over traditional paper-based currencies. A remarkable property of Bitcoin is that it provides no support for identity management and authentication of parties who act as payers, payees, and miners. All parties preserve their anonymity in transactions (some think of Bitcoin as "personal offshore bank"). Another advantage of the Bitcoin system is lack of transaction fees associated with a fund transfer since transactions take place over a peer-to-peer network.

Bitcoin keeps middlemen away not only from profiting from transaction fees but also from "invading" transaction privacy.

Despite the potential advantages of decentralized currencies, their widespread adoption faces a number of obstacles. The main one is uncertainty surrounding their operation and growth. People can easily download the Bitcoin application and start using digital money although they do not fully understand how the system works and which risks they take. Cybersecurity is also a constant concern. A large-scale theft of bitcoins from many users could create a confidence crisis. Digital currencies also face the problem of network externalities. The benefit of using a digital currency depends on the number of other people using it. As Bitcoin is not pegged to any real currency and its exchange rate is determined solely by supply and demand in the market, the whole system could collapse if people try to get rid of their bitcoins and are not able to do so because of its illiquidity. As Bitcoin is susceptible to irrational bubbles, a loss of confidence may collapse demand relative to supply.

Before investigating tax implications of digital currency, it is necessary to determine its nature. Can digital money be regarded as "money"? Can it be treated in the same way as EUR or USD? To answer those questions, one must first have an idea of what constitutes money.

Regardless of the form, money is traditionally associated with three different functions (Macintosh, 1998; European Central Bank, 2012). First, money is a medium of exchange used as an intermediary in trade to avoid the inconveniences of a barter system. Second, money provides a unit of account. It acts as a standard numerical unit for the measurement of value of goods and services to make different offerings on the market more comparable. However, to serve as an efficient unit of account, a currency must be more than decimal and readily divisible. It must provide a measure of relative worth that users can understand on a nearly intuitive level. Otherwise, users must expend time and effort to determine what the currency and its associated unit of account really mean. Moreover, a currency can serve as an effective unit of account only if users accept its legitimacy. Third, currency serves as a store of value of current earnings for future spending. Noncirculating money can circulate in the future and that potential for future circulation represents wealth or value that an individual participant can take advantage of.

Undoubtedly, Bitcoin can act as a medium of exchange. However, given the limited number of venues accepting digital currency, it is still a weak barter catalyst. It is questionable whether digital currencies can be considered intrinsically and intuitively valuable. To determine how much digital currencies are worth, users usually translate their value into value expressed in a familiar unit of account. By looking at the string of data, hardly anyone can identify its value. It is impossible to determine the value of particular goods in Bitcoin without knowing the bitcoin exchange rate at a particular time. The question arises as to whether Bitcoin fulfills the "store of value" function in terms of being reliable and safe. At any moment, regulators from various jurisdictions may take action against Bitcoin and its participants. At any moment, the Bitcoin market may collapse due to changing sentiments among bitcoin users: a technically stronger decentralized currency may appear and degrade Bitcoin to a mere historic incident. And of course at any moment, technical problems may bring Bitcoin down without any advance warnings. Given the enormous volatility of bitcoin, possible technical problems, the lack of oversight, and legal uncertainty surrounding Bitcoin, it is questionable whether Bitcoin can be a reliable store of value. After all, storing wealth in any medium that is easily susceptible to collapse or price fluctuations is unwise.

To sum up, at present, Bitcoin cannot be regarded as money in the economic sense. It is still surrounded by significant legal and factual uncertainty, which questions its ability to store value. Due to its limited use and enormous volatility, it cannot serve as a unit of account (its value must be first translated into the value of a traditional currency). However, Bitcoin has the potential to become economic money in the future. Time will tell whether Bitcoin will be reliable and stable enough to achieve this aim.

It is important to mention that when law refers to the concept of money (e.g., when it requires to remit monetary amounts to settle tax liabilities), it does not use the economic definition. For legal purposes, money has three additional features: legal tender status, central management, and a physical carrier (coins and banknotes). Due to its decentralized nature and lack of physical carrier, Bitcoin does not meet the necessary criteria of money in the legal sense. Although it is designed to act as a traditional currency (and maybe even replace it in the future), it cannot be treated as such.

The owner of a bitcoin can use it in any way he sees fit. This is similar to what generally can be done with commodities: the owner of precious metals can either sell or keep them. Thus, a reasonable perspective on Bitcoin is to view it as a steadily evolving piece of software or an asset that can be held as a part of an investment portfolio, alongside traditional currencies and other commodities.

14.3 INCOME TAX
14.3.1 Concept of taxable income

Income tax is levied on persons who have earned taxable income for the relevant tax period. Whether an individual generating or trading in bitcoins can be regarded as having taxable income depends on the income definition of a particular country.

From a structural viewpoint, two basic types of income tax systems can be distinguished: schedular and global (Burns and Krever, 1998). In a schedular tax system, income tax is levied tax on selected income categories. If a benefit does not fit into any categories, it is not subject to tax. In contrast, in a global tax system, all receipts, irrespective of their source, are subject to tax. In practice, most existing income tax systems lie on the spectrum between global and schedular (mixed systems).

An example of a country with an income tax system of a global nature is the United States. Under the Internal Revenue Code (IRC), receipts from whatever source derived are subject to tax. In such a system, a receipt qualifies as taxable income without having to meet any additional criteria (such as periodicity, profit motive, and market participation). Thus, in the United States, the receipt of bitcoins gives rise to gross income.

An example of a country with a schedular income tax system is Germany. It imposes income tax on seven categories of receipts and there is no all-encompassing provision that would tax income from whatever source derived. If a taxpayer's income does not fall into any of the categories, it is not subject to income tax. Among benefits that are not covered by the income categories are gifts, bequests, lottery winnings, and prizes granted for personal achievements or a successful participation in an event. Thus, before tax can be imposed on income in the form of bitcoins derived from a particular transaction, it is necessary to examine whether such income meets the criteria of any of the income categories. In Germany, income generated from bitcoin transactions could fall within the business income or the miscellaneous income category.

There are some income categories that are common to many jurisdictions. Almost all countries distinguish between business activity (which gives rise to business income) and sales transactions performed in a private capacity (which may give rise to capital gains).

The starting point in determining whether an item of income is business income is to determine whether the underlying activity is properly characterized as a business. In the absence of a definition in the income tax law, the term "business" has its ordinary meaning. In broad terms, a business is a commercial or industrial activity of an independent nature undertaken for profit (Burns and Krever, 1998).

The rules on taxation of gains from transactions performed in a private capacity vary from country to country. In the United Kingdom, there is a separate capital gains tax on disposal of assets (which also include intangibles and currency other than sterling). In Germany, casual sales of assets give rise to taxable miscellaneous income provided that the asset is sold within a year from its purchase and the total profit from disposal of private assets has exceeded the threshold of EUR 600 in a calendar year.

The fact that Bitcoin does not constitute money (either in the economic or in the legal sense) does not prevent profits expressed in bitcoins from taxation. Sales of goods and services for bitcoins constitute barter transactions, which are subject to the general income tax rules. In transactions where the consideration does not involve monetary amounts but benefits in kind, the determination of value of the exchanged objects becomes a pivotal issue. The basic valuation standard in many countries is market value, defined as the amount for which an asset could be exchanged between knowledgeable individuals in an arm's length transition. Market value is based on a hypothetical transaction (ordinary) and hypothetical participants (knowledgeable and willing) and assumes informational symmetry and profit maximization. Under perfect competition, there would be only one market price in a long-term equilibrium. However, as most markets are characterized by informational asymmetry, uncertainty, and imperfect competition, an asset can have more than one market value.

14.3.2 Challenges to income tax compliance

Income in the form of bitcoins is generally taxable. However, the fact that income is taxable does not mean that it is *actually* taxed. People who have "virtual" income do not pay tax on that income for two reasons: They are not aware that such income is taxable and they deliberately avoid paying tax knowing that this noncompliance is unlikely to be detected and punished.

The first issue (unawareness of tax liability) results from lack of clear guidance on the tax treatment of digital currency. If taxpayers turn to the Internet for tax help, they may find a lot of misinformation there. There are a number of websites, wikis, and blogs that provide differing opinions on the tax treatment of digital currency, including some that could lead taxpayers to believe that transacting in digital currencies relieves them of their responsibilities to report and pay taxes. For example, after the Danish tax authorities ruled that profits from casual bitcoin trading are not subject to tax, but taxpayers who trade in bitcoins in the ordinary course of business are subject to the general tax rules, one website posted the following statement:

> Trading Bitcoins in Denmark is exempt from taxes in Denmark. "Skatterådet", the Danish commission for taxes, decided that virtual currencies are not "real" money, so they will not charge taxes.

The second issue (deliberate noncompliance) stems from the characteristics of digital currencies: transactions take place anonymously usually in a multijurisdictional setting. A seller that accepts payments in bitcoins is not required to identify himself when establishing his online Bitcoin wallet. Although the entire history of bitcoin transactions is publicly available, it is extremely difficult to trace the earnings accumulated in a particular wallet back to a particular taxpayer. Thus, it is unlikely that tax authorities will know about the income, unless the taxpayer voluntarily reports it.

Some scholars claim that decentralized currencies possess the traditional characteristics of tax havens: earnings are not subject to taxation and taxpayers' anonymity is maintained. They assume that tax evaders who use bank accounts in tax-haven jurisdictions opt out of traditional tax havens in favor of cryptocurrencies (Marian, 2013). Traditional anti-tax-evasion mechanisms cannot successfully address Bitcoin-based tax evasion since Bitcoin's operation is not dependent on the existence of a sovereign jurisdiction that could provide information. Given the growing popularity of decentralized currencies, tax evasion associated with them may become more common in the future. The Federal Bureau of Investigation (FBI) issued a report on Bitcoin, in which it expressed its concerns about Bitcoin's popularity with criminals engaged in money laundering and other illicit activities (FBI, 2012). This report was probably motivated by the fact that Bitcoin became associated with the website Silk Road, a "digital black market" accessible only through the anonymized browsing service. However, the unfortunate fact that Bitcoin has been used for illegal transactions should not create a general pattern of discrimination against those who want to use Bitcoin for legitimate trade: there is hardly any financial system that would not have been used for illegal purposes.

14.4 CONSUMPTION TAX
14.4.1 Initial comments

The objective of consumption tax is to tax expenditures made by persons for their private purposes. It is the final consumer who should bear the tax burden. The most widespread consumption tax is the value-added tax (VAT), also called goods and services tax (GST). Limited to fewer than ten countries in the late 1960s, it has now been implemented by over 150 jurisdictions, where it often accounts for a large part of the total tax revenue (OECD, 2012).

This section discusses VAT aspects of transactions in digital currencies based on the EU VAT system. In simple terms, the functioning of the EU VAT system can be described as follows. All supplies of goods and services carried out for consideration by a taxable person in the EU territory are subject to VAT, unless a specific exemption applies. VAT charged by the supplier to his customers is known as "output VAT." The supplier is generally responsible for the remittance of output VAT to the tax authorities. VAT paid by the supplier to other businesses on goods and services that he receives is known as "input VAT." A taxable person is generally able to recover input VAT attributable to his taxable transactions by setting it off against the output VAT in his VAT return, provided that all the requirements for an input VAT deduction are met. The main source of the EU VAT legislation is the VAT Directive (2006/112). The provisions of the VAT Directive (2006/112) are clarified in the VAT Implementing Regulation (1042/2013).

14.4.2 Taxable person

In order to determine the personal scope of VAT, it is necessary to establish who may be regarded as a taxable person. "Taxable person" is an autonomous VAT concept. It does not exist in civil or trade law. Under Article 9 of the VAT Directive, a taxable person is anyone who independently carries out in any place any economic activity, whatever the purpose or result of that activity. The definition of the taxable person is very broad: it is not limited to EU residents ("any person in any place") or to persons acting for profit motives ("whatever the purpose"). This is in line with the objective of VAT as a general consumption tax. The argument that no profits are or will be made cannot be used to deny the status of a "taxable person." However, the statement "whatever purpose or result" cannot be interpreted as that a hobby purpose is sufficient. According to the settled ECJ case law, the economic nature of the activities is decisive.

Bitcoin mining and trading may start as a hobby. Once successful, it can be turned into a business activity. The problem is to determine when leisure activity ceases and a taxable venture begins. In most countries, registration thresholds are used to relieve taxpayers with low turnover ("small enterprises") from levying and collecting tax. The registration thresholds vary significantly among member states. They can be as low as EUR 1450 (the Netherlands) or reach EUR 93,300 (the United Kingdom). However, it is important to keep in mind that small enterprises have to register irrespective their turnover if they render services to taxable persons established in other member states and those services are deemed to be supplied in the customer's country or if they receive services from abroad that are subject to VAT under Article 44 of the VAT Directive. No monetary threshold applies to supplies of those cross-border services. Since digital currency qualifies as a service under the EU VAT (see Section 14.4.3), the small enterprise exemption is not likely to exclude VAT liability of Bitcoin traders.

It is not possible to give a clear answer to the question when a person trading in digital currency becomes a taxable person. If an activity has a hobby component, a case-by-case analysis that has to weigh many different circumstances against each other is necessary. Although some indicators can be found, it is not possible to consider their existence to be an unequivocal sign that taxable activities are likely to occur. Giving the wrong answer to the question of whether or not a person acts as a taxable person for VAT purposes may have dramatic financial consequences because the tax authorities normally check a person's VAT liability retrospectively over a period of several years and, if it exists, the VAT liability is a substantial percentage of the person's total gross proceeds. If a person does not register for VAT under the assumption that he is not engaged in economic activities but the tax authorities take a different position, that person will be liable for payment of the VAT that he has not declared and remitted on the output transactions, especially where the initial input tax claim is nil or relatively low. On top of having to pay the unpaid tax, without having the possibility to recharge the tax to his customers, the person may incur a penalty for having committed tax fraud.

14.4.3 Taxable transaction

Transactions are usually stated to be within the scope of VAT if they are "supplies of goods or services." A supply of goods is defined as the transfer of the right to dispose of tangible property as owner. The supply of services is defined residually as any transaction that is not a supply of goods. Due to their intangible nature, digital currencies are considered services for EU VAT purposes. They fall within the category of electronically supplied services, which are defined as services delivered over the Internet or an electronic network, the nature of which renders their supply essentially automated, involving minimum human intervention and impossible in the absence of information technology.

A supply of services will only occur if the taxable person receives payment (consideration) for the effects of a transaction. There must be a direct link between the service provided and the consideration received. A supply is taxable only if there is a legal relationship between the service provider and the recipient (a reciprocal performance). However, VAT liability does not depend on the existence of an enforceable and binding obligation according to domestic law of a member state. This would be contrary to the principle of VAT neutrality. Decisive is the mutual agreement, that is, that the parties agree to exchange some items and not a valid legal relationship between them.

It cannot be disputed that a bilateral legal relationship exists between the parties who trade in digital currencies. The transaction is performed in order to obtain consideration from the other party. However, a link between services provided and consideration received cannot be assumed in the case of bitcoin mining. Although it may appear that bitcoin miners perform a service (solving cryptographic algorithms to verify bitcoin transactions) for which they get paid in Bitcoin, not every miner is rewarded with new bitcoins. As more and more miners compete for a limited supply of blocks to verify, fewer receive reward for their mining efforts. Thus, mining activities are outside the scope of VAT.

14.4.4 Place of supply

Since VAT is an indirect tax focusing on the transaction rather than on the person performing it, the primary determination of the territorial scope of the charge to VAT is by reference to the location of a transaction. There are two principles on which the territorial scope of a VAT can be based: the destination principle and the origin principle. Under the former, the total tax paid in relation to a supply is determined by the rules applicable in the jurisdiction of consumption (exports are zero-rated and imports are taxed on the same basis and at the same rates as local production), whereas under the latter, each jurisdiction where a value is added collects the tax on this value at the local rate. The origin-based approach is said to distort competition in favor of business activity in low-tax countries, whereas the destination principle is regarded as the conceptually ideal approach to taxing consumption. For this reason, as of January 1, 2015, all supplies of electronic services follow the destination principle, that is, they will be taxed at the place where the customer is established or resident.

To determine who has to account for VAT on the supply, it is necessary to distinguish between business-to-business (B2B) and business-to-consumer (B2C) supplies. Cross-border B2B supplies are subject to the reverse-charge mechanism. This means that the VAT liability is shifted to the customer, that is, the supplier issues an invoice without

VAT and the customer accounts for VAT on the supply in his VAT return. If the recipient of a service is a private individual, it is not possible to shift the VAT liability to him since private individuals are not registered for VAT purposes and do not submit VAT returns. Thus, the supplier must account for VAT and remit it to the tax authorities in the customer's country. To prevent that suppliers have to register for VAT in all countries where their nontaxable customers are located (the transaction is deemed to take place in the customer's country, so it should be properly accounted for there), suppliers of cross-border B2C supplies can benefit from a simplified electronic registration, declaration, and payment system (the one-stop-shop scheme). This means that they can be registered and submit VAT returns only in one country. Until December 31, 2014, the one-stop-shop scheme is available only to non-EU suppliers. As of January 1, 2015, it also applies to EU businesses supplying electronic services to private individuals in other EU member states.

However, the one-stop-shop regime does not relieve suppliers of electronic services from the burden of locating their customers on a transaction-by-transaction basis. Such suppliers must comply with VAT legislation of the member states where their nontaxable customers are resident. Unlike supplies of goods under the distance selling regime, there is no turnover threshold for supplies of cross-border electronic services: even if the volume of such services supplied in a particular member state is insignificant, the service provider must be aware of the local VAT legislation. Finally, enforcing the one-stop-shop regime is difficult in a digital context where multiple transactions are carried out anonymously. Tax authorities have limited possibilities to sanction suppliers who fail to register and report their supplies to EU customers. According to statistics provided by the UK Treasury in March 2012, 453 non-EU providers of electronic services had registered under the one-stop-shop scheme at the end of 2011 (207 in the United Kingdom, 83 in the Netherlands, 65 in Luxembourg, 36 in Germany, 25 in Ireland, 14 in Italy, and 23 in nine other member states) (Lamensch, 2012). It is questionable whether the fact that VAT collection is reliant on voluntary compliance is acceptable from a neutrality and competition perspective in the long term. Without effective supervision and enforcement, there is a risk of nontaxation that threatens to distort competition. If tax rules are not linked to a real possibility of enforcement, taxpayers are unlikely to comply.

The VAT law provides that the location of the customer can be determined on the basis of two of noncontradictory evidence items, such as the customer's billing address, the customer's Internet protocol (IP) address or any method of geolocation, the customer's bank details, and other commercially relevant data obtained by the supplier. The items of evidence used to identify the location of the customer must be different and should not duplicate each other. For example, the fact that the customer gives his bank details and those details are confirmed by a payment service provider is considered one piece of evidence. If each piece of evidence points to a different country, the supplier must decide which item of evidence is more reliable in determining the customer's location. Priority should be given to the country that best ensures taxation at the place of actual consumption.

To establish the location of the customer is undoubtedly the biggest challenge for suppliers of electronic services. Since such services can be provided at a distance, the supplier may not obtain enough information to identify where the customer is resident or established. Given the multitude of low-value transactions in the electronic services sector, the determination of the customer's location on a transaction-by-transaction basis may result in a large compliance burden for suppliers. Consider the following example. Seller S (who is registered for VAT purposes in an EU member state) supplies two bitcoins (i.e., provides electronically supplied services) to buyer B in exchange for cash (EUR 200). B has received the bank details of the supplier to transfer EUR 200. After the payment is received, the seller sends the bitcoins to B's digital wallet. The only information he needs for that purpose is the buyer's bitcoin address: for example, 31uEbMgu-nupShBVTewXjtqbBv5MndwfXhb. He has no indication where B is located.

14.4.5 Exemptions

There is an extensive use of VAT exemptions across the European Union. Member states exempt some categories of goods and services considered as essential for social reasons: healthcare, education, and supplies by charities. In addition, they also use exemptions for practical reasons (e.g., in the case of financial and insurance services due to the difficulties in assessing the taxable amount).

Under Article 135(1)(d) and (e) of the VAT Directive, transactions involving currency (used as legal tender), accounts, debts, payments, and other negotiable instruments must be exempt from VAT. As shown in Section 14.2, digital currencies cannot be regarded as money in the legal sense. Neither can they be regarded as "accounts," "debts," or "negotiable instruments." Although the word "payment" may have a wide connotation and include all transfers of goods or services in exchange for another form of goods or services, this broad meaning may be limited by the statutory context. As the term "payment" is used in article 135 of the VAT Directive, it seems logical that "payment" or "transfer" must be made by way of one of the instruments listed there. Thus, the exemption of Article 135(1)(d) and (e) of the VAT Directive cannot be applied.

14.5 NATIONAL APPROACHES

Although digital currency is ignored by the tax authorities in the majority of countries where no guidance is provided on the tax consequences of mining and trading in bitcoins, recently, some countries have published their views on the status and taxation of Bitcoin. This section summarizes their approaches.

The Dutch Finance Ministry (*Ministerie van Financiën*) presented its opinion on Bitcoin in a April 10, 2013 letter. According to its view, Bitcoin cannot be regarded as a currency (legal tender) since it lacks central supervision and stability. Neither can it be treated as electronic money or financial product. The letter also mentioned that taxpayers earning their profits in bitcoins are subject to the general income tax rules and bitcoin transactions are governed by the general VAT rules.

In April 2013, the Canada Revenue Agency (CRA) reportedly announced that bitcoin users have to pay tax on transactions in this digital currency. According to the CRA, different rules apply depending on whether bitcoins are used as money to purchase goods and services or whether they are bought and sold for speculative purposes. Rules on barter transaction apply in the former case, while the latter is governed by provisions on trade in securities.

On December 3, 2013, the Central Bank of China and four other central government ministries and commissions jointly issued the Notice on Precautions against the Risks of Bitcoins. Defining it as a special "virtual commodity," the notice said that Bitcoin is not a currency and should not be circulated and used in the market as a currency. Banks and payment institutions in China are prohibited from dealing with bitcoins and from using it to price goods and services. The notice also required strengthening the oversight of websites providing bitcoin registration, trading, and other services and warned about the risks of using the bitcoin system for money laundering purposes.

The Finnish Tax Authority (*Vero Skatt*) clarified the treatment of Bitcoin for income tax purposes in its notice issued on August 28, 2013. This notice is quite comprehensive and provides several numerical examples showing how to calculate taxable income in bitcoin transactions. In the view of the *Vero Skatt*, profits from sales of bitcoins for traditional currency may be taxed as capital gains. The value of bitcoins generated through mining is also subject to income tax. The *Vero Skatt* regards Bitcoin neither as a traditional currency nor as a security.

In November 2013, the Norwegian Directorate of Taxation (*Skatteetaten*) published a statement explaining that Bitcoin is an asset (not a currency) and income tax can be charged on gains from its sale. For VAT purposes, supplies of bitcoins constitute taxable supplies of electronic services. Since Bitcoin does not have the status of a legal tender, the exemption for financial services cannot apply.

On December 13, 2013, the Slovenian Ministry of Finance (*Davčna uprava Republike Slovenije*) issued a formal opinion about the status of Bitcoin and other digital currencies. The opinion states that Bitcoin is neither a currency under Slovenian law nor a financial instrument. Profits from both sales of bitcoins and bitcoin mining are subject to tax. According to the Ministry of Finance, the existing legislative framework does not contain provisions applicable to businesses involved in bitcoin trading.

On December 19, 2013, the German Federal Financial Supervisory Authority (*Bundesanstalt für Finanzdienstleistungsaufsicht*, BaFin) issued a statement explaining the status of Bitcoin for the purposes of the German Banking Act (*Gesetz über das Kreditwesen*) and the risks of using this digital currency. The BaFin recognizes bitcoins as financial instruments that fall into the category "unit of account" and are comparable to foreign exchange accounting units. Although Bitcoin does not have legal tender status, it is similar to private or regional money (i.e., it can be used in transactions on the basis of legal agreements of private law). The BaFin statement does not say anything about tax consequences of transactions involving digital currencies.

The UK tax authorities (Her Majesty's Revenue and Customs, HMRC) set out their position on the tax treatment of income received from activities involving bitcoins and other similar cryptocurrencies in Revenue and Customs Brief 09/14 of March 3, 2014. The brief states that such income is subject to the general rules of income tax and capital gains tax. The question whether any profit on bitcoin transactions is chargeable must be answered on the basis of the individual facts of each case, taking into account the relevant legislation and case law. For VAT purposes, the HMRC is of the opinion that mining is outside the VAT scope, exchanges of bitcoins into traditional currencies are exempt, and supplies of goods and services for bitcoins are subject to VAT under the general rules. The HMRC observed that, given the evolutionary nature of cryptocurrencies, the position outlined in Revenue and Customs Brief 09/14 is provisional and pending further developments, especially in respect to EU VAT.

On March 25, 2014, the Danish tax authorities (SKAT) published a ruling on the tax treatment of Bitcoin. The ruling was issued in response to a taxpayer's request on whether he could use the exchange rates posted on the then-operating website Mt. Gox for the purposes of calculating his income tax and whether changes in the value of accumulated bitcoins due to exchange rate fluctuations have tax consequences. The SKAT observed that Bitcoin cannot be regarded as a currency (legal tender) since it is not subject to regulation by a central bank and cannot be withdrawn from circulation. Consequently, neither the Danish tax return nor invoices can use values expressed in Bitcoin. The SKAT ruled that profits from casual bitcoin trading are not subject to tax and the corresponding losses cannot be deducted. Taxpayers who trade in bitcoins in the ordinary course of business are subject to the general rules (profits are taxable and losses are deductible). However, changes in the value of accumulated bitcoins due to exchange rate fluctuations should not have any tax consequences.

In March 2014, the Estonian Tax and Customs Board (*Maksu- ja Tolliamet*) presented its views on taxation of Bitcoin. In its opinion, Bitcoin is neither electronic currency nor a security but property, the alienation and exchange of which give rise to capital gains. Income from trading in bitcoins is taxed as business income that, in addition to individual income tax, is also subject to social security contributions. Bitcoin transactions are subject to the standard VAT rate. They cannot benefit from the exemption for financial services since such exemption does not apply to the provision of services of alternative means of payment.

The Inland Revenue Authority of Singapore (IRAS) explained its position on the treatment of bitcoin transactions for GST purposes. In its view, digital currencies do not constitute money, currency, or goods but services and do not qualify for GST exemption. GST-registered businesses selling bitcoins need to charge GST on those sales, except for sales to a customer outside Singapore. If digital currencies are used to pay for goods or services, the transaction will be regarded as a barter trade. As a concession, if taxpayers use digital currencies to buy digital goods or services within the gaming world, they need not charge GST until those virtual goods and services are exchanged for real moneys, goods, or services.

The Brazilian tax authority (*Receita Federal*) reportedly does not consider Bitcoin a currency. According to various news sources, the *Receita Federal* has announced that taxpayers who sell bitcoins with a value of over BRL 35,000 will have to pay a 15% capital gains tax and those who possess than BRL 1000 in digital currency holdings must file annual account declarations. Neither the Brazilian government nor the Brazilian Central Bank is planning to issue special regulations on digital currencies unless the currency becomes frequently used in transactions.

The Unites States is the country that paid most attention to tax issues of digital currency. In its 2013 Annual Report to Congress, the United States Taxpayer Advocate considered need to issue guidance addressing the tax treatment of digital currencies to be one of the most serious problems facing the IRS. This report noted that the use of digital currencies is growing and that it is the government's responsibility to inform the public about the rules they are required to follow. The National Taxpayer Advocate recommended that the IRS answer, inter alia, the following questions: When will receiving or using digital currency trigger gains or losses, will these gains be taxed as ordinary income or as capital gains, and what information reporting, withholding, and record-keeping requirements apply to digital currency transactions?

In March 2013, another department of the US Treasury, the Financial Crimes Enforcement Network (FinCEN), issued interpretive guidance clarifying some obligations of persons creating, obtaining, distributing, exchanging, accepting, or transmitting digital currencies. Such persons must be registered as "money transmitters" with the FinCEN under the regulations relating to money-services businesses. The FinCEN guidance does not discuss the tax treatment of digital currency transactions.

In May 2013, the Government Accountability Office (GAO) published a report exploring potential tax compliance risks associated with digital currencies. The GAO recommends that IRS find relatively low-cost ways to provide information to taxpayers on various matters regarding digital currencies. In commenting on a draft of this report, the IRS agreed to implement this recommendation.

Finally, on March 25, 2014, the IRS issued a notice containing 16 questions and answers on various aspects of convertible digital currencies. According to this notice, digital currency is treated as property (and not as a currency) for US federal tax purposes. General tax principles that apply to property transactions apply to transactions using digital currency. A taxpayer who mines or receives digital currency as payment for goods or services must include the fair market value of the digital currency in computing gross income. A person who settles payments made in digital currency on behalf of merchants that accept digital currency from their customers may be subject to the reporting requirements for third-party settlement organizations.

The provision of guidance by tax authorities is a positive development. It promotes compliance among taxpayers who want to report their transactions in digital currency properly and reduces the risk that users of digital currency will be confronted with tax consequences that they did not anticipate. It also demonstrates that tax authorities are able and willing to respond to innovations in the digital marketplace. However, the guidance should not be limited to the statement that the general rules apply. Such a statement is insufficient as it presupposes that individuals know precisely what those general rules are. An individual who is only familiar with, for example, tax on employment income may not know what rules apply to entrepreneurs. Moreover, the general rules apply be default, so there is no need to state that fact explicitly.

14.6 CONCLUSIONS

This chapter reviewed some of the tax implications of mining and trading in bitcoins. Based on the analysis in the previous sections, it can be concluded that, whereas the current law is generally able to capture transactions in digital currencies, taxpayers need more practical guidance on how the rules apply to their particular situation.

As regards income tax, tax authorities should provide information on the income characterization, allowable deductions, ways of income calculation, and records to be kept. As the range of potential income-generating situations is broad (there are bitcoin miners who treat their currency as stock in trade, users who cultivated their hobby into a business venture, and professional entrepreneurs who accept virtual currency as a means of payment), taxpayers need be able to determine when their activity can be categorized as trade or business, a for-profit activity, or a hobby. Assistance could be provided by means of examples, in a way similar to that used by the HMRC to educate its taxpayers about the tax consequences of online sales.

Comprehensive guidance can help taxpayers but it does not solve all their problems. Given the variety of digital currency schemes and different personal situations of taxpayers, advice on the individual circumstances would be greatly appreciated. Taxpayers would like to have certainty that the chosen income characterization and the method of income calculation will not be challenged by the tax administration. For those reasons, taxpayers should have the possibility to request advice and tax authorities should handle those requests in a timely manner.

The main practical problems faced by trade in digital currencies under the EU VAT system are as follows. First, the concept of taxable person lacks clarity. The definition contained in the VAT Directive is very broad. The CJEU gives general guidelines and recommends a case-by-case analysis. The VAT registration thresholds help prevent unexpected assessments, but they do not solve all the problems as small businesses are required to register irrespective of their turnover if they perform certain cross-border services.

Second, the location of the customer in B2C scenarios is difficult to establish. The VAT Implementing Regulation recommends determining it on the basis of two noncontradictory evidence items (such as bank details and IP address). It is unclear what should be done if two noncontradictory pieces of evidence cannot be found. The Explanatory Notes issued by the European Commission simply recommend the suppliers to "continue to seek" them.

The one-stop-shop arrangement was introduced to avoid multiple registration and reporting obligations. While it clearly reduces the compliance burden, its operation is not free from flaws. The use of the one-stop-shop arrangement by non-EU suppliers depends on their willingness toward voluntary compliance. In the absence of effective enforcement mechanisms and sanctions, many non-EU suppliers will not register, which will lead to distortion of competition and violation of the principle of legal neutrality (since digital products offered by nonresidents will be tax-free).

The study from the European Central Bank (2012) suggests that the use of digital currencies is expected to grow in the future. If the future of electronic commerce entails an increasing use of digital currencies, it is critical that our economic, political, and legal institutions are prepared to deal with them and to incorporate them into the existing legal framework.

REFERENCES

Burns, L., Krever, R., 1998. Individual income tax. In: Thuronyi, V. (Ed.), Tax Law Design and Drafting. International Monetary Fund, Washington, USA, pp. 495–563.

European Central Bank, October 2012. Virtual Currency Schemes, available at: http://www.ecb.europa.eu/pub/pdf/other/virtualcurrencyschemes201210en.pdf.

FBI, 24 April 2012. Bitcoin Virtual Currency: Unique Features Present Distinct Challenges for Deterring Illicit Activity, available at: http://www.wired.com/images_blogs/threatlevel/2012/05/Bitcoin-FBI.pdf.

Lamensch, M., 2012. Proposal for implementing the EU one-stop-shop scheme from 2015. Intl. VAT Monitor 23 (5), 312–315.

Macintosh, K.L., 1998. How to encourage global electronic commerce: the case for private currencies on the Internet. Harvard J. Law Technol. 11 (3), 733–796.

Marian, O., 2013. Are cryptocurrencies super tax havens? Mich. Law Rev. 112 (19), 38–48.

Nakamoto, S., 2009. Bitcoin: A Peer-to-Peer Electronic Cash System, available at: https://bitcoin.org/bitcoin.pdf.

OECD, 2012. Consumption Tax Trends 2012. OECD, Paris (Chapter 1).

CHAPTER 15

Cryptocurrency and Virtual Currency: Corruption and Money Laundering/ Terrorism Financing Risks?

Kim-Kwang Raymond Choo
University of South Australia, Adelaide, South Australia, Australia

Contents

15.1 CORRUPTION: A SOCIAL EVIL

Bribery and corruption have been the subject of study by scholars, policymakers, and international organizations such as Transparency International. There are various levels of bribery and corruption (which will be simply referred to as corruption in the remainder of this chapter), ranging from petty corruption by individuals to systemic or "grand" corruption by institutions or governments (e.g., in the case of state capture—see Hellman et al., 2003). Corruption may also involve nonmonetary instruments such as art and antiques and precious metals (see FATF, 2013). In January 2014, for example, it was reported that the former Anhui Deputy Governor in the People's Republic of China allegedly accept carved jade in return for mining rights and land for a businessman's metal business (Associated Press, 2014).

In recent years, there has been an increase focus on criminalizing corruption at both the international (e.g., UN Convention against Corruption[1]) and national levels. For example, in Australia, Australian citizens or residents and legal entities incorporated

---

[1] According to the UN Convention against Corruption progress report 2013, 168 countries have ratified the convention (Transparency International, 2013b).

by, or under a law of, the Commonwealth or of a state or territory found guilty of bribing, or attempting to bribe, foreign public officials are liable to criminal penalties. For an individual convicted under *Criminal Code Act 1995* (Cth), the maximum penalty is a term of imprisonment of up to 10 years, a fine not more than 10,000 penalty units (currently AU$ 1,700,000 as each penalty unit means AU$ 170—see Section 4AA, *Crimes Act 1914* (Cth)), or both. For a body corporate, the maximum penalty is a fine of up to 100,000 penalty units or three times the value of benefits obtained by the act of bribery, whichever is greater. If the court cannot determine the value of that benefit, the penalty is a fine of up to 100,000 penalty units or 10% of the annual turnover of the body corporate during the period (the turnover period) of 12 months ending at the end of the month in which the conduct constituting the offense occurred, whichever is greater.

In the United Kingdom, Sections 1 and 6 of the *Bribery Act 2010* make it an offense to bribe another person and a foreign public official, respectively. For an individual convicted under *Bribery Act 2010* (United Kingdom), the maximum penalty is a term of imprisonment of up to 10 years (12 months on summary conviction in England and Wales or Scotland or 6 months in Northern Ireland) and/or a fine of up to the statutory maximum (currently £5000 in England and Wales or Northern Ireland and £10,000 in Scotland) if the conviction is summary and unlimited if it is on indictment—see Section 11 of the Act. If the offense is committed by a person other than an individual, the maximum penalty is punishable by a fine of up to the statutory maximum.

Despite the increased emphasis in the fight against corruption, recent studies such as Transparency International (2013a)'s Corruption Perceptions Index suggest that corruption remains a serious problem in both developed and developing countries and that public trust of politicians is low in several of these countries—see Table 15.1. This is consistent with the findings of Global Financial Integrity, which estimated that illicit financial outflows from developing countries due to crime, corruption, and tax evasion are "US$946.7 billion in 2011, with cumulative illicit financial outflows over the decade between 2002 and 2011 of US$5.9 trillion" (Global Financial Integrity, 2013: iii).

In recent years, there has been increasing concern about money laundering cases involving high net-worth individuals who are, or who have been, entrusted with prominent public functions—commonly referred to as politically exposed persons (PEPs)—where their wealth has been obtained by illegal means, such as bribery and corruption. As recently as March and May 2014, more than US$458 million allegedly stolen by the former Nigerian dictator was frozen by the US Department of Justice (FBI, 2014) and Israel ex-PM Ehud Olmert was reportedly jailed for 6 years for bribery (BBC, 2014), respectively.

FATF (2012) defines foreign PEPs as individuals who are or have been entrusted with prominent public functions by a foreign country (e.g., heads of state or of government, senior politicians, senior government, judicial or military officials, senior executives of state-owned corporations, and important political party officials) and domestic PEPs as individuals who are or have been entrusted domestically with prominent public functions (e.g., heads of state or of government, senior politicians, senior government, judicial or

Table 15.1 Control of corruption for 2012

Country/territory	Governance score	Percentile rank	Country/territory	Governance score	Percentile rank
Afghanistan	−1.41	2	Liberia	−0.57	34
Albania	−0.72	27	Libya	−1.40	2
Algeria	−0.54	36	Liechtenstein	1.80	94
American Samoa	0.35	68	Lithuania	0.31	66
Andorra	1.29	87	Luxembourg	2.12	96
Angola	−1.29	5	Macao SAR, China	0.45	70
Anguilla	1.29	87	Macedonia, FYR	0.02	59
Antigua and Barbuda	1.29	87	Madagascar	−0.61	31
Argentina	−0.49	39	Malawi	−0.45	40
Armenia	−0.53	37	Malaysia	0.30	66
Aruba	1.11	83	Maldives	−0.44	41
Australia	2.00	96	Mali	−0.76	25
Austria	1.35	89	Malta	0.96	80
Azerbaijan	−1.07	13	Marshall Islands	−0.14	54
The Bahamas	1.34	88	Martinique	0.82	77
Bahrain	0.39	68	Mauritania	−0.60	32
Bangladesh	−0.87	21	Mauritius	0.33	67
Barbados	1.66	93	Mexico	−0.41	43
Belarus	−0.52	37	Micronesia, Fed. Sts.	−0.11	55
Belgium	1.55	91	Moldova	−0.60	33
Belize	0.01	59	Monaco	#N/A	#N/A
Benin	−0.92	19	Mongolia	−0.52	38
Bermuda	1.29	87	Montenegro	−0.10	55
Bhutan	0.82	78	Morocco	−0.41	42
Bolivia	−0.70	27	Mozambique	−0.59	33
Bosnia and Herzegovina	−0.30	49	Myanmar	−1.12	11
Botswana	0.94	79	Namibia	0.32	67

Continued

Table 15.1 Control of corruption for 2012—cont'd

Country/territory	Governance score	Percentile rank	Country/territory	Governance score	Percentile rank
Brazil	−0.07	56	Nauru	0.05	60
Brunei Darussalam	0.64	72	Nepal	−0.83	23
Bulgaria	−0.24	52	Netherlands	2.13	97
Burkina Faso	−0.52	38	Netherlands Antilles (former)	0.82	77
Burundi	−1.46	1	New Caledonia	#N/A	#N/A
Cambodia	−1.04	14	New Zealand	2.32	100
Cameroon	−1.24	7	Nicaragua	−0.78	25
Canada	1.92	95	Niger	−0.69	28
Cape Verde	0.81	74	Nigeria	−1.13	11
Cayman Islands	1.35	89	Niue	#N/A	#N/A
Central African Republic	−0.89	20	Norway	2.24	99
Chad	−1.25	6	Oman	0.08	61
Chile	1.56	91	Pakistan	−1.06	14
China	−0.48	39	Palau	−0.28	50
Colombia	−0.43	42	Panama	−0.39	44
Comoros	−0.73	26	Papua New Guinea	−1.04	15
Congo, Dem. Rep.	−1.30	4	Paraguay	−0.84	22
Congo, Rep.	−1.19	10	Peru	−0.39	43
Cook Islands	#N/A	#N/A	The Philippines	−0.58	33
Costa Rica	0.58	71	Poland	0.59	72
Côte d'ivoire	−0.91	20	Portugal	0.93	78
Croatia	−0.04	57	Puerto Rico	0.57	71
Cuba	0.30	65	Qatar	1.19	84
Cyprus	1.24	85	Réunion	0.82	77
Czech Republic	0.23	64	Romania	−0.27	51
Denmark	2.39	100	Russian Federation	−1.01	16
Djibouti	−0.38	45	Rwanda	0.66	73

Corruption and Money Laundering/Terrorism Financing Risks   287

Continued

Country			Country		
Dominica	0.69	73	Samoa	0.15	62
Dominican Republic	−0.83	23	San Marino	#N/A	#N/A
Ecuador	−0.66	28	São Tomé and Principe	−0.39	44
Egypt, Arab Rep.	−0.57	34	Saudi Arabia	−0.06	57
El Salvador	−0.38	44	Senegal	−0.32	48
Equatorial Guinea	−1.56	0	Serbia	−0.31	48
Eritrea	−0.65	29	Seychelles	0.33	67
Estonia	0.98	80	Sierra Leone	−0.94	19
Ethiopia	−0.60	32	Singapore	2.15	97
Fiji	−0.44	41	Slovak Republic	0.07	60
Finland	2.22	98	Slovenia	0.81	75
France	1.42	90	Solomon Islands	−0.44	40
French Guiana	1.11	83	Somalia	−1.59	0
Gabon	−0.55	36	South Africa	−0.15	54
Gambia, The	−0.64	30	South Sudan	−1.34	4
Georgia	0.25	64	Spain	1.05	82
Germany	1.78	94	Sri Lanka	−0.24	52
Ghana	−0.09	56	St. Kitts and Nevis	0.98	81
Greece	−0.25	51	St. Lucia	0.96	79
Greenland	1.21	85	St. Vincent and the Grenadines	0.98	81
Grenada	0.40	69	Sudan	−1.51	1
Guam	0.82	77	Suriname	−0.37	45
Guatemala	−0.61	31	Swaziland	−0.33	47
Guinea	−1.11	12	Sweden	2.31	99
Guinea-Bissau	−1.22	9	Switzerland	2.15	98
Guyana	−0.75	26	Syrian Arab Republic	−1.17	11
Haiti	−1.24	6	Taiwan, China	0.72	74
Honduras	−0.94	18	Tajikistan	−1.18	10
Hong Kong SAR, China	1.71	93	Tanzania	−0.85	22

Table 15.1 Control of corruption for 2012—cont'd

Country/territory	Governance score	Percentile rank	Country/territory	Governance score	Percentile rank
Hungary	0.28	65	Thailand	−0.34	47
Iceland	1.86	95	Timor-Leste	−0.98	17
India	−0.57	35	Togo	−0.99	17
Indonesia	−0.66	29	Tonga	−0.07	56
Iran, Islamic Rep.	−0.82	24	Trinidad and Tobago	−0.29	50
Iraq	−1.23	8	Tunisia	−0.18	53
Ireland	1.45	90	Turkey	0.17	63
Israel	0.83	78	Turkmenistan	−1.34	3
Italy	−0.03	58	Tuvalu	−0.30	49
Jamaica	−0.36	46	Uganda	−0.95	18
Japan	1.61	92	Ukraine	−1.03	16
Jersey, Channel Islands	1.21	85	United Arab Emirates	1.18	83
Jordan	0.07	61	The United Kingdom	1.64	92
Kazakhstan	−0.88	21	The United States	1.38	89
Kenya	−1.10	12	Uruguay	1.32	88
Kiribati	0.00	58	Uzbekistan	−1.23	9
Korea, Dem. Rep.	−1.37	3	Vanuatu	0.45	69
Korea, Rep.	0.47	70	Venezuela	−1.24	7
Kosovo	−0.62	30	Vietnam	−0.56	35
Kuwait	−0.16	53	Virgin Islands (the United States)	0.82	77
Kyrgyz Republic	−1.09	13	West Bank and Gaza	−0.78	24
Lao PDR	−1.04	15	Yemen, Rep.	−1.23	8
Latvia	0.15	63	Zambia	−0.36	46
Lebanon	−0.87	22	Zimbabwe	−1.27	5
Lesotho	0.11	62			

Governance score ranges from approximately −2.5 (weak) to 2.5 (strong) governance performance and percentile rank among all countries ranges from 0 (lowest) to 100 (highest) rank.
Source: Compiled from http://info.worldbank.org/governance/wgi/index.aspx (last accessed 25.06.14).

military officials, senior executives of state-owned corporations, and important political party officials). The definition includes a person who is or has been entrusted with a prominent function by an international organization—referred to as members of senior management (i.e., directors, deputy directors, and members of the board or equivalent functions), and the definition is not intended to cover middle-ranking or more junior individuals in the foregoing categories.

Although the majority of PEPs do not abuse their position for illicit financial gain, they are vulnerable in that they have the capacity to control or divert funds and to award or deny large-scale projects for illicit gain (Choo, 2010). A recent investigation by the International Consortium of Investigative Journalists (2014), for example, revealed that "[c]lose relatives of China's top leaders have held secretive offshore companies in tax havens that helped shroud the Communist elite's wealth." Individuals named in the study include the brother-in-law of China's President Xi Jinping, the son and son-in-law of former Premier Wen Jiabao, and daughter of former Premier Li Peng.

15.2 REVIEW OF FINANCIAL ACTION TASK FORCE ON MONEY LAUNDERING COMPLIANCE ON PEPs

Financial Action Task Force (FATF) is an intergovernmental body established in 1989, which sets international standards and develops and promotes policies to combat money laundering and terrorist financing. In 1990, a set of 40 recommendations were introduced to guide the fight against money laundering. These 40 recommendations set out the framework for anti-money laundering efforts and provide a set of countermeasures covering the criminal justice system and law enforcement, the financial system and its regulation, and measures to enhance international cooperation (Walters et al., 2012).

Since the terrorist attacks against the United States on 11 September 2001, FATF has expanded its mandate to deal with the financing of terrorism. Eight additional, and subsequently one further, recommendations aimed at combating the funding of terrorist acts and terrorist organizations were created. These nine special recommendations include recommendations for dealing with financing channels specific to terror groups, such as nonprofit organizations or cash couriers (in bulk cash smuggling activities). FATF 40 + 9 recommendations were designed to combat increasingly sophisticated money laundering techniques and the increased use of professionals to advise and assist in money laundering (FATF, 2004) and are widely regarded as the international anti-money laundering/counter terrorism financing (AML/CTF) standard and constitute a comprehensive regime that has been endorsed and adopted by member countries and by a number of international bodies including the United Nations and the International Monetary Fund.

The three primary objectives of the FATF 40 + 9 recommendations are

1. to support the criminalization of money laundering and the financing of terrorism,
2. to ensure that assets linked to money laundering or the financing of terrorism can be frozen and confiscated, and

3. to ensure that financial institutions and other regulated businesses comply with the recommendations (FATF, 2004).

In addition to performing normal due diligence measures, FATF Recommendation 6 requires that financial institutions should, in relation to PEPs,

    (a) have appropriate risk management systems to determine whether the customer is a PEP,

    (b) obtain senior management approval for establishing business relationships with such customers,

    (c) take reasonable measures to establish the source of wealth and source of funds, and

    (d) conduct enhanced ongoing monitoring of the business relationship.

Countries are also encouraged to extend the requirements of Recommendation 6 to individuals who hold prominent public functions in their own country (i.e., domestic PEPs).

One of the main changes in the most recent revision of FATF standards in February 2012 (referred to as the 2012 FATF Recommendations in this chapter, FATF, 2012) is the introduction of stronger requirements when dealing with PEPs. The new recommendation (2012 FATF Recommendation 12) now requires that financial institutions should be required, in relation to foreign PEPs (whether as customer or beneficial owner), in addition to performing normal customer due diligence measures, to

(a) have appropriate risk management systems to determine whether the customer *or the beneficial owner* is a PEP,

(b) obtain senior management approval for establishing (*or continuing, for existing customers*) such business relationships,

(c) take reasonable measures to establish the source of wealth and source of funds, and

(d) conduct enhanced ongoing monitoring of the business relationship.

Financial institutions should be required to take reasonable measures to determine whether a customer or beneficial owner is a domestic PEP or a person who is or has been entrusted with a prominent function by an international organization. In cases of a higher-risk business relationship with such persons, financial institutions should be required to apply the measures referred to in items (b)-(d). In other words, the specific rules and procedures envisaged in 2012 FATF Recommendation 12 cannot be simplified on the basis of an institutional risk-based analysis.

In this chapter, the discussions are based on the FATF 40 + 9 Recommendations as only one jurisdiction (i.e., Austria) has been assessed using the 2012 FATF Recommendations at the time of this research. Although there have been criticisms of the mutual evaluation process, the intention of this chapter is neither to critique/evaluate the effectiveness of mutual evaluations nor to examine the politics involved in this process and/or the composition of the mutual evaluation team. This is similar to the approach we took in our previous studies (Choo, 2010, 2013, 2014b) and that of Johnson (2008).

As of June 25, 2014, there are 34 member jurisdictions[2], 2 regional organizations, and 8 FATF FATF-style regional bodies.[3]

15.2.1 Noncompliant and partially compliant jurisdictions

Thirty-one jurisdictions were assessed to be noncompliant with FATF Recommendation 6—see Table 15.2.

Of the 75 jurisdictions, nearly a third was assessed to be partially compliant—see Table 15.3.

It is clear from both Tables 15.1 and 15.2 that a number of jurisdictions remain either noncompliant or partially compliant several years after their first mutual evaluation. Not surprisingly, a number of the jurisdictions assessed to be either noncompliant or partially compliant were also perceived to have high levels of corruptions in the Corruption Perceptions Index compiled by Transparency International (2013b) and low governance score (see Table 15.1)—for example, Afghanistan, Guinea-Bissau, Haiti, Republic of Angola, Turkmenistan, Uzbekistan, and Venezuela. Our findings echoed the findings in our previous study (Choo, 2013)—most of the jurisdictions that were assessed to be partially or noncompliant were also assessed to have a low level of compliance for FATF Recommendation 20 (other measures to deter money laundering and terrorist financing).

The low average compliance level of jurisdictions highlighted in this review could potentially create a favorable situation for corrupted PEPs looking to infiltrate the global financial system or for individuals looking to bribe (senior) government officials to advance their economic interests.

The remaining 19 jurisdictions were assessed to be largely compliant, but no jurisdiction was assessed to be fully compliant.

15.2.2 Recommendations

We observed from this review that the level of details in the mutual evaluation and follow-up reports varies between jurisdictions and between years, and it is at times

---

[2]Argentina, Australia, Austria, Belgium, Brazil, Canada, China, Denmark, European Commission, Finland, France, Germany, Greece, Gulf Cooperation Council, Hong Kong (China), Iceland, India, Ireland, Italy, Japan, Republic of Korea, Luxembourg, Mexico, the Netherlands, Kingdom of New Zealand, Norway, Portugal, Russian Federation, Singapore, South Africa, Spain, Sweden, Switzerland, Turkey, the United Kingdom, and the United States (http://www.fatf-gafi.org/pages/aboutus/membersandobservers/).

[3]Asia/Pacific Group on Money Laundering, Caribbean Financial Action Task Force, Council of Europe Committee of Experts on the Evaluation of Anti-Money Laundering Measures and the Financing of Terrorism, Eurasian Group, Eastern and Southern Africa Anti-Money Laundering Group, Financial Action Task Force on Money Laundering in South America, Inter Governmental Action Group against Money Laundering in West Africa, and Middle East and North Africa Financial Action Task Force (http://www.fatf-gafi.org/pages/aboutus/membersandobservers/).

Table 15.2 Noncompliant jurisdictions

Jurisdiction (mutual evaluation reports (MER)/follow-up reports, year)	Factors underlying a rating of noncompliance
Afghanistan (MER, 2011)	• The absence of requirement to determine whether a potential customer or a beneficial owner is a PEP • No requirement to obtain senior management approval to continue the business relationship, where a customer has been accepted and the customer or beneficial owner is subsequently found to be, or subsequently becomes, a PEP • No requirement to take reasonable measures to establish the source or wealth and the source of funds of beneficial owners identified as PEPs
Albania (4th follow-up, 2011)	Weaknesses in identification of beneficial owners and the lack of any customer due diligence (CDD) measures for customers that are foreign politically exposed persons (PEPs). In addition, the effectiveness of implementation of preventive measures remains a concern, with uneven understanding of the provisions among financial institutions and a lack of suspicious transaction reports
Algeria (MER, 2010)	The absence of obligation to put in place appropriate risk management systems to determine whether a potential customer, customer, or beneficial owner is a PEP
Antigua and Barbuda (4th follow-up, 2012) Aruba, Kingdom of the Netherlands (8th follow-up, 2014)	No information provided in both follow-up reports
Benin (MER, 2010) Bermuda (2nd follow-up, 2011) Brunei Darussalam (MER, 2010)	No legal or regulatory obligations related to PEPs No information provided in the follow-up report There are no obligations for financial institutions to • put in place appropriate risk management systems to determine whether a potential customer, a customer, or the beneficial owner is a politically exposed person, • obtain senior management approval for establishing business relationships with a PEP, • take reasonable measures to establish the source of wealth and the source of funds of customers and beneficial owners identified as PEP, • conduct enhanced ongoing monitoring on PEP.
El Salvador (4th follow-up, 2012) Greece (10th follow-up, 2011)	The absence of provisions related with PEPs No information provided in all five follow-up reports

Grenada (4th follow-up, 2011) Guinea-Bissau (2nd follow-up, 2011) Haiti (3rd follow-up, 2012) Honduras (6th follow-up, 2012) Kingdom of Swaziland (MER, 2010)	There are no requirements for financial institutions to apply enhanced due diligence when dealing with foreign PEPs clients
Lao People's Democratic Republic (MER, 2011)	There are no legislative, regulatory, or other enforceable requirements in respect to politically exposed persons
Liberia (MER, 2011)	PEPs not addressed in the law: • No requirement to establish source of wealth and source of funds of customers and beneficial owners identified as PEPS • No requirement to conduct enhanced ongoing monitoring of the relationship with PEPs • No requirement to get senior management's approval before establishing or continuing a business relationship with a PEP
Maldives (MER, 2011)	There are no obligations for financial institutions to • put in place appropriate risk management systems to determine whether a potential customer, a customer, or the beneficial owner is a PEP, • obtain senior management approval for establishing and continuing business relationships with a PEP or where the beneficial owner is a PEP, • take reasonable measures to establish the source of wealth and the source of funds of customers and beneficial owners identified as PEPs. There are no requirements for banks, other money transfer businesses, and institutions licensed by the MMA to conduct enhanced ongoing monitoring on PEPs
Nepal (MER, 2011)	The limited PEP provisions are unenforceable • Foreign PEPs not considered high risk • No reference to beneficial owners • No guidance to financial industry on development of PEPs policies and procedures • No senior management approvals required on PEP accounts

Continued

Table 15.2 Noncompliant jurisdictions—cont'd

Jurisdiction (mutual evaluation reports (MER)/follow-up reports, year)	Factors underlying a rating of noncompliance
Papua New Guinea (MER, 2011)	• No specific mandates on sources of funds or wealth for PEPs • The absence of effective PEP procedures at all financial institutions • There is no requirement to identify foreign PEPs • No requirement for senior management approval to establish a business relationship with a foreign PEP • No requirement to take reasonable measures to establish the source and wealth of foreign PEPs • No provisions require ongoing monitoring of transactions of foreign PEPs
Saint Lucia (5th follow-up, 2012)	No information provided in the follow-up report
Solomon Islands (MER, 2010)	There are no requirements for financial institutions to have in place risk management system and due diligence measures for politically exposed persons
Spain (4th follow-up, 2010)	No information provided in the follow-up reports
Suriname (2nd follow-up, 2012)	
Togo (MER, 2011)	• Financial institutions have not put in place adequate systems for AML/CFT-associated risk management to determine whether a potential customer or beneficiary owner is a politically exposed person • In practice, some banks that belong to international banking groups prepare and update the list of PEPs and get approval from their senior management before establishing new relations with this type of person. Other banking institutions have practices closer to marketing goals than to FATF objectives for AML/CFT risk management systems
Trinidad and Tobago (6th follow-up, 2012)	No information provided in the follow-up reports
Turkmenistan (3rd follow-up)	
Turks & Caicos Islands (6th follow-up, 2012)	
Union of Comoros (MER, 2010)	• Failure to apply provisions on PEPs to insurance companies • No requirement to obtain authorization from senior management in order to continue a business relationship with an existing client that subsequently appears to be a PEP • No clear definition of PEPs
Uzbekistan (2nd follow-up, 2012)	No information provided in the follow-up reports
Venezuela (5th follow-up, 2012)	

Table 15.3 Partially compliant jurisdictions

Jurisdiction (mutual evaluation reports (MER)/follow-up reports, year)	Factors underlying a rating of noncompliance
Anguilla (2nd follow-up, 2011)	No information provided in the follow-up report
Argentina (MER, 2010)	There is no requirement in law, regulation, or other enforceable means for financial institutions of the securities and insurance sector to identify and apply enhanced CDD for foreign PEPs
	• The approval by the head of the branch office (local branch) to establish a business relationship with a PEP does not constitute approval by senior management level. In addition, there is no requirement to require such approval when an existing customer becomes a PEP
	• Banking and foreign exchange institutions are not required to take reasonable measures to establish the source of wealth of customers or beneficial owners identified as PEPs
	• The absence of STRs related to foreign PEPs and the low number of STRs submitted on domestic PEPs suggest a lack of effectiveness of the system in place
Austria (3rd follow-up, 2014)	• Some shortcomings in the requirements concerning PEPs (DNFBPs)
	• The absence of AML/CFT requirements for all casinos operating in Austria
	• No legal framework for CDD requirements concerning Internet casinos
	• No rules to determine the basis upon which Internet casinos are subject to AML/CFT requirements
	• No legal obligation for casinos to perform CDD for all customers when they engage in financial transactions equal to or above EUR 3000
	• No specific review for higher-risk categories and no enhanced due diligence for higher-risk categories of customers, such as nonresident customers
	• R.12 (Deficiency 7): No legal obligation to record keeping of transactions
	• R.12 (Deficiency 8): No enforceable requirements for Internet casinos in order to address the specific risks related to non-face-to-face transactions
	• R.12 (Deficiency 9): No appropriate management systems to determine whether a potential customer, a customer, or the beneficial owner is a PEP
Bahamas (3rd follow-up, 2011) Barbados (7th follow-up, 2012)	No information provided in both follow-up reports
Canada (6th follow-up, 2014)	Requirements for financial institutions in relation to politically exposed foreign persons (PEFPs) were introduced in June 2008 through amendments to the PCMLTFA and PCMLTFR, which specified the enhanced customer identification and due diligence requirements for this category of clients

Continued

Table 15.3 Partially compliant jurisdictions—cont'd

Jurisdiction (mutual evaluation reports (MER)/follow-up reports, year)	Factors underlying a rating of noncompliance
Czech Republic (4th follow-up, 2011)	• Does not include certain types of PEPs included in the glossary of definitions in the methodology • No requirement to consider whether a beneficial owner may also be a PEP • Lack of comprehension in some cases of what constitutes a politically exposed person • Approval is not specified to be at the level of senior management • Limited effectiveness and implementation
Dominican Republic (7th follow-up, 2012)	No information provided in the follow-up report
Germany (MER, 2010) Guatemala (2nd follow-up, 2011) Guyana (2nd follow-up, 2012) Holy See (MER, 2012)	Provisions do not apply to foreign PEPs residing in Germany No information provided in the follow-up reports • The requirement to put in place appropriate risk management systems to determine whether the counterpart is a politically exposed person does not extend to the case of the beneficial owner • Beyond the requirement to establish the source of funds of customers and beneficial owners identified as PEPs, there is no express requirement to establish the source of their wealth *Effectiveness* The following requirements have been introduced or clarified too recently to be considered fully effective: • The requirement to apply PEP requirements irrespective of the residence • The requirement to obtain senior management approval, where a customer has been accepted and the customer or beneficial owner is subsequently found to be, or subsequently becomes, a PEP. The requirement to determine a PEP in all instances, irrespective of "risky situations"
Kazakhstan (MER, 2011)	• The requirements set forth in the AML/CFT legislation of Kazakhstan do not apply to consumer credit unions, pawnshops, microcredit organizations, leasing companies, insurance agents, and organizations accepting from public cash as payment for the provided services received by a trustee who acts on behalf and at instructions of a trustor (service provider) under an agency contract, inter alia, via electronic terminals • No identification of existing customers is performed for recording information on them as well as for determining whether they are politically exposed persons

- Measures for enhanced ongoing monitoring of the relationships with PEPs are not developed
- No timeline is established for regular verification of information of customers to identify PEPs among them

Kingdom of Saudi Arabia (MER, 2010)

- Definition of PEPs only covers current and recent PEPs, with no definition of "recent"
- Financing companies are not explicitly required, in addition to performing the CDD measures, to put in place appropriate risk management systems to determine whether a potential customer, a customer, or the beneficial owner is a politically exposed person
- Insurance companies, authorized persons, and financing companies are not explicitly required to seek senior management approval for continuing the relationship in cases where a beneficial owner is subsequently found to be, or subsequently becomes, a PEP
- Insurance companies are not required to determine the source of wealth and source of funds for beneficial owners identified as PEPs, as well as source of wealth for customers identified as PEPs
- Financing companies are not explicitly required to determine source of wealth and source of funds for clients or beneficial owners identified as PEPs
- Inadequate implementation of several components of the due diligence requirements toward PEPs, notably with respect to the risk management systems in place to spot PEPs at insurance companies and money exchange businesses, senior management approval for continuation of business relationship, verification of source of wealth, and enhanced ongoing monitoring

Luxembourg (6th follow-up, 2014)

- Not all financial institutions are covered
- The definition of PEP is not consistent with that of the FATF: not all important public functions and certain direct family members are not covered with the result that the PEP definition in Luxembourg is more restrictive than that of the FATF
- The enhanced due diligence obligation with respect to PEPs applies only to those PEPs who reside outside Luxembourg
- Lack of a legal or regulatory obligation to have a risk management system for determining whether the beneficial owner is a PEP

Continued

Table 15.3 Partially compliant jurisdictions—cont'd

Jurisdiction (mutual evaluation reports (MER)/follow-up reports, year)	Factors underlying a rating of noncompliance
	• Lack of a legal or regulatory obligation to obtain senior management approval before opening an account. Only "high-level" approval is required without this being specified in an enforceable provision
	• There is no obligation to obtain senior management approval to continue a business relationship with a customer who has become a PEP
	• The effectiveness of the system has not been demonstrated, given the lack of obligation to determine whether a PEP is the beneficial owner and the scope of CDD exemptions
Netherlands (2nd follow-up, 2014)	• There is no requirement for institutions to ascertain source of wealth and to identify the beneficial owner when the source of wealth is a PEP
	• The PEP-related requirements do not apply to non-Dutch PEPs resident in the Netherlands
	• The obligation for financial institutions to have risk-based procedures to determine whether a customer is a PEP does not extend to the case of the beneficial owner
	• There is no requirement to obtain senior management approval to continue a business relationship when a customer/beneficial owner becomes a PEP or is found to be a PEP during the course of an already established business relationship
	• The notion of close associate in the explanatory memorandum is limited to those who are "publicly known"
Nicaragua (4th follow-up, 2012)	No information provided in the follow-up report
Niue (MER, 2012)	• There is a definition of a PEP in the guidelines, but this definition is not in line with that provided in the FATF Recommendations
	• There is no requirement to apply the stricter CDD measures to beneficial owners who themselves qualify as a PEP
	• No requirement to obtain senior management approval to continue a business relationship where a customer or beneficial owner has been accepted and is subsequently found to be a PEP
	• Effectiveness not tested
Portugal (Second Biennial, 2010)	• The deficiencies in the implementation of Recommendations 5, 6, and 11 that apply to financial institutions also apply to designated nonfinancial business or profession (DNFBP)
	• There are few implementation measures that clarify the specific obligations of DNFBPs (similar to regulations and circulars for financial institutions)
	• Portugal has not implemented explicit AML/CFT measures concerning PEPs applicable to DNFBPs

Republic of Angola (MER, 2012)	• There is no evidence of risk management systems in financial institutions to enable the identification of foreign PEPs, with the exception of a few private banks
Russia (6th, 2013)	• There is no implementation of the legal rules regarding PEPs • Definition of PEPs does not extend to those who were entrusted with public functions • No requirement for obtaining approval from senior management for existing customers found to be PEPs • Lack of clarity relating to establishing the source of wealth and enhanced ongoing due diligence
Slovak Republic (4th follow-up, 2011)	• No provision to verify if the beneficial owner is PEP in the Slovak law is present • Provisions do not apply to foreign PEPs residing in Slovakia • The definition of PEPs is not sufficiently broad to include all categories of senior government officials • No provision for senior management approval to continue business relationship where the customer subsequently is found to be or becomes PEP

Timor-Leste (MER, 2012)	• Although the account of a customer who is or becomes a PEP is classified as a "high-risk" account, there is no explicit requirement in the law for financial institutions to obtain senior management approval to continue the business relationship when an existing customer becomes a PEP (see criterion 6.2.1)
	• No enforcement of PEP requirements for MTOs, which are not yet regulated or supervised
	• Definition of PEP for nonbank financial institution does not extend to family members, persons, or companies
	• No requirement for no-bank financial institutions to
	  • obtain senior management approval for establishing business relationship with a PEP
	  • obtain senior management approval for existing PEPs to continue the business relationship
	  • take reasonable measures to establish the source of wealth and the source of funds of customers and beneficial owners identified as PEP
	    • conduct enhanced ongoing monitoring on PEPs
	• Effectiveness concerns: doubt as to whether all financial institutions have effective systems to identify foreign PEPs

Tonga (MER, 2010)	• Requirements are set out in other enforceable means, which are only enforceable for a small minority of FIs/cash dealers, albeit the larger financial institutions. • Deficiencies noted within the financial institutions' AML/CFT policies and manuals provided

unclear about how a particular rating was given. It does not appear that there is consistency in the format of mutual evaluation and follow-up reports (e.g., identification of common underlying factors), although there has been a push to improve the quality and consistency of FATF evaluation reports in recent years (Nechaeve, 2013).

Recommendation 1: It is suggested that a uniform and transparent mutual evaluation process and a standard mutual evaluation and follow-up report template be adopted to ensure consistency of approach undertaken by FATF and FATF-style regional bodies and to avoid mutual evaluation reports from being "softened" for political reasons.

Recommendation 2: It would be useful for the international community if there is an online Web site displaying up-to-date FATF compliance (rather than undertaking this exercise manually such as in Choo, 2010, 2013, 2014b, and Johnson, 2008).

15.3 CRYPTOCURRENCIES AND VIRTUAL CURRENCIES AND THEIR POTENTIAL TO BE MISUSED FOR MONEY LAUNDERING

There is a wide range of virtual currencies including cryptocurrencies. The Web site http://coinmarketcap.com/, for example, provides an up-to-date view of 349 cryptocurrencies and virtual currencies in 740 markets (as of June 26, 2014). Bitcoin, one of the most well well-known cryptocurrencies, is a peer-to-peer cryptocurrency that uses a very complex cryptographic algorithm that requires connected network of computers to conduct computationally expensive mathematical operations (Peck, 2012; Velde, 2013). The design of the Bitcoin system ensures that there is no double-spending, without relying on a single authority such as a government and a bank. The currency can be exchanged because all the potential recipients have the means to verify past transactions so that there is no double-spending and validate new ones since all transactions are fully public.

Cryptocurrencies and virtual currencies are unlike buying precious metals such as gold, and they are useful only when they are widely accepted by both consumers and businesses (i.e., an ecosystem). If the user stores the bitcoins on his/her mobile device (e.g., iOS device and a portable hard drive) and the device is lost or stolen, all the bitcoins stored on the device will also be lost. This is somewhat similar to fact in the real world that if a user loses his/her wallet, he/she will also lose the cash in the wallet. Theft of bitcoins can occur due to a rash of reasons, including criminals exploiting technical vulnerabilities of the online virtual currency exchange—as we have seen in the case of Mt Gox (Villar, 2014)—as well as of our computers or mobile devices where the bitcoin software applications are installed. Examples of such malware include Pony, which is a malware designed to compromise virtual currency wallets installed on a phone or a computer. The malware reportedly steals the credentials in order to steal the virtual currencies, including bitcoins (Chechik and Davidi, 2014).

Cryptocurrencies and virtual currencies such as bitcoins do not generally have legal tender status, and the broad acceptance of currencies such as bitcoins does not have a requirement upon any government or country. This is also its weakness. Because of the lack of regulations and oversight, cryptocurrencies and virtual currencies lack consumer protection. For example, a consumer is unlikely to be insured against incidents such as the closure or the compromise of a virtual currency exchange such as Mt Gox (Villar, 2014), unlike users of a traditional banking and financial system. In addition, the value of these currencies is very volatile and such currencies can easily devalue overnight or even over a security incident such as the Mt Gox incident (see Greenberg, 2014).

A number of jurisdictions have recently introduced legislation to regulate such currencies. For example, the US Internal Revenue Service (2014) has recently issued a notice that virtual currencies such as bitcoins will be treated as property for US federal tax purposes. This regulation, according to some commentators, may be a good thing for consumers (Abrams, 2014). Under this new regime, bitcoin users in the United States who lost money due to, say, the collapse of Mt Gox might be able to consider this loss as a capital loss on their tax forms.

According to a report released by the Institute of International Finance (2014, p. 2), several other jurisdictions have also introduced or have plans to introduce legislation to regulate cryptocurrencies and virtual currencies:

> While the German finance ministry has formally acknowledged Bitcoin as a "unit of account" (meaning it can be used for tax and private trading purposes in the country), the German Bundesbank has become the latest big central bank to warn about the risks of Bitcoin, amid rising concerns from regulatory authorities around the world as the virtual currency grows in popularity.
>
> China has banned the country's Bitcoin exchanges from accepting new inflows of cash, putting the virtual currency in danger in its biggest market. Regulators were concerned that people could use Bitcoins to skirt the country's capital controls, and about the wide-spread speculative demand for Bitcoins and potential for a price bubble. However, transaction activity is reportedly continuing, with some exchanges finding ways to work around the controls.
>
> Bitcoin exchanges in India shut down late December 2013, days after the Reserve Bank of India (RBI) warned users of virtual currencies against security and financial risks associated with them. The RBI stated that it fears users could unintentionally breach anti-money laundering and financing of terrorism laws; it continues to study the status of Bitcoin under current law.
>
> In July 2013, Thailand banned the buying and selling of Bitcoins, as well as sending or receiving the currency from other jurisdiction.
>
> Bitcoin-friendly sovereigns such as Denmark, Poland, and Singapore are currently taking a laissez-faire approach claiming that no regulation is needed presently, though the issue will be revisited in the future.
>
> Norway classifies Bitcoin not as money but rather as an asset subject to capital gains tax.

In addition to consumer protection, financial stability, monetary policy, and taxation concerns, a policy area of concern to governments is the potential for cryptocurrencies and virtual currencies to be used in money laundering and terrorist financing and the financing of illegal activities (e.g., bribery of government officials).

To disguise the origins of illicit proceeds, individuals involved in bribery or corruption can perform a series of business transactions prior to integrating the corruption proceeds into the legitimate financial system. The money laundering process is typically segmented into three stages, as explained by Choo (2013):

- In the *placement* stage, the money launderer introduces corruption proceeds into the financial system or acquires nonmonetary instruments of value such as art and antiques, precious metals, and cryptocurrencies and virtual currencies.
- After the corruption proceeds have entered the financial system or used to acquire nonmonetary instruments of value, the money launderer may engage in a series of transactions to distance the funds from their source. In this *layering* stage, the funds might be channeled through the purchase of cryptocurrencies and virtual currencies or by transferring money electronically through a series of cryptocurrencies and virtual currency accounts. The money launderer might also seek to disguise the transfers as payments for goods or services, thus giving them a legitimate appearance. Money launderer can also recruit individuals or establish front companies to purchase cryptocurrencies and virtual currencies under the reporting thresholds in countries where such currencies are regulated to avoid triggering identification or reporting requirements.
- Integration: Disguised funds (cleaned money) would appear to have been legally earned, and it is extremely difficult to discern between legal wealth and illegal wealth at this stage.

As of March 2014, Singapore (one of the key financial hubs in East Asia) announced that Singapore-based virtual currency intermediaries will be regulated to address potential money laundering and terrorist financing risks. Under this new regime, virtual currency exchanges, if they are based in Singapore, are required to verify the identities of their customers—in short, conduct customer due diligence (CDD) and know your customer (KYC) and report any suspicious transactions to the Suspicious Transaction Reporting Office, the country's financial intelligence unit. In other words, the requirements will be similar to those already imposed on money changers and remittance businesses that undertake cash transactions in the country (Monetary Authority of Singapore, 2014).

The general risk factors and associated money laundering and terrorism financing risks can be summarized using the risk categorization developed for mobile payment/money by the GSMA and World Bank (see Table 15.4, adapted from Chatain et al., 2011).

15.4 THE WAY FORWARD: A CONCEPTUAL INTELLIGENCE-LED AML/CTF STRATEGY

In investigating the potential criminal exploitation of information and communications technologies (ICT), particularly new payment methods such as cryptocurrencies and

Table 15.4 Money laundering and terrorism financing risk categorization for cryptocurrencies and virtual currencies

General risk factors	Potential exploitation of vulnerabilities at each stage		
	Placement	Layering	Integration
Near anonymity	Cryptocurrencies and virtual currencies and/or accounts can be opened by criminals and their associates	Suspicious names, particularly if money mules are involved, cannot be flagged by system, making it a safe zone for known criminals and terrorists	Allows for cashing out of proceeds of crime and/or legitimately obtained funds for terrorism financing activities at automated teller machines (ATMs), etc. In addition, cryptocurrencies and virtual currencies can easily be passed on to anonymous individuals who are the (true) beneficial owner and whose names do not appear on the account
Elusiveness and high negotiability	Criminals can structure the proceeds of crime into multiple accounts or multiple cryptocurrencies and virtual currencies to avoid triggering reporting requirements (if applicable)	Multiple transactions can be performed to confuse the money trail and obscure the true origin of funds	Funds from multiple accounts or multiple cryptocurrencies and virtual currencies can be withdrawn at the same time
Real-time transaction and utility and withdrawal of funds	Proceeds of crime can be quickly deposited and transferred to another account or currency in another country	Transactions occur in real time, allowing for little time to stop them if there is a suspicion of money laundering and/or terrorist financing	Proceeds of crime money can be moved rapidly through the system and withdrawn from another account in another country

virtual currencies, it is important to consider a wide variety of information in order to provide a broader picture to be used by stakeholders and decision makers in different sectors. One potential approach is the intelligence-led policing model where criminal intelligence (e.g., of organized crime and corruption activities) and data analysis are used to provide valuable input to a decision making framework in an effort to reduce, disrupt, and prevent crime through strategies and management (Ratcliffe, 2007).

Figure 15.1 describes a conceptual intelligence-led AML/CTF strategy, adapted from Choo (2014a), to study and understand the complex threat landscape faced by governments, government agencies (e.g., financial intelligence units and AML/CTF regulators), and cryptocurrency and virtual currency providers and intermediaries.

In order to do so, one would need to understand the interplay between the objects (e.g., threat actors such as corrupted individuals seeking to exploit cryptocurrencies and virtual currencies to launder corruption proceeds and victims such as government agencies) and their environment (e.g., technologies, political, geographic, socioeconomic, legal and regulatory, and cultural) and how this interplay is further shaped and can be integrated as part of a governance and risk management strategy that should evolve as circumstances require.

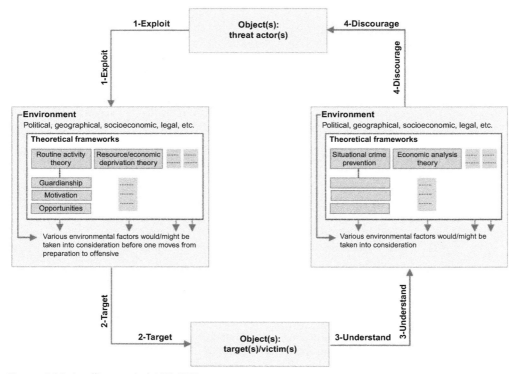

Figure 15.1 Intelligence-led AML/CTF strategy.

Any effective AML/CTF strategy should be a dynamic document to be regularly reviewed by stakeholders. Therefore, the fundamental aim of the conceptual intelligence-led AML/CTF strategy is to ensure the effective use of up-to-date intelligence (broadly defined) in a combined top-down/bottom-up approach to

- provide situational awareness;
- make careful predictions about future trends in ICT, particularly new payment methods including cryptocurrencies and virtual currencies, scale of the threat landscape at both localized and international levels, the impact of corruption, and the potential for ICT to be exploited to launder corruption proceeds on the society; and
- ensure that appropriate controls (e.g., resources and investment) are put in place to ensure that the criminal exploitation of ICT, particularly new payment methods, is minimized.

Future work would include a multimethod approach from different disciplines and different countries that would provide a strong quantitative cum qualitative balance and deliver both theoretical and evidence-based contributions, by addressing the following research questions:

1. What is the nature of corruption and money laundering/terrorism financing threats and the emerging trends and challenges, and how can we measure corruption, money laundering, and terrorism financing using academically robust methods?
2. What academic theories can be collectively used to explain and mitigate corruption and money laundering/terrorism financing threats and modify the environment (see Figure 15.1) to reduce the opportunities for corruption and money laundering/terrorism financing activities to occur and enhance policing?
3. What (policy) strategies, techniques, and (operational) best practices can be collectively used to explain and mitigate corruption and money laundering/terrorism financing threats and modify the environment to reduce the opportunities for corruption and money laundering/terrorism financing threats activities to occur and enhance policing?

A combination of theoretical and evidence-based methodologies from different disciplines will need to be adopted in order to answer the above research questions. Example research activities include the following:

Research activity 1: Policy discourse and analysis of the different theories, strategies, techniques, and best practices will be the key theoretical methodologies. Policy discourse analysis is an approach based on the work of French philosopher Michel Foucault (Foucault, 1982) and subsequently expanded by well-known critical linguist Norman Fairclough (Fairclough, 1995). While there are variations of this methodology, this approach is deemed useful for policy and regulatory research because it does not only analyze the crux of a policy position or directive but also seeks to delve beneath the intents or spirit of a clause or position to uncover the actual effect(s) and outcome(s). In other words, policy discourse analysis can cut through to the core of regulatory positions and determine feasibility and practicability.

Research activity 2: Online survey and panel study involving in-depth interviews, round tables, and focus groups with key stakeholders in countries across a broad geographic spread (e.g., Asia Pacific, North America, and Europe) will gauge change and monitor emerging corruption and money laundering/terrorism financing trends and review prevalent risk assessment metrics and mitigation models. This would also include a comprehensive review of current sources of data and research initiative, so that we could contribute to the development of clear national and international definitions and procedures for the collection of data on corruption and money laundering/terrorism financing threats and activities.

REFERENCES

Abrams, R., 2014. I.R.S. takes a position on bitcoin: it's property. NYTimes (25 March). http://dealbook. nytimes.com/2014/03/25/i-r-s-says-bitcoin-should-be-considered-property-not-currency/(last accessed 26.06.14).

Associated Press, 2014. Former Chinese provincial official accused of accepting vast amounts of jade in bribes. Fox News (7 January). http://www.foxnews.com/world/2014/01/07/former-chinese-provincial-official-accused-accepting-vast-amounts-jade-in/(last accessed 25.06.14).

BBC, 2014. Israel ex-PM Ehud Olmert jailed for six years for bribery (13 May 2014). http://www.bbc.com/ news/world-middle-east-27387568.

Chatain, P.L., Zerzan, A., Noor, W., Dannaoui, N., de Koker, L., 2011. Protecting Mobile Money: Against Financial Crimes Global Policy Challenges and Solutions. The International Bank for Reconstruction and Development/The World Bank, Washington, DC.

Chechik, D., Davidi, A.F., 2014. Look what I found: Pony is after your coins! SpiderLabs (24 February). http://blog.spiderlabs.com/2014/02/look-what-i-found-pony-is-after-your-coins.html (last accessed 28.06.14).

Choo, K.K.R., 2010. Challenges in dealing with politically exposed persons. Trends Issues Crime Crim. Justice 386, 1–6.

Choo, K.K.R., 2013. New payment methods: a review of 2010-2012 FATF mutual evaluation reports. Comput. Secur. 36, 12–26.

Choo, K.K.R., 2014a. A conceptual interdisciplinary plug-and-play cyber security framework. In: Kaur, H., Tao, X. (Eds.), ICTs and the Millennium Development Goals—A United Nations Perspective. Springer, New York, USA, pp. 81–99.

Choo, K.K.R., 2014b. Designated non-financial businesses and professionals: a review and analysis of recent financial action task force on money laundering mutual evaluation reports. Secur. J. 27 (1), 1–26.

Fairclough, N., 1995. Critical Discourse Analysis: The Critical Study of Language. Longman, London.

FBI, 2014. U.S. freezes more than $458 million stolen by former Nigerian dictator in largest kleptocracy forfeiture action ever brought in the U.S. Media release 5 March. http://www.fbi.gov/ washingtondc/press-releases/2014/u.s.-freezes-more-than-458-million-stolen-by-former-nigerian-dictator-in-largest-kleptocracy-forfeiture-action-ever-brought-in-the-u.s (last accessed 25.06.14).

Financial Action Task Force (FATF), 2004. The Forty Recommendations. FATF/OECD, Paris.

Financial Action Task Force (FATF), 2012. International Standards on Combating Money Laundering and the Financing of Terrorism & Proliferation: The FATF Recommendations. FATF/OECD, Paris.

Financial Action Task Force (FATF), 2013. Money Laundering and Terrorist Financing Through Trade in Diamonds. FATF/OECD, Paris.

Foucault, M., 1982. Afterword: the subject and power. In: Dreyfus, H., Rabinow, P. (Eds.), Michel Foucault: Beyond Structuralism and Hermeneutics. Harvester Wheatsheaf, New York, pp. 208–226.

Global Financial Integrity, 2013. Illicit Financial Flows from Developing Countries: 2002–2011. Global Financial Integrity, Washington, DC.

Greenberg, A., 2014. Bitcoin's price plummets as Mt. Gox goes dark, with massive hack rumored. Forbes (25 February), http://www.forbes.com/sites/andygreenberg/2014/02/25/bitcoins-price-plummets-as-mt-gox-goes-dark-with-massive-hack-rumored/.

Hellman, J.S., Jones, G., Kaufmann, D., 2003. Seize the state, seize the day: state capture and influence in transition economies. J. Comp. Econ. 31 (4), 751–773.

Institute of International Finance, 2014. Bitcoin—Tulip mania or revolution. www.iif.com/cem201401_1. pdf (last accessed 26.06.14).

International Consortium of Investigative Journalists, 2014. Leaked records reveal offshore holdings of China's elite. http://www.icij.org/offshore/leaked-records-reveal-offshore-holdings-chinas-elite (last accessed 25.06.14).

Johnson, J., 2008. Third round FATF mutual evaluations indicate declining compliance. JMLC 11 (1), 47–66.

Monetary Authority of Singapore, 2014. MAS to regulate virtual currency intermediaries for money laundering and terrorist financing risks. Media release 13 March. http://www.mas.gov.sg/news-and-publications/press-releases/2014/mas-to-regulate-virtual-currency-intermediaries-for-money-laundering-and-terrorist-financing-risks.aspx (last accessed 25.06.14).

Nechaeve, V., 2013. Commitment to improve AML/CFT in the MENA region. In: Speech at the 18th Middle East and North Africa Financial Action Task Force (MENAFATF) Plenary Meeting, Kingdom of Bahrain. http://www.fatf-gafi.org/topics/fatfgeneral/documents/speech-menafatf-dec-13.html (last accessed 25.06.14).

Peck, M.E., 2012. Bitcoin: the cryptoanarchists' answer to cash. IEEE Spectr. 49 (6), 50–56.

Ratcliffe, J., 2007. Integrated Intelligence and Crime Analysis: Enhanced Information Management for Law Enforcement Leaders, second ed. Police Foundation, Washington, DC.

Transparency International, 2013a. UN Convention Against Corruption Progress Report 2013. Transparency International, Berlin, Germany.

Transparency International, 2013. Corruption perceptions index 2013. http://files.transparency.org/content/download/700/3007/file/2013_CPIBrochure_EN.pdf (last accessed 25.06.14).

U.S. Internal Revenue Service, 2014. Notice 2014–21. http://www.irs.gov/pub/irs-drop/n-14-21.pdf (last accessed 25.06.14).

Velde, F.R., 2013. Bitcoin: a primer. Chicago Fed Lett. 317, 1–4.

Villar, R., 2014. Bitcoin exchange Mt. Gox goes dark in blow to virtual currency. Reuters (25 February). http://www.reuters.com/article/2014/02/25/us-mtgox-website-idUSBREA1O07920140225 (last accessed 28.06.14).

Walters, J., Budd, C., Smith, R.G., Choo, K.K.R., McCusker, R., Rees, D., 2012. Anti-money laundering and counter-terrorism financing across the globe: a comparative study of regulatory action. In: Research and Public Policy Series No. 113, Australian Institute of Criminology, Canberra, ACT.

CHAPTER 16

A Light Touch of Regulation for Virtual Currencies

Lam Pak Nian, David LEE Kuo Chuen
Sim Kee Boon Institute for Financial Economics, Singapore Management University, Singapore

Contents

16.1 INTRODUCTION

The wave of decentralized virtual currencies, especially Bitcoin and its derivatives, has received attention by regulators and entrepreneurs alike. The attention is split among two popular narratives (Financial Action Task Force, 2014): excitement, with virtual currencies being the future of financial innovation, and caution, with virtual currencies

Handbook of Digital Currency

providing a powerful tool to facilitate the activity of criminals, money launderers, and terrorist financiers beyond law enforcement. This chapter considers the virtual currency landscape from a market supervisory perspective. First, Bitcoin is introduced as a type of virtual currency known as a decentralized cryptocurrency, and the main participants in such a market are identified. A brief on the legitimate uses and potentially regulable risks of virtual currencies is then provided before the wide-ranging spectrum of existing regulatory approaches and opinions is surveyed. Finally, this chapter concludes by recommending a light-touch approach to the regulation of cryptocurrencies like Bitcoins. While Bitcoin will be the most frequently used example in this chapter, the issues and ideas discussed will also apply to many of the other decentralized virtual cryptocurrencies similar to Bitcoin.

16.1.1 Virtual currency

There are many definitions of virtual currency, but we shall adhere closely to the criteria used by most regulators. Broadly, virtual currency (1) is a digital representation of value; (2) functions as a currency, with the three requirements of being a medium of exchange, unit of account, and store of value accordingly; but (3) is currently not legal tender in any jurisdiction (Financial Action Task Force, 2014). However, some jurisdictions, especially those with some form of regulation on virtual currencies, have more specific definitions. Virtual currency is usually not legal tender because it is not fiat currency, that is, the money that is issued by a particular country. Virtual money that transacts within the virtual world and not convertible to fiat currency is not, in strict legal sense, defined as virtual currency. It should also not be confused with e-money, which is a digital transfer mechanism for fiat currency (Financial Action Task Force, 2014), of which PayPal is an example. The most well-known virtual currency, with the largest trading volume and market capitalization (defined as price of each unit multiplied by the total number of units of issued currency), is Bitcoin. As a virtual currency, Bitcoin is also known for its open convertibility with fiat currency; indeed, it is this feature of Bitcoin that is often exploited at physical points of sale to make Bitcoin a viable payment method.

16.1.2 Decentralized cryptocurrency

Bitcoin is a type of virtual currency that is also commonly referred to as a decentralized cryptocurrency. It is *decentralized* in the sense that there is neither a *central* administering authority nor *central* monitoring, while the *crypto-* prefix refers to its incorporation of principles of *cryptography* in its operation. Cryptography is key to Bitcoin (pun unintended)—Bitcoin uses public and private keys to authenticate transactions, and the proof-of-work system used to verify transactions and maintain the block chain depends on cryptography. While Bitcoin is the first major cryptocurrency, Bitcoin alternatives, called altcoins, have mushroomed in recent years. These altcoins are essentially derivatives of Bitcoin, their developers having taken advantage of the open-source nature of Bitcoin as a base from which to code. Altcoins often offer improvements on the Bitcoin model based on different policy objectives. For example, some of the modifications in Litecoin over Bitcoin are faster block generation, which at 2.5 min is four times faster than Bitcoin, and an intentionally different proof-of-work algorithm, using scrypt, to shift mining from application-specific integrated circuits (ASICs) back to the usual central processing units (CPUs) in most computers today.

16.1.3 Market participants in a virtual currency system

There are various participants in a virtual currency system, some of whom operate entirely within the system, such as an administrator, user, miner, and wallet provider, while others, like an exchange, operate as an interface between the virtual currency and other currencies. It is important to understand the characteristics of the participants involved in order to, if desired, better regulate the system.

Administrator. An administrator is a person who issues the virtual currency, establishes the rules for its use, and may also redeem the currency. There is no central administrator, however, for Bitcoin, as the rules for its use is subject to consensus-based modification in the network, and there is neither a single issuer nor redeemer of the currency. The party closest to an administrator in Bitcoin is likely to be the pseudonymous Satoshi Nakamoto, who created the cryptocurrency and its rules of operation with the publication of his paper (Nakamoto, 2008). However, he is not known to be able to exert any other form of control as the network runs on its own according to a decentralized, consensus-based model. However, there is an identified group of core developers, but they are not considered at his moment as responsible administrator. Neither is the open-source software an entity that is considered as administrating in the legal sense. The current interpretation is that the nodes, the software, and the core development team are not deemed to be in control of the system.

User. A user is a person who obtains virtual currency for personal uses, which include purchasing real or virtual goods and services, making personal fund transfers, and holding as a personal investment. In computing terms, this is most similar to an end user. In Bitcoin, users often purchase them with fiat currency from an exchange, receive them from providing real or virtual goods and services, or obtain them through participating in mining.

Miner. A miner is a person who participates in a decentralized virtual currency network by doing the heavy processing for the network. In a way, they are the backbone of a decentralized cryptocurrency like Bitcoins. Miners run special software, often on special hardware, to solve complex mathematical problems in a distributed proof system with the objective of verifying transactions, recording them onto a ledger known as the block chain, possibly for a fee or self-generated reward in Bitcoins. Miners may be end users themselves, or they may be a business entity seeking to profit from mining through keeping the fees or rewards as investments or through exchanging them for a commission.

Wallet: A wallet is a means of holding, storing, and transferring virtual currency, much like a physical wallet holding cash. It is usually based on a software application on either a computer or mobile device. A wallet must be kept securely because it holds a user's private keys, which are essential to a user's access to his or her Bitcoins. Instead of maintaining a wallet by himself or herself, end users often turn to a wallet provider who provides a user-friendly interface to the wallet, likely with the ease of access to spend, transfer, and obtain more Bitcoins from an exchange and with matters of security of the keys handled by the wallet provider.

The few participants outlined above are not an exhaustive list. As more entrepreneurs see the potential of virtual currencies like Bitcoins, more entities may participate in a given system, possibly developing products and services either to increase ease of use or to avoid regulatory scrutiny.

16.2 LEGITIMATE USES

The genesis of Bitcoin was borne with low transaction costs in mind (Nakamoto, 2008). Virtual currencies like Bitcoins therefore have huge potential in improving the efficiency of payments, which are traditionally centrally processed by financial institutions at a high price of providing the payment processing service and at a high cost of maintaining their centralized payment infrastructure. Using Bitcoin is currently cheaper than using traditional credit and debit cards (Financial Action Task Force, 2014). However, if the mining costs continue to rise, then the entire system as a whole can be costly to maintain from an administrative perspective. Businesses and users, however, do not view the entire system costs as input of their decision making. In terms of a transaction fee or mining costs, the Bitcoin system is still considered cheap to use.

The low transaction cost also facilitates micropayments (Lam, 2014). This allows businesses to monetize very low-cost goods and services, like music downloads, at a more appropriate and lower price than present, especially after eliminating the higher transaction costs with traditional payment methods like credit cards.

The decentralized cryptocurrency concept also has the potential for further innovation, particularly in the financial services industry. Being a data-driven platform, Bitcoin technology may be adapted for the secure transfer of other types of data, like stocks or bets, in the future (Brito, 2013).

Regulators need to consider the legitimate uses of virtual currencies carefully, especially to ensure that regulatory requirements do not destroy the advantages and uses of virtual currencies like Bitcoins while still controlling the risks. Preexisting law and regulation did not envision a technology like Bitcoin, so there are many aspects that lie in a legal gray area.

16.3 POTENTIALLY REGULATED RISKS
16.3.1 Counterparty risk in a virtual, decentralized system

Transactions in a decentralized cryptocurrency like Bitcoins are handled by many parties without centralized control. In Bitcoin, a single transaction is broadcast to the entire network of users, of whom the miners then compete to process it in the shortest possible time. It is difficult to pin liability for counterparty risk on these miners, despite them being the very parties who have undertaken the processing work.

However, it is also clear that payment transactions, whether using legal tender or not, do not operate in a complete legal vacuum. The use of virtual currencies as a means of payment for goods and services, if agreed upon, is likely to fulfill requirements for contracts, whether as good consideration or through mutual expression of intent. As the development of the law often lags behind novel technological developments, there has yet to be a clear holding on these issues.

16.3.2 Consumer protection: loss and theft

A major criticism against virtual currencies like Bitcoins, or indeed any novel type of currency, is the risk of loss. There are two possible types of losses: First, a user may lose his private keys, which means access to those Bitcoins will be lost forever. Second, virtual currencies, and especially their service providers, are vulnerable to hacker attacks, as seen in the example of Bitcoin exchange in Mt Gox, with losses amounting to USD 500 million (Federal Council, 2014). Users who poorly secure their computers and Bitcoin wallets may also risk their private keys and Bitcoins getting stolen. Other possible risks arise from information asymmetry: users using virtual currencies as investments may suffer losses as a result of unreliable price and exchange rate data, or worse still, as a result of manipulation or fraudulent schemes. There are therefore considerable risks for consumers and investors dealing with virtual currencies.

16.3.3 Financial crime

Like fiat currency, virtual currencies can be used for both lawful and unlawful activities. Black markets for illegal goods and services may choose to accept Bitcoins as a means of payment. For example, the now-defunct Silk Road website, used to trade drugs and counterfeit goods, only accepted Bitcoins as a payment method.

With fast transactions and pseudoanonymity, the use of virtual currencies may also stymie legal efforts in confiscation of assets because enforcement authorities may not be able to trace particular transactions or target-specific entities. The pseudoanonymous nature of virtual currencies may also present difficulties in identification and investigation.

16.3.4 Risk of facilitating money laundering and terrorist financing

Openly convertible virtual currencies like Bitcoins are also vulnerable to the risk of money laundering and terrorist financing. The initial exchange of fiat currency from criminal proceeds into Bitcoins fulfills the first stage of classic money laundering. Various transfer transactions can then be made within Bitcoin, often using new Bitcoin addresses for each transaction, to layer the transactions. Finally, the illicit funds may be exchanged back into fiat currency, laundered, and integrated into the economy. The layering efforts are also useful to terrorist financiers in transmitting money to terrorists with limited regulatory scrutiny. In particular, there are fears among regulators that if the mining activities are penetrated by organizations that conduct illicit activities, the newly mined coin by unknown miners can be cashed out via the fiat system, thus making detection and tracing of money laundering a much harder task.

16.4 SURVEY OF REGULATORY APPROACHES IN TACKLING THESE RISKS

With the fast development and spread of virtual currencies, countries are beginning to consider the regulation of virtual currencies like Bitcoins and alternative coins (altcoins). However, there is neither comprehensive regulation nor uniformity of approaches. There has been commentary that the regulatory situation is similar to the uncertainty faced by other new technologies in the past, like Voice over Internet Protocol (VoIP) (Brito and Castillo, 2013). The US Federal Communications Commission grappled with the issue of regulation, especially with the original laws then having envisioned only voice communications over a traditional telephone network. The experience with VoIP is similar to the extent that VoIP also competed with a highly regulated legacy network. The US lawmakers and regulators later clarified the regulatory gray area for VoIP without "saddling the new technology with the legacy regulatory burden" intended for a monopoly service (Brito and Castillo, 2013). This allowed VoIP to flourish, being a less expensive competitor to a stagnant monopoly in the telephony market. It has been suggested that the policymakers should aim for a similar achievement with Bitcoin.

Bitcoin has the various properties that do not allow it to fit existing regulatory definitions of electronic payments, currencies, commodities, etc. (Brito and Castillo, 2013). Below is a suggested nonexhaustive summary of the range of regulatory responses that Bitcoin has received.

Spectrum of regulatory approaches

Restrictive					Permissive
Restrictive regulation	Participation discouraged	Regulate under existing structures	Encouragement with self-regulation	Active engagement for coexistence	Laissez-faire or no regulation
• China • Russia	• European Banking Authority	• The United States: FinCEN and NY's BitLicense • Singapore • Canada	• The United Kingdom	• Ireland's Gareth Murphy	• Australia • Brazil

Lack of international uniformity

16.4.1 Restrictive regulation

China has one of the most restrictive practices against virtual currencies like Bitcoins. In late 2013, its central bank and government agencies issued a joint statement requiring that all financial institutions cease all services involving Bitcoins (People's Bank of China, 2013). The government predicates this on the basis that Bitcoins is not a currency in China. Prior to these restrictions, the trade in Bitcoins was growing in China, with a 500% jump in value of a bitcoin in the month prior to the announcement (Hill, 2013). Following the announcement, the Bitcoin market reacted negatively, resulting in a fall in value from USD 1200 to USD 830. The government's restrictions also spread through the market in China, with online marketplace websites like Taobao also clamping down on Bitcoins. Taobao subsequently banned trade in bitcoins, Bitcoin tutorials, and mining software and hardware on its platform (Taobao, 2014). These restrictions, however, do not necessarily mean that Bitcoins is no longer used in China; rather, it likely means that its use is now driven underground.

Similarly, in February 2014, Russia's general prosecutor declared that the ruble was the only official currency and that using "money substitutes" such as bitcoins is illegal (Ostroukh, 2014). The central bank had also warned that using Bitcoins to pay for goods and services or exchanging it into fiat currency could be construed as money laundering and terrorist financing. However, the central bank's highly restrictive stance has now softened; in a response to a letter from a private citizen, the Bank of Russia now says that the central bank will be observing the situation while not rejecting these "instruments" (Ostroukh, 2014).

16.4.2 Discourage participation to allow time to develop comprehensive regulation

European central authorities have been interested in virtual currencies like bitcoins for quite a few years. In 2012, the European Central Bank issued an exploratory report on virtual currencies. The report defined virtual currency as a type of unregulated, digital money, which is issued and usually controlled by its developers and used and accepted among the members of a specific virtual community. Depending on their interaction with traditional, "real" money and the real economy, virtual currency schemes can be classified into three types (European Central Bank, 2012).

Type 1 is used to refer to closed virtual currency schemes, basically used in an online game.

Type 2 virtual currency schemes have a unidirectional flow (usually an inflow); that is, there is a conversion rate for purchasing the virtual currency, which can subsequently be used not only to buy virtual goods and services but also exceptionally to buy real goods and services.

Type 3 virtual currency schemes have bidirectional flows, that is, the virtual currency in this respect acts like any other convertible currency, with two exchange rates (buy and sell), which can subsequently be used not only to buy virtual goods and services but also to purchase real goods and services.

More recently, in July 2014, the European Banking Authority (EBA) issued its considered opinion on virtual currencies. From its perspective as a prudential banking policy authority for the European Union, the EBA highlighted a lengthy list of risks to virtual currency participants, existing financial institutions, and regulators (European Banking Authority, 2014). The EBA opinion concluded that in the short term, only the certain risks that arise during the interaction between virtual currencies and regulated financial institutions are able to be regulated. These presently regulable risks would include the risk of money laundering and financial crime, contagion risk to conventional payment systems, and user-related informational risks. For these risks, the EBA has recommended that existing financial institutions should be discouraged from dealing with virtual currencies, thereby "shielding" them (European Banking Authority, 2014) while at the same time mandating that virtual currency exchanges comply with anti-money laundering and counter terrorist financing requirements.

The EBA prefers this discourage-to-shield approach so that it has time to formulate a comprehensive regulatory model to deal with virtual currencies in the long term. The issued opinion makes it seem that the EBA wants to regulate virtual currencies by addressing the risks similar to those faced by regulated financial services. The long-term EBA proposal is based on identifying certain virtual currency participants as "scheme governance authorities" who will be accountable to regulators. The targeted participants will then be required to fulfill many regulatory requirements similar to those faced by existing regulated financial services. For a start, the EBA recommends mandatory incorporation of scheme governance authorities and market participants. They will then be subject to capital requirements, payment guarantees and refunds, and customer due diligence requirements, among many others.

16.4.3 Regulate under existing structures

The United States has been regulating service providers who deal with virtual currencies like bitcoins since 2013 (Lam, 2014). As US regulatory efforts were a hot topic at the time of writing, the information on US regulation in this subsection is only introductory for brevity, with more details of US regulation explored in a separate section in this chapter.

The main risks targeted by its Financial Crimes Enforcement Network (FinCEN) are the criminal risks, especially the money laundering and terrorist financing risks. In March 2013, FinCEN issued interpretative guidance applying money services business (MSB) regulation to virtual currency businesses, requiring them to also register, report, and keep records of transactions and customers (FinCEN, 2013).

In terms of consumer protection, the Government Accountability Office's report issued in May 2014 criticizing the government's lack of efforts in protecting American consumers (Government Accountability Office, 2014) may spur greater emphasis by federal agencies on protecting its consumers from theft and fraud in virtual currencies, although there are no specific calls for greater regulation (Quentson, 2014).

Of note is that the US state of New York has begun to consider creating a "BitLicense" for Bitcoin businesses (New York State Department of Financial Services, 2014a), the details of which are beginning to emerge. The proposed regulations have broad coverage, having defined "virtual currency" as "any type of digital unit that is used as a medium of exchange or a form of digitally stored value or that is incorporated into payment system technology" (New York State Department of Financial Services, 2014b). A license is required for receiving or transmitting virtual currency on behalf of customers, storing virtual currency on behalf of customers, buying and selling virtual currency as a customer business, performing retail conversation services or controlling, and administering or issuing a virtual currency. Consumers or merchants who use virtual currency solely for the purchase or sale of goods and services and firms chartered under the New York banking law to conduct exchange services and approved by the superintendent to engage in virtual currency business activity are exempted from licensing. The main changes to the virtual currency landscape are that a license is now required and that licensees will have to comply with standards intended to, among others, prevent money laundering, ensure consumer protection, and enhance cyber security (New York State Department of Financial Services, 2014a,b).

Elsewhere, regulators in Singapore and Canada are likely moving toward an approach similar to that of the federal government of the United States, but they are likely to focus on the money laundering and terrorist financing risks for a start.

In March 2014, Singapore's central bank announced that while it does not regulate Bitcoin per se, it intends to address the risks of money laundering and terrorist financing by requiring "virtual currency intermediaries that buy, sell or facilitate the exchange of virtual currencies for real currencies to verify the identities of their customers and report suspicious transactions to the Suspicious Transaction Reporting Office" (Monetary Authority of Singapore, 2014a). These "intermediaries" were left undefined, although operators of exchanges and vending machines are especially targeted. The central bank has also issued alerts about virtual currencies on its financial literacy website to help consumers make informed decisions about the risks involved and protect themselves (Monetary Authority of Singapore, 2014b).

More recently, in June 2014, Canada has also started to regulate virtual currencies for criminal risks, with the amendment to the Canadian anti-money laundering and counter-terrorist financing laws bringing registration, reporting, and recordkeeping requirements onto businesses "dealing in virtual currencies" (Economic Action Plan, 2014 Act, No. 1, 2014).

16.4.4 Encouragement with self-regulation

The regulatory atmosphere in the United Kingdom is considerably more relaxed at present, with no formal requirements imposed by its financial conduct regulator. This hands-off approach has not stopped many Bitcoin businesses operating in the United Kingdom from self-regulation; many have voluntarily imposed their own anti-money laundering and countering of terrorist financing measures (Jankelewitz, 2014). In an unusual step, the government also appears to be encouraging further innovation in virtual currencies, having also met with industry representatives to identify the potential ways in lowering the barriers to entry and growth for innovative businesses like those dealing in virtual currencies (Hajdarbegovic, 2014). One suggestion that is presently under consideration is a tax exemption for income from cryptocurrencies like Bitcoins.

16.4.5 Active engagement for multicurrency coexistence

Perhaps, the most optimistic view of the future of virtual currencies comes from Gareth Murphy, a representative from Ireland's central bank. In July 2014, he suggested the possibility of a coexistence of multiple currencies in a financial system during his speech at the Bitcoin Finance 2014 Conference and Expo in Dublin (Murphy, 2014). Although his remarks were made in his personal capacity, they were significantly received as he was the world's first government-backed representative to speak at a virtual currency conference (Rizzo, 2014a,b).

He had suggested that rapid advancement in information technology and the various benefits of virtual currencies meant that they could evolve well in a multicurrency economy. At the same time, he emphasized that the monopoly in economic activity held by existing financial institutions and central banks is challenged by virtual currencies. In particular, virtual currencies directly challenge a central bank's ability to collect data and set monetary policy, exchange rates, and the price of credit. Finally, he advocated that these issues of challenge were unique to virtual currencies and the industry would do well to actively address regulatory concerns instead of having a cat-and-mouse chase.

In Murphy's eyes, therefore, the future of virtual currencies will be found in active engagement and coexistence among stakeholders—the virtual currency industry, the regulators, and traditional financial institutions—with each continuing in their niche areas while meaningfully coexisting with one another to the betterment of the economy.

16.4.6 Laissez-faire or no regulation yet

At the other end of the spectrum, there are countries that have yet to take a firm stand on the regulation of cryptocurrencies and have therefore left them unregulated while also often still keeping the door to regulation open.

Australia at present does not regulate virtual currencies, although its financial literacy website has consumer alerts on them (Australian Securities and Investments Commission, 2014). It is expected, however, for the government to eventually explain its tax treatment of virtual currencies and its future plans for regulation (Federal Council, 2014).

Brazil, on the other hand, has consciously decided not to regulate virtual currencies at this point in time. Although Brazil's law on payments was amended in 2013, with terms like "payment arrangements" and "electronic currency" potentially applying to virtual currencies, the central bank declined to regulate virtual currencies (Banco Central do Brasil, 2014). It explained that virtual currencies like Bitcoins do not pose significant risks to Brazil's economy and therefore does not warrant regulation.

16.4.7 Lack of international uniformity

International bodies have also begun to seriously consider regulating virtual currencies, although much of the discussion centers on the money laundering and terrorist financing risks. The Financial Action Task Force, which deals with anti-money laundering and the countering of terrorist financing, has issued a paper on the subject, but the discussion is only beginning. The International Monetary Fund, which deals with currencies issued by nation states, is said to be unable to recognize virtual currencies like Bitcoins as currencies. Commentators have suggested indirect control as a workaround (Plassaras, 2013), but again, discussions have only just begun.

16.5 HIGHLIGHT ON US REGULATION
16.5.1 FinCEN

FinCEN, in its role in ensuring smart regulation for virtual currency that is not too burdensome but also protects the US financial system from illicit use (Calvery, 2013), has a much narrower definition for virtual currency from the general definition mentioned in the beginning of this chapter. To recap, let us consider the definition in more details before discussing the BitLicense regulatory framework proposed by the New York State Department of Financial Services (NYSDFS).

In a speech before the US Senate, Jennifer Calvery, director of FinCEN explained FinCEN's position:

Virtual currency is a medium of exchange that operates like a currency in some environments but does not have all the attributes of real currency. In particular, virtual currency does not have legal tender status in any jurisdiction. A convertible virtual currency either has an equivalent value in real currency, or acts as a substitute for real currency. In other words, it is a virtual currency that can be exchanged for real currency. At FinCEN, we have focused on two types of convertible virtual currencies: centralized and decentralized.

Centralized virtual currencies have a centralized repository and a single administrator. Liberty Reserve, which FinCEN identified earlier this year as being of primary money laundering concern pursuant to Section 311 of the USA PATRIOT Act, is an example of a centralized virtual currency. Decentralized virtual currencies, on the other hand, and as the name suggests, have no central repository and no single administrator. Instead, value is electronically transmitted between parties without an intermediary. Bitcoin is an example of a decentralized virtual currency. Bitcoin is also known as cryptocurrency, meaning that it relies on cryptographic software protocols to generate the currency and validate transactions.

It is important to note that by generally defining virtual currency as any type of digital unit used as a medium of exchange or stored value that is integrated into any type of *payment* system, any online currency that is used for online gaming, customer affinity, or reward programs such as airline miles, as long as these cannot be converted into or redeemed for cash, is excluded.

FinCEN's 2013 guidance has also clarified that virtual currency payment systems and trading platforms are considered MSBs (FinCEN, 2013). The guidance considered three categories of participants a virtual currency system: a user, exchanger, and administrator, who have been similarly defined in the introduction to this chapter.

Users, who obtain Bitcoins for purchasing goods and services, are not regulated.

Exchangers, or rather exchanges in the Bitcoin world, are considered as money exchangers and will be regulated as MSBs.

The regulation of administrators, which was then unclear in a decentralized crypto-currency like Bitcoins—FinCEN's definition depended upon their capacity to issue units of the currency—was later clarified in a 2014 administrative ruling, which considered the question of miners. FinCEN held that miners who obtained Bitcoins through mining and who subsequently used them to purchase goods and services or converted them into other currencies were not MSBs if these actions were intended to be for one's own benefit. Here, the miner is construed to be a user and is therefore not regulated (FinCEN, 2014).

The effect of FinCEN's regulation at the federal level is that Bitcoin exchanges serving American customers are required to fulfill the registration, reporting, and record-keeping requirements of MSBs. With the initial compliance cost of MSBs in all states going up to USD 2 million, such a high compliance cost is a major deterrent for start-ups to engage in such activities given that most seed money hardly exceeds USD 500,000.

At the federal level, nothing is confirmed about the tax treatment of bitcoins although some states are already planning their own regulatory frameworks specific to virtual currencies, which very likely includes tax aspects.

16.5.2 New York's BitLicense

On July 17, 2014, the NYSDFS proposed a new set of codes, rules, and regulations for virtual currencies. The definition of "virtual currency" and "virtual currency business activity" is given below.

> Virtual Currency *means any type of digital unit that is used as a medium of exchange or a form of digitally stored value or that is incorporated into payment system technology. Virtual Currency shall be broadly construed to include digital units of exchange that (i) have a centralized repository or administrator; (ii) are decentralized and have no centralized repository or administrator; or (iii) may be created or obtained by computing or manufacturing effort. Virtual Currency shall not be construed to include digital units that are used solely within online gaming platforms with no*

market or application outside of those gaming platforms, nor shall Virtual Currency be construed to include digital units that are used exclusively as part of a customer affinity or rewards program, and can be applied solely as payment for purchases with the issuer and/or other designated merchants, but cannot be converted into, or redeemed for, Fiat Currency.

Note that it is the business activity of virtual currencies, rather than the virtual currency software technology, that is required to be licensed; the NYSDFS went further to define what business activity means:

Virtual Currency Business Activity *means the conduct of any one of the following types of activities involving New York or a New York Resident:*

(1) *receiving Virtual Currency for transmission or transmitting the same;*

(2) *securing, storing, holding, or maintaining custody or control of Virtual Currency on behalf of others;*

(3) *buying and selling Virtual Currency as a customer business;*

(4) *performing retail conversion services, including the conversion or exchange of Fiat Currency or other value into Virtual Currency, the conversion or exchange of Virtual Currency into Fiat Currency or other value, or the conversion or exchange of one form of Virtual Currency into another form of Virtual Currency; or*

(5) *controlling, administering, or issuing a Virtual Currency.*
Statutory Authority: Financial Services Law, Sections 102, 201, 301, and 3026.

A license is required to undertake virtual currency business activity (Section 200.3), and a licensed business should not deal with any other unlicensed agent or agency, but rather, deal with merchants or consumers or any other approved exchange service providers.

While the response to New York's proposal has been varied, the growing consensus in the Western world suggests that the New York's regulatory proposal has overreached to the extent of stifling innovation to protect consumers (Rizzo, 2014a,b), although it is admittedly a work in progress. Subjecting companies that deal with virtual currencies to almost full-scale compliance requirements to the extent of those requirements faced by well-capitalized financial institutions will put many virtual currency start-ups into financial difficulties and expose licensees to liability that many entrepreneurs may not want to be exposed to. This potentially has the effect of stifling business activity in virtual currencies. Many critical comments, unsurprisingly, have therefore been submitted during the consultation period.

In terms of compliance requirements, the licensee is required to have a qualified compliance officer with compliance policy for anti-fraud, anti-money laundering, cyber security, private and information security, and others (Section 200.7). There are requirements for minimum amount of capital to be maintained (Section 200.8). The licensee has to maintain a bond or trust account (Section 200.9). The licensee has to seek approval for material changes to business and change of control and mergers and acquisitions (Sections 200.10 and 200.11).

First, the licensee is required to establish an anti-money laundering program that includes risk assessment, recordkeeping, suspicious transaction reporting, and customer identification and verification processes. The firm is also required to block transactions that violate the law (New York State Department of Financial Services, 2014a,b).

Second, for the protection of customer assets, the licensee is required to maintain a bond and trust account in USD for the benefit of customers and hold virtual currency of the same type and amount as that that is owed to customers who have entrusted the storage of their virtual currency to the licensee. The licensee is also required to disclose the material risks of virtual currency to customers in writing in the English language and any other predominant language of the customer at the beginning of the customer relationship and prior to entering into an initial transaction. There are also capital requirements to be determined on a case-by-case basis and a quarterly and annual financial audit and reporting requirement. A complaint resolution policy is also required, and the licensee must state that the potential complainant may also complain to the Department of Financial Services (New York State Department of Financial Services, 2014a,b).

Third, bearing in mind that virtual currencies are processed electronically, the cyber security requirements include designating a qualified employee to serve as the chief information security officer who will be responsible for the licensee's cyber security program to identify cyber risks, protect its electronic systems, detect unauthorized access, and recover from cyber security events. A written business continuity and disaster recovery plan is also required to be maintained, and penetration testing needs to be conducted quarterly.

16.5.3 Commentary on BitLicense

Our commentary is that the BitLicense perspective brings together the some pertinent issues of virtual currency companies. These issues can be generalized to be (1) consumer protection; (2) anti-money laundering and counterterrorist financing; and (3) cyber security improvement for virtual currency business.

As the definition of "business activities" includes the conduct of certain activities with a New York resident, the proposal has extraterritorial effect, subjecting any US or non-US companies and their employees to BitLicense regulation. Furthermore, each licensee will have to provide, upon request, immediate access to all facilities, books, records, documents, or other data maintained by the licensee or its affiliates, wherever located. As the compliance cost is expected to be high, many businesses may in turn decide to instead avoid dealing with New York customers.

These regulations are meant for companies providing virtual currency financial services, rather than merchants or consumers that use virtual currency solely for the purpose of sale of goods or services. But it has placed disclosure, recording, and capital requirements on these businesses. Businesses also have to detail consumer protections and create a system to resolve complaints for consumers using virtual currencies. Furthermore, they have to outline disaster recovery mechanisms, merger rules, and licensee advertising rules. These will impose a cost and equity structure that start-ups are unlikely to be able to comply. The most difficult areas for smaller outfits to comply with are keeping books and records for 10 years, reports and financial disclosures, anti-money laundering program, cyber security programs, business continuity and disaster recovery, advertising and marketing, consumer protection, and management of complaints, which appear more suited for large-scale businesses. In the meantime, while discussions and consultations are still ongoing, the transitional license may provide an adequate period of time to comply or exit. However, that the high compliance cost and liability have a stifling effect on the market has not been adequately addressed makes New York's BitLicense an interesting case study sometime in the future.

16.6 TOWARD A LIGHT-TOUCH APPROACH TO REGULATION

Having surveyed the spectrum of existing regulatory approaches, I further develop the regulation ideal by arguing for a light-touch approach with three main lenses.

16.6.1 General policy considerations

As virtual currencies may be the way for the future, it is important for regulators to view it with less hostility, but instead be constructively involved. The challenge here is to meaningfully minimize the risks posed by virtual currencies while still encouraging their beneficial uses and future innovation. It is impulsive (Brito and Castillo, 2013) to clamp down on disruptive technology simply as a knee-jerk reaction to its association with unlawful activity (Lam, 2014). The use of virtual currencies for unlawful purposes needs to be viewed in perspective with their use for legitimate purposes. For example, BitPay, which provides Bitcoin point-of-sale payment services for merchants, has reportedly processed a transaction volume of USD 5.2 million, which far exceeds the USD 2 million transferred on the notorious Silk Road black market website.

16.6.2 A light touch with three lenses

Three main questions, or lenses, of regulation are to be considered: the micro lens for addressing specific risks first, the macro lens for developing prudential regulation and stability, and the international lens for coordinating meaningful regulation.

In the micro lens for addressing specific risks first, the most immediate risks are the facilitation of criminal activity, including money laundering and terrorist financing, with virtual currencies. A possible way to tackle this risk is FinCEN's approach, which targets certain participants in the virtual currency system, such as the exchanges, as the gatekeepers. These designated gatekeepers are regulated for the criminal risks because they are the best placed to identify customers and report suspicious transactions (Lam, 2014).

Zooming out from the micro lens, the macro lens considers prudential regulation. Such regulation looks at market confidence as the basis for a functioning market.

Well-honed prudential regulation should address information asymmetry, promote systemic stability, and allow laws and rules to develop.

Financial literacy programs are a method for addressing information asymmetry, especially for consumers. They can be undertaken by the regulator, as has been done in Australia and Singapore, or by the virtual currency industry, with Bitcoin Wiki and CoinDesk leading the way online.

Systemic stability is more difficult to regulate for. Virtual currencies, if integrated into the economy alongside traditional financial institutions, risk being a contagion when they fail. Perhaps, a possible prudential regulation tool is self-disclosure—parties dealing with financial institutions and virtual currencies should disclose their level of dealings and their risk management policies—which dovetails with the efforts to reduce information asymmetry.

Given the possible cross-border nature of virtual currencies, international cooperation is necessary for virtual currency regulation to be meaningful. There have been limited efforts by international bodies at working out the details, but discussions have started. The Financial Action Task Force and the International Monetary Fund present possible forums for coordination. Alternatively, there are calls for a forum specific to virtual currencies to better engage with the various stakeholders and participants unique to a virtual, decentralized (crypto)currencies (Tay et al., 2014).

16.6.3 This is only the beginning

The final and most important takeaway from the regulation literature is that virtual currencies are only in their infancy. The development of more innovative services built on Bitcoin technology is rapidly being carried out, especially by extending the use of the block chain concept to offer various services, such as crowd funding. In particular, with the development of Bitcoin 2.0 and side chains, regulations are way behind technology innovation. Crowd funding involving crypto equity and retail investors have not received much attention from regulators. This is an important area to focus on, especially for the development of social businesses, so that the masses can participate. Crypto crowd funding with equity participation will benefit those at the bottom of the wealth pyramid and thus lead to improvement in their welfare as equity owners. The property right of digital asset is another area that regulation has not addressed. Regulation and guidance are crucial for the benefits of these innovations to spread across the wealth pyramid.

Ultimately, if regulators remain oblivious and the industry to continue to leapfrog them, both sides would have lost a valuable opportunity to learn about and understand the issues and concerns of a burgeoning technology that could be the way of our future. The message is best conveyed that a win-win and sustainable situation for the regulator and industry will be that there is an appropriate balance between protecting the consumers and rooting out illicit activities, without stifling beneficial innovation.

REFERENCES

Australian Securities and Investments Commission, 2014. Virtual currencies. Retrieved from MoneySmart by ASIC: https://www.moneysmart.gov.au/investing/investment-warnings/virtual-currencies.

Banco Central do Brasil, 2014. Policy statement on the risks related to the acquisition of the so-called "virtual currencies" or "encrypted currencies" and to the transactions carried out with these currencies. Retrieved from Banco Central do Brasil: http://www.bcb.gov.br/pom/spb/ing/IComunicado25306.pdf.

Brito, J., 2013. The top 3 things I learned at the bitcoin conference. Retrieved from Mercatus Center Expert Commentary: http://mercatus.org/expert_commentary/top-3-things-i-learned-bitcoin-conference.

Brito, K., Castillo, A., 2013. Bitcoin: a primer for policymakers. Retrieved from Mercatus Center: http://mercatus.org/publication/bitcoin-primer-policymakers.

Calvery, J. S., 2013. Statement of Jennifer Shasky Calvery, Director, Financial Crimes Enforcement Network, United States Department of the Treasury, Before the United States Senate.

Economic Action Plan 2014 Act, No. 1, 2014. Canada. Retrieved from: http://www.parl.gc.ca/LEGISInfo/BillDetails.aspx?Language=E&Mode=1&billId=6483626.

European Banking Authority, 2014. EBA Opinion on "virtual currencies" European Banking Authority. Retrieved from: http://www.eba.europa.eu/documents/10180/657547/EBA-Op-2014-08+Opinion+on+Virtual+Currencies.pdf.

European Central Bank, 2012. Virtual Currency Scheme. Available from: http://www.ecb.europa.eu/pub/pdf/other/virtualcurrencyschemes201210en.pdf (retrieved 25.01.15.).

Federal Council, 2014. Federal Council report on virtual currencies in response to the Schwaab (13.3687) and Weibel (13.4070) postulates. Retrieved from: http://www.news.admin.ch/NSBSubscriber/message/attachments/35355.pdf.

Financial Action Task Force, 2014. Virtual currencies—key definitions and potential AML/CFT risks. Financial Action Task Force, Paris. Retrieved from: http://www.fatf-gafi.org/media/fatf/documents/reports/Virtual-currency-key-definitions-and-potential-aml-cft-risks.pdf.

FinCEN, 2013. Application of FinCEN's regulations to persons administering, exchanging, or using virtual currencies. Retrieved from FinCEN: http://www.fincen.gov/statutes_regs/guidance/html/FIN-2013-G001.html.

FinCEN, 2014. Application of FinCEN's regulations to virtual currency mining operations. Retrieved from FinCEN: http://www.fincen.gov/news_room/rp/rulings/html/FIN-2014-R001.html.

Government Accountability Office, 2014. Virtual Currencies: Emerging Regulatory, Law Enforcement, and Consumer Protection Challenges. United States Government Accountability Office, Washington, DC. Retrieved from: http://www.gao.gov/assets/670/663678.pdf.

Hajdarbegovic, N., 2014. UK financial regulator's new initiative encourages bitcoin innovation. CoinDesk, Retrieved from: http://www.coindesk.com/uk-financial-conduct-authority-fca-launches-bitcoin-initiative/.

Hill, K., 2013. Bitcoin in China: the fall-out from Chinese government banning real world use. Forbes, Retrieved from: http://www.forbes.com/sites/kashmirhill/2013/12/06/bitcoin-in-china-the-fall-out-from-chinese-government-banning-real-world-use/.

Jankelewitz, E., 2014. Bitcoin regulation in the UK. CoinDesk, Retrieved from: http://www.coindesk.com/bitcoin-regulation-uk/.

Lam, P.N., 2014. Bitcoin in Singapore: A Light-Touch Approach to Regulation (LLB Thesis). National University of Singapore, Faculty of Law, Singapore. Retrieved from: http://ssrn.com/abstract=2427626.

Monetary Authority of Singapore, 2014a. MAS to regulate virtual currency intermediaries for money laundering and terrorist financing risks. Retrieved from Monetary Authority of Singapore: http://www.mas.gov.sg/News-and-Publications/Press-Releases/2014/MAS-to-Regulate-Virtual-Currency-Intermediaries-for-Money-Laundering-and-Terrorist-Financing-Risks.aspx.

Monetary Authority of Singapore, 2014b. Virtual currencies. Retrieved from MoneySENSE: http://www.moneysense.gov.sg/Understanding-Financial-Products/Investments/Consumer-Alerts/Virtual-Currencies.aspx.

Murphy, G., 2014. Address by director of markets supervision Gareth Murphy at the BitFin 2014: digital money and the future of finance conference. Retrieved from Central Bank of Ireland: http://www.centralbank.ie/press-area/speeches/Pages/GarethMurphyBitFin2014.aspx.

Nakamoto, S., 2008. Bitcoin: a peer-to-peer electronic cash system. Retrieved from: https://bitcoin.org/bitcoin.pdf.

New York State Department of Financial Services, 2014a. NYDFS virtual currency hearing. Retrieved from: NYDFS: http://www.dfs.ny.gov/about/hearings/vc_01282014_indx.htm.

New York State Department of Financial Services, 2014b. Proposed New York codes, rules and regulations. Retrieved from: http://www.dfs.ny.gov/about/press2014/pr1407171-vc.pdf.

Ostroukh, A., 2014. Russia softens stance on bitcoin. Wall Street J, Retrieved from: http://online.wsj.com/articles/russia-softens-stance-on-bitcoin-1404305139.

People's Bank of China, 2013. Prevention of risks associated with bitcoin (in Chinese). Retrieved from People's Bank of China: http://www.pbc.gov.cn/publish/goutongjiaoliu/524/2013/20131205153156832222251/20131205153156832222251_.html.

Plassaras, N.A., 2013. Regulating digital currencies: bringing bitcoin within the reach of the IMF. Chicago J. Int. Law, Retrieved from: http://ssrn.com/abstract=2248419.

Quentson, A., 2014. Federal agencies criticized for failing to protect bitcoin users. Cryptocoins News, Retrieved from: http://www.cryptocoinsnews.com/news/federal-agencies-criticized-failing-protect-bitcoin-users/2014/06/30.

Rizzo, P., 2014a. Irish central banker envisions hybrid bitcoin-fiat future. CoinDesk, Retrieved from: http://www.coindesk.com/irish-central-banker-envisions-hybrid-bitcoin-fiat-future/.

Rizzo, P., 2014b. New York's BitLicense proposal: the view from China. CoinDesk, Retrieved from: http://www.coindesk.com/new-yorks-bitlicense-proposal-view-china/.

Taobao, 2014. Amended taobao rule against the trade of bitcoin and other virtual currencies (in Chinese). Retrieved from Taobao: http://rule.taobao.com/detail-1358.htm.

Tay, D., et al., 2014. A Comparative Study on the Governance Practices of BitCoin in China and USA (BA Dissertation). National University of Singapore, Faculty of Arts and Social Sciences, Singapore.

CHAPTER 17

Real Regulation of Virtual Currencies

Richard B. Levin[a]**, Aaron A. O'Brien**[b]**, Madiha M. Zuberi**[c]
[a]Bryan Cave, LLP, Denver, Colorado, USA
[b]Baker & Hostetler, LLP, PNC Center, Cleveland, Ohio, USA
[c]Baker & Hostetler, LLP, New York, New York, USA

Contents

17.1 INTRODUCTION

Bitcoin has been described by Bill Gates as a "techno tour de force" (Munger/Buffet, 2013). Peter Thiel, the co-founder of PayPal and an early investor in Facebook, believes Bitcoin has "world-changing" promise for online transactions without fees (Hill, 2013b; Simonite, 2014). Fred Wilson of Union Square Ventures believes "Bitcoin represents something fundamental and powerful . . ." (Yarow, 2013). Leading Silicon Valley investors, including Andreessen Horowitz, Lightspeed Ventures, and Hong Kong Billionaire Li Ka-shing's Horizon Ventures, are supporters of the virtual currency (Simonite, 2013; Karkaria, 2013). Bitcoin is a digital, private cryptocurrency that is exchanged by means of the Internet (Kaplanov, 2012).

Virtual currencies are monetary units of exchange stored or represented in a digital or other electronic format that operate like currency in some environments, but that do not have legal tender status in any jurisdiction (FinCEN, 2013). Bitcoin is a leading virtual currency that is not backed by any tangible real asset and without specie, such as coin or precious metal. According to Dion (2013) "Bitcoin is a decentralized store of value and open-ledger payment network that operates securely, efficiently, and at low cost without the need for any third-party intermediaries. The Bitcoin protocol allows individuals or service providers' access to a global financial system that will see rapid innovation."

Supporters of virtual currency believe Bitcoin has the potential to support more efficient global commerce and to help combat poverty. Marc Andreessen of Andreessen Horowitz has invested nearly $50 million in Bitcoin-related startups and believes the virtual currency solves what he calls the "Byzantine Generals Problem" or how to establish trust between otherwise unrelated parties over an untrusted network like the Internet (Andreessen, 2014). Andreesen noted, "practical consequence of solving this problem is that Bitcoin gives us, for the first time, a way for one Internet user to transfer a unique piece of digital property to another Internet user, such that the transfer is guaranteed to be safe and secure, everyone knows that the transfer has taken place, and nobody can challenge the legitimacy of the transfer" (Andreessen, 2014).

Critics of Bitcoin, however, have been equally as vocal in their skepticism of the virtual currency and concern about its long-term viability as a unit of exchange as well as its potential impact on financial services and commerce. Bitcoin has been derided as a "shady online currency" and as "a virtual Wild West for narcotraffickers and other criminals" (Sanati, 2012). The New York State Department of Financial Services Notice of Inquiry on Virtual Currencies noted that "the Department of Financial Services (NYDFS) has launched an inquiry into the appropriate regulatory guidelines that it should put in place for virtual currencies" (NYDFS, 2013). Senator Charles Schumer has described Bitcoin as a form of money laundering (Schumer, 2011). Leading economist, Paul Krugman, has been critical of Bitcoin, suggesting that the structure of the currency incentivizes hoarding (Krugman, 2014). Other analysts have raised concerns of a Bitcoin bubble (Isidore, 2013; Salmon, 2013a,b). Former Secretary of the Treasury Larry Summers has been more circumspect in his evaluation of the virtual currency and appears to be waiting to judge its potential (Myhrvold, 2012).

The debate over the long-term potential of Bitcoin has been influenced in part by the regulatory scrutiny of virtual currencies by the Federal Bureau of Investigations (FBI), the U.S. Securities and Exchange Commission (SEC), the Commodity Futures Trading Commission (CFTC), the United States Department of the Treasury (Treasury), the Internal Revenue Service (IRS), the United States Senate, and state governments like the State of New York and its Department of Business Oversight (FinCEN, 2013; NYDFS, 2013; Zabel, 2014). Despite the disagreement over the future of the virtual currency, Bitcoin is described as the "Internet's favorite virtual currency" (Boesler, 2013b).

Bitcoin "may finally be going mainstream" (Wingfield, 2013) based in part on the involvement of firms like Silicon Valley Bank, a commercial banking entity (Boesler, 2013a). The involvement of a leading bank marks a milestone in the development of virtual currencies because banks are subject to the anti-money laundering (AML) compliance requirements of the Bank Secrecy Act (BSA) (Currency and Foreign Transactions Reporting Act of 1970, 31 U.S.C. § 5311 et seq.). The BSA requires money transmitters to register with FinCEN, adopt an AML compliance program, and keep records of client transactions. Firms involved in the exchange of Bitcoin must remain vigilant.

Research analysts from leading investment banks, including Bank of America Merrill Lynch have started to cover Bitcoin (Hill, 2013c; Luria and Turner, 2014). Growing acceptance of Bitcoin is also evidenced by the recent announcement from Pantera Bitcoin Advisors that it had raised nearly $150 million for a fund that will invest in Bitcoin (Primack, 2013; Flitter, 2013; Gandel, 2013). The Sacramento Kings of the NBA have also announced the team will become the first professional sports franchise to accept Bitcoins (Rovell, 2014). Despite the growing enthusiasm within the financial services industry and acceptance of Bitcoins, generally for commercial transactions, the model for the regulation of this virtual currency remains unclear.

In this chapter, we provide an overview of virtual currencies, including Bitcoin and the most prominent actions by the Department of Justice (DOJ) against operators of virtual currency platforms. The chapter discusses the current state of regulation of virtual currencies by three agencies: Treasury (through the Office of Foreign Asset Control (OFAC) and the Financial Crimes Enforcement Network (FinCEN)); the SEC; and the CFTC. This chapter does not address the current and potential regulation of Bitcoin and other virtual currencies by the states and foreign jurisdictions. The New York Department of Financial Services recently proposed rules for the regulation of New York-based nonmerchant virtual currency businesses (NYDFS, 2013, 2014a,b; Library of Congress, 2014). The chapter concludes with a discussion of the efforts of the U.S. Congress and other agencies with respect to virtual currencies.

17.2 BACKGROUND

Bitcoin is an open-source decentralized virtual currency that may be traded through online exchanges for conventional fiat currencies, such as the U.S. dollar and the Euro, or used to purchase goods and services online (Levin et al., 2014a,b,c). The term virtual currency refers to electronic money that operates like a currency in some environments, but does not have all the attributes of real currency (Levin et al., 2014a,b,c). Virtual currencies can be created by an individual, corporation, or organization, or can arise from use and acceptance by people as currency (Turpin, 2014). Virtual currency is distinguished from electronic money produced by government-endorsed central banks and backed by national currency, and that goes through electronic banking and payment system. Traditional currencies are generally either backed by the faith and credit of the national governments that recognize the currency (the fiat system) or by real assets or hard commodities, such as gold, silver, or minerals (the commodity system). Bitcoin, however, exists purely as bits of computer code and is neither backed by fiat nor a commodity (Yermack, 2014). Bitcoin is not regulated by a central bank or any other form of governmental authority. The supply of Bitcoins is based on an algorithm that structures a decentralized peer-to-peer transaction system (Nakamoto, 2008; Turpin, 2014).

Bitcoins were purportedly developed in 2008 by an anonymous computer programmer known as "Satoshi Nakamoto."[1] The complex computer algorithm, when "mined" successfully, creates new Bitcoins. The exchange rate for Bitcoins is somewhat volatile

---

[1] The name Satoshi Nakamoto is most likely a pseudonym since his or her identity is unknown. Jon Randoff, "Bitcoin Mining: The Free Lottery" (Jon Randoff's Internet Wonderland. June 3, 2011), available at www.zimbio.com/BitCoin/articles/BsLT5LZu_mv/Bitcoin+Mining+Free+Lottery.

and fallen as low as $2 but has also exceeded $600 per Bitcoin. Presently, fewer than 12 million Bitcoins with a total value of about $1.5 billion are in circulation.

17.2.1 How Bitcoin works

Bitcoin is revolutionary in that, unlike any prior online payment system, it is not administered by a central authority. There is no middleman between the buyer and the seller as there is with, for example, PayPal, traditional payment cards, bank wires, or other payment systems. Bitcoin is thus referred to as a "decentralized" virtual currency. There is no Bitcoin company that manages or controls the software or its operation. Instead of a central authority, the Bitcoin transaction network consists of computers around the world running the Bitcoin software, which operates the protocol for administering Bitcoin transactions. The software can be downloaded and run by anyone, and any computer running the software can join the network. Each computer on the network also maintains a copy of the universal public ledger known as the "block chain" (Levin et al., 2014a,b,c).

17.2.1.1 The public ledger

The public ledger is a crucial component of Bitcoin. The ledger records all transactions occurring in the system. The ledger is broken into blocks of transactions, and each new block of transactions is linked to the previous block, forming what is called the "block chain." The newest block at the end of the chain links back to every block that precedes it. Having access to the most recent block allows one to follow the chain backward to observe every Bitcoin transaction ever made (Brito and Castillo, 2013).

17.2.1.2 Mining

New blocks of Bitcoins are created by "mining." Mining is the process of verifying and adding transaction records to the Bitcoin public ledger [or block chain] and is done by solving a complex mathematical algorithm that creates the next block incorporating recent transactions. Mining is costly in terms of computer processing (hardware, electricity, and time). The difficulty of the math problem becomes more complex as additional miners join the network. This controls the pace at which new Bitcoins are added to the system, and it reduces the chance that any one miner or group will take control of the block chain. The number of Bitcoins to be mined is limited to 21 million. Miners expect that the last Bitcoin will be mined in 2140 (Brito and Castillo, 2013).

17.2.1.3 Peer-to-peer network

Bitcoin relies on a peer-to-peer network and complex cryptography to establish the payment mechanism. Individuals who want to own or transact in Bitcoins can either (1) run a program on their computer which implements the Bitcoin protocol or (2) establish an account on a Web site (or exchange) that has already implemented the Bitcoin protocol and runs the program for its users. The Bitcoin client is essentially a virtual wallet that stores an individual user's Bitcoins into an electronic file folder (Brito and Castillo, 2013).

The block chain described earlier is used to record all Bitcoin transactions. Transactions involving the exchange and transfer of Bitcoins are broadcast across the Bitcoin network, which is visible to all network members. Computer participants then communicate with each other to validate the transaction by checking the block chain to confirm that the transaction has not already occurred. This peer-to-peer network of computers harnesses the transparency of an open peer-accessible network to maintain the integrity of Bitcoin, the accuracy of the ledger, and the payment system, generally. Bitcoin is defined by a chain of digitally signed transactions. Each Bitcoin owner transfers Bitcoins to the next owner by digitally signing the Bitcoins over to the next owner (Brito and Castillo, 2013).

17.2.1.4 Cryptography

Bitcoin has been called a crypto currency because it uses cryptography to control transactions and prevent double-spending, a problem for virtual currencies. Once validated, every individual transaction is permanently recorded in the block chain (Brito and Castillo, 2013). Payment processing is done by a network of private computers often specially tailored to this task (Brito and Castillo, 2013). The operators of these computers, the "miners," are rewarded with transaction fees and newly minted Bitcoins. However, new Bitcoins are created at an ever-decreasing rate (Brito and Castillo, 2013).

17.2.1.5 Speculation

Speculators have been attracted to Bitcoin, fueling volatility and price swings. As of July 2013, the use of Bitcoin in the retail and commercial marketplace was relatively small compared with the use by speculators (Grocer, 2013).

17.2.1.6 Wallets

Bitcoins are stored by associating them with addresses called "wallets." Wallets can be stored on Web services, on local hardware like personal computers and mobile devices, or on paper print-outs. A Bitcoin wallet takes the form of a cryptographic "public key," which is a string of numbers and letters roughly 33 digits long. Each public key has a matching "private key," known only to the user. Control of the private keys is what assures one of control of the Bitcoins at any Bitcoin address, so collections of private keys must be protected by passwords or other means of securing them. While wallets can be created and maintained using the Bitcoin open-source software, in practice many users have accounts with one or more Bitcoin service providers and store Bitcoins at addresses provided though their accounts (Brito and Castillo, 2013).

Thefts of Bitcoins from Web services and online wallets have been covered in the media, prompting assertions that the safest way to store Bitcoins is on secure paper wallets. As recent as August of 2014, Bitcoin mining pools have become the targets and victims of hackers seeking to steal Bitcoins (Osborne, 2014). There have also been technology issues that have impacted the ability of Bitcoin users to access their wallets.

17.2.1.7 Using Bitcoins

Any Bitcoin user can transact directly with any other Bitcoin user. To initiate a transaction, the software or service sends a message to the other computers on the network announcing the transfer of a certain value in Bitcoins from the user's public key to the recipient's public key. The sending user's private key is used to "sign" the transaction. The private key is mathematically paired with the public key, and through a standard cryptographic process of the sort used to secure Web site connections, every computer on the network can verify that the transaction is signed with the correct private key. The private key signature thus serves to confirm that the transaction originated with, and was approved by, the actual owner of the originating public key, and therefore that the transaction is valid.

17.2.2 Major vendors dealing Bitcoins

Bitcoins are increasingly used as payment for legitimate products and services, and merchants have an incentive to accept the currency because transaction fees are lower than the 2–3% typically imposed by credit card processors (Lomas, 2014). Notable vendors include WordPress, OkCupid, and Reddit (Hill, 2013a). Chinese Internet giant Baidu stopped accepting Bitcoins following the announcement of the People's Bank of China prohibiting the use of the virtual currency by Chinese institutions (Kelion, 2013). In effort to comply with applicable laws, a leading Bitcoin exchange is in the process of registering with the Treasury as money services business (Sparshott, 2014). The SEC has also reported several recent filings by individuals and companies interested in taking advantage of a growing Bitcoin trading industry.

17.3 BITCOIN PROSECUTIONS

The anonymity offered by Bitcoins and the lack of regulatory and exchange infrastructure that lower the operating cost of the Bitcoin system, make it highly attractive to users. The model also creates a unique payment system that can be used for illegal means such as money laundering, trading in illegal goods and services, financing terrorism, fraud, and tax evasion. In addition to the efforts of other regulatory agencies, the DOJ has prosecuted several virtual currency vendors.

17.3.1 E-Gold

In 2007, the DOJ first took action against a virtual currency provider when it indicted E-Gold Ltd, an Internet-based digital currency business, and its three principal owners on charges related to money laundering and operating an unlicensed "money transmitting business" (Department of Justice 2007; Lowery, 2013). According to information contained in plea materials, the E-Gold operation provided digital currency services over the Internet through two Web sites.

E-Gold was founded in 1996 and backed virtual currency with gold coins stored in a safe-deposit box in Florida. Users were required to supply a valid e-mail address to set up an account, but otherwise did not have to provide their true identity, and blatantly used false names such as "Mickey Mouse" and "Donald Duck"(Department of Justice, 2007; Lowery, 2013). Once users opened E-Gold accounts, the accounts could be funded through the use of exchangers who converted U.S. currency into E-Gold. Users with funded accounts could gain access through the Internet and conduct anonymous transactions with other E-Gold users throughout the world (Department of Justice, 2012; Lowery, 2013). However, this anonymity made E-Gold attractive to users with criminal intentions. E-Gold allowed users to engage in such illicit activities including child exploitation, investment scams, credit card fraud, and identity theft.

Ultimately, the DOJ liquidated E-Gold's reserve for $90 million to allow legitimate account holders to claim their assets (Department of Justice, 2012). "As of December 18, 2012, over $10.8 million contained in 12,869 accounts has been to forfeited to the Federal Government as part of an on-going asset forfeiture process" (Department of Justice, 2012).

17.3.2 Liberty Reserve

In May 2013, the DOJ indicted Liberty Reserve and its executives, including Arthur Budovsky, for running a $6 billion money laundering operation (Department of Justice, 2013b; Lowery, 2013). Liberty Reserve was a Costa Rica-based centralized digital currency service that provided real-time currency for international commerce for users around the world (Department of Justice, 2013b). Before it was shutdown, Liberty Reserve was:

> [A]lleged to have had more than one million users worldwide, including more than 200,000 users in the U.S, who conducted approximately 55 million transactions—virtually all of which were illegal—and laundered more than $6 billion in suspected proceeds of crimes including credit card fraud, identity theft, investment fraud, computer hacking, child pornography, and narcotics trafficking.
> **(Department of Justice, 2013a).**

Consequently, the United States charged Budovsky and six others with money laundering and operating an unlicensed financial transaction company (Lowery, 2013). Liberty Reserve is alleged to have been used to launder more than $6 billion in criminal proceeds during its history (Lowery, 2013).

Like E-Gold, the service allowed users to send and receive funds with a high level of anonymity by not requiring users to validate their identities. Many of the transactions were sent to or from users in the United States, but Liberty Reserve never registered with the appropriate U.S. authorities. Because of these characteristics, Liberty Reserve became a primary choice for criminal activity such as credit card fraud, identity theft, investment fraud, computer hacking, and child exploitation.

17.3.3 Western Express

Western Express International was a Manhattan-based corporation that exchanged conventional currency to E-Gold and WebMoney (Murck, 2013; Lowery, 2013). The company's loose standards catered to Eastern European criminals supporting global cybercrime by acting as a digital currency exchanger, illegal money transmitter, and money launderer. To date, 16 individuals have been found guilty in the case, including citizens of Eastern Europe (Lowery, 2013). The corporation and its officers ultimately pleaded guilty to laundering about $2 million dollars in connection with the scheme (Lowery, 2013). Nine of Western Express' customers were convicted by guilty plea in the conspiracy, which trafficked nearly 100,000 stolen credit card numbers and was responsible for identity theft resulting in losses of more than $5 million (Lowery, 2013). After a two-and-a-half month jury trial, the remaining three defendants were convicted of every count (Lowery, 2013). This case demonstrates how digital currency has allowed criminals around the globe to do their criminal business together while cloaked in anonymity, and despite never meeting each other in person.

17.3.4 Silk Road

Launched in 2011, Silk Road was an online marketplace that allowed online users to browse it anonymously and securely without potential traffic monitoring. Allegedly operated by a U.S. citizen living in California at the time of his arrest, Silk Road accepted Bitcoins exclusively as a payment mechanism on its site. The DOJ complaint alleges that, in less than 3 years, Silk Road served as a venue for over 100,000 buyers to purchase hundreds of kilograms of illegal drugs and other illicit goods from several thousand drug dealers and other criminal vendors (FBI, 2013). As of March 2013, the site had 10,000 products for sale by vendors, of which 70% were drugs of 340 varieties, including heroin, LSD, and marijuana. On October 2013, the FBI shut down Silk Road and arrested its founder, Ross William Ulbricht who used the pseudonym Dread Pirate Roberts, on numerous allegations (Segal, 2014). By early 2013 an estimated $15 million in transactions were made on Silk Road, with buyers and sellers conducting transactions with Bitcoin, which provided another layer of anonymity. In addition to arresting the site's operator and shutting down the service, the DOJ to date has seized over 170,000 Bitcoins, valued as of November 15, 2013, at over $70 million. A separate indictment charged Silk Road's operator with drug distribution, conspiracy, attempted witness murder, and using interstate commerce facilities in the commission of murder-for-hire.

On February 4, 2015, the founder of Silk Road, Ross Ulbricht was convicted (Weiser, 2015). Mr. Ulbricht faces a minimum prison sentence of 20 years and the four most serious convictions, including distributing narcotics on the Internet and engaging in a continuing criminal enterprise, carry potential life sentences. Mr. Ulbricht will be sentenced on May 15, 2015 (Weiser, 2015).

17.4 FinCEN REGULATION OF VIRTUAL CURRENCIES

Virtual currencies are not created or overseen by a central bank in the manner of traditional currencies. The fact that virtual currencies are not subject to traditional regulatory oversight has drawn the attention of federal regulators including the Treasury (through FinCEN), the SEC, and the CFTC (FinCEN, 2013).

FinCEN is delegated authority under U.S. Department of Treasury Order 180-01 to administer the BSA and to thereby regulate money transmission to detect and prevent money laundering, fraud, and other illegal practices.

17.4.1 Virtual currency and Money Service Businesses

FinCEN regulates money services businesses (MSBs) and money transmitters. The BSA and FinCEN regulations considers each of the following to be MSBs: currency exchangers; issuers, redeemers, or cashiers of travelers' checks, checks, money orders, or similar instruments; the United States Postal Service; a person who engages as a business in the transmission of funds; and any business or agency which engages in any activity determined by regulation to be an activity similar to, related to, or a substitute for these activities (FinCEN, 2013). The term "money transmitter" includes a person that engages in the acceptance of currency, funds, or other value that substitute for currency from one person and the transmission of currency, funds, or other value that substitutes for currency to another location or person by any means (*Code of Federal Regulation.* Chapter 31. Section 1010.100(fff)). It is important to note that the definition of a money transmitter does not differentiate between real currencies and convertible virtual currencies.

A person accepting or transmitting anything of value that substitutes for currency (such as Bitcoin) will be viewed as a money transmitter. Any entity or person, including certain foreign-located persons that engage in money transmission in any amount is subject to the BSA rules. Persons operating money transmitting businesses must register as such with FinCEN. The failure to register a money transmitting business is a federal offense punishable by civil and criminal penalty. The jurisdiction of FinCEN is proscribed under the BSA.

17.4.2 Real currency and virtual currency

Transactions involving the exchange of Bitcoin for goods, services, or investments accordingly have drawn the attention and regulatory scrutiny of FinCEN as it seeks to exercise its jurisdiction over these exchanges and the Bitcoin exchange. FinCEN's ability to regulate transactions in Bitcoin is, however, subject to an authoritative determination by FinCEN that Bitcoins are "money" (or "currency").

FinCEN's regulations define currency (also referred to as "real" currency) as "the coin and paper money of the United States or of any other country that (i) is designated as legal tender and that (ii) circulates and (iii) is customarily used and accepted as a medium of exchange in the country of issuance" (United States. *Code of Federal Regulation*. Chapter 31. Section, 1010.100(m)).

Bitcoins clearly fall outside of the definition of "real currency" not simply because they are neither coin nor paper, but primarily because Bitcoins are not recognized as the legal tender of any country. Bitcoins are virtual currency. The BSA does not define virtual currency but FinCEN guidance, rather broadly, states that "virtual currency is a medium of exchange that operates like a currency in some environments, but does not have all the attributes of real currency."

Virtual currencies can be divided into two primary categories: (1) convertible virtual currencies and (2) nonconvertible virtual currencies. Nonconvertible virtual currencies are essentially credits that can only be redeemed for products or other services. Nonconvertible virtual currencies, like Facebook credits, generally cannot be converted into state-issued or government backed currency. Convertible currencies, on the other hand, may act as a substitute for real currency and have an equivalent value in real currency. These virtual currencies are frequently converted into and exchanged for real currency. Bitcoin is a convertible virtual currency.

17.4.3 Regulated persons and entities

FinCEN regulation is less about the type of currency involved in a transmission or transaction and more about the process by which the currency is transmitted, the purpose of the transmission and the participants involved in the transmission. FinCEN has stated that "[w]hat is material to the conclusion that a person is not an MSB is not the mechanism by which a person obtains the convertible virtual currency, *but what the person uses the convertible virtual currency for, and for whose benefit*" (United States. *Code of Federal Regulation*. Chapter 31. Section, 1010.100(m)). FinCEN has stated activities that do not constitute accepting and transmitting currency, funds or the value of funds do not fit within the definition of "money transmission services" and are not subject to FinCEN's registration, reporting, and recordkeeping regulations for MSBs (United States. *Code of Federal Regulation*. Chapter 31. Section, 1010.100(m)). However, a Bitcoin user that wants to purchase goods or services with Bitcoins it has mined, that pays Bitcoins to a third party at the direction of a seller or creditor, may be engaged in money transmission.

17.4.4 Users, exchangers, and administrators

FinCEN refers to the participants in generic virtual currency arrangements, using the terms "user," "exchanger," and "administrator" (United States. *Code of Federal Regulation*. Chapter 31. Section, 1010.100(m)). A user is a person that obtains virtual currency to purchase goods or services. How a person engages in "obtaining" a virtual currency may be described using any number of other terms, such as "earning," "harvesting," "mining," "creating," "auto-generating," "manufacturing," or "purchasing," depending on the details of the specific virtual currency model involved. For purposes of the guidance, Fin-CEN has noted the label applied to a particular process of obtaining a virtual currency is not material to the legal characterization under the BSA of the process or of the person engaging in the process. An exchanger is a person engaged as a business in the exchange of virtual currency for real currency, funds, or other virtual currency. An administrator is a person engaged as a business in issuing (putting into circulation) a virtual currency, and who has the authority to redeem (to withdraw from circulation) such virtual currency.

17.4.4.1 Users of virtual currency

A user who obtains convertible virtual currency and uses it to purchase real or virtual goods or services is not an MSB under FinCEN's regulations. Such activity, in and of itself, does not fit within the definition of "money transmission services" and therefore is not subject to FinCEN's registration, reporting, and recordkeeping regulations for MSBs (United States. *Code of Federal Regulation*. Chapter 31. Section, 1010.100(ff)(1-7)).

17.4.4.2 Administrators and exchangers of virtual currency: generally

An administrator or exchanger that (1) accepts and transmits a convertible virtual currency, or (2) buys or sells convertible virtual currency for any reason is a money transmitter under FinCEN's regulations, unless a limitation to or exemption from the definition applies to the person. FinCEN's regulations provide that whether a person is a money transmitter is a matter of facts and circumstances. The regulations identify six circumstances under which a person is not a money transmitter, despite accepting and transmitting currency, funds, or value that substitute for currency (United States. *Code of Federal Regulation*. Chapter 31. Section, 1010.100(ff)(5)(ii)(A)-(F)).

FinCEN's regulations define the term "money transmitter" as a person that provides money transmission services, or any other person engaged in the transfer of funds. The term "money transmission services" means "the acceptance of currency, funds, or other value that substitutes for currency from one person and the transmission of currency, funds, or other value that substitutes for currency to another location or person by any means" (FinCEN, 2013). The guidance also notes that the definition of money transmitter excludes any person, such as a futures commission merchant, that is "*registered with, and regulated or examined by . . . the Commodity Futures Trading Commission*" (FinCEN, 2013). This definition appears to create a regulatory model for the operator of a Bitcoin platform that registers with the CFTC.

The definition of a money transmitter does not differentiate between the form of money transmitted, but rather, will reach both real currencies and convertible virtual currencies. Accepting and transmitting anything of value that substitutes for currency makes a person a money transmitter under the regulations implementing the BSA (FinCEN, 2013).

FinCEN has reviewed different activities involving virtual currency and has made determinations regarding the appropriate regulatory treatment of administrators and exchangers under three scenarios: (1) brokers and dealers of e-currencies and e-precious metals; (2) centralized convertible virtual currencies; and (3) decentralized convertible virtual currencies.

Administrators and exchangers for purposes of FinCEN regulation are comparable to the broker-dealers for purposes of securities regulation under federal and state securities laws. FinCEN regulates brokers and dealers of currency, whether an e-currency, centralized convertible virtual currency or a decentralized virtual currency. Administrators and exchangers are generally only participants found in the context of centralized virtual currencies.

Centralized virtual currencies are currencies that utilize a central repository and an administrator over the centralized repository. These currencies are subject to FinCEN regulation. The administrator, in such instances, will be considered a money transmitter to the extent the administrator allows transfers of value between persons or from one location to another. Likewise, exchangers that use access to the convertible virtual currency services provided by the administrator to accept and transmit the convertible virtual currency on behalf of others, including transfers intended to pay a third party for virtual goods and services, are also money transmitters.

Exchangers convert real currency into virtual currency, oftentimes held on account by an administrator, and vice versa. Exchangers oftentimes act as the "seller" of the convertible virtual currency and the user functions as the "purchaser." An exchanger that accepts currency or its equivalent from a user and privately credits the user with an appropriate portion of the exchanger's own convertible virtual currency held with the administrator of the repository is engaged in money transmission and thereby a money transmitter. The exchanger in these instances will often step into the shoes of an administrator to transmit credited value to third parties upon the user's direction and request.

Exchangers, unlike administrators, frequently participate in Bitcoin transactions. Bitcoin is a decentralized currency because it does not utilize a centralized repository or an administrator. Bitcoin units are traded over a decentralized peer-to-peer network that allows for the proof and transfer of ownership without the need for a trusted third party. A person that creates units of convertible virtual currency and sells those units to another person for real currency or its equivalent is engaged in transmission to another location and is a money transmitter. Likewise, a person is an exchanger and a money transmitter if the person accepts such decentralized convertible virtual currency from one person and transmits it to another as part of the acceptance and transfer of currency, funds, or other value that substitutes for currency.

An administrator or an exchanger that (1) accepts and transmits a convertible virtual currency, or (2) buys or sells convertible virtual currency for any reason is a money transmitter under FinCEN's regulations, unless a limitation to or exemption from the definition applies to the person. FinCEN's regulations provide that whether a person is a money transmitter is a matter of facts and circumstances.

Bitcoin exchanges and retailers which accept Bitcoin may be considered money transmitters. The term "money transmitting" includes transferring funds on behalf of the public by any and all means including domestic and foreign transfers by wire, check, draft, facsimile, or courier.

17.4.5 Persons and entities excluded from regulation

FinCEN excludes entities or persons engaged in certain limited activities from the definition of a money transmitter. These exclusions include persons that only (1) provide delivery communication, or network access services used by a money transmitter to support money transmission services; (2) act as a payment processor to facilitate the purchase of, or payment of a bill for, a good or service; (3) operate a clearance and settlement system or otherwise acts as an intermediary solely between BSA-regulated institutions; (4) physically transports currency, other monetary instruments, other commercial paper, or other value that substitutes for currency as a person primarily engaged in such business, such as an armored car; (5) provide prepaid access; or (6) accept and transmits funds only integral to the sale of goods or the provision of services, other than money transmission services, by the person who is accepting and transmitting the funds.

In evaluating the money transmission exemptions, and specifically whether a certain transmission constitutes "money transmission," it is important to determine whether the transmission of funds is a fundamental element of the actual transaction. If the transmission of funds is not a fundamental element of the transaction then the transmission will not be considered money transmission for the purposes of FinCEN regulation.

Brokers and dealers in real currency and commodities that accept and transmit funds solely for the purpose of affecting a bona fide purchase or sale of the currency or commodity for or with a customer are not acting as money transmitters. FinCEN does not regulate "users," as defined above. FinCEN does not have the authority to regulate transactions in consumer goods by ordinary persons. In January 30, 2014 guidance, FinCEN noted that to the extent that a user mines Bitcoin and uses the Bitcoin solely for the user's own purposes and not for the benefit of another, the user is not an MSB under FinCEN's regulations, because these activities involve neither "acceptance" nor "transmission" of the convertible virtual currency and are not the transmission of funds within the meaning of the Rule (FinCEN, 2014a,b).

A user who obtains convertible virtual currency and uses it to purchase real or virtual goods or services is not an MSB under FinCEN's regulations. Such activity, in and of itself, does not fit within the definition of "money transmission services" and therefore is not subject to FinCEN's registration, reporting, and recordkeeping regulations for MSBs (FinCEN, 2014a,b). Thus, in a transaction in which a purchaser uses 15 Bitcoins to purchase furniture for a home, neither the purchaser nor the transaction will be subject to the regulation of FinCEN.

Transactions in Bitcoins are broadcast to the Bitcoin network, and recorded in "blocks" which are published in "block chains." This publication mechanism maintains the integrity of the system while allowing control to be decentralized. The BSA excludes from the definition of money transmitter, providers of prepaid access. This exclusion is limited to real currency transactions and therefor does not apply to persons providing prepaid access in connection with Bitcoin.

Based on the FinCEN guidance, Bitcoins would fall within the scope of the definition of a decentralized virtual currency. A Bitcoin miner would be deemed a person that creates units of this convertible virtual currency. If the Bitcoin miner uses the Bitcoins to purchase real or virtual goods and services, the miner would not be subject to regulation as a money transmitter. A miner that sells Bitcoins to another person for real currency or its equivalent would be deemed to be engaged in transmission to another location, and would be a money transmitter. Finally, a person would be an exchanger and a money transmitter if the person accepts Bitcoins from one person and transmits Bitcoins to another person as part of the acceptance and transfers of currency, funds, or other value that is a substitute for currency.

17.4.6 Duties of money transmitters

If a Bitcoin exchange or retailers is deemed a money transmitter, the business will be subject to the requirements of the BSA. MSBs are generally required to (1) establish written AML programs that are reasonably designed to prevent the MSB from being used to facilitate money laundering and the financing of terrorist activities; (2) file Currency Transaction Reports (CTRs) and Suspicious Activity Reports (SARs); and (3) maintain certain records, including those relating to the purchase of certain monetary instruments with currency, transactions by currency dealers or exchangers (to be called "dealers in foreign exchange" under this rulemaking), and certain transmittals of funds. Most types of MSBs are required to register with FinCEN and all are subject to examination for BSA compliance by the IRS.

The BSA requires money services businesses to establish AML programs that include "an independent audit function to test programs." Any AML program established by a money service business must be in writing and provide for independent review to monitor and maintain an adequate program. Bitcoin merchants must identify and assess the money laundering risks that may be associated with its unique products, services, customers, and geographic locations. Regardless of where risks arise, money services businesses must take reasonable steps to manage them.

17.4.7 Recent FinCEN administrative rulings

FinCEN recently published two administrative rulings regarding whether companies must register as an MSB. In both instances FinCEN concluded the proposed systems were money transmitters required to register as MSBs. FinCEN's analysis in each ruling provides useful guidance.

17.4.7.1 The hotel payment system

The first administrative ruling involved a company that proposed to establish a virtual currency payment system (FinCEN, 2014d). The company proposed to set up a system that would provide virtual currency-based payments to merchants in the United States and Latin America, who wanted to receive payment for goods or services sold in a currency other than that of legal tender in their respective jurisdictions. The company would receive payment from the buyer or debtor in currency of legal tender (real currency), and transfer the equivalent in Bitcoin to the seller or creditor, minus a transaction fee. The company proposed to offer the system to the hotel industry in several Latin American countries where, because of currency controls and extreme inflation, merchants face substantial foreign exchange risks when dealing with overseas customers.

The company proposed to use the system and the company's Web site to permit customers purchasing the merchant's goods or services to pay for the purchase using a credit card. Instead of the credit card payment going to the merchant, it would go to the company, which would transfer the equivalent in Bitcoin to the merchant. The company would then pay the merchant using the reserve of Bitcoin it acquired from wholesale purchases from virtual currency exchangers at the company's discretion. The company would assume any exchange risk that occurred during the time between the company's wholesale purchases and its payment to a merchant. The company had no agreement with the customer and would only make payment to the merchant.

The company claimed it should not be regulated as a money transmitter because it did not conform to the definition of virtual currency exchanger, due to the fact that the company made payments from an inventory it maintained, rather than funding each individual transaction. The company also claimed that, should the company be considered an exchanger of convertible virtual currency, the company's business should be covered by an exemption that applies to certain payment processing activities, and/or the company's transmissions should be deemed integral to the transaction and thereby covered under another exemption from money transmission.

FinCEN rejected the company's claim that it did not convert the customer's real currency into virtual currency because the company purchased and stored large quantities of Bitcoin that the company then used to pay the merchants. FinCEN concluded the company was an exchanger because it engaged as a business in accepting and converting the customer's real currency into virtual currency for transmission to the merchants. FinCEN noted the fact that the company used its cache of Bitcoin to pay the merchant was not relevant to whether it fits within the definition of money transmitter. FinCEN concluded the company would be a money transmitter because it was acting as an exchanger of convertible virtual currency.

FinCEN also rejected the company's claim that it was covered by the payment processor exemption from registration. FinCEN identified four conditions to the application of the payment processor exemption:

- The entity providing the service must facilitate the purchase of goods or services, or the payment of bills for goods or services (other than money transmission itself);
- The entity must operate through clearance and settlement systems that admit only BSA-regulated financial institutions;
- The entity must provide the service pursuant to a formal agreement; and
- The entity's agreement must be at a minimum with the seller or creditor that provided the goods or services and receives the funds.

FinCEN found that the company failed to satisfy one of the conditions—the company was "not operating through clearing and settlement systems that only admit BSA-regulated financial institutions as members" (FinCEN, 2014d). FinCEN noted that payments of the Bitcoin equivalent to the merchants would take place outside such a clearing and settlement system, either to a merchant-owned virtual currency wallet or to a larger virtual currency exchange that admits both financial institution and nonfinancial institution members, for the account of the merchant.

FinCEN also rejected the company's claim that money transmission was integral to the provision of the company's service. FinCEN noted there are three fundamental conditions that must be met for the exemption to apply:

- The money transmission component must be part of the provision of goods or services distinct from money transmission itself;
- The exemption can only be claimed by the person that is engaged in the provision of goods or services distinct from money transmission; and
- The money transmission component must be integral (that is, necessary) for the provision of the goods or services (FinCEN, 2014d).

FinCEN believed the payment service met the definition of money transmission and that such money transmission was the sole purpose of the company's system. FinCEN did not believe the payment service offered by the company was a necessary part of another, non-money transmission service being provided by the company. For the reasons noted above, FinCEN concluded the company was engaged in money transmission, and such activity was not covered by either the payment processor or the integral exemption.

17.4.7.2 The convertible virtual currency trading system

In the second administrative ruling FinCEN addressed whether a proposed convertible virtual currency trading and booking platform was a money transmitter under the BSA

(FinCEN, 2014c). The company proposed to establish a platform that consisted of a trading system to match offers to buy and sell convertible virtual currency for currency of legal tender (real currency), and a set of book accounts in which prospective buyers or sellers of one type of currency or the other customers can deposit funds to cover their exchanges. The company proposed to maintain separate accounts in U.S. dollars and a virtual wallet, both segregated from the company's operational accounts and protected from seizure by the company's creditors (the "Funding Accounts"), in which customers would deposit their U.S. dollars or convertible virtual currency to fund the exchanges. The company planned to maintain the funding received from each customer in its separate book entry account (the "Customer Account").

Once the exchange was funded, the customer would submit an order to the company to purchase or sell the currency deposited at a given price. The platform would automatically attempt to match each purchase order of one currency to one or more sell orders of the same currency. If a match was found, the company would purchase from the customer acting as seller and sell to the customer acting as buyer, without identifying one to the other. If a match was not found, the customer could elect to withdraw the funds or keep them in its Customer Account to fund future orders.

The company would not allow inter-account transfers, third-party funding of a Customer Account, or payments from one Customer Account to a third party. Payments to or from the customer would be sent or received by credit transmittals of funds through the Automatic Clearinghouse (ACH) system or wire transfers from U.S. banks. The platform would not allow any customer to know the identity of another customer, and customers would be required to conduct transactions exclusively through their formal agreements with the company.

The company claimed that because it was already registered with FinCEN as a money transmitter and a dealer in foreign exchange, that it should not be regulated as a money transmitter for the following reasons:

- The company acts in a similar manner to securities or commodities exchanges, and there is no money transmission between the company and any counterparty.
- If FinCEN was to find that the company is engaged in money transmission, then such activity would be integral to the company's business or eligible for the payment processor exemption.
- Last, should FinCEN find that the above exemptions do not apply, the company fits the definition of "user" rather than "exchanger" or "administrator" pursuant to FinCEN's guidance (FinCEN, 2014c).

FinCEN rejected these arguments and concluded the proposed platform would be a money transmitter. FinCEN noted that "a person is an exchanger and a money transmitter if the person accepts convertible virtual currency from one person and transmits it to another person as part of the acceptance and transfer of currency, funds, or other value that substitutes for currency" (FinCEN, 2014c). FinCEN concluded the payment service that the company intended to offer met the definition of money transmission.

FinCEN found that while the company was registered with FinCEN as a dealer in foreign exchange, it was subject to regulation as a money transmitter. FinCEN noted the company's platform consisted of two parts: (1) an electronic matching book for offers of buying and selling virtual currency and (2) a set of book accounts that pre-fund the transactions ordered by customers that want to exchange virtual currency for real currency. FinCEN concluded that because of the foregoing, each trade conducted through the platform involved two money transmission transactions—one between the company and its customer wishing to buy virtual currency, and another between the company and its other customer wishing to sell such virtual currency at the same exchange rate. FinCEN did not consider providing virtual currency for real currency or vice versa as a nonmoney transmission-related service.

FinCEN rejected the company's claim the money transmission was integral to the provision of the company's service, and eligible for exemption. FinCEN concluded: (1) the company was facilitating the transfer of value, both real and virtual, between third parties; (2) that such money transmission was the sole purpose of the company's system; and (3) that such services were not a necessary part of another, nonmoney transmission service being provided by the company.

FinCEN also rejected the company's claim that it was exempt from registration under the payment processor exemption. Citing the same criteria discussed above, FinCEN concluded the company failed to satisfy two of the conditions. First, the customer was "not receiving payment as a seller or creditor from a buyer or debtor for the provision of nonmoney transmission related goods or services." FinCEN stated that it does not consider providing virtual currency for real currency or vice versa as a nonmoney transmission-related service. Second, that the company was "not operating through a clearing and settlement system that only admits BSA-regulated financial institutions as members" (FinCEN, 2014c).

FinCEN also rejected the company's assertion that it was eligible for the payment processor exemption because payments to or from the Customer Accounts could take place in part using a clearing and settlement system such as EPN, FedACH, or FedWire. FinCEN noted the platform was not a clearance and settlement system that admits only BSA-regulated financial institutions, and the payments of convertible virtual currency to and from the customers, were to take place outside such a clearance and settlement system (FinCEN, 2014c).

Finally, FinCEN rejected the company's argument that it should be considered a user and not an exchanger because "a true virtual currency exchange would have its own reserve of virtual currency and dollars that it would buy and sell in order to fund exchanges with users" (FinCEN, 2014c). FinCEN noted that:

a person is an exchanger and a money transmitter if the person accepts convertible virtual currency from one person and transmits it to another person as part of the acceptance and transfer of currency, funds, or other value that substitutes for currency. The method of funding the transactions is not relevant to the definition of money transmitter. *An exchanger will be subject to the same obligations under FinCEN regulations regardless of whether the exchanger acts as a broker (attempting to match two (mostly) simultaneous and offsetting transactions involving the acceptance of one type of currency and the transmission of another) or as a dealer (transacting from its own reserve in either convertible virtual currency or real currency).*

(Yermack, 2014; FinCEN, 2014c).

FinCEN found that the company was acting as an exchanger of convertible virtual currency and must register with FinCEN as a money transmitter.

17.5 SEC REGULATION OF VIRTUAL CURRENCIES

17.5.1 What is a security?

The definitions of "security" under the Securities Act of 1933 (the "Securities Act") and the Securities Exchange Act of 1934 (the "Exchange Act") are virtually identical and each is broad enough to include the various types of instruments that are used in commercial marketplaces that one might suspect to fall within the ordinary concepts of a security. This would include common instruments like stocks, bonds, and notes, as well as the various collective investment pools and common enterprises devised by persons seeking to generate profits from the efforts and investments of others (i.e., investment contracts and instruments commonly known as securities).

Section 2(a)(1) of the Securities Act (*Securities Act*) defines a "security" as:

[A]ny note, stock, treasury stock, security future, security-based swap, bond, debenture, evidence of indebtedness, . . . transferable share, investment contract, . . . *any put, call, straddle, option, or privilege on any security, certificate of deposit, . . . or any put, call, straddle, option, or privilege entered into on a national securities exchange relating to foreign currency, or, in general, any interest or instrument commonly known as a "security", or any certificate of interest or participation in, temporary or interim certificate for, receipt for, guarantee of, or warrant or right to subscribe to or purchase, any of the foregoing.*

The definition of "security" under the Securities Act does not include currencies. However, the SEC has argued that investments in Bitcoin-related schemes are investment contracts—a contract, transaction, or scheme involving (1) an investment of money, (2) in a common enterprise, (3) with the expectation that profits will be derived from the efforts of the promoter or a third party (*Securities Exchange Commission v. W.J. Howey, Co.* (1946) 328 U.S. 293; *Brotherhood of Teamsters v. Daniel* (1979) 421 U.S. 837, 852).

17.5.2 Is Bitcoin a security?

Any investment in securities in the United States remains subject to the jurisdiction of the SEC regardless of whether the investment is made in U.S. dollars or a virtual currency.

Individuals selling investments are typically subject to federal or state licensing requirements. Whether a Bitcoin is a security for the purposes of the Securities Act and the Exchange Act has been at the heart of recent Bitcoin controversies and government actions against persons engaged in the trading of Bitcoins.

17.5.3 SEC treatment of Bitcoins

In *Securities Exchange Commission v. Trendon T. Shavers and Bitcoin Savings and Trust* (BST) (2013), a well-publicized case involving the SEC's regulation of Bitcoin investment schemes, the SEC alleged that Shavers and BST engaged in the fraudulent offer and sale of securities without registration under the Securities Act. The SEC claimed that, during the relevant period, Shavers obtained at least 700,467 Bitcoins in principal investments from BST investors, or $4,592,806 in U.S. dollars, based on the daily average price of Bitcoin when the BST investors purchased their investments. In Shavers (2013), the alleged organizer of a Ponzi scheme advertised a Bitcoin "investment opportunity" in an online Bitcoin forum. The SEC claimed investors were promised up to 7% interest per week and that the invested funds would be used for Bitcoin arbitrage activities in order to generate the returns. Instead, the invested Bitcoins were allegedly used to pay existing investors and exchanged into U.S. dollars to pay the organizer's personal expenses (*Securities Exchange Commission v. Trendon T. Shavers and Bitcoin Savings and Trust*, 2013).

In a memorandum regarding the court's subject matter jurisdiction, the court analyzed whether as a matter of law, BST's solicitations to entice persons to invest in Bitcoin-related investments opportunities constituted the sale of securities. The court analyzed whether the investment opportunities fell within the scope of the term "security," noting that the term "security" is defined as "any note, stock, treasury stock, security future, security-based swap, bond ... [or] investment contract ... " United States (*United States Code: Section 77b*). The court applied the three part test articulated by the U.S. Supreme Court in *Howey* (1946), to determine whether an offering, contract, transaction, or scheme constitutes an investment contract.

Many headlines and online articles interpreting Shavers (2013) have mistakenly proclaimed "*Bitcoins are a form of currency* subject to federal securities laws" (Greene, 2013). Misleading statements like these fail to recognize a key legal distinction made in the *Shavers* case. The question before the court in *Shavers* was whether the BST investments being offered by Shavers constituted securities under federal securities laws. Accordingly, the opinion of the court focused on the characterization of the investments and not the underlying commodity—Bitcoins.

The court in Shavers (2013) evaluated the investments in BST and held that all three prongs of the Howey (1946) test were satisfied and thereby, the sale of interests in the trust constituted the sale of securities. In its analysis, the court found that:

- Because Bitcoin can be used as money to purchase goods or services and also can be exchanged for conventional currencies, Bitcoin is in fact a currency or form of money;
- The investors and the promoter were interdependent because the investors were dependent on Shavers's expertise in Bitcoin markets and his local connections and in addition, Shavers allegedly promised a substantial return on their investments as a result of his trading and exchanging Bitcoin; and
- Investors participating in the BST investments were expecting profits from Shavers's efforts.

Noting, "it is clear that Bitcoin can be used as money" the court found that the BST investments met the definition of investment contract, and as such, were securities (*Shavers v. BST, 2013*; Sandler, 2013).

The court did not address the issue of whether Bitcoins constitute securities, but rather focused on the system or scheme through which the investments in Bitcoins were being made. The dicta from the court's opinion, however, makes clear that at least one federal court considering the issue acknowledged the utility of Bitcoins as a form of money.

17.5.4 The SEC's concerns

The mission of the SEC is to protect investors; to maintain fair, orderly, and efficient markets; and to facilitate capital formation (U.S. Securities and Exchange Commission, 2014a). As securities markets evolve, the SEC must focus on how to regulate new forms of capital formation. The SEC has focused on the potential for Bitcoin and virtual currency proprietors to mislead and defraud investors. Like other regulatory agencies, the SEC is concerned with the potential for virtual currencies to be used to solicit and trap investors in fraudulent or otherwise misleading investment scams. This concern was addressed by the SEC in a July 2013 investor alert which states "the rising use of virtual currencies in the global marketplace may entice fraudsters to lure investors into Ponzi and other schemes in which these currencies are used to facilitate fraudulent, or simply fabricated, investments or transactions" (Securities and Exchange Commission, 2013). The alert explains a fraud involving virtual currencies may also involve an unregistered offering of securities or the operation of an unregistered trading platform.

While it is unclear if Congress or the U.S. Supreme Court would treat Bitcoins as securities, the Shavers (2013) case is evidence of the SEC's intention to closely monitor investments that involve the sale of Bitcoins and other virtual currencies. If the SEC believes the investment constitutes an investment contract that involves fraud or other misconduct, an SEC enforcement action is likely.

17.5.5 The SEC's focus

While Bitcoin may not be a "security," certain transactions in Bitcoin involve investment contracts as described above and thereby will be subject to the federal securities laws. The

SEC recently charged the co-owner of two Bitcoin-related Web sites for publicly offering shares in the two ventures without registering the securities under the Securities Act. "All issuers selling securities to the public must comply with the registration provisions of the securities laws, including issuers who seek to raise funds using Bitcoin" (Securities and Exchange Commission, 2014b).

Those who use or invest in virtual currency are exposed to risks that do not affect national currencies. The anonymity and irrevocability of transactions in virtual currencies, while valuable to the user because of the limited transactional expense, expose users to fraud and theft, and virtual wallets do not benefit from any deposit insurance.

17.6 CFTC REGULATION OF VIRTUAL CURRENCIES

Sale of Bitcoins could also be characterized as futures contracts, commodity futures, forwards, swaps, or options (Shadab, 2014). This would bring Bitcoin within the jurisdiction of the CFTC, which has authority to regulate commodity futures contracts and certain foreign exchange instruments. Recent comments by then CFTC Commissioner, Bart Chilton suggest the CFTC is considering exercising jurisdiction over virtual currency transactions.

On May 6, 2013, then Commissioner Chilton noted "there is more than a *colorable argument* to be made that derivative products relating to Bitcoin fall squarely in [the CFTC's] jurisdiction" (Alloway et al., 2013). In another interview the same day, he stated: "Here's what we know for sure: [the CFTC] could regulate [Bitcoin] if we wanted. That is very clear" (Miedema, 2013). Former Commissioner Chilton explained: "if you're buying Bitcoin and you are hoping that their value increases . . . and you could purchase something with them in a day or a week or a month or a year, that is clearly a derivative of the actual Bitcoin" (Miedema, 2013).

If the CFTC chooses to regulate Bitcoin transactions, it may do so under its commodity futures or foreign exchange authority.

17.6.1 Bitcoins as commodity futures

The Commodity Exchange Act (CEA) defines commodities as "all goods and articles . . . and all services, rights and interests . . . in which contracts for future delivery are presently or in the future dealt in . . . except for onions and motion picture box office receipts" (Commodities Exchange Act, 7 U.S.C. § 1a(9) (2013)). By this definition, Bitcoins could qualify as commodities because they are articles that can be made subject to futures contracts. Despite this, decisions explaining why certain commodities are not securities highlight that commodities are generally "tangible" and have "inherent value," unlike securities (Bromberg, 1975).

Commodity futures are not defined in the CEA (2013). In *Dunn v. Commodity Futures Trading Commission*, the U.S. Supreme Court explained that futures contracts are "agreements to buy or sell a specified quantity of a commodity at a particular price for delivery at a set future date" (*Dunn v. Commodity Futures Trading Commission*, 519 U.S. 465, 470 (1997)). All terms of a futures contract except for price are standardized.

Commodities are distinguished by the CFTC on "whether they are financial or non-financial in nature" (Shadab, 2014). The CFTC also distinguishes between "tangible commodities (such as crops and currencies) and intangible commodities (such as price indices, pollution allowances, and contractual rights)" (Shadab, 2014).

Should Bitcoins come within the CEA's definition of commodity, it is unclear what category of commodity may apply. Bitcoins may be deemed an excluded commodity if they are viewed as being a type of currency or other financial interest (Shadab, 2014). Bitcoins may also be deemed an exempt commodity because the are similar to precious metals that are mined. Finally, Bitcoins may be treated as exempt intangible commodities because "ownership of the commodity can be conveyed in some manner and the commodity can be consumed" (Shadab, 2014). If Bitcoins are deemed commodities, the CFTC may regulate Bitcoins as commodity futures. Such regulation would apply only to circumstances in which parties entered a contract for Bitcoins for delivery at a future date.

17.6.2 Bitcoins as foreign exchange, currency swaps, or forwards

Under revisions to the CEA mandated by Title VII of the Dodd-Frank Wall Street Reform and Consumer Protection Act of 2010 (the "Dodd-Frank Act"), the CFTC's authority was substantially expanded to include regulation of derivatives, in addition to commodity futures. The CEA defines a derivate, commonly known as a "swap," to include foreign exchange or currency swaps and forwards (Commodities Exchange Act 7 U.S.C. § 1a(47)).

The CFTC has exclusive jurisdiction over most swaps, including those based on commodities, currencies, and interest rates. The SEC has exclusive jurisdiction over swaps based on securities and narrow-based indices. Generally, Swaps must be cleared by a regulated central counterparty clearinghouse and be traded on a swap execution facility ("SEF").

A foreign exchange swap is defined as "an exchange of *two different currencies* on a specific date at a fixed rate that is agreed on at the inception of the contract covering the exchange; and a reverse exchange of those two currencies at a later date at a fixed rate that is agreed on at the inception of the contract covering the exchange" (Commodities Exchange Act 7 U.S.C. § 1a(9), 2013). A foreign exchange forward is defined as "a transaction that solely involves the exchange of *two different currencies* on a specific future date at a fixed rate agreed on at the inception of the contract covering the exchange" (Commodities Exchange Act, 2013). Despite defining the foregoing terms, the CEA does not define "foreign exchange" or "foreign currency." For the

CFTC to assert its foreign exchange authority over Bitcoin transactions, it will have to take the position that Bitcoin is considered a "foreign currency." However, such a determination would be "at odds with the common understanding of foreign currency, as the money coined by foreign governments" (Brito and Castillo, 2013).

Although "foreign exchange" is not defined for purposes of Title VII of the Dodd-Frank Act, such term is defined for purposes of Dodd-Frank Act Title X, which creates the Consumer Finance Protection Bureau. Under Title X, "foreign" exchange is defined as "the exchange, for compensation, of currency of the United States or of a foreign government for currency of another government" (12 U.S.C. § 5481(16)). If this definition gives any indication of Congress' interpretation of the term "foreign exchange," Bitcoin is likely to fall outside of the definition due to the fact that it is not government issued.

Bitcoin contracts may also be deemed options. A call option gives the purchaser the right to purchase an asset at predetermined price and only has value if that price is below the market price. A put option works in the opposite manner. A party could use a call option to sell goods denominated in Bitcoins and to be protected if the price increases. A party could use a Bitcoin put option for protection from a decline in the price of Bitcoins by guaranteeing the option to sell at a predetermined price.

The CFTC could treat Bitcoin options as swaps under the CEA. However, the CFTC's jurisdiction would be limited in instances where the options involve physical delivery and the counter parties are financially sophisticated commercial users.

While the authority of the CFTC to regulate Bitcoins is unclear, former Commissioner Chilton's statements are an important indication of the agency's belief that it has the authority to regulate Bitcoin transactions. In light of the lack of regulatory clarity, operators of Bitcoin platforms should proceed with caution to minimize the risk of an enforcement action by the SEC or the CFTC.

17.6.3 Regulation of Bitcoin "Spot" transactions

As a commodity, "spot" Bitcoin transactions could also give the CFTC oversight authority under its antimanipulation rules. Also called cash trades, spot trades are the opposite of futures contracts and they are commodities traded on the spot market. They are traded with the expectation of actual delivery, as opposed to a commodity future that is usually not delivered (Zerenga and Watterson, 2014). Because manipulation in the spot market can affect the prices in the derivatives market, the CFTC has regulatory authority. The CFTC has historically limited the exercise of its jurisdiction of the spot market toward manipulation that affects futures prices, and under the Dodd-Frank Act, the agency has enforcement authority with respect to market manipulation. The CFTC's first enforcement action in the spot market was with respect to a Ponzi scheme involving spot market silver contracts (*CFTC v. Atlantic Bullion & Coin, Inc., C.A.* (2014)). The CFTC's regulation of spot Bitcoin transactions may be similar to its regulation of crude oil, which is a commodity frequently bought and sold on the spot market.

17.6.4 Bitcoin as foreign exchange or derivatives

The Dodd-Frank Act expanded the CFTC's authority over derivatives expanded. The CEA defines a derivative, commonly known as a "swap," to include foreign exchange or currency swaps and forwards. 7 U.S.C. § 1a(47). The creation of a platform for buying and selling swaps linked to Bitcoin may be the first step toward regulatory oversight by the CFTC. Swaps let investors, companies, and institutions exchange one kind of payment for another. These can be speculative based on prices or hedge risk from trading. Certain swap contracts can also spur derivatives trading by offering investors multiple structure deals, including deals in foreign currency. Such platforms would fall with the CFTC's jurisdiction. In fact, Tera Group, creator of a Bitcoin swap market, submitted a report to the CFTC for its TeraExchange platform.

According to the Dodd-Frank Act, the CFTC would have authority over Bitcoin transactions were it to define Bitcoin as a "foreign currency." This determination would be at odds with the current definition of foreign currency, which is, "money coined by foreign governments" (Brito and Castillo, 2013). Nevertheless, on May 6, 2013, then Commissioner Chilton noted "there is more than a colorable argument to be made that derivative products relating to Bitcoin fall squarely in [the CFTC's] jurisdiction" (Alloway et al., 2013).

With respect to Bitcoin transactions, it may be appropriate for the CFTC to analogize the virtual currency to foreign exchange swap transaction since Bitcoin shares characteristics with currencies in their use and exchange. A "foreign exchange swap" is defined as "an exchange of two different currencies on a specific date at a fixed rate that is agreed on at the inception of the contract covering the exchange; and a reverse exchange of those two currencies at a later date at a fixed rate is agreed on at the inception of the contract covering the exchange" (Commodities Exchange Act, 7 U.S.C. § 1a(47) (2013)). Whereas a "foreign exchange forward" is defined as a "transaction that solely involves the exchange of two different currencies on a specific future date at a fixed rate agreed on at the inception of the contract covering the exchange" (Commodities Exchange Act, 2013).

17.6.5 CFTC and BSA compliance

The CFTC also has the authority to examine firms for BSA compliance, including futures commission merchants (FCMs) and other futures market intermediaries accepting virtual currency as payments. FCMs are entities that solicit or accept orders for the purchase or sale of a commodity for future delivery on or subject to the rules of any exchange and that accept payment from or extend credit to those whose orders are accepted. Nonetheless, the CFTC would have to make a determination about the capital treatment of virtual currencies if the merchants held virtual currencies for their own account or an account of a customer (Evans, 2014).

In order to carry out its regulatory responsibilities, the CFTC will have to determine whether the derivatives were susceptible to manipulation, review applications for new exchanges seeking to offer derivatives, and examine exchanges offering the derivatives to ensure compliance with the applicable commodity exchange laws (Evans, 2014).

17.6.6 Recent CFTC statements on Bitcoin

While the authority of the CFTC to regulate Bitcoins is unclear, former Commissioner Chilton's statements are an important indication of the agency's belief that it has the authority to regulate Bitcoin transactions. In light of the lack of regulatory clarity, operators of Bitcoin platforms should proceed with caution to minimize the risk of an enforcement action by the SEC or the CFTC.

While FinCEN has been the most active regulator in the United States with respect to the regulation of virtual currencies, the CFTC's has become increasingly active. After several months of speculation by the media and Bitcoin observers of the agency's potential plans for regulating virtual currencies, Mark Wetjen, the CFTC's acting Chairman, indicated that CFTC staff are examining the regulation of virtual currencies and derivatives linked to virtual currencies (Miedema, 2014). Chairman Wetjen stated the CFTC has not completed its analysis of whether Bitcoin and other virtual currencies meet the definition of a commodity under CFTC rules against manipulation (Miedema, 2014). He also noted that "there is a pretty good argument that [Bitcoin] would fit" the definition of a commodity and that the CFTC is looking at platforms that are seeking to offer derivatives tied to Bitcoin (Miedema, 2014).

In October 9, 2014, acting Chairman Wetjen acknowledged that "[o]nly with additional understanding can the CFTC be confident that it can effectively execute on its mission of preserving the proper functioning of a cryptocurrency derivative market, which includes enforcing rules intended to prevent manipulation of these markets." The CFTC's increasing focus on the regulation of virtual currencies was evidenced by the CFTC's Global Advisory Committee meeting on October 9, 2014, which addressed Bitcoin and the implications for the derivatives markets.

17.6.7 CFTC approval of TeraExchange

The same day as the CFTC's Global Markets Advisory Committee Meeting, TeraExchange—a New Jersey based swap execution facility—announced the first Bitcoin derivative transaction to be executed on a CFTC regulated exchange. TeraExchange was recently approved by the CFTC to offer a Tera Bitcoin Price Index swap.

It is unclear how the CFTC will proceed with respect to the regulation of Bitcoin. During the October meeting, the CFTC sidestepped the larger questions about Bitcoin's classification as a currency or commodity. However, the CFTC has repeatedly indicated that the agency has the authority to regulate virtual currencies and will continue to follow Bitcoin's development. Wetjen made clear that, "it would be a real mistake for . . . [the] commission to not make sure [they] are staying on top of these developments" (Wetjen, 2014).

17.7 IRS TREATMENT OF VIRTUAL CURRENCIES

The old adage that there are only two truths in life, death and taxes, has come to the world of virtual currency. The well-publicized $400 million failure of Mt. Gox, a leading Bitcoin platform, has produced fevered new calls for regulation of virtual currencies. Following the death of Mt. Gox, on March 25, 2014, the IRS provided guidance to miners, users, and traders of virtual currencies, such as Bitcoin. The IRS guidance discusses the U.S. federal tax implications of transactions involving virtual currency. In the guidance the IRS noted that:

> [virtual currency] operates like "real" currency—i.e., the coin and paper money of the United States or of any other country that is designated as legal tender, circulates, and is customarily used and accepted as a medium of exchange in the country of issuance—but it does not have legal tender status in any jurisdiction.
>
> **(Internal Revenue Service (2014)).**

Having concluded that virtual currencies are like "real currency," the IRS (2014) noted "virtual currency is treated as property for U.S. federal tax purposes." Accordingly, this means that:

- Wages paid to employees using virtual currency are taxable to the employee, must be reported by an employer on a Form W-2, and are subject to federal income tax withholding and payroll taxes;
- Payments using virtual currency made to independent contractors and other service providers are taxable and self-employment tax rules generally apply;
- The character of gain or loss from the sale or exchange of virtual currency depends on whether the virtual currency is a capital asset in the hands of the taxpayer; and
- A payment made using virtual currency is subject to information reporting to the same extent as any other payment made in property.

17.8 FINRA CONCERNS REGARDING VIRTUAL CURRENCIES

Concerns regarding the risks of using virtual currencies have also been raised by FINRA, the self-regulatory organization charged with supervising broker-dealers and protecting investors. In a recently published alert, FINRA identified the following risks of using the virtual currency:

- Bitcoins may become worthless because Bitcoin is not legal tender and its use is limited to businesses and individuals that are willing to accept Bitcoins;
- The loss of Bitcoins due to the illegal hacking of Bitcoin platforms used to store the virtual currency;
- The operators of platforms used to store Bitcoins are not subject to the requirements placed on banks and credit unions to protect client assets; and
- The fact that Bitcoin transactions cannot be reversed (Finra.org, 2014).

17.9 CONGRESSIONAL CONCERNS REGARDING VIRTUAL CURRENCIES

Not to be out done by the regulators, U.S. Senator Joe Manchin of West Virginia has called for a Bitcoin ban. In a letter to regulators, Senator Manchin described Bitcoin as "disruptive to our economy" (Manchin, 2014). The Senator believes Bitcoin is used for "either transacting in illegal goods and services or *speculative gambling* . . . " (Manchin, 2014). Senator Manchin urged "regulators to work together" and to "act quickly," to "prohibit this *dangerous currency* from harming hard-working Americans" (Manchin, 2014).

However, in a nod to the technologists that support the growth of virtual currencies, and in a light hearted retort to Senator Manchin's call for banning Bitcoin, Congressman Jared Polis of Colorado called on the Treasury to ban physical dollars (Polis, 2014). The Congressman noted, "[t]he exchange of dollar bills, including high denomination bills, is currently unregulated and has allowed users to participate in illicit activity, while also being highly subject to forgery, theft, and loss" (Polis, 2014). Congressman Polis (2014) also noted that:

> [t]he clear use of dollar bills for transacting in illegal goods, anonymous transactions, tax fraud, and services or speculative gambling *make me wary of their use. Before the United States gets too far behind the curve on this important topic, I urge the regulators to work together, act quickly, and prohibit this dangerous currency from harming hard-working Americans* . . .

While the statements of Congressman Polis were meant to serve as a satirical response to Senator Manchin's letter, the letters reflect the divergent views in Congress and within the Democratic Party with respect to the potential risks and benefits of the use of virtual currencies.

17.10 CONCLUSIONS

Virtual currencies such as Bitcoin represent an innovation in financial services products and technology that has the potential to support more efficient and transparent global commerce. Since Bitcoin does not rely on intermediaries, it may lower transaction costs for businesses and emerge as a major means of electronic payment processing. In the authors' opinion, Bitcoin has a clear potential for growth in light of these attributes. Of course, virtual currencies, like traditional currencies, can also be used for money laundering and other criminal activities.

Despite the many benefits and drawbacks highlighted by supporters and detractors of Bitcoin, it is clear that presently, virtual currencies exist in a legal gray area. Though certain regulators, including FinCEN, have sought to clarify this regulatory framework, further clarification by regulators and policymakers is necessary to foster widespread acceptance of virtual currencies.

The authors appreciate the desire of Congress and the regulators to protect the public from fraudulent schemes that make use of virtual currencies. However, the fact that Bitcoin has been used by parties as part of a fraud does not mean virtual currencies are inherently fraudulent or flawed. We are encouraged by the statements by regulators, including the CFTC that they plan to issue guidance on the regulation. However, as always, the devil will be in the details.

REFERENCES

Alloway, T., Meyer, G., Foley, S., 2013. US regulators eye Bitcoin supervision—FT.com. Financial Times, Available at: http://www.ft.com/intl/cms/s/0/b810157c-b651-11e2-93ba-00144feabdc0.html#axzz3CAKRXT5B (accessed 02.09.14).

Andreessen, M., 2014. Why Bitcoin matters. New York Times, Available at: http://dealbook.nytimes.com/2014/01/21/why-bitcoin-matters/?_php=true&_type=blogs&_r=0 (accessed 23.08.14).

Boesler, M., 2013a. ANALYST: Bitcoin took a key step towards going mainstream, and that's why it's been going crazy the last two days. Business Insider, Available at: http://www.businessinsider.com/reason-behind-bitcoin-surge-2013-3 (accessed 26.08.14).

Boesler, M., 2013b. ANALYST: the rise of Bitcoin teaches a tremendous lesson about global economics. Business Insider, Available at: http://www.businessinsider.com/global-economics-lesson-from-bitcoin-2013-3 (accessed 26.08.14).

Brito, J., Castillo, A., 2013. Bitcoin: A Primer for Policymakers, first ed. Mercatus Center at George Mason University, Arlington, VA, Available at: http://mercatus.org/sites/default/files/Brito_BitcoinPrimer.pdf (accessed 02.09.14).

Bromberg, A., 1975. Commodities law in securities law-overlaps and preemptions. J. Corp. L. 1, 217.

Brotherhood of Teamsters v. Daniel (1979) 421 U.S. 837, 852.

CFTC v. Atlantic Bullion & Coin, Inc., C.A. No. 8:12-1503-JMC (D. S.C., June 6, 2010), 2014.

Commodity Exchange Act. 7 U.S.C. § 1a(9), 2013.

Commodity Exchange Act. 7 U.S.C. Sec. 1a(47), 2013.

Commodity Futures Trading Com. v. U. S. Metals Depository Co. (1979) 468 F.Supp.1149.

Currency and Foreign Transactions Reporting Act of 1970, 31 U.S.C. § 5311 et seq.

Department of Justice, 2007. Indictment of E-Gold, Ltd., et al., Available at: http://www.justice.gov/criminal/pr/2007/04/CRM_07-301_042707_egold_indict.pdf (accessed 07.01.2015).

Department of Justice, 2012. More than $10.8 Million in E-Gold, Ltd Accounts Traceable to Criminal Offenses to Be Forfeited, Available at: http://www.justice.gov/usao/md/news/2012/Morethan10.8MillioninE-GoldAccountsTraceabletoCriminalOffensestoBeForfeiteda2012_template.html (accessed 07.01.15).

Department of Justice, 2013a. Manhattan U.S. Attorney Announces Charges Against Liberty Reserve, One of World's Largest Digital Currency Companies, and Seven of Its Principals and Employees for Allegedly Running a $6 Billion Money Laundering Scheme, Available at: http://www.justice.gov/usao/nys/pressreleases/May13/LibertyReservePR.php (accessed 07.01.15).

Department of Justice, 2013b. Indictment of Liberty Reserve S.A., et al., Available at: http://www.justice. gov/usao/nys/pressreleases/May13/LibertyReserveetalDocuments/Liberty%20Reserve,%20et%20al. %20Indictment%20-%20Redacted.pdf (accessed 07.01.15).

Dion, D., 2013. I'll gladly trade you two bits on Tuesday for a byte today: Bitcoin, regulating fraud in the E-conomy of hacker-cash. Univ. Illinois J. Law Technol. Policy, Available at: http://illinoisjltp.com/ journal/wp-content/uploads/2013/05/Dion.pdf (accessed 23.08.14).

Dunn v. Commodity Futures Trading Commission, 519 U.S. 465, 470 (1997).

Evans, L., 2014. [pdf] United States Government Accountability Office, first ed, Available at: http://www. gao.gov/assets/670/663678.pdf (accessed 02.09.14).

FBI: New York Field Office, 2013. Manhattan U.S. Attorney Announces Seizure of Additional $28 Million Worth of Bitcoins Belonging to Ross William Ulbricht, Alleged Owner and Operator of "Silk Road" Website, Available at: http://www.fbi.gov/newyork/press-releases/2013/manhattan-u.s.-attorney-announces-seizure-of-additional-28-million-worth-of-bitcoins-belonging-to-ross-william-ulbricht-alleged-owner-and-operator-of-silk-road-website (accessed 26.08.14).

Financial Crimes Enforcement Network, 2014a. Guidance: FIN-2014-R001: Application of FinCEN's Regulation to Virtual Currency Mining and Operations, FIN-2014-R001, Available at: http:// www.fincen.gov/news_room/rp/rulings/pdf/FIN-2014-R001.pdf (accessed 26.08.14).

Financial Crimes Enforcement Network, 2014b. Guidance: FIN-2014-R002: Application of FinCEN's Regulations to Virtual Currency Software Development and Certain Investment Activity, FIN-2014-R002, Available at: http://www.fincen.gov/news_room/rp/rulings/pdf/FIN-2014-R001.pdf (accessed 26.08.14).

Financial Crimes Enforcement Network, 2014c. FIN 2014–R011: Request for Administrative Ruling on the Application of FinCEN's Regulations to a Virtual Currency Trading Platform. FIN-2014–R011, Available at: http://www.fincen.gov/news_room/rp/rulings/pdf/FIN-2014-R011.pdf (accessed 08.12.14).

Financial Crimes Enforcement Network, 2014d. FIN-2014-R012: Request for Administrative Ruling on the Application of FinCEN's Regulations to a Virtual Currency Payment System. FIN-2014-R012, Available at: http://www.fincen.gov/news_room/rp/rulings/pdf/FIN-2014-R012.pdf (accessed 08.08.14).

Financial Crimes Enforcement Network (FinCEN), 2013. Guidance FIN-2013-G0001: Application of Fin-CEN's Regulations to Persons Administrating, Exchanging, or Using Virtual Currencies. United States Department of the Treasury, New York, Available at: http://www.fincen.gov/statutes_regs/guidance/ pdf/FIN-2013-G001.pdf (accessed 23.08.14).

Finra.org, 2014. Investor Alert—Bitcoin: More than a Bit Risky—FINRA, Available at: http://www.finra. org/Investors/ProtectYourself/InvestorAlerts/FraudsAndScams/P456458 (accessed 02.09.14).

Flitter, E., 2013. Bitcoin fund raises $65 million after first two months, founder says. Reuters, New York, Available at: http://www.reuters.com/article/2013/12/11/us-etf-bitcoin-secondmarket-idUSBRE9BA15520131211 (accessed 26.08.14).

Fox Business, 2013. Munger/Buffett disagree on corporate tax rates. Fox Business, Available at: http:// video.foxbusiness.com/v/2359385547001 (accessed 02.09.14).

Gandel, S., 2013. Bitcoin start-up nabs Goldman board member. Fortune, Available at: http://fortune.com/ 2013/12/27/bitcoin-start-up-nabs-goldman-board-member/ (accessed 26.08.14).

Greene, K., 2013. Bitcoins are currency subject to securities laws, judge says. Law360, Available at: http:// bitcoinaware.com/article/355/bitcoins-are-currency-subject-to-securities-laws-judge-says/ (accessed 26.08.14).

Grocer, S., 2013. Beware the risks of the Bitcoin: Winklevii outline the downside. WSJ, Available at: http:// blogs.wsj.com/moneybeat/2013/07/02/beware-the-risks-of-the-bitcoin-winklevii-outline-the-downside/ (accessed 02.09.14).

Hill, K., 2013a. Bitcoin says goodbye to Silk Road and hello to Baidu, China's Google. Forbes, Available at: http://www.forbes.com/sites/kashmirhill/2013/10/16/bitcoin-says-goodbye-to-silk-road-and-hello-to-baidu-chinas-google/ (accessed 28.08.14).

Hill, K., 2013b. Bitcoin companies and entrepreneurs can't get bank accounts. Forbes, Available at: http:// www.forbes.com/sites/kashmirhill/2013/11/15/bitcoin-companies-and-entrepreneurs-cant-get-bank-accounts/ (accessed 23.08.14).

Hill, K., 2013c. Bitcoin valued at $1300 by Bank of America analysts. The Bitcoin Channel, Available at: http://www.thebitcoinchannel.com/archives/29131 (accessed 26.08.14).

In re Stovall, [1977–1980 Transfer Binder] Comm. Fut. L. Rep. (CCH) (CFTC December 6, 1979), 2014.

Internal Revenue Service, 2014. IRS Virtual Currency Guidance: virtual currency is treated as property for U.S. Federal Tax Purposes; General Rules for Property Transactions Apply, Notice 2104–21, Available at: http://www.irs.gov/pub/irs-drop/n-14-21.pdf (accessed 02.09.14).

Isidore, C., 2013. Bitcoin bubble may have burst. CNNMoney, Available at: http://money.cnn.com/2013/04/12/investing/bitcoin-bubble/ (accessed 26.08.14).

Kaplanov, N.M., 2012. Nerdy money: Bitcoin, the private digital currency, and the case against its regulation. Temple University Beasley School of LawLoy. Cons. L. Rev. 25, 111–174, Available at: http://luc.edu/media/lucedu/law/students/publications/clr/pdfs/kaplanov.pdf (accessed 23.08.14).

Karkaria, U., 2013. Hong Kong billionaire invests in Atlanta startup BitPay. Atlanta Business Chronicle, Available at: http://www.bizjournals.com/atlanta/blog/atlantech/2013/12/hong-kong-billionaire-invests-in.html (accessed 23.08.14).

Kelion, L., 2013. Bitcoin sinks after Chinese action. BBC News, Available at: http://www.bbc.com/news/technology-25428866 (accessed 02.09.14).

Krugman, P., 2014. Golden cyberfetters. New York Times, Available at: http://krugman.blogs.nytimes.com/2011/09/07/golden-cyberfetters/?_php=true&_type=blogs&_r=0n (accessed 26.08.14).

Levin, R., O'Brien, A., Osterman, S., 2014a. Dread Pirate Roberts, byzantine generals, and federal regulation of Bitcoin. J. Tax Reg. Fin. Inst. 27, 5–20, Available at: http://www.civicresearchinstitute.com/online/article_abstract.php?pid=2&iid=867&aid=5685 (accessed 06.09.14).

Levin, R., OBrien, A., Zuberi, M., 2014b. The Empire State Strikes Back: New York Proposes Rules for Virtual Currency. Baker & Hostetler, LLP—Client Alert, Washington, DC, Available at: http://bakerlaw.com/alerts/the-empire-state-strikes-back-new-york-proposes-rules-for-virtual-currency (accessed 06.09.14).

Levin, R., Mosier, M.A., Zuberi, M., 2014c. Bitcoin Investment Vehicles Beware—The SEC Is Watching. Baker & Hostetler, LLP—Client Alert, Washington, DC, Available at: http://bakerlaw.com/alerts/bitcoin-investment-vehicles-beware-the-sec-is-watching (accessed 06.09.14).

Library of Congress, 2014. Regulation of Bitcoin in Selected Jurisdictions, Available at: http://www.loc.gov/law/help/bitcoin-survey/?loclr=bloglaw (accessed 26.08.14).

Lomas, N., 2014. BitPay Passes 10,000 Bitcoin-Accepting Merchants on Its Payment Processing Network. TechCrunch.com, Available at: http://techcrunch.com/2013/09/16/bitpay-10000-merchants/ (accessed 02.09.14).

Lowery, E., 2013. Hearing—Beyond Silk Road: Potential Risks, Threats, and Promises of Virtual Currencies" Testimony of Edward Lowery III, U.S. Secret Service, U.S. Senate Committee on Homeland Security and Governmental Affairs, Available at: http://www.dhs.gov/news/2013/11/18/written-testimony-us-secret-service-senate-committee-homeland-security-and (accessed 06.09.14).

Luria, G., Turner, A., 2014. Digitalizing Trust: Leveraging the Bitcoin Protocol Beyond the "Coin", first ed. Wedbush Securities: Equity Research, Los Angeles, Available at: https://equities.wedbush.com/clientsite/Research/ActionAlertFilePreview.asp?UUID=8F27B170-5C0F-4A17-8A59-A33229236B04 (accessed 26.08.14).

Manchin.senate.gov, 2014. Manchin Demands Federal Regulators Ban Bitcoin—Press Releases—Newsroom—Joe Manchin, United States Senator, West Virginia, Available at: http://www.manchin.senate.gov/public/index.cfm/press-releases?ID=237cbd66-6a26-4870-9bcb-20177ae902b0 (accessed 02.09.14).

Miedema, D., 2013. Regulator Mulls Setting Rules for Digital Currency Bitcoin, Available at: http://www.reuters.com/article/2013/05/06/net-us-bitcoin-regulation-idUSBRE9450Y520130506 (accessed 28.08.14).

Miedema, D., 2014. U.S. Swaps Watchdog Says Considering Bitcoin Regulation. Reuters, Boca Raton, FL, Available at: http://www.reuters.com/article/2014/03/11/us-bitcoin-regulation-idUSBREA2A1W020140311 (accessed 28.08.14).

Murck, P., 2013. Hearing—Beyond Silk Road: Potential Risks, Threats, and Promises of Virtual Currencies: Testimony of Patrick Murck. The Bitcoin Foundation, U.S. Senate Committee on Homeland Security and Governmental Affairs, Washington, DC, Available at: http://www.hsgac.senate.gov/hearings/beyond-silk-road-potential-risks-threats-and-promises-of-virtual-currencies (accessed 06.09.14).

Myhrvold, C., 2012. Larry Summers and the technology of money. MIT Technol. Rev., Available at: http://www.technologyreview.com/news/427348/larry-summers-and-the-technology-of-money/ (accessed 26.08.14).

Nakamoto, S., 2008. Bitcoin: A Peer-to-Peer Electronic Cash System, Available at: http://bitcoin.org/bitcoin.pdf (accessed 02.09.14).

New York Department of Financial Services (NYDFS), 2013. New York State Department of Financial Services Notice of Inquiry on Virtual Currencies. New York, Available at: http://www.dfs.ny.gov/about/press2013/memo1308121.pdf (accessed 26.08.14).

New York Department of Financial Services (NYDFS), 2014a. Press Release—July 17, 2014: NY DFS Releases Proposed Bitlicense Regulatory Framework For Virtual Currency Firms, Available at: http://www.dfs.ny.gov/about/press2014/pr1407171.html (accessed 02.09.14).

New York Department of Financial Services (NYDFS), 2014b. Remarks of Benjamin M. Lawsky, Superintendent of Financial Services for the State of New York, on the Regulation of Virtual Currencies at the New America Foundation in Washington, DC, Available at: http://www.dfs.ny.gov/about/speeches_testimony/sp140212.htm (accessed 26.08.14).

Osborne, C., 2014. Hacker Swipes $83,000 from Bitcoin Mining Pools—CNET, Available at: http://www.cnet.com/news/hacker-swipes-83000-from-bitcoin-mining-pools (accessed 28.08.14).

Polis, J., 2014. Polis Calls for Ban of U.S. Dollar Bills in Response to Manchin Letter Calling for BitCoin Ban—U.S. Representative Jared Polis, Available at: http://polis.house.gov/news/documentsingle.aspx?DocumentID=371808 (accessed 02.09.14).

Primack, D., 2013. Fortress Is Forming a Bitcoin Fund. Fortune, Available at: http://fortune.com/2013/12/31/fortress-is-forming-a-bitcoin-fund/ (accessed 26.08.14).

Rovell, D., 2014. Sacramento Kings to Be Accept Bitcoin. ESPN.com, Available at: http://espn.go.com/nba/story/_/id/10303116/sacramento-kings-become-first-pro-sports-team-accept-bitcoin (accessed 26.08.14).

Salmon, F., 2013a. The Bitcoin Bubble and the Future of Currency. Medium, Available at: https://medium.com/@felixsalmon/the-bitcoin-bubble-and-the-future-of-currency-2b5ef79482cb (accessed 26.08.14).

Salmon, F., 2013b. Why Bitcoin's Rise Is Nothing to Celebrate. Reuters, Available at: http://blogs.reuters.com/felix-salmon/2013/04/03/why-bitcoins-rise-is-nothing-to-celebrate/ (accessed 02.09.14).

Sanati, C., 2012. Bitcoin Looks Primed for Money Laundering. Fortune: CNNMoney, Available at: http://fortune.com/2012/12/18/bitcoin-looks-primed-for-money-laundering/ (accessed 24.08.14).

Sandler, B., 2013. Federal District Court Holds Bitcoin Is Money, SEC Can Pursue Bitcoin-Based Securities Charges | BuckleySandler's InfoBytesBlog. Infobytesblog.com, Available at: http://www.infobytesblog.com/federal-district-court-holds-bitcoin-is-money-sec-can-pursue-bitcoin-based-securities-charges/ (accessed 26.08.14).

Schumer, C., 2011. Schumer Wants Underground Drug Website Shut Down. WKBW News 7, Available at: http://www.wkbw.com/news/Schumer-Wants-Underground-Drug-Website-Shut-Down-123196923.html (accessed 26.08.14).

Securities and Exchange Commission, 2013. Investor Alert: Ponzi Schemes Using Virtual Currencies, Available at: http://www.sec.gov/investor/alerts/ia_virtualcurrencies.pdf (accessed 26.08.14).

Securities and Exchange Commission, 2014a. The Investor's Advocate: How the SEC Protects Investors, Maintains Market Integrity, and Facilitates Capital Formation, Available at: http://www.sec.gov/about/whatwedo.shtml (accessed 26.08.14).

Securities and Exchange Commission, 2014b. SEC Charges Bitcoin Entrepreneur with Offering Unregistered Securities, Available at: http://www.sec.gov/News/PressRelease/Detail/PressRelease/1370541972520#.VAY1HqHnaUk (accessed 26.08.14).

Securities Exchange Commission v. Trendon T. Shavers and Bitcoin Savings and Trust ("BST"), 2013. 4:13-cv-00416-RC-AL. [online], Available at: http://www.sec.gov/litigation/complaints/2013/comp-pr2013-132.pdf (accessed 02.09.14).

Securities Exchange Commission v. W.J. Howey, Co. (1946) 328 U.S. 293.

Segal, D., 2014. Eagle Scout. Idealist. Drug Trafficker? New York Times, Available at: http://www.nytimes.com/2014/01/19/business/eagle-scout-idealist-drug-trafficker.html (accessed 26.08.14).

Shadab, H., 2014. Regulating Bitcoin and Block Chain Derivatives, Available at: http://www.cftc.gov/ucm/groups/public/@aboutcftc/documents/file/gmac_100914_bitcoin.pdf (accessed 29.03.2015).

Simonite, T., 2013. Big-name investors back effort to build a better Bitcoin. MIT Technol. Rev., Available at: http://www.technologyreview.com/news/513606/big-name-investors-back-effort-to-build-a-better-bitcoin/ (accessed 23.08.14).

Simonite, T., 2014. Bitcoin hits the big time, to the regret of some early boosters. MIT Technol. Rev., Available at: http://www.technologyreview.com/news/515061/bitcoin-hits-the-big-time-to-the-regret-of-some-early-boosters/ (accessed 23.08.14).

Sparshott, J., 2014. Web money gets laundering rule. WSJ, Available at: http://online.wsj.com/news/articles/SB10001424127887324373204578374611351125202 (accessed 28.08.14).

Turpin, J., 2014. Bitcoin: the economic case for a global, virtual currency operating in an unexplored legal framework. Ind. J. Global Legal Stud. 21 (1), 335–368, Available at: http://www.repository.law.indiana.edu/ijgls/vol21/iss1/13/ (accessed 05.09.14).

United States. Code of Federal Regulation. Chapter 31. Section 1010.100(fff), (m), (fff)(1-7), (5)(ii)(A)-(F). Washington, DC, 2013.

United States. United States Code: Section 77b. Washington, DC, 2012.

Weiser, B., 2015. Man Behind Silk Road Website Is Convicted on All Counts, New York Times, Available at: http://www.nytimes.com/2015/02/05/nyregion/man-behind-silk-road-website-is-convicted-on-all-counts.html?_r=0.

Wetjen, M., 2014. CFTC Global Markets Advisory Committee Meeting, Available at: http://www.cftc.gov/PressRoom/Events/opaevent_gmac100914 (accessed 21.01.15).

Wingfield, N., 2013. Bitcoin Pursues the Mainstream. New York Times, Available at: http://www.nytimes.com/2013/10/31/technology/bitcoin-pursues-the-mainstream.html?pagewanted=all&_r=0 (accessed 02.09.14).

Yarow, J., 2013. Here's Why I'm Investing in Bitcoin. Business Insider, Available at: http://www.businessinsider.com/fred-wilson-heres-why-im-investing-in-bitcoin-2013-5 (accessed 02.09.14).

Yermack, D., 2014. Is Bitcoin a Real Currency? An Economic Appraisal. New York University Stern School of Business and National Bureau of Economic Research, New York, NY, Available at: http://online.wsj.com/public/resources/documents/NBER.pdf (accessed 21.01.15).

Zabel, R., 2014. The New York State Department of Financial Services Hearing on Law Enforcement and Virtual Currencies Prepared Testimony of Deputy U.S. Attorney Richard B. Zabel. United States Department of Justice, Available at: http://www.justice.gov/usao/nys/pressspeeches/2014/DFSLawEnforcementandVirtualCurrenciesHearing2014.php (accessed 26.08.14).

Zerenga, T., Watterson, T., 2014. Bitcoin and the CFTC: "Spot"ing the Jurisdictional Hook: The Swap Report. Theswapreport.com, Available at: http://www.theswapreport.com/2014/03/articles/general/bitcoin-and-the-cftc-spoting-the-jurisdictional-hook/ (accessed 02.09.14).

CHAPTER 18

A Facilitative Model for Cryptocurrency Regulation in Singapore

Jonathan W. Lim[a,b]

[a]National University of Singapore Centre for Banking and Financial Law, Singapore
[b]Wilmer Cutler Pickering Hale & Dorr (WilmerHale) LLP, London, UK

Contents

18.1 INTRODUCTION

Cryptocurrencies such as Bitcoin have received much attention of late. They are, at bottom, simply computer protocols; and like other computer protocols such as the Transmission Control Protocol/Internet Protocol (TCP/IP) and HyperText Markup Language (HTML)—which birthed the Internet and its myriad modern uses—cryptocurrencies are said to have the potential for similar global impact, including by revolutionizing the existing e-payments and e-commerce sectors through a process of "disruptive innovation."[1]

---

[1]Disruptive innovation is a term coined by Clayton Christensen, a management professor at the Harvard Business School, and describes a process by which an innovation transforms an existing market or sector, initially taking root in simple applications at the bottom of a market, and then relentlessly moves upward and completely redefines the industry as it creates entirely new markets with different value networks. See Christensen, C., 1997. The Innovator's Dilemma: When New Technologies Cause Great Firms to Fail. Cambridge, MA, USA.

Unsurprisingly, these developments have not gone unnoticed by regulators. Law-makers and regulatory agencies around the world are considering introducing, and indeed some have already introduced, some form of regulation for cryptocurrencies. This momentum for regulation has also been motivated, in part, by recent high-profile events such as the failure of the Mt. Gox Bitcoin exchange based in Tokyo, Japan, and the public prosecutions in the United States and Australia for Bitcoin-related transactions of illicit goods on the Silk Road marketplace.

Regulatory responses and proposals have, of course, not been uniform but have instead differed greatly across the board. Some jurisdictions, such as Vietnam and Iceland, have instituted some form of ban on the use of digital currencies. Other jurisdictions, such as Germany and the United States, have introduced limited forms of regulation intended to address targeted regulatory interests such as antimoney laundering and counter-terrorist financing (AML/CTF). Still, more jurisdictions are taking a wait-and-see approach, with regulators keeping silent on the issue of regulation. As yet, no consensus has emerged on an optimal or ideal approach to regulating this new technology.

This chapter reflects on a number of key issues that arise from cryptocurrency regulation—and attempts to articulate what the optimal features of such regulation might look like. It situates this discussion in the Singapore context, which provides a useful case study for several reasons. Singapore is an international financial and wealth management center, with significant flows of funds passing through its shores; at the same time, it is also a rapidly growing regional hub for technology start-ups and innovation. In addition, Singapore has always shown a willingness to modify its laws or regulations to obtain a pragmatic or economic advantage and is well known for its market-leading regulatory practices and laws in relation to commercial matters—particularly matters with a strong transnational and competitive dimension, such as foreign investment, finance, and inter-national commercial arbitration. Recent announcements by regulators from the Monetary Authority of Singapore (MAS) suggest that a similar approach will be followed with regard to cryptocurrency regulation.

In these circumstances, this chapter articulates and develops a "facilitative" model for cryptocurrency regulation in Singapore. This approach recognizes that, while some form of regulation of cryptocurrencies is desirable and even necessary, there is a real risk that blunt, heavy-handed regulation would impede the development of a nascent and pro-ductive cryptocurrency industry and ecosystem.

Indeed, regulation need not be anti-industry; cryptocurrency regulation can, if well calibrated, reduce business and end-user uncertainty, encourage and incentivize innova-tion, and enhance the legitimacy of cryptocurrencies for use in a variety of real-world applications. This is consistent with the view espoused by Mr. Ravi Menon, managing director of the MAS, at a recent interview with centralbanking.com, where he opined that, in Singapore, "digital currencies have a role to play, which is why [the MAS has] not sought to ban them, or make it more difficult for them to operate... while there is reason to be cautious about the risks, we have chosen to address these risks in a targeted way so that innovation can continue to take place."

Facilitative cryptocurrency regulation should therefore, by design, ensure appropriate space for innovation and legitimate competition while clamping down on and disincentivizing misconduct and harmful behavior. This would support Singapore in becoming a global leader in the development and marketization of cryptocurrency technology, especially if it gains widespread mass-market adoption. Ensuring this balance will of course be difficult in practice and the devil will likely lie in the details; the purpose of the facilitative model outlined below is to suggest a useful blueprint or starting point for discussion.

Three aspects of this model or framework will be discussed in the sections below:

a. *First*, clear and targeted regulations, backed by the force of law, are needed to tackle core regulatory concerns raised by the new technologies, such as fraud and AML.

b. *Second*, a self-regulatory framework involving effective partnership between the industry and regulators must form an integral part of the regulatory architecture for cryptocurrencies.

c. *Third*, and finally, effective cryptocurrency regulation will require coordination and harmonization with other regulators and jurisdictions, given the decentralized and often transnational character of cryptocurrency transactions and protocols.

18.2 BACKGROUND TO CRYPTOCURRENCIES

Cryptocurrencies are a subset of virtual currencies. Virtual currency may be defined as a "digital representation of value that can be digitally traded and functions as (1) a medium of exchange; and/or (2) a unit of account; and/or (3) a store of value, but does not have legal tender status... in any jurisdiction" (Financial Action Task Force, 2014, p. 4). In other words, virtual currencies are digital objects that hold economic value and are functionally similar to fiat currencies that are issued by governments, but are not issued as such and are instead created pursuant to, and governed by, private agreement among a community or users and other network participants.

Cryptocurrencies are decentralized (i.e., issued without a central administering authority) and cryptography-based virtual currencies that are distributed and open source, and thereby function on a peer-to-peer basis (Financial Action Task Force, 2014, p. 5). Cryptocurrencies are also by definition *convertible* virtual currencies, meaning that they have an equivalent value in real fiat currency and can be exchanged for such fiat currency. In contrast, nonconvertible virtual currencies, such as World of Warcraft gold or airline miles, are specific to a particular domain or virtual world under particular rules governing their use and cannot be exchanged for fiat currency.

The combination of these features allows cryptocurrencies to function both as currency and as a peer-to-peer payments platform. Understanding these features is crucial to the design of facilitative regulation that accords appropriate space for innovative potential of cryptocurrencies and their many commercial applications.

18.2.1 Bitcoin

Bitcoin is in many ways *the* archetype cryptocurrency. It was the first of its kind when it was introduced in 2009, and the technology has spawned many imitators since. Bitcoin is also today the most widely adopted cryptocurrency, with the most obvious potential for commercial and business application to real-world goods and services. Much has been written about Bitcoin, and it provides a useful case study for understanding what cryptocurrencies are and how they work.

Unlike traditional currencies, Bitcoins are not issued or backed by any government or central bank, and their value does not derive from precious metals or other similarly tangible proxies of value. Instead, like all cryptocurrencies, Bitcoins are essentially digital units of account that are composed of unique strings of characters and that can be traded electronically via a cryptography system that verifies and records transactions. They are intangible, exist only digitally, and have no intrinsic value.

Instead of a central administrator, the Bitcoin system is run by a decentralized network consisting of over 20,000 independent computers (or nodes) around the world running Bitcoin software and operating the protocol for administering Bitcoin transactions. Bitcoins are issued to nodes in the network that succeed at being the first to solve a difficult mathematical problem that requires a tedious amount of computation. Not unlike precious metals, the supply of Bitcoin increases at a predetermined rate that gets progressively slower over time, with total supply capped at 21 million Bitcoins.

The decentralized network validates and verifies transactions using a math-based proof-of-work scheme. Whenever a new block of transactions is created, it is added to the "blockchain" where it will be verified by competing nodes in the network through a process that involves solving a mathematical problem that is difficult to solve but easy to verify. The first node in the network that succeeds in solving the problem receives a reward in Bitcoins, and the solution is broadcasted throughout the network; this solution is then quickly verified by a majority of other nodes in the network.

The use of a proof-of-work concept to generate and administer digital money has been rightly recognized as a technological breakthrough. Because of the competition for mining Bitcoins, and the scarcity of computational resources, proof of work ensures that decentralized, independent agents collaborate to maintain the integrity of the system and builds in incentives for honest users within the network to protect the system from attack by potentially malicious participants.[2] There is thus no need for a central administrator or issuer in such a system. Cryptocurrencies other than Bitcoin (also referred to as

---

[2]It has been described as an "elegant universal solution to the Byzantine Generals' Problem," which is one of the core problems of reaching consensus in distributed systems. See http://www.quora.com/Is-the-cryptocurrency-Bitcoin-a-good-idea.

Altcoins) use different distributed proof systems, including proof-of-stake algorithms, which require validation of transactions not through mathematical computations, but through proof of ownership.

As a payments' platform, the Bitcoin protocol is capable of transferring value between users on a peer-to-peer basis, thus requiring no middleman between sender and receiver or between buyer and seller. Transfers can be done almost instantaneously and either for free or for a low transaction fee in exchange for additional functionality. Transactions are secured by a dual-key system. All users have a Bitcoin address that has both a cryptographic public key and a matching private key known only to the user. When a transaction is initiated, all nodes in the network will be notified of the transfer from the sender's public key to the recipient's public key. The private keys are then used to sign the transaction through a cryptographic process. These processes are handled invisibly, and are not noticeable by the end users, for whom the direct peer-to-peer transaction proceeds almost instantly and in a frictionless manner.

Bitcoin technology records all transactions occurring in the system in a "blockchain," which functions as a kind of universal public ledger, with each new block of transactions linked to a preceding block. Every Bitcoin transaction *ever* made can be observed by following this chain backward. Because the blockchain makes available to all a record of every single Bitcoin transaction, attempts to spend the same Bitcoin after it has already been transferred can be easily detected by the network. Bitcoin transactions are irreversible the same way that cash transactions are irreversible (Grinberg, 2011, p. 165).

18.2.2 The ecosystem

A sizable and vibrant cryptocurrency ecosystem has developed over time in several leading jurisdictions—including Singapore—with a number of prominent venture capital firms having invested, and continuing to invest, in various cryptocurrency start-ups and businesses. This ecosystem broadly comprises participants such as miners, users, exchangers, and transaction service providers and software developers, among many other stakeholders:

a. *Miners* are persons or entities that run specialized software to generate solutions to complex algorithms and verify transactions in the cryptocurrency network.

b. *Users* are persons or entities that obtain cryptocurrency and use it to purchase goods or services, or to transfer value to another person, or to hold for investment purposes.

c. *Exchangers* are persons or entities in the business of exchanging cryptocurrencies for real or fiat currency, such as the US dollar or the Japanese yen, or for other cryptocurrencies or virtual currencies.

d. *Transaction service providers* are websites that provide transaction services, allowing individuals to store and transact Bitcoins without having to run the Bitcoin client on their own computers. This includes wallet and vault providers.

e. *Software developers* are persons or entities that are involved in researching, designing, making, or testing computer software that makes use of cryptocurrencies.

Other participants in the cryptocurrency ecosystem include market information and chart providers and merchants that accept cryptocurrencies in exchange for real goods and real services. Indeed, an increasing number of merchants also now accept Bitcoin as payment, including a number of established household names across the spectrum such as Dell, Target, Expedia, Bloomberg, PayPal, and Tesla Motors. Several food and drink establishments in the United States, Europe, and Singapore also now accept Bitcoin as payment.

Complex cryptocurrency-based financial products are also emerging in the market, particularly with more established cryptocurrencies such as Bitcoin. Trading in cryptocurrency futures is now possible with derivatives exchanges or trading platforms such as ICBIT and OKCoin. As recently as September 2014, TeraExchange, a Bitcoin derivatives exchange, announced that it had received approval from the US Commodity Futures Trading Commission to trade dollar-denominated Bitcoin currency swaps—the first ever Bitcoin swap approved in the United States. Proposals for a Bitcoin exchange-traded fund (ETF) are currently being considered by US regulators. Some businesses have also introduced interest-bearing cryptocurrency accounts and cryptocurrency-based peer-to-peer lending services. These developments will likely boost liquidity in cryptocurrencies and potentially reduce volatility in cryptocurrency prices. They also increasingly blur the line between the cryptocurrencies and the traditional financial system.

18.2.3 Benefits and future applications

Much of the discussion about cryptocurrency regulation has tended to focus on the dangers posed by cryptocurrencies. It is true that these risks exist, and there is a need for targeted regulation to address potential harms that flow from this. However, it is equally important not to overemphasize these risks and lose sight of the substantial benefits, economic or otherwise, that may be gained through legitimate applications of the technology.

To begin with, cryptocurrencies can significantly reduce the costs of fund transfers across international borders. The capability for direct peer-to-peer transfers, without the need for an intermediary, can eliminate or substantially reduce transaction costs and time lag. This technology has the potential to disrupt existing payment systems that involve intermediaries and associated agency costs, such as debit or credit card networks, by providing a platform for more efficient or frictionless mobile or electronic transfers in the future. Even if cryptocurrency payments do not become widespread and ubiquitous, competition with existing payment systems and intercryptocurrency competition are likely to bring down costs or improve the quality of payment services. Efficient and secure payment systems are vital to any well-functioning economy.

A frictionless mode of international money transfer is also particularly valuable in poorer developing countries, where remittance transaction costs tend to be the highest. Cryptocurrencies could potentially revolutionize the existing $600 million annual global remittance market. By way of example, Africa's diaspora pays around 12% in fees to send $200 in funds. The use of Bitcoin or other cryptocurrencies could significantly cut both the time and costs of such remittances. This would in turn raise the quality of life for migrant workers and their families and have a positive effect on the world's poorest countries.

Cryptocurrencies also make micropayments easy and viable, where such payments would previously have not been cost-effective because of prohibitive transaction costs. This would allow businesses to extract value from low-cost goods or services on the Internet through calibrated and targeted pricing policies that use micropayments, such as one-time article downloads from newspapers or one-time game or music downloads. Cryptocurrency may support financial inclusion through new cryptocurrency-based products that serve the unbanked and can also facilitate crowdfunding for small and medium enterprises.

More generally, cryptocurrencies—and related blockchain technologies—have the potential to be enablers of innovation on a much larger scale, just like other computer protocols such as TCP/IP and HTML. They can provide a platform for further financial or technical innovation and enable a wide variety of different uses—even ones that have not yet been conceived of—transforming entire industries and markets just as the Internet did. As some commentators have written, because cryptocurrencies are protocols for exchanging values over the Internet without an intermediary, these protocols can be adapted to potentially transform any transaction that has traditionally required an inter-mediary or third-party validation, including (1) property transfer, (2) contract execution, and (3) identity verification and management (Wan and Hoblitzell, 2014).

18.3 CLEAR AND TARGETED REGULATION

The emergence of new technologies, with accompanying new markets and new market actors, has always posed challenging issues for regulation. While it is said that technolog-ical innovation "disrupts" and transforms markets and industries, the effects of such dis-ruptions invariably extend also to the regulatory and legal spheres. Pertinent legal issues raised by such technological disruption often encompass the uncertainty of applicability of existing rules and the potential need for new rules to ban, restrict, or encourage the new technology.

The cryptocurrency industry has had to grapple with much regulatory uncertainty of late, which has not been helped by some of the recent negative press coverage, including news surrounding the failure of Mt. Gox—at the time, the world's largest Bitcoin exchange—and the disappearance of 844,000 Bitcoins (worth about US $480 million) held by it. In addition, Bitcoin's early association with the Silk Road marketplace, and its use for trading in illicit goods, also helped foster an impression among laypersons that Bitcoin and other cryptocurrencies were somehow less than legitimate and less than legal. Even if this was not actually correct in most jurisdictions, which do not ban the use of Bitcoin or other cryptocurrencies, mixed signals and divergent proposals from regulators in jurisdictions around the world have further contributed to an uncertain regulatory environment.

Such uncertainty has tangible negative effects. Uncertain regulatory treatment makes it difficult for cryptocurrency start-ups to access funding and to establish banking relationships. Regulatory uncertainty impedes the flow of institutional money and much-needed investment capital into the cryptocurrency industry. Consumers also tend to be wary given the uncertain legal status of cryptocurrencies and the lack of endorsement or backing by any government.

Clear and targeted regulations can do much to remedy this and clarify the legal environment, providing the framework for wider adoption of cryptocurrencies by businesses and consumers. Targeted laws addressing specifically identified cryptocurrency risks or regulatory interests are appropriate and consistent with the facilitative framework: targeted cryptocurrency regulation would ensure that products or practices that are harmful are appropriately contained while at the same time preserve the benefits of innovation and allow new business models to experiment, compete fairly, and flourish. This section explores these issues in the Singapore context, with three specific areas of regulatory focus: (1) AML/CTF, (2) securities and financial regulation, and (3) theft, misappropriation, and fraud.[3] It aims to capture a snapshot of the salient concerns in each area, although a full treatment of the issues raised will not be possible given the prevailing constraints of time and space.

18.3.1 Antimoney laundering and counter-terrorist financing

In March 2014, the MAS announced that it would be taking a "targeted regulatory approach" to regulating virtual currencies (which include cryptocurrencies), in order to "specifically address money laundering and terrorist financing risks." This is within its mandate as central bank and financial regulator to issue regulations in the area of AML/CTF, as expressly authorized by Section 27B of the MAS Act.

18.3.1.1 Justification for AML/CTF regulation
Decentralized cryptocurrency systems have obvious and real AML/CTF risks because they are convertible to real fiat currency and characterized by a high degree of

---

[3]These are not exhaustive of the regulatory landscape that determines the cryptocurrency business environment. Other regulatory issues such as tax treatment are relatively settled and are in any event not the subject of this chapter due to constraints of space and time.

anonymity—certainly a higher degree of anonymity than traditional payment methods such as credit cards. The Bitcoin protocol does not require identification of participants and is not set up to monitor suspicious transaction patterns (Financial Action Task Force, 2014, p. 9). This system has been more accurately described as "partially anonymous," because although the trail of all transactions made from all accounts can be seen on the "blockchain," nothing in the system allows one to tie specific accounts or transactions to real-world individuals (Grinberg, 2011, p. 164).

The upshot is that cryptocurrencies such as Bitcoin permit completely anonymous transfers on a peer-to-peer basis, with no requirement for the sender and recipient to be identified, and the decentralized nature of the network means that no one individual or entity can be singled out easily for investigation or asset seizure. AML/CTF risks are also particularly heightened because of the global reach of cryptocurrencies through the Internet, which allows them to be used to make almost instantaneous cross-border transfers that are difficult to detect and trace.

There is thus a clear and present justification for AML/CTF regulation of cryptocurrencies. Indeed, many jurisdictions have imposed or are exploring regulations in this regard. The question is not, then, whether or not to impose AML/CTF regulation, but what kind of AML/CTF regulation is appropriate.

18.3.1.2 AML/CTF regulation in Singapore

Like most developed jurisdictions, Singapore's AML/CTF regime involves a two-prong regulatory strategy, involving criminal sanction for offenses on the one hand and prevention through a regulatory licensing regime on the other. Thus, at least two types of issues are implicated in considering AML/CTF regulation for cryptocurrencies: first, in relation to AML/CTF offenses and sanctions, whether the existing rules and regulations extend to cryptocurrency-related transactions, and, second, in relation to licensing regimes, which entities should be subject to money transmission licensing requirements and what rules or regulations should apply to such licensed cryptocurrency entities.

On the first issue, the governing AML/CTF statutes in Singapore are the Corruption, Drug Trafficking and Other Serious Crimes (Confiscation of Benefits) Act (the "CDSA") and the Terrorism (Suppression of Financing) Act (TSOFA). Both statutes are drafted in technologically neutral terms and adopt very broad, all-encompassing definitions of "property" that are likely to cover cryptocurrencies and cryptocurrency transaction.

The CDSA sets out four types of money laundering offenses, namely, directly or indirectly acquiring, possessing, using, concealing, or transferring property that represents the benefits of drug trafficking or criminal conduct; assisting another person in doing the former; failing to disclose or report any knowledge or suspicion to the Suspicious Transactions Reporting Office (STRO) that any property represents the proceeds of drug trafficking or criminal conduct; and tipping off and disclosing information likely to prejudice an investigation under the Act (CDSA Sections 39, 43, 44, 46, 47, and 48). These offenses will likely apply in the context of cryptocurrencies and cryptocurrency transactions: the Act defines "property" as "money and all other property, movable or immovable, including things in action and other intangible or incorporeal property" (CDSA Section 2).

Similarly, the TSOFA sets out a number of terrorism financing offenses, namely, providing or collecting property for terrorist acts; making available, using, or possessing property for terrorist purposes; direct or indirect dealing with property of terrorists; failing to disclose information about transactions involving property belonging to any terrorist or terrorist entity; and tipping off and disclosing information likely to prejudice an investigation under the Act (TSOFA Sections 3-6, 8, and 10B). Like the CDSA, the TSOFA is also likely to apply to cryptocurrencies and cryptocurrency transactions, as it adopts a similarly broad definition of "property" as "assets of every kind, whether tangible or intangible, movable or immovable, however acquired" (TSOFA Section 2(1)).

On the second issue, the MAS had announced in March 2014 that it would be introducing regulations for "virtual currency intermediaries that buy, sell, or facilitate the exchange of virtual currencies for real currencies," to require them to verify customer identities and report suspicious transactions to the STRO. No regulations have been formally introduced as of the time of writing of this chapter, but it is anticipated that the regulations would cover a number of existing and future cryptocurrency businesses.

As discussed above, a licensing regime for AML/CTF regulation is justified considering the risks posed by decentralization and anonymity. Licensing requirements can establish accountability structures and allocate responsibility for the policing of the decentralized cryptocurrency network for AML/CTF activity. This will boost consumer and institutional confidence in cryptocurrencies. At the same time, such licensing and accompanying regulation will mean increased costs of compliance for businesses and may have the unintended effect of increasing barriers to entry and punishing smaller businesses and start-ups—an outcome inimical to promoting innovation in the cryptocurrency industry.

A thoughtful balancing of costs and benefits is therefore necessary in deciding which entities to license and what regulations to impose on licensed entities. Regulators will need to weigh the potential costs and calibrate any proposed regulation accordingly, in order not to stifle innovation and the potential economic and productivity benefits of a thriving cryptocurrency industry. This is well encapsulated by the "risk-based approach" recommended by the Financial Action Task Force (FATF)—an intergovernmental standard setting and body, of which Singapore is a member state, with an AML/CTF mandate—which counsels in favor of applying preventive measures that "are commensurate to the nature of risks" (FATF Guidance, 2013, paragraph 89).

This is also encapsulated in Tenet 5 of the MAS's Tenets of Effective Regulation, which are internal guiding principles for the development and review of the MAS's regulatory framework. Tenet 5 requires MAS regulation to be "impact-sensitive," and this requires that the "costs and impact of regulation" not be "disproportionate to the benefits" and that regulation be "targeted clearly at specific and material risks" and to avoid "unintended and unnecessary disruption to market practices."

The definition of the relevant "intermediaries," which are subject to licensing and regulation, will become decisive. Two possible approaches are available to the regulators. The first is to extend the existing regime under the Money-Changing and Remittance Businesses Act (MRBA) via interpretive guidance from the MAS, potentially clarifying that certain cryptocurrency businesses, particularly exchanges, fall within the MRBA definition of a "remittance business."[4] This is similar to the approach taken by the US Treasury Department's Financial Crimes Enforcement Network (FinCEN), which issued interpretive guidance documents in March 2013 and January 2014 to extend existing registration, reporting, and record keeping requirements for "money services business" under the US Bank Secrecy Act to cryptocurrencies. The second approach is to enact *sui generis* regulations for cryptocurrencies, similar to New York's recently proposed "BitLicense" proposal. Which approach Singapore regulators choose may ultimately be a matter of form, rather than substance, although the latter approach would allow for greater customization of rules to fit the needs and risk profile of the cryptocurrency industry and ecosystem.

Regardless of which approach is taken, what is vital is that regulators calibrate the scope of the licensing regulatory regime such that participants in the cryptocurrency ecosystem, which are *not* in the business of exchanging, transmitting, or trading cryptocurrencies for real fiat currency or for other cryptocurrencies—that is, miners or users using cryptocurrency to purchase real goods and services, and merchants accepting cryptocurrency—are not regarded as money transmission *intermediaries* and therefore not unduly subject to potentially onerous compliance requirements. This is consistent with both FATF's risk-based approach and current international best practices, as reflected by the US FinCEN guidance and German BaFin rules. AML/CTF regulation that covers miners and end users would be overinclusive, contrary to best practice, and significantly bog down the cryptocurrency ecosystem in Singapore with unnecessary costs.

As regards the specific regulations applicable to licensed entities, the MAS had announced in March 2014 that it would be introducing basic AML/CTF rules such as customer due diligence requirements, transaction reporting, and recordkeeping requirements. These would likely be similar to those that exist under the MRBA, which stipulates all of the above requirements in relation to transaction amounts of SGD $5000 and above (Sections 21 and 32-33). These rules are appropriate, justified, and consistent

---

[4]Defined in Section 2(1), Money-Changing and Remittance Businesses Act (Cap. 187), as "the business of accepting moneys for the purpose of transmitting them to persons resident in another country or a territory outside Singapore."

with international best practices as crystallized in the FATF Guidance (2013, paragraphs 63-70).

It is unclear from the MAS announcements whether Singapore regulators will extend to cryptocurrency-related businesses the existing rules under the MRBA that are meant to apply to "remittance businesses" or "money changers"—in particular, the rules stipulating requirements for a minimum capital of SGD $100,000 and a SGD $100,000 bond (Sections 9 and 10) or rules requiring licensees to have a "permanent place of business" in Singapore in order to operate (Section 11).

Applying such rules to cryptocurrencies would be inappropriate: those rules are designed for and are rooted in a different contextual background, and extending them to the cryptocurrency ecosystem will have unintended costs and consequences. For instance, the requirement for a physical "place or location in Singapore" for business activities is both unnecessary and awkward when applied to cryptocurrencies, especially given that a large diversity of cryptocurrency business models do not involve or necessitate brick-and-mortar premises. Similarly, the rules requiring a minimum capital or bond sum were expressly introduced in order to create "higher entry requirements" so that only large or well-established remittance firms remained, thus "weed[ing] out the weaker players in the industry."[5] This stated justification is at odds with the promotion of Singapore as an innovation-friendly hub or ecosystem for cryptocurrency start-up companies.

An optimal AML/CTF regulatory regime for cryptocurrencies should be facilitative, with customized rules appropriate for the industry and with suitable breathing space for innovation; it should not disincentivize or exclude small, nimble, and innovative business models from legitimately participating in business activities within the regulatory umbrella.

18.3.2 Securities and financial regulation

Another mode of potential cryptocurrency regulation is through securities or financial regulation. Such rules target and deal with very different regulatory interests from AML/CTF regulation: securities regulation deals with consumer protection and market integrity issues in the financial services sector, while financial regulation is concerned more fundamentally with issues of systemic risk and financial stability.

Singapore regulators have expressed that cryptocurrencies would not be considered "securities" under the Securities and Futures Act (the "SFA") (Shanmugaratnam, 2014). This is consistent with Section 2(1) of the SFA, which defines "securities" as, inter alia, debentures or stocks issued by governments or private corporations, any right or option or derivative in respect of any such debentures or stocks, any unit in a collective investment scheme, or any unit in a business trust or its derivative. Cryptocurrencies are thus

---

[5]Second reading, *Money-Changing and Remittances (Amendment) Bill*, 15 August 2005, columns 1227-1228.

not subject to the investor protection and market integrity regulation under the SFA and the Financial Advisers Act in Singapore, including the various registration, disclosure, and antifraud obligations under those statutes.

However, this does not preclude investment products or investment schemes that are based on cryptocurrencies from being regulated under securities regulations. Distinct from the purchase and exchange of cryptocurrencies themselves, cryptocurrency-based financial products, such as ETFs or derivatives, involve the use of regulated investment structures and therefore attract the application of the relevant securities regulations.

For instance, cryptocurrency ETFs would constitute "collective investment schemes" under the SFA, with the shares of such ETFs qualifying as "securities" under the SFA. Similarly, cryptocurrency derivatives will likely fall within the regulatory umbrella of Parts VIA and VIB of the SFA and the requirements therein. Even though cryptocurrency derivatives are not currently defined as "specified derivatives' contracts" under existing guidelines, according to the Securities and Futures (Reporting of Derivatives' Contracts) Regulations 2013, which limits such contracts to interest rate and credit derivatives, Sections 124 and 125 of the SFA clearly envisage that the MAS may prescribe the regulations to apply to such derivatives. In any event, these cryptocurrency-based financial products are only at a very early stage of development and do not raise significant regulatory concerns yet.

As for financial regulation, the effects of cryptocurrencies on monetary policy and financial stability are currently unclear. Cryptocurrencies are not issued or backed by any governmental authority and, at current adoption levels, do not have sufficient market capitalization to significantly impact the supply of money or otherwise affect macroeconomic policy. In addition, cryptocurrency businesses, unlike banks, do not have access to public safety nets or central bank liquidity, and therefore, there is little or no justification for prudential regulation for safety and soundness concerns.

Cryptocurrency firms and businesses also do not pose the same systemic risks as banks do in the form of a structural vulnerability to "runs," because they do not carry out maturity transformation, that is, the conversion of short-term liquidity needs of depositors into long-term funding commitments for borrowers. As the Diamond-Dybvig model (Diamond and Dybvig, 1983, p. 404) illustrates, it is the structural mismatch between the liquidity and maturity profiles of a bank's funding structure—that is, the fact that banks borrow short to lend long—that gives rise to the potential for systemically destabilizing "runs" (Lim, 2014, pp. 83-84). Since cryptocurrency firms are not generally in the business of performing maturity transformation, and do not pose the same systemic risks as banks, financial regulations such as capital requirements or public insurance schemes are not appropriate.

That said, drawing the line between typical cryptocurrency firms and banks will become less clear-cut over time, as lending in cryptocurrencies and cryptocurrency fractional reserve banks becomes possible and more widespread. It is too early to tell whether this "financialization" trend will continue, but at present, cryptocurrency banking and lending services remain quite niche and do not yet pose any real regulatory concerns. Hasty regulation in this area would be both unwarranted and unwise and poses more risks than benefits.

18.3.3 Theft or misappropriation

Like cash or other forms of money, cryptocurrencies function as a store of value and a medium of exchange and contain or signify a degree of economic value for its owner. Similarly, just like cash, cryptocurrencies can be lost or stolen (from virtual wallets), thus resulting in effective destruction of that economic value for the owner. However, while there are clear civil and criminal laws that protect one's property rights in tangible hard currency or cash, it is unclear under existing laws whether such private remedies or criminal sanctions extend to the theft or misappropriation of cryptocurrencies.

Under Singapore law, it is uncertain whether private remedies for theft or misappropriation apply to cryptocurrencies. Conversion is the principal civil remedy under English or Singapore law in respect to theft or misappropriation of personal property (including money) and provides the original owner with a means of vindication where those rights have been interfered with, including through tracing his original property and demanding the return of the property or its equivalent in-kind from third parties (*Kuwait Airways Corporation v Iraqi Airways Co (No 3)*). However, the current state of Singapore case law has left undetermined the question of whether conversion remedies are available for intangible property—a category that includes cryptocurrencies.

As the Singapore High Court recently held in *Tjong Very Sumito v Chan Sing En* (2012), it "remains an open question in Singapore whether intangible property can form the subject matter of conversion" (p. 985). Likewise, in *Alwie Handoyo v Tjong Very Sumito*, the Singapore Court of Appeal—Singapore's apex court—cited to the approach by the majority of the English House of Lords in the *OBG v Allan* case, which had held that conversion protects only interests in physical chattels, and that there cannot be conversion of intangible property such as choses in action (paragraph 131). However, the Singapore Court of Appeal held in that case that narrow exception documentary intangibles (i.e., where the intangible property in question has a corporeal representation, such as in the case of checks or share certificates) applied in that case and that it was therefore not necessary to determine whether conversion could apply to purely intangible property (paragraphs 132-137).

Cryptocurrencies need not have their existence reflected in a physical document and would therefore be classified as purely intangible property. It is unclear whether conversion remedies would be available for theft or misappropriation of cryptocurrencies. Practically, this means that a victim of cryptocurrency misappropriation or theft might only have a personal remedy against the relevant exchange or counterparty (under contract, tort, or other related personal actions such as unjust enrichment), but not a proprietary remedy that can be used to make recovery against the third parties that come into possession of the intangible online property.

A number of prominent legal commentators have rightly criticized the distinction between tangible and intangible properties as arbitrary and without basis. Indeed, a fixation with physical possession as the traditional criterion for the availability of the remedy of conversion is inappropriate and out of place in a modern economy, where many things of value are intangible (Shaw, 2009, pp. 434-435). As a matter of principle, conversion should apply to protect property interests—whether tangible or intangible—that are excludable from others and capable of being controlled in a broader and not just physical sense (Green, 2008, p. 117). Unfortunately, this is not yet the current state of the law in Singapore; however, it is hoped that the realities of a functioning cryptocurrency and significant peer-to-peer economic activity will shape the law toward abolishing this distinction between tangible and intangible properties.

As for criminal sanctions, Singapore law has equally little to say about theft or misappropriation of cryptocurrencies: intangible property is not covered by criminal offenses for theft or misappropriation of property under Singapore law. Theft is defined under Section 378 of the Penal Code with reference to dishonest taking of "movable property," which is defined in Section 22 as including "corporeal property of every description." The same goes for criminal misappropriation of property under Section 403 of the Penal Code, which also makes reference to "movable property." Thus, unlike other jurisdictions such as the United Kingdom, whose 1968 Theft Act expressly defines protected "property" to include "things in action and other intangible property," Singapore's criminal legislation does not address theft or misappropriation of intangible property. The one exception is the offense of "cheating," which is defined under Section 415 of the Penal Code to include dishonestly inducing the delivery of "any property." This has, however, only a limited scope and will not cover all instances of theft or misappropriation.

Singapore's cybercrime legislation, the Computer Misuse and Cybersecurity Act, does little to address the above lacunae in relation to theft or misappropriation of intangible online property. That Act relies on a predicate offense approach and punishes the use of a computer to commit certain crimes or offenses involving "property, fraud, dishonesty or which causes bodily harm" (Section 4). Without a predicate offense for theft or misappropriation under the Penal Code, all the cybercrime legislation does is criminalize very narrow classes of online misdemeanors, including "unauthorized access to computer material" and "unauthorized modification of computer material" (Sections 3 and 5-8). While these provisions may address to some extent particular hacking and cybersecurity breach concerns, they do not address many situations of theft or misappropriation of cryptocurrencies—which may not necessarily involve a breach or lack of authorization.

Under existing Singapore law, therefore, it remains unclear whether (or which) private remedies or criminal sanctions will be available in a case of theft or misappropriation of cryptocurrency. The laws in this area appear to be still grappling with an old-world distinction between tangible and intangible properties, with protection from interference largely available only for the former. As stated above, this is unsustainable in a modern economy where, as is the case in the cryptocurrency system, systems of value and commerce are built upon intangible, but highly valuable, property. A developed and flourishing cryptocurrency business sector requires commercial certainty and clearly defined and enforceable property rights in respect to cryptocurrencies; this is currently lacking under the current legal landscape in Singapore and will require further clarification or reform, whether through courts or legislators.

18.4 A SELF-REGULATORY FRAMEWORK

In addition to clear and targeted regulations, effective cryptocurrency regulation requires a robust self-regulatory framework involving effective partnership between industry and regulators. This is a matter of regulatory architecture or structure and not simply a matter of substantive content, as with the specific regulatory norms discussed in the preceding section. A self-regulatory process or framework involves the setting, policing, and enforcement of standards governing firms or individuals within an industry by *private* actors or industry professionals, rather than by external *public* regulators. In other words, self-regulation involves, structurally, a degree of private sector involvement in the regulatory process, by the regulated industry itself.

There are a number of benefits to this approach. Self-regulation is said to lower monitoring and enforcement costs: A self-regulatory body will usually have more technical expertise and know-how than external regulators, and this is especially true in fast-moving industries with a high rate of technological change, which by nature often involve regulators playing catch-up with industry know-how. It is also said to create incentives for voluntary compliance by the industry, reduce costs of amending and adapting standards, and also increase collaborative behavior and positive interaction between the industry and regulators. Self-regulation can also help to foster trust between consumers, regulators, and the industry and can thereby encourage further investment and innovation (Castro, 2011, p. 3).

Self-regulation has thus proved suitable in industries characterized by dynamism, complexity, or innovation. For instance, self-regulation has been used as a regulatory tool in connection with complex financial markets with significantly fast-moving financial innovations, such as the regulation of financial derivatives, as in through the use of swap execution facilities and futures exchanges acting as self-regulatory organizations in post-2008 US Dodd-Frank Title VII regulations. Self-regulation reflects a regulatory attitude of accommodating disruptive innovation and is premised on innovation being a necessary component of a competitive and productive economy.

In addition, self-regulation is particularly appropriate for regulating Internet-based activities and businesses, such as in the cryptocurrency ecosystem, because it allows for regulatory structures that "mirror" the Internet as a global, private, and decentralized network. Indeed, regulation of the "code" layer (as distinct from the "physical" or "content" layer) of the Internet is and has always been carried out through the self-regulatory initiatives of the Internet Corporation for Assigned Names and Numbers (Lessig, 2001, p. 23).

Varying degrees of self-regulation are possible, depending on the degree of collaboration between the self-regulatory organization and government agencies, the powers granted to the self-regulatory organization, or the legal or binding character (or lack thereof) of the self-regulation norms. Indeed, depending on various calibrations of these factors, self-regulatory organizations can play a gap-filling interpretive role within a legal framework with "hard" enforceable rules, exercise a rule-making function but without any formal supervisory or enforcement functions, or take on full-fledged regulatory functions that cover the entire gamut of rule making, supervising compliance, and enforcement.

Self-regulation tends to work best when paired with government involvement or support. Indeed, commentators have stated that "self-regulation cannot function without the support of public authorities," whether that support is found in willful noninterference, endorsement or ratification, or through active collaboration and enforcement support (Bertelsmann Foundation, 1999, p. 22). Self-regulation should not be seen as a substitute for traditional regulation through legislation and formal enforceable rules, but rather as a complement to such a legal framework.

Self-regulation may involve the use of "soft" norms through nonbinding codes of conduct or informal guidelines. Such norms do not come attached with legal sanctions for noncompliance and instead rely more on reputational sanction and market incentives for compliance. In certain industries involving sophisticated participants, soft norms can be more effective than binding and enforceable rules. Indeed, the "regulatory uncertainty principle" holds that when a rule crystallizes as a binding financial regulation, it will cause adaptive behaviors and changes in the regulated institutions' risk management practices such as to water down the rule's effectiveness—in other words, it will result in regulatory arbitrage to circumvent the rule (Caruana, 2014, p. 3). In such an environment, the flexibility and adaptability of soft norms may be more effective in incentivizing voluntary compliance, especially when normative content is generated from within the industry.

These principles are not merely abstract; they are readily applicable in the Singapore context. Indeed, self-regulation is consistent with the MAS's Tenets of Effective Regulation, which expressly recognize that a "self-regulatory approach" can be "effective and appropriate" when applied in the right circumstances (p. 31). Thus, the "Stakeholder-Reliant" principle "acknowledge[s] and encourage[s] the contribution that financial institutions individually, the financial industry collectively and other stakeholders" can make in "achieving outcomes aligned with the MAS' supervisory objectives" (p. 10). Likewise, the "Business-Friendly" principle espouses due regard to "business efficiency and innovation" and calls for regulators to "adopt a consultative approach to regulating the industry" (p. 10).

MAS's Tenet 2 on "Shared Responsibility" clearly articulates the MAS's regulatory philosophy that "[t]he design of regulation should wherever appropriate provide for rather than take away from financial institutions and stakeholders' responsibility and incentives to contribute towards regulatory outcomes"—specifically, with the regulated institutions, including their "board and senior management" and the "industry collectively," taking on such responsibility for regulatory outcomes. The MAS does rely, in practice, on self-regulatory organizations to carry out several regulatory functions; for example, the Singapore Foreign Exchange Market Committee and the Singapore Exchange carry out self-regulation in relation to conduct or market integrity issues in foreign exchange and securities markets.

In relation to cryptocurrencies, the Association of Crypto-Currency Enterprises and Start-ups, Singapore (ACCESS) presents a ready candidate for a cryptocurrency self-regulatory organization. ACCESS was formed on May 30, 2014 as a registered society with the Registry of Societies in Singapore, and its objectives are, first, to promote dialog with regulators and other stakeholders and, second, to conduct "self-regulation" of the cryptocurrency industry, including through establishing a code of conduct for firms that will become a criterion for membership. ACCESS appears ready and willing to take on the mantle of self-regulation, although it is still unclear at this stage what kind of regulatory role it could play within the system and what degree of collaboration with regulators would be possible.

For the reasons above, a robust self-regulatory framework involving effective partnership between ACCESS and regulators such as MAS would produce contextually adaptable regulations that complement the legal framework, lower regulatory costs, and support innovation—and should be encouraged if Singapore is to augment its position as a regional or global hub for cryptocurrencies and next-generation financing.

18.5 INTERNATIONAL COORDINATION AND HARMONIZATION

Finally, the international dimension of any cryptocurrency regulation warrants attention. Owing to the deterritorialized and often international nature of cryptocurrency transactions, effective regulation will require a significant amount of coordination and harmonization among regulators and jurisdictions.

Indeed, the Internet and cryptocurrency transactions are by nature borderless, and this sits uncomfortably with traditional regulatory boundaries of jurisdiction and sovereignty. This is particularly so in the case of cybercrime and online misdemeanors: they can originate in one jurisdiction, but have deleterious effects in another, and sometimes on nationals of yet another jurisdiction.

Thus, no single jurisdiction can guarantee a protected cybersecurity environment on its own: crimes in one territory can go without detection or punishment because they cannot be effectively monitored or enforced against persons outside the jurisdiction. Coordination and cooperation among regulators and law enforcement authorities to address such issues are thus essential. The importance of such cooperation is underscored by the recent failure of Mt. Gox, where reportedly more than US $480 million of customers' cryptocurrency had disappeared as of February 2014, allegedly due to large-scale hacker attacks, which have to this date gone unpunished.

However, international cooperation on cybersecurity issues can be as complicated as it is necessary, particularly as different countries can take very different approaches in their national laws, policies, or attitudes on issues of cybercrime and cybersecurity. Some countries see vital state and national security interests as implicit in such cybersecurity issues and have regulatory or legal structures that allow extensive governmental intrusion into the sender and recipient details of every single transmission and the contents of such transmissions. Other countries see that proper Internet governance requires balancing security concerns against certain constitutionally protected freedoms and accordingly have legal structures that emphasize privacy and data protection (Satola and Judy, 2011, p. 1750). These differences are fundamental and may be difficult to reconcile in specific cases, as the recent WikiLeaks episode illustrates.

In Singapore, regulators have pursued more partnerships with other regulators on the cybersecurity front in recent years, including through the signing of information sharing and collaborative agreements with other regulators in jurisdictions such as Japan and South Korea. Commentators believe that international cooperation will continue to scale upward with the opening of the INTERPOL Global Complex for Innovation in Singapore in 2014 and the deepening of cooperative ties with the European Cybercrime Centre (Chang, 2013).

Effective cryptocurrency regulation will require further and more detailed cooperation arrangements with foreign regulators and particularly on cryptocurrency- and Bitcoin-specific cybersecurity issues. This will go some way to creating a stable regulatory environment that will boost consumer confidence and support the cryptocurrency industry.

Aside from cybersecurity issues, many cryptocurrency regulations in foreign jurisdictions, such as in the United States or Canada, are expressed to have extraterritorial effect, and this subjects cryptocurrency firms in Singapore to a "double deontology" risk, where they may be subject to potentially conflicting and irreconcilable rules at the same time. For instance, Canada's recently released virtual currency regulations, issued by the Financial Transactions and Reports Analysis Centre of Canada, are stated to have extraterritorial effect and capture foreign firms that either have a place of business in Canada or are offering services to Canadians. Thus, a cryptocurrency firm operating in Singapore may have to comply not only with Singapore regulations but also with Canadian cryptocurrency regulations, to the extent that it has a Canadian office or markets to Canadian customers. In a case of conflict, the firm may have no choice but to comply with the stricter standard, even though its competitors may not be similarly constrained; worse still, in cases of more fundamental conflict, complying with either standard may put a firm in breach of the other standard it is subject to.

As such, the extraterritorial reach of foreign regulations could impose particularly onerous compliance obligations on cryptocurrency firms and have a significant impact on their costs and competitiveness. This also adds to the existing regulatory uncertainty, especially when the applicable laws to any particular transaction may be different and potentially in conflict. Given the inherently cross-border nature of most cryptocurrency business models, this creates very real risks for firms operating in this space.

A facilitative regulatory model should accommodate the decentralized, diverse, and international nature of the cryptocurrency markets. This requires that cross-border harmonization of regulations in Singapore and other leading jurisdictions be prioritized and pursued to the extent possible, in order to minimize regulatory uncertainty, reduce unnecessary costs, and eliminate opportunities for rent-seeking and regulatory arbitrage.

18.6 CONCLUSION

With the globalization of commerce and the increasing porosity of territorial boundaries, the use of cryptocurrencies will only continue to grow. There is a real demand for private currencies that are not necessarily tied to any particular government and for a frictionless payment system that accommodates and best suits the increasingly decentralized and transnational character of modern e-commerce. This is a technology that has the potential to transform the way people buy and sell services across the world, with almost limitless economic potential flowing from this.

Thoughtful and well-designed regulation can play a large part in this development, by clarifying the business environment and boosting both consumer and investor confidences. This requires, on one hand, the weeding out of real and present dangers, such as money laundering, terrorist financing, cybercrimes, and other misdemeanors. On the other hand, this also requires a regulatory approach that recognizes the risks of over-regulation, including its negative effects on productivity and innovation. The facilitative model outlined in this chapter aims to strike the appropriate balance between promoting innovation and preventing illegitimate use and outlines the legal, extralegal, and international aspects of how such a balance would be struck. This will provide a foundation for cryptocurrencies to flourish in the real world, such that the industry's much-talked-of potential will become an economic and commercial reality.

REFERENCES

Alwie Handoyo v Tjong Very Sumito and another [2013] 4 SLR 308.
Bertelsmann Foundation, 1999. Self-Regulation of Internet Content (https://www.cdt.org/files/speech/BertelsmannProposal.pdf).

Caruana, J., 2014. Speech: financial regulation, complexity and innovation. In: Bank of International Settlements' Promontory Annual Lecture.

Castro, D., 2011. Benefits and Limitations of Industry Self-Regulation for Online Behavioral Advertising. The Information Technology & Innovation Foundation, Washington, DC.

Chang, W., 2013. Amendments to the Computer Misuse Act. E Finance Payments Law Policy, Singapore.

Diamond, D.W., Dybvig, P.H., 1983. Bank runs, deposit insurance, and liquidity. J. Polit. Econ. 91, 401.

Financial Action Task Force, 2013. Guidance for a Risk-Based Approach, Prepaid Cards, Mobile Payments and Internet-Based Services (http://www.fatf-gafi.org/media/fatf/documents/recommendations/Guidance-RBA-NPPS.pdf).

Financial Action Task Force, 2014. Virtual Currencies Report—Key Definitions and Potential AML/CFT Risks.

Green, S., 2008. To have and to hold? Conversion and intangible property. Mod. Law Rev. 71 (1), 114.

Grinberg, R., 2011. Bitcoin: an innovative digital currency. Hastings Sci. Technol. Law J. 4, 160.

Kuwait Airways Corporation v Iraqi Airways Co (No 3) [2002] UKHL 19.

Lessig, L., 2001. The Future of Ideas: The Fate of Commons in a Connected World. Vintage Books, New York.

Lim, J., 2014. Untangling the money market fund problem: a public–private liquidity fund proposal. Stanford J. Law Bus. Finance 19, 63.

Monetary Authority of Singapore, 2014. MAS to Regulate Virtual Currency Intermediaries for Money Laundering and Terrorist Financing Risks. Press release.

OBG Ltd v Allan [2008] 1 AC 1.

Satola, D., Judy, H.L., 2011. Towards a dynamic approach to enhancing international cooperation and collaboration in cybersecurity legal frameworks: reflections on the proceedings of the workshop on cybersecurity legal issues at the 2010 United Nations Internet Governance Forum. William Mitchell Law Rev. 37 (4), 1743.

Shanmugaratnam, T., 2014. Reply to parliamentary question on virtual currencies. MAS Notice Paper 62 of 2014.

Shaw, S.L.K., 2009. Conversion of intangible property: a modest, but principle extension? A historical perspective. Victoria Univ. Wellington Law Rev. 40, 419.

Tjong Very Sumito and Ors v Chan Sing En and Ors [2012] 3 SLR 953.

Wan, T., Hoblitzell, M., 2014. Bitcoin's promise goes far beyond payments. Harv. Bus. Rev. (https://hbr.org/2014/04/bitcoins-promise-goes-far-beyond-payments/).

Financial Innovation and Internet of Money

CHAPTER 19

Advancing Egalitarianism

Gavin Wood, Aeron Buchanan
Ethereum Foundation, Switzerland

Contents

19.1 INTRODUCTION

Egalitarianism is a central motivation in the development and use of Bitcoin, cryptocurrencies, and blockchain technologies; broadly speaking, they represent the best system yet seen to achieve the decentralization of power. Centralization precipitates several problems, particularly in the realm of commerce, such as vulnerability and trust in gateway institutions. In this chapter, we will discuss these problems, look at examples, and see how blockchain technologies provide a way of avoiding such problems through decentralized organization.

19.2 DEVELOPMENT OF CENTRALLY CONTROLLED MONEY SYSTEMS

To help give a background for the original motivations and future potential of blockchain technology, we start with a brief narrative description of the development of the ledgerized fiat money system we use today.

The exchange of goods and services was revolutionized with the introduction of money. Money provides a universal reference for value and a concise way of transferring that value or, similarly, debt. An implementation of a system of money needs to possess a set of particular attributes. These can be expressed in several ways (Mankiw, 2007), but the most relevant to this discussion are the following:

- Fungibility: interchangeable and divisible—all dollars are equal and two 50 cent coins are worth exactly one dollar.
- Stable value: a roughly stable value over time—due to a known, limited creation rate, for example.
- No double-spending: following from above, individuals should not be able to give their money (debt) to more than one recipient.

Physical commodity money initially made for an excellent way to implement a money system: Due to the physical necessity of communication, historically, having to transfer physical objects to represent the transfer of debt was an acceptable inconvenience. Physical objects can necessarily only be held by one entity at a time, so double-spending is impossible. For a long time, commodities universally accepted to be limited by a sufficient difficulty of production but undifferentiable at any practical scale, for example, silver, gold, or potatoes, served very well and did so without the need for any central authority, only the consensus taken on the natural self-evident characteristics fulfilling the requisite attributes. However, as convenience demanded the use of commodities of high-value density, small amounts came to possess a lot of value leading to the problem of determining the quantity of material being presented for a transaction. This problem was solved by looking to a trusted institution (e.g., a government mint), to create standardized coins, for example. Eventually, the inconvenience of using raw commodities brought about the innovation of representative money: namely, notes and checks. These do not have the intrinsic commodity value and so need a guarantee of issuance by way of sufficiently sophisticated antiforgery devices, which require trust in the issuing authority that they will make good the debt on demand. In the last 100 years or so, the link to commodities has been dropped and fiat money is now the norm, which, with no commodity backing, requires a consensus of trust in the issuing authority; historically achieved by government enforceable laws to ensure it remains viable money. Fiat currency makes plain the implicit *social contract* that money systems work on: If you want others to value your fiat money, you must respect everyone else's right to expect you to value their money equally. The worth of this social contract comes from a money system's ability to fulfill the attributes listed above. Fungibility of fiat money is intrinsic, but maintaining a stability of value is harder because the participants using the money must be happy about the net amount of money that is being created over time, which requires a level of trust outside the social contract, namely, trust in the institutions that are authorized to create money, for example, via lending (McLeay et al., 2014).

In parallel to the development above was the invention of ledger money, also known as *demand deposits*, which is controlled by banks in the form of account balances kept on record. Using ledger money means trusting banks to prevent people from double-spending their balance. It is now hard to participate in Western society without having a bank account of ledger money. This suits the banks as it makes their services more popular. It also suits governments because it means that a citizen's participation in society can be more easily controlled, through bureaucratic demands on banking institutions. Furthermore, since the advent of telecommunications, the physical transfer of money has become increasingly inconvenient, fueling the utility of ledger money. This is reflected in the increase in the number of institutions that manage the money system, for example, credit cards and online payment service companies (Capgemini, 2013). In the OECD, the transfer of money through direct interbank (electronic) ledger money exchanges is now the majority of transactions (at least by value) and by all accounts will only rise (Federal Reserve System, 2013). This has increased the power of banks as the gatekeepers of the money system (Carlton and Frankel, 1995). Using gatekeepers to manage the money system has provided a way to keep transactions private (though not completely), but part of the flip side is that this gives the gatekeepers the power over participation.

There are several concerns arising from relying on a small number of institutions (relative to the number of participants) to manage the money system, the most prominent of which derive from

- a concentration of power,
- conflicts of interest,
- inept operators.

This has led to a system that is vulnerable to the following:

- Single targets for attack: while attacks are mostly more theoretical than practical, we do continually see announcements by credit card companies in particular that large blocks of account numbers have been stolen.
- Arbitrary exclusion of participants: exclusion is well documented and ranges from individuals, to organizations (such as WikiLeaks or legal marijuana merchants), to entire countries (making online payments in many African countries practically impossible) (Molyneux et al., 2005).
- Cartel-bolstered fees: analysis of international money transfers (remittances) has revealed that the highest fees are paid on transfers to the poorest countries, because pricing can be geographically segmented (Watkins and Quattri, 2014).
- Subversion of processes: as demonstrated by the recurring fines imposed by regulators for dishonest behavior such as misselling (Inderst and Ottaviani, 2009).
- Creation of self-serving instruments: with the profit-making entities having the power to create money in new ways faster than the regulators (and indeed the institutions themselves) can come to understand them, problems can be silently built up and catastrophically revealed (Brunnermeier, 2008).

For a modern ledger-based fiat money system to be successful, it is important that the gatekeeper institutions are seen to obey the rules and act responsibly. However, being in positions of trust, the system depends on them and so they have become "too big to fail," which, in practice, only lowers the cost to them of misdemeanors. This was observed notably in the 2008 "banking crisis," which had repercussions around the world and for many years afterward. Further scandals, such as Libor in the United Kingdom in

2012 (Hall, 2013), emphasize the inadequacies of the centralized "behind closed doors" system.

Together, the centralized and trust-based issues of the currently predominant money systems have driven the desire for, and development of, a decentralized way of achieving the same ends: Blockchain technology provides a solution. Bitcoin (Nakamoto, 2009) was the first realization of this technology and provides the decentralized, democratically administered, trustlessly traded currency that is seen as the way forward by many. Within only a few years of going live, it has delivered on many of the expectations placed upon it: Anyone with an Internet connection can participate and can obtain Bitcoin in an increasing number of ways; transaction fees are very low and tend to be fixed; sending money across borders is being made increasingly cheaper; its rules are transparent and consistently enforced; it is yet to succumb to any kind of cyber-attack. It is leading the way for a new system of interaction.

19.3 A NEW PARADIGM: DECENTRALIZATION OF AUTHORITIES

From an individual citizen's point of view, the principal concern in relation to a practical money system for society can be summarized as
• the utility of one's own money in the eyes of others
which, being the mutual concern of all participating citizens, is inductively equivalent to the externally defined *functions of money* described in economy textbooks. However, by viewing money in this way, that is, as a social contract, we can more readily discuss the relationship between citizens and the money system and hence the emergent effects on society. Note that we are using the term "citizen" here to refer to any entity that may reasonably want to participate with the rest of society through the money system, that is, including both real people and entities such as companies, charities, and groups. We can use the mutuality of participation to expand the principal above as comprising all citizens' concerns of
• the ability to participate (being barred from the system by definition makes one's money inaccessible or worthless in the eyes of others),
• the level of faith in the legitimacy of funds being received (one is unlikely to be able to spend invalid funds),
• the level of faith in the control of the money supply (as the money supply is increased, the value of one's funds decreases),
• the privacy of transactions (a more subtle influence, but one's reputation could invalidate one's funds),
• convenience (one's funds will be less acceptable (i.e., worthless) to others in inconvenient forms).

The penultimate point regarding privacy is more complex for drawing in issues technically beyond the realm of money systems. However, while the core of the discussion here does not rely on civil rights, disregarding the further operation of society is illogical because of the fact that money systems must be implemented within a society and as such are an integral part of that society and all aspects of it.

It is important to note at this stage that all of the above points require the participants to trust the combined centralized administration. As such, participation in the current system is actually only partly the implicit agreement between a citizen and society: It is also a reliance of the citizen on the administration. In other words, the current ledger-based fiat money system we use relies heavily on trust in a few institutions by the many participants. This is barely sustainable as is evidenced by their conduct being regularly called into question. The government, banks, and auxiliary companies can (and do)

1. bar participation,
2. fail to correctly verify the legitimacy of funds,
3. fail to act in the interests of the participants in the control of the money supply,
4. reveal the details of transactions,
5. employ more convenient systems that end up making all of the above worse.

Blockchain technology provides the ability to implement money systems that have

1. a universally undiscriminatory threshold to entry (an Internet connection),
2. a mathematically provable legitimacy of funds,
3. a mathematically provable mechanism of money creation,
4. a cryptographically secure privacy of transactions (even from the other transacting party),
5. a digital implementation allowing for arbitrarily convenient methods of usage.

The underlying principle of blockchain technology is to have the enforcement of the social contract as part of the social contract itself.

	Centralization	Blockchain
Social contract (implicit in participation, i.e., trustless)	Recognition of value	Recognition of value; legitimization of funds, money supply, privacy
Centralized administrators (extraparticipatory oversight, i.e., trustful)	Legitimization of funds, money supply, privacy	

This is achieved with the following two fundamental components to the technology:

1. Cryptographically anonymized accounts
2. A public ledger

The only way to remove the requirement for centralized administration is to make all participants take part in the administration; blockchains provide a way to achieve this. Exactly how will be explained in the next section, but on the face of it, the process of spending money is the same in a cryptocurrency as it is using a debit or credit card. The common elements are the following:

1. Someone signals that they authorize a recipient to receive some of their money.
2. The recipient seeks confirmation that the funds are available.
3. An exchange takes place.

When banks are involved, the authorization signals and confirmation requests are sent to the bank, which holds all the information and updates the records accordingly. With a blockchain, the authorization signal is sent to everybody in the system, because the system is administered by all participants, that is, there is a public announcement that someone wants to give money to someone else. The recipient, also being part of the system, has a record of all past transactions, because in order to make a transaction, it has to be made public, and so, the recipient can check for themselves whether the account that the money is coming from has enough money in it or not. If it does, they can be satisfied that, with enough other participants acknowledging they have received notice of the transfer, they alone are eligible to spend that money in the future. It might be a concern that all transactions are made public, but cryptography allows account holders to remain anonymous. The only information that needs to be made public for an account to authorize a payment is a cryptographic public key and the details of the payment itself (amount and recipient). The recipient's identity can also be hidden behind their public key. In practice, accounts can gain or lose reputation by being associated with other accounts, but there is no restriction on account creation and so an individual can create an account for every transaction if desired. Note that a key element is that "enough other participants" must acknowledge a money transfer before it can be taken as being a fully confirmed transaction. While a participant need not trust any single other participant they may have blockchain dealings with, they do still need to trust the blockchain network as a whole. It is important to see at this point how, by becoming a participant in the blockchain system, one becomes part of enforcing that system and that what is being enforced is a set of strong conventions, known to everyone, which are precisely defined and which can be expected to be honored by everyone else, that is, a social contract.

We are witnessing the next step in the progression of monetary record keeping:

1. Fragmented physical ledgers (the currency in people's pockets)
2. Centralized ledger (written or electronic and held privately by very few entities)
3. Public ledger (held by all participants)

However, a money system is only one example of a social contract. With blockchain technology, it is possible to broaden the possible uses of the system from just currency to anything that can be expressed in the form of a contract, that is to say, anything at all.

By social contract, we mean a system for which to be part of it means obeying the rules. In societies to date, "obeying the rules" has meant suffering penalties for noncompliance. Individuals therefore have the ability to weigh the penalties against the perceived gains of cheating the social contract, and as such, the social contract has evolved to weigh the penalties according to some assessment of the cost of noncompliance to the society. It appears that implementing anything approaching objectively quantified costs is very difficult, mainly due to the centralization of power leading to conflicts of interest between the government and society, worsened occasionally by inept execution and sometimes exaggerated by the anti-wisdom of the populace. Apart from the last point, we can see that the discussion of the problems of the money system can be extended to the general case. With blockchain technology, by contrast, we have that by being part of it, one has a small share of authority to enforce the rules. Unlike with the use of a centralized police force, the rules are enforced by consent (thus, exclusion from the system, not violence, is the punishment) and are enforced precisely and correctly from the point of view of the majority of participants, which, due to strong convention being the only point of authority, is the fair and expected way. Up to now, societies have used the threat of physical action/exclusion (punishment/prison), but on the blockchain, the rules cannot be broken and so exclusion is implicit. As such, we can view Bitcoin, Litecoin, and other cryptocurrencies as being proofs of concept, not only of a decentralized money system but also of a blockchain-based decentralized social contract platform. With this comes the possibility of using blockchain technology to allow for enforceable contracts to be created, for even just a single individual transaction that will be precisely executed without further intervention of the parties to the transaction and without the need to bring in external arbitrators to resolve discrepancies. For example, the registration of unique URL domain names could be managed on a well-defined "first come, first served" basis on a blockchain. Hedging contracts can be set up with preagreed limits that are guaranteed to pay out as initially specified. Crowdfunding with money-back guarantees will be transparently honored. The range of applications is hard to predict, but because anything is possible, it is fair to describe the systems that will be developed as being crypto law.

Nick Szabo was discussing the idea of crypto law using the term "Smart Contracts" in 1997 (Szabo, 1997), but the technology was not then available to implement them. With the invention of the blockchain, the development of the required technology is now surfacing.

We use the term crypto law to effect the understanding that with blockchain technology, we have the potential for systems, not just for trustless monetary transactions, but for trustless agreements regarding anything at all. The term emphasizes the intrinsic enforceability of the contracts that participants enter into and the generality of what those contracts can be used for. We have given a few examples already, but we will expand on the uses and implications later in the chapter.

In summary, cryptography in general and blockchain technology in particular are bringing about an entirely new way for individuals to communicate and societies to operate. The main attributes of the system they create provide the following:
- Anonymity for participants, if desired
- No need for trust of any individual entities
- Enforcement by the whole community, that is, no reliance on centralized entities

For commerce, this means that we can have a money system that vastly shifts the emphasis of control and so has the potential to radically reduce ambiguity, exclusion, and the dangers of abuse and mistrust. After 5 years of Bitcoin and also in an increasing number of other blockchain-based systems, this is being observed, albeit at the expense of stability. With the distributed mechanism of operation, decentralization provides
- no single point of vulnerability,
- democratically guaranteed social contract.

In short, we will be able to go beyond cryptocurrency and have crypto law. The resulting crypto-societies will operate in ways that we are yet to foresee.

19.4 PRACTICALITIES

Many explanations start with a description of the blockchain and understandably so, given its vital importance to current cryptocurrency implementations. Here, we have intentionally held back on describing what blockchains are, to emphasize that they are, nevertheless, an implementation issue, albeit the first and currently the only implementation.

Giving examples of the use of blockchains to date is limited by the fact that a full crypto law platform is yet to be finalized. However, there exist a good range of blockchain networks ranging from pure cryptocurrencies through information lookup services to distributed exchanges.

Satoshi Nakamoto was the first to combine the three fundamental techniques we will describe—consensus blockchains, proof of work, and digital signatures—to create Bitcoin (The Bitcoin Wiki). However, Bitcoin and indeed the other altcoins are very restricted in the enforceable information that can be added to their blockchain, namely, information on the transfer of ownership of currency. Their social contract rule that everyone obeys is limited to no double-spending. There are many projects extending the utility of the blockchain, such as Namecoin, providing a decentralized DNS lookup system, and the likes of Mastercoin, Counterparty, and NXT who provide currency and the ability to track and exchange user-defined resources.

19.4.1 Blockchains

In the previous section, we talked about how cryptocurrencies use a public database of information so that everyone can check for themselves that a payment coming to them is money that has not already been spent. Blockchains provide a way to achieve this: a way of recording an ordered sequence of packets of information, such that anyone can trust (in a mathematically reliable way) the information contained within and, importantly, the order in which the information was added. Each packet of information, the "block" in blockchain, can contain any information at all, but it must contain the *hash* of the block it is to come after, making that previous existing block its *parent*.

19.4.2 Cryptographic hashing

A *cryptographic hash*, or simply *hash*, given the cryptographic context, is the result of a special process, called *hashing*, which takes in any information and quickly returns a mathematically derived number between zero and a very large upper limit, for example, 2^{256} (1 followed by 77 zeros). What is special about the outputted number is that it is completely different to the point of looking random with even the smallest change in the input, and as a result, it is effectively impossible to guess what information was used to generate that hash. Hashing functions are also known as *one-way functions*.

As part of a blockchain, the hash is a vital component in the blockchain's role as a public database: Not being able to invent information that will give a particular hash means that one can trust that all the information used to generate a particular hash was actually known at the time. Therefore, by including the hash of all the information in the previous block, any block of interest necessarily came after the block before it and so on back to the very start.

19.4.3 The blockchain as consensus data

The blockchain can be taken as a database that everybody can access. The universal accessibility is possible because, in principle, anybody can have their own copy. Indeed, everybody having their own copy is part of the robust nature of the blockchain. Whenever anyone would like to join a blockchain, they simply connect to that blockchain's network and ask any or all of the participants for the blocks and collect the responses until all the blocks have been saved locally and an up-to-date copy of the blockchain is complete. Whenever a participant wants to add data to the database, they create a block and send it to everyone on the network so that everyone is aware of the new block. Because every block includes the unique hash of the block it follows from (its *parent* block), the new block is a *vote* for its parent (and indeed for every ancestor of that parent). Participants receiving a new block have two choices. After inspecting the new data contained within it, they can either accept the update to the database that the new data represent or reject it as being undesirable. New data can be undesirable for being inconsistent with existing data, for breaking the rules that updates must obey or because it contains data a particular recipient does not like. For cryptocurrencies, a block will be rejected if, for example, it includes a transaction involving money that has already been spent. In order for a participant to publicly vote for the inclusion of a new block, they simply include its hash (or that of any acceptable block that has this block as an ancestor) in their next addition to the blockchain. While a participant has no information to add, they can reject any new blocks that do not have their preferred blocks as a parent or ancestor and keep track of those that do.

Because any block can only have one parent, any particular block is the head of a chain of blocks leading back to the first, or *genesis* block. This means that participants who want to add data must add it with a parent that the rest of the network will accept as a preferred block: If they add it to a parent block that is being rejected by most of the network or even a parent block that has an ancestor that most of the network has rejected, then their block, and their data, will in turn be rejected. This is because only one chain of blocks can be taken as the canonical database of information, that is, the *main chain*. However, at any one time, there will be several blocks that a participant could take as the head block and use as their block's parent. In practice, it is actually easy to keep track of the network's preferences because of strong conventions on how to prioritize blocks for inclusion in the main chain. A blockchain platform's convention typically uses a scoring system for blocks: When there is more than one valid candidate for the new head block, everyone agrees to accept the candidate with the highest score. For example, the blocks that are added sooner could be given higher priority. This is applied on top of the implicit voting system in which blocks with more descendants are taken as being better, implying that head blocks with more ancestors, that is, longer chains, are more important. If someone who has added new information to the blockchain sees that their block is going *stale*, that is, not receiving any more descendants (i.e., votes), and that another chain is going to become the main chain to the exclusion of their block and the information it holds, they must resubmit their information using the new main-chain head block as the parent.

At this point, one should note that blockchain systems are secured by having many participants add new blocks continually. Broadly speaking, more participation means more voting, more independent oversight, and therefore a greater reassurance for any one participant to trust the system, without having to trust any particular participants that help run it.

19.4.4 Proof-of-work and proof-of-stake voting

In a real network system, information is not propagated instantaneously, and so, a participant may not receive notification of the latest blocks for some time. The danger here is that in the time it takes for someone to receive notification of a new block, those with superior network connections and processing capabilities could have added any number of new blocks onto the blockchain, making it impossible for some participants to ever have the chance of voting or even adding their own data. This is because they never know about the head block in time to include its hash in their block before it is too late.

Their block will not get any votes because enough people in the network will have already accepted the new blocks from the superior networked participants and will therefore overlook any blocks that do not have all of the new blocks as their ancestors.

A solution comes in the form of *proof of work*. The idea is to make it take, on average, an amount of time, significantly greater than the time to propagate information across the whole network, to create a new block. In this way, all participants can have a chance to know about all the proposed blocks currently on the network and so can know about all the heads to vote on and grow the blockchain from.

Adam Back proposed a method of achieving this, in the context of e-mail systems that were suffering from excessive quantities of spam messages, and called it *hashcash* (Back, 1997). A cost must be paid before a submission to the network can be made. This means spending time and computer processing power on solving a problem and including the proof in the information of the block being submitted. It must take a specified amount time to find the solution, but it must be quick and easy for others to verify the solution for them to be able to accept that the work has been done. The problem is to find an extra number that when included in the information for the block will mean that the hash of the block is itself a number that is lower than a target threshold. The threshold is set by the system to control the average time it takes to find an acceptable solution. Remember that hashing produces an unpredictable number so the extra number must be guessed: Each attempt has a low probability of success and so a very large number of attempts will be needed before a solution is found. However, each attempt requires the sophisticated hashing algorithm to be executed, using up time and energy. Because the result of any particular attempt is effectively random, occasionally, a participant will be lucky and get a qualifying proof of work very quickly. Other times, it will take a very long time. On average, however, it takes the desired time for someone to solve the proof-of-work problem and be able to add a block to the blockchain. Verification takes only the time of a single attempt and so is very fast.

Another view of the utility of proof of work is a way to distribute voting power. Adding a block is voting for a particular blockchain, and so, having to pay a processing cost to add a block is having to pay for a vote. Without proof of work, having better network connectivity would mean having greater voting power, which is very undesirable from being too geographic and difficult for individuals to obtain. Instead, processing power can be chosen as a superior mechanism to allocate votes, with the view that anyone wanting to join the cryptocurrency network necessarily already has computing power.

Most cryptocurrencies created so far, including Bitcoin, use the hashcash proof of work. As a result, we have seen the proliferation of cheap ASICs (hardware whose only purpose is computing proofs of work), which are considered detrimental, because they give disproportionately more votes to those able to make significant investments in otherwise useless hardware. The dominance of ASICs in the participation of a blockchain's voting system skews the democratic credibility of its consensus mechanism.

The second most popular cryptocurrency, Litecoin, uses a proof of work called *scrypt*, invented by Colin Percival to be *memory-hard*. It was adopted by Litecoin in an effort to overcome ASIC bias. It extends the operation to find a solution from being a single hash to being a large number of hash operations, which must be applied in a pseudorandom order. However, being also based on a particular hash function, scrypt has not saved Litecoin from ASIC dominance.

Proof of resources other than processing power can also be used. For example, MaidSafe uses a participant's network bandwidth and digital storage capabilities to determine voting power.

Proof of stake is an alternative to proof of work that allocates voting power in proportion to one's stake in the system. For example, owning 1% of all active currency on the NXT network gives you 1% of the voting power. Proof of stake more closely binds the oversight of the system with the usage of the system. A participant with more of a stake in the system and so who would suffer a greater loss if the system were to fail gets more voting power. In contrast, proof of work rewards external investment, rather than internal investment, making the cost of an attack less dependent on the internal value of the system.

Peercoin is an example of a hybrid system drawing on both proof of work and proof of stake. Its measure of stake incorporates both the holdings of the peercoin currency and the time a participant has been holding that currency.

Adding a block to the blockchain is both the inclusion of information in the public record and a vote for existing information. As such, it is important for any blockchain platform to have a robustly democratic way for the participants on its network to add blocks. It is likely that proof-of-stake schemes become the accepted way to achieve this efficiently.

19.4.5 Public-private key pair cryptography aka digital signatures

The last element required for cryptoplatforms is a way to be sure that data or a message added to the blockchain really came from a particular identity and not an impostor. For example, everyone must be able to agree that it was really you who sent those Bitcoins before the beneficiary can accept that your gift is honorable. This can be achieved using public-private key pairs: You have two mathematical keys (which are just numbers, although very special ones), one of which you must keep secret (your private key) and one which you let everybody know (your public key). A message encoded using your public key can only be decoded using your private key (for people wanting to send messages only to you), and more importantly, your public key will only decode messages encoded using your private key (the feature of importance here). As such, by sending a message tagged with that same message (or its hash) encoded using your private key, everybody is mathematically guaranteed that only you could have sent it, assuming that no one has been able to steal your private key, of course. Tagging a message in this way is called digitally *signing* that message.

Wei Dai presented a way of using this concept to secure electronic payments in a system he called *b-money* (Dai, 1998). Each electronic coin is owned by whoever can prove that they have the private key matching the public key that the coin has been tagged with. In order to give a coin you own to someone else, you relinquish your ownership by appending their public key and proving you were entitled to do that by signing it using your private key. Afterward, only the beneficiary is able to assign new ownership and so owns that coin himself or herself. Nakamoto added an extra innovation that allowed the spending of fractions of a currency unit.

Ultimately, however, the important characteristic is the ability for proving identity in a decentralized system.

19.5 THE FUTURE OF BLOCKCHAIN-BASED SYSTEMS

Bitcoin and its sister altcoins present a very specific example of what is possible with blockchain technology. They provide a way of keeping track of a spendable "account balance" at a practically unlimited number of "account numbers" represented by public keys. The rules of their social contract are effectively limited to ensuring that a transaction must increase account balances only by the amount that it reduces others. They are the initial foray in what is becoming a fruitful source of innovation and implementation.

The first additional functionality was an arbitrary key-value database storage platform implemented as Namecoin. In the Namecoin system, participants recognize the currency and, additionally, must respect the unique use of data labels, such as domain names, and the data stored in association with them, such as IP addresses. Being a consensus blockchain, it is robust to centralized censorship and so is an important platform for free speech. When used as a decentralized DNS lookup system, mapping domain names to IP addresses (it is currently used for ".bit" top level domains), it represents two main advantages over the official ICANN registry system, both coming from the blockchain's main characteristic of enacting a social contract. Firstly, the blockchain is more secure than ICANN's registry databases and so would not suffer from redirection attacks that have affected the likes of The New York Times (when Melbourne IT was hacked in August 2013); those wanting to add or change entries in the Namecoin network must get approval from the majority of the network for that change, so an attacker (being someone wishing to update the public database in a way contrary to the rules) must in some way gain influence of over half the network's resources (and in practice, a much higher percentage to be effective for any significant length of time), which would be half of the entire Internet if this system were deployed as the official DNS lookup mechanism. Secondly, the blockchain is effectively immune to political pressure (in whatever form, be it regulation or bribery) to change the system. Such change could be at a high level, affecting the rules governing which names can be registered and who can register them, or at a low level, meaning that a particular name is not allowed or a particular entity is given special registration rights. The rules of a blockchain are specified as part of its creation (and can include rules governing how they are updated) and those rules become the social contract that everyone joining the system unavoidably agrees to respect, simply by using the system. As a result, if the initial social contract espouses free speech by stating that everyone has the right to register whatever new domain name they wish, then no single participant can go against that, because it is the majority decision that dominates and any minority desire contrary will be overruled. Thus, through consensus, the strong convention as defined by the rules of the blockchain maintains and enforces the social contract all the participants have signed up to.

Mastercoin and NXT have created platforms on which participants can create their own currencies, representing whatever assets they choose, from gold to personal reputation, and decentralized exchange mechanisms (atomic transactions) so that trade between them is easy.

However, most projects realized to date attempt to provide a single additional functionality or small set of extra functionalities, to the basic use as a currency platform. For blockchain technology to truly advance, a new, fully capable system is needed: a blockchain technology that could serve natively as a platform for development in and of itself. Rather than create a new blockchain platform for each new idea, we will eventually have blockchain platforms on which the new ideas could be implemented *in situ*. This is a development analogous to advancing from the digital calculators of cryptocurrencies to the full computing power of crypto law.

To explain this further, let us look at a few more examples.

Escrow mechanisms are a necessary service when two parties want to exchange value without trusting the other. One of the parties places their value, usually money, in the escrow where it is inaccessible to either party until either they both agree or one agrees with the designated arbitrator to release it. The preblockchain solution as to who should hold the escrowed value is a trusted third party, such as a bank or credit card provider. The trusted third party usually acts as the arbitrator as well, but in most jurisdictions, arbitration ultimately falls to the judiciary. With a crypto law platform, the system itself can act as the escrow, with a "two-of-three" signature release mechanism automatically built in. Only trust in the system is required. In most cases, the two parties can sign the release themselves, without anyone else ever needing to be explicitly involved. In the case of a dispute, the third signatory, being the arbitrator, can be contacted as before. Technically, this can already be accomplished with Bitcoin, although it is not yet common. However, this is just the simplest example of an automated escrow. With the ability to create enforceable, yet bespoke contracts, one could devise a set of conditions, which could be automatically evaluated to resolve a potential dispute without having to involve a human arbitrator service and thus save money. For example, a taxi service could offer time-based escrows, where a client puts down a deposit for a given destination, thus reassuring the taxi driver that they will be paid, but the amount that will be paid depends on the time it takes to get to the destination, with longer times incurring a lower fee perhaps. Time-stamped GPS tracking data in the client's phone and the taxi itself can be sent to the escrow contract and so it knows when the destination has been reached, thus when to release the funds, and in what time, thus how much to release.

Broader commercial contracts, such as mergers and acquisitions, would also be radically transformed if conducted on a crypto law platform. The current approach tends to involve armies of lawyers reading through reams of legalese, checking that updates proposed by the other party have only affected the parts of the contract that their client expects to have changed while hoping that the other party's lawyers will not notice a subtle effect of one of the clauses they have added, which would give them an advantage if particular outcomes arise. This process, if conducted on the blockchain, would be made much more efficient, because updates to the contract during negotiation would be fast and each party could rely on the contract they were looking at, being the contract the other party would be signing, and it would be much more transparent, because being in computer code, there would be no ambiguities in the contract's interpretation. The transition would dramatically reduce the risk of the merger and acquisition process, particularly for the party with less money, making badly organized, malevolent, or hostile acquisitions less likely and so would benefit both business in general and society as a whole. Note that there is no need for law firms to feel that they will lose out with the move to the blockchain: Their service is the organization, creation, and interpretation of the contracts between the parties and that service will still be required. The only difference is that the contracts are written in precise computer code instead of ambiguous language, and so, the current verbosity seen in modern legal contracts employed in the attempt to overcome the ambiguity will be supplanted by long computer programs designed to accurately cover a list of necessarily well-described eventualities.

Further into the future, we could see the blockchain being used to represent the people politically with the development of crypto law parties and, eventually, governments. Through the creation of enforceable policies, voters would be able to vote for representatives or decrees that would act or be enacted as promised at the time of the election or vote. This is in contrast to the present system where voting for a politician is at best a vote for a party manifesto, which despite being written to sound detailed tends to represent little more than vague descriptions of the general tendencies of a party. In practice, the elected politicians have no obligation to vote in line with the expectations of the voter or indeed to stay with the party they campaigned under. The basic concept of contractual representation has already been enacted; for example, South East England had the option to vote for the YOURvoice party in the 2014 European elections, which is a party that promises to survey its members on every vote that its MEPs would be called upon to attend. This is an implementation of direct democracy and as such is at the inefficient end of the scale, but is an example of a trend that blockchain technology can help to realize. If we reached the point where a national currency was a cryptocurrency, then spending allocations, or the ways in which they would be determined, could be transparently presented under the guarantee of their application if selected by the electorate. Note that free and fair elections become trivial on a crypto law platform: A special VoteCoin currency is created for any particular vote and one coin is given to each citizen. They can then cast their vote by giving it to their favored candidate, through an automatic time-lock relay system so that everyone's votes are cast simultaneously. The entire society is administering the system and so the final counts are seen by everyone and fraud is a practical impossibility.

With the decentralized systems we are describing here comes increased trust of an individual in society, without the need for that individual to trust any other particular individual. In economic terms, this reduces the risk of all interactions within a society and so makes the whole society more efficient and more productive. Blockchain technology provides for platforms of crypto law, which are robust to dishonest actors to the maximum extent permitted by democracy. This robustness, together with the ability to create and execute contracts programmatically, paves the way for entirely new systems of interaction, a paradigm shift for society and arguably the next step in egalitarianism.

19.6 CONCLUSION

The development of blockchain technology was initially motivated by the desire to have a decentralized system of authority that can operate with only a trust in the system and not of any particular participants. It allows for a social contract in its purest form, whereby participation alone requires and ensures adherence to whatever rules the contract describes. This is implemented by everybody having a copy of all the information held by the system and uses cryptography to provide a way to be both open and private, thus breaking the prima facie contradiction. The distributed nature of operation makes the system robust through redundant duplication and democratic consensus.

Bitcoin was the first system implemented using blockchain technology. It was designed as a money system with a very simple set of rules making up a social contract allowing for its use as a currency. Its growth has been phenomenal and after 5 years has come to represent an economy worth billions of dollars. Bitcoin represents convenience without centralization and has been dubbed "banking without the banks." However, currency is just the start: the technology provides a way for a generalized system of agreement without need for interparticipant trust.

The advantages of blockchain technology in its resilience to attack and its distributed democratic oversight mean that it will become attractive to anyone who requires a safe record of time-ordered data entries, including the very institutions that the current proponents of the technology are hoping to supersede. However, the disruptive motivations of the current developers of the technology have caught the attention of governments and financial institutions. The current level of activity is relatively low, but it is on the rise. Therefore, it is, in many arenas, being seen as a threat. The United States of America, whose currency is the most widely accepted internationally and who derives soft power from the fact, could see widespread adoption of cryptocurrencies that its regulators and power brokers cannot control as potentially undermining. China tacitly supported Bitcoin, possibly for exactly the same reason, but has since banned its banks from dealing with it at all. Sub-Saharan Africa, whose countries have much to gain from remittance-boosting money-transfer-channel competition, is only in the early stages of developing regulatory frameworks for cryptocurrencies, if they are aware of them at all.

However, as technologists and developers come to see the breadth of applications for blockchain technology and the wider social implications of those visions, it becomes increasingly important to have a blockchain-based system providing a generalized state with the ability to specify state updates codified with a general-purpose programming language. This will drive the development of the use of blockchain technology and take it well beyond the realm of virtual money: even now, there is the possibility for the creation of systems that can administer bespoke contracts, digitally authored and signed by anyone. This, in turn, is going to change social and business interactions in ways not yet predicted, both locally and internationally.

We have talked about money systems as a specific example of a social contract between all participants and have done so in order to be able to more easily describe the full generalized potential of blockchain technology, not as a base limited to the creation of cryptocurrencies, but as a platform for crypto law.

REFERENCES

Back, A.H., 1997. http://www.hashcash.org/papers/announce.txt.

Brunnermeier, M.K., 2008. Deciphering the liquidity and credit crunch 2007–08. National Bureau of Economic Research Working Paper No. 14612, November 2008.

Capgemini, 2013. World Payments Report 2013. http://www.capgemini.com/resources/world-payments-report-2013, September 2013.

Carlton, D.W., Frankel, A.S., 1995. The antitrust economics of credit card networks. Antitrust Law J. 63, 643–668, http://faculty.chicagobooth.edu/dennis.carlton/research/pdfs/AntitrustEconomicsCreditCardNetworks.pdf.

Counterparty, 2014. http://counterparty.io/.

Dai, W.B., 1998. Money. http://www.weidai.com/bmoney.txt, November 1998.

Federal Reserve System, 2013. The 2013 Federal Reserve Payments Study: Recent and Long-Term Payment Trends in the United States: 2003–2012. http://www.frbservices.org/files/communications/pdf/research/2013_payments_study_summary.pdf.

Hall, C., 2013. Anything for you big boy: a comparative analysis of banking regulation in the United States and the United Kingdom in light of the LIBOR scandal. Northwestern J. Int. Law Business 34, 154–180.

Inderst, R., Ottaviani, M., 2009. Misselling through agents. Am. Econ. Rev. 99 (3), 883–908.

Litecoin. https://litecoin.org/.

Maidsafe. http://maidsafe.net/.

Mankiw, N.G., 2007. Macroeconomics, sixth ed. Worth Publishers, New York, ISBN 0-7167-6213-7, pp. 22-32.

Mastercoin. http://www.mastercoin.org.

McLeay, M., Radia, A., Thomas, R., 2014. Money creation in the modern economy. The Bank of England's Monetary Analysis Directorate, http://www.bankofengland.co.uk/publications/Documents/quarterlybulletin/2014/qb14q1prereleasemoneycreation.pdf.

Molyneux, P., Gardener, E.P.M., Carbo, S., 2005. Financial Exclusion. Palgrave Macmillan, Hampshire, UK and New York, NY, ISBN 1-4039-9051-4.

Nakamoto, S., 2009. Bitcoin: a peer-to-peer electronic cash system. https://bitcoin.org/bitcoin.pdf.

Namecoin. http://namecoin.info/.

Nxt. http://nxter.org/.

Peercoin. http://peercoin.net/.

Szabo, N., 1997. The idea of smart contracts. http://szabo.best.vwh.net/smart_contracts_idea.html.

The Bitcoin Wiki. https://en.bitcoin.it/wiki/Main_Page.

Watkins, K., Quattri, M., 2014. Lost in Intermediation: How Excessive Charges Undermine the Benefits of Remittances for Africa. Overseas Development Institute, London, UK, http://www.odi.org/sites/odi.org.uk/files/odi-assets/publications-opinion-files/8901.pdf.

CHAPTER 20

How Digital Currencies Will Cascade up to a Global Stable Currency
The Fundamental Framework for the Money of the Future

Gideon Samid
Case Western Reserve University, Cleveland, Ohio, USA

Contents

20.1 INTRODUCTION

The amazing and earthshaking potential of digital currency is so far clouded by the follies of its illustrious flagship: bitcoin. Favored by criminals, terrorists, and fraudsters, bitcoin invokes condemnation and warnings issued by "the money royalty." Innocent youngsters treat bitcoin as the means to take power away from bankers and other "exploiters"— reminiscent of the youthful reaction to The Communist Manifesto, in 1848. And much as capitalists all over the world saw Karl Marx as a threat, so they see Satoshi Nakamoto, the mysterious author of the bitcoin protocol, as bad news.

Today's passenger jets look totally different from the contraption that the Wright Brothers used in 1903. So will digital money 2020 bear only a faint resemblance to bitcoin. The Wright brothers pioneering act made a statement: air travel is here. And bitcoin makes a statement: *digital money arrived*.

Before air travel, you had to negotiate wriggly roads, steep hills, and stormy water in order to go from point A to point B. The airplane flew over these obstacles and made transportation frictionless to a great degree. That is exactly what digital money does: it makes payment frictionless and storing money quick and easy. When Alice prevails on Bob to agree to pay her $X, the execution of this concurrence should be smooth and painless and versatile too: payment should be carried out efficiently whether Alice and Bob are merchants, bankers, private citizens, or government agencies. Transactions should be executed lightning fast whether Alice and Bob meet face to face or reside a city, even an ocean apart, crossing several international borders. Nonrepudiation fixtures should accompany payments, so that both Alice and Bob can prove to themselves, to their accountants, to their shareholders, and to their governments that this transaction took place. In short, once a decision to effect a payment has been made, the implementation thereto should be quick, automatic, and painless.

Today, payment is an elaborate dialogue, payer and payee need to expose their identity and many private attributes, and banks make it cumbersome to open an account to move money around and to understand the barrage of new rules coming down the pike. International transfer is Kafkaesque, and currency exchange is a maze.

Digital currency, once omnipresent and mature, will do away with most of those inhibitors. Digital cash is paid by confirming its validity, not by forcing the payer to expose himself or herself. Digital money—a bit sequence—is stored on a pinhead, secured by unbreakable encryption, and paid as easy as a text message, an email attachment, or a direct file transfer.

Historically, whenever payment became easier and smoother, commerce flourished and civilization jolted up. It happened when barter was replaced by primitive money, when precious metal became standard money, and then again when scales were replaced by preminted coins, and of course, we have seen the medieval period end and the Renaissance bud up when the first promissory notes became popular and introduced the notion of paper money. Expect no less now when digital money is media-free, weightless, volumeless, and frictionless. We probably do not have the imagination to foresee what will happen, much as the house of Medici in Florence could not foresee today's paper money when they started issuing their paper claim checks for deposited gold.

But a few things loom clear: (1) volatility will need to dry up, (2) payment platform will become global, and (3) currencies cascade up.

Volatility: the underlying idea of money is that its value is stable and predictable. When a farmer sold eggs in the spring in order to buy a plough shed in the summer and managed to do so by exchanging his eggs against some form of money, his or her expectation was that that money will keep its value until the summer when he would wish to use it to buy the plough shed. If people would have expected money (any form of money) to appreciate, they would stop trading with it, waiting for it to be worth more. If people suspected the other way that money will inflate, then they would get rid of it as fast as they could, and nobody will be eager to accept it. Money—essentially—must be a stable store of value. So, whether bitcoin will be sufficiently modified to lose its unacceptable volatility or it would be replaced by something like BitMint or by any other nonspeculative currency, volatility should be dried out before digital currency is a currency.

In antiquity, gold and silver transcended political boundaries and served as the currency of choice for international transactions. In the more recent history, states guard their power to mint their own currency, and as a result, international trade requires a resolution of the rate of exchange. Researchers like Cohen (2003) highlight the competing efforts of states to elevate their currency as a reference option. Some, like Greco (2009), highlight the claim that money became the instrument of political power, which hampers its utility. Lewis (2007), on his part, argued that in order to achieve monetary stability across the trading globe, it is necessary to honor the historical role of gold and pull back from the free money-printing option claimed by modern states. Lietaer (2002) went further in pointing out that our global money system is sick, strained, and in a position to destroy global economic well-being. Perhaps, the most credible warning with regard to world finance comes from Roubini (2010) who was the only serious voice that unsuccessfully warned about the 2008 debacle. He claimed that while bailing up the banks saved the world from a financial collapse, it failed to eradicate the root causes, creating a ticking bomb toward the next financial shake-up. His account points out to the power of inertia. It leads one to regard a profound technological breakthrough, like digital money, as a much needed game changer. Wray (2012) represented the voices that are apprehensive of the efforts to fuse currencies across political borders, claiming that each nation should mint its own currency. Surrendering this power will unleash destabilization. Chittenden (2010) was an excellent source for a broad scope of opinions over the issue of the money of the future. Vince Cable asserts in his introduction that one should not forecast the future, but rather think of many possible scenarios—that is the spirit that should guide the reader of this chapter.

The Internet turned us all into villagers who meet in the cyber town square and exchange goods and services. The need to pay across international borders has been growing for years and keeps growing with accelerated momentum. Digital money flows across the room or across the globe with equal ease, so digital money will have to rise into international acceptability to allow everyone to pay anyone.

And the last premise of the big change is cascading. Imagine two digital currencies, A and B. It is so very easy to use these currencies as building blocks for a third currency, C, defined as, say, 50% A and 50% B. You buy a C coin by paying half its value with A bits and half its value with B bits. The bits flow lightning fast and the exchange is equally fast.

In another corner of the world, two different digital currencies, D and E, have been used in commerce. Upon them, one could establish another currency, F, defined as follows: an F coin is composed of half a D coin and half an E coin.

But that is only the beginning. Anyone could create another currency, G, and define it as composed of half C and half F (or a third C and a two-third F, as the choice may be).

Since C is composed of currencies A and B and F is composed of currencies D and E, it figures then that G is composed of A, B, D, and E.

Digital currency G expresses a diversification of wealth that ranges through A, B, D, and E—giving it stability and trust that are higher than any placed in either A, B, C, D, E, or F by themselves. In other words, by using the ease in which one cascades up digital currencies, we can readily continue this process and cascade G with a similarly composite currency, H, and yield a super currency, I, defined over G and H.

By keeping the cascading protocol iteratively, one approaches a super currency *that is anchored upon the entire wealth of the trading society*, and hence, this currency is inherently stable!

And once we have this super currency to trade with, we have exactly what is needed for the credit market to flower. Money that comes with poor expectation of stability is money that chokes credit because lenders do not wish to lend money that would be worthless when paid back and borrowers do not wish to commit to pay a loan that would require a much higher payback when payback is due. The emerging super currency therefore will be an excellent basis for global credit and global prosperity.

And all that because digital money is so naturally cascading up. That is the message. Details ahead.

20.2 COMMODITY-BACKED DIGITAL MINT

A digital mint is an operation that issues digital strings that represent both value and identity. So digital string A of value X is distinct from digital string B, which may also be of value X.

Bitcoin has captured the fancy of traders on account of its daring proposition for value. Given that President Nixon in 1971 has decoupled the US dollar from its base—gold, without a collapse of the currency—this triggered far-reaching thoughts that the value of money is established by trader's consent, which in turn is anchored on nothing substantial. If the US dollar that is backed only by itself is so widely accepted and overall holds its value, then why not bitcoin—anchored to nothing, substantiated by no commodity, and guaranteed against no universal value—why should it not enjoy a stable value just on account of the desire of its traders for currency stability? This was a daring proposition that overreached its bounds. The US dollar is backed by the US federal government, which has the power to tax US citizens, and it has a central bank that can control the supply of the US dollar and thereby influence its value. Bitcoin, by contrast, has no taxing authority and no central bank. In fact, bitcoin is designed to insure that no coordinated minority will ever take over the currency and impose its will on the majority of traders. It sounds very appealing at first glance, but quite troubling at further thought. The rule of majority implies rigidity of control. Should the value rise or fall in an accelerating mode, there would be no power to arrest that movement. By design, bitcoin has no central bank, no power center, and no leadership. So, it is only a matter of time before bitcoin will swing up or down or oscillate between high up and low down that traders will be forced to abandon it in favor of a more stable currency. This dire future for this pioneering currency is also shared by Robinson (2014) and Samid (2014). But unlike most detractors, these two authors point out that the trading protocol and other bitcoin ideas may fit into the evolving digital money solution—a case in point is offered by Samid (2014).

Calming down from the fanciful idea of "*money that is hooked on nothing will hook us all,*" we revisit the notion of money backed by a commodity.

The operation is simple: a digital mint accepts a measure of the backed commodity and issues a digital claim check for the same amount, allowing for the holder of the claim check to forward it back to claim the measure of the backup commodity. A digital mint will have to define strict rules and procedures for handling the challenge of double-spending, of theft, coercion, or splitting of value, etc. And for our account here, we will assume that any digital mint we talk about did indeed develop a satisfactory solution for these challenges.

The backing commodity against which the digital claim check is issued may also be submitted through another coin, at its value equivalent at the time of the exchange.

While the value of the claimed commodity may rise or fall, the relationship between the digital claim check and the measure of the backing commodity is fixed and nonspeculative.

20.3 DERIVED COMMODITIES

Taking a broad definition of the term "commodity," one would regard fiat currencies as a bona fide commodity. Fiat currencies serve as a basis for an array of financial instruments. The full set of business shares, stocks, bonds, tradable promissory notes of all kind, mutual funds, and more recently loyalty money issued by stores for purchases there or even for restricted purchases are all derived commodities. We see derived commodities in the form of tradable air miles, health-care dollars, community dollars, etc. The 2008 severe economic recession gave a bad rap to elaborate and sophisticated packages of a large assortment of debt instruments designed to achieve enhanced securitization. Any such device can be identified as a commodity to be used as a backup for a nonspeculative digital mint.

One might note that the difference between the collateralized debt obligation (CDO), collateralized loan obligation (CLO), and digital minted money backed by them is that money is much easier to handle, freer (less regulated), and highly frictionless. Also, money is trading with a much finer resolution than these complex financial packages.

20.4 CASCADING

The essential process in this account is the process of cascading digital mints. We shall first define the process to be called composite backing or "ground cascading."

20.4.1 Composite backing (ground cascading)

Let C_1 and C_2 be two commodities within a given society of traders. One could build a digital mint M_1 to issue digital claim checks against C_1 and build digital mint M_2 to issue claim checks against measures of commodity C_2. However, one could build a digital mint $M_{1,2}$ that would issue digital coins, of type $d_{1,2}$, (digital strings) against a measure c_1 of commodity C_1 and a measure c_2 of commodity C_2. Upon redemption of d_{12}, the redeemer will collect from the mint c_1 quantity of C_1 and c_2 quantity of C_2.

Since commodity C_1 and commodity C_2 are both traded in the same relevant trading society, they do have an exchange ratio:

$$C_2 = E_{2,1} \times C_1$$

where $E_{2,1}$ represents how many units of C_2 are traded against a single unit of C_1. Naturally, the value of $E_{2,1}$ depends on the choice of units for C_1 and C_2. Respectively, we may define $E_{1,2}$ as the reverse value so that

$$E_{21} \times E_{12} = 1$$

We can therefore say that mint M_{12} is backed by commodities C_1 and C_2 at a ratio, r_2:

$$r_2 = E_{1,2} \times c_2/c_1$$

The cross-commodity exchange values $E_{2,1}$ reflect the relative desirability between these two commodities at a given moment of time, as reflected by a majority of actual trades between commodities C_1 and C_2 (directly or indirectly), and they reflect the desirability force in an average way across the trading society.

Assume that a time measure t passed from time point regarded as "0" when the mint issued its digital coin to the trader and the time point t when a redeemer of that digital coin came to redeem it. Then, we may register $E_{2,1}(0)$ the exchange value at the time of purchase of the digital coin and $E_{2,1}(t) \neq E_{2,1}(0)$ at the time the coin was redeemed.

According to definition of the digital coin (digital string) d_{12}, when it is being redeemed, it will claim the same quantities of the backup commodities: c_1 and c_2. Since $E_{2,1}(t) \neq E_{2,1}(0)$ if the redeemer changes his or her c_2 measure to equivalent measure of commodity C_1, or vice versa, he or she will net a different measure of c_1 (or c_2 as the case may be) than the measure he or she would have netted if exchanged at time 0.

This dual backing of a digital currency may be extended to multiple backing: let C_1, $C_2, \ldots, C_n$ be n commodities traded in the relevant society. One could establish a mint $M_{1,2,\ldots,n}$ that would issue a digital coin $d_{1,2,\ldots,n}$ purchased and redeemable against quantities $c_1, c_2, \ldots, c_n$ of the respective commodities.

Since stability is the primary attribute of money, the popularity of a currency reflects its stability. Traders shy away from unstable money. Therefore, a cascaded currency based on the more popular currencies has a clear stability edge because not only does it reflect the better stability of its constituent currencies but also it offers enhanced stability owing to its partial or complete immunization against fluctuations among these constituent currencies. This argument can be developed with mathematical rigor, and so, it can be shown that $d_{1,2,...,n}$ is a digital coin that in general is more stable than some random d_i ($i = 1,2,...,n$) from the mix. This added stability is the motivation for this ground cascading process.

This procedure ("composite backing" or alternatively "ground cascading") may be applied not only to primary commodities but also to derived commodities, for example, fiat currencies.

Any number of commodities among the n, as defined above, may, in fact, be fiat currencies of some particular country or any other currency that trades well in the relevant society.

20.4.2 Digital cascading

By regarding digital currencies (defined above) as bona fide commodities and applying the above procedure to such currencies, one extends this ground cascading into digital cascading.

Let one identify n resources of tradable value within a given trading society. Let there be m digital mints defined over these n resources as backup commodities. For $i = 1,2,...,$ n, let mint M_j be issuing a d_j coin against measures $c_{1j}, c_{2j}, ..., c_{ij}, ..., c_{nj}$ of the n tradable commodities $C_1, C_2, ..., C_n$. Naturally, any (but not all) measures c_{ij} for any $i = 1,2,...,n$ and $j = 1,2,...,m$ may be zero.

One of the n resources will be arbitrarily chosen to be used as benchmark and regarded as C_1, against which the $(n-1)$ exchange values will be defined $E_{2,1}, E_{3,1}, ..., E_{n,1}$—these are all functions of time per the relevant trading society.

Any number of these resources may be a derived commodity. We have regarded fiat currency as a derived commodity, but similarly, we may regard any of the m digital coins defined over the same trading society as derived currencies. The validity of a digital coin d_j issued by M_j is based on the trust associated with M_j for it to be able to redeem the specified quantities $c_{1j}, c_{2j}, ..., c_{nj}$ for any redeemed coin d_j.

We may now consider a second set of m' digital mints $M'_1, M'_2, ..., M'_{m'}$, defined over the n primary resources $c_1, c_2, ..., c_n$, and in addition over the m digital coins $d_1,$ $d_2, ..., d_m$. For $j' = 1, 2, ..., m'$, mint $M'_{j'}$ will be defined over the quantities $c_{1j'}, c_{2j'},$ $..., c_{nj'}, d_{1j'}, d_{2j'}, ..., d_{mj'}$. The new m' mints are defined over a larger set of commodities $(n+m)$, compared to the first round of m defined over the n primary resources.

The first set $M_1, M_2, ..., M_m$ mints will be regarded as the zero set of digital mint or the ground set. The second set of digital mints $M'_1, M'_2, ..., M'_{m'}$ will be regarded as the first "aboveground" set or the "first cascading set."

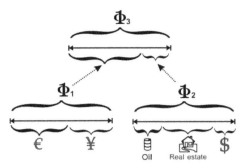

Figure 20.1 Graphic depiction of currency cascading.

This process may be repeated, and a second cascading set composed of m'' digital mints may be defined: M''_1, M''_2, ..., $M''_{m''}$ over the combined $(n+m+m')$ backup commodities.

Cascading may be repeated as many times as desired, resulting in k-count cascading set, composed of $m^{(k)}$ mints $M^{(k)}_1$, $M^{(k)}_2$, ..., $M^{(k)}_{m^{(k)}}$, defined as below over the available commodities counted as $n+m'+m''+\cdots+m^{(k-1)}$.

The values for m, m', m'', and $m^{(k)}$ may be very large. They are limited only by the resolution of the original commodities c_1, c_2, ..., c_n, since one assumes that a digital coin can be issued at any desired resolution. The original resources that are used in the minting process c_1, c_2, ..., c_n have a natural maximum practical resolution, which is much coarser than their theoretical resolution (see Figure 20.1).

20.4.3 Illustration

Four nonspeculative digital mints 1, 2, 3, and 4 are established. Mint 1 mints a digital currency with units (coins) defined as 500$ plus 500€ plus 20 ounces of silver, plus 1 ounce of gold. At time point $t=0$, the euro is worth 1.15$, an ounce of silver trades for 20$, and an ounce of gold fetches 1600$. Hence, the dollar value of a single digital coin minted by mint 1 is $500+500 \times 1.15+20 \times 20+1 \times 1600=3075$$. This implies that a trader could buy a mint 1 coin for 3075.00$ because the mint will parcel these dollars to buy and deposit the set amount of euros, gold, and silver, so that the mint can redeem its coin per its defined entity.

At some later times, $t=1$ and $t=2$, the relative values of the backup commodities change as follows:

Commodities cross pricing ($)

Time points	$	€	Silver	Gold
$t=0$	1	1.15	20	1600
$t=1$	1	1.35	22	1500
$t=2$	1	1.55	28	1300

Accordingly, the dollar values of the mint 1 coin are

Mint 1

Time	$/Coin	$/Appreciation (%)
$t=0$	3075	0
$t=1$	3115	1
$t=2$	3135	2

That means that a holder of mint 1 coin should redeem it at $t=1$ and opt to retain its value in dollars and will net 3115\$ or mark a gain of 1%. That will also be the purchase price of the mint -1 coin at $t=1$. Similarly for $t=2$, the dollar gain is now 2%.

In parallel to mint 1, three more mints defined their own digital currencies as follows:

Mints	$	€	Silver	Gold
1	500	500	20	1
2	250	300	0	4
3	800	0	50	2
4	0	2500	125	10

Yielding the following dollar values over time,

Time	$/Coin	$/Appreciation (%)
Mint 2		
$t=0$	6995	0
$t=1$	6655	−5
$t=2$	5915	−15
Mint 3		
$t=0$	5000	0
$t=1$	4900	−2
$t=2$	4800	−4
Mint 4		
$t=0$	21,375	0
$t=1$	21,125	−1
$t=2$	20,375	−5

Traders who chose mint 1 enjoyed the most stable choice in the time space $t=0$ to $t=2$, while traders who picked mint 2 lost 15% of the dollar value of their investment.

A cascade can now be formed. Indeed, three more mints come to existence (mints 5, 6, and 7), and they refer to the four commodities ($, €, silver, and gold) as backups, but they also regard the four existing mints (mints 1, 2, 3, and 4) as backup commodities. These three mints in turn issue their unique digital coin as defined below:

Mints	$	€	Silver	Gold	Mint 1	Mint 2	Mint 3	Mint 4
5	5000	0	8	2	4	0	1	0
6	3000	0	0	15	4	0	0	4
7	0	0	0	3	0	1	2	2

So, for example, mint 7 is defined over gold and mints 2, 3, and 4.

The corresponding values of these three cascading mints over the same time periods are readily computed as

Time	$/Coin	$/Appreciation (%)
Mint 5		
$t=0$	25,660	0
$t=1$	25,536	0
$t=2$	25,164	−2
Mint 6		
$t=0$	124,800	0
$t=1$	122,460	−2
$t=2$	116,540	−7
Mint 7		
$t=0$	64,545	0
$t=1$	63,205	−2
$t=2$	60,165	−7

This shows that mint 5 is the most stable among the three. Cascading may continue. For example, mint 8 may be defined as a digital coin backed by three coins issued by mint 5 and one digital coin minted by mint 6. Mint 8, in dollar value over time, will then be

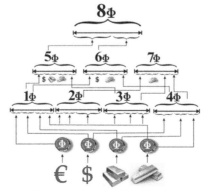

Three layers cascading illustration
12 Mints InterMint
4 Base Mints (Dollar, Euro, Silver, Gold)
Eight cascading mints (4 @level1, 3 @level2, 1 @level3)

Time	$/Coin	$/Appreciation (%)
Mint 8		
$t=0$	201,780	0
$t=1$	199,068	-1
$t=2$	192,032	-5

20.4.4 Cascading stability

Suppose that somebody is smart enough to account for every piece of asset, value, and wealth owned by every single human being on the face of the Earth. Let's call this sum that represents the total wealth of humanity H. What unit will H be measured by? US dollar? Really, what if the US central bank prints oodles of money and the US dollar inflates? H then will rise. For good reason? Hardly. Nothing will change in the real world: the same amount of food, clothing, housing, cars, boats, toasters, and TVs. Say then that the US dollar is not a very good metric for H. What then? Gold? What will happen if a meteorite composed of a million tons of gold will land on planet Earth. Gold will instantly inflate—it will again look like H rose in value, but surely not. It will be the same for the case of an earthquake under Ft Knox, where tons of gold will be lost and gold will appreciate overnight, pulling H down—accounting-wise, not in any real sense. We may conclude then that H, the wealth of humanity, cannot be reliably measured. But why do we need to attach, say, a dollar figure to H? Is there a buyer for it? Are we going to sell H to some extraterrestrial and demand so much gold?

While H is not really measurable, it itself can serve as a unit of measurement. We may say that the upper 10% of rich countries own 90% of H, while the other 90% own 10% of H. If over time, your fraction of H increases, you truly will get richer. While if your bank account got fatter, you might in fact be poorer because of inflation.

Since we have no scale to measure H, we also have no indication whether H itself changed over time. From our point of view, H—the total wealth of humanity—is a reference point, stable, reliable, and durable. It is the natural anchor to hook our accounting to. We care not whether H rises or falls in some theoretical sense of how much, say, a Martian will pay for H; we do care if we individually, our family, our company, or our country has a bigger or a smaller piece of H.

It does not take much thinking to realize that if we figure out a currency that measures fractions of H, then we will have a fundamentally stable currency. What is the source of instability for currency C_1? Its value with regard to some other currency C_2 is changing. If C_1 accounts for apples and C_2 for oranges and people over time like apples more and oranges less, then $C_1:C_2$ fluctuates. But if $C_1=H$ and people like oranges less, will we say that H is appreciating? No! H is H; C_2 depreciates. H then is inflation- and deflation-immunized.

Having concluded that H is our desired stable currency, how now do we go about it? The above cascading process is the answer. And that is the profound attraction of cascaded digital currencies; they evolve over time to define higher-up and higher-up currencies, and each successive currency gets closer to H and becomes more stable and less insecure. The process is asymptotic. By cascading up from a wide as possible range of commodities, we gradually and surely approach the ideal of a theoretically and practically stable super currency.

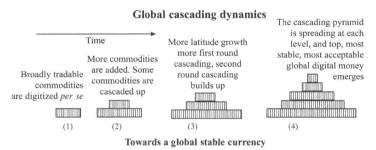

Global cascading dynamics

Time

Broadly tradable commodities are digitized *per se*

(1)

More commodities are added. Some commodities are cascaded up

(2)

More latitude growth more first round cascading, second round cascading builds up

(3)

The cascading pyramid is spreading at each level, and top, most stable, most acceptable global digital money emerges

(4)

Towards a global stable currency

20.5 OUTLOOK

Here is an outlook scenario for evaluation: the global bitcoin flare-up has positioned digital currencies on the discussion tables of major financial institutions. The realization that crypto money plucked from the air is bound to fade away as a side game currency, will focus attention on nonspeculative digital money like BitMint. This focus will undermine the fear of the new, crack the power of inertia, and bring to bear a pioneering step by a financial institution that will digitally mint the prevailing fiat currencies. Such a financial institution is most likely to be US-centric, and the digital currency it would mint will be digitized US dollars, using the BitMint protocol. Following a period in which the mere trade with BitMint digitized dollars becomes a norm, this institution or a competing financial institution will start cascading and mint a composite digital coin composed of a proportion of US dollar and euro. This cocktail currency will become the one quoted and specified in bilateral US-European contracts. From there, the idea of mixed fiat currencies will spread to the Yuan, the Yen, etc. At the next stage, entrepreneurs around the world will come up with well-thought-out combinations of minerals like gold, silver, and oil, food supplies, fertile land, real estate complexes, and increasingly mint currencies contending to reflect the wealth of the Earth. Later on, the assortment of competing currencies will be sorted out to a few prevailing ones, and enterprising agents will combine those winners into higher cascaded money options, which again would compete, and over time, perhaps two decades, the world will see a contender "super money"—a currency that is backed by a vast majority of "earthlings" offering stability, tradability, and a robust framework to secure sound banking, effective credit, and accelerated prosperity.

20.5.1 Financial Panacea

Imagine a world where money is stable and universal. You can put your digital money into your digital device, back it up, encrypt it, secure it to your heart's delight, and then be assured that its buying power will not erode. What will it do for our quality of life? But mostly, what will it do for credit?

A word about credit: Wealth distribution within humanity is not consistent with talent distribution and ability distribution. Some very talented and able people simply do not have the money to exercise their gifts. On the other hand, some very wealthy people are too old, too sick, to depressed, or too something else and cannot put their money to good use. The credit market is the ingenious mechanism to allow the latter to lend to the former and benefit in part from the eventual success of the borrower. Progress and prosperity depend therefore on the availability of credit. We witness today and for a long time a big battle raging between two opposite economic schools: One says let the government tax the wealthy and then give credit, loans, grants, and gifts to the poor, especially to the talented poor (or to the voting poor, rather). Other say let the rich find ways to lend money, extend grants, and offer gifts to the nonrich, so that wealth distribution will be more productive. Either way or with regard to any way in between, society will advance via the mechanism of credit extension. But for credit to flower, it has to be extended in super stable currency since money that rises in value hinders borrowers and money that loses value discourages lenders. Say then that the increased stability of the upper currencies in the cascading ladder will be increasingly more fitting to serve for credit extension. And as this top currency approaches H, it ignites further the credit market, and the blessing of global prosperity will be here sooner. There will be more on that vision in Samid (2013).

Now all that we have to do is to conquer our fear of the new media-independent form of money, choose a robust secure nonspeculative digital currency protocol (BitMint is one serious candidate), and start cascading toward our bright joint future.

REFERENCES

Chittenden, O., 2010. The Future of Money. Virgin Digital, London.
Cohen, B., 2003. The Future of Money. Princeton University Press, Princeton, NJ.
Greco, T., 2009. The End of Money and the Future of Civilization. Chelsea Green Publishing, White River Junction, VT.
Lewis, N., 2007. Gold: The Once and Future Money. Wiley, Hoboken, NJ.
Lietaer, B., 2002. The Future of Money: Creating New Wealth, Work and a Wiser World. Random House, London.
Robinson, J., 2014. BitCon: The Naked Truth About Bitcoin, ©Jeffrey Robinson.
Roubini, N., 2010. Crisis Economics: A Crash Course in the Future of Finance. Penguin Books, USA.
Samid, G., 2013. Tethered Money: Digital Currency & Social Innovation. DGS Vitco McLean, Virginia.
Samid, G., 2014. bitcoin.BitMint: Reconciling Bitcoin with Central Bank. https://eprint.iacr.org/2014/244.
Wray, R., 2012. Modern Money Theory: A Primer on Macroeconomics for Sovereign Monetary Systems. Palgrave Macmillan, London.

CHAPTER 21

Bitcoin-Like Protocols and Innovations

Ignacio Mas[a,*], David LEE Kuo Chuen[b,†]
[a]Saïd Business School, University of Oxford, Oxford, UK
[b]Sim Kee Boon Institute for Finance Economics, Singapore Management University, Singapore

Contents

*Funding for the author's fellowship at the Saïd Business School and for this chapter comes from the Bill & Melinda Gates Foundation. The author would like to thank both organizations for their support and to Colin Mayer of the Saïd Business School for the very useful conversations.
†Funding for the author is provided by the Sim Kee Boon Institute for Financial Economics.

In this chapter, we examine the protocols of Bitcoin and its innovations (based mainly on the original paper by Mas, 2014 and Podcast by Lee, 2014). We argue that the role of any cryptocurrency and especially bitcoin is likely doomed as an alternative to fiat currencies, but its role as a system providing financial services may have been grossly underestimated. In particular, the Bitcoin key engineering elements (Nakamoto, 2009) offer the possibility of a radically different approach for architecting electronic payment systems (EPSs) among other more sophisticated systems such as crowd sales, crowd funding, peer-to-peer exchanges, and other side-chain capabilities. The technologies embedded within the Bitcoin system have the potential to develop into very open, contestable, and interconnected ecosystems for the delivery of new and existing form of financial services.

The most salient feature is its distributed architecture with the following characteristics:

1. All transactions are peer to peer, and therefore, Bitcoin is decentralized with no gatekeepers.
2. All transactions are through the Internet, and therefore, Bitcoin requires no additional specialized networking infrastructure.
3. All Bitcoin nodes have access to the same information and therefore are distributed. The main advantage of the Bitcoin system over traditional financial services is lower infrastructure and network costs. This will be the main driver for innovation at the edge of the network. The adoption of pseudo Bitcoin, also known as Bitcoin 2.0 or Bitcoin-like protocols, could radically expand access and relevance of financial services globally, especially across borders and in developing countries. Immediate examples of Bitcoin cost advantage are Bitcoin as a low-cost payment system that disrupts traditional remittance and credit card businesses, cloud funding with peer-to-peer exchanges that disrupt the traditional second or emerging boards of stock exchanges, and pseudo (centralized) peer-to-peer institution network that can reduce the backroom and operating costs of financial institutions, which enhances the traditional financial business models. We shall elaborate on the last innovation in a later section.

Given its novelty and inherent complexity, Bitcoin and the broader family of cryptocurrencies are not well or widely understood by many. Therefore, the first part of this chapter is to explain the Bitcoin system and the critical components in a Bitcoin service and ecosystem. The motivation is to provide an intuition of how the underlying technology and monetary framework are supposed to work. The second part of this chapter reviews the benefits and risks from using Bitcoin as a platform for payment and financial services. The third part examines the prospects for Bitcoin and in particular to discuss the likely drivers of demand for Bitcoin in its present form and the ways the system will evolve to address some of its shortcomings.

21.1 THE BITCOIN SYSTEM AND THE ELEMENT OF TRUST

The Internet is known to be a mechanism to store and transfer packet data. Satoshi's original configuration (Nakamoto, 2009) of the Bitcoin system is a complex mechanism for strong and transferring digital value with almost no need of trust. Since Bitcoin is both a currency and a protocol, we have adopted the convention throughout this chapter to use *Bitcoin (singular with an upper case letter B) for the system and technologies and bitcoins (with a small letter b) to label units of the digital currency.*

When we refer to bitcoins, they are purely digital records of ownership over a certain quantity of monetary value. One bitcoin refers to just a monetary value of one unit of the digital currency. The digital currency bitcoins are not backed by any commodity or assets and have no legal claim on any underlying assets. It is similar to the fiat currencies that we use except that a bitcoin is a set of numbers stored on the register. It is one of over 300 cryptocurrencies, and this class of cryptocurrency is a subset of the entire digital or virtual currency class.

21.2 A NEW DIGITAL COMMODITY

The digital currency bitcoins have value only insofar as other people are ready to accept them for transaction purposes and are ready to accept them in exchange for something else—including for national currency. The value of bitcoins lies in their relative scarcity, public trust in the endurance and security of the protocols used to store and exchange them, the convenience of handling them digitally, and the demand from transaction motives.

The standard abbreviation of a bitcoin is BTC, and one-thousandth of a BTC is referred to as a *millibit*. Bitcoins can be subdivided into up to eight decimal places, so the minimum trading amount is 0.00000001 of a BTC (referred to as a *satoshi*), though this limit could be raised or eliminated in the future if bitcoins price deflation made that necessary.

The supply of bitcoins is determined by a fixed and known set of rules. These rules are enforced through a complex computational procedure with cryptography known as mining (Bhaskar and Lee, 2014a). The supply of bitcoins initially grew at 50 bitcoins every 10 min. This number will be halved every 4 years. By 2140, the maximum number of 21 million bitcoins will have been issued. Since the first bitcoin transaction occurred in January 2010, more than 4 years ago, at present, 25 bitcoins are created at 10-min intervals.

21.3 PSEUDONYMOUS OWNERSHIP AND TRADES

Cash is, in principle, both anonymous and untraceable. Similarly, banknotes and coins bear no indication of who their legal owner is. They carry no information about the history of transactions that have been conducted with them. Bank money is not associated with legal identities, and banks maintain a record of previous transactions conducted for at least in the last 5-10 years.

The cryptocurrency bitcoins, on the other hand, are somewhere in between cash and banknotes. They can be held against user-defined pseudonyms rather than legal identities. But transactions can be traced through the blockchain that is publicly available, for example, on the website www.blockchain.info. Each bitcoin user has a **bitcoin address**. In cryptographic terms, this is known as a **public key**. The user can share the address with anyone. There is a **matching key**. In cryptographic terms, this is known a **private key**. The bitcoin user must keep this key confidential.

Bitcoin private keys are 256 bits (binary characters) long, which can be represented as a 64-character hexadecimal string text. They can also be represented in a *wallet import format* that uses a shorter 52-alphanumeric character string and incorporates error-checking codes so that typos can be immediately detected. Bitcoin addresses are 27-34 alphanumeric character sequences. Both can be encoded as a QR (for quick response) code, so it can be captured photographically by a mobile phone.

The public address and the private key are mathematically linked, such that it is very easy to check that the two match. But to infer the private key from the bitcoin address, it is almost impossible. The currency bitcoins associated with your bitcoin address belong to the owner only because he is the only holder of the key that is matched to that address. Everyone gets to see the bitcoins associated with that bitcoin address, but only the owner can "unlock" and dispose of them using the private key.

There is no need to exchange any identity- or account-related information when trading bitcoins. This is because the authenticity of individual bitcoins can be established cryptographically and therefore they can be traded pseudonymously. In other words, all bitcoin transactions can be conducted totally anonymously. This is in contrast with the existing retail EPSs. EPS requires the disclosure of buyer's account or card information, thereby potentially exposing the buyer's full balance to fraud by the merchant. In the event of *card not present* transactions, there is also a need to disclose the billing address to reduce the merchant's risk that the buyer is not the authorized user of the card.

21.4 AN OPEN AND DECENTRALIZED LEDGER SYSTEM

One key feature of Bitcoin system is the way it deals with double-spending. Given that digital records can be freely copied, the system needs to prevent bitcoin holders from *double-spending* bitcoins. The system has to prevent a bitcoin holder from transferring his bitcoin to two different parties. In order to prevent this from happening, there must be accurate timestamping of all transactions. There must be incontrovertible evidence of which transaction came first and hence which are valid.

In traditional digital payment systems (whether operated by a bank, a card association, an online payment provider, or a mobile money operator), a central player takes on the role of timestamping and maintaining a ledger of all transactions that have occurred. This allows them to maintain up-to-the-second set of accounts reflecting the value held by each user in the system based on their past transactional history. The central player must authorize each and every transfer based on these accounts.

In the case of Bitcoin, it is totally decentralized and the digital register is maintained by the peer-to-peer network. The ledger is not maintained by a central authority, and in consequence, there is no central authorization of transactions. Instead, these functions are completely delegated to the community of bitcoin users as a whole. The entire history of creation and transfers of bitcoins can be found in the public record known as block-chain. Any user can be a node in the Bitcoin network and can independently check the validity of any bitcoin by consulting the blockchain. For this decentralized transaction validation system to work requires a consensus-building mechanism, such that all users in the network can come to collectively agree on the validity of the *past* transactions.

21.5 BLOCKCHAIN, MINING, BLOCK TIME, AND FORKS

Blockchain is constructed via a mining process, and the resulting digital register is the consensus on the precise history of past transactions. Approximately every 10 min (we termed it a Block Time), a new block summarizing all the transactions will be appended to a preexisting block on the blockchain. The new block captures all the validated transactions that have occurred over those 10 min or so.

Bitcoin system can be viewed as a competitive accounting ledger system. Any node in the network can compete to earn the right to be the one who defines the next block. The winner of the competition will define the precise record of transactions that have occurred in the previous 10 min or Block Time. The competition is on the basis of some computationally complex puzzle that aspiring nodes (called *miners*) need to solve. Bhaskar and Lee (2014a) give a technical overview of Bitcoin mining of which we will describe briefly here.

The complexity of the puzzle is regularly adjusted so that a winner can be expected to emerge in approximately 10 min. If the Block Time is more than 10 min, the difficulty of the problem will increase. Conversely, the difficulty will be less if the Block Time exceeds 10 min. The puzzle cannot be solved logically, only by trial and error and in some sense by brute force (i.e., guessing an answer, checking whether it solves the puzzle, and trying a new guess if not). Thus, the probability of winning the competition is a function of the amount of computational power used by a miner as well as his luck.

The winners have two rewards, the newly created bitcoins and the transaction fees. These provide the incentives for the nodes to take part in the mining activities. It is a very powerful incentive, and it has an implication for cost reduction for centralized digital register. There are incentives for nodes to take on the mining challenge and exert this hard computational work. The winning miner is granted an allocation of new bitcoins (the 25 bitcoins referred to above) and in addition gets to keep all the transfer fees that users may have set aside for miners in order to make sure that their transactions are duly picked up in the latest block. It can be an innovation for pseudo Bitcoin or semi-Bitcoin system for cost reduction purpose. There is no reason that such a system cannot be modified for a more than 51% pseudo Bitcoin system compared to a licensed controller or multiple stakeholders owning more than 51% of the computing power yet enjoying the cost reduction by having miners carry some of the costs.

It usually takes six blocks to confirm a transaction. In other words, even if a block is added to the blockchain, a transaction may not be confirmed until five additional blocks. The winning miner must attach his new block to an existing block on the blockchain, typically but not necessarily the previously mined one (i.e., the one created in the immediately preceding 10 min). If the new block is attached to the previously mined one, the existing blockchain gets elongated and the miner is in effect validating the previous block, in addition to extending it to cover the transactions in the subsequent Block Time. The expanded blockchain will propagate through the network so that any node can now use it to independently validate any new transactions in the next Block Time.

But a winning miner might choose to *fork* the blockchain and ignore the previously mined one(s), simply by attaching the new block onto an earlier block. When there is a fork, the Bitcoin protocol interprets the longest chain as the valid blockchain. The longest is defined as the one that incorporates most cumulative computational power expended in mining each block on it. Any winning miner can fork the blockchain, but for his efforts to succeed in overturning previous blocks, he must get sufficient number of *future* blocks to be attached onto the forked chain so that cumulatively, they have embodied more computational power than the original line of blocks. Consequently, the further back the block is in the blockchain (i.e., the older it is), the more difficult it would be for anyone to overturn its validity.

Thus, it is very important to note that Bitcoin transaction history is not necessarily cast in stone even though it can be viewed as confirmed. The validity of older blocks in the blockchain can be challenged and overturned. To do so, you would require more computational effort than the accumulated work that previously gone into mining that and every subsequent block. The cost of doing so makes it highly improbable that nodes would attempt to change the blockchain for nefarious reasons. In other words, it is just too costly to negate transactions that had occurred in the past in order to respend those bitcoins. It is therefore good to acknowledge that the transactions that were deemed to be confirmed are not necessarily cast in stone.

21.6 VALIDATION OF TRANSACTION OVER A PEER-TO-PEER NETWORK

All previous bitcoin transactions are captured by the blockchain. A transaction is defined by

(i) a value (number of bitcoin),

(ii) the bitcoin address of the owner of the bitcoin, and

(iii) a link to the previous transaction on the blockchain from which these bitcoins were gotten.

These bitcoin will be deemed valid by all nodes on the Bitcoin network if

(i) the sequence of prior transactions from which these bitcoins arose are all valid, that is, their origin is fully accountable within the blockchain, and

(ii) there are no subsequent transactions (on the blockchain or any recent ones that are still not recorded there) that point *back* to this transaction, that is, they have not been already spent.

The sender or owner of the bitcoin communicates to the entire community much like sending an e-mail to each other. To do so, they must associate the required number of bitcoin with the bitcoin address of the intended recipient, link it to the immediately preceding transaction through which they obtained the bitcoin, and sign that with their private key (which must match with the previous bitcoin address associated with those bitcoins).

A new transaction may need to be linked to more than one earlier transaction if the transfer amount does not coincide with the number of bitcoins received on an earlier transaction. Also, any fractional amount left over must be treated as a transfer back to oneself, such that the total amount transacted completely exhausts the value of claimed past transactions.

To recap, bitcoins are really just entries in a global ledger representing monetary value. This ledger is the result of unpacking the entire history of prior bitcoin transactions that is contained within the blockchain. A bitcoin address is a way of identifying the location of an amount of value written into the global ledger, but that value can only be used (i.e., passed on to a different bitcoin address) by whoever holds the private key that matches the bitcoin address to which the value is currently assigned in the ledger. When bitcoins are transferred from A to B, nothing is materially transferred between their wallets; instead, a set of bitcoins that were previously associated with A's public address in the ledger now come to be associated with B's public address. A announces this transfer to all nodes on the Bitcoin network, not just to B, so that the network can collectively validate it through the mining process and it gets embedded within the blockchain.

21.7 OPERATION VIA OPEN-SOURCE PROTOCOLS

The entire set of Bitcoin protocols is offered on an open-source basis, such that anyone can gain direct access to the source code. This means that each user can independently assess the adequacy of the system (in terms of its security, the fairness of the mining process, etc.), and no player enjoys privileged access to information or functionality. Thus, there is as much transparency about the software as there is about the history of transactions that run over it.

The Bitcoin Foundation-sponsored website (https://bitcoin.org/en/development) contains documentation, the name of the core developers, and other information on the open-source Bitcoin software known as Bitcoin Core. The site maintains the code and regularly issues new releases (for free). The core developer team (according to the website, the current 2014 team consists of Wladimir J. van der Laan, Gavin Andresen, Jeff Garzik, Greogory Maxwell, Pieter Wuille, and of course Satoshi Nakamoto whom no one knows the exact identity) is therefore in an asymmetrical position since they are the only ones who can implement changes in the Bitcoin code. Bitcoin Core is released under the terms of the MIT license. However, its open-source nature places natural limits to potentially arbitrary action by the Bitcoin Foundation. Anyone, who disagrees with the direction the Bitcoin Foundation is imparting on the protocol, can relatively easily create a competing (or, in the jargon, *forked*) cryptocurrency simply by modifying the Bitcoin protocols however he or she sees fit. There are already many other virtual or cryptocurrencies in existence today, beyond the bitcoin (such as, to name only a few, the namecoin, mastercoin, and litecoin; see Ong et al., 2014). In this chapter, we refer only to the bitcoin, though that could represent whatever cryptocurrency becomes dominant in the future (Box. 21.1).

BOX 21.1 Useful Online Reference Resources Relating to Bitcoin

- A short animated video from WeUseCoins and a longer one explaining how Bitcoin works and a series of blackboard videos from the Khan Academy explaining the technological components in more detail.
- A particularly engaging set of videos by Andreas Antonopoulos describing how Bitcoin is the "Internet of money" and how it can be used to expand access to finance to all.
- A wiki maintained by the Bitcoin community and a Bitcoin news service offered by CoinDesk.
- Bitcoin trading data and analysis are available from The Genesis Block and from Blockchain. Trading volume by country is available from BitcoinCharts. Comparisons against other payment methods are available from Coinmetrics.
- An online map showing merchant globally where bitcoin is accepted is provided by CoinMap. A list of Bitcoin exchanges in the world is provided by BitcoinEAST and in Bhaskar and Lee (2014b).
- An evolving online description of regulatory landscape across all countries, by BitLegal.
- A chronology of Bitcoin, including its record of thefts and frauds.
- An evolutionary map of all the cryptocurrencies that have evolved from bitcoin; market statistics for the ones still trading, including exchange rates against the US dollar; and live exchange rates between cryptocurrencies.
- Listings of Bitcoin start-ups from Creandum and AngelList.

21.8 THE ANATOMY OF BITCOIN

Having gained a basic understanding of the mechanics of Bitcoin, we can now formally deconstruct its core elements and identify what is truly unique—even revolutionary—about Bitcoin.

21.8.1 Key components of bitcoin

Bitcoin can be defined at three levels:

A consistent set of technologies (how)	Bitcoin is a protocol that combines the following key technologies, all of which are designed to create trust on the integrity of digital properties exchanged between independent parties: • *Public key cryptography*, which allows for messages to be passed securely (i.e., confidentially, without interception or tampering) between two nodes in an insecure network. This implements the public addressing and private key systems described above • *Proof-of-work routines*, which create an incentive structure so that all the nodes in a network can create a consensus as to the timing (and hence validity) of transactions, in a way that makes it difficult to manipulate by rogue nodes. This is known mathematically as the *Byzantine Generals' Problem*, which refers to the difficulty of coordinating a common battle plan by an army when some of the generals that are in the chain of communication might in fact be traitors and hence the generals as a class cannot all be trusted. The proof-of-work routines are implemented through the mining procedure described above • *Peer-to-peer file synchronization*, so that the new transactions and the consensual transaction history that emerges through the mining process can propagate through the entire Bitcoin network sufficiently quickly and reliably, such that every node can independently validate transactions • *Open-source software*, so that every aspect of the protocol can be independently scrutinized and verified
A network of nodes (who)	Bitcoin is also a network of computers operating on the Bitcoin protocol and fulfilling the various functions and roles envisioned in the Bitcoin protocol. There are fundamentally two types of nodes: • *Miners* who compose the blockchain and in the process create new bitcoins • *Wallets* holding the private keys and implementing the signing and validation process to effect bitcoin transactions The Bitcoin network can be used by nodes to transfer any piece of digital property securely, without fear of tampering, misappropriation, or duplication. It is fundamentally a record of transferable ownership
A currency (what)	Finally, bitcoin is a representation of value, which, due to its tradable nature through a Bitcoin network, can be used as a digital currency. It is therefore a very specific type of digital property that can flow through a Bitcoin network. As a currency, Bitcoin has an additional set of rules relating to its *denomination* (any positive number up to the eighth decimal digit) and *supply* (which is predetermined, exhibiting a period of decreasing rate of growth and then settling at zero growth)

21.8.2 Uniqueness of bitcoin

The key characteristic of Bitcoin is its decentralized nature. This can be related to the above three aspects:

- *As a technology*: The protocol is free and open source and hence collectively owned by the Bitcoin community, although the Bitcoin Core software development team is charged with managing new releases of the Bitcoin protocol. By determining how the Bitcoin protocol evolves, the development team (Gavin Andresen is seen to be the spokesperson) is the closest there is to a central authority for Bitcoin.
- *As a network*: Bitcoin does not require any specific infrastructure to operate since it can run entirely on standard devices connected to the Internet. Importantly, Bitcoin has no central ledger or database, since the blockchain is distributed to all nodes on the network. Bitcoin is often referred to as an *infrastructureless* network: It does use network resources (memory to store the blockchain and computational power to validate transactions), but these need network resources that do not need to be dedicated exclusively or specifically for Bitcoin.
- *As a currency*: There is no official issuer of money since new bitcoins are issued by the protocol itself, under prespecified rules through the mining process. There is no central bank with the responsibility for managing the supply or liquidity of bitcoins. Some economists are fascinated about the idea of the Bitcoin protocol being a virtual decentralized monetary system with a decreasing growth rate of approaching zero over 30 years.

21.8.3 Monetary anachronism or a Harbinger of financial innovations?

The noted economist Robert Shiller dismissed Bitcoin as "a return to the dark ages," and most economists would likely agree with that. Martin (2013) gave an interesting broad historical perspective on legal and economic arguments concerning the fixing of money supply. Bitcoin does ignore a millennium or two of monetary history. Before the emergence of macroprudential policy that places emphasis on the control of individual's exposure to systematic risk and in particular the prevention of overleverage of individuals and households, monetary policy is seen to be effective in managing inflation expectations. Prior to the global financial crisis, a decade of great moderation in price increases and steady growth was attributed to new classical economists who believed that growth could continue indefinitely with the focus on financial and technological innovations. These beliefs have undermined the traditional economics policy analysis, which has mostly shown the difficulty of grappling with the question of how to control the money supply and in particular how to strike a balance between allowing policymakers the wiggle room they need to respond to changing economic circumstances and preventing them from doing so arbitrarily for some narrow gain.

Every decade seems to have its faddish prescription: in more recent times, monetarism (rule-based fixing of the growth in a higher-level monetary aggregate), price or inflation targeting (setting a single, clear policy objective rather than a strictly monetary goal), central bank independence (removing this crucial matter from the political rough-and-tumble and delegating it to a committee of wise elders), monetary boards (fully reserved currency), and international monetary unions (irrevocably fixed exchange rates). None seem to provide a sufficiently robust answer over time, and no doubt, many new ideas will continue to be put forth.

But it is unlikely that the answer to the money supply control problem lies at either extreme: giving the sovereign uncontested access to the coin foundries or printing presses or tying our fortunes arbitrarily to a single shiny commodity with a fixed supply. In fact, Bitcoin is as extreme as it gets, in the latter direction.

As stated above, there is an entirely predictable growth trajectory in the bitcoin supply, which entails a steadily falling rate of growth over time until it hits zero growth. It's like a strict monetarist rule stuck on M0 and trending towards zero growth. It's like an even stricter version of a gold standard,[1] dispensing with the noisy oscillations from arbitrary luck (gold mine discoveries), steady technological progress (better mining equipment reducing the cost of extraction), and cyclical production incentives (more mining when the gold price is high and less when it is low).

There is therefore no particular mechanism linking the demand for bitcoin to its supply other than the pure price mechanism.[2] If Bitcoin is successful and experiences the kind of adoption S curve that is typical of new technological innovations,[3] there is a natural strong deflationary effect built in: Demand will tend to accelerate over time as network effects kick in, and yet, supply will tend to decelerate per the fixed nominal growth rule. The deflationary bias built into Bitcoin runs the risk of feeding periodic speculative bubbles and price volatility. Price instability is not something most people want to associate with their money.

Against this pessimistic monetary view, the noted Internet entrepreneur and venture capital investor Marc Andreessen sees Bitcoin as standing in equal importance to and a logical continuation of the trends brought on by the emergence of personal computers in 1975 and the Internet in 1993. He argues: *"Bitcoin offers a sweeping vista of opportunity to reimagine how the financial system can and should work in the Internet era,*

---

[1] It's not a coincidence that the process of creating new bitcoins is called *mining*.

[2] This weakness is pounced on by Paul Krugman (The New York Times blog post) and Brad DeLong (Equitablog post) both dated December 28, 2013 and is further picked up by Mark Williams (comment here).

[3] For a description of adoption S curves and why they arise, see Rogers, E.M., 2003. Diffusion of Innovation, fifth ed. Free Press.

and a catalyst to reshape that system in ways that are more powerful for individuals and busi-nesses alike."[4]

What Andreessen is seeing is a migration of power from the center of the financial grid (represented by the main banks and payment associations) to its edge (represented by its users and a range of superusers we can refer to as developers), creating much more room for decentralized innovation. This leads to a flattening of service delivery hierarchies, making it harder for individual players to exert a stranglehold on what services are offered to customers or to extract monopolistic rents.

Most recent trends in networked industries have indeed followed the centripetal force pushing intelligence away from the core networks and centralized network providers, relegating these to mere utilities operating standard pipes and empowering a range of developers and businesses to independently position new services and applications running on those networks. This was made possible by the Internet protocol (IP), which broke telecom operators' control over what kinds of applications customers could run on their networks. The brilliance of the IP is precisely that it is entirely network- and application-agnostic, or, to be more specific, it allows communications networks and applications to be provided totally independently of each other. In the same way that the IP does not assume what services users wanted to consume, it does not assume anything about the security, quality, and reliability of the underlying communications networks.

The IP and its associated higher-level networking protocols concern themselves with the correct transmission of information between two network nodes according to the standards of precision, speed, integrity, security, and confidentiality that the application that uses that information requires, but not with the validity of the information itself. The Bitcoin protocol adds a mechanism through which the two nodes can trust the nature of the information itself, even if they have no reason to trust each other. Thus, the Bitcoin protocol may be to digital value (or, more generally, digital property) what the IP was to digital information.

If users can trust the information delivered via the Bitcoin protocol, it can be used as a representation of value, that is, as currency. But the real opportunity is not only in having replicated yet another form of money. It is that this form of cryptomoney can now be held by anyone and freely exchanged with anyone on an IP cloud, without requiring a central institution to manage his holdings and interactions. Moreover, just as the IP spawned higher-level protocols (e.g., UDP/TCP to string packets together, RTP to control real-time transmission, and HTTP to structure text and hyperlinks) and applications, Bitcoin is likely to spawn a broad range of money management tools, automated payment applications, and higher-level financial protocols.

[4]New York Times OpEd, January 21, 2014.

BOX 21.2 Some Key Approximate Bitcoin Statistics
- 60,000 transactions per day, or 40 per minute, or 400 per 10-min block.
- USD 100 million transacted per day, or USD 70,000 per minute.
- 12.5 million bitcoins issued, which is 60% of the total that will ever be issued.
- The entire blockchain occupies 14 gigabytes of memory.
- Bitcoin market cap of USD 8 billion (i.e., the current market price of all bitcoins in circulation).
- The USD price of a bitcoin posted on four online exchanges, on February 9, 2014 at 5:18 pm, according to bitcoinity.org: 672 on Mt. Gox, 701 on Bitstamp, 708 on BTC-e, 700 on Bitfinex, and 1088 on LocalBitcoins. The prices quoted on BitCoinWisdom 1 min later: 672 on Mt. Gox, 700 on Bitstamp, 711 on BTC-e, and 741 on Huobi.

As of February 2014 (Source: www.blockchain.info).

This is the notion that has been termed *programmable money*: the ability for anyone to software-encode not only their money but also a variety of various potential actions around it. Programmable money represents a shift from a situation where money services can only be designed and provided centrally by powerful financial service providers to one where money services can be run automatically by a user-controlled application or provided by any of a number of hosted service providers selected by the user. One could develop a Bitcoin wallet that implemented all the money management rules that we now pay banks to do time deposit, recurrent deposits, alerts, etc.

Still, one has to wonder, can all this goodness happen if people do not fundamentally want to hold bitcoins because of a fear of unstable value? Is there a way to reconcile its inherent monetary anachronism with the futuristic programmable possibilities? That hinges on the interplay between two ancillary services around the Bitcoin protocol, wallets and exchanges, to which we turn next (Box. 21.2).

21.9 BITCOIN ECOSYSTEM

For all its potency, the Bitcoin protocol is merely a mechanism for validating and passing around bitcoins. Converting it into usable services requires the creation of a whole range of complementary capabilities. There is already an emerging constellation of service providers who aim to create a role for themselves by making the process of managing bitcoins more useful and convenient for users. The following is meant to be an illustrative rather than a complete list of innovations being developed, and the highlighted providers are again meant to be illustrative rather than necessarily the leading ones in each area.

21.9.1 Bitcoin exchanges

In order for bitcoins to become widely accepted, people will need the reassurance that they can liquidate their bitcoin holdings at will. Bitcoin exchanges are online marketplaces at which bitcoins can be bought and sold against one or more *fiat* currencies. A survey of the exchanges and their sites are given in Bhaskar and Lee (2014b).

Some websites, such as Localbitcoins, merely facilitate the meeting of bitcoin buyers and sellers. They act as dealers, much like eBay works: Sellers post their offers online, and buyers select the particular seller they want to buy from. Buyers pay the seller directly through a mechanism proposed by the seller. Because the transfer of fiat money and bitcoins is not coincident in time, there is a specific counterparty risk.

The larger exchanges, such as BTC China and the recently bankrupted Mt.Gox of Japan, operate bitcoin markets on a continuous basis, with the exchange assuming the counterparty risk. Before transacting, market participants need to fund an account at the exchange with the currency they wish to sell: depositing bitcoins if they wish to dispose of bitcoins or depositing *fiat* currency if they want to buy bitcoins. Exchanges typically accept both market orders (buy/sell transactions to be executed at the prevailing market-clearing price) and limit orders (to be executed if the price reaches a certain threshold). Once transactions are completed, users can withdraw their newly acquired currency: sending bitcoins to their personal bitcoin wallet if they bought bitcoins or transferring money to their bank account if they sold bitcoins. Transacting at the exchanges is relatively quick, but depositing and withdrawing cash in a user's account at the exchange can take longer, depending on the interbank money transfer arrangements in each country.

Bitcoin exchanges would need to operate in every jurisdiction where bitcoins are used, though in practice, they tend to operate very thin markets in developing countries. Buttercoin has developed a white-labeled platform for creating Bitcoin exchanges and aims to partner with locally licensed players in developing markets in order to accelerate the spread Bitcoin exchanges.

Most exchanges do not work with debit or credit cards. However, CoinMama lets users buy bitcoins through Western Union or MoneyGram money transfers. Since these transfers can be funded from a debit or credit card, this offers an indirect channel for funding bitcoin purchases with bank cards. AurumXchange, an exchange that went bust, was offering a Withdraw2Cash service that allowed cash from the sale of bitcoins to be sent directly to any debit or credit card.

PawnCoin aims to provide liquidity for bitcoins through a process analogous to pawning. Users send bitcoins to a secure bitcoin wallet owned by PawnCoin, in return for which they get a cash advance. Users can then reclaim their bitcoin by returning the cash with the agreed interest.

Given that exchanges are the most important intermediaries that link the fiat currencies with cryptocurrencies, it is likely to be the first target of regulation. The cost of compliance is envisaged to increase once regulation is in place. On the revenue side, it is anticipated that profit margin will be squeezed as in most exchanges. The largest threat, ironically, will come from within the Bitcoin protocol with peer-to-peer trading in Bitcoin and Bitcoin-fiat/fiat-Bitcoin space. This sector is clearly at the forefront of margin squeeze with increasing cost and decreasing margin. It is anticipated that the age of consolidation will come a lot faster than anticipated. Unless revenue growth or velocity of Bitcoin use is increasing at a faster rate than cost, the consolidation will be most severe in this segment of the ecosystem.

21.9.2 Bitcoin wallets

Bitcoin wallets are software applications that facilitate the process of buying, selling, and managing one's bitcoins. The wallet application can be downloaded into the user's terminal (computer or smartphone), or hosted by a provider in the cloud. Some players focused on emerging markets, such as Kipochi and BitPesa, are developing "lightweight hosted wallets" with SMS, USSD, and HTML5 front ends. So far, no Bitcoin-based service has successfully integrated into a preexisting mobile money service.

The kinds of customer convenience elements introduced by wallets include (i) being able to send bitcoins to e-mail addresses rather than bitcoin addresses; (ii) QR code generation and scanning capabilities to be able to share bitcoin addresses conveniently; (iii) integration with exchanges, such that transactions can be denominated in either bitcoin or national currency; and (iv) a variety of charting and analytic tools to view one's bitcoin history.

In addition, cloud-based wallets have additional advantages: (i) The wallet is available from any device, through a secure log-on procedure; (ii) all bitcoin validations are done by the provider in the cloud, so it is not necessary for users to download large blockchain files into their devices; and (iii) incoming bitcoins can be accepted by the wallet provider in the cloud, even if the user is off-line, and the user can be notified of that fact through prespecified communication channels.

The two official wallets proposed by the Bitcoin Foundation are MultiBit for Windows, Mac, and Linux devices and Bitcoin Wallet for Android phones and tablets. Other popular wallets are Coinbase, Circle, and Blockchain.

21.9.3 Specialized security services

A key concern for bitcoin users is the secure storage of private keys. The Bitcoin protocol incorporates many security features preventing theft as bitcoins travel through the network. But there are vulnerabilities on the client side and in particular with the safe storage of Bitcoin private keys. A number of providers are tackling this risk in a number of ways:

- Bitcoinpaperwallet is a software solution for generating secure Bitcoin keys and for printing on any connected printer. Printouts hold the public and private keys, in both text string and QR formats. Printouts are designed to be folded up and taped shut to avoid casual snooping. There is the possibility of taping them with tamper-evident and serialized holographic strips available for purchase from the same company. This procedure allows users to keep their private Bitcoin keys in bits of paper, which are easy to store securely and are entirely beyond the reach of hackers.
- Piper is a dedicated hardware computing device that generates secure Bitcoin keys using its own high-standard random number generator. The keys can then be stored within the device, printed out using an incorporated thermal paper printer, or transferred via a USB port to a USB memory stick or an external printer. Thus, it allows for safekeeping of keys in paper format or on off-line digital storage devices.
- Bitbills are Bitcoin key holders in a plastic card rather than printed on paper. The private key is printed on a QR code that is placed between plastic layers inside the card and cannot be read without physically destroying the plastic card. There is no digital record of the private keys other than on the card itself, limiting potential double-spending or fraud but exposing its holders to full loss of value if they lose the plastic card.
- Trezor is a much smaller piece of hardware that not only generates and holds Bitcoin private keys but also lets users sign transactions using those keys. It can be attached to the USB port of a user's computer, and through that, it allows for more secure off-line signing of Bitcoin transactions processed through online wallets.

Another security concern for some bitcoin users is preserving their anonymity, that is, keeping their Bitcoin pseudonym totally separate from their real identity. The concern is that with the high degree of traceability of Bitcoin transactions, their identity can be worked out, either by analyzing transaction patterns or by tracing the pseudonym back to previous transactions where identity was disclosed (e.g., for regulatory reasons).

Commercial services have arisen that promise to raise the barriers to tracing identity. Bitcoin *mixers* or *laundries* combine the funds of many users into a collection of shared bitcoin addresses in order to obfuscate the trail of bitcoin back to individual users. The larger ones are operated by Blockchain.info and BitLaundry. Mixing services require users to trust the intermediary that is mixing the addresses, since they rather than the users need to hold the private Bitcoin keys in order to shift money around. Mixing services can of course be used by money launderers.

21.9.4 Prepaid card, merchant, and ATM solutions

Several solutions aim to replicate the typical debit card and point of sale (POS) solution for Bitcoin. This way they can offer a user experience that people are familiar with, as well as access to an installed infrastructure of card-reading point-of-sale terminals and ATMs. These include the following:

- Coinkite plans to create a closed-loop network of customers and merchants who maintain a bitcoin-denominated account with Coinkite. Customers will be offered a pin-and-chip debit card linked to their Bitcoin account, usable at Coinkite-approved merchants. Merchants can use a conventional POS terminal to accept these cards and their payments and receive the funds into their Bitcoin account with Coinkite.
- Virtex also plans to issue bitcoin-denominated debit card, but because it has a money transfer license and operates its own Bitcoin exchange, its service will be open loop, enabling direct conversion of bitcoins into national currency. Therefore, they can be accepted at any ATM or merchant POS, much like a prepaid card.
- Casascius is developing a stand-alone POS terminal that lets merchants accept bitcoins and dispense (i.e., sell) bitcoins.
- Robocoin has deployed the first ATMs that allow immediate purchases and sales of bitcoins for cash, without needing to have a bank account or a bank card. The ATM can send purchased bitcoins to an existing user wallet (which the user can enter by scanning its QR code) or to a new wallet with the private key printed on the ATM receipt. Likewise, bitcoins can be sold by scanning the QR code of the wallet that contains them.

Bitcoin ATMs are therefore a retail front end to a Bitcoin exchange, where the transaction happens much faster because they do not depend on bank clearing and settlements. Bitcoin purchases and sales at the ATM are anonymous, but the system can limit total transaction volumes by any given user to combat money laundering; this is done by scanning the palm of every user and matching that against a database of previous transactions.

Bitcoin addresses, to which payments are made, are represented by very long character strings. To make the in-store payment experience simple and quick for buyers, the most likely scenario is that stores would display a QR (Quick Response) code at the counter containing the payment address. The buyer would seize this information automatically using the camera on their smartphone in order to complete the payment.

BitPay is a virtual payment processor that is developing a range of specialized Bitcoin payment solutions for various merchant verticals. It operates an escrow mechanism through which customer-merchant disputes can be handled. It also recently launched a solution for payroll-bulk distributions through Bitcoin (Box. 21.3).

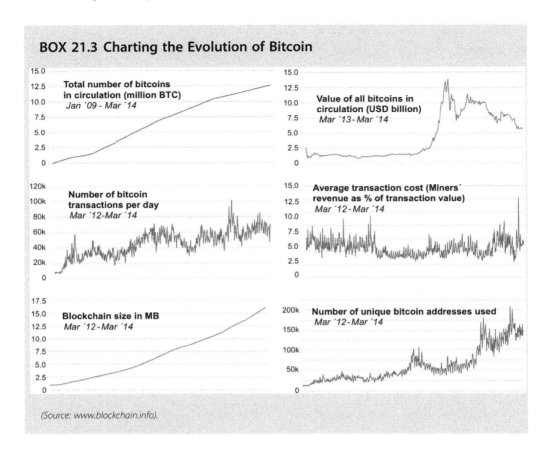

BOX 21.3 Charting the Evolution of Bitcoin

(Source: www.blockchain.info).

21.10 BENEFITS OF BITCOIN: AN ASSESSMENT

Advocates of Bitcoin see a number of benefits stemming from its decentralized and *infra-structureless* nature, relative to established payment mechanisms. Some of these claimed benefits, however, may not be inherent to Bitcoin but to a particular way of using, while other benefits entail trade-offs that need to be taken into account as well. The following discussion evaluates four arguments that are commonly made in favor of Bitcoin, in each case stating first the claimed advantages and then following up with the reasons why the benefits may be less than anticipated.

21.10.1 Transaction irreversibility

Current digital merchant payment systems typically allow transactions to be reversed in case of a dispute between the buyer and the seller, even weeks after the payment had been authorized by the payer's bank. This so-called *chargeback* process introduces uncertainty in merchants' revenues and cash flows. Worse, it can be abused by fraudsters disowning payments after having acquired the corresponding goods and services.

Bitcoin proponents argue that Bitcoin entirely eliminates the chargeback process as there is no central authority who can mediate disputes between the buyer and the seller. Bitcoin transactions are final and irreversible, so it operates strictly under a *buyer beware* policy. This reduces opportunities for fraud. However, there are three reasons why this claimed benefit may not in fact be that significant.

First, chargebacks do represent protection for customers, and the costs incurred by banks and merchants to manage the chargeback process (along with the fraud it may engender) may in fact be economically optimal. If there are no chargebacks, the risk of fraud on the buyer side is reduced, but it then reintroduces consumer protection risks (e.g., the risk of having been sold faulty goods). These two types of risks need to be balanced.

Second, while the Bitcoin protocol itself does not contemplate chargebacks, they can be provided by specialized players offering more sophisticated Bitcoin-based payment solutions to merchants. Merchants may feel it is necessary to adopt such solutions in order to offer a more attractive payment option to customers, thus reintroducing the attendant costs and risks.

Third, it should be mentioned that bitcoin transactions are not immediate: Full validation takes 10-20 min, so the notion of transaction finality is itself a bit ambiguous in a Bitcoin payment setting (this is further discussed below). During this transaction validation period, a merchant may choose to withhold the goods for a certain period of time after the buyer has sent the bitcoins. This introduces inconvenience to the buyer in an in-store setting and will engender distrust by the buyer in an online setting. But releasing the goods earlier will expose merchants to fraud if the bitcoins turn out to be invalid.

21.10.2 Identity theft

Digital money based on centralized ledgers (i.e., bank money) requires that a trusted third party (a bank) authorize transactions. Fraud can occur by someone other than the legal account holder representing himself as the account holder, in what constitutes identity theft. Banks combat this by issuing credentials that can be used to identify their customers (cards, PINs, and tokens). Merchants, especially in non-face-to-face (or *card not present*) situations, protect themselves from the consequences of such fraud by asking for more personal information about their customers (address, CVV code, etc.), a practice that in fact makes it easier for malevolent agents to acquire that information. It therefore feels like a security arms race, severely inconveniencing customers and merchants in the process.

Bitcoin proponents argue that using bitcoins eliminates the need to prove identity in order to access one's money. This is because Bitcoin is a bearer instrument, and its ownership is defined strictly by who has the private key that corresponds to the bitcoin address that holds the value.

However, it can be argued that the possibility of theft of account or identity credentials is merely replaced by the possibility of theft of Bitcoin private keys (and hence of bitcoins themselves). Moreover, people are likely to use bitcoin wallets that handle the bitcoin signage process in the background, without the user ever knowing or even having access to their Bitcoin private keys. These wallets will be secured through identity credentials that prove that you are the legal owner of the wallet and hence of the bitcoins within it—much like how Internet banking works today.

However, the critical distinction is that to pay with bitcoins, one never needs to reveal any private information to the payee or merchant, which makes the stealing of the private keys or wallet identification credentials harder.

21.10.3 Cheaper transactions

Proponents of Bitcoin argue that bitcoins can be traded or paid out as simply and as cheaply as by attaching a bitcoin address to an e-mail. It may be necessary to provide a small fee to incentivize miners to validate the transaction promptly by inserting it into the next block. But because bitcoin transactions do not require authorization by any central institution, there is no player with the capacity to arbitrarily set bitcoin transaction costs. This should result in a much more competitive market, with lower transaction costs.

In principle, decentralized solutions ought to be more expensive to provide than optimally designed centralized solution because of the duplication of effort involved (Think of the blockchain that must be stored by all nodes or the vast amount of computing power expended by unsuccessful miners.) Thus, any Bitcoin pricing advantage arises not because of an inherent cost advantage but from the elimination of market power.

In fact, bitcoin is not so cheap to use today, at least for smaller transactions. The minimum fee that is payable is 0.0001 BTC, which is about 20¢ at the current exchange rate.[5] The transaction size would need to be larger than USD 20 in order for the cost to be less than 1%.

There is a further hidden cost of maintaining the blockchain through mining, which is borne by bitcoin holders. The 25 bitcoins that miners currently get per 10-min block (which were worth over USD 20,000 at December 2013 bitcoin prices) represent a dilution in the capital value of all previously issued bitcoins—a kind of inflationary tax.

In addition, exchange fees to buy and sell bitcoins may be several percentage points of the amount transacted, and there are substantial bid-ask spreads involved, as well as

---

[5]As of January 23, 2014, according to Glen Fleishman, "On the Matter of Why Bitcoin Matters," The Magazine. Note that it is not mandatory to pay a fee, but then the transaction may be deprioritized by miners and it may take longer to have it validated. These fees may become more significant in the future as rewards to mining, since miners are scheduled to get progressively fewer new bitcoins per block mined every 4 years.

substantial price differences between the various exchanges. So transacting inside the Bitcoin cloud may be cheap, but accessing it is not.

More generally, it is possible, and even likely, that some degree of market power will creep back into the Bitcoin realm, as wallet providers, exchanges, merchant solution providers, and others seek to lock in Bitcoin users through their value-added services as they recreate familiar banking experiences. Thus, the total cost of using bitcoins by users may rise well above the basic bitcoin transaction cost.

Finally, it should also be remembered that the higher direct cost of traditional payments is due in large part to the system of consumer protections (such as the chargebacks) and the extra customer functionality (such as credit) embedded within them. Therefore, direct price comparisons between current card-based and Bitcoin-based payments are misleading.

21.10.4 More and faster innovation

In traditional electronic banking and payment systems, the scope for innovation is tightly controlled by a range of players who have bottleneck control over payment channels and networks. Given their high margins, they may not have much appetite for innovation themselves and may seek to limit innovation by others who might threaten to commoditize their business.

Bitcoin is a platform for innovation because anyone is free to program services that run on the open Bitcoin standard, without requiring any permission from any central authorities. Developers can record instructions directly on bitcoin transactions using a limited scripting system within the Bitcoin protocol. They can also embed information in a transaction by combining it into the transaction hash during the signing process. The competitive nature of the Bitcoin network means that players with unique customer experiences will be in the best position to monetize their services, creating strong incentives for innovation.

On the other hand, while Bitcoin should engender much innovation on top of the basic Bitcoin protocol, the protocol itself will prove hard to evolve because of its distributed, public-good nature. Therefore, its innovation friendliness will be limited in the long run by the quality of the Bitcoin standard itself.

It is possible to have platform-level innovation by creating new cryptocurrencies based on a modification of the Bitcoin standard. Bitcoin's open-source code makes this simpler to occur and may in fact lead to excessive fragmentation of the cryptocurrency space. Uncertainty on which will be the winning platform(s) may also reduce the pace of innovations on each.

Also, the decentralized nature of Bitcoin may make it harder and more expensive to market new services, as these are more likely to need to be pitched directly to users rather than to a fewer set of intermediaries. Innovators without much marketing clout may not be able to sustain their innovations.

21.11 FUTURE-PROOFING BITCOIN: ADDRESSING KEY RISKS

Based on the above discussion, we can focus on three key questions that will determine the development of Bitcoin, and cryptocurrencies more generally, going forward: bitcoin price stabilization (how comfortable will users be to hold bitcoins), encroaching regulation (how open and anonymous it will remain), the efficiency of the mining process, and the technical security and robustness of the Bitcoin protocol. We next analyze each of these questions in turn.

21.11.1 Stabilizing bitcoin value

The observed volatility in bitcoin value is an important impediment to its widespread adoption. If bitcoin prices continue exhibiting significant volatility, confidence in bitcoins as a store of value will be undermined. This would reduce savings-based use cases for bitcoins and would also limit the role of bitcoins in payments to that of a shadow currency, a mere technicality, where users specify transaction values in terms for national currency and there is automatic conversion of national currency into bitcoins and vice versa.

There is a particularly nefarious scenario where big bitcoin hoarders attempt to manipulate bitcoin prices in the future. The ownership of bitcoins is presumed to be highly concentrated, especially in the hands of early miners, and statistics show clearly that the majority of bitcoins are being hoarded and not traded. Bitcoin will remain vulnerable to willful price manipulations while the holdings remain so concentrated. The number of bitcoins that are scheduled to be issued from the present forward is less than the number of bitcoins already issued, so current holdings will not naturally be diluted enough through sheer issuance.

There are two ways forward for a Bitcoin system to evolve, beyond the simple monetary construct it is today:

Developing a more optimal money supply rule	It is possible that in the future, a Bitcoin-like cryptocurrency will emerge that has a more sophisticated, market-supporting money supply growth rule. Such a rule would have to incorporate automatic feedback loops that allow for variations in money supply to achieve general price (or inflation) stability, improve economic performance (compensating for business cycles), and avoid asset pricing bubbles (in stocks, real estate, and other markets). It is not clear that a sufficiently benign prescriptive rule could be devised with current economic knowledge, but if it were, then it could sustain a truly mathematical currency
Becoming a medium for fiat currency	An alternative is to allow for sufficient policy discretion in the determination of money supply so that what cannot be achieved mathematically can be achieved through expert judgment. It is hard to imagine society delegating enough trust in a private body to exercise such discretion, if that body is not accountable through a democratic process. This function is traditionally vested in governments, through the central bank. There is a scenario, then, where a Bitcoin-like platform is used by central banks to issue and manage the national fiat currency. It becomes just one more format for national currency, alongside coins, banknotes, and bank credit

21.11.2 Regulating bitcoin use

A second set of issues relates to how Bitcoin (or the cryptocurrencies that may replace it in the future) will be treated from a legal and regulatory point of view. Regulators are already taking a keen interest in Bitcoin, as they do not want it to become an open channel for funding or hiding the proceeds of illicit activities or to avoid taxes. Measures to bolster the integrity of bitcoin transactions will inevitably raise the cost of accessing, if not using, Bitcoin payment networks. This needs to be done carefully so that it does not yet again result in the shutting out of large segments of the population.

The policy thinking, let alone the legal and institutional practice, around this topic remains very incipient. But we can already identify what the main issues are likely to be the following:

Monetary and exchange regulation	Bitcoins are as yet not regulated as legal currency in any jurisdiction in the world, though trading in bitcoins is tolerated in most. However, regulators have sought to dampen market activity in bitcoins in several major countries. The Bank of Thailand, then the Reserve Bank of India, and more recently the Bank of Russia have all declared that the use of bitcoins is not authorized, and its users can be exposed to legal risks. The People's Bank of China banned the trading of bitcoins by financial institutions and payment companies, in order to insulate the financial system from potential volatility in bitcoins
Anti-money laundering (AML) and law enforcement	As the volume and value of bitcoins grow, bitcoin transactions will increasingly be subjected to AML rules. This regulation is likely to apply at the *perimeter* of the Bitcoin network, that is, on transactions that involve buying and selling bitcoins against national currency. In the United States, for instance, transactions worth more than USD 10,000 need to be reported by companies involved in issuing or exchanging online currencies[a]
Consumer protection	We can also expect in the future more application of consumer protection rules, given the inherent complexities in understanding how cryptocurrencies work and the substantial risks that arise for consumers. There are likely to be at least three drivers for such regulation. The first one will be protection against fraud. There have been a number of high-profile bitcoin theft cases that highlight the vulnerability of less technology-savvy customers to hackers. Second, the principle of transaction finality under which Bitcoin operates exposes users to abuses by unethical sellers, and appropriate mediation dispute mechanisms will need to be put in place. Third, there need to be mechanisms for the ownership of bitcoins to be transferred when their legal owner dies, along the lines of wills and common law, but this will not be possible if the private keys are not properly stored and recorded

Continued

Taxation	The tax treatment of bitcoin transactions will also need to be clarified, especially relating to the following three specific issues. First, tax authorities will want to make sure that they can track the commercial transactions happening on bitcoins, especially those occurring cross border, so that they can be effectively taxed; tax authorities will resist bitcoins if it can be used to disguise or hide transactions that ought to be subject to general income or sales taxes. Second, as long as bitcoin is not recognized as a currency, it may attract capital gains taxation and possibly also deductible tax losses $=$ when bitcoins are spent or sold. In the context of a highly volatile price, this can produce onerous and unpredictable tax burdens. Third, tax authorities may want to subject bitcoins earned by miners to income taxation, as long as the activity generates significant revenue. In the United States, the IRS recently stated the position that bitcoin is treated as a commodity, not a currency, and hence is taxable along these three lines[b]

[a]This is under a new rule issued in March 2013 by the US Treasury's Financial Crimes Enforcement Network (FinCEN). The rule does not specifically mention bitcoins by name; it clearly implied that bitcoin exchanges must operate under a money transmitting business (MTB) license and report significant transactions. It could also be interpreted to apply to miners as issuers of bitcoins, as long as the bitcoin price exceeds USD 400 (since the mining award of 25 new bitcoins would take them over the reporting threshold).
[b]See the IRS's guidance issued in March 2014 here.

21.11.3 Efficiency of the mining process

The mining process is the key to maintaining the trust in a Bitcoin system. (i) The inherent delays in and lingering uncertainty about the validation of transactions through the mining process, (ii) the potential for manipulation of the blockchain by powerful miners, and (iii) the apparent wastefulness of resources employed in the mining relate to the efficiency of the mining process. These are discussed below, in turn.

*Temporal **uncertainty** about the validity of transactions*	Transactions can propage immediately across the entire Bitcoin network, but their validity will take some time to get established. Moreover, because the consensus represented by the blockchain can always be challenged, there is no agreed standard on what constitutes irreversible acceptance. Each user has to decide formiku himself when bitcoins received can be trusted to be valid (i.e., not having been previously spent). There are several approaches that a node can take before declaring acceptance of bitcoins it has received: • The node can check the bitcoins against the blockchain and against the collection of as-yet unvalidated transactions that have been propagated through the network since the time that the last block was appended on the blockchain. This enables potentially the fastest validation but at a higher computational cost

- The node can wait until the transaction is picked up in the blockchain, which will be a signal that the bitcoins are thought to be valid. This transfers the work from the node to the miners, but it can take up to 10 min for a new transaction to be picked up by a miner into the next block—longer if the miner misses it
- The node could decide to wait even longer, if it wants to make sure that the block containing his transactions does not get overturned as new blocks are subsequently mined. If the node waited another 10 min, it could be sure that the next miner didn't fork the blockchain, thereby potentially eliminating the prior block on which the node's transaction got captured

In practice, nodes are likely to make their own decisions as to when and how to accept bitcoins, based on the size of the payment, their prior history with the sender/payer of the bitcoins, and the nature of the underlying transaction

To address this temporal ambiguity over acceptance, Litecoin, the second most traded cryptocurrency after bitcoin, has reduced the block to a 2.5-min interval. This increases the size of the blockchain but speeds up transaction validation times. Bitcoin could in future go in the direction of shortening mining time frames as well

Rogue users with sufficient computing resources gaining control of the blockchain	Rogue users with enough sustained computing resources could in principle dominate the mining process, that is, put themselves in a position of systematically winning the mining contest and hence having the right to define a significant number of blocks. Through that, they could in effect commandeer the blockchain, impose "their" version of bitcoin transaction history by forking off the preexisting blockchain, and decide which transactions are valid and which are not. This would give them the license to double spend bitcoins freely
	Because the blockchain can only be written—and rewritten—one 10-min block at a time, commandeering a portion of the blockchain would require as much computing power as what went into creating it in the first place, and it would take just as long in elapsed time. For instance, to undo the last year's worth of transactions in the blockchain, a rogue miner would need to win the mining contest and fork the blockchain at a point 52,560 (=365 days/year × 24 h/day × 6 blocks/h) blocks ago. He would then need to win systematically a roughly similar number of blocks in order to exceed the total amount of work that went into creating the original blockchain—and only then would *any* of the forked blockchain take effect. This of course means that as soon a miner forks the chain, all nodes would be on notice that someone might be trying to tamper with history, and measures could be taken to stop the rogue miner
	In order to have a reasonable chance of taking control of the blockchain, a rogue user would need to command at least 51% of the computing power of all mining nodes. It is not thought likely that any individual player could garner sufficient computational power to seek to overturn the consensus blockchain, though some might succeed in controlling the more recent transaction blocks

Continued

	However, there are strong incentives for miners to pool their computational resources in order to maximize their individual expected payoff from mining. It recently surfaced that a pool got so large that it managed to control 42% of all the mining power. This creates a dangerous scenario where the blockchain may be controlled by a pool rather than by individual rogue users.[a] Rules will likely need to be added to cap the size of such mining pools
Environmental footprint	A final consideration relates to the environmental impact of the mining process. This relates to the efficiency of the new currency relative to the resources that are consumed in the process of producing and maintaining it. Because miners receive a fixed allocation of bitcoins with each new block they compose, the monetary rewards to mining have increased tremendously: in December 2013, the 25-bitcoins reward for successfully mining a block was worth over USD 20,000—to be won every 10 min
	The incentives built into the Bitcoin mining process have resulted in a vast amount of computational power—estimated to be the equivalent of the top 500 supercomputers in the world—being dedicated to the building out of the blockchain under its proof-of-work logic.[b] This has proved to be extremely expensive in terms of hardware and electricity consumption. Many argue the resources devoted so far in excess to what would be required to maintain the integrity of the mining process. Given the Bitcoin experience, many alternative cryptocurrencies limit miners' rewards, and Bitcoin could as yet alter its policy. However, it needs to be done in such a way as to not undermine the basic *proof-of-work* principle of Bitcoin

[a] *Source:* Business Insider, January 10, 2014.
[b] *Source:* Fleishman, *op. cit.*

21.11.4 Technical robustness

It is beyond the scope of this chapter to conduct a technical analysis of the Bitcoin protocol, so here, we merely record risks that are commonly highlighted in the burgeoning popular literature on Bitcoin:

Reliability and scalability of Bitcoin's security protocols	From a technical point of view, the integrity of the Bitcoin protocol hinges on two key aspects: (i) the unassailability of the cryptographic protocol used (which prevents bitcoin theft) and (ii) the scalability of the blockchain mechanism as the transaction history balloons (which is essential to ensure against bitcoins double-spending)
	The risk of security breaches on the Bitcoin protocol can be reduced to infinitesimal proportions. But still, the question will always arise as to what can be done in the event of such a breach. It is hard to see how the system would recover in such an eventuality given that there are no central actors through which some *status quo ante* can be recreated

Risk of loss or theft of Bitcoin keys	Even if the underlying Bitcoin protocols are entirely secure, cases will arise where users lose bitcoins, either because they accidentally lost their private key (for instance, through a hard disk wipeout) or because they did not store their private key securely enough (for instance, through a malicious software bot snooping in their hard disk). Similarly, hosted wallet providers could potentially be hacked, compromising the bitcoins of all wallet holders. If these situations arise often enough, it could trigger a wave of mistrust of bitcoins—even if the protocol itself is not violated
Recentralization of network power through control of wallets and exchanges	The Bitcoin promise is one of reducing the power of established financial intermediaries to exert market power and limit innovation. However, such control over consumers and the services they are offered can still be exerted from the edge of the network if particular wallet providers or exchanges can establish a controlling position. The Bitcoin ecosystem could develop in a way that undermines the principle of neutrality and decentralization with which it was conceived. This is more likely to be a problem in developing countries, where competition at the wallet and exchange level might be a lot less
Capture of the Bitcoin protocol and rule-setting by commercial interests	The Bitcoin community does have an apex: the Bitcoin Foundation, which is the guardian of the Bitcoin protocol and, through that, of all the policies and rules that govern it. It is possible that the Bitcoin Foundation, or others to whom it chooses to give delegated powers, becomes captured by commercial interests as they seek funding or industry support. The protocol could then be modified to reinstate centralizing tendencies (reestablishing opportunities for some to exert market power or control innovations) or to erode the principles of neutrality (the notion that how transactions are handled by the network should not depend on the characteristics of the transaction or who is behind them). If that happened, the confidence in Bitcoin, and even its very *raison d'être*, could be undermined in a very fundamental way

21.12 POTENTIAL DEMAND DRIVERS FOR BITCOIN

For all these reasons, for all its attractive architectural features, one can foresee a very rocky evolution of bitcoin prices even in the best of circumstances. Where, then, can demand for holding bitcoins come? Below, we discuss four potential drivers of demand for bitcoins: for its expected value appreciation, for its anonymity, for its safety relative to national currencies, and for its convenience in making payments.

21.12.1 Speculative motive: value appreciation

One potential source of demand for holding bitcoins comes from an investment belief that over time, bitcoins will appreciate more in value than financial investments denominated in national currency. This is a speculative motive, under which bitcoins are viewed as a normal commodity investment.

444 Handbook of Digital Currency

This demand scenario represents a composite bet that Bitcoin will

- prove to be a secure platform for holding and exchanging digital value,
- gain sufficiently trading volume so as to generate enough liquidity to be able to acquire and unwind investment positions in bitcoins on a reasonably timely and efficient basis,
- experience a sustained growth in demand that continues to outstrip its growth in supply, thus resulting in value appreciation (of these, the third is in principle the easiest to assume given the in-built deflationary bias of Bitcoin, though as noted earlier, that is likely to come with wide swings in its price).

21.12.2 Anonymity motive: privacy

A second potential source of demand for holding bitcoins is to evade detection by authorities, whether out of principle, for tax evasion or to cover up illicit activities. As stated earlier, bitcoins are held against pseudonyms and cannot be directly traced to individuals. However, once a bitcoin pseudonym is successfully linked to an individual, authorities can then reconstruct the entire bitcoin trading history by examining the bitcoin blockchain that is in the public domain. Anonymity is most likely to be broken through the Bitcoin exchanges and other ancillary services used to access the Bitcoin network.

Thus, preserving anonymity requires users exercising extreme care in not leaving any traces that link their bitcoin pseudonym to their real identities. Avoiding all possibilities of identification requires

- foregoing the convenience of public wallet hosting and exchange services, which are likely to come under stricter KYC rules from regulators, and possibly using bitcoin address mixing services as described above;
- using anonymizing communications protocols over the Internet (such as TOR), so that bitcoin transactions cannot be traced back to the computer from which they were made;
- storing the Bitcoin private key off-line, maybe even hiding it in printed format, to minimize the risk that it is ever found in your possession. These measures would be difficult and inconvenient to take by most ordinary citizens.

21.12.3 Precautionary motive: capital flight

This demand scenario combines elements of the previous two. Demand for bitcoins may stem from an urge by nationals of economically and/or politically unstable countries to abandon investments denominated in the national currency or legally domiciled in the country for risk of capital value erosion through inflation, punitive taxation, or outright government confiscation. Bitcoins might represent a convenient mechanism for moving and holding capital beyond the reach of the national authorities. This is a precautionary flight-to-safety motive rather than a speculative one, insofar as the option of investing in bitcoins, while in itself inherently risky, is deemed to be safer than the alternative of keeping the money in-country.

This demand scenario assumes that bitcoins represent a safer and more convenient route to capital flight than other available mechanisms such as US dollars or foreign exchange. However, one can assume that governments' bent on stemming capital flight would attempt to restrict and regulate the market for bitcoins on the same basis as other foreign currencies. The relative advantage of bitcoins versus US dollars as a vehicle for capital flight would depend on two key factors:

Relative ease of procuring them locally	US dollars are likely to enjoy a more liquid local market (whether of an official, parallel, or black nature) since local supplies are likely to be more naturally replenished through the daily processes of international commerce, international remittances, and foreign investment. Bitcoins, in contrast, may not enjoy a similar naturally offsetting base of transactions (at least not for a while), in which case they will sell locally at a larger premium than US dollars (i.e., at a higher implicit US dollar-per-Bitcoin price) in order to attract bitcoin sellers and speculators
Relative ease of moving and investing them abroad	On the other hand, once procured, bitcoins are automatically offshore (residing in cyberspace) and can be moved across borders at minimal cost, and holding them does not require traveling and opening accounts abroad. Offshoring US dollars, on the other hand, requires physically transporting bank notes or having access to a receiving bank account abroad, which is beyond the means of normal citizens in many countries. Thus, bitcoins would have an advantage because they serve as a direct store of value in themselves—provided that one can procure them locally at a reasonable price and has confidence in their future preservation of value

21.12.4 Convenience motive: payments

Even if people do not have an inherent preference for *holding* bitcoins over national currency, they may still have a preference for paying with them. Three particularly likely payment scenarios for bitcoins are as follows:

International remittances: price arbitrage	International remittances typically incur high charges, in the form of explicit commissions and implicit foreign exchange conversion costs, which well exceed the marginal cost of undertaking the transfer. These high-charging practices by established players are protected by the difficulty of replicating the retail distribution network requirements at both the originating and the destination countries. In thicker remittance corridors (such as US-Mexico) where alternative distribution networks have been built, we have seen significant reductions in charges. Charges are particularly high for money transfers to smaller and poorer countries in Africa

Continued

	Because bitcoins can be sent directly from sender to recipient at minimal cost, they present a very significant price arbitrage opportunity over more established services. However, remittance services on bitcoins are likely to be offered by intermediaries who manage the website through which senders can make and track their payments, as well as the process for converting national currency and bitcoins at least at the receiving end (where Bitcoin exchanges are likely to be less liquid or not operational at all). Thus, there is still likely to be an intermediary driving a wedge between the price and the cost, especially on thinly traded routes.[a] Bitcoin will deliver a much cheaper service only if there is effective competition for such services
Micropayments: cost-effectiveness	Most established online payment mechanisms entail sufficiently high costs as to be ineffective for very small-denomination (under one dollar) payments. Thus, the market for micropayments tends to be dominated by off-line smartcard solutions that do not work for remote (i.e., nonpoint-of-sale) transactions. Bitcoins, on the other hand, can be exchanged online at much lower cost, in a process analogous to sending an e-mail. Thus, Bitcoins could become an effective platform for enabling a variety of micropayment services that today are too expensive and clunky to contemplate. Unlike for international remittances, this is not about price arbitrage but a basic market enablement argument
	Micropayments based on Bitcoin could be used to pay for public services such as parking and to enable new pay-as-you-go charging models for utilities. In a developing country context, where daily wages may be as low as a dollar or two, the ability to make subdollar money transfers would enable electronic payments to enter into most people's daily lives. This would be in sharp contrast with today's mobile money solutions in Africa, which because of their cost tend to cater to transactions of more than USD 10 and to be done less frequently
Merchant payments: cashlessness	Existing electronic merchant payment solutions are heavily intermediated through merchant acquiring institutions. Merchants have to incur upfront costs to deploy the necessary point-of-sale infrastructure, pay a hefty discount (typically in the 1.5-5% range) every time they ring a sale electronically, and incur the risk of transaction reversals if customers subsequently repudiate the payment. These costs discourage merchants from promoting electronic payments and dissuade many smaller merchants from accepting them altogether
	Bitcoin in principle enables merchants to accept electronic payments without having to enter into any merchant acquiring contract with intermediaries and hence without having to accept merchant discounts or customer chargebacks. It can therefore help propagate electronic payment-enabled merchants at the base of the pyramid. Buyers would not have to incur very low cost in order to pay with bitcoins at the store, but they would need to accept the finality of all payments at the point of sale

[a] An example of such a company is BitPesa, which plans to launch remittance services in March 2014 on the UK-Kenya and US-Somalia corridors and is reported to intend to charge around 3% of transmitted value (*Source*: Bloomberg Technology News, November 28, 2013). Another one is Buttercoin, which plans to initially offer services into India and is reported to intend to charge around 1% of transmitted value (*Source*: TechCrunch, August 20, 2013).

It is worth repeating that the cost advantages of these payment scenarios are greatest when there is a direct interaction between sender/buyer and recipient/seller and they are both comfortable holding bitcoins. In this case, transaction costs are circumscribed to the connectivity with the Bitcoin network and the transaction fees attached to bitcoin transactions. However, in practice, other costs are likely to crop up:

- If either or both parties are loath to hold bitcoins because they are not comfortable with its storage-of-value properties, they will need to access Bitcoin exchanges to fund the Bitcoin payment and/or to liquidate the bitcoins obtained in payment. Many payment applications will be premised on seamless (meaning: quick and cheap) conversion of national currency into bitcoins and vice versa. In so doing, they will incur additional exchange fees, which could possibly eliminate the price advantage of transacting through Bitcoin. If exchanges are inefficient (high bid/ask spreads and long settlement delays), convenience and confidence will both be undermined. This is likely to be more of a problem in developing countries, where interbank settlement systems may be costly or lacking altogether.

- To the extent that intermediaries enter the picture in order to facilitate the emergence of these markets (such as international remittance portals and merchant acquirers handling customer complaints and chargebacks), they will introduce new costs that will need to be absorbed by one of both of the payment parties, and there may again be opportunities for these intermediaries to extract margins over and above their costs.

21.13 CONCLUSIONS: THE NEW VISTAS OPENED UP BY BITCOIN

The question is why should anyone even care about Bitcoin? The disruptive protocol has many shortcomings and substantial resistance from the incumbencies. One of the major weaknesses remains the fear of not so much of a 51% attack, a situation when enough computing power can render the digital register unreliable, but the danger of a gold finger that with his ulterior motive can bring the whole experiment to a sudden halt. Such a catastrophe will bring about an unimaginable systematic risk and nightmare to regulators especially if Bitcoin successfully prospers with network effect brought about by a successful incubation of an ecosystem.

However, if one were to move away from pure fascination of bitcoins but focuses on the Bitcoin protocols, the future would not be as bleak but in fact, on the contrary, it would be very promising. A pseudo Bitcoin protocol, a protocol lying somewhere in between the centralized controlled digital register and the centralized peer-to-peer fully distributed network, has a much promising future. Whether it is a more than 50% centralized business-to-peer network or a less than 50% decentralized peer-to-business distributed network, there will be cost advantages for financial business. There is a clear advantage in being decentralized peer-to-peer fully distributed network where trust is not needed. However, a pseudo network that provides varying degree of trust has its advantages too. One possibility is the proof of identity that allows for immediate encrypted identification for individual or business entity to address the regulatory issue for anti money laundering (AML) and counterterrorism financing (CTF). There is a possibility of the advancement of a regulatory financial architecture that allows for the same cost advantages of Bitcoin system but addresses the issues of concerns to regulators, in particular consumers' protection.

With mining activities and proof of identity, financial institutions such as banks will be able to reduce the cost of data storage and compliance by a substantial amount. This makes micropayments a viable business proposition allowing for the provision of mobile payments services with pre-identified e-wallet. Given that the number of underbanked and unbanked are in region of 2 billion people out of the entire global population of 7 billion, this is a growth area for financial institutions. In Asia, with close to 1.2 billion people in India, 1.4 billion in China, 300 million in Indonesia, 60 million in Myanmar, and many more in ASEAN countries without fixed telephone lines, scalable financial innovations with pseudo Bitcoin system are sought-after business ideas.

There are other innovative ideas such as the creation of a Pan Asian Coin or a Cross Country Coin that can be a joint venture among various financial institutions, sovereign wealth funds, and regulators that seek to achieve the purpose of financial integration. A Pan Asian Coin could be the bridge to the integration of capital, debt, and derivative markets besides stimulation of economic trades. Such a concept or an initiative, with support from regulators or financial market, can lead to reduction in business costs and the formation of a common market in finance and economics. Given the low GDP per capita in ASEAN countries and yet large economy, the potential of a Pan Asian Coin with micropayment capabilities will certainly be a stimulus to increase consumption of the lower income group, improving the welfare of the underserved and underconsumed population. When we stretch this idea of a Pan Asian Coin further west to India and further east to China, the potential is clearly huge. Other interesting innovations are discussed in Bhaskar et al. (2014).

A new currency requires that there be trust in the process by which units of the currency are created or destroyed. This can be broken down into several challenges: (i) It must offer reasonable certainty that its *nominal* value will be readily accepted in exchange and upheld over time; (ii) it must be able to hold its worth against other measures of value in *real* terms; and (iii) the medium in which the currency is expressed and exchanged needs to be forgery- and tamper-resistant. Bitcoin represents a breakthrough solution to the latter challenge: ensuring that digital claims to money cannot be misappropriated or spent multiple times, without requiring any kind of proprietary hardware solutions (like smartcards).

But Bitcoin exhibits serious shortcomings on the first two issues. The consensus on the validity of transactions that builds through the mining process is not immediate, and in fact, it is never definitive. Its usefulness in face-to-face transactions is limited by the speed with which blocks are formed. Moreover, there is a nonnegligible risk that a sufficiently large coalition of miners could successfully rewrite Bitcoin history, and that goes to the heart of Bitcoin's trust system. Also, Bitcoin offers no innovation in regard with the monetary stability issue: its deterministic money supply growth rule is extremely rudimentary. The observed price volatility of bitcoins is not just due to its newness: it is likely inherent in unmanaged monetary systems.

You can dismiss Bitcoin as a doomed monetary experiment, but you must not pass over the opportunity to let your imagination run with it as it can shake some basic assumptions you have on how financial systems must work. Might there be some lessons in there for how to "fix" what's wrong or broken in our financial system? Take Bitcoin as an invitation to dream about the following two questions:

- What if digital money was something that I could hold for myself and pass onto others, without necessarily having to go through a licensed financial institution? You can't do that now: You cannot hold digital money without becoming a customer of Citibank, PayPal, or M-PESA, and yet you can hold coins and bank notes by yourself; there is decentralized management of that. With digital money, we've been delivered into the hands of a select group of institutions, and in this context of complete dependence, it's not hard to see how a range of financial risks and consumer protection abuses are likely to arise. But what if we held the *option* to serve ourselves financially, even if only as a countervailing power or last resort?

- What if we could build an entire digital money network that did not require any specialized infrastructure? Modern finance is burdened by ever more complex core banking platforms. Most other forms of digital content have gotten off specialized networks and converged onto the Internet, simply by layering higher-level protocols on top of the basic IP, which take into account the unique technical needs of different applications. In the case of money, higher-level protocols would ensure that the digital value carried over the ubiquitous Internet is uniquely and securely owned by someone and cannot be freely copied or double-spent by their owner.

Combine these two thoughts and what we have is *fiat* (i.e., government-issued) money, which can be held and passed on in a peer-to-peer fashion and operates over the open Internet. Centralized issuance but decentralized day-to-day management of money once it's out there.[6] This would preserve a role for the central bank in ensuring monetary stability and would position the central banker as an arbiter that could step in if there ever emerges a coalition of miners seeking to subvert the currency. This new architecture of

---

[6]Of course, in so doing, the mining process and rewards would need to be redesigned to accommodate discretionary currency issuance by the central bank. It is beyond the scope of this chapter to discuss how; here, we only present the scenario of bolting national currencies onto bitcoin-like protocols as a thought experiment.

money would take out the traditional banking gatekeepers (per the first point) and massively reduces the cost of moving money around (per the second point).

This would have the result of opening up the floodgates of innovation, because financial services could then be implemented at the customer wallet application level, without necessarily having to touch or even consult any central services or centralized providers. (A crude example: you could set up a time deposit by telling your wallet rather than your bank to not give you access to your money.) This is the rise of programmable money: empowerment at the edge of the network.

In addition to more service innovation, the cost of achieving financial inclusion would be vastly reduced, as people could gain financial access simply by downloading a secure application on their smartphone (which are coming for all) without requiring any provider's consent. Transaction pricing would be reduced down toward the underlying cost, as the ability of users to pay themselves on a peer-to-peer basis would set a new lower cap on what service providers could charge. This would likely affect international remittances most significantly, where entrenched service providers are today able to exercise significant market power. But it would also lower the cost to provide, as sending money need not cost much more than sending an e-mail. This could economically extend electronic transactions down to very small transaction sizes, creating a new digital *nanoeconomy*.

A decentralized payments fabric inspired on Bitcoin principles would also create complete transparency of payment histories through the public blockchain. This should lead to new peer-to-peer credit models and should give authorities more traceability on criminal activities.

Finally, such a system would also go in the direction of giving policymakers more options to prevent or deal with financial crises, by increasing market discipline on banks. There would be a much more credible flight-to-safety option for people if they suspected a weak bank or a bubble. And in the event of banking distress, there would be a more credible let-it-fail option for regulators since our economy need not be so dependent on them.

This is not about doing away with banks; they will still have a big role to play intermediating funds. Even in a Bitcoin-like scenario, they can try to win customers over with attractive deposit interest rates and on-demand loans, which my wallet may not be able to negotiate on a peer-to-peer basis. But anyone should be able to opt for a self-service option whenever we like—or when banks are failing to include us. As it is, there are other forms of shadow banking, investment banking, or digital banking alternatives mushrooming all over the Internet such as Lending Club, Venmo, Apple Pay, Google Wallet, Klarna, Dragonpay, Square, Stripe, Alipay, PayLah, DASH, Moven, mBank, First Direct, Fidor Bank, Simple, Circle, Kickstarter, Indiegogo, and SWARM. This is the same service-versus-application dichotomy that has played out between telecom providers and Skype to such advantage to end users.

We are a long way from being able to implement this sort of solution, from a technical, regulatory, and customer acceptance point of view. For once in history, technology has the potential to seriously disrupt the financial services sector that has been ironically protected by regulation. The process of profit margin squeeze is slowed down only by regulation, but it is hard to imagine that it will not accelerate when financial technology is popularized. Unbundling banking and financial services presents opportunities for regulatory arbitrage as regulators tighten regulation. Bitcoin is certainly in the space of reinventing these services using the distributed network, and more interestingly, profit opportunities are abundant in between centralized and distributed networks, simply to decentralize the banking and financial services in order to facilitate payments, lending, and fund raising (Lee, 2014). But shouldn't these issues be at the heart of the ongoing financial architecture debate? We need to think of financial systems much more as a seamless fabric and less as a restricted collection of connected institutions. Bitcoin system if viewed as a scalable financial innovation will have a future only limited by our imagination.

REFERENCES

Bhasker, N.D., Lam, P.N., Lee, D.K.C., 2014. Bitcoin IPO, ETF and Crowdfunding. Sim Kee Boon Institute for Financial Economics, Singapore Management University, Singapore.

Bhaskar, N.D., Lee, D.K.C., 2014a. Bitcoin Mining Technology. Sim Kee Boon Institute for Financial Economics, Singapore Management University, Singapore.

Bhaskar, N.D., Lee, D.K.C., 2014b. Bitcoin Exchanges. Sim Kee Boon Institute for Financial Economics, Singapore Management University, Singapore.

Lee, D.K.C., 2014. Cryptocurrency: The Future. Podcast by Singapore Management University, Singapore.

Martin, F., 2013. Money: The Unauthorized Biography. Bodley Head, UK.

Mas, I., 2014. Why Should You Care About Bitcoin. University of Oxford, Said Business School, United Kingdom.

Nakamoto, S., 2009. Bitcoin: A peer-to-peer electronic cash system. https://bitcoin.org/bitcoin.pdf.

Ong, B., Lee, T.M., Li, G., Lee, D.K.C., 2014. Evaluating Potential of Alternative Cryptocurrencies. Singapore Management University, Singapore.

CHAPTER 22

Blockchain Electronic Vote

Pierre Noizat
Co-founder of Paymium, Bitcoin Exchange and provider of e-commerce solutions, Paris, France

Contents

22.1 THE PROBLEM WITH PROPRIETARY VOTING SYSTEMS

Existing electronic voting systems all suffer from a serious design flaw: They are proprietary, that is, centralized by design, meaning there is a single supplier that controls the code base, the database, and the system outputs and supplies the monitoring tools at the same time.

The lack of an open-source, independently verifiable output makes it difficult for such centralized systems to acquire the trustworthiness required by voters and election organizers.

This design flaw is therefore limiting electronic vote applications at a time when growing computer literacy and usage should in fact foster their widespread adoption.

Without an easy, free access to effective, secure electronic voting technology, political participation is limited to on-site elections that are few and far between, given the high setup cost of election preparation, supervision, and postelection operations.

Electronic voting is not meant to replace traditional elections but can provide a much-needed complementary voting method.

22.2 OPEN-SOURCE, FREE SOFTWARE ELECTRONIC TRANSACTION AND VOTING SYSTEMS

Since the invention of the Bitcoin protocol (Nakamoto, 2008), the Bitcoin network has grown to become today the most powerful distributed computing network on Earth, providing a very secure, free software, database infrastructure to store electronic transaction data of any kind.

The complete Bitcoin transaction database is referred to as the blockchain because bitcoin transaction records are paginated in blocks appended to the database every 10 min on average.

An electronic vote is essentially an electronic transaction whereby a voter, given some voting credits, will spend them in favor of one or more candidate recipients.

Candidate recipients can be people like in a presidential election or options to choose from like in a referendum election.

This chapter describes how to leverage the availability of the Bitcoin blockchain as a secure transaction database, to log votes and audit vote results. The proposed method involves Merkle trees (Merkle, 1980) for voters' list verification and block explorers for vote count check.

The solution protects the privacy of the vote by using a simple form of Bitcoin pay-to-script-hash scripts (Andresen, 2012) (https://github.com/bitcoin/bips/blob/master/bip-0016.mediawiki) with 2-of-3 multisignature addresses.

I have developed a demo voting application based on my proposal to assess usability and performance, but testing has only begun and is far from over: I am sharing here early results to get the discussion going. The application is deployed on the web site: www.unchain.voting.

Here is how the whole process unfolds in five steps.

22.2.1 Preelection: Know the list of candidates

Each candidate (C) assigns a public key *KeyC* to the voter and publishes everywhere a Bitcoin address like 1Martin.., that is, a vanity address (https://en.bitcoin.it/wiki/Vanitygen) prepared by the organizers for candidate Martin.

For the secrecy of each ballot, each KeyC is different for each voter, so the candidate must generate n public keys KeyC for n voters.

Each candidate should be required by the organizers to publish the Merkle root of a hash tree comprising all of his public keys KeyC.

Alternatively, the voting application can generate the keys KeyC on behalf of the candidate, although this option could be avoided to reduce the need to trust the organizers.

Using the voting application, each voter should be able to check her branch of the hash tree, linking the key KeyC to the root.

22.2.2 Check the list of voters

Each voter (B) is also assigned by the election organizers (e.g., an association A) a public key *KeyA* and a nonce value that can be used by the voter as a secret access key to log on to her account.

These access keys will be sent securely by the organizers to each voter.

The voters' list can be represented in a Merkle tree (Figure 22.1): The application gives each voter the list of interior hashes, linking her public key KeyA to the Merkle root.

With the Merkle tree published by the application and with the standard computation formulas below, the voters' list can be independently verified by all parties because every voter can check the path from her leaf node to the Merkle root and make sure that the number of leaf nodes is equal to the number of voters.

This is how interior hashes are calculated as 64-character string, using Ruby scripting:

sha256_base64   "#{sum_of_upper_left_and_right_nodes}|#{upper_left_hash}|#{upper_right_hash}"

Likewise, leaf node hashes are calculated as follows:

sha256_base64 "#{voter_name}|#{voter_credit_balance}|#{voter_nonce}"

The voter credit balance can be initialized to one in the simple case of a presidential election or to n if the voter can choose n of m candidates like in the election of n board members. Voter credit is updated when the voter casts her vote, spending all or part of her voting credit.

sha256_base64 is the standard method for generating the 64-character hash of a string:

sha256_base64(string)   =   OpenSSL::Digest::SHA256.new.digest(string).unpack ('H*').first

The path to the root for one of the voters in the above example tree would look like this:

Voter name: stephan

Voter credit balance: 0.01 ฿

Account Nonce (voter access key): 958a78b68c8f53f89c3433c1fde98152

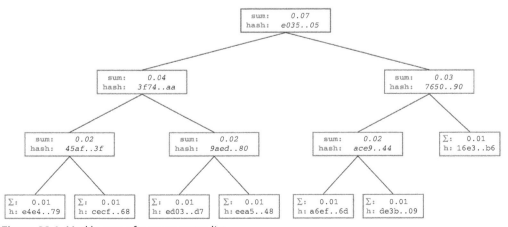

Figure 22.1 Merkle tree of a seven-voter list.

Account Hash (leaf node hash): eea58cf19ed83072a9ea650e1c71a100f8f22129196cf52 d1d91c4ecf68bdc48

Interior Hash #1: 9aed30f6447d11e852873d4896d43a13152773b7ba2dae65b1eb342854c9de80

Interior Hash #2: 3f74cef73f11bbc2eca69e70b985f7a3e6a69d292f4dc0fb9d0fbcdd5453dfaa

Interior Hash #3 (Merkle Root): e035cfb7615443b4e49bc1a0bd4b16bdb28ec79ad8c409f5bbf55dea9cbf7f05

As a precautionary option, the public key KeyA should be random and should not be on the Bitcoin elliptic curve bitcoin, for instance, using a side chain, to prevent the organizers (A) from producing a valid signature.

This precaution is also independently verifiable and reduces the need to trust the organizers. However, the complexity of using a side chain instead of the blockchain should not be underestimated.

Additionally, the application assigns a unique public key *KeyB* to the voter.

As an option, to further reduce the need to trust the organizers, KeyB can be generated independently by the voter herself. However, opening this option would entail some voter education, support efforts, and less usability.

As usual, the choice for an optimal convenience/security trade-off should be guided by common sense and knowledge of the voters' demographics, including computer literacy. Generally speaking, organizers should not expect that people will be able to handle private keys themselves in a secure manner.

22.2.3 Prepare the ballot

Before election day, with the A, B, and C public keys recorded by the application, the application can create a *2-of-3 multisignature address* and a transaction sending to it a bitcoin micropayment (about the price of a postage stamp) upon the voter's confirmation of her vote.

The voter's ballot now has a cryptographically secure representation in this transaction, which is broadcast to the bitcoin network nodes by the application.

At this point, it should be noted that the voter can check independently and immediately that her vote has been submitted to the bitcoin network by looking up the multisignature address with any block explorer such as blockchain.info or blockr.io: Although unconfirmed yet, the transaction is showing 2–3 s at most after she confirmed her vote.

After a few hours, the ballot is securely logged on the blockchain with an increasing number of network confirmations.

The output script (destination) of her micropayment transaction looks like this: OP_HASH160 Hash OP_EQUAL

Where *Hash* is the hash calculated by her bitcoin wallet from the following (*SerializedScript*) script:

OP_0 OP_2 KeyA KeyB KeyC OP_3 OP_CHECKMULTISIG

This transaction is compliant with BIP-16.

Each key is a concatenation of the x and y coordinates of a point. If the point is on the bitcoin Koblitz curve, then it is a Bitcoin public key and there is a corresponding private key. Coins sent to the multisignature address can be spent only if at least two of the keys are Bitcoin public keys. A key is represented as a 128-hexadecimal character string, each coordinate being represented as 32 bytes.

Here is an example:

KeyA:

7d56d13563243998e4934e189574db4eca3b1ac1e0f20f8e136ec047a202151da60a38 a561bc4debd28c0433c51b2f21f1df58c53d4e69c828351dfff4ce1eca

KeyB:

d3363437960978fef861678d9ae0e18544cf999892c0375e7b2856a5258d740f0dfd31 d3b1547b0847c1e65f4d7228a2e7223cc18e42b4271bf7421a54f03d48

KeyC:

2fdede700db4d7c5e40cbe90d61961240e6fab869270c21d024614b83803adfc84e001 d313a24910317ec3a7e73c6dcdf828acb639d8048cc4efed95b77c8eb9

The following is the multisignature address whose funding represents the vote of B in favor of C: 3NSxmhDPpYak4HH5BYJdsNDq5s1bE121oH.

Because this address was funded, it can be found in a transaction output of the blockchain by anyone using a block explorer. More precisely, the address is derived from the 20-byte hash of the redeem script of the transaction recorded in the blockchain. The redeem script itself, a simple concatenation of the three public keys, will not be visible until the output is spent on a subsequent transaction, after election day.

The application displays a list of all the funded multisignature addresses as an indicator of the vote participation rate.

There is no way to guess neither the voter (B) nor the candidate (C) from a multi-signature address without knowing all three public keys (KeyA, KeyB, and KeyC) and knowing to whom they belong.

In particular, the candidates have no way of knowing their rankings at this point.

A voter can check if the multisignature address representing her vote appears in the list.

In the demo application, organizers generate and fund a separate address for each voter in the preelection period. This address (Address B) is derived from KeyB to keep things simple.

On election day, the unspent output of Address B can be used by the application to fund the multisignature address corresponding to the voter's choice.

If multiple choices are offered in the election like in a board member election, several multisignature addresses can be linked to the voter's account to reflect her selection, each address representing a selected candidate or chosen option.

Since we want the multisignature address funding transactions to show up in the blockchain, preferably before the vote count, organizers must consider the settings of transaction fees. If transaction fees were set too low, a funding transaction could end up being left in limbo, stuck in the memory pool of the miners, and ultimately dropped.

According to the Bitcoin Wiki (https://en.bitcoin.it/wiki/Transaction_fees), a transaction may be sent without fees if the following conditions are met:

- It is smaller than 1000 bytes.
- All outputs are 0.01 BTC or larger.
- Its priority is large enough, where

priority = sum(input_value_in_base_units * input_age)/size_in_bytes

The typical size of a transaction from one standard address to one multisignature address is around 223 bytes.

As of core client version 0.3.21, *transactions needed to have a priority above 57,600,000 to avoid the enforced limit. This threshold is written in the core client code as COIN * 144 / 250, suggesting that the threshold represents a one day old, 1 btc coin (144 is the expected number of blocks per day) and a transaction size of 250 bytes.*

*So, for example, a transaction that has 2 inputs, one of 5 btc with 10 confirmations, and one of 2 btc with 3 confirmations, and has a size of 500bytes, will have a priority of (500000000 * 10 + 200000000 * 3) / 500 = 11,200,000*

Therefore, the recommended setup process to avoid paying fees to the miners is to use 0.01 BTC as the transaction amount for each voter and to fund Address B at least 1 day before election day.

The challenge is about paying minimal mining fees while ensuring that the transactions will be confirmed.

It should be anticipated that, in the future, miners' fees will evolve from rule-driven fees to market-driven fees, turning the above fee-avoiding recommendation into a fee-minimizing strategy.

Because the time period when the coins are needed equals roughly 2 days, the amount of the transaction should be scaled according to the number of voters: As the amount is driven lower by a large number of voters, mining fees will start to kick in. As a result, organizers may be able to find an optimal trade-off combining financial costs and mining fees.

In fact, as noted in the description of Section 22.2.3, there is no strong requirement for a fast confirmation time as long as the voter can see that her vote transaction has been broadcast to the network nodes.

Confirmations are needed only to etch the transaction in the blockchain forever and to make verifications possible at any time in the future.

If large-scale operations like a national election are on the agenda, the organizers should consider mining themselves to ensure that the vote transactions will eventually make their way to the blockchain: the more hashing power harnessed by the organizers, the lower the statistical cap on the maximum confirmation time.

22.2.4 Counting votes on election day

At the end of election day, the application can simply display the compiled results from its database.

Compared to a traditional, proprietary system, the added feature is the ability to display a funded multisignature address for each vote record.

The blockchain does not say much about this address yet until its coins are spent to another address.

The election results will be made independently verifiable in the next and final step.

22.2.5 Postelection: Showing independently verifiable results

Now is the time to show the world a lasting, easily verifiable proof that the vote count was not rigged in any way.

Let's say one of the candidate is Martin: Martin has advertised a special bitcoin vanity address 1Martin.. on social networks during the election campaign.

For each voter, the application uses the two private keys corresponding to KeyB and KeyC, respectively, to sign a transaction, spending the coins from the 2-of-3 multisignature address to the address 1Martin.., unequivocally linking the vote to the candidate.

The transaction from the multisignature address to 1Martin.. includes the following input:

SignatureB SignatureC SerializedScript,

where SerializedScript designates the redeem script converted from its binary form to a hexadecimal string.

Looking up the multisignature address in the blockchain using any block explorer, it is easy to find the redeem script in the spending transaction, in other words the serialized input script of the transaction sending coins from 3NSxmh..., revealing the three public keys.

An observer can use the Merkle tree published by the candidate before the election to check the validity of the interior hashes connecting KeyC to the Merkle root. Similar verifications applied to KeyA and KeyB will allow the observer to assert the validity of the multisignature address.

A discrepancy between the vote count provided by the application on election day and the blockchain transactions could be spotted easily with any block explorer software.

However, it is impossible for an observer to link a multisignature address to a voter insofar as KeyB cannot be linked to the voter identity by the observer.

Incidentally, this system uses an advantage of a digital signature compared with a manual signature: a digital signature identifies its author only with her consent, if and when she reveals her identity.

The votes, while preserving the secrecy of the ballots, are perfectly verifiable by candidates and voters, independently of any organization.

To complete the postelection operations, the organizers collect the funds from address 1Martin.. and from the other candidates' vanity addresses that were prepared in the preelection period.

Would it be simpler to just create a new blockchain and wallet for each election cycle?

It is in fact simpler to use an existing blockchain.

Besides, no other blockchain comes close to the Bitcoin blockchain in terms of protection against a 51% attack led by one of the candidates.

Creating a new blockchain dedicated to a particular vote amounts to requesting the voters to trust more the organizers and all the candidates: the organizers or some candidate could take control of the new blockchain, mine some votes, and drop some other votes. This would seriously disrupt the verification of the vote count.

22.3 CONCLUSION

Before the invention of Bitcoin, electronic voting solutions were not satisfactory because they were not easily auditable and not sufficiently transparent neither for candidates nor for voters. In addition, they require a costly, labor-intensive setup.

With the Bitcoin blockchain, any community can organize a free, secure electronic voting.

Initially, communities, associations, or listed corporations should consider using this technology for local elections, board elections, or general assembly voting of their members or shareholders.

Scaling up to national elections might require direct involvement of the organizers in mining operations or some level of cooperation with miners.

The proposed system does not solve all the issues associated with electronic voting, but it does provide a valuable alternative to current, proprietary electronic voting systems with the following benefits:
- Free, open-source peer-reviewed software
- Ubiquitous
- Secure
- Protecting the secrecy of the ballots
- Allowing free, independent audits of the results
- Minimizing the trust level required from the organizers

REFERENCES

Andresen, G., 2012. BIP-0016 (Bitcoin Improvement Proposal), January 2012.

Merkle, R.C., 1980. Protocols for public key cryptosystems. In: Proceedings of the 1980 Symposium on Security and Privacy, April 1980. IEEE Computer Society, pp. 122–133.

Nakamoto, S., 2008. Bitcoin: a peer-to-peer electronic cash system, November 2008.

CHAPTER 23

Translating Commons-Based Peer Production Values into Metrics: Toward Commons-Based Cryptocurrencies

Primavera De Filippi
CERSA/CNRS/Université Paris II—Berkman Center for Internet & Society at Harvard Law School, Cambridge, Massachusetts, USA

Contents

23.1 INTRODUCTION

Since the 1990s, increasing reliance on socialized forms of collaborative knowledge production (Florida, 2002; Peck, 2005), user-driven innovation (von Hippel, 2004), and shared, open, free forms of productive relations (Bauwens, 2005; Kelty, 2008; O'Neil, 2009) has raised questions about the meaning and measurement of value in commons-based peer production (CBPP) communities.

Academic theory is still young in this field. Scholars have looked at the values that structure online forms of CBPP (Benkler, 2006), such as free and open-source software (Coleman, 2005; Kelty, 2008; O'Neil, 2009), and many researchers have underlined the growing and important role of value and reputation metrics (Arvidsson, 2012; cf. Lury and Atkins, 2012). Yet—given the multifaceted notion of "value" (discussed in

Value metrics		Immaterial reward mechanisms	
Reputation in the system based on the trust by other users(Ebay)		Real reputation (real-world volunteer networks)	
		Power and status in the community, administrative permissions	
Quantitative measures : number of contributions, size (Stackoverflow), popularity of content, visits, likes, shares (Facebook, Youtube)		Privileges in the community, more space, speed (FTP media sharing)	
		Qualitative rewards, e.g., congratulation from individuals (Wikilove)	
Online social network service analytics (Klout, Kred)		Material reward mechanisms	
		Tokens exchangeable for services within the community (Farm Ville)	
Calculation of "karma" based on "helpfulness" algorithm (Slashdot)		Donations from individuals, crowdfunding (Kickstarter)	
		Distributed donations from the community (Flattr)	
Token (medals/badges) received from other's appreciation: Wikipedia, P2PUniversity		Offers from others to contribute to projects (Free/open source)	

Figure 23.1 Value metrics and rewards system in CBPP platforms. *(Source: P2Pvalue.eu.)*

Section 23.3.3)—there is, to date, no consolidated analytical framework capable of measuring the overall value of CBPP outside of the market economy.

Over the past centuries, market mechanisms have been used to evaluate the market value of a large variety of resources and price tag them into goods to be exchanged. The market is, however, incapable of understanding the value of nonmarket resources (Shiller, 2012). While such an indicator might not be necessary for the successful operation of the CBPP ecosystem, it might, nonetheless, be useful to identify a new proxy for value—other than price—so as to be able to better evaluate (and compare) the value generated by CBPP communities.

At present, a number of value metric systems have been proposed, including a diversity of reward systems and reputational rewards (see Figure 23.1). However, these systems do not stem from any systematic research on the different conceptions of value in CBPP. Conversely, considerable research has been done on reputation economies and reputation systems (Castells et al., 2012; Marwick et al., 2010), but this research has generally not been married to the practical development of any usable tools.

23.2 COMMONS-BASED PEER PRODUCTION

Today, an alternative model of production is emerging—both on the Internet and elsewhere—that does not rely on market transactions, but rather on sharing and cooperation among peers. The deployment of Internet and Web 2.0 technologies spurred the development of online platforms for the production and dissemination of information resulting from voluntary collaboration between a community of peers (the so-called peer production platforms). In the realm of information, Wikipedia is perhaps the most popular example, along with Github, Reddit, Slashdot, Kune, and so forth. But the same applies also in the physical realm, with a growing number of initiatives such as the Open Source Ecology and Fab Labs. All these platforms facilitate peer production by providing interactive applications allowing for synchronous/asynchronous collaboration and community coordination. Some of them also rely on specific licenses—such as Free/Libre Open-Source Software (FLOSS) and Creative Commons—in order to promote the creation and preservation of "information commons": immaterial and collectively owned informational resources that can be freely used and reused by everyone (Hess and Ostrom, 2007). This new model of production—sometimes referred to as CBPP (Benkler, 2006)—represents the building block of the new "commons-based ecosystem" that is progressively establishing itself, both online and off-line.

A distinction needs, however, to be made between traditional physical commons (which mostly relate to material goods) and digital or information commons (which are inherently intangible). While commons of both kinds exist, the production, management, and use thereof may significantly differ from one type to the other (Frischmann, 2004). Information commons can exist with ease and without boundary due to their nonrival nature. Conversely, physical commons—while existing without a private owner, produced and consumed by a community, and outside of a market logic—must still organize to regulate their consumption and production (Dietz et al., 2003). In order to avoid creating unnecessary confusion, we will focus here only on the latter kind of commons—information commons—which constitutes the principal output of CBPP (Beagle et al., 2006).

A specific characteristic of CBPP is that both the production and dissemination of information are increasingly done outside of the market economy. Production is achieved through voluntary collaboration among a distributed network of peers that cooperate to produce content or information, without relying on hierarchical organization or market pricing for coordination. The output of production is, itself, less directly affected by the traditional mechanisms of supply and demand, given that informational resources are released under liberal licensing schemes ("some rights reserved" as opposed to "all rights reserved") so that they can be freely used and reused by everyone. As opposed to material resources (which are inherently scarce and rival in consumption), information commons (because of their nonrival nature) lend themselves to a different economic system based on the notions of "abundance" and "sharing."

As such, CBPP does not properly fit within the framework of the most conventional economic theories based on the notion of "scarcity" and "exchange." Economic value is based on scarcity and/or needs. As most commons-based products or services are nonrival and nonexcludable (i.e., based on abundance), the concept of value breaks down in its traditional sense. Market mechanisms might still work, as value shifts from product to service (e.g., the FLOSS community often sells its consulting expertise, whereas Wikipedia could implement a Twitter-style business model based on API). Yet, even where there is economic value, conventional market mechanisms are unable to estimate the overall social value of the resources produced by CBPP communities that operate outside (or at the edges) of the market economy. Indeed, traditional market mechanisms—such as pricing and the law of supply and demand—do not correctly operate in a commons-based ecosystem, because the market is incapable of understanding the value of nonmarket transactions. In a market economy, the key concern is to assess the economic value (or market value) of things through the mechanism of supply and demand. Everything else (such as friendship, solidarity, or even deeper ideological values such as freedom and justice) is regarded as mere externalities, which will only be accounted for to the extent that they can be or have been translated into monetary value.

Alternative theories have been elaborated as an attempt to understand the dynamics subtending nonmarket processes and interactions in the context of both online and off-line communities. In terms of commons-based resources, to contrast Hardin's tragedy of the commons, according to which the selfish motivations of community members will inevitably lead to the destruction of the resources they depend upon (Hardin, 1968), Ostrom had shown, through her comprehensive research on the governance of commons-based resources (Dietz et al., 2003; Ostrom, 1990; Ostrom et al., 1999), that specific communities are capable of self-organizing in order to protect and preserve the long-term sustainability of the commons by relying on an internal system of community governance that operates outside of traditional market mechanisms. By moving property into commonly held constructions, accumulated wealth and its purchasing power are no longer at play. Instead, earning access to a given commons-based resource is the reward available for contributing to the commons. One's right to consume resources is, there-fore, limited to what the particular community is willing to give back to every individual member or contributor (Cardenas and Ostrom, 2004).

With regard to nonmarket transactions, Cheal (1988) introduced the notion of the "gift economy," defined as a system whereby resources are not traded for money or another commodity, but rather are given away for free, without any explicit agreement for immediate or future rewards. Reciprocity might nonetheless be expected, either directly or indirectly: Deferred reciprocity means that whoever has given away some-thing expects to receive something else in exchange, at a later moment in time, whereas circular reciprocity emerges when people are giving away things without any expectation of returns but for the fact that those who have received a gift will eventually pass it for-ward to someone else (Boyd and Richerson, 1989). The notion of the "sharing econ-omy" (also known as the peer-to-peer economy or collaborative economy) appeared only later, in the mid-2000s, as new business structures emerged, inspired from the prac-tices of "collaboration" and "sharing" that had become pervasive in the digital world (Gold, 2004). As an attempt to transpose these practices in the physical realm (which is essentially made up of tangible resources impossible to copy and paste), the "sharing economy" established itself as a new socioeconomic model of production, driven by the desire to overcome the ongoing trend toward resource depletion through the sharing of both human and physical assets (Kranton and Kranton, 1996). More recently, Botsman and Rogers (2010) analyzed the motivations underlying the recent growth in popularity of the so-called collaborative consumption, a model whereby access replaces ownership as the key economic concern. In this context, resources are no longer exchanged on the market, but rather shared among different people and organizations, who merely provide access to certain goods or services, rather than claiming individual ownership over them.

Beyond economic theories, new theoretical frameworks have also been devised in the last decade, with a view to understand the social norms and governance rules regulating the production and distribution of resources within specific communities that operate outside of the market economy. While Benkler (2002) applied Coase's theory of the firm to describe the innovative governance structures adopted by CBPP communities, Bauwens (2005) relied on commons theory to describe the political economy of peer productions, whereas Shirky (2010) employed a variety of motivation theories to understand the intrinsic motivations subtending the infrastructures of peer production. Yet, the CBPP theory is still young and there is, to date, no consolidated analytical framework that could be applied—either directly or indirectly (by analogy)—to properly measure or estimate the value generated by CBPP communities.

23.3 VALUE METRICS

Today, CBPP constitutes an important source of value to society as a whole (Seppänen et al., 2007). In spite of its recent origins (mid-1980s), CBPP is already playing an important role in the Internet economy (Rajala et al., 2012). Wikipedia, Creative Commons, and the various FLOSS communities represent today an important driver for online innovation and cultural development (Bauwens, 2005). However, while their overall contribution to the well-being of society cannot be denied (Ghosh, 2007), estimating—or quantifying—the actual value generated by CBPP communities is an extremely difficult task, whose solutions are yet to be explored.

23.3.1 Universal indicator of value

Over the past centuries, money has been an extremely useful and important medium to help human society develop into modernity. Today, all dominant social systems featuring a market economy are, for the most part, based on a monetary system.

Money, including all currencies and their derived formats (gold, cash, bonds, securities, etc.), plays three core functions in the market economy. To begin with, money is a medium of exchange. Provided that a particular currency is accepted and recognized as such by a specific community, trade is facilitated by virtue of the transferability and divisibility of money. But money also constitutes a standard measure of value, which provides a common (and neutral) unit of account to assess and compare the value of different resources. By virtue of the pricing mechanism, money can be used to evaluate the market value of a large variety of resources and price tag them into goods to be exchanged. Finally, to the extent that it can be stored, money provides a means for people to accumulate value, so as to expend it at a later time. As such, money can also be used to indicate one's wealth, estimating the societal value of individuals according to how much money they have accumulated over time.

Exploring how CBPP and the logic of money intersect can help us better understand the difference between market-based and commons-based economies and their respective approaches to wealth and property.

The first function (medium of exchange) becomes to a large extent irrelevant in the context of a commons-based ecosystem, composed for the most part of nonrival resources, which are made freely available to everyone. This is all the more true in the context of online CBPP communities, which exclusively produce or manage information commons. As access trumps ownership (Gansky, 2010), the value of a particular resource can be uncoupled from the ownership thereof. We are moving away from a system of exchange toward a system that relies almost exclusively on *collaboration* and *sharing*. Resources need no longer be traded before they can be consumed, and those that are not shared are likely to be ultimately wasted or underused.

The third function (value store) also becomes less relevant in a commons-based ecosystem, as scarcity is shifting away from the *output* of production (which is nonrival) toward the actual *act* of production (i.e., the creative act), which only needs to happen once. Thus, the logic of accumulation characteristic of a capitalist economy does not properly apply in a commons-based ecosystem characterized by a growing abundance of (nonrival) resources. However, while accumulation might no longer be required for mere consumption, accumulation of wealth might still be necessary in order to set up and manage organizations or communities of creators. Creative work time is (and will always remain) inherently scarce. Yet, in the context of CBPP, even though there is scarcity of work, individuals generally contribute to the production of commons-based resources in a voluntary manner—whatever their underlying reasons might be. Wealth accumulation becomes, therefore, to a growing extent, unnecessary, ultimately lessening the function of money as a storage of value.

Conversely, the second function (indicator of value) remains an extremely useful tool that could significantly contribute to supporting the commons-based ecosystem, to the extent that it would provide a means for people to estimate or compare the value of commons-based resources and to assess productivity gains (or losses) over time. The challenge is, therefore, to identify an alternative proxy for value (other than price) that is universally applicable and that can be used as a means of comparison between different CBPP projects, in spite of their heterogeneity (i.e., ideally, the same indicator would apply in the context of physical and digital commons).

A key difficulty in assessing the overall (social) value of CBPP is the inadequacy of conventional market mechanisms in estimating the value of nonmarket resources—that is, one can't simply use money to evaluate people's social values, from their credibilities to their social responsibilities, or creativities. Indeed, as opposed to market resources, whose value is determined by the mechanisms of supply and demand, the value of resources produced within CBPP communities is more difficult to establish, in that there is no single common denominator of value capable of understanding the overall social value of commons-based resources.

For instance, how can we estimate the overall value of Wikipedia? Does it have a monetary value? And, if so, would it make sense to evaluate Wikipedia (solely and exclusively) in monetary terms? What are the other indicators that could be used to quantify (or qualify) the value of Wikipedia? We know it has a high social value because of the perceived value others give to it, but how can this value be effectively measured? And what are the tools we can rely upon in order to express such value to others?

The problem is that without the traditional system of "pricing," one can no longer rely on a universal unit of analysis (value proxy) to assess and compare the value of different CBPP platforms and the value contributed by various individuals to these platforms. There is, therefore, a need for a universal denominator of value (other than price) capable of understanding and measuring the value generated by CBPP. In the remainder of this chapter, we will, therefore, investigate alternative frameworks of analysis that could help us reframe the notion of value in the context of CBPP, so as to eventually come up with more relevant indicators of value or value metrics.

23.3.2 Alternative value metrics

Comparing the nature and relevance of different indicators that can be (and have been) used to measure the value generated within a variety of CBPP platforms might help us understand how well can we estimate the value that each platform provides to society and whether there are some common or universal metrics we can rely upon. We will focus here on two popular cases—Wikipedia and the FLOSS community—whose values are mostly generated outside of the market economy and cannot therefore be assessed through conventional market mechanisms.

Wikipedia is perhaps the most notorious example of a successful CBPP platform. Created in 2001, Wikipedia has become the sixth most visited Web site in the world (according to Alexa), with over 30 million articles written in 250 languages by over 20 million contributors, as of June 2014. The value of Wikipedia can be estimated by a variety of indicators, which might be either quantitative (e.g., the number of articles, contributors, and visitors) or qualitative (e.g., the quality of articles and the reputation of the platform). Yet, none of these indicators are actually capable of expressing the overall value of Wikipedia as it is perceived by society nor estimating the value of every individual contribution to the project. In this regard, while Wikipedia refused to adopt a formal reputation system within its own institutional framework, it did nonetheless implement internal value metrics—through Wikipedia's "service awards," which are, in fact, merely self-declaratory badges (Ashton, 2011)—and immaterial P2P reward mechanisms through the "WikiLove" extension, a way of democratizing the old *barnstars* (typically rewarded from librarians to merit users) by letting users acknowledge an editor's level of contribution by sending a gesture of appreciation. Other services (external to Wikipedia) have also been deployed with a view to estimate the value of Wikipedia contributions according to different criteria or value metrics (see, e.g., WikiTrust, the most commonly used metric of quality in Wikipedia). Yet, none of these services actually purport to evaluate the social value of Wikipedia in terms of "value" *per se*.

Similarly, the majority of FLOSS projects—regardless of their scale—provide neither mechanism for assessing the value of the contributions they receive nor any internal mechanism of rewards for contributors. Most projects rely on an informal meritocratic system, whereby contributions are evaluated, internally and in a purely informal manner, by other contributors according to the value that they have contributed to the project (Amant and Still, 2007). Even the larger FLOSS projects, such as the GNU project or the Linux kernel, rely on an informal system of participation based on a meritocratic structure, which is often not rigidly defined. The case of Linux is particularly emblematic in this regard. Linus Torvalds—the archetype of a "benevolent dictator"—does not have any authority to exercise hierarchical command nor to impose his criteria onto the community (which might refuse to comply), yet Torvalds retains control over the core Linux repository, which can only be updated by a (relatively large) number of trusted developers, to which Linus has delegated his powers. Everyone else needs to obtain authorization in order to submit a patch to the kernel (Malcolm, 2008). Likewise, in spite of its more decentralized structure, the Debian community relies on a highly formalized and meritocratic system of governance, whereby contributors have to fulfill a certain number of steps (laid out in a detailed policy document) before they can become formal "developers" (Malcolm, 2008). Yet, the community does not provide any internal indicator or value metrics to evaluate the contributions of community members. The reason for this might be that only a small proportion of FLOSS developers regard reputation as an important driver for motivation, whereas the majority of them actually reject reputation as a motivational factor for contribution (Ghosh, 2007).

To date, the most interesting evaluation system for individual contributions is the one elaborated by Stackoverflow, which combines a sophisticated reputation system (where users can gain or lose reputation based on the quality and popularity of their answers) with a set of badges to reward the most helpful users (Bosu et al., 2013). More specific to the context of software development, Ohloh.net is another evaluation system for estimating the value of different software projects and the contributions to these projects. Ohloh operates as an independent umbrella application, aggregating data from multiple FLOSS repositories (such as Github and Sourceforge). Its goal is to map the landscape of software development by means of both software metrics (such as lines of code and commit statistics) and social metrics, measuring developers' skills and productivity on the basis of quantitative metrics (e.g., number of contributions and commit statistics) or qualitative metrics (e.g., badges, mutual ratings, or "kudos"). While they are not formally connected to any specific project or community, Ohloh ratings are well recognized by a large number of institutions and communities and are often relied by individual developers in order to showcase their contributions to the overall software community. As such, while it does not implement a system of affordances or rewards, Ohloh nonetheless constitutes a useful tool for personal marketing, allowing software developers to understand (and to communicate) the value of their contributions in the context of a particular ecosystem. Yet, its applicability remains limited insofar as it is constrained to the realm of software development and that it does not properly take into account the whole plethora of contributions that cannot be objectively/subjectively quantified.

23.3.3 Competing value systems

The main difficulty derives from the fact that "value" is not primary and cannot, as such, be understood devoid of its context. In other words, value is subjective. Every individual and every community and every culture has its own idea of value, which can be interpreted in different ways by many different people, according to the contingencies at stake. Hence, the value generated by CBPP is not uniform; rather, it is the result of a complex system of interconnected value systems, each with their own value metrics.

In this regard, it is important to distinguish between the "transactional value" of commons-based resources and the "transcendental value" of the commons as a more inherent attribute or quality. The former is an extrinsic value, which can be determined by the traditional mechanisms of supply and demand, whereby people's willingness to pay for a particular resource indicates their perceived value for that resource. Hence, depending upon their individual preferences or characteristics, different people may assign a different value to a same commons-based resource. The latter type—the transcendental value—is intrinsic to the commons-based resource. It may be acknowledged (or appreciated) at different degrees by different individuals or group of individuals (according to their own value systems) but cannot be altered or modified without affecting the nature of the resource itself.

Another distinction to be made, in the context of CBPP, is between the utilitarian or social value (singular) of a particular resource and the ideological values (plural) underlying the production or use of that resource. Distinguishing between three competing value systems might help us achieve a better understanding of the overall value of CBPP:

1. *Functional value*, that is, what are the benefits that can be derived from the production or use of commons-based resources? This particular type of value—also known as technical or technological value—is, to a large extent, objectively quantifiable by looking at the overall utility that can be extracted from CBPP by society as a whole (von Hippel, 2007). Given that software is inherently functional, estimating the value of FLOSS is likely to be easier than estimating the value of other types of commons-based resources, such as music and poetry, whose value is ultimately

subjective. Large collaborative projects, such as Wikipedia or major FLOSS projects, generally assume an important function in society, and—while their functional value might be difficult to establish, to the extent that it cannot be translated in economic terms—a basic approximation thereof can be derived by looking at the value of other similar (commercial) projects on the market.

2. *Social value*, that is, what are the positive, emotionally satisfying experiences that result from the social interactions surrounding the collaborative production and/or use of commons-based resources? Users of and contributors to a commons-based resource participate actively in the CBPP ecosystem (Ostrom, 1990), from which they might gain a significant amount of social capital. For instance, developers working on FLOSS projects automatically become part of a larger community of individuals collaborating toward a common goal; Wikipedia contributors necessarily engage into a joint and collaborative process of edits and revisions, which turns them into an integral part of the Wikipedia community. Yet, as opposed to the former, this particular type of value—an emotional value—can only be qualitatively (and subjectively) assessed by looking at the social value emanating from the complex network of interpersonal relationships resulting from CBPP.

3. *Ideological values* (plural), that is, what are the underlying values that the CBPP community is trying to promote? These include not only abstract values, such as freedom or autonomy, cooperation, and sharing, but also more personal values such as individual enjoyment or political satisfaction and personal enhancement or self-actualization. As opposed to the former two types of value (which can be, to a certain extent, observed in the real world), the problem with this latter category of values is that, because of their transcendental character, they cannot be translated into economic terms nor can they be expressed—in either objective or subjective terms—into a quantifiable value. They represent "ethical" or "moral" principles or ideals related to a normatively structured worldview, whose fulfillment depends on people's ability to live well according to the horizons of the community at stake.

These different value systems are of a radically different nature and must therefore be analyzed and described by means of different indicators or value metrics (some of which might not be capable of producing an objective assessment nor a quantifiable result). Besides, even for those value systems, which can be effectively described by means of quantifiable value metrics, there subsists no guarantee that their respective values might actually be comparable with each other. Indeed, in some cases, assessing the value of CBPP according to one particular value system might actually reduce the value of another system—that is, the mere fact of assigning a functional or social value to a given commons-based resource might actually work at the expense of the underlying ideological values subtending it. For example, in the context of FLOSS, some people value the software functionalities and others value the underlying values of freedom and autonomy—yet, in a market economy, the monetized values usually win. Any system designed to provide an interface between competing value systems must, therefore, necessarily account for the possible tyranny of a group imposing its own set of values over the others.

23.4 COMPLEMENTARY CURRENCIES

Today, the most widely used currencies are issued by national governments. Yet, historically, a large number of "local currencies"—specific to a particular community—have been created and deployed by a variety of actors, including local banks, companies, communities, and individuals. Especially at times of economic hardship, when official currencies fell short, alternative (and complementary) currency models have been devised as an attempt to revive the economy. These currencies are not legal tender (i.e., they are not recognized by law as a method of payment that can be used to meet a financial obligation). And although there is no guarantee that a business (or a peer) will accept them in exchange for specific goods or services, many of them have been successful in reviving the economy of local communities.

There has been, for instance, a long history of self-depreciating currencies deployed in the context of local communities suffering from economic downturn. From the Bavarian "wära" to Alberta's velocity dollar and other Gesellian currencies, all demurrage-based currencies share a common characteristic: their value decrease over time, so as to discourage the accumulation of capital by making it unattractive for people to hoard money. The result is a more lively economy and a better distribution of capital among market players (Marchini, 2013).

Conversely, in countries whose official currencies were subject to really high inflation rates, complementary currencies have been regarded as an attractive solution to the need for citizens to store value, that is, through savings, without fear of losing all or most of their capital. In this regard, following the hyperinflationary period during the Argentinean great economic depression (from 1998 to 2002), more than 2000 local currencies were deployed in different areas of the country and employed as a mechanism for barter in a limited area (Place, 2010). Most of these, however, failed to find a way to remain sustainable in the long term (Gómez, 2009).

In Europe, we have witnessed, as well, the deployment of a large number of complementary currencies, aimed at empowering communities through the creation of parallel markets for the exchange of goods and services outside of traditional market economies (Seyfang, 2000). More than hundreds of local currencies have been deployed thus far in countries suffering from a damaged economy, such as in Spain, Greece, and Portugal (Blanc, 2011). While many of them were created in the early 2000s (before the financial crisis blew up), most of these currencies experienced a significant spike in popularity in the years following the crisis, mainly due to the greater need for money flow.

Today, on the Internet, we are witnessing the emergence of a new "complementary currency" movement, driven by a variety of online communities eager to create their own money. Multiple experiments were made during the 1990s and the early 2000s with the deployment of digital currencies such as E-gold and the Liberty Dollar. Yet, most of them were highly centralized and eventually failed because of instability, frauds, and scalability problems. A variety of virtual currencies also emerged in the context of online games (e.g., Second Life's Linden dollar) or social networks (e.g., Facebook's credits), but none of them actually manage to become widely adopted and recognized as an actual currency beyond their particular community.

For the remainder of this chapter, we will focus on cases, such as Bitcoin and other decentralized cryptocurrencies, whose potential threats and opportunities—when applied to the realm of CBPP—are yet to be fully explored.

23.4.1 Commons-based cryptocurrencies

Cryptocurrencies are digital currencies that rely on cryptographic algorithms to provide users with a secure medium of exchange: money creation and transactions are controlled by mathematical algorithms (the so-called mining) implemented within the underlying protocol. As opposed to other digital currencies (such as E-Gold or Linden dollars), which are issued by a central authority, most cryptocurrencies are based on distributed online architectures: they incorporate principles of cryptography directly into their protocol to establish a worldwide, highly secure payment system that does not rely on any government, company, or central bank, but rather on a decentralized network of peers that contribute, through mining, to achieve distributed autonomous consensus (DAC) as to the current state of the network.

Created in 2009 by pseudonymous author Satoshi Nakamoto, Bitcoin was the first cryptocurrency that eventually got traction in the real world. Today, Bitcoin is regarded as the "gold standard" of cryptocurrencies (Grinberg, 2012), but many other cryptocurrencies have been created since then, each with their own characteristics and peculiarities. Indeed, while Bitcoin is a scarcity-based cryptocurrency that merely mimics gold, it has spurred the deployment of a large number of derivative cryptocurrencies, some of which are specifically meant to promote sharing and cooperation among the members of a specific community.

Already a considerable number of such currencies have been deployed so far, yet most of them are still in their early stage of deployment, and it is difficult to say whether or not they will eventually take off. This section will illustrate the objectives and underlying technicalities of some of these cryptocurrencies, which implement a hybrid approach to value creation and distribution by merging the principles of CBPP with more conventional economic thinking. We will refer to these currencies as commons-based cryptocurrencies (CBCC), not because they are themselves commons-based resources (although some of them might be) but because they have been created with a view to support, promote, or incentivize CBPP.

Freicon is one of the first CBCC that was designed not only to create a more stable and sustainable economy but also to support commons-based projects. The cryptocurrency implements an approximately 5% annual demurrage fee, so as to encourage the circulation of money in the economy and discourage hoarding. Moreover, only 20% of the money created is assigned to the miners and the other 80% is assigned to the Freicon Foundation, which redistributes these funds over the most socially or ethically valuable community projects.

A clearer example of CBCC is CommunityCoin proposed by the Guifi community network. CommunityCoin is a cryptocurrency designed for network communities, which features a mechanism of rewards based on the contribution and participation of community members. This currency can, however, only be used for the internal community work-around: users contributing their resources to the network will be able to spend the CommunityCoins they receive in order to, e.g., buy a secondhand hardware from another community member. The goal is, ultimately, to incentivize the members to work for the community (installing new nodes, creating new services, etc.) and make the community network self-sustainable.

Finally, a few CBCC have managed to incorporate their own commons-based agenda directly within the mining protocol itself. This is the case, for instance, of Curecoin (whose mining protocol consists in protein folding computations) and Gridcoin (contributing to solving scientific problems to the Berkeley Open Infrastructure for Network Computing). The opportunities are endless, as cryptocurrencies can be designed to implement any sort of cryptographic protocols and money creation policies whatsoever.

23.4.2 Translating CBPP values into metrics

After having analyzed the possible dynamics or interactions that subsist between CBPP and CBCC, this section will investigate whether (and how) the latter can be used to translate the functional, social, and ideological values of the former into quantifiable terms. CBCC could, in fact, be used as a potential proxy to assess the value produced within a particular CBPP community or to compare the values of different CBPP platforms—thereby benefiting from a universal indicator of value without (necessarily) falling within the scope of conventional economic theories.

Before we begin, it is important to note that we are not trying to compare the value generated by CBPP with the market value of these cryptocurrencies. Market mechanisms are only interesting to us to the extent that they implement, at least in theory, some form of DAC. In modern society, the market represents a useful way to interface between competing values. Indeed, in a free and competitive market system—with no barriers to entry and no asymmetries of power—market players act independently and contribute, through their aggregate actions, to setting the overall market price. The mechanism of supply and demand is such that each and every market player is allowed to express their own voice as to what the value of different goods or services is, ultimately (and collaboratively) establishing the market price, without having to rely on any centralized authority or institution. These principles have been transposed from the market into the realm of the firm, with the deployment value economics tools, such as the Sensorica's open value network (OVN), allowing employees to vote in order to determine which job should have priority over the others and who should be paid more or less.

What we suggest here is to build upon these concepts, to create an alternative mechanism (separate from the market) that would instantiate the same DAC principles (but not the same market principles) within the CBPP ecosystem—so as to eventually come to a consensus as to the overall (systemic) value of commons-based resources.

23.4.2.1 Systemic value of CBPP

Let us imagine a world with a flourishing commons-based ecosystem that operates alongside the market economy. At the macro level, commons-based entities (be they individuals, communities, or institutions) interact with each other, on a daily basis, creating a complex network of interdependent relationships and interactions. We describe here a reputation-based value system—which each of these entities could potentially join—that will help us determine the overall systemic value of CBPP.

In order to be effective and to ensure that the system is a proper representation of the CBPP ecosystem, Sabir's relative determination of value requires careful control of its boundaries. The main issue is to ascertain which projects truly support the commons and which are merely open platforms on which value-producing sharing and collaboration may occur (in ways that may be monetizable). In order to address this issue, participation into the Sabir system is based on a network-of-trust model, where previously endorsed institutions can vouch for new institutions to join but only to the extent that these are also regarded by others as providing a valuable contribution to the commons (i.e., an institution needs to be endorsed by at least n institutions before it can join the system). Starting such a network would, of course, take serious care and caution, since the initial selection of players might have a significant impact on the subsequent population of the ecosystem.

Once the system has been populated, the value of each commons-based entity must be established and regularly updated by other entities in the system, according to their corresponding value (or weight) in the commons-based ecosystem as a whole. To measure (and compare) the weight of different CBPP platforms, we have devised an algorithm inspired simultaneously from

- Flattr, understood as a meter of individual appreciation that translates into donations,
- Google's PageRank, as a means to ponderate the importance of a Webpage based on its incoming links.

In this model, commons-based entities may designate others as being more or less valuable by assigning them some weight. The more weight an entity accumulates, the more socially valuable it will be considered (quantity matters). Yet, the value of every one of these weights will ultimately depend on the social value of the entity assigning them (quality matters).

As an algorithm, in its simplest form, we can implement it as follows:

- Every entity assigns a particular weight to the other entities in the system, whose sum must be equal to 1.
- For any given entity X, its social value (SV) at time t is expressed by the function $SV(X,t)$. $SV(W,t)$ indicates the total amount of weight (w) received by X from other entities in the system (A, B, C), ponderated by the SV of these entities:

$$SV(X, t + 1) = w(A, X) \times SV(A, t) + w(B, X) \times SV(B, t) + w(C, X) \times SV(C, t)$$

- More generally, the complete formula can be expressed as:

$$SV(X, t + 1) = \sum_{i \in U_x} w(i, X) \cdot SV(i, t),$$

$$\text{where } \forall i \in U_x, \left(\sum_{k \in V_i} w(i, k) \right) = 1 \text{ and } 0 \leq w(i, k) \leq 1$$

where U_x = the universe of all the entities assigning a weight to X and SV_x = the universe of all the entities that were assigned weight by X.

The result is a numeral, which describes the influence, or the weight that every CBPP entity has acquired in the commons-based ecosystem in which it operates, as perceived by the other actors of the same ecosystem.

23.4.2.2 Value of CBPP contributions

Once the systematic value of CBPP entities has been established (at the macro level), it becomes necessary to understand the value of CBPP contributions (at the micro level). We propose here a mechanism—akin to a karma system—that relies on the deployment of several CBCC issued by a variety of CBPP entities or communities and assigned to individual contributors as an expression of gratitude for the work they have done.

Whoever contributes to the commons is rewarded with a particular set of tokens from the CBPP entity or community they have contributed to. Each CBPP entity or community is free to decide on the number of tokens to produce and on the manner in which these tokens will be redistributed to their contributors, according to their own preferences or specific needs. Different CBPP communities will, therefore, issue different amounts of tokens (whose quantity might increase over time) and rely on different value systems and reward mechanisms based on their own internal metrics for gratitude or appreciation.

Individuals contributing to the commons will collect these tokens, which serve as a proxy for the value of their contribution (expressed by the amount of gratitude they received). Yet, every one of these tokens might have a different value (from both a global and an individual perspective): in order for people to compare the value of their contributions to different CBPP communities, the value of each token must be translated into a common denominator of value.

This common denominator (which we call Sabir—as a reference to "lingua franca") represents an interface between these different CBPP value systems. It translates individual contributions into a common numeric value, according to the following formula:

1 token issued by a CBPP platform = Systemic value of the CBPP platform/
Total number of tokens issued by the CBPP platform in Sabir value

This formula is useful for contributors not only to understand the value they have contributed to the commons (from a systemic view) but also to easily express this value to others, who might not be acquainted with the particular CBPP communities to which the contribution was made. Most importantly, given that Sabir is an open value system, not everyone has to rely on the standard value metrics. Certain people, institutions, or communities could (theoretically) assign weights to the entity, which are part of CBPP ecosystem according to their own specific value metrics (e.g., schools or universities could apply the "education" matrix—giving more importance to Wikipedia and Creative Commons—whereas a local restaurant might apply the "slow food" matrix, giving more weight to local farmers and producers).

As such, Sabir acts as a proxy for value in the commons-based ecosystem. Just like the price does in the market economy, Sabir allows for individual contributions to be assessed and compared according to a common denominator of value (which remains distinct from market value). While price is linked to a particular service or product of exchange, Sabir is an expression of the value that a particular individual contributed to the commons over a lifetime and should therefore remain linked to that individual over the whole lifetime (i.e., it is not transferable).

But Sabir also constitutes an interface (or a bridge) between the commons and the market economy, so that the two can benefit from each other, without one actually taking over the other. Indeed, to the extent that it introduces a quantifiable unit of value for commons-based contributions, Sabir makes it easier for market entities to understand the value that individuals contributed to the common good—and reward them accordingly, if they so wish. Commercial players that recognize the value of individuals' contribution to the commons might provide free and/or discounted goods or services to them, as a form of appreciation to their work. As a result, CBPP contributors operating outside of the market economy acquire the capacity to protect and reproduce their value creation, while also being able to interact with the market, without being subordinate or vulnerable to it (i.e., eliminating the need to implement any kind of business model for the community or themselves).

Sabir is also useful from a more commercial perspective, in that it enables market players to price discriminate between standard customers and CBPP contributors, potentially restricting their offers only to those people who contributed at least *x* Sabir to the commons. For instance, software companies might provide free licenses to some of their software to anyone who contributed more than 10 Sabirs to the FLOSS community, whereas an airplane company might provide a number of standby tickets for anyone who contributed over 100 Sabirs to the overall CBPP ecosystem (regardless of the CBPP community they contributed to).

23.5 CONCLUSION

The value of CBPP has been widely acknowledged over the past few years (Bauwens, 2005; Benkler, 2006; Cheal, 1988; Gold, 2004; etc.). Accounting for the value produced by different CBPP communities and determining the relative value of each contribution is a worthy endeavor, which is however difficult to achieve insofar as there are—to date—no proper tools capable of understanding the value of CBPP communities or quantifying the value generated by their community members.

The problem is mostly due to the complex system of values that CBPP entails. While the market is only concerned with the economic value of goods or services, understanding the value stemming from CBPP cannot be done without accounting for multiple value systems, which are not always compatible with one another: the functional value (i.e., the utility it brings to society), the social value (i.e., the social capital produced within the community), and the ideological values (i.e., freedom or autonomy—which cannot be measured nor quantified).

From an economic perspective, it is virtually impossible to set an equilibrium between these competing value systems. Sabir successfully bypasses the problem, by simply delegating the task to the community. Instead of trying to assess the value of CBPP according to these different value systems, the system relies on a decentralized system of tokens—implemented in the form of a CBCC—issued by a variety of CBPP entities or communities and distributed to anyone contributing to the commons according to the amount of gratitude triggered by their contributions. The value of each token is then determined by the weight of these entities, which is a function of their influence or value within the CBPP ecosystem as a whole, as perceived by the other actors in the system.

In this sense, the mechanism described in this chapter is, to some extent, quite similar to standard market mechanisms. In a market economy, the value of things is determined by their price (which is set by the law of supply and demand). In this proposed model, the value of people's contribution to the commons is determined by their Sabir (which depends on the amount of gratitude they each have received, ponderated with the weight of the CBPP institution issuing it). Hence, both mechanisms are fundamentally the same: There is no central authority responsible for setting the value of a resource; the value is established, indirectly, through a distributed consensus stemming from the actions of the market players (in the former case) or the contributors in the CBPP community (in the latter case).

The idea, however, is not to mimic the market, but rather to explore the potential of measuring contributions to the commons without commodifying or privatizing its wealth. In other words, if price constitutes the outcome of DAC in a market economy, then Sabir represents the outcome of DAC in a nonmarket ecosystem. Thus, traditional market mechanisms (supply and demand) and the mechanisms described in this chapter (weighted gratitude) are comparable only to the extent that they both represent a separate implementation of DAC, instantiated in a different ecosystem (market vs. nonmarket).

The main advantage of this model is that, by creating an interface between the commons and the market economy, Sabir allows for CBPP communities to benefit from some of the goods and services provided by the market, without necessarily having to interact (directly) with the market economy. Instead, individuals can choose whether to work for the market (earning money) or for the commons (earning Sabirs), without having to give up one for the other. As more and more market entities recognize the value of Sabir (and reward CBPP contributors accordingly), people will be able to spend more time doing what they love—contributing to the commons while also benefiting from some of the goods and services offered by the market economy. As a result, Sabir might actually encourage people to contribute to the commons in order to benefit from the advantageous deals provided by certain market entities to CBPP contributors.

Over time, a positive feedback loop will therefore be established, as market entities that support (or sponsor) the commons will gain reputation within the commons ecosystem. This might, ultimately, bring more and more market players (whether or not they are themselves CBPP contributors) to purchase their goods or services on the market, knowing that, by doing so, they are also helping the commons.

And yet, an important question remains. While it might be useful to rely on traditional market mechanisms to measure and compare the value of CBPP, measuring the value of CBPP within a nonmarket economy nonetheless raises an important question: can CBPP values (such as freedom, sharing, and cooperation) actually be translated into quantifiable terms, without incurring a loss?

As the fathers of neoclassical economy have put it, measurement is at the very center of how we look at the economy today (cf. Edgeworth, 1925; Fisher, 1950). But how can such measurement be transposed into a nonmarket commons-based ecosystem, and why?

Before engaging into such a complex endeavor, it might be worth considering the risks and/or challenges that might result from any attempt at quantifying values (such as emotional or ideological values) that are, at least theoretically, not quantifiable. In particular, one of the major challenges to be addressed is the effect of explicit rewards on the psychology and sociology of participation.

A lot of research has been done in this regard, most notably with regard to the practices of sharing endorsed by the hippie movement in the late 1960s (Crowe, 1969;

Howard, 1969; Levin and Spates, 1970) and the generalized gift economy at Burning Man (Chen, 2011; Kozinets, 2002; Sherry and Kozinets, 2007). Extensive literature has been made on the nonseparability of motivational vectors in the context of CBPP (Benkler, 2014), focusing specifically on the issues of intrinsic vs. extrinsic motivations (Bitzer et al., 2007; Lakhani and Wolf, 2005), money versus love (Folbre and Nelson, 2000; Kass, 1988), crowdsourcing (Brabham, 2010; Kaufmann et al., 2011), and so forth. After having thoroughly analyzed the question, Deci and Ryan (Deci and Ryan, 2010; Deci et al., 1999; Ryan and Deci, 2000a,b) suggested that all explicit and extrinsic rewards enjoy either a direct relationship with intrinsic rewards or—at least—a complex system of dependencies and effects. It is unclear, at the moment, whether the introduction of a system like Sabir, offering a formalized, personal (albeit nontransferable) indicator of value, is likely to increase or reinforce the motivations for people to contribute to the CBPP ecosystem or whether it might, on the contrary, disrupt that particular set of motivations, which have been established thus far.

REFERENCES

Amant, K.S., Still, B. (Eds.), 2007. Handbook of Research on Open Source Software: Technological, Economic, and Social Perspectives. IGI Global.

Arvidsson, A., 2012. General sentiment. How value and affect converge in the information economy. In: Lury, C., Atkins, L. (Eds.), Measure and Value. Sociological Review Monographs. Wiley, London, pp. 39–59.

Ashton, D., 2011. Awarding the self in Wikipedia: identity work and the disclosure of knowledge. First Monday 16 (1).

Bauwens, M., 2005. The political economy of peer production. CTheory. December, www.ctheory.net.

Beagle, D.R., Bailey, D.R., Tierney, B., 2006. The Information Commons Handbook. Neal-Schuman, Chicago.

Benkler, Y., 2002. Coase's Penguin, or, Linux and "The Nature of the Firm". Yale Law J. 112, 369–446.

Benkler, Y., 2006. The Wealth of Networks. How Social Production Transforms Markets and Freedom. Tale University Press, New Haven.

Benkler, Y., 2014. Peer production and cooperation. In: Bauer, J.M., Latzer, M. (Eds.), Handbook on the Economics of the Internet. Edward Elgar, Cheltenham and Northampton.

Benkler, Y., Shaw, A., Hill, B.M., 2014. Peer production: a modality of collective intelligence (working paper).

Bitzer, J., Schrettl, W., Schröder, P.J., 2007. Intrinsic motivation in open source software development. J. Comp. Econ. 35 (1), 160–169.

Blanc, J., 2011. Classifying 'CCs': community, complementary and local currencies' types and generations. Int. J. Community Curr. Res. 15, 4–10.

Bosu, A., Corley, C.S., Heaton, D., Chatterji, D., Carver, J.C., Kraft, N.A., 2013. Building reputation in stackoverflow: an empirical investigation. In: Proceedings of the 10th Working Conference on Mining Software Repositories. IEEE Press, pp. 89–92.

Botsman, R., Rogers, R., 2010. What's Mine Is Yours. Harper Business, New York.

Boyd, R., Richerson, P.J., 1989. The evolution of indirect reciprocity. Soc. Netw. 11 (3), 213–236.

Brabham, D.C., 2010. Moving the crowd at threadless: motivations for participation in a crowdsourcing application. Info. Commun. Soc. 13 (8), 1122–1145.

Cardenas, J.C., Ostrom, E., 2004. What do people bring into the game? Experiments in the field about cooperation in the commons. Agr. Syst. 82 (3), 307–326.

Castells, M., Caraca, J., Cardoso, G. (Eds.), 2012. Aftermath. The Cultures of the Economic Crisis. Oxford University Press, Oxford.

Cheal, D., 1988. The Gift Economy. Routledge, New York, pp. 1–19.

Chen, K.K., 2011. Lessons for creative cities from burning man: how organizations can sustain and disseminate a creative context. City Cult. Soc. 2 (2), 93–100.

Coleman, G., 2005. Three Ethical Moments in Debian. Available at: http://anthropology.usf.edu/cma/ssrn-id805287.pdf, accessed 23 December 2012.

Crowe, B.L., 1969. The Tragedy of the Commons Revisited. American Association for the Advancement of Science, Pennsylvania, US.

Deci, E.L., Ryan, R.M., 2010. Self-Determination. John Wiley & Sons, Inc., New York.

Deci, E.L., Koestner, R., Ryan, R.M., 1999. A meta-analytic review of experiments examining the effects of extrinsic rewards on intrinsic motivation. Psychol. Bull. 125 (6), 627.

Dietz, T., Ostrom, E., Stern, P.C., 2003. The struggle to govern the commons. Science 302 (5652), 1907–1912.

Edgeworth, F.Y., 1925. Papers Relating to Political Economy.

Fisher, A.G., 1950. Alternative techniques for promoting equality in a capitalist society. Am. Econ. Rev. 356–368.

Florida, R., 2002. The Rise of the Creative Class. Basic Books, New York.

Folbre, N., Nelson, J.A., 2000. For love or money—or both? J. Econ. Perspect. 14 (4), 123–140.

Frischmann, B.M., 2004. Economic theory of infrastructure and commons management. Minn. L. Rev. 89, 917.

Gansky, L., 2010. The Mesh: Why the Future of Business Is Sharing. Penguin, New York.

Ghosh, R.A., 2007. Economic Impact of Open Source Software on Innovation and the Competitiveness of the Information and Communication Technologies (ICT) Sector in the EU.

Gold, L., 2004. The Sharing Economy: Solidarity Networks Transforming Globalisation. Ashgate Publishing, Ltd, Surrey, UK.

Gómez, G., 2009. Argentina's Parallel Currency: The Economy of the Poor (No. 11). Pickering & Chatto Ltd, London, UK.

Grinberg, R., 2012. Bitcoin: an innovative alternative digital currency.

Hardin, G., 1968. The tragedy of the commons. Science 162 (3859), 1243–1248.

Hess, C., Ostrom, E. (Eds.), 2007. Understanding Knowledge as a Commons: From Theory to Practice. MIT Press, Cambridge, MA.

Howard, J.R., 1969. The flowering of the hippie movement. Ann. Am. Acad. Pol. Soc. Sci. 382 (1), 43–55.

Kass, L., 1988. Neither for love nor money: why doctors must not kill. Public Interest 94, 25–46.

Kaufmann, N., Schulze, T., Veit, D., 2011. More than fun and money. Worker motivation in crowdsourcing—a study on mechanical turk. In: AMCIS 2011 Proceedings.

Kelty, C.M., 2008. Two Bits. The Cultural Significance of Free Software and the Internet. Duke University Press, Durham, North Carolina.

Kozinets, R.V., 2002. Can consumers escape the market? Emancipatory illuminations from burning man. J. Consum. Res. 29 (1), 20–38.

Kranton, R., Kranton, R., 1996. Reciprocal exchange: a self-sustaining system. Am. Econ. Rev. 86 (4), 830–851.

Lakhani, K.R., Wolf, R.G., 2005. Why hackers do what they do: understanding motivation and effort in free/open source software projects. Persp. Free Open Source Softw. 1, 3–22.

Levin, J., Spates, J.L., 1970. Hippie values: an analysis of the underground press. Youth Soc. 2 (1), 59–73.

Lury, C., Atkins, L., 2012. Measure and value. Sociological Review Monographs, Wiley, London.

Malcolm, J.M., 2008. Multi-stakeholder public policy governance and its application to the Internet Governance Forum (Doctoral dissertation), Murdoch University.

Marchini, K., 2013. The curious case of the disappearing money: demurrage-based currencies in theory and practice. Economic Colloquium, Fall, 2013.

Marwick, A., Murgia-Diz, D., Palfrey, J., 2010. Youth, privacy and reputation: a literature review. Berkman Center Research Publication 2010-2015. Available at: http://papers.ssrn.com/sol3/papers.cfm?abstract_id=1588163, accessed 6 January 2013.

O'Neil, M., 2009. Cyber Chiefs. Autonomy and Authority in Online Tribes. Pluto Press, London.

Ostrom, E., 1990. Governing the Commons: The Evolution of Institutions for Collective Action. Cambridge University Press, UK.

Ostrom, E., Burger, J., Field, C.B., Norgaard, R.B., Policansky, D., 1999. Revisiting the commons: local lessons, global challenges. Science 284 (5412), 278–282.

Peck, J., 2005. Struggling with the creative class. Int. J. Urban Reg. Res. 29 (4), 740–770.

Place, C., 2010. Creative Monetary Valorization. SSRN working paper.

Rajala, R., Westerlund, M., Möller, K., 2012. Strategic flexibility in open innovation–designing business models for open source software. Eur. J. Mark. 46 (10), 1368–1388.

Ryan, R.M., Deci, E.L., 2000a. Intrinsic and extrinsic motivations: classic definitions and new directions. Contemp. Educ. Psychol. 25 (1), 54–67.

Ryan, R.M., Deci, E.L., 2000b. Self-determination theory and the facilitation of intrinsic motivation, social development, and well-being. Am. Psychol. 55 (1), 68.

Seppänen, M., Helander, N., Mäkinen, S., 2007. Business Models in Open Source Software Value Creation. Handbook of Research on Open Source Software: Technological, Economic, and Social Perspectives, p. 578.

Seyfang, G., 2000. The euro, the pound and the shell in our pockets: rationales for complementary currencies in a global economy. New Political Econ. 5 (2), 227–246.

Sherry, J.F., Kozinets, R.V., 2007. Comedy of the commons: nomadic spirituality and the burning man festival. Res. Consum. Behav. 11, 119–147.

Shiller, R.J., 2012. The Subprime Solution: How Today's Global Financial Crisis Happened, and What to Do About It. Princeton Academic Press, New Jersey, USA.

Shirky, C., 2010. Cognitive Surplus: Creativity and Generosity in a Connected Age. Penguin.

Von Hippel, E., 2004. Democratizing Innovation. MIT Press, Cambridge, MA.

Von Hippel, E., 2007. Horizontal innovation networks—by and for users. Ind. Corporate Change 16 (2), 293–315.

CHAPTER 24

The Confluence of Bitcoin and the Global Sharing Economy

Alyse Killeen
March Capital Partners, Santa Monica, California, USA

Contents

24.1 2008 STIMULUS

I've been working on a new electronic cash system that's fully peer-to-peer, with no trusted third party.

Satoshi Nakamoto, November 1, 2008, Saturday

Bitcoin The peer-to-peer network, also known as the blockchain network or blockchain protocol, that allows for the proof and transfer of ownership of digital currency without the verification of a trusted third party, but instead through the cryptographic verification provided by the network's miner nodes.

bitcoin The unit of digital currency that may be transmitted by the blockchain peer-to-peer network.

Note, in the text to follow the term Bitcoin is used to reference both the blockchain peer-to-peer network infrastructure alone, and to the blockchain peer-to-peer network along with the digital currency transacted upon it. The context will make clear the intention of the term Bitcoin when used, or a footnote will be added to facilitate disambiguation.

2008 was a dynamic year for cultural change both nationally and globally, as well as a historically significant year for computer science innovation as the distributed ledger system of the blockchain protocol was introduced. The transactional marketplace is quick to reflect both cultural change and relevant technology innovation, and in 2008, a confluence of events and changing sentiment radically impacted marketplace evolution.

Handbook of Digital Currency

Peer-to-peer transaction and infrastructure gained importance and a position of ever-increasing relevance to the marketplace. The distributed peer-to-peer network emerged.

Historically, a marketplace is an arena of competitive or commercial dealings; it is the world of trade and value exchange facilitated by currency. Through currency, value can be stored and represented so that the flexible exchange of value may occur where there would otherwise be a system of barter. For example, food supplies are paid for in currency rather than traded for coincidental labor or exchanged for a good. We do not exchange our own produced crafts for food supplies owned by the grocer; we exchange currency for our food, and this creates a flexible marketplace. At the most fundamental level, a marketplace is a meeting of resource supplier and resource procurer. As such, it is immediately responsive to change on either or both sides of that supplier-to-procurer exchange.

Change in the cultural zeitgeist spread broadly in 2008 as the economy rebuffed the trend of hyper consumption of both consumers and enterprises. At the same time, the Satoshi white paper "Bitcoin: A Peer-to-Peer Electronic Cash System (Nakamoto, 2008)" was quietly published to *The Cryptography Mailing list* at melzdowd.com. Three days later, on November 4th 2008, Barack Obama was elected to become the 44th President of the United States, and millions of people across the globe tuned in to view his historic acceptance speech. In an election largely centered upon the economy and 2008 recession, Obama earned 365 electoral votes to the 173 votes earned by John McCain. Exit polls showed that 62% of voters considered the economy to be the top issue of the election (CNN, 2008).

The 2008 presidential election occurred on the heels of 2008s global Great Recession, also referred to as the Second Great Depression. The recession was catalyzed by the U.S. subprime mortgage crisis that resulted from the decline in home prices, resulting mortgage delinquencies and foreclosures, and associated devaluation of housing-related securities. Subprime loans are those offered to borrowers at an interest rate above that charged to the most credit-worthy customers, as such borrowers have a higher likelihood of defaulting on debt repayment.

Increased subprime mortgage lending may be a symptom or cause of hyper consumption in the housing market. In 2003, 8% of total mortgage loans issued were subprime mortgage loans, and in 2005 and 2006 the rate reached 20% (Joint Center for Housing Studies of Harvard University, 2008). If subprime mortgage lending is a cause of nonpractical house purchase, then financial institutions increased loan incentives[1] to mortgage candidates in order to encourage candidates to take on higher risk mortgages

---

[1] Loan incentives incorporated into subprime mortgage contracts included interest-only debt repayment during an initial period, discounted interest rates that reset after an initial period, eased underwriting standards in loan attainment, low or no down-payment requirement, and no requirement of income documentation.

that the candidate likely expected could be quickly refinanced at manageable terms. As housing prices declined and mortgage interest rates rose, many subprime borrowers and housing speculators defaulted on debt repayments. Serious delinquencies skyrocketed in late 2006 through 2007 (Joint Center for Housing Studies of Harvard University, 2008). The demand for subprime mortgage backed securities halted (Joint Center for Housing Studies of Harvard University, 2008) and these securities, held widely by financial firms worldwide, lost most of their value. Credit markets constricted and the Great Recession was inexorable. As a result, at least in part, of mortgage lending decisions made by institutions and borrowing decisions made by individuals, the economy fell into crisis.

In 2008 in the United States, home foreclosure fear, unemployment fear, and job loss was widespread. Foreclosure filings surpassed 3 million; one in 54 homes received at least one foreclosure filing in 2008 (RealtyTrac, 2014). Unemployment rose from 5.0% to over 7.5% (Economic Research and Federal Reserve Bank of St. Louis, 2014) and Millennials, those between the age of 13 and 30 in 2008, were the hardest hit. Housing prices fell, the stock market tumbled, and the net worth of households and nonprofit organizations declined from over 65 trillion in January 2008 to less than 56 trillion in December (Economic Research and Federal Reserve Bank of St. Louis, 2014).

While people managed the anxiety associated with the conditions and uncertainty of the Great Recession, U.S. citizens were tasked to evaluate their beliefs and values, as it was a contentious election year. Presidential candidates Barack Obama and John McCain, and running mates Joe Biden and Sarah Palin, were polar opposite contenders. All voters, but especially campaign-targeted New Voters and Swing Voters (groups comprised in significant part by Millennials), had much to reflect on in the months preceding their vote. It was a time of heightened consciousness and active contemplation.

As a result, the 2008 global recession profoundly changed consumption, and a younger generation's thought on their own consumption. People began to define themselves more as Users and Makers, and less as Consumers. The preference to collaboratively share resources, set against the preference to singularly own those same resources, increased. Conscious consumption of resources was desirable, while conspicuous consumption was not. A widely reported presidential campaign gaffe centered upon this tension between the new modernity of consumer discretion and the antiquated nature of hyper consumption.

In an interview with Politico conducted on August 2008, presidential candidate John McCain said that he was uncertain of how many houses he owned in response to an exploratory question, "I think—I'll have my staff get to you." This inspired a Democrat campaign video titled *Seven*, for the number of houses McCain was immediately identified and then reported to own. Ownership and consumption for the sake of excess became symbolized by McCain's apparent inability to even recall the residences he owned. Although the culture of previous decades may have admired this casualness of riches, it was out of step with the evolving culture of 2008. An old economy was collapsing, a new economy was forming, and culture was responding.

Old guard subprime mortgage originator New Century Financial Corp filed for Chapter 11 bankruptcy (April 2007), followed by Bank of America acquiring Countrywide Financial in an all-stock deal (January 2008), The Federal Reserve Bank of New York providing $29 billion in financing to allow JPMorgan to buy Bear Sterns (March 2008), the U.S. government placing Fannie Mae and Freddie Mac into conservatorship (September 2008), and Lehman Brothers collapsing (September 2008), among other catastrophic events (Reuters, 2011). Concurrently, Sharing Economy collaborative marketplaces TaskRabbit and Airbnb emerged in February and August of 2008, respectively. Sharing Economy crowdfunding platform IndieGoGo officially launched in January 2008. With the crises of old guard centralized institutions providing the backdrop, the Internet-enabled Sharing Economy emerged. Similarly to the presidential campaigns, these sharing companies targeted Millennials. The Economy's, Democrat's, and sharing companies' message were consistent: hyper consumerism is old-fashioned and peer-to-peer collaboration is cool.

Peer-to-peer collaboration was so cool that it was leveraged and lauded for Barack Obama's successful 2008 fundraising campaign. The Obama campaign organization reported that over 80% of donations made were from small donors contributing less than $200. Both the fundraising message and the retrospective report of the process were framed as peer driven, rather than institutional. Obama became the crowdfunding candidate of 2008, and this collaborative fundraising process and campaign brand were successfully carried over to the 2012 presidential election cycle. In 2008, the popular Presidential vote split 53% for Barack Obama. Voters age 18-24 chose Obama 68% of the time versus McCain 30% of the time, and voters age 25-29 split 69% for Obama and 29% for McCain. In exit polling, first-time voters indicated an overwhelming preference for Obama over McCain, at a 72-27% split (CNN, 2008).

The early growth in Internet-enabled Sharing Economy companies continued in 2009, as popular peer-to-peer sharing companies Getaround, Uber, Rent The Runway, and Kickstarter launched.

24.2 CONFLUENCE OF BITCOIN AND THE GLOBAL SHARING ECONOMY

The connectivity that exists between nations and between socioeconomic groups was made evident by the cascading repercussions of the economy's collapse. In 2008, it was evident that people are connected to one another across groups and nations through their reliance upon centralized institutions. The connectivity between peers is the infrastructure of Bitcoin, the Sharing Economy, and ultimately, the Internet of Things. This peer connectivity empowers the disintermediation of centralized institutions in peer-to-peer relationships.

There exists a complementary nature between the three movements of (1) bitcoin, the cryptographic currency, and the decentralized ledger technology of the Bitcoin blockchain, (2) the Sharing Economy (i.e., the Efficiency Economy), the network of collaborative consumption and the network of collaborative creation, and (3) connected autonomous devices, commonly referenced as the Internet of Things or IoT. The technical infrastructure, underlying psychology of each network, and the cultural impetus are similar or shared by these three named movements. Their confluence by means of time and nature will drive the broad adoption of each of the three movements.

In July 2014, an estimated 5 million people use or own bitcoin, although 2.9 billion (Live Stats, 2014) people have Internet access, the resource necessary for simple bitcoin transaction or purchase.[2,3] The expansion of Bitcoin's user base from 5 million to several hundred million people and more will be driven in large part by Bitcoin innovation's application to the Sharing Economy, and Bitcoin's ability to merge Sharing Economy marketplace dynamics with IoT level resources.

24.3 SHARING ECONOMY

The Sharing Economy term, while broadly used, is most appropriately used to refer to collaboration that results in efficiency. The Sharing Economy is an Efficiency Economy. It is the network of collaborative consumption and/or collaborative creation. The term is inclusive of centralized marketplaces in which resources owned, managed, or aggregated by a third-party institution are shared by marketplace users in a manner that results in a higher rate of resource usage than would be expected of a sole user owned resource. The term is also inclusive of distributed systems, in which peer-to-peer transactions occur without the intermediation of a third-party institution. Peers are on both sides of the exchange in each instance.

In either form, collaborative consumption or creation is not Internet or World Wide Web dependent, but global Internet penetration allows the Sharing Economy to scale. With the World Wide Web accessible to facilitate inexpensive and borderless communication, peer-to-peer connection can occur across geographies, socioeconomic groups, and affinities, even when these groups or group members are otherwise unfamiliar with each other. As this communication is available, the primary limiting factors to Sharing

---

[2]In Q2 2014, upon a regional Internet-connected gateway, it is possible to transmit value via SMS from Internet access-less feature phone to Internet access-less feature phone; in this way, people may use or own bitcoin without their own owned or traditionally secured Internet access point (i.e., without securing use of a community shared physical Internet access point, such as that available in an Internet café or library).

[3]In Q2 2014, mesh-network shared Internet connection (i.e., multiple users sharing Internet access owned or secured by a single or multiple consumer suppliers, or gateways) is accessible through mobile application, which could greatly increase global Internet penetration. See Shalunov (2013).

Economy permeation are (1) resource characteristics, especially as they relate to ease of sharing, and (2) secure payment transmission.

24.4 RESOURCE OWNERSHIP VERSUS ACCESS

In the domain of the Sharing Economy, ownership of a resource is set against the ability to access (i.e., share) that same resource on a metered basis by need. For metered access to be traded, the resource utility must be discreetly defined and units of consumption must be measurable. Consequently, resource characteristics impact the ease of sharing and the network within which a resource may be shared. The centralized, technology-enabled Sharing Economy has made easily measurable resources accessible to peers who are co-located, and popular modern collaborative consumption has been aggregated around several marketplaces. Getaround for car sharing, LiquidSpace for office sharing, Lyft for car service sharing, and Airbnb for living quarters sharing, are well-known Sharing Economy marketplaces in the United States. These platforms have accustomed people to sharing cars, working space, and living space; these are common goods for sharing. It is reported that in 2014 in the United States, approximately 23% of the population has participated in the organized Sharing Economy, sharing common goods.

Getaround, LiquidSpace, Lyft, TaskRabbit, and Airbnb are examples of centralized sharing platforms for common goods and services whose utility may be understood, measured, accessed, and priced by common units: hours, days, time, or distance. The procurer can easily judge the quality of these resources and their ranked preference for these resources. Importantly, each resource's accessibility is made transparent to users through the public marketplace. Consider Lyft's in-app map visualization of available drivers (i.e., suppliers) in the procurer's local geography, or Airbnb's searchable marketplace and transparent calendar of availability tool. As a result, procurers may easily estimate the future accessibility of preferred resources. Ability to simply evaluate personal preference for a resource, as well as the future accessibility of that shared resource permits an individual to forgo resource ownership and choose resource access sharing.

Access sharing marketplaces may be centralized, such as the hub companies previously listed, or distributed peer-to-peer networks. In 2014, the latter form is rare, as the provision of (1) aggregated supply and/or demand, (2) customer relationship management tools, and (3) payment processing, is highly valuable to both suppliers and procurers. Because of the value of these (1–3) standard offerings of centralized Sharing Economy companies, users are willing to pay for use of the marketplace and associated tools.

Centralized sharing platforms take various forms, including marketplaces for aggregated peer-owned resources and marketplaces for hub company managed contract-based resources. Getaround, LiquidSpace, and Airbnb are examples of Sharing Economy companies whose marketplaces aggregate resources owned by individual suppliers to rent access to peer procurers. Differently, Lyft and TaskRabbit are examples of Sharing

Economy companies whose marketplace comprises managed contract-based resources that may be accessed by peer procurers. Although a third-party arbiter exists in each marketplace form, peers share resources in order to create a viable market of what would otherwise be dormant resources.

Here, a resource is available to be accessed by unit that, in the absence of aggregated demand, would need to be wholly owned by each individual if access to the resource was required or preferred. In the centralized Sharing Economy, community need is aggregated in such a manner that consumption of a resource may be made more efficient through sharing. The total quantity of wholly owned resources needed to fulfill the community's demand is reduced through sharing, and the average utilization of each resource is increased.

24.5 MENTAL ACCOUNTING

In marketplaces in which a centralized intermediary (e.g., Getaround, LiquidSpace, Airbnb) aggregates resources owned by marketplace users to be rented to marketplace users, peers are on both sides of the transaction: resource supplier and procurer. The same is true of distributed peer-to-peer networks. Market pricing drives both marketplace types. Essential to the function of market pricing is that both sides of a transaction must be able to mentally plot resource price to the value obtained or rendered, so that parties to the transaction can adjust behavior according to price (Szabo, 1996). This is also true in merchant-to-consumer transactions. Ultimately, the lower bound of transaction price is established by technological transaction costs and mental transaction costs, also referred to as mental accounting costs.

Nick Szabo describes mental accounting cost as a barrier to micropayments (Szabo, 1996). It is a "cognitive bottleneck" that must be surpassed if the benefits of low technological transaction costs are to be captured. The ability to account for price, value, and preference for resources is necessary in a transaction for both sides of the transaction, the supplier and the procurer, and this cognitive burden is the mental accounting cost of the transaction.

The market pricing of metered access to a Sharing Economy resource must uniquely allow the procurer to estimate and plot the price for the quantity of access that is needed, to the value obtained from that access. The more discreet the unit of meter, the more difficult to account for the number of units of resource access that is needed. But the larger the unit of meter, the more likely that the procurer pays for some amount of access that the procurer doesn't need; inefficiency results. The balance between inefficiency and the mental hurdle of accounting must be struck with the goal in mind that resource pricing drives marketplace activity; it catalyzes or stymies activity.

The Airbnb marketplace provides supplier-users' rooms or living quarters for rent, metered by day. In this way, 24 h of use (i.e., demand) of the space is priced at the same rate as 6 h of demand of the space, and pricing is fully transparent. The minimum unit of purchase is one day's time, regardless of the smaller meter units of hours that are needed by the procurer. The benefit of this pricing system is the ease of which a procurer and supplier may mentally account for the exchange. The drawback is the inefficiency of the overcharge of the procurer, who pays for access that is not needed, and the fallow time of the asset in the period that it remains unused.

Would the allowance of living space rental by the hour, so that a weekend trip could be booked for 36 h rather than 2 days, for example, increase or decrease the average usage rate of marketplace resources? How would this impact marketplace supply and demand? These are the question types that marketplace managers must consider when defining the unit of resource access to be priced and offered on the market.

The 2014 marketplace for Lyft competitor Uber, offers on-demand car service in a more obfuscated pricing schema (in a similar pricing schema as is proposed by Lyft). In 2014, Uber pricing is the sum of a base fee plus price per minute or per mile and a "surge" multiple. Procurers pay for precisely the resource access they consume, along several variables of measure. First, and easiest to mentally account for, procurers pay for the connection to the resource provider; this is the base fee. Second, procurers pay for the minutes of time travelled, or the miles travelled, or a combination of both; this is discreetly metered access. Third, a surge multiple is applied or not to compensate for dynamic marketplace supply and demand characteristics, thus decreeing that units of access are not fungible.

In the instance that event, holiday, weather, or other circumstance may have or may be imagined to have such impact as to result in an decreased supply to demand ratio, a surge multiple is applied to the market price. This may rationally be considered a manner of metering the percentage share of supply accessed (e.g., distinguishing between access to 0.05% of the supply and 0.10% of the supply). The benefit of this pricing system is the efficiency at which resource access is allocated to optimize for supply and demand dynamics; the procurer pays for precisely what is accessed. However, such pricing dynamics create a significantly greater mental accounting challenge, and Uber user-procurers have repeatedly expressed distress (Kovach, 2014).

While the procurer must be able to plot price to value and mentally account for the price of access, suppliers of the resource must be able to do the same; resource suppliers must be able to measure the value received in return for availing access. The mental accounting hurdle of transacting has been a barrier to the type of resource transacted in the Sharing Economy for this reason. We do not seek efficiencies when "they're not worth the brain cycles (Szabo, 1996)."

Mental accounting cost, also known as mental transaction cost, is a critical category of transaction cost for the growing Sharing Economy. The value assigned to resource units of access must incentivize both procurers and suppliers to participate in peer-to-peer transactions. For procurers, the market price of access allows personal budget to be plotted against personal values (Szabo, 1996), including resource needs and desires.

This mental plotting process requires the comparison of the procurement price of a resource to its personal value (Szabo, 1996) to both sides of the transaction. The supplier must judge if the market price (i.e., compensation or reward) for the resource rental is worth the temporary loss of access to the resource. The procurer must judge if the market price and loss of budget is worth access to the resource. Most importantly, the effort required to make these judgments must be minimal; the judgment process must be sufficiently intuitive.

It is the mental transaction costs that set the lower bound for price granularity, and thus the lower bound for resource metering unit. It is easier to account for the cost of a kilometer than the cost of 100,000 cm. Because mental accounting costs may ultimately prohibit an exchange, pricing for metered access may best be bundled or simplified (Szabo, 1996). Visual metaphors of the exchange presented by the user interface may also be used to lower mental transaction costs (Szabo, 1996).

In addition to mental transaction costs, payments also incur technological transaction costs. The technological costs of the traditional payment system are high enough to make micropayments illogical. This is because the technological cost is assumed as a transaction fee and the percentage of the total price that the transaction fee represents impacts a user's decision to transact. The user generally expects that a transaction fee will be a low percentage of the total fee, regardless of the size of the transaction. Technological costs must be significantly lower than the cost to access the resource.

The digital currency bitcoin and the protocol of the Bitcoin blockchain technologically enable micropayments, thus allowing the metering of access of smaller units. The technological cost of a transaction processed on the Blockchain is relatively very low and is based on the volume of data transmitted rather than on the value transmitted. This differentiates Bitcoin payment from payments made through the traditional financial system. Now that micropayments are technically possible, mental accounting costs are the primary barrier to microtransactions. A user interface and purchase decision automation or simplification through the user interface, will reduce mental accounting costs allowing for the advantage of low technological costs to be made useful to the sharing market.

24.6 BITCOIN

Bitcoin is the ability to securely transact to transfer value without intermediaries and is valuable in contexts in which distribution of influence in preferred or valuable against centralized influence.

Digital currency is not a new phenomenon, but bitcoin is differentiated from earlier digital currencies by the blockchain's ability to prevent the double spend of digital currency without reliance upon a centralized third party. The bitcoin currency's transactional ledger is kept by a distributed network, rather than balanced by a central institution. The blockchain protocol is a trust-not-needed infrastructure upon which people may transact to exchange value. Without the need to consider the trustworthiness of a central institution or the trustworthiness of the owner-sender of the currency, transactions may occur between unfamiliar actors, including both people and connected autonomous devices. Consumers may be on both sides of a transaction, and connected devices may be on both sides of a transaction. Consumers may transact with merchants or with connected devices, and devices may do the same. The global Internet-enabled marketplace opens up as the challenge of trust is removed.

In the twenty-first century, driven by rising Internet penetration and the associated ability to communicate instantly without the constraint of geography, a global village and marketplace began to take form. In July 2014, total global population penetration of the Internet reached 41% (Census Information, 2014; Live Stats, 2014) with annual Internet growth expected to be approximately 9%, driven by emerging markets (Meeker, 2014). Although the world has been wired to connect and communicate, the infrastructure to broadly transact and transmit value has been limited. Bitcoin wires this connected global village to transact, and to share value.

Prior to the introduction of bitcoin, and without access to the blockchain, traditional financial institutions gate access to the global Internet economy. These institutions are generally very difficult to disintermediate. Further, consumers (i.e., resource procurers) relying upon the financial institution as a third-party arbiter to transactions, expect for the institution to insure their position in transactions. The merchant (i.e., resource supplier) is less protected, or unprotected in the same transaction. On a peer-to-peer level, the same dynamic between procurer and supplier exists when an Internet transaction is facilitated by the traditional financial system. When the third-party institution assumes the responsibility of consumer insurance, that institution is incented to broadly restrict access on both sides of the transaction in order to reduce their financial risk. The result is such that suppliers of a resource may not be permitted to accept purchase of that resource from certain interested groups. The global economy is circumscribed.

One group without clear access to online commerce is the unbanked (i.e., adults that do not have access to a bank account). There are 2.5 billion unbanked adults globally (Chaia et al., 2010). This includes 2.2 billion unbanked people in Africa, Asia, Latin America, and the Middle East (Chaia et al., 2010), and 103 million unbanked people in the United States. One-third of the U.S. population exists without access to an individually controlled bank account (Ashoka, 2013). Beyond the evident social, ethical, and cultural implications, the global ecommerce economy and the Sharing Economy are crippled by the lack of access to one-third of the world's population. Such mass exclusion from the global village marketplace will become intolerable as the level of resources that can be shared becomes more discreet, mental accounting costs are lowered through better user interface, and sharing becomes more easily automated.

The Sharing Economy often has a more restrictive standard than the traditional financial system imposes. Sharing Economy marketplaces commonly use social media platforms as a measure of reputation, and reputation is used as a proxy to transactional trustworthiness. A person without the required social media account is not permitted access to the centralized sharing marketplace that requires it. And so, not only must a person have access to traditional banking and be deemed low risk by the transaction-relevant banks, they must also have a Facebook account (or the designated social account(s) permitted by the particular Sharing Economy company) to participate in the Internet-enabled Sharing Economy. 2014s most dominant social platform, Facebook, has 1 billion active users (New Age Media, 2014). Over 6 billion people do not use Facebook. This includes the currently, or previously, domestic-government-banned national populations of Iran, China, Cuba, North Korea, Bangladesh, Egypt, Syria, Mauritius, Pakistan, and Vietnam (Kirkland, 2014).

Regardless of whether one or several social platforms gate the Internet Sharing Economy, the ownership of a profile(s) on a popular platform is an inadequate proxy for transaction trustworthiness. Demographics unrelated to transactional trustworthiness are indeed related to social platform community membership. Most importantly, in defining rules of access to the global village Sharing Economy, discreet person-by-person evaluation is necessary, and group affiliation is too indiscriminate. More rationally inclusive transaction access is critically important to the Sharing Economy.

Bitcoin opens the global marketplace to more inclusive participation in many ways, and the distributed network kept ledger and irreversibility of transactions are two key properties.

First, when the transactional ledger is taken out of the purview of the trusted central institutions (e.g., JP Morgan Chase & Co., Bank of America, Wells Fargo, Citigroup, PNC Financial Services Group, etc.) and is distributed among many network nodes, the central institutions lose the ability to gate access. The central institution(s) also loses the ability to be used as a point of attack for others seeking to impose a gate to the network for regulatory purposes or otherwise.

The distributed blockchain protocol network as designed by Satoshi does not discriminate against participants. However, if a portion of the mining nodes that compose this network work together, they may effectively discriminate against participants. This may be either in contradiction of their interests as mining nodes or in their own interests. Such an organized effort can be the result of (1) mining node collusion or (2) the organizational efforts of a third-party unbeknownst to the involved nodes. Miners may be incented to not process transactions from certain points of origination. Dangerously, as the network of nodes grows, or those involved in an organized effort of exclusion grows, each involved miner may feel less responsible for the outcome of the organized behavior; behavior becomes less ethical as miners are able to cognitively distance themselves from produced outcomes.

The distributed nature of the network, and the long tail mining node network participants, are vital to maintain the nondiscriminatory inclusion of transactional participants.

Satoshi references the role of the network long tail on November 3, 2008, and Hal Finney reinforces the value to explain his interest in Bitcoin on November 8, 2008:

I like the idea of basing security on the assumption that the CPU power of honest participants outweighs that of the attacker. It is a very modern notion that exploits the power of the long tail. When Wikipedia started I never thought it would work, but it has proven to be a great success for some of the same reasons.

Hal Finney

Later reciting the long tail as a key characteristic to explain the protocol's value on November 13, 2008:

The long tail of node operators is sufficiently large that no small collection of nodes can control more than a small fraction of overall resources. (Here, the "tail" refers to a ranking based on amount of resources controlled by each operator.)

Hal Finney

In this distributed blockchain network, protected by the network of nodes' long tail, the traditionally unbanked can participate in the global Internet economy.

Further, because transactions are not reversible once committed and confirmed, a resource supplier in the Sharing Economy or a merchant in the ecommerce economy may confidently transact without regard to the risk of the procurer or consumer. Suppliers may share and receive compensation for sharing from procurers without assuming the financial risk of chargebacks.

24.7 DISTRIBUTED NETWORK

The distributed network is both (1) resistant to and (2) resilient against attack. First, as Paul Baran purported in his 1962 On Distributed Communications Networks paper, the distributed network is resilient against attack and will continue to perform even after a portion of nodes are rendered unable to contribute to the network following an attack. This differs from the centralized system, which may be destroyed if the central node is attacked. Baran's work was foundational to the development of the Internet. Among other contributions, Baran argued that the distributed network format was valuable relative to the centralized format as the distributed network was resilient.

The decentralized network illustrated by the center image in Figure 24.1 is a blend of the centralized and distributed systems. In this type of network the attack of a small number of nodes can destroy or devalue the system (Baran, 1962). Further, as the relative size of central hub nodes changes (as defined by number of links to the hub), the number of nodes that must be attacked to destroy the network changes; it may increase or decrease. A decentralized network may be destroyed or rendered vulnerable by the attack of a single node if that single node links to a majority or large share of the decentralized network's nodes. In Satoshi's white paper "Bitcoin: A Peer-to-Peer Electronic Cash

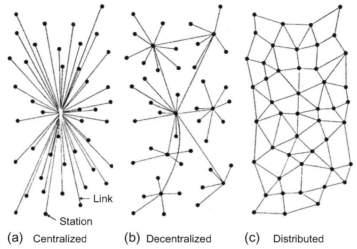

(a) Centralized   (b) Decentralized   (c) Distributed

Figure 24.1 The image included in Paul Baran's On Distributed Communications Networks (1962) illustrates the two basic systems of data transmission networks: centralized and distributed, also known as grid or mesh (Baran, 1962).

System (Nakamoto, 2008)" decentralization is not once referenced. The blockchain mining network is designed and referenced by Satoshi at distributed. It is not designed or referenced as decentralized.

Paul Baran discussed network system and attack in terms of physical attack, and specifically in terms of the physical attack threat associated with combat between nations. However, Baran's argument is relevant to a broad definition of attack, including the attack form of network corruption, third-party influence, taxation, co-option, and data siphoning.

Additionally, while the Figure 24.1 image was created to reference data transmission networks leveraged for communication, it translates well to reference data transmission networks leveraged for financial transactions. Figure 24.1 may also be used to visualize the marketplace network dynamics of the Sharing Economy.

24.8 TOKEN LIFECYCLE

Token, Oxford Dictionary A thing serving as a visible or tangible representation of a fact, quality, feeling, etc.; a voucher that can be exchanged for goods or services, typically one given as a gift or offered as part of a promotional offer.

Within this text, reference to bitcoin as a token is meant to reference bitcoin's function to incentivize and facilitate certain system behaviors; fiat currency, reward points, etc., may all be used to do the same.

To catalyze Sharing Economy activity and participation, shared resource access may be represented by a token. In this application, a lifecycle of the token emerges as

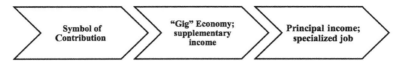

Figure 24.2 The resource token begins as a Symbol of Contribution to the resource network, may evolve to be a source of supplementary income for the resource supplier, creating a Gig Economy, and may finally evolve to be a source of principal income. At this final stage, the provision of the tokenized resource is a specialized job. Software development decisions impel each progressive lifecycle stage.

illustrated in Figure 24.2. The resource token begins as a Symbol of Contribution to the resource network. It may next evolve to be a source of supplementary income for the resource supplier, creating a Gig Economy. At the next stage, it may evolve to be a source of principal income, making the provision of the tokenized resource a new specialized job. Each progressive lifecycle stage following the token as a Symbol of Contribution stage is an optional stage impelled by software development decisions.

Bitcoin the digital currency originated as a token representing the compute power applied to the blockchain mining network; bitcoin was born as a token of stored compute power that incentivized the collaborative creation of the mining network. The ability to represent and store labor and contribution as a token or currency allows for the flexible trading of labor. The value created by an individual can be tracked and used by that individual to obtain resources flexibly at their convenience.

The bitcoin token has differentially incentivized behavior based on mining network maturity. The Sharing Economy is invigorated by bitcoin innovation in part due to Satoshi's introduction of digital tokens that function as an evolving representation of stored value based on the lifecycle stage of the network.

Digital tokens like bitcoin are either network or marketplace agnostic, or network or marketplace specific, and this distinction impacts the token's role in the network and its role as a catalyst to behavior. Network agnostic currency or token, like bitcoin, can be used across purposes and platforms. Network-specific currency can be used only within the network it was earned, or if transferrable, can be traded on an exchange and thus indirectly applied outside of the network. If token ownership may be transferred, the token can represent stored labor of any form, just as fiat currency may represent stored labor of any form.

Token lifecycle of bitcoin:

At first, most users would run network nodes, but as the network grows beyond a certain point, it would be left more and more to specialists with server farms of specialized hardware.

Satoshi Nakamoto, November 2, 2008, Sunday

At first release and operation of the blockchain open source software and protocol, the bitcoin token was a Symbol of Contribution; at this stage bitcoin's utility as a currency was insignificant. Instead, bitcoin functioned as a token that effectively symbolized a miner's contribution to the blockchain network. When a whole single unit of bitcoin was equivalent in monetary value to a few cents USD, the bitcoin token did not function to motivate a Gig Economy, but functioned merely to track participant and community behavior (e.g., an individual's increasing or decreasing relative effort, and individual's relative time spent contributing to the network, relative power resource contributed, etc.). Bitcoin was a method of gamifying[4] the blockchain mining node network. It was a powerful tool of behavioral incentivization, catalyzing the early growth of the network.

Hal Finney referenced early mining node incentivization in the late 2008 forum posts in dialogue with Satoshi, "[If] the bitcoin system turns out to be socially useful and valuable, so that node operators feel that they are making a beneficial contribution to the world by their efforts ... In this case it seems to me that simple altruism can suffice to keep the network running properly." If a behavior is either (1) altruistic and aligned with a participant's value system or (2) a form of entertainment, it can be incentivized through the tokenization of contributed resource or effort.

Effective incentivization increases or sustains emergent behavior. Prior to bitcoin gaining significant purchasing power and utility as a currency, bitcoin tracked a miner's contribution and this psychologically motivated the network. Miners that began to compete to process blocks because the process intrigued or entertained them, or because the core values of the system resonated with them, were more likely to continue mining because their contribution was tokenized; their contribution was tracked. Several block reward characteristics made this possible.

First, on average, the bitcoin block reward received by an individual miner over a time period is based on the percentage share of total network power that a miner contributes to the network during that period. Therefore, by representing compute power as bitcoin token, early miners were able to assess concretely the community's progress and their relative standing in the community through the bitcoin award process and schedule. This is prototypical gamification: progress or accomplishment tracking through predictable and concrete reward.

Second, in early mining the average reward over time was predictable rather than random. While the timing of the reward and an individual's own reward was and is still based on chance, the distribution of reward has always been logical and unbiased. Participating in the early mining network, miners could expect to have their work recognized and rewarded.

---

[4]Gamification, Oxford Dictionary def., the application of typical elements of game playing (e.g., point scoring, competition with others, rules of play) to other areas of activity, typically as an online marketing technique to encourage engagement with a product or service.

Once a market to exchange the bitcoin token for other currencies emerged, and bitcoin gained greater value against fiat, the token moved from the Symbol of Contribution stage to the Gig Economy stage. In this stage of the token lifecycle, the accumulation of tokens does more than symbolize contribution, it also generates a supplementary income stream. Here, miners in the Bitcoin network derive ancillary income from their contribution to the network. Sharing Economy networks commonly build their marketplace by aggregating resources from suppliers that will derive only secondary or supplementary income from the sale of access to their contributed resource. Consider the 2014 Getaround and Airbnb marketplaces; the vast majority of resource suppliers to these marketplaces earn revenue that is secondary to their primary source of income.

The Gig Economy is a key element of the Sharing Economy. The term Gig Economy refers to a network or marketplace fueled by the generation of alternative micro or supplementary streams of income, each of which would not sustain the individual singly. Often this form of income is created through the sharing or renting of an individual's owned resources; this is the Sharing Economy.

In the early twenty-first century, the Gig Economy is generally dependent upon institutionally operated marketplaces such as Getaround, LiquidSpace, Lyft, TaskRabbit, and Airbnb. These marketplace examples are all centralized. Distributed network marketplaces within which people may share and transact without dependency upon intermediation or institutionally controlled structure are also possible and present (Economic Research and Federal Reserve Bank of St. Louis, 2014).[5] For instance, earlier methods of mining the blockchain that relied upon the application of dormant CPU or GPU compute power are an example of a distributed Gig Economy market. Once bitcoin gained a level of relative value against fiat currency, and thus block reward could be considered supplemental income, contributing the resource asset of compute power from currently owned hardware, or acquiring a single or a few new devices to mine in the background, could be considered a "Gig."

Finally, as the market value of the token rises, the provision of the resource in exchange for the token can become a principal, specialized job. Satoshi predicted this evolution in Bitcoin mining. As the market value of bitcoin grew, specialized machines were developed and promoted for the mining of bitcoin, and CPU or GPU power could no longer compete. A new type of miner emerged, and mining pools that centralize power formed.

---

[5]The concept of distributed networks is critical to Bitcoin. The existence of institutional competition, and thus optionality through decentralization, is not akin to the existence of peer-to-peer distributed networks; market competition and decentralization are not synonymous to distributed network. A distributed market is one that exists independent of the control or intermediation of one or many institutions. If an organization may impart disproportionate advantage to its members, the system in which it participates is centralized.

24.9 DEVICE LEVEL RESOURCES

The Internet of Things is the connection of the Internet to the physical world through ubiquitous sensors. It is the network of connected autonomous devices. Empowered by Bitcoin, the Sharing Economy and the Internet of Things converge.

In 2014, shared resources may be divided into the categories of common and uncommon resources. Common resources are those that Millennials and others are culturally accustomed to sharing, such as living space, office space, automobiles, and time. Marketplaces now exist to support the exchange of many common resources. Uncommon resources are sharable resources for which no popular exchange practice now exists; people are unaccustomed to sharing such resources.

The development and application of bitcoin the currency to the blockchain mining process is a first example of the tokenization of a shareable uncommon resource—the resource of compute power. The value of dormant resources is unlocked through sharing, opening up opportunities for greater efficiency in the global economy.

For uncommon resources, and especially those that are of minimal exchange value in fiat currency when contribution is tracked by the popular Sharing Economy units of hours or days, the ability to represent the portion of the resource shared in fiat currency is likely not incentivizing to resource owners; it will not drive sharing. Using a network-specific token to represent the shared unit of uncommon resources will catalyze the sharing of many more dormant resources, including data storage space, bandwidth, and energy generation. Alternatively, the low cost of bitcoin transmission and divisibility of the digital currency unit also allow it to be applied as a currency token for the exchange of uncommon resources.

Another option for token application to a Sharing Economy network exists. If token ownership may not be transferred, a token may be used to represent resource contribution at time X that may be used to obtain that same resource in the same quantity at an undefined time in the future. In such a system, greatest stability is assured in the absence of inflation.

The impact of tokenizing a resource is significant; the price of resource access is now knowable. A market-driven price for resource access facilitates a consumer's ability to plan for the allocation of wealth for future needs or priorities. If the token remains within the network because ownership may not be transferred, a user can plan for how sharing extra owned (or controlled) resources now will allow them to access extra resource in the future, matching planned need with known capacity.

Ownership today is largely motivated by the need for reliable, on-demand access to a resource. This is particularly true for device level resources. The dependable understanding of obstacles to, or price of access, makes ownership less necessary.

The first condition of successfully tokenizing a resource is to compensate each resource supplier in proportion of their contribution to the total aggregate contribution of all suppliers. This allows for the accurate assessment of the resource supply. Resource supply and cost may be projected by the consumer, and in this manner consistent access can be achieved without ownership and instead through sharing.

The tokenization, or digital currency pricing of a resource, provides people consistent access to the resource without ownership and is the foundation for a broader and deeper Sharing Economy. Device level resources may be shared. Connected devices now communicate to exchange data, and relying upon bitcoin and the blockchain, will transact to exchange value. Devices may assign value to the data or resources exchanged so that shared information or other device level resources will be a source of Gig Economy revenue.

Things may transact on the blockchain under several conditions. The device or thing must have a unique identity, must be able to communicate with other things, and must have some form of sensory ability. Initially and perhaps indefinitely, the things must be able to respond to the dynamic rule set imposed or implied by its owner.

The parameters of speed and cost are central. The parameter of speed refers to the average time required for the blockchain or similar distributed system to process the transaction. The parameter of cost refers to the fee imposed by the network to process the transaction. For metered device level resources of low per unit value, quick transaction processing and low cost per transaction is paramount. The transaction fee must be low in terms of percentage of total transaction value.

Culture is moving away from dependence and preference for asset ownership, and away from the use of ownership to define self-identity. Concurrently, the need to own a resource in order to be able to count on resource access is eroding. The existence of a distributed ledger for peer-to-peer transaction processing and (depending on resource conditions) the tokenization of shared resources is the mainstay to the Sharing Economy movement.

REFERENCES

Ashoka, 2013. Banking The Unbanked: A How To. http://www.forbes.com/sites/ashoka/2013/06/14/banking-the-unbanked-a-how-to/.

Baran, P., 1962. On Distributed Communications Networks.

Census Information, 2014. U.S. and World Population Clock. http://www.census.gov/popclock/ (last accessed July 2014).

Chaia, A., Goland, T., Schiff, R., 2010. Counting the World's Unbanked. http://www.mckinsey.com/insights/financial_services/counting_the_worlds_unbanked (last accessed July 2014).

CNN, 2008. Exit Polls: Obama Wins Big Among Young, Minority Voters. http://www.cnn.com/2008/POLITICS/11/04/exit.polls/ (last accessed July 2014).

Economic Research, Federal Reserve Bank of St. Louis, 2014. Federal Reserve Economic Data. http://www.research.stlouisfed.org (last accessed July 2014).

Internet Live Stats. 2014. http://www.internetlivestats.com/internet-users/ (last accessed July 2014).

Joint Center for Housing Studies of Harvard University, 2008. The State of the Nation's Housing 2008. http://www.jchs.harvard.edu/research/publications/state-nations-housing-2008 (last accessed July 2014).

Kirkland, A., 2014. 10 Countries Where Facebook has been Banned. http://www.indexoncensorship.org/2014/02/10-countries-facebook-banned/ (last accessed July 2014).

Kovach, S., 2014. Uber Did Its Best to Warn you About New Year's Eve Surge Pricing, but Everyone Complained Anyway. http://www.businessinsider.com/uber-new-years-eve-surge-pricing-2014-1 (last accessed July 2014).

Leverage New Age Media, 2014. Social Media Comparison Infographic. https://leveragenewagemedia.com/blog/social-media-infographic/(last accessed July 2014).

Meeker, M., 2014. Internet Trends 2014. http://www.kpcb.com/internet-trends (last accessed July 2014).

Nakamoto, S., 2008. Bitcoin: A Peer-to-Peer Electronic Cash System. https://bitcoin.org/bitcoin.pdf (last accessed July 2014).

RealtyTrac. http://www.realtytrac.com (last accessed July 2014).

Reuters, 2011. Timeline: Most Impactful Events of the Financial Crisis. http://www.reuters.com/article/2011/03/31/us-usa-fed-lending-timeline-idUSTRE72U4E720110331(last accessed July 2014).

Shalunov, S., 2013. Multi-hop Wi-Fi Offload. https://opengarden.com/Multi-hop_Wi-Fi_Offload.pdf.

Szabo, N., 1996. The Mental Accounting Barrier to Micropayments. http://szabo.best.vwh.net/micropayments.html (last accessed July 2014).

CHAPTER 25

What Does Cryptocurrency Mean for the New Economy?

David G.W. Birch
Consult Hyperion, Guildford, Surrey, UK

Contents

25.1 INTRODUCTION

A currency is a form of money. In the modern economy, most moneys take the form of bank deposits. The principal way these deposits are created is through commercial banks making loans. Whenever a bank makes a loan, it simultaneously creates a matching deposit in the borrower's bank account, thereby creating new money (Mcleay et al., 2014). So, modern money, with the exception of the cash "rump," is in the form of bank deposits. It is institutional and it is overwhelmingly digital.

Almost all of the pounds, euros, dollars, and yen in the world are already digital, created and managed by central banks under the control of national governments. There have already been a number of attempts to replace that cash rump ("the last mile" of money) with digital alternatives in order to create a wholly digital national money stock, a digital currency, in other words. One of the most recent attempts, the MintChip experiment at the Royal Bank of Canada, uses microSD cards and mobile phones to do this, but there have been other attempts using a variety of cryptographic techniques, going back a couple of decades to the days of Mondex and DigiCash (Levy, 1994).

In a strange way, these schemes were essentially conservative: Their purpose was to make the use of fiat currency more efficient and cost-effective for consumers, retailers, and banks. Such cryptographic technologies could, however, be used to create wholly private currencies (Birch and Mcevoy, 1996) issued by a range of different entities (i.e., not only central banks). Let us label these "X$."

In this chapter, I will look at what kinds of private currencies these might be and how X$ might evolve to actually remove money from some kinds of transactions. I predict that at the end of the transition to X$, the marginal cost of introducing another kind of money will be approximately zero. So, we will be in the "let a thousand flowers bloom" mode and might reasonably expect a rush to evolutionary dead ends followed by mass extinction. Private currencies give us a starting point to explore the flowering (if not the extinction!) by first asking who might want to issue these private currencies and what kinds of private currencies they might want to issue before we move on to ask whether X$ might be the best way of implementing those new kinds of digital money, setting to one side whether anyone would want to issue physical private money, like casino chips or the Liberty Dollars described by Dowd (2014).

We therefore start from the premise that X$ makes the cost of entry into the currency-issuing "market" quite small. This dynamic means that many organizations may then wish to enter this market, for example, as a means of supplying credit (as discussed by Friedrich Hayek and others), of raising finance, or of encouraging customer loyalty (as envisaged by Edward de Bono and others) or perhaps as for community or social purposes (as explored by Bernard Lietaer and others). Whereas the world's currencies are currently organized on territorial lines, these actors adumbrate a future in which currencies occupy (overlapping) niches according to the "virtual," as well as geographic, communities to which people belong and a vigorous "foreign" exchange market where people (or, more likely, their mobile phones) trade these currencies. The ramifications of such a widespread deployment have long deserved serious examination and debate (Birch and Mcevoy, 1997), as the apparently widespread assumption that the fiat currency system that has been in place since 1971 represents that the optimal monetary arrangement is lazy and flawed. Thus, broadly speaking, and for the sake of simplicity in covering some key concepts, we can use these three different kinds of private money that I will label (imperfectly but conveniently) bank money, company money, and community money to test the impact of X$.

25.1.1 Bank money

The issue of private bank money under what is generally referred to as a "free banking" regime, which means the unrestricted competitive issue of currency and deposit money by private banks on a convertible basis (White, 1989), is comparatively well known and well understood. The famous case study of Scottish banks before the Bank of England monopoly was extended in Victorian times is illuminating. For a couple of hundred years, England had gradually been folding the control of money into the Bank of England monopoly, whereas in Scotland, private banks continued to issue their own money and competed to keep the value of their money up. The result was a period of incredible innovation when the more tightly regulated London and country banks failed more often than the less tightly regulated Scottish banks (Under Threat, 2008). The competition resulted in many of the innovations that we take for granted as part of modern banking. Indeed, it is surprising how many of these innovations (colored banknotes, overdrafts, checkbooks, and so on) date specifically from this competitive period in Scottish banking history. Bank failures in Scotland were fewer and less catastrophic than bank failures in England, supporting a kind of ecological argument that diversity provides strength.

The argument for this kind of private money was developed more recently by economists of what is known as the "Austrian School." A good example is Hayek's *The Denationalisation of Money—The Argument Revisited*, which was first published in the 1970s. In this, Hayek presented the case for a diverse monetary base, with private banks once again creating money through credit but each creating their own money (Hayek, 2007). With great foresight, Hayek noted the problem with using tens or hundreds of different currencies in practice and speculated that within a community (e.g., a country or a city), perhaps one currency would predominate or (with amazing prescience) that ingenious technologists might develop "plastic or similar tokens with electronic markings which every cash register and slot machine would be able to sort out, and the 'signature' of which would be legally protected against forgery as any other document of value." This is a pretty good description of a Bitcoin app on a mobile phone!

There are lots of different kinds of digital money that a bank could choose to issue and X\$ is only one kind (and Bitcoin is only one kind of X\$). If we make the assumption that the primary use of bank money will be for retail transactions of one form or another, then we are not drawn toward an obvious conclusion that X\$ is the best choice. I think there are many scenarios based on an improved identity infrastructure that lead to an exactly opposite conclusion. That is, if new technology helps with identification and authentication, then, frankly, payments are easy. Once you know that the counterparties to a transaction are Alice and Bob, then changing a few bytes in a bank database to transfer money from Alice to Bob is simple, cheap, and fast.

25.1.2 Company money

The issue of private company money was intriguingly explored by the famous lateral thinker Edward de Bono, who wrote a fascinating pamphlet for the London-based think tank, the Centre for the Study of Financial Innovation back in the 1990s. His central point was that if the cost of issuing currency falls, then it makes economic sense for companies to issue their own money, rather than use equities (Bono, 2002), and he went on to write that he looked forward to a time when "the successors to Bill Gates will have put the successors to Alan Greenspan out of business." Dr. de Bono was arguing that companies could raise money just as governments now do—by printing it. He put forward the idea of private currency as a claim on products or services produced by the issuer, rather than the bank credit of Hayek. So IBM might issue "IBM Dollars" that would be not only theoretically redeemable for IBM products and services but also practically tradable for other companies' moneys or for other assets. To make such a scheme work, IBM would have to learn to manage the supply of money to ensure that (with too many vouchers chasing too few goods) inflation does not destroy the value of their creations. But companies should be able to manage that trick at least as easily as governments do, particularly as they don't have voters to cope with.

The idea might sound odd at first, but I think it is quite easy to imagine how such a system might work. A start-up launches, and instead of issuing equity, it issues money that is redeemable against some future service. So, for example, a wind farm start-up might offer money in the form of kilowatt-hours that are redeemable 5 years from now. In the early days, this money would trade at a significant discount to take into account the risks inherent in the venture. But once the wind farm is up and running and producing electricity, then the value of the money will rise. There might, in this case, be a demand for renewable energy that drives the value of the money higher than its original face value.

With millions or even tens of millions of these currencies in circulation and constantly being traded on foreign exchange markets, it might sound as if the situation would be unbearably complex for anyone trying to actually pay anyone else. But remember that this is not analogous to me taking notes out of my wallet and handing them to you. This is my computer, or more likely my mobile phone, talking to your computer, or more likely your mobile phone. And our mobile phones are entirely capable of negotiating between themselves to work out the deal. In his original work, de Bono put it quite nicely by saying that

> Pre-agreed algorithms would determine which financial assets were sold by the purchaser of the good or service according to the value of the transaction. And the supplier of that good or service would know that the incoming funds would be allocated to the appropriate combination of assets as prescribed by another pre-agreed algorithm. Eligible assets will be any financial assets for which there were market clearing prices in real time. The same system could match demands and supplies of financial assets, determine prices and make settlements.

I cannot resist pointing out that de Bono also wrote that the key to any such developments "is the ability of computers to communicate in real time to permit instantaneous verification of the creditworthiness of counterparties," an early vision of what we might now call the reputation economy that I explore further in my recent book, where I note that identities and credentials are easy to create and destroy, but reputations are much harder to subvert since they depend not on what *anyone* thinks but on what *everyone* thinks (Birch, 2014). Now that the combination of mobile phones, social networks, and strong authentication makes the calculation of reputations (including credit worthiness) cost-effective even for small transactions, all of the technology needed to deliver the IBM Dollar is in place.

Here, the X\$ technology may make a real difference. The de Bono assumption that trading in money (essentially) is cheaper than trading in equities or other kinds of corporate paper is challenged by shifting to blockchain technology. Therefore, I can see that the spirit of de Bono's proposals can be implemented in an attractive and practical manner but not in the way that he imagined. If you can move IBM paper around without expensive clearing and settlement infrastructure, then to all intents and purposes, that is the IBM money that he was thinking about. Corporate paper that is a cross between private money and loyalty scheme (so that if you hold the paper, you obtain some benefits in terms of products or services) strikes me as being something of an opportunity.

There is another factor in favor of this approach, which is the drive for transparency in company ownership. One might imagine a kind of stock exchange where start-ups launch as previously described, but instead of issuing money, they create equities that are "coins" on a blockchain. The trading of these coins is indistinguishable from the trading of money (because there is no clearing or settlement), but there is an additional transparency in corporate affairs because all of the transactions are public. And while the company and observers may not know the beneficial owner of the coins (because the wallets are identified only by keys), the stock exchange will be set up to issue wallets after appropriate KYC. In the general run of things, transactions are private but where there is suspicion of wrongdoing, the ownership can be exposed under appropriate legal conditions.

These kinds of ideas, combined with the smart contract and other innovations, suggest the basis for elements of the new economy. Smart contracts combine protocols, interfaces, and "promises" expressed via those interfaces to deliver new ways to formalize the digital relationships that are more functional than their inanimate paper-based ancestors and reduce transaction costs (Szabo, 1997) and when combined with the blockchain form an entirely new, entirely unprecedented platform for business.

25.1.3 Community money

While there is a tradition of looking at social, alternative, and complementary moneys as a means to achieve social good, it has been at the margins of economic thinking. The idea of using such community-based money to, for example, create economic activity where there is none—set out in, for example, Lietaer's *Future of Money* (Lietaer, 2001)—is very attractive, and there have been a great many such experiments around the world. However, the issue of community money has been given renewed thrust by the global financial crisis, and there are examples in countries such as Italy and Greece where the absence of conventional money has pushed communities into thinking more radically roles.

A useful case study is the "TEM" currency in Volos in Greece (Donado, 2011). A TEM is equal in value to one euro, and it can be used to exchange goods and services. Community members start their accounts with zero and get TEM by offering goods and services. They also receive books of physical currency itself, which are printed with a special seal that makes it difficult to counterfeit. Businesses in the town will accept TEM (generally in part payment). They can also borrow up to 300 TEMs, but they are expected to repay the loan within a fixed period of time.

It may be tempting to belittle alternative currencies as limited, unrealistic, or maybe a little kooky, but they do work, so long as they don't run into counterfeiting problems and supply is intelligently controlled to avoid inflation. Nothing but perception makes the issuing authority of the US government more legitimate than, say, the Ithaca HOURs Circulation Committee. Both try to supply users with real money, and both do their best to wisely steer monetary policy in a way that promotes growth (Wolman, 2012).

This is, again, a vision of multiple currencies. A single currency is more efficient for transactions, but it stops economic managers from tailoring the institutions of money to local circumstances (Castronova, 2014), hence the attractive notion of more communities tied to specific currencies, thus minimizing their transaction costs between members. If we divide alternative currencies into local and global (Kenny, 2014), this perspective tends to privilege the local and there is evidence to support the idea that such currencies are better suited to support growth within communities (Groppa, 2013), largely because they mitigate against hoarding (which plagues the nascent Bitcoin economy). But more than economic efficiencies, community currencies may embody values (e.g., environmental policies) that are important to the community and therefore drive usage. One might imagine a gold-backed currency for the Islamic diaspora or a renewable energy currency for the green movement and so forth.

25.2 BITCOIN

Now, let's move on to the most widespread X$ implementation today. Why would people use Bitcoin to implement a new kind of money? There seem to be three key reasons: One is that they want a cheap, irreversible online means of exchange (cash for the twenty-first century), another is that they want an anonymous means of exchange (coins for the twenty-first century), and another is that they want to use nongovernment currency because they don't trust governments to manage money properly (gold for the twenty-first century).

25.2.1 Frictionless low-value payments

Now, having been involved in a previous attempt to create a global, decentralized, peer-to-peer means of exchange that addressed the first two of these issues (the Mondex scheme, mentioned previously), I'm naturally interested to see how Bitcoin attacks the cash rump. I am sympathetic to the goals of "frictionless" means of exchange for the online world because I think it would stimulate trade and therefore prosperity.

Is Bitcoin a good X\$ implementation for these purposes? It may work in some online environments, but I don't think it is. Retail payments aren't really what Bitcoin is all about. Bitcoin does not work as an alternative to handing a £1 coin to a market trader or tapping a contactless card on a reader on a London bus. At the beginning of 2014, there were some 30,000 merchants that accepted Bitcoins (XBT) for payment. By the end of the first quarter, this had doubled, and approximately 60,000 merchants accepted XBT, but there was no commensurate growth in the transactions on the blockchain, so I strongly suspect that the overwhelming majority of merchants are accepting X\$ for marketing purposes.

In fact, it is not clear to me that Bitcoin was ever intended to be a retail payment mechanism, so it is not surprising that it is less than optimal in such an environment. After all, credit cards were never designed to work on the Internet, which is why they are less than optimal there and people are investing considerable effort in developing digital wallets. My point is that we shouldn't be surprised that Bitcoin is clunky when buying noodles in a fast-food restaurant because that's not what it is for.

25.2.2 Anonymity

While Bitcoin advocates often advance anonymity as a driving force in adoption, I postulate that what the general public want is privacy, rather than anonymity. Privacy is vital to democracy. It is valuable in its own right. It contributes to the "marketplace of ideas" and the promotion of the truth (Solove, 2007). While it is certainly possible to construct anonymous electronic payment systems or electronic payment systems that deliver anonymity to honest participants (Camenisch et al., 2006), in practical terms, anonymity in payment systems has many drawbacks.

The most obvious drawback is around loss and theft. If I lose my wallet, I want my money back. This is why I always carry prepaid cards when I travel, rather than carrying cash. In fact, I've just been through the process of getting my money back because I gave my son a prepaid euro card to use on a school trip he was on and he lost it when there was a €70 balance. No one else can use that card (they don't know the PIN and it has no name on it so they can't pass AVS online) and I am getting the money back. Personally, I think this is closer to the kind of cash that makes sense in the new economy. It is economically infeasible (although not computationally infeasible) to track and research every payment, but when something goes wrong, it can be restored. And if I did use the card for some illegal purpose, the police could get a warrant and the issuer would direct them to me.

I might go further and observe that a great many people would not to want to live in a society that allows anonymity for all but the smallest transactions. They want to live in a society that provides the *appropriate* level of privacy. If all transactions are anonymous, then the rich and the powerful are not accountable. It seems to me that privacy-enhanced payments are the way forward, not anonymity. Money remains private in the normal course of events, but if there is a fraud or some other crime or if the police have a warrant following due process, then the veil can be peeled back and the transaction details revealed. I think that when it comes to anonymous cash, the bad outweighs the good.

Bitcoin, in an odd way, is a step in the right direction. The blockchain tells me that wallet X sent XBT to wallet Y, but I don't know to whom wallet X and wallet Y belong to. One might imagine a future blockchain where I don't know whom wallet X and wallet Y belong to, but (say) the "system" does and will reveal so under warrant. This would stop the use of Bitcoin for criminal activity, the exemplar of such being assassination markets. These provide an interesting diversion and a means to reflect on the issue of anonymous money.

25.2.3 Assassination markets

Here is how an assassination market works (Greenberg, 2013). Someone runs a public book on the anticipated death dates of public figures. I hate a particular pop star or politician or business rival, so I place a bet on when they will die. When the person dies, whoever had the closest guess wins all of the money, less a cut for the house. Let's say I bet $10 that a particular TV personality is going to die next New Year. Other people really hate this TV personality too and so they put down bets as well. The more hated the person is, the most bets there will be and the larger the pot for the winner and the larger the incentive to act to win it.

New Year's Day comes around. There's a $1 million bet on this particular personality. I pay a hit man half a million to murder the personality. I've won the bet, so I get the $1 million and give half to the hit man. I don't have to prove that I was responsible for the assassination to get the money: I'm just the lucky winner of the assassination bet. If someone else had bet the 30th of December and murdered the television personality themselves the day before, then I wouldn't get the payoff but it would only have cost me $10 and that would have been a spent in a good cause (to me).

This is actually a rather old idea but will it work with the Bitcoin? Bitcoin is a poor choice of payment mechanism for an assassination market that has to have unconditional anonymity to work properly. The placing of the bets, and the collection of the winnings, must be untraceable. Completely untraceable. If you obtain your winnings in Bitcoin, the "trail of breadcrumbs" through the public ledger will sooner or later lead back to you. There are people who examine these trails in detail, and this examination will get more automated and better informed in time.

The proponents of cash argue that if X$ is to mount a serious effort to eradicate fiat currencies, then they must replicate anonymity, as it is a key property of cash. I couldn't disagree more. X$ should aim to set a higher bar: money with privacy built in.

25.2.4 Beyond government control

This may well be the most contentious area for debate, and I do not want to make it a focus of this chapter because it is, largely, a political discussion. Nation-state fiat currencies are an artifact of a vanishing postindustrial world, rather like national airlines. We no longer think that each country should have a national airline: Some countries have many and some share. Similarly, it might be time for the post-Bretton Woods world to abandon some of its fiat currencies, replacing them with dollars, euros, and new, as yet to exist subnational and regional currencies (Steil, 2007).

I would prefer to see a system of competing private currencies, rather than government monopolies, because I think that sound money is an important base for the economy. But this issue is, to my mind, orthogonal to the two issues noted above. You could implement competing bank, company, or commodity currencies in anonymous, pseudonymous, or unconditionally traceable ways, and you could implement the mechanism for exchange using all sorts of systems that are more or less suited to day-to-day retail payments.

25.3 A MONEY NARRATIVE

What does this analysis tell us about this future? I think we can summarize in three main points: Firstly, Bitcoin may not, after all, be the best way to replace cash; secondly, new currencies associated with communities have a dynamic beyond economic efficiency; and finally, the use of the blockchain to go beyond corporate money looks attractive.

I think it would be useful to develop a shared narrative around X$ to foster communication between the X$ community and business, organizations, governments, and individuals to build on this analysis. We had a narrative for mobile phones because of Star Trek, but it did not provide a narrative for money. In fact, in science fiction, the subject of money is rarely handled well, probably because many people don't really understand what money is or how it works, so speculating on where it might go is just too far outside their envelope. (I'm the other way around: I find it hard to imagine time travel but easy to imagine Facebook issuing its own currency!)

To build a functional narrative that will facilitate communication about, and help creative thinking about, the future, we need to look away from technologists. To illustrate a narrative for the purposes of this chapter, I've chosen two nontechnological "big picture" inputs to compare and contrast.

I will begin with *The Future of Money* by Benjamin Cohen from the University of California, Santa Barbara, because he set out some of the key issues around money very clearly. One of the questions that he addressed was whether the dynamic of monetary evolution is a tendency to one currency (the galactic credit beloved of science fiction authors) because the minimization of global transaction costs is the dominant, driving factor or whether an explosion of currencies is likely because new technology minimizes transaction costs inside multiple communities. Cohen concluded that "the power of scale economies notwithstanding, monetary geography is set to become more, not less, complex" and he compared the future to the "heterogenous, multiform mosaic that existed prior to the era of territorial money" (Cohen, 2004). I agree, and for fundamental reasons related to the functions of money in society. Why would one "money" provide the means of both exchange and stability (Schlichter, 2011)?

Cohen also talks about geography, and I think that this will also be a key factor in shaping the monetary landscape. This shift means that nearly half of the economic growth expected over the next decade will take place in just 400 cities in the world's global growth markets. It will create an urban consumer class of four billion people by 2025, up from one billion as recently as 1990. These are large numbers. And our traditional way of viewing the world as a collection of national economies cannot provide a clear view of this transformation. To make wise decisions, investors and policy makers need to view the world not so much as a collection of countries but as a network of cities (Naqvi, 2014). Therefore, city-based currencies make more sense that national currencies and cities form a dynamic class of community that will be driven to acquire its own currency.

There is an interesting connection between Cohen's conclusion in his *The Future of Money* and the work of social anthropologist Jack Weatherford who wrote *The History of Money*, in which he also looked at the sweep of monetary evolution. Weatherford observed (The Fiscal Frontier, 1998) that the future of money looks more like it did in "the neolithic world economy before the invention of money than it looks like the market as we have known it in the past few hundred years."

In other words, Weatherford said that advanced technology means that money as we know it might well disappear to be replaced by obligations that are memorized and accounted for without the use of money, a view that resonates with the company currency ideas discussed above.

To see two experts from diverse fields come to similar conclusions that we need to look to the past not the present to see the future, especially since this is the same conclusion that I draw from a technological perspective, leads me to conclude that we are heading into an era of monetary experimentation, fragmentation, and innovation. As a technologist, I suspect that there will be more different kinds of money, not just more currencies, than ever before.

If this comes to pass, and we find ourselves in the neo-neolithic economy with a wide variety of currencies, what will the narrative then be? Cohen's cogent work plus the analysis of company and community currency leads me to speculate that perhaps in the future, all money will be local, it's just that local will mean something different in the connected world. Whether the community is Totnes or World of Warcraft will not make a difference, because the shared desire to minimize transaction costs for "us" at the possible expense of transaction costs from "them" will dominate. Since the overwhelming majority of retail transactions are local, most people's transactions most of the time will be in their local currency with minimal transaction costs. A small number of transactions will be in "foreign" currencies (i.e., someone else's local currency).

There's another refinement to this vision. These currencies may not be money in the conventional sense at all but what might be termed "near money." Cohen referred to the cross elasticity of demand between currencies, but if the cost of using near money is low enough (because of new technology), then just as tally sticks switched from being a mechanism for deferred payment into a temporary store of value and then a means of exchange, so technology might go down the same path again but with some more modern implementation. If we take de Bono's ideas of community money and project them on to the blockchain, we can see that the cost/benefit equation around equity vs. money changes again, in interesting and desirable ways.

25.4 BEYOND MONEY

If this analysis is anything like correct, then it tells us that Bitcoin is not the future of money. Instead, we should think of Bitcoin as the key piece of technology that allows us to begin assembling a future economy that in many of its dynamics takes us to a richer and more diverse version of the past, rather than a simplified version of the present.

Will Bitcoin make it into the mainstream? I don't think so. But something like it will, and it won't be for currency. I think that the Bitcoin technology is, indeed, a revolution, an entirely new way of doing things. It is this aspect of Bitcoin that will be the lasting legacy. I am unconvinced about the currency, but I'm sold on the cryptography. I am convinced about the technology because it is part of an evolving family of technologies that will continue to adapt and find new niches. You are not going to be using Bitcoin to get on the subway or buy a pair of shoes, but you are going to be using the Bitcoin technology in all sorts of other services.

The media attention is on bitcoin the currency (XBT), not Bitcoin the protocol. Hence, the media focus on Bitcoin stories such as the Mt. Gox collapse. What does the Mt. Gox collapse mean for the long-term evolution of X$? Well, as far as I can tell, the answer is almost nothing. This might mean a hiccup for XBT but not for the underlying technology and not for the family of X$ to come, which will be used to build great new financial services around transaction systems, even though retail payments are almost certainly not one of them.

I can see many reasons why people might prefer to trade in community currencies, to store value-based currencies, to put energy-based currencies into their pension plans, and so on. Given the incredible new technology platforms, it would be amazing if money remained fundamentally unchanged. It didn't in the agricultural revolution, it didn't in the industrial revolution, and it won't in the information revolution.

25.5 CONCLUSIONS

When people are asked to imagine the future of money, they tend to think of novel implementations of existing payment instruments, rather than new kinds of money; electronic versions of existing institutions, rather than new institutions; and further centralization, rather than decentralization, experiment, and diversity. So, when people think of X$, they think of a cheaper and faster way to buy things on the web. But if this is all that X$ will do for the coming economy, it's hardly worth writing a chapter about, let alone a book!

Let us think harder. Taking as a starting point, the well-known and tolerably well-understood phenomenon that technologists overestimate the speed of technology-induced change but underestimate the scale of impact.

The long-term outcome will surely be that technology is used not to develop replicants—electronic means of exchange that simulate, as perfectly as possible, physical means of exchange—but to develop new means of exchange that are better for society as a whole. Thus, X$ as a vehicle for synthetic currencies that could be used directly in contracts as payments ought to be the science fiction writers' new monetary paradigm. No more "that will be ten galactic credits, thank you" and more "you owe me a return trip to Uranus and a kilogram of platinum for delivery in 12 months." Well, that's what my payments autodroid bot (i.e., mobile phone) and your payments autodroid bot will agree between themselves anyway.

X$ means a world of communities (geographic in neolithic times and virtual in postmodern construction) in which money is little used within communities, but a variety of both types of money and currencies are used between communities. Within communities, blockchains will manage digital assets and remove money from a great many transactions. Perhaps, it is better to see X$ not as the whole future of money themselves but as the flux capacitor of *Back to the Future* fame, the key piece of technology that allows us to begin assembling a future economy that in many of its dynamics takes us to a richer and more diverse version of the past, rather than a simplified version of the present.

ACKNOWLEDGMENT

Many thanks are due to Jon Matonis, executive director at the Bitcoin Foundation, for 20 years of discussion, debate, argument, and learning about the future of money.

REFERENCES

Birch, D., 2014. Identity Is the New Money. LPP, London.
Birch, D., Mcevoy, N., 1996. DIY Cash, Wired UK (April 1996).
Birch, D., Mcevoy, N., 1997. Technology Will Denationalise Money. Financial Cryptography. Springer Berlin Heidelberg, Berlin.
Bono, E.D., 2002. The IBM Dollar. In: Boyle, D. (Ed.), The Money Changers. Earthscan, London.

Camenisch, J., Hohenberger, S., Lysyanskaya, A., 2006. Balancing accountability and privacy using e-cash. In: Prisco, R.D., Yung, M. (Eds.), Security and Cryptography for Networks. Springer Berlin Heidelberg, Berlin.

Castronova, E., 2014. Wildcat Currency. Yale University Press, New Haven.

Cohen, B., 2004. New frontier. In: The Future of Money. Princeton University Press, Princeton.

Donado, R., 2011. Battered by economic crisis, Greeks turn to barter networks. The New York Times, A8, 2 October.

Dowd, K., 2014. New Private Monies—A Bit-Part Player? IEA, London.

Greenberg, A., 2013. Meet the 'assassination market' creator who's crowdfunding murder with Bitcoins [Online]. Available: http://www.forbes.com/sites/andygreenberg/2013/11/18/meet-the-assassination-market-creator-whos-crowdfunding-murder-with-bitcoins/ [Accessed 23 November, 2013].

Groppa, O., 2013. Complementary currency and its impact on the economy. Int. J. Commun. Curr. Res. 17, 45–57.

Hayek, F.A., 2007. Denationalisation of Money. Profile, London.

Kenny, C., 2014. Alternative Currencies. Parliamentary Office of Science and Technology, London.

Levy, S., 1994. E-money (That's What I want). Wired, December 1994.

Lietaer, B., 2001. Work-enabling currencies. In: The Future of Money. Century, London.

Mcleay, M., Radia, A., Thomas, R., 2014. Money creation in the modern economy. In: Mcleay, M., Radia, A., Thomas, R. (Eds.), Money Creation in the Modern Economy. Bank of England, London.

Naqvi, A., 2014. Cities, not countries, are the key to tomorrow's economies. Financial Times, 25 April.

Schlichter, D., 2011. Beyond the cycle: paper money's endgame. In: Paper Money Collapse. John Wiley, Hoboken.

Solove, D., 2007. Anonymity and accountability. In: The Future of Reputation. Yale, New Haven.

Steil, B., 2007. The end of national currency. Foreign Affairs, May 2007.

Szabo, N., 1997. Formalizing and security relationships on public networks. First Money, 2.

Weatherford, J., Davis, P., Gregory, C., Kocher, P., Minsky, M., Lederman, L., Sapolsky, R., 1998. The Fiscal Frontier: speculations on the future of money. Discover, October 1998.

Under Threat, 2008. Under threat in The Economist 386 (8566), 41 (9 February 2008).

White, L., 1989. Free banking as an alternative monetary system. In: Competition and Currency—Essays on Free Banking and Money. New York University Press, New York.

Wolman, D., 2012. Time for cash to cash out? Wall Street J., 11 February.

CHAPTER 26

Bitcoin: A Look at the Past and the Future☆

Anton Cruysheer
ABN AMRO Bank, Amsterdam, The Netherlands

Contents

Much has been written about the bitcoin, a digital currency and an encrypted unit of computer data (bit). Many articles have been written about what it is, how it works, and what the pros and cons are. This chapter is not about how the bitcoin functions—there is enough to be found on this topic on the Internet—but about the function of money in relation to the bitcoin, a link that cannot be found sufficiently in discussions as of yet. Furthermore, some developments will be discussed and suggestions will be given for the future.

Money has always been seen primarily as a means for barter or payment facilitating the exchange of goods or services. It is a means for economic communication. By using money, barter becomes commerce thus stimulating the economy. Money is also a means to calculate and save (Van Gelder, 1986, G-14). In light of the discussion about the bitcoin, it is interesting to note the following (provisional) characteristics of money: generally coveted (useful and valuable), generally accepted, anonymous (unidentified owner), legal (value set by authorities), easily moved, long-lasting, divisible, of constant quality, set value, and recognizable (Polanyi, 1957, pp. 264-266; Van Gelder, 1986-2002, G-14).

It seems that banks originated even earlier than coins (as is seen in the photograph of the coin of electrum, from Lydia), the oldest reference being found in ca. 700 BC in Babylon. The original function of banks was not much different to that of today: opening

---

☆This chapter is translated by Barbara Mees.

an account, renting safety deposit boxes, taking out loans, writing checks, etc. Even personal trading and speculation were not shunned (Van Beek, 1986–2002, p. 38).

The first "western coin," electrum (naturally occurring alloy of gold and silver), 1/6 stater Lydian (western Turkey), about 650-600 BC. Weight: 2560 g. Diameter: 10 mm (photo: British Museum).

Semiofficial, physical bitcoin, encrypted, value to be retrieved via the Internet (source: https://www.casascius.com).

It is interesting to note that throughout history, coins existed next to other forms of barter. At some point in time, completely different materials were more desirable than coins. In the seventeenth and eighteenth centuries, international trade used cowry shells and glass beads, among others. These were also used as decorations in gardens and country houses (Van Beek et al., 1984; Cruysheer, 2013, pp. 159-160). Today, our money is divided in tangible and abstract currency: currency and demand deposits. The latter is made up of directly claimable credit from the bank via a withdrawal, credit card, check, mobile or Internet banking. All these have a so-called fiduciary character, in other words, fiat money, whereby the value is derived from the trust invested in it by the users—similar to the bitcoin, but more about that later. Both cash and deposits are legal tender in the sense of government and bank money.

On the other hand, there are many illegal tender that have been around for centuries, for example, tokens of all kinds (for machines and prisons), Medieval charity tokens, eighteenth-century plantation tokens, cafeteria tokens, ship's money (valid on-board international ships), and seed money (for special ceremonies) (Van Gelder, 1986-2002, G-14-15). Let's not forget complementary monetary units popular in southern Europe. For example, in Spain, there are more than 30 of these types of currencies in use such as the Màlaga Común, Boniato, Pita, and BilbòDiru. Although some of these have existed for more than 15 years, they seem to be coming to the forefront due to the ongoing economic crisis. Bartering is increasingly being used by people who cannot or do not want to participate in the official economy, especially by the homeless or those who use it as a form of protest. Thus, it looks like these countries are in a state of doom and gloom while actually social environments are creating and using alternative solutions. People are becoming creative and self-reliant, whether out of necessity or not. Furthermore, in Spain, we see the so-called timebanks. Timebanks do not use currencies but time. If someone delivers a service (cutting someone's hair or mowing a lawn), he is paid in minutes. This is an alternative form of bartering, not to be overlooked (Spain already has more than 300 timebanks) (Knack, April 8, 2013), and it is growing, often at the cost of the formal economy, for example, consider the reduction in tax income. However, virtual bitcoin currency is not completely unexpected. In the past years, we have seen a number of variations on this theme. An example is the digital Linden dollars in the computer game *Second Life* in which ABN AMRO Bank conducted an experiment by opening a virtual branch in order to contact (potential) new clients. Another extremely successful example is the mobile payment system in Kenya, the M-Pesa. Some 17 million Kenyans make use of this service while only 5 million of them have an actual bank account (Volkskrant, October 7, 2011).

The bitcoin as cryptocurrency for that matter is not a new phenomenon either. In 1983, *DigiCash* and *eCash* tried to combine electronic currency with encryption (Chaum, 1983, pp. 199-203). The first bitcoin is also already a few years old, having been first introduced in 2009 under the pseudonym Satoshi Nakamoto according to rumors on the Internet.

The aforementioned lets us see that the bitcoin is not as exceptional as people suggest. In fact, it is in line with the ancient tradition of alternative currencies of which many different varieties existed and exist, even today. All these crypto tender—there are many more than bitcoins alone—remind us of all the different coins and tokens of the twelfth and thirteenth centuries in Europe. Users were completely unsure of the value and exchange rates on the local markets. The difference is that the bitcoin operates on a worldwide scale, is exchanged quickly, and has digital possibilities as compared to the physical possibilities of the coin or token. As we saw in the beginning of this chapter, the bitcoin only partly meets the requirements set for cash or demand deposits. It is not generally coveted—like gold or its value. Furthermore, it is based entirely on trust and therefore has the character of a Ponzi scheme: it works as long as people continue to participate. Also, there is no constant or set value and it is not "legal" in the sense that the value is not guaranteed by the central government.

26.1 REASONS FOR SUCCESS AND FAILURE

Contrary to the many different regional and national phenomena—as in Spain—the bitcoin can be seen as the first successful digital, nonlegal coin that works with encryption worldwide. This success is due to a number of underlying conditions: social dissatisfaction of large numbers of people with state and bank currencies, the worldwide continuing media hype, the popularity with the online underworld (e.g., money laundering), the investment hype in China due to state television broadcasts, and finally the increasing intertwining of the formal and informal economy leading to all kinds of innovative possibilities. A long list of companies already exists where one can pay for services with bitcoins. But there are also failures:

- The development of the bitcoin is insufficient for it to comply to the qualities of legal tender (see above).
- Extreme speculation and inflation of the bitcoin exchange rate can cause the bubble to burst.
- Government intervention, for example, if the official economy were threatened.
- If use of the bitcoin remains too technical causing worldwide acceptance to fail.

26.2 A NUMISMATIC APPROACH

Interesting from the point of view of academics who study money (numismatics) is that people continue to feel a need for actual, physical money. Various initiatives have met this need. For example, Mulligan Mint created a copper and silver bitcoin medallion with a QR code that, when scanned, brings the user to the online company shop. The launch had an unforeseen effect for director Rob Gray: the company bank Capital One immediately closed the company's bank account. No reason was given but the reason may be the text stamped into the silver edition of the coin: "Commodity banks and crypto currencies will render central banks desolate—Free the currency, free the people."

A second, more serious producer is Casascius that produces copper-, silver-, and gold-plated coins worth Ƀ1, Ƀ0.5, and Ƀ0.1. Pictures of these coins are used most often in the media. Each coin has a redeemable/convertible private code placed under the hologram that can be deciphered via the Web site http://blockexplorer.com to exchange the value of the coin.

Bitcoins (source: https://www.casascius.com).

A third initiative is seen on the channel island of Alderney that would like to make a name for itself by producing physical coins in cooperation with the Royal Mint, the producer of Great Britain's official coins. Alderney would like to do this in agreement with antilaundering legislation, but how this will be done was unsure at the time of writing of this chapter (De Telegraaf, November 30, 2013).

26.3 THE END OF MONEY

There are two interesting books, partially with the same title, that each has its own point of view with regard to the worldwide development of currency in the past years. In *The End of Money and the Future of Civilization*, written in 2009, the author Greco places the "problem of money" in a wide historical and political context. He sees the control of money and banking as the most important mechanism for the concentration of power and thus disregard for the democratic principle. The book has a revolutionary character, evident in the summary. If we look at the virtual development of currency, Greco seems to be able to predict the future in his book, although the success of the bitcoin is mostly based on old-fashioned speculation without underlying value. This can be seen as contradictory in view of the fundamental cause of the economic crises of our official money system, which the author is reacting against.

On the cover of *The End of Money* by David Wolman, we see a dollar bill folded into a Stegosaurus. This book takes us on an anecdotal journey to money, a journey that surprises the reader again and again (Wolman, 2007). In this book, contrary to many of the other texts that have been written, the author argues for regulation of the bitcoin by a central authority, which will stabilize the exchange rate thus creating more trust. If bitcoin users don't agree, according to Wolman, a new type of cryptocurrency should be made (Wismans, 2013, p. 5).

26.4 THE ROLE OF THE GOVERNMENT

On November 28, 2013, the Dutch newspaper *De Telegraaf* wrote that De Nederlandsche Bank (the Dutch Central Bank) is not necessarily negative when it comes to virtual currencies, such as the bitcoin. At the time of publishing, the DNB is researching potential risks involved with this currency such as risks of integrity and risks for the financial system. According to the DNB, the bitcoin falls outside the scope of the legal framework, such as the Electronic Money Directive and the Payment Services Directive. This notice complies with the characteristics of cryptocurrencies such as the bitcoin—they purposely withdraw from this supervision—and may have potentially large consequences for (income and profit) taxes that can be consciously avoided. The difficulty lies in the increasing entanglement with the formal economy (see above). It is therefore possible that governments will criminalize or forbid the bitcoin if problems increase. However, forbidding the bitcoin will probably lead to users finding other cryptocurrencies that they can use.

26.5 THE ROLE OF BANKS

By definition, central banks do not have formal influence on digital currencies as they do not fall under present regulations. If financial institutions, such as banks, were to support cryptocurrencies for their clients, the tax authorities would certainly arrive quickly to ask for bank account details. However, this does not mean that banks cannot do anything, on the contrary. They can inform, give advice, and facilitate. Informing their clients is the least they can do—it is not customer-friendly to not (be able to) answer questions that clients have. They can advise their clients by warning them about market depreciation of the bitcoin or by exchanging the received bitcoins into euros on a daily basis. Facilitating may mean saving the code that the bitcoin represents in a secure (bank) environment so that loss through theft or (computer) failure is minimized.

Let's look at the Web site http://www.thuisbezorgd.nl, a Dutch takeaway Web site. It is fascinating to see that at the bottom of the payment page, you can pay not only via the regulars such as Ideal, PayPal, and credit card but also, since 2013, with bitcoins. The next step is a "VC" logo for "virtual currency" through which various virtual currencies can be chosen, among which the bitcoin.

"Ideal"–one of the many currencies in the online world (source: http://www.thuisbezorgd.nl).

As mentioned before, it seems that more and more companies are accepting bitcoins as a means of payment, whether from a marketing standpoint or for other reasons. Related developments can also be seen here. For example, HEMA (a large

Dutch retail chain) is researching various business possibilities far beyond their core business such as health insurance, notary services, mortgages, and other bank services. HEMA also accepts PayPal as a means of payment although this does not apply to "cakes and chocolate orders with photo," according to the Web site.

26.6 FUTURE POSSIBILITIES

What makes the bitcoin innovative is the unique network as payment platform, the low-cost payment traffic, and the fact that there are hardly transaction fees and international transactions can be done much faster than via traditional routes through banks. The short-comings of the bitcoin are the degree of difficulty, value fluctuations, lack of central supervision of the payment platform, and thus safety. Only time will tell if these are fundamental issues or just teething problems. Because stable money has always had underlying value, it seems to be a key requirement for long-term trust. The bitcoin has neither at the moment, but both must be reached if the bitcoin, or any other cryptocurrency, is to have a future.

It might be that there will be more alternatives, as in Spain. One possibility is that the cryptocurrency is restricted to a geographic area and no longer anonymous (e.g., connected to a passport number). With regard to accessibility, it is likely that obtaining (new) bitcoins will be linked to online performance, such as Internet games, as Linden dollars in *Second Life*. Nxt-id.com's "MobileBio, biocloud, and Authentication and Identity Management Services" is an example of a means to identify people, something that is becoming increasingly important in view of safety. The near future will undoubtedly see a rise in the development of safely identifying people. For example, a bankcard with pin code is almost out of date. Biometric identification is the future, whether through the voice, iris/eye, fingerprint, or eventually DNA. There are also many developments in transaction traffic such as the interesting concept of money exchange service of Mycelium's "Bitcoincard." This system, with which messages and payments can be sent worldwide, works via radio frequencies and is therefore free from network administrators, banks, or government authorities (*CoinDesk.com*, May 22, 2013; with special thanks to Céline Pessers, Innovation Manager, ABN AMRO Bank). The Web site states "The Bitcoincard moves bitcoin economic interaction offline, which significantly expands both turnover and the target audience. But, most importantly, it makes the clustered local growth of a new free economy possible," thus calling upon economic freedom of thought.

REFERENCES

Chaum, D., 1983. Blind signatures for untraceable payments. Adv. Cryptol. Proc. Crypto 82 (3), 1983.
Cruysheer, A.T.E., 2013. Geldtuinen bij buitenplaatsen. De Beeldenaar 4, 113–118.
Greco, T.H., 2009. The End of Money and the Future of Civilization. Chelsea Green Publishing.

Polanyi, K., 1957. The economy as instituted process. In: Polanyi, K., Arensberg, C.M., Pearson, H.W. (Eds.), Trade and Market in the Early Empires. Glencoe, New York, pp. 36–118.

Van Beek, E.J.A. (Ed.), 1986-2002. Geschiedenis van het geld. Encyclopedie van munten en bankbiljetten. Bohn Stafleu van Loghum, Houten.

Van Beek, B., Jacobi, H., Scharloo, M., 1984. Geld door de eeuwen heen.

Van Gelder, H.E., 1986-2002. Geld. In: Van Beek, E.J.A. (Ed.), Encyclopedie van munten en bankbiljetten. Samsom, Utrecht.

Wismans, L., 2013. Bitcoin. Daar was toch iets mis mee? Of niet? NRCNext, Netherlands, November 19th (4-5).

Wolman, D., 2007. The End of Money.

SOURCES

This chapter is published previously in the Dutch numismatic journal "De Beeldenaar" (April 2014, 38, No. 3, pp. 113-118).

A large number of (company) websites such as http://www.bitcoinfoundation.org, http://www.bitcoinexaminer.org, https://www.casascius.com, Wikipedia, De Telegraaf, Amazon, HEMA, Volkskrant, and http://www.bitcoincard.org.

Investments and Crowdfunding

CHAPTER 27

Bitcoin IPO, ETF, and Crowdfunding

Nirupama Devi Bhaskar, Lam Pak Nian, David LEE Kuo Chuen
Sim Kee Boon Institute for Financial Economics, Singapore Management University, Singapore

Contents

Handbook of Digital Currency

27.1 INTRODUCTION

There is money to be made in the business of cryptocurrency, and money is being put in to support businesses dealing in them. In the Bitcoin world, two well-known financing efforts are Digital CC, an initial public offering (IPO) on the Australian Stock Exchange (ASX), and the Winklevoss Bitcoin Trust (WBT), an exchange-traded fund (ETF) on NASDAQ. The first part of this chapter considers Digital CC's IPO and the WBT as case studies for the legal structure of their respective investment vehicles. The discussion in the first part of this chapter will present a summary insight of how the investment vehicle was structured and, as far as was disclosed, how the business is run or expected to be run. The second part then presents an alternative view—that cryptocurrencies have the potential to be used in crowd financing efforts. As discussed elsewhere in this book, cryptocurrency is a form of virtual currency, digital currency, or electronic money. However, it is not merely electronic but is also programmable, allowing creators and later even the users to dictate how the cryptocurrency—colloquially also referred to as a "coin"—should behave. The unrestricted potential for modification allows programmers to design a new torrent of innovations that are built on top of the Bitcoin system. Often referred to as Bitcoin 2.0, the new protocols that innovatively build upon the Bitcoin platform for a myriad of purposes are a whole new game of financial innovations that we will explore in the later part of this chapter.

More interestingly, platforms for alternative ways of fundraising are emerging. The most prominent has been the emergence of Crypto Initial Crowd Offer (IWO), a form of crypto crowd sales (CSs), which rides on the Bitcoin protocol using the blockchain technology. Several successful IWOs and CSs have raised awareness of what Bitcoin 2.0, a layer protocol, can disrupt the financial industry. While these fundraising technologies are still in their infancy in terms of development, the possibilities for disruption to traditional business and finance are giving traditional financial institutions much to think about. We will also discuss in detail later in this chapter the various technology and platforms that may be of interest to finance professionals.

27.2 IPO: DIGITAL CC

27.2.1 History

The major parties involved were Macro Energy and Digital CC. Macro Energy was an Australia-based investment company listed on the ASX. It had a varied portfolio of investments, which included an operating segment in investments in oil and gas exploration in the United States and Africa. Digital CC was a nonlisted, recently incorporated Australian company in the digital currency sector that focused on Bitcoin, generating its revenues from digital currency mining, its digital arbitrage and liquidity desk, and the development of retail digital currency products and applications. Digital CC's performance at the time of the IPO saw it generate in excess of 1700 Bitcoins in its first 42 days from the first installment of mining hardware on March 20, 2014, valued at US $1,000,000.

On May 12, 2014, Macro Energy Ltd lodged a prospectus with the Australian Securities and Investments Commission for a reverse IPO (Macro Energy Ltd, 2014). In summary, the reverse IPO involved inviting investors to acquire shares in Macro Energy Ltd, which in turn proposed to acquire all of the issued shares of Digital CC Holdings Pty Ltd. Macro Energy Ltd would then be renamed to Digital CC Ltd.

It invited applications for 45,500,000 shares, priced at AU $0.20 per share, to raise a total of AU $9,100,000. This sum represented the net gain, as up to AU $1,335,675 was to be raised through the conversion of loans by the vendors (i.e., provided by the then-shareholders of Digital CC to the company) to equity, thus reducing Digital CC's liabilities following the closure of the IPO and the completion of the acquisition.

The IPO was subject to two conditions precedent, which were the full subscription of its shares to raise the full subscription expected and the obtaining of regulatory approval for the Digital CC to resume trading shares on the ASX.

27.2.2 Effect of Macro Energy acquiring Digital CC

The effect of Macro Energy's acquisition was to change the nature and scale of the company's operations, to focus on digital currency and developing the Digital CC business. It was an event that required regulatory approval for Macro Energy to relist on the ASX. In particular, the company was required to comply with the requirements for new listings in Chapters 1 and 2 of the ASX Listing Rules, including seeking shareholder approval of the acquisition of Digital CC, and the change in the nature and scale of the company's business, the issuance of a prospectus, and obtaining a sufficient number of shareholders with the requisite number of shares in accordance with those rules.

Therefore, prior to seeking the IPO, Macro Energy had executed a conditional share purchase agreement to acquire 100% of the issued capital in Digital CC. Macro Energy then convened a general meeting to seek shareholder approval of the acquisition and the change in nature and scale of Macro Energy's business. An example of a listing requirement was the profit test, which required that the company had been a going concern for three full financial years, making an aggregated profit of at least AU $1,000,000, would have been fulfilled as well.

The acquisition also changed the capital structure of the company. Prior to consolidation, its issued capital was 217,607,664 shares and 16,000,000 options. Assuming no existing options were exercised, postconsolidation issued capital was estimated at 38,076,581 shares and 3,849,518 options. In exchange for the acquisition, Macro Energy was to issue to the Digital CC shareholders a set of vendor consideration securities, which are detailed later in Section 27.2.4.1. As part of the payment for consultancy services in arranging this IPO, the company was also expected to incur a capital raising fee of 1,600,000 in issuing shares to the company's consultants for this IPO. On completion, its estimated capital structure therefore consisted of 167,941,236 shares, 12,166,228 options, and 24,950,130 performance rights.

27.2.3 Proposed business

Digital CC was incorporated in Australia in January 2014 and was actively involved in earning new coins through investments in dedicated mining pools and hardware. The mining process enabled Digital CC to participate in seeking to earn new coins through the dedication of computing processing power to the Bitcoin verification and processing. Digital CC mined bitcoins and may also launch alternative cryptocurrencies (known as "altcoins").

Digital CC planned to use its listing on the ASX to gain access to capital for the purpose of growing its mining and hashing capabilities, trading in digital currencies, developing new products that relate to digital currency trading and use, and considering the acquisition of other existing digital currency businesses that might complement or assist Digital CC to grow its size and scale. Its business activities are summarized below.

27.2.3.1 Bitcoin mining

Digital CC already had invested in dedicated pooled mining platforms and hardware using specialized equipment. It proposed to invest in new technology increasing its own hash rate, improving its chances of mining. Its business model consisted of acquiring hashing power for rates that are below market rates through strategic hardware and contracting agreements, utilizing hashing power and participating in mining, and on-selling the computer power at market rates. This would be enabled by the close relationships it had developed with its key supplier, BitFury (Malta); and the location of its data centers in Iceland, where electricity is cheap.

After the announcement of the reverse IPO, Digital CC signed a strategic agreement with CloudHashing.com, one of the world's largest Bitcoin mining providers (and a company associated with a proposed director of Macro Energy) for CloudHashing. com to manage Digital CC's mining hardware. An agreement was also signed with Bitfury, one of the leading hardware manufacturers for Bitcoin mining hardware, for the supply of the same. Digital CC then used that hardware to mine more than 1700 new Bitcoins and traded them with a return of approximately 31% up to April 30, 2014.

Digital CC still intended to hire hashing power, but only as an alternative to the extent that manufacturers cannot provide sufficient hardware or that Digital CC has excess cash that it wishes to invest at short notice.

27.2.3.2 Digital currencies trading and investment

Digital CC proposed to trade digital currencies with specialized strategies including arbitrage, buying long positions, selling short positions, future contracts, and market making of exchanges. Its trading operations were managed by its chief investment officer, who was also proposed to sit on the board.

Digital CC's arbitrage proposal would take advantage of the price differences between Bitcoin exchanges that arise from the illiquidity of the nascent Bitcoin markets. Digital CC also planned to forecast the rise and fall of Bitcoin prices and to buy and sell Bitcoin futures accordingly.

Digital CC was engaged with two of the six major Bitcoin exchanges (Bitfinex and ICBIT) to act as a market maker, by completing buy/sell orders at prices that other participants are unwilling to transact at. Digital CC would generate revenue from the difference in the price at which it buys and sells Bitcoins. It would only engage in market making once it completed its internal trading platform.

27.2.3.3 Consumer products

Digital CC planned to release some of its initial suite of retail products in the first quarter of 2014. Digital CC disclosed two examples of products that it might be working on: a digital wallet, which would facilitate digital and real-world purchases using digital currency via a mobile and Web application, and a digital API, which would enable third-party developers to integrate Digital CC's payment services into their own applications, allowing any Web site to accept digital currency payments and issue refunds.

27.2.3.4 Others

Digital CC also planned to consider the acquisition of complementary businesses. It planned to adopt the "first-mover" strategy, integrating emerging and alternative digital currencies, although it remained primarily focused on Bitcoin.

27.2.4 Corporate structure and material business contracts

There are various subsidiaries under Digital CC that, while potentially shielding the parent Digital CC Ltd and one another from liability, further increase the complexity of commercial arrangements. This section visualizes the corporate structure before listing the material business contracts entered into both internally and externally.

Digital CC Limited:
Parent company listed on ASX
*Digital CC **Holdings** Pty Ltd*:
Holding company incorporated in Australia

*Digital CC **Trading** Pty Ltd*:	*Digital CC IP Pty Ltd*:	*Digital CC Management Pty Ltd*:	*Digital CC USA Holdings, Inc.*:	*Digital CC IP Limited (HK)*:	*Digital CC Limited (HK)*:
Company incorporated in Australia with right to trading accounts and leased hardware and hashing capacity from Digital CC Management Pty Ltd	Company incorporated in Australia owning Digital CC's intellectual property rights	Company incorporated in Australia owning hashing capacity, bitcoins, litecoins, cash, and hardware	Company incorporated in Delaware for US-based operations and employees and will be parent to two further limited liability companies	Company incorporated in Hong Kong that will license intellectual property rights from Digital CC IP Pty Ltd	Company incorporated in Hong Kong

---

There were a number of material agreements that the company entered into, which included the following.

27.2.4.1 Share purchase agreement between the company and the vendors

Macro Energy agreed to acquire 100% of the issued share capital of Digital CC from the existing shareholders. The conditions precedent were Macro Energy's completion of the offer, undergoing consolidation of its existing capital, the parties obtaining all third-party consents, approvals or waivers to the transaction, the lack of any material adverse change in respect of either party, and Macro Energy obtaining ASX approval to relist, to be satisfied by June 30, 2014.

In consideration of completion of the agreement, the company would issue after consolidation to all vendors, a set of vendor consideration securities: 82,764,655 shares, 8,316,710 options, 16,633,420 class A performance rights, and 8,316,710 class B performance rights. For both classes of performance rights, each nontransferable performance right vests to one share, but on different vesting conditions for each class. Class A rights vest on July 1, 2015 upon earnings before interest, tax, depreciation, and amortization (EBITDA) from January 1, 2014 to June 30, 2014 amount to at least AU $9,000,000, while class B rights vest a year later if EBITDA from July 1, 2015 to June 30, 2016 amount to at least $30,000,000. The 8,316,710 unlisted options in the company are exercisable at $0.28 each expiring 2 years after completion of the acquisition. These were expected to be subjected to escrow rules by the ASX. The agreement also entitled either party to a break fee of $150,000 and contained standard terms and conditions considered standard for an agreement of this nature.

27.2.4.2 Loan facility agreement between the company and Digital CC

Macro Energy agreed to provide an unsecured loan facility to Digital CC of up to $2,000,000 prior to completion of the acquisition, to enable Digital CC's subsidiary to contract with BitFury (Malta) for mining hardware. The interest rate is 15% per annum. The contract is on standard commercial and arms' length terms, repayable within 3 months if the acquisition fails to proceed or on any other date that parties agree to in writing.

27.2.4.3 CloudHashing agreement between Digital CC and Technology IQ

As mentioned in its proposed business, this agreement was for the purchase of hashing power and the provision of hosting facilities by Digital CC. Technology IQ Ltd, which is one of the vendors, is based in the United Kingdom and trades under the name Cloud-Hashing. Its proprietary mining management software is proposed to be deployed on Digital CC's hardware. Digital CC is also to undertake Bitcoin trading for the account of Technology IQ Ltd.

27.2.4.4 BitFury agreement

Digital CC Management Pty Ltd and BitFury (Malta) entered into a master agreement under which parties will from time to time enter into contracts with each other for the purchase of computing hardware for mining, specifications and pricings of which will be negotiated on an order by order basis. BitFury (Malta) is not a related party, and the agreement was negotiated at arms' length terms. Besides terms on the calculation of compensation for delayed delivery or warranty claims, the agreement contains terms considered standard for an international agreement of this nature.

27.2.4.5 Lease of goods agreement

Digital CC Trading Pty Ltd and Digital CC Management Pty Ltd entered into an agreement under which the latter will lease to the former such hardware, equipment, contractual rights, and other goods as determined from time to time, for which the former must pay the latter a lease fee equal to market value, payable annually on arrears. The agreement contains terms considered standard for an international agreement of this nature.

27.2.4.6 Development agreement between Digital CC IP Pty Ltd (a wholly owned subsidiary of Digital CC) and Mpire Media Pty Ltd

Digital CC IP Pty Ltd engaged Mpire Media to develop systems, content, and branding on behalf of Digital CC IP Pty Ltd, in exchange for a development fee agreed by parties on a per job basis at the then applicable market rate. The development agreement otherwise contains terms that are considered standard for an agreement of this nature including standard rights to intellectual property developed under the agreement. One of the proposed directors is the sole director and sole ultimate shareholder of Mpire Media.

27.2.4.7 Intellectual property license agreements

Digital CC IP Pty Ltd entered into three separate licensing agreements with Digital CC Trading Pty Ltd, with Digital CC Management Pty Ltd and with Digital CC IP Limited, incorporated in Hong Kong. Each involves Digital CC IP granting a nonexclusive license over the IP it holds to the other company, in exchange for a license fee equal to market value payable annually in arrears. Each otherwise contains terms that are considered standard for an agreement of this nature.

27.2.4.8 Shareholders' and directors' loan agreement and deed of variation between Digital CC and the entities associated with certain vendors and proposed directors

Under these loan agreements, entered into on March 7, 2014, the lenders, which comprise two vendors and two companies each controlled by a different proposed director, are to provide unsecured funding to Digital CC to continue with its activities prior to completing the reverse takeover. Digital CC is to pay interest at 63% of any profits derived from the use of the funds until the loans are repaid in full. Digital CC may repay the funds in its discretion, but before the completion of the offer or 6 months following the date of the agreement. The agreement otherwise contains terms that are considered standard for an agreement of this nature including in relation to default rights except that in the event of default a single lender cannot itself commence recovery proceedings against Digital CC, requiring at least one other lender to join with them.

Some lenders assigned their debts to their related entities, such that each of the creditors of Digital CC is now vendors. Digital CC later requested more funds from the lenders, and the parties entered into an agreement to provide additional funds on demand subject to a cap for each lender. These funds are proposed to be repaid by way of converting the amounts outstanding during the offer into shares in Macro Energy pursuant to the offer for each of the lenders, at the deemed issue price of AU $0.20 of the principal amounts of the respective loans per share. Digital CC has the right to repay the loans earlier in cash. For any loan amounts exceeding the caps, they are to be repaid within 6 months after the date of advancement. Interest accrues either by way of an in-specie transfer, for loans to purchase equipment or mining contracts, of 5% of the hashing power attributable to the relevant equipment or contract or at 10% per annum calculated and payable monthly for monies loaned for any other purpose.

27.2.4.9 Facility agreement between Digital CC and one of the vendors, Lydian Enterprises Pty Ltd ATF Lydian Trust

One of the vendors advanced a further unsecured loan facility to Digital CC, in the sum of up to $2,800,000 to fund the Bitfury purchase during the time beginning from the date of announcement of the transaction and the completion of the transaction and relisting. Interest is at 15% of the principal outstanding, payable on the last day of each month until borrowed funds are repaid in full. The principal of $2,800,000 and any outstanding interest were proposed to be repaid by a lump sum cash payment out of funds raised from the offer.

27.2.4.10 Trading account agreements between Digital CC Management Pty Ltd (a wholly owned subsidiary of Digital CC) and Alex Karis, NRB International LLC, and William Brindise

Digital CC Management entered into separate trading account agreements with two proposed directors (who were also controlling vendors), under which parties confirmed that trading exchange accounts are held on trust for Digital CC Management Pty Ltd and that each account holder is only to deal with the accounts at the direction of Digital CC Management under a bare trust agreement.

Following in time to the trading account agreement, Digital CC Trading entered into a trading account transfer agreement with Digital CC Management Pty Ltd, under which the latter party transfers the accounts in the first agreement to the former party, which confirms that account balances will be held (and invested) on trust for the benefit of Digital CC Management Pty Ltd.

These agreements otherwise contain terms that are considered standard for an agreement of this nature including in relation to rights to vest the trust and indemnities and default.

27.2.4.11 Other agreements

Some other agreements are domain transfer agreements with Zhenya Tsvetnenko and Alex Karis; a line of credit agreement for Digital CC Holdings Pty Ltd to permit Digital

CC Management to borrow up to $10,000,000 to be repaid on the expiry of 36 months or such later date as agreed by parties, without interest; a general security agreement in respect of the line of credit; and executive employment agreements for various directors and the agreements executed between vendors for the acquisition of shares.

27.3 ETF: WBT

27.3.1 Introduction

The WBT, as an ETF proposed to be available to mainstream investors, presents a more novel financial product. The legal structure for the WBT is for a trust to be created to hold bitcoins. WBT proposed to issue 10,000,000 Winklevoss Bitcoin Shares, which represented units of "fractional undivided beneficial interest in and ownership of the Trust," with no par value (Math-Based Asset Services LLC, 2014). These shares were to be listed and traded on the NASDAQ.

Like commodities-based funds, like those in gold, silver, or precious metals, a bitcoin ETF makes it "significantly easier to gain exposure to bitcoins" (Popper and Lattman, 2013). At the time of writing, WBT has yet to receive regulatory approval. However, bitcoin analyst Gil Luria suggests that the fact that the US Securities and Exchange Commission (SEC) has allowed the filing of the WBT's extensive registration statement in Form S-1 is an indication of a possible regulatory approval in the future (Abrams, 2014).

The WBT is intended to be a common law trust, formed on under New York law pursuant to the trust agreement between Math-Based Asset Services LLC, as sponsor, and the trustee, to be appointed. The trust agreement will give effect to the legal structure explained in the filing by setting forth the respective rights and duties of the sponsor and the trustee and establishing the segregated custody account of the trust to hold the bitcoins deposited with the WBT.

27.3.2 How the trust operates

The WBT is managed as a passive vehicle, unlike a corporation. Bitcoins held by the trustee would only be transferred out of the trust custody account for certain authorized purposes, which excludes holding or trading in commodities futures or other derivatives contracts or engaging in other activities regulated by the US Commodity Exchange Act.

Broadly speaking, the WBT will offer shares backed by bitcoins. How this works is that behind the scenes, the WBT will, from time to time, issue baskets of shares (baskets) in exchange for bitcoin deposits and distribute bitcoins in connection with redemptions of baskets, both activities combining to result in fluctuations in outstanding shares. Creating and redeeming baskets require delivery into and distribution out of the WBT of the bitcoins represented by the baskets being created and redeemed. The bitcoins required for basket creation were to be calculated on the combined net asset value of the number of baskets being created or redeemed.

On the first day of trading, each share in the baskets will compose of 0.20 bitcoins, and each basket comprises 10,000 bitcoins. When selling all or part of the shares in the basket, every creation or redemption is subject to a transaction fee.

WBT was to reflect the performance of the price of bitcoins on the Winklevoss Index (WinkDex) after deduction of the expenses incurred by the WBT. Institutional and retail investors were expected to be attracted to the convenience and price point in accessing exposure to bitcoins while minimizing their credit risk.

27.3.3 Reasons for investing in WBT

27.3.3.1 Reduced risks of holding bitcoins

Ordinarily, a large direct investment in bitcoins is expensive because bitcoins would be acquired, stored, and safeguarded. While not identical to a direct investment, the WBT shares were proposed as an alternative opportunity to investors to participate in the bitcoin markets via securities investing. The logistics of acquisition, storage, and safekeeping would be dealt with by the trustee using a proprietary system, the expenses of which were built into the share price.

WBT distinguished itself from other digital math-based asset exchange-traded products by highlighting that it used a proprietary security system involving the cold storage of private keys to protect against bitcoin theft or loss. WBT intends to locate these private vaults, at least initially, within the United States and to allow periodic inspections of the security system and vaults by third-party consultants. The trustee holds the private keys for the WBT's digital wallet as a custodian, and through the trustee, the WBT has direct and actual ownership of bitcoins. It is also intended for the share price to reflect the performance of the price of bitcoins not through derivative instruments or future contracts but by the WinkDex with the sponsor's fee. As these shares represented units of fractional undivided beneficial interest in and ownership of the trust and the bitcoins, as assets owned by WBT, are not subject to borrowing arrangements with third parties, WBT shares were marketed as carrying little credit risk.

27.3.3.2 Transparency

There were other reasons for investors to be attracted to investing in WBT. Investors are free to implement their own various investment strategies using the WBT exchange-traded shares. As WBT was not to hold or employ any derivative securities and the value of WBT's holdings was to be published daily on WBT's Web site, it was also marketed as transparent.

27.3.3.3 Cheaper

WBT shares were expected to also trade in NASDAQ's secondary market at prices lower or higher than their net asset value, depending on factors such as the variations in trading hours and liquidity between NASDAQ and other bitcoin exchanges.

The WBT was expected to incur a single ordinary recurring expense, which was the sponsor's fee. In return, the sponsor undertook to assume certain administrative and marketing expenses incurred by the trust. Details of fees and payments are covered in Section 27.3.4.1.

As a result of recurring bitcoin transfers to pay sponsor's fees and other fees incurred by the trust, WBT's net asset value, and therefore the fractional number of bitcoins represented by each share, was expected to decrease over time, a trend that would not be reversed by fresh bitcoin deposits into the trust custody account received for fresh baskets issued by WBT.

27.3.4 Trust structure

27.3.4.1 Roles of the sponsor and the trustee

Math-Based Asset Services LLC is a limited liability company formed in 2013 in Delaware and is wholly owned by Winklevoss Capital Management LLC. Under Delaware corporate law and the Math-Based Asset Services LLC's governing documents, Winklevoss Capital Management LLC is not responsible for the debts, obligations, and liabilities of the sponsor solely by reason of being the sole member of the sponsor. The trust was to be administered using a proprietary system owned by Winklevoss IP LLC, exclusively licensed to the sponsor for the purposes of operating an ETF.

The sponsor, Math-Based Asset Services LLC, was to arrange for the creation of the trust, the registration of the shares for their public offering in the United States, and the listing of the shares on the NASDAQ. It would assume certain administrative and marketing expenses incurred by the WBT: the trustee's monthly fee and expenses reimbursable under the trust agreement, exchange listing fees, US Securities and Exchange Commission registration fees, printing and mailing costs, audit fees, marketing and legal expenses subject to a per annum cap, and the costs of the WBT's organization and the initial sale of the shares. The sponsor had the discretion to waive its fee. The fee is calculated by the trustee and to be paid by transfer of bitcoins from the trust custody to the sponsor custody accounts on a monthly basis, calculated at the WinkDex spot price at the time.

The trustee is yet to be appointed. In its capacity as trustee of the trust, the trustee is generally responsible for the day-to-day administration of the trust. The trustee would receive and process orders to create and redeem baskets in coordination with the Depository Trust Company (DTC) and calculate the net asset value of the trust and per share. It was to transfer the bitcoins it held out of the trust custody account in certain circumstances: paying the sponsor's fee and any extraordinary trust expenses not assumed by the sponsor out of WBT's bitcoins and selling WBT's bitcoins at termination of WBT and distributing the cash proceeds to the shareholders of record. The trustee could sell bitcoins in the trust expense account to cover WBT's expenses and liabilities not assumed by the sponsor or as required by law or regulation. Every delivery, transfer, or sale of bitcoins by the trust to pay any trust expense was to be a taxable event to shareholders.

The trust's custodian is also the trustee. Although the trust's bitcoins are not stored in a physical sense, the transaction records included in the blockchain assign a location for each of the trust's bitcoins to digital wallets established by the trustee using the trust's proprietary security system, which wallets digitally hold the bitcoins and permit the trust to move its bitcoins. Access to those digital wallets, and the bitcoins they hold, is restricted through the public–private key pair relating to each digital wallet. As custodian, the trustee is responsible for the safekeeping of the trust's private keys used to access the digital wallets. The trustee also facilitates the transfer of bitcoins into and out of the trust custody account through the bitcoin custody accounts it will maintain for authorized participants and the sponsor. In accordance with the procedures of the security system and the provisions of the trust agreement, the trustee will store all of the trust's digital wallet private keys in US vaulting premises on a segregated basis and will deliver such private keys to the trustee's authorized administrative operations to permit access to the digital wallets on an as-needed basis.

27.3.4.2 Custody of WBT bitcoins in cold storage

WBT's digital wallets, comprising both public and private keys, are maintained by the trustee under cold storage mechanisms through the lease of the proprietary security system. Wallets held in cold storage can receive bitcoin deposits but require activation in order to send bitcoins. Activation includes retrieving the public and private keys and entering them into a program that reconstructs the wallet.

The trustee is the custodian of WBT's private keys per the terms and conditions of the trust agreement. Under the license agreements, the sponsor was to administer periodic updates and procure periodic reviews of the security system, and it also undertook to pay up to a certain limit per annum for such expenses.

The trustee may accept bitcoin deposits on behalf of WBT under the standing instructions in the trust agreement. These transferred bitcoins are only available to the trust to the extent that they have been transferred to the digital wallets held in cold storage, and generally, deposits are expected to be made directly into the wallets.

27.3.4.3 Segregated custody accounts for temporary live storage

The trust custody account was established by the trust agreement, which enjoins the trustee to maintain daily reports and produce monthly statements on bitcoin movements in and out of the trust custody account, to hold bitcoins for the trust custody account in digital wallets in the security system's administrative portal. Those wallets were to be used only for that purpose. The public and private keys of every wallet were to be in cold storage except for those wallets created solely to temporarily hold bitcoins. The trustee was also to keep backup data relating to the keys.

WBT's bitcoins in the trust custody account were to be kept segregated from all other assets that the trustee owns or holds for others. Segregation was achieved by storing

WBT's bitcoins in the proprietary security system. The sponsor and the security consultant it engaged were authorized to visit the trustee's premises and inspect the security system and the vaults and records.

The trustee was also expected to adhere to a transfer confirmation protocol. Transfers into the account could only be made from an authorized participant custody account or from an account authorized by the sponsor for that purpose. Transfers out of the account would only be made in the three circumstances outlined in Section 27.3.4.1.

The trustee was empowered to refuse or accept instructions to transfer if as custodian, it believed such instructions had unacceptable form (or illegal) or threatened the security of WBT's assets and to amend the rules and procedures of transfer necessary for compliance or security, notifying the sponsor of the same.

The trustee limited its liability for loss or damage suffered by WBT to that directly resulting from gross negligence, fraud, or willful default of its duties and furthermore to the market value of the lost or damaged bitcoins at the time of the trustee's discovery of that gross negligence, fraud, or willful default, on prompt notification of the sponsor of such discovery. The trustee would also indemnify on demand its custodial operations out of WBT's assets except where those costs, expenses, damages, liabilities, and losses were directly due to its gross negligence, fraud, or willful default. The trustee was also protected by a force majeure clause.

27.3.4.4 Valuation

Net asset valuation of WBT and of each share would be conducted by the trustee around the close of each trading day based on the WinkDex spot price or such publicly available price as the sponsor may deem fairly to represent the bitcoins' commercial value. In valuing shares, where the WinkDex spot price is not available and the next most recent spot price is determined to be no longer reliable by the sponsor, then fair value pricing by the trustee will be used, which involves subjective factors, thus a different bitcoin price than current market valuations.

These prices were to be published as soon as practicable after determination of the net asset value on the WBT Web site. Investors could also turn to financial service providers such as Bloomberg financial terminals or other information sites for bitcoin pricing information or with bid/ask spreads directly from bitcoin exchanges. The WinkDex spot price itself was constituted of three bitcoin exchanges.

27.3.4.5 Share arrangements

Under the trust agreement, the trustee may create and issue unlimited shares. It could only do so in blocks of 50,000 and only to certain authorized participants, at the net asset valuation for 50,000 shares. These authorized participants would then distribute these shares to the public through sale on the NASDAQ, at prices to be determined by reference to the price of bitcoins represented by each share and the trading price of shares at the time of the sale. More information on authorized participants is contained in Section 27.3.4.6.

The prospectus contained a registration statement stating an upper limit on the creation and issuance of shares, which when exceeded required the additional shares to be registered.

All shares were of equal class, transferable, fully paid, and nonassessable. Rather than individual certificates issued for the shares, global certificates would evidence all shares outstanding at any time and would be deposited by the trustee with the DTC.

Shareholders had limited rights. Shareholders did not have the statutory rights of a corporate shareholder, such as the right to bring claims in oppression or derivative claims. Shareholders also had limited conversion or preemptive rights and did not have redemption rights or the right to distribution. They could, however, vote on certain matters as provided for in the trust agreement. For example, the trust may be terminated by the trustee where shareholders owning 75% of outstanding shares agree. However, shareholders need only be notified of amendments to the trust, and their approval thereto is not required.

On termination and liquidation of WBT, shareholders of record (on a record date set by the trustee) would receive from the trustee a pro rata portion of the cash proceeds remaining, after settling WBT's outstanding liabilities and setting aside reserves for government taxes, charges, and future and contingent liabilities determined by the trustee.

Under the trust agreement, only three categories of shareholders were permitted: DTC participants, those maintaining a custodial relationship with a DTC participant (known as "indirect participants"), and others who hold interests in the shares through DTC participants and indirect participants. Shares could only be transferred by DTC's book-entry system.

27.3.4.6 Redemption of shares by authorized participants

Redemption of shares would only be in whole baskets and only by or through an authorized participant.

The access and withdrawal of bitcoins for redemption would follow the same procedure as for the deposit of bitcoins in reverse. Where an authorized participant wishes to withdraw bitcoins, the trustee's administrative operations would instruct its custodial operations to deliver the relevant public and private keys from cold storage, thus activating and reconstituting the wallets on the security system's administrative portal. Remaining bitcoins not transferred for withdrawal would then be transferred to another wallet still in cold storage. Wallets previously activated from cold storage would be discarded and not reused.

Authorized participants had to be registered broker-dealers or institutional security market participants who did not need broker-dealer registration or DTC participant. They had to enter into an authorized participant agreement with the sponsor and trustee, setting out procedures for the creation and redemption of baskets and for the delivery of bitcoins, whole and fractional, required for creation and redemption. Deposits made by authorized participants would receive no compensation or inducement from the sponsor or WBT, and no person would have any obligation to the sponsor or trust to affect any share sale or resale. Authorized participants took the risk that they would be subject to securities regulation as statutory underwriters.

Before starting a creation or redemption order, an authorized participant had to enter into an authorized participant custody account with the trustee to establish an authorized participant custody account to hold bitcoins with the trustee. Bitcoins held in each of these accounts are segregated from all other assets held by the trustee; therefore, the authorized participant has a proprietary interest in those specific bitcoins, rather than being assets of WBT. Deposits made thusly are safe from the risk of the trustee's insolvency. No fees applied to such deposits where the authorized participant custody account is used only to transfer bitcoins to and from the trust custody account, and the trustee is compensated for its custodial operations in the trust custody account.

Authorized participants may act for their own accounts or as agents for other securities participants who wish to create or redeem baskets.

To create a basket, bitcoins would be transferred to the trust custody account from the authorized participant custody accounts. To redeem a basket, the transfer would happen in reverse. Creation procedures largely mirror those for redemption, but in reverse.

Redemption is initiated when an authorized participant places an order with the trustee to do so, no later than 3:59:59 p.m. on each business day that NASDAQ is open for regular trading, in the correct form. Such an order is effective on the date of receipt. The authorized participant thereby agrees to deliver the basket(s) to be redeemed through DTC's book-entry system to the trust and to transfer the transaction fee to the authorized participant, by 9:00 a.m. New York time on the third business day following the order's effective date. Redemption distribution is triggered on completion of the confirmation protocol and comprises transferring the bitcoins held in the trust custody account to the redeeming authorizing participant's authorized participant custody account, ignoring fractions of a bitcoin smaller than a Satoshi (i.e., 0.00000001 of a bitcoin). Redemption distribution is subject to taxes or other governmental charges. If some baskets have not yet been credited, the redemption distribution will be delivered to the extent of whole baskets and subject to receipt of a fee to extend the redemption distribution date, the remaining whole baskets the next business day. The trustee would be able to determine this extended date from time to time, and any further outstanding amount would be canceled. If the authorized participant has "collateralized its obligation to deliver the baskets" on terms that the sponsor and trustee agree on and the baskets to be redeemed are not credited to the trustee's DTC account by 9:00 a.m. New York time on such third business day, the trustee may still deliver the redemption distribution. To facilitate delivery, the trustee shall calculate the bitcoins required for delivery and instruct its custodial operations to deliver the private keys for the activation of the relevant digital wallets, on a "first in, first out" basis.

The trustee has the discretion, and will on the sponsor's direction, to suspend the right of redemption or postpone the redemption settlement date when the NASDAQ is closed by reason other than customary weekend and holiday closings, when NASDAQ trading is suspended or restricted or during emergencies resulting from the impracticability of bitcoin delivery, disposal, or evaluation or from a potential compromise of the security system, in the view of the sponsor, trustee, or their agents. The sponsor, trustee, and their agents are not liable for loss or damage resulting from these suspensions or postponements.

27.3.5 Risk factors

As a recent technological development, bitcoins may be likened to assets such as commodities and currencies. Although governments and regulators across various countries have not made specific promulgation on the subject of commodities, tax, and security laws applicable to bitcoins, the sponsor discussed the assets as such, and this regulatory uncertainty is a source of risk for WBT and its shares.

27.3.5.1 Private key loss or destruction

There is the risk that a private key safeguarded and stored by WBT using the security system were to be lost or destroyed; WBT would not be able to access the bitcoins held in that wallet. Such loss or destruction of the private key may be irreversible.

27.3.5.2 Exchange market and WinkDex risks

WBT share value is pinned to bitcoin prices as measured by WinkDex. WinkDex is calculated from transaction prices of bitcoins on high-volume bitcoin exchanges, where participants use "fiat currency to trade, buy, and sell bitcoins based on bid-ask trading." Several factors contributed to high bitcoin price volatility over the three years preceding the publishing of the prospectus. They include the global bitcoin demand and supply, investors' expectations on inflation, currency exchange rates, service disruptions of the bitcoin exchanges, regulatory actions, and the maintenance of the bitcoin network's open-source software.

Because of the disproportionate amount of investor and speculative demand for bitcoins relative to the currently limited adoption of bitcoins in retail and commercial markets, bitcoins are subject to price volatility. Retail and commercial acceptance of Bitcoins for payment could even contract in the future.

Bitcoin exchanges are themselves a source of risk, being vulnerable to hacking attacks and regulatory clampdowns, reducing liquidity and increasing price volatility.

WBT itself might acquire so many bitcoins and grow to the extent that WBT itself impacts global bitcoin supply and demand, independent of other factors affecting the global bitcoin market.

Other factors also contribute to the volatility of the price of bitcoins or the WinkDex spot price, including political and economic crises, competition from other means of bitcoin investment, other DMBA ETPs tracking bitcoin prices, purchase and sale of bitcoins in the bitcoin exchange market associated with basket creation and redemption and nonoverlapping trading hours of NASDAQ, and the bitcoin exchange market.

27.3.5.3 Trust risks

The sponsor and its management operating the trust investment vehicle, the mechanisms and procedures governing share creation, redemption and offering, and governing bitcoin storage were all constituted specifically for the WBT, and they have never been tested before. As a result, there might be unexpected operational or trading issues to which the sponsor may be ill-suited to deal with, resulting in a decrease in share value.

Besides the fact that shareholders would not be protected by the Investment Company Act or the Commodities Exchange Act, future regulatory actions taken by US and foreign governments might adversely affect the nature of an investment in WBT shares or restrict or prohibit the use of bitcoins or the operation of the bitcoin network. These may directly affect the price of bitcoins or significantly increase the operating costs of WBT. Where such costs become untenable, the sponsor will instruct the trustee to terminate the trust, which could result in liquidation of bitcoins at a time adverse to investors.

Although discounts or premiums in the share trading price relative to net asset value per share may widen due to nonoverlapping trading hours, the prospectus predicted that the authorized participants would be motivated to exploit arbitrage opportunities, causing the public trading price to tend to track net asset value in the longer run. However, a large-volume arbitrage may still distort the trading price whether temporarily or in the longer run. Arbitrage also depended on the smooth running of the basket creation and redemption procedures to preserve liquidity. Liquidity could also be affected by the withdrawal of an authorized participant holding a substantial interest in shares. Arbitrage could be stymied by the postponement, suspension, or rejection of creation and redemption orders, which is permitted in certain scenarios under the trust agreement. Arbitrage depended on maintaining the integrity of and confidence in the security system. Finally, arbitrage depended on the existence of an active trading market developing on NASDAQ and WBT's assets reaching a suitable size, which could not be guaranteed as WBT was a new fund.

NASDAQ may halt trading on the shares.

A significant risk relating to the trust vehicle is the shareholders' limited recourse against WBT, the trustee, and the sponsor under New York law, combined with WBT's lack of insurance protection. There is therefore the risk that a loss is occasioned to WBT's bitcoins for which no party can be held responsible. Depositor protection rules applicable to banks or to members of the Federal Deposit Insurance Corporation or Securities Investor Protection Corporation do not apply to WBT, leaving WBT shareholders vulnerable to losses in bitcoins held by WBT. Moreover, the trustee had limited its liability for loss or damage sustained by WBT under the trust agreement. Even if held liable, that party may lack the financial resources to restore lost, damaged, or stolen bitcoins.

Other risks relating to the trust vehicle may adversely affect share value, for example, where WBT assets are sold in the indemnification of the trustee or sponsor for their liabilities or expenses, to pay expenses not borne by the sponsor when bitcoin prices are low, to pay extraordinary expenses from unexpected events, or where the trustee makes an incorrect determination of net asset value per share and of WBT. Moreover, shareholders are taxed on every delivery or transfer of bitcoins by WBT to satisfy the sponsor's fee and other expenses. The trust may be forced to terminate and liquidate, including upon the events specified in the trust agreement, when prices are disadvantages to shareholders.

27.3.5.4 Conflicts of interest

Conflicts of interest may arise between the sponsor, responsible for managing WBT, its related entities, and WBT. No fiduciary duties are owed by the sponsor and its related entities to WBT and the shareholders, which could allow them to favor their own interests at the expense of WBT and the shareholders, such as directly competing with WBT or abusing the indemnification clause in the trust agreement. The sponsor is not required to serve as a sponsor for WBT for any length of time; discontinuation may lead to a liquidation where a substitute has not been appointed, and even if a substitute is appointed, he or she may lack the expertise to manage WBT.

27.3.6 Termination events

There was no fixed termination date. On 90 business days' prior notice, the trustee or the sponsor may terminate the trust for any reason. WBT may also be terminated with immediate effect by the sponsor if the trustee ceased to offer the contemplated custodial services, by either party if the trust agreement is found to be illegal, by the trustee if it reasonably thinks that the trust is insolvent or about to be so, and by either party if the trust agreement ceases to be in full force and effect.

On termination, the trustee shall enter into a trust custody account agreement with a sponsor-approved custodian, which shall set forth largely identical terms to the custody of WBT's bitcoins with the new custodian. If no acceptable redelivery arrangements are made, then the trustee can continue to store bitcoins and keys and to charge for those services, and 6 months from the date of termination, the trustee can sell the bitcoins and the account for the proceeds.

"Termination events" include the delisting of shares from NASDAQ and failure to secure listing approval on another national securities exchange, the agreement of shareholders holding 75% of assets; the elapsing of 60 days from the trustee's notice of resignation and when a willing successor has not been put in place; the determination of WBT to be an "investment company" under the US Investment Company Act by the Securities Exchange Commission; the determination of WBT to be a "commodity pool" under the Commodity Exchange Act or a "monetary transmitter" under FinCEN regulations and when the sponsor informs the trustee that termination is therefore advisable; a change in its current tax treatment as a grantor trust; forced shutdown or liquidation by a US regulator; the aggregate market capitalization of WBT falling below a specified figure within 6 months of the last trading date on which it was at that figure and the sponsor decides to terminate; the elapsing of 60 days since DTC stops being a depository for the shares and the sponsor has not appointed another willing depository; or when the trustee elects to terminate when the sponsor is deemed conclusively to have resigned effective immediately as a result of bankruptcy, insolvency, receivership, or liquidation.

27.4 CROWDFUNDING

As an alternative to seeking funding on the stock exchanges, the second part of this chapter explores the increasing use of crowdfunding Web sites and the growth in cryptocurrency-related technologies in this area.

27.4.1 History of crowdfunding

Crowdfunding is the latest form of social lending. It originated from the friendly societies of eighteenth century and has developed eventually to the crowdsourced lending platforms of today (Everett, 2014). Crowdfunding gained traction with the launch of ArtistShare, the first online platform to raise funds from the public via Internet. Following this, many other reward- and donation-based crowdfunding platforms like IndieGoGo, Kickstarter, RocketHub, EquityNet, GoFundMe, MicroVentures, and FundaGeek were launched. Such Web sites charge a commission amounting to a certain percent of the funds raised and often do not claim ownership of the projects. More than 700 crowdfunding sites currently exist and new platforms with improvised features and services offered are still being launched. Yet, very few platforms remain as a large and dominant crowdfunding sites, unlike the very popular crowdfunding Web site Kickstarter. It hosts creative projects to raise funds by crowdsourcing individual investors. On the Kickstarter platform, the creators of the project receive the contributed funds only if the defined funding goal is met within a certain period of time, unlike IndieGoGo that allows the creators to use any amount of funds received without the need to meet the specified monetary funding goal. The contributors of the funds are offered special rewards of some sort for their investment, which may also possibly constitute a goodie bag. The current security laws and SEC regulations do not govern reward-based crowdfunding, as the so-called reward may not qualify as a security in most cases. Like Bitcoin, Kickstarter does not have any intermediary and is not responsible for the funded projects that either fail or deliver on a delayed basis. Fortunately, the reported fraud rate in crowdfunding has been very low over the years. In addition to the cost and security issues concerned with such centralized platforms, they impose restrictions on project creators that add to their burden. Though crowdfunding schemes pose many risks to both contributors and the project creators, they continue to surge in popularity.

While many crowdfunding sites hesitate to accept funds in bitcoins, few of them have started accepting bitcoins along with most major fiat currencies, following the requests from its users. A Sydney-based crowdfunding platform with the highest success rate named Pozible accepts Bitcoin, as it considers cryptocurrencies as an unavoidable method of payment transactions, owing to its gaining momentum over the Internet.

A new development in the crowdfunding sector is equity crowdfunding, which provides not only unlimited upside return but also internal governance control mechanism. Investors in equity crowdfunding fund businesses that have the potential to be successful for which they receive equity interest in the start-up. The JOBS (Jumpstart Our Business Start-ups) Act in the United States facilitates equity crowdfunding by allowing investors to receive a financial return without registering the offering with the SEC while investing in business ventures. As the frictional costs of raising new capital through this method are low, it even has the potential to disrupt or even replace the traditional equity financing schemes. Both virtual currencies and crowdfunding represent risks because current rules and regulations impose restrictions on traditional equity-based funding models. Such restrictions inhibit emerging enterprises' business activities to a certain extent. The research work of Groshoff (2014) details the new business possibilities for crowdfunded entities and also addresses the unnecessary constraints imposed on enterprises by law, regulators, and policymakers. Seedrs, the first equity crowdfunding platform to receive regulatory approval, supports the start-ups throughout Europe. It is also an "all or nothing" platform like Kickstarter, where the project creators do not receive any funds unless the defined investment target is reached.

27.4.2 Developments in crypto crowdfunding

As the price of Bitcoin and cryptocurrencies becomes more stable by the day, entrepreneurs can no longer rely on the increasing value of this asset to fund their ideas. This creates a new need for crowdfunding in crypto community. Crypto crowdfunding platforms provide a novel way to invest in new projects without the barriers to entry as in the case of conventional funding methods.

Bitcoin 2.0 technology that serves as a protocol and a platform is based on the idea that the blockchain can be used for many other applications than just for the purpose of payment transactions. Therefore, Bitcoin 2.0 can be seen as a second-layer protocol or a derivative protocol. In the Bitcoin 2.0-based crowdfunding applications, people can leverage the Bitcoin protocol to raise funds for launching new cryptocurrencies.

The price of a particular coin however depends on the success of the project, and investors will be rewarded with additional coins from successful campaigns. The initial asset pool may also be distributed as shares to the users (initial investors) of the project as in the case of equity crowdfunding. In most cases, the users/investors will end up having both the new crypto coins and the crypto equity. A new wallet application will usually be created in the process even though the coins may be traded thinly in a created exchange or other friendly exchanges. Such innovative decentralized models of Cryptocurrency 2.0 technologies are expected to revolutionize many sectors in the near future. Adding layers of complexity to the existing Bitcoin protocol has paved the way to developments in corporate governance, financial, and information markets.

Numerous noncurrency applications are also being built on the blockchains. Some of the Bitcoin 2.0 technologies include Counterparty, Maidsafe (Safecoin and Mastercoin), Swarm, Ethereum, Namecoin, BitShares, and Colored Coins. The concept of BitShares, which uses distributed consensus technology to create more efficient payment network, is based on crypto equity where the units issued by Bitcoin or other cryptocurrencies resemble shares in start-ups. A digital public ledger allows for the creation of Distributed Autonomous Companies (DAC) that are global, efficient, and profitable and, most importantly, some may argue, provide "better-quality" services at a fraction of the cost incurred by their centralized counterparts.

Some of the donation-based bitcoin crowdfunding sites include nestorbooster, Ignition-Deck, and BitcoinChipin. CoinFunder and Bitcoinstarter are Bitcoin-only donation-based crowdfunding platforms. Cryptostocks is an active and much sought after equity-based crowdfunding platform, while the site BankToTheFuture that is yet to be launched promises a range of features. The site BTCJam, which provides P2P microlending services, is based on the transaction protocol of Bitcoin and a global credit scoring model.

We will highlight in the rest of this chapter some of the more recent, controversial, and high-profile examples either because the ideas are novel or innovative or that the crowdfunding exercise deserves a discussion.

27.4.3 Counterparty

Counterparty is a multipurpose platform riding on the Bitcoin blockchain by inserting additional data into normal bitcoin transactions. The blockchain is a digital ledger with additional space for information and Counterparty is simply a protocol to display additional notes or information in these spaces. Each action on counterparty requires a Bitcoin transaction, and each counterparty address is a Bitcoin address. It is a "Bitcoin 2.0" platform because it allows financial activities to happen. These are some of the features of Counterparty:
1. Creating new tokens or coins
2. Issuing a crypto security or crypto equity

3. Trading of BTC directly for any Counterparty-created asset

4. Creating financial derivatives such as contracts for difference or binary outcome

The native token is named XCP and the functionality is enabled by Counterwallet. The platform allows custom tokens to be created at the cost of 0.5 XCP each. This essentially allows for crypto securities or shares to be created and can tie in with issuance of dividends, creation of electronic tickets, access to content, etc.

Counterparty Distributed Exchange is an exchange using the Bitcoin protocol to announce buy and sell orders and attempt to match the orders within individual user-specified period. Once the buy and sell orders are matched, it will be executed automatically or with the consent of the seller as specified. The sellers are encouraged to offer a commission of 1% for announcing the offer and buyer. Once the order is made, the Counterparty protocol will debit the necessary funds from the client's wallet (address) and hold them in escrow. An address cannot make an order to sell a quantity of an asset it does not already have. The protocol sends the escrowed funds to the appropriate party. Counterparty has announced that it is now working with Overstock.com to create a virtual exchange.

27.4.4 Maidsafe, Safecoin, Mastercoin

Maidsafe's digital initial coin/cryptocurrency offering (ICO) is by far the most successful crowdfunding that has raised close to USD 6mil (between USD 5.5-7mil depending how one measures) worth of Mastercoins and Bitcoins in just 5 hours out of the intended amount of USD 8mil in April 2014. The amount raised was even more than other ventures that did an initial crowd sale via Kickstarter, even though there are a couple of other ventures that raised more than that amount in a longer time frame. However, majority of its ICO was raised in a cryptocurrency called Mastercoin, which is illiquid and its price crashed after the ICO raised some concerns.

The theme of the MaidsafeICO was to create a decentralized Internet platform with open-source programs. As data on this platform are heavily "shredded" into chunks and then encrypted, Maidsafe (Massive Array of Internet Disks) keeps track of the allocation of hard disk space and communicates between the computers. Those who rent out their hard disk storage space to the network, known as farmers, will get Safecoin in return. Safecoin is another cryptocurrency that can be used to store information on the network. Developers who make their applications available on the network, known as builders, are paid according to how often their applications are used. Those core developers who improve core SAFE network code by fixing bugs and adding new features can also earn Safecoin. While Safecoins give users and developers a stake in the Secure Access for Everyone (SAFE) network, MaidSafeCoin uses a proof of resource (hard drive storage, CPU power, and bandwidth) for miners to earn coins. It is intended that miners trade their computing resources for MaidSafeCoin. Managed by network's transaction manager, the records are unchained and different from blockchain in the sense that only the existing and previous owner records are kept. If the concept is workable, the SAFE network will be able to cannibalize Internet services currently available today and decentralized them. All the servers will have privacy, anonymity, and security given the "shred, encrypt, and store in chunks" on peer nodes or vaults. Out of the 4.3 billion Safecoins, 10% has been released. Maidsafe was a not a new idea but was the brain child of David Irvine for a few years before the fundraising.

27.4.5 Swarm

Swarm, by using Bitcoin's second-generation protocol Counterparty and crowdsourcing engagement, takes a widespread approach to crypto equity and crowdfunding of early projects and business ventures. Counterparty, as mentioned above, being a peer-to-peer distributed, open-source Internet protocol built on top of the Bitcoin network, serves as the world's first decentralized digital currency exchange that allows creating virtual assets, derivatives, bets, prediction markets, and issuing dividends. Assets can be created and issued on top of the Bitcoin blockchain and traded for its native currency (XCP) or Bitcoins. Crowd-incubator-like systems such as Swarm use technology built on Bitcoin to allow start-ups to raise money by launching their own cryptocurrencies. This platform's motive is to make the Kickstarter concept accessible, transparent, and rewarding in the crypto world by introducing cryptoshares to raise funds. As this distributed crowdfunding platform is powered by Bitcoin 2.0 technology, it is viewed as the future of next-generation crowd sales. Swarm also facilitates fundraiser participation and coin issuance with its the crowd intelligence features such as decentralized due diligence, programmable governance including profit shares and voting rights, Y Combinator style application, legal advocacy across jurisdictions for allowance of crypto equity, and distribution of perks to the Swarmcoin holders on the success of new cryptocurrencies. Unlike the current accelerator models, every holder of a Swarmcoin owns an equity share and receives a portion in the success of the company or project (DAC), which launches a coin throughout the network. Swarmcoin holders are also rewarded for trying out additional projects associated with each new coin. One of the main advantages with Swarm is that it has been designed to be compliant with the existing legal framework with respect to security offerings. The users need not have a legal entity, enabling them to fund all sorts of open-source software projects. The equity aspect is the same as in the conventional setting except the advantage of no burden of red tape. The Swarm community chooses the new business ventures that are eligible to be included in the network by due diligence and voting.

27.4.6 Ethereum

Ethereum is another Bitcoin 2.0 distributed application software platform, scheduled for launch in 2014 or 2015. In addition to supporting monetary transactions, this platform provides diverse functionality where one can securely code, decentralize, and trade anything. It supports crowdfunding through bitcoins, voting systems, domain name registries, financial exchanges, company governance, contracts and agreements, intellectual property, and smart property. Ethereum has its own tokens called ether, with which one can build and distribute decentralized applications or pay for its usage. Each ether is further divided into smaller units of currency in the order of finney, szabo, shannon, babbage, lovelace, and wei, where every larger unit on the left is equal to 1000 subsequent lower unit of currency (Buterin, 2014). A contract in Ethereum is a computer program that acts as the building blocks of the network. Its blockchain is similar to Bitcoin with one additional feature to store the recent state, which eliminates the need to store the entire history of blockchain for reference, thereby saving significant storage space. This platform is directed toward replacing certain aspects of the Web in a decentralized and pseudonymous manner by introducing four components to it including static content publication, dynamic messages, trustless transactions, and an integrated user interface. Many promising crypto crowdfunding platforms are currently being developed to effectively replace the centralized crowdfunding platforms. One of the upcoming projects is Lighthouse, a bitcoin-powered app that projects Bitcoin as an application platform. It leverages the Bitcoin protocol to build decentralized applications for crowdfunding campaigns without relying on any trusted third parties.

27.4.7 Storj

Storj network, a decentralized peer-to-peer file storage platform, closed their Initial Crowd Offering in mid-October 2014 and raised 910 BTC, just 9% of its goal of 9800 BTC. Similar to the centralized file storage competitors such as centralized provider Dropbox, it provides file storage space. The difference is that it is a distributed network, using the blockchain technology with encryption. By being part of the network and using the DriveShare apps, participants are able to earn free Strojcoin X, SJCX, by renting out whatever amount of their free disk space after the initial testing period. Data are uploaded using the Web application MetaDisk and store by those running the DriveShare program. Files are encrypted prior to uploading and access to the stored files is via a private key. Users of the storage will pay in SJCX, and those who rent out the disk space will get paid in SJCX by an equivalent amount of stored data. Storjcoin X stores information about who can access what data and where it is at any time. It is unknown whether the crowd sale was undersubscribed, but as in earlier ICOs, there are multitiers of offering. After the initial tier of offering is taken up, the next tier will be offered at a higher price. The strategy worked well for earlier ICOs, but public interest seems to have waned. It remains to see whether the new tranches will be oversubscribed.

27.4.8 Gems, BitShares Music Foundation

Gems is a social network currency. By owning the cryptocurrency and earning additional gems through introduction of new members, owners of the cryptocurrency can accumulate and trade on selected exchanges. The general idea of most of the ICOs is to reward the ones that contribute to the network and hopefully the exit comes from a sale of the coins on an exchange, from an eventual IPO, or via merger and acquisition. In the case of gems, 25,000 gems are air-dropped daily to the "Exodus, Address" (addresses that were given the coins), and the ecosystem automatically credits those accounts according to their contribution. The revenue model is payment by gems for unsolicited content or advertisement. The value of gem will increase as the network effect of the number of users and advertisements kick in. The air drop share is multiplied by the total gems owned to entice investors to accumulate gems.

For gems, 100 million coins will be issued with 45 million distributed to stakeholders and 45 million as daily airdrops for 5 years; the balance is reserved for bonus block rewards, promotion, marketing, bounties, network R&D, and operation costs.

BitShares Music Foundation is a nonprofit organization whose purpose is to form a decentralized peer-to-peer music network. The funds raised are for developing the front- and back-end projects that can give value to the BitShare Music blockchain or DAC. PeerTracks is a company that plugs into the BitShare Music blockchain. It allows for a user-friendly way for artists and fans to interact with each other by being a music track exchange that the buying and selling currency is DAC notes, with a maximum of 1.5 billion BitShares music notes. Artists will be able to create his or her own digital currency. The bitcoin raising period is from 6 October until 4 December 2014. It remains to be seen how this crowd sales will perform.

Ideas such as gems and PeerTracks can be extended for any other digital assets such as API using XAP and others. Basically, digital assets are easy to do crowd sale and likely to be sustainable given that monitoring is online.

27.4.9 Namecoin, BitShares, Colored Coin, and Ripple

Just like Bitcoin that cannot be shut down, Namecoin is the "basis" of a decentralized domain name system (DNS) that cannot be censored or shut down. The DNS is the Internet-wide address book that is linked with the numerical addresses or IP addresses. The top-level domain (TLD) such as the .com in an URL address is controlled by central authority ICANN in the United States, and it allows third-party companies or registrars to provide customer service and administer.

A decentralized DNS means that TLDs such as .bit can exist that are not owned by anyone, and the DNS lookup tables are shared on a peer-to-peer system. Namecoin and Bitcoin, while not interacting or interfering with each other, are similar in that it is based on the idea of a blockchain and reward for mining. Of course, with programming, there can be defined expiry dates for the domain names.

BitShares is a protocol for issuing DAC shares with millions of shareholders working together to secure the system. The business plan can be encoded in open-source software that operates automatically in a transparent manner. As we have seen above, it has the potential to disrupt music, insurance, derivatives, banking services (deposits, loans, and securitizations), and industry that deals with assets that can be digitized or collateralized. Business can then easily produce profits by providing services that they can charge transaction or usage fees. These profits can in turn be distributed to the holders of BitShares.

Colored Coins is based on the blockchain technology and focuses on using the technology to hold real assets. Since the blockchain is public, it allows color-specific addresses. These addresses hold colored bitcoins. One can track the assets simply by knowing the first Colored Coins and tracking them throughout the transaction history. There are legal issues such as the responsibility of trustee that have to be resolved.

Ripple Labs, Inc., previously known as OpenCoin, Inc., is a payment system. The 100 billion native currency XRP (no one knows why XRP) was created or premined at inception. Of the 100 billion, 20% were retained by the creators, seeders, venture capital companies, and other founders. The balance is given to Ripple Labs with intention of 55% distributed to users and strategic partners. For the Ripple native currency XRP-denominated transactions and its use in house ledger and for transactions in other assets, the Ripple ledger only records the amounts owed by one user to another. Ripple is only a debt recording, clearing, and settlement agent and has no real-world enforcement power. It is a digital version of the hawala system and has been known as "Facebook for money." The user will have to define who they trust as peer and set the limit of lending for different instruments. The users themselves are responsible for the counter party risk and they can act as market maker. A small transaction fee is charged for each transaction as an antispam measure and the fee paid in XRP is destroyed. The gateway to redemption and subscription is via the Ripple network.

27.5 CONCLUSION

This chapter has presented two major models of obtaining large-scale financing in the cryptocurrency field: first, with the traditional methods of listing and trading on a stock exchange and, second, with a distributed crowdfunding effort with growth in crypto crowdfunding.

These recent events are merely the beginning of many more to come, whether in terms of big firms getting listed or firms experimenting with technology-based approaches in seeking funding. Time is needed for firms to grow organically to a size and profit level sufficient enough for them to get listed on its own; the Digital CC case study is after all a reverse IPO. At the same time, the Winklevoss case study is still not a reality at the time of writing.

On the crowdfunding front, even with significant developments in the crypto crowdfunding sector, fiat currency crowdfunding sites may continue to attract quality projects, albeit smaller ones, and dominate the crowdfunding sector for the next few years until cryptocurrencies are widely used around the world. Though some of the bitcoin crowdfunding platforms are currently performing well with considerably good success rates in raising funds, crypto crowdfunding has a long but optimistic way to go.

More importantly, as corporate governance is a common concern among the public and regulators, given that there is no sure-fire method of supervising corporate behavior, perhaps, the sustainable companies of the future will be those that are dealing with easy-to-track digital assets. In such cases, these companies would be fairly transparent and no manual update or reporting is required as the blockchain itself will contain all the information required. It is likely in the future that there could be a "smart" contract to engage an external agent to handle some of the administrative duties of the company, not unlike the property management company today who is contracted by a real estate investment trust (REIT) manager to handle day-to-day activities of the REIT. The REIT manager itself can determine what assets to acquire or dispose through a voting system via the blockchain, effectively eliminating the role of the exchange as a middleman between the company and external stakeholders. However, if the REIT or property manager misbehaves, it remains to be seen how the problems can be resolved. So in practice, like how it is done presently, there still remains a requirement for some sort of a supervisory Digital Council to devise and enforce rules for the digital manager and property manager. There is therefore a role for a council in this financial space of cryptocurrency.

There are still other unresolved issues despite the success of some these Initial Crowd Offerings. Accountability is an issue especially if the use of funds and expenses are not transparent. It is also unclear how decentralized due diligence can be done. Some of crowdfunding in many countries today, like in the United States, is restricted by net worth or annual income requirements of investors, which limit the pool of potential investors. Besides the intrinsic kinks of crowdfunding and crypto crowdfunding that need to be worked out, regulatory support is just as important. In the meantime, companies have an increasing array of methods to raise funds, whether in the traditional or new crypto-related manner, and it remains to be seen how the future of fundraising will pan out.

ACKNOWLEDGMENT

The authors thank Ms. Cheryl Kwok for her useful points on traditional fundraising methods.

REFERENCES

Abrams, R., 2014. Winklevoss twins to list bitcoin fund on Nasdaq. The New York Times Dealbook, 4 May.
Buterin, V., 2014. A next generation smart contract and decentralized application platform. https://github.com/ethereum/wiki/wiki/%5BEnglish%5D-White-Paper.

Everett, C.R., 2014. Origins and Development of Credit-Based Crowdfunding. Graziadio School of Business and Management, Pepperdine University, California, CA.

Groshoff, D., 2014. Kickstarter my heart: extraordinary popular delusions and the madness of crowdfunding constraints and bitcoin bubbles. Wm. Mary Bus. L. Rev. 5, 489.

Macro Energy Ltd, 2014. Prospectus.

Math-Based Asset Services LLC, 2014. Winklevoss Bitcoin Trust: Amendment No. 4 to Form S-1 Registration Statement (1 July 2014).

Popper, N., Lattman, P., 2013. Winklevoss twins plan first fund for Bitcoins. The New York Times Dealbook, 1 July.

RELEVANT WEBSITES

http://bitcoinmagazine.com/14947/how-crypto-opened-software/.

http://bitcoinmagazine.com/15919/completely-decentralize-internet/.

https://bitcointalk.org/index.php?topic=664071.0.

http://www.buyxap.com/#whitepaper-economics-wallet.

http://en.wikipedia.org/wiki/MaidSafe.

http://www.followthecoin.com/swarm-dawn-cryptoequity/.

http://www.forbes.com/sites/kashmirhill/2014/06/03/mastercoin-maidsafe-crowdsale/.

https://github.com/DavidJohnstonCEO/TheValueofAppCoins.

http://maidsafe.net/safecoin.

http://www.mastercoin.org/.

http://swarmcorp.com/.

CHAPTER 28

Bitcoin Exchanges

Nirupama Devi Bhaskar, David LEE Kuo Chuen

Sim Kee Boon Institute for Financial Economics, Singapore Management University, Singapore

Contents

28.1 INTRODUCTION

Advancements in technology that allow businesses to innovate and develop are crucial to a country's economic success. Cryptocurrencies have the potential to improve payment efficiency by reducing transaction costs. The increase in the number of companies that adapt to the world of digital currencies may directly affect several sectors of the financial services industry. Bitcoin has received positive attention from venture capital community and many other early movers in the market. Bitcoin-related technologies are expected to disrupt the payment markets in the coming years, including the credit card companies, money transfer companies, payment hardware companies, securities exchange companies, payment processors, trust and escrow companies. With the increasing popularity of Bitcoin, cryptocurrency exchanges that are third-party intermediaries like mining pools have emerged to support Bitcoin-related services.

28.2 BITCOIN EXCHANGES

Bitcoin exchanges are marketplaces where people can exchange a cryptocurrency for real money or other cryptocurrencies and vice versa. These exchanges serve as the main

Handbook of Digital Currency

559

source of access to Bitcoin network, and so, they truly have a substantial amount of power and influence over Bitcoin markets. Bitcoin is inextricably linked to fiat currency that is the main commodity traded against bitcoins. The value of bitcoins is largely determined by the buying and selling that takes place on the exchanges. At a Bitcoin exchange, a client can buy, sell, or store bitcoins at the exchange rate and in the currency supported by that particular Bitcoin exchange. A client can communicate with the exchange over its Web site through a secure SSL connection. The exchange holds the identity and the bank information of the client. When a client wants to sell bitcoins through an exchange, he or she has to transfer those bitcoins to the wallet of the exchange. An exchange creates a wallet for every user in their system and one can trade bitcoins with this wallet. However, exchanges possess the private keys of the users' wallets, and it is highly important for the users to choose exchanges that are trustworthy of depositing large amounts. Bitcoin deposits and withdrawals are real transactions that are recorded in the blockchain, whereas selling (trades) bitcoins are recorded only in the trade history of the Bitcoin exchange. Transactions recorded in the blockchain are only identified as those sent from the exchange, and the concerned client cannot be specifically identified as the details of the clients' transactions are present in the exchange's database. There are hundreds of Bitcoin exchanges around the world that provide services like trading, digital currency exchange, information, gift cards, currency tracking, mining, and merchant services. The following are some of the exchanges that form the majority of the market share. The popularity of these exchanges depends on their services provided and the fees charged by them for the services. Their fee schedule may include a portion of the deposit or withdrawal funds and a commission for the trading services. While some of the exchanges follow different strategies for the fee schedule, few other exchanges charge no fee in order to attract more customers to invest or trade through their exchange (Table 28.1).

28.3 EXPOSURE TO RISK OF EXCHANGE FAILURE

28.3.1 Bitcoin exchange closure due to security breach

Exchanges are highly exposed to cybersecurity threats. Those that handle a sheer quantity of trade are successful, yet they face the highest number of cyber-attacks. Every exchange has to maintain the transaction volume above a certain level in order to survive in the competitive market, but once it reaches that level, hackers find it worthwhile to launch an attack on that particular exchange. In examining 40 Bitcoin exchanges, Moore and Chrisitin (2013) have found that transaction volume is positively correlated with experiencing a breach. At the same time, average transaction volume is negatively correlated with the probability it will close prematurely.

Table 28.1 Bitcoin exchanges

Exchange	Origin	Currency	Fees		
			Transaction	Deposit	Withdrawal
OKCoin	China	CNY	—	—	—
Huobi	China	CNY	—	—	0.0001 BTC
Anxbtc	Hong Kong	AUD, CAD, CHF, EUR, GBP, HKD, JPY, NZD, SGD, USD	—	2.5%	0.5%
Btcchina	China	CNY	—	—	0.0001 BTC
Bitstamp	UK	USD	0.2–0.5%	—	SEPA— 0.09 €Intl— 0.09%
Bitfinex		USD	0.2–0.3%	—	—
Btce	Unknown	EUR, RUR, USD, CNH, GBP	0.2% USD/ RUR— 0.5%	—	—
Localbitcoins	Finland	ARS, AUD, BRL, CAD, CHF, CZK, DKK, EUR, GBP, HKD, INR, MXN, NOK, NZD, PLN, RUB, SEK, SGD, THB, JPY, USD, ZAR, ILS	0.0001– 0.0004 BTC	—	—
Itbit	Singapore	EUR, SGD, USD	0.12–0.2%	—	—
Kraken		EUR, KRW, USD	0.05–0.3%	—	—
Bitcoinde	Germany	EUR	0.1%	—	
Bitcurex		EUR, PLN	0.4%	SEPA— 30 Euros Intl— 50 Euros	SEPA— 115 Euros Intl— 0.3% (5–50 Euros)

Continued

Table 28.1 Bitcoin exchanges—cont'd

Exchange	Origin	Currency	Fees		
			Transaction	Deposit	Withdrawal
Cavirtex	Canada	CAD	0.2–0.75%	—	—
Mercadobitcoin	Brazil	BRL	0.3–0.7%	—	—
Justcoin	Norway	EUR, NOK, USD	0–0.5%	—	—
Btcarkets	Australia	AUD	0.1–0.85%	—	—
Paymium (Bitcoinentral)	France	EUR, GBP	0.59%	—	—
Campbx	USA	USD	0.55%	—	—
Bit2c	Israel	ILS	0–0.6%	—	0.0001 BTC
Rmbtb	China	CNY	—	—	—
Icbit	SE	USD	0.005 BTC	—	—
Bitquick	USA	EUR, USD	0–2%	—	—
1Wbe	Cyprus	EUR, USD	0.2%	—	0.01%
HitBTC	Denmark	EUR, USD	0.1%	—	—
Bter	China	CNY, AUR, BC, BQC, BTB, BUK, CENT, CDC, CMC, CNC, COMM	0.2%	—	0–0.5%
The Rock Trading	Malta	EUR, USD	1%	—	0.001 BTC
Bitex	Holland	EUR, USD	0.2%	—	—
Cryptsy	USA	USD	0.25%	—	—
Indacoin	UK	USD	0.15%	—	0.0001 BTC
Vault of Satoshi	Canada	CAD, USD	0.3–1%	—	—
Cryptotrade	Hong Kong	EUR, USD	—	—	0.001 BTC

One of the biggest attacks was on Mt. Gox, the leading Bitcoin currency exchange that handled about 70% of all the bitcoin transactions around the world in 2013. There were a few security breach incidents, because of which the exchange had to face significant losses. In June 2011, a hacker used the credentials from the exchange auditor's computer illegally to transfer a large number of bitcoins to his account. The hacker manipulated the exchange's software to create a massive "ask" order and sold all the bitcoins. This temporarily increased the prices, after which it subsequently returned to the normal user-traded prices. As was reported, the incident affected the accounts in the exchange by a value of $8,750,000. Mt. Gox, in order to restore the confidence of the clients and to prove that it was in control of the situation, moved 424,242 bitcoins from the cold storage to one of its addresses (transactions of Block 132749; see https://blockchain.info/tx/ 3a1b9e330d32fef1ee42f8e86420d2be978bbe0dc5862f17da9027cf9e11f8c4 with a total block size of 550,000). A similar incident occurred in October 2011, where a total of 2609 BTC were transferred to an "invalid" address (transactions of Block 150951). This is equivalent to destroying the bitcoins, as no private key is assigned to that invalid address and hence would be extremely difficult to restore.

---

12 Jan 2009—block 170, transaction f4184fc5 spends 50.00000000
14 Jan 2009—block 496, transaction a3b0e9e7 spends 61.00000000
15 Jan 2009—block 586, transaction 4d6edbeb spends 250.00000000
19 Jan 2009—block 1055, transaction 8897ea9c spends 500.00000000
22 Jan 2009—block 1296, transaction 59bf8acb spends 500.00000000
24 Jan 2009—block 1586, transaction 3a5c037f spends 500.00000000
26 Jan 2009—block 1945, transaction 5559270f spends 1000.00000000
31 Jan 2009—block 2518, transaction 2ccc3f59 spends 1000.00000000
08 Feb 2009—block 3510, transaction 92f55c2c spends 1000.00000000
09 Feb 2009—block 3645, transaction cec658ac spends 2200.00000000
16 Mar 2009—block 7677, transaction e6f00fa6 spends 2400.00000000
20 Apr 2009—block 11666, transaction eebd343e spends 3500.00000000
20 Jul 2009—block 19863, transaction 123a3968 spends 6049.67000000
16 Oct 2009—block 25095, transaction 4aa98b18 spends 9700.00000000
22 Oct 2009—block 25618, transaction 1aae9d58 spends 11950.00000000
24 Oct 2009—block 25788, transaction 5d793270 spends 12250.00000000
27 Oct 2009—block 25969, transaction 3cd9410f spends 13000.00000000
04 Nov 2009—block 26402, transaction 6029e51c spends 15500.00000000
11 Nov 2009—block 26814, transaction 1043eb5c spends 15500.00000000
19 Nov 2009—block 27525, transaction f2e5fdd3 spends 21850.00000000
19 Nov 2009—block 27528, transaction 67fc73c7 spends 22500.00000000
06 Mar 2010—block 44006, transaction 23709241 spends 23247.39000000
12 Jul 2010—block 65566, transaction ba62e528 spends 35000.00000000
26 Jul 2010—block 70527, transaction b9d69463 spends 46754.31000000

28 Jul 2010—block 70870, transaction 73ac0fdc spends 50000.95000000
06 Nov 2010—block 90003, transaction 70dab592 spends 55000.00000000
08 Nov 2010—block 90505, transaction 1ec28eee spends 96999.00000000
27 Jan 2011—block 104770, transaction 8f821069 spends 400000.33000000
12 Jun 2011—block 130281, transaction a09ac44c spends 432110.10745232
23 Jun 2011—block 132749, transaction 3a1b9e33 spends 442000.00000000
16 Nov 2011—block 153509, transaction 29a3efd3 spends 550000.00000000

Source: http://bitcoin.stackexchange.com/questions/3287/what-is-the-largest-transaction-by-value-to-date-for-bitcoin-currency.

A few other such breaches led to delayed or refused withdrawals and suspension of trading in the subsequent years. Eventually, in February 2014, all bitcoin transactions were halted by the exchange due to the issue of transaction malleability and therefore to obtain a clear technical view of the currency processes. The withdrawals remained halted for more than a couple of weeks, raising the concerns of the customers about the security of the exchange. An alleged internal information disclosed that the exchange lost 744,408 bitcoins in a theft undetected for years. The exchange had lost approximately 750,000 of the clients' bitcoins and 100,000 of its own, which totals about 7% of all bitcoins worth $473 million at the time of filing. Mark Karpeles, the CEO of Mt. Gox, resigned followed by suspension of all trades and filing for bankruptcy protection in Tokyo as it had debts of over $63.6 million. Currently, the exchange faces lawsuits from its clients and has requested the Tokyo court for liquidation.

The fall of Mt. Gox was indeed digital currency's biggest crisis. In fact, 730,000 bitcoins were already found missing prior to Mt. Gox's collapse, owing to theft, cyber-crime, and other criminal pursuits. This number accounts for 6% of the total supply of bitcoins and doesn't include the unreported cases of individuals who lost bitcoins to the hackers. Bitfloor, the fourth largest Bitcoin exchange of 2013, also shut down its operations due to security breaches by the hackers. It lost more than 24,000 BTC in the attack. In addition to these exchanges, many others have closed owing to security attacks and poor management.

28.3.2 Lost/stolen BTCs

The ownership of a private key can be identified, but it is difficult to prove if the private key has been lost. So it is not possible to differentiate between lost and saved coins. A bitcoin is lost forever when it is sent to a bitcoin address with an unknown private key. A private key cannot be derived from the address as it is time-consuming for any amount of hashing power to guess from 2^{160} possible private keys. Bitcoins can also be destroyed intentionally by sending them to a nonexistent private key. Such a private key can be obtained using an invalid public key from which a valid bitcoin address can be generated. Every valid public key begins with the 0×04 byte. This fact can be utilized to create an invalid public key and the corresponding private key. For instance, a series of zeroes (64 bytes) would make an invalid public key. The combination of SHA-256 and RIPEMD-160 functions is used to generate a valid bitcoin address from an invalid public key. A list is given in https://bitcointalk.org/index.php?topic=576337.

As of June 2014, there are 12.4 million bitcoins in circulation, of which approximately 818,485.77 bitcoins have been stolen. This accounts for about 6.6% of the total bitcoin supply and its present worth is $502,018,166.11. In other words, one in every 16-17 bitcoins is stolen. The following is a list of the major bitcoin thefts over the years. While most of the events had a toll on the digital currency exchanges, the other victims include individuals, mining pools, online Web sites, or savings trusts. The approximate value (it is not an audited number but a guesstimate depending on the time of the theft and the prevailing price) USD equivalent of the stolen bitcoins is with respect to the exchange rate at that specific period (Table 28.2).

28.4 SURVIVAL TIME OF AN EXCHANGE

Hundreds of cryptocurrency exchanges are present worldwide, but approximately 45% of them shut down eventually. Some of the important factors on which their survival time depends include transaction volume, security breach, compliance capabilities, backroom and settlement support, and financial strength.

28.4.1 Transaction volume

The average daily transaction volume is an important factor in determining if the operations of an exchange are profitable, and profitability depends on achieving scale in the number of fee-generating transactions performed. Exchanges with larger volume prove to be attractive to the liquidity-seeking traders and gain popularity. Those with low transaction volume are more likely to shut down. This serves as the main reason for exchanges to inflate the volume data as there is no method to verify the trading volume figures. Although these figures can be manipulated, they are significant, and until there exist independent audits to verify these data, investments made by venture capitalists and other companies serve as a close approximation. Hence, bigger exchanges and longer lived exchanges are richer targets for the cyber-attacks.

28.4.2 Experiencing a security breach

Apart from the value of bitcoins, anonymity is the main reason for criminals to embrace digital currencies. They use digital currencies for money laundering purposes and

Table 28.2 Bitcoin thefts

Event	Circumstances	Period	Bitcoins stolen	USD equivalent
Stone Man Loss	Loss private key	9 August 2010	8999	$539.94
Ubitex Scam	Investors of Ubitex on GLBSE unregulated stock exchange	April–July 2011	1138.98	$11,668.7
Stefan Thomas Loss	Lost coins together with three copies of his wallet	June 2011	7000	$128,000
Allinvain Theft	User Allinvain: stolen	13 June 2011	25,000.01	$502,750.2
June 2011 Mt. Gox Incident	Mt. Gox: hacks and withdrawals	19 June 2011	2643.27	$46,970.91
Mass MyBitcoin Thefts	MyBitcoin: weak account passwords	20 June 2011	4019.43	$69,777.31
MyBitcoin Theft	MyBitcoin	July 2011	78,739.58	$1,110,544
Bitomat.pl Loss	Bitomat.pl: wallet was wiped and bitcoins lost	26 July 2011	17,000	$236,000
Mooncoin Theft	Mooncoin.in	11 September 2011	4000	$24,000
Bitcoin7 Hack	Bitcoin7	5 October 2011	11,0000	$50,000
Oct 2011 Mt. Gox Loss	Mt. Gox	28 October 2011	2609.36	$8115.12
Bitscalper Scam	Bitscalper users: an arbitrage engine gone wrong	January–April 2012	1000	$5000
Andrew Nollan Scam	Shades Minoco and BitArb: investors and creditors lost money	February 2012	2211.08	$10,978
Linode Hacks	Bitcoinica, Bitcoin faucet, Bitcoin.cz	01 March 2012	46,653.47	$230,468
Betcoin Theft	Betco.in	11 April 2012	3171.5	$15,509
Tony Silk Road Scam	Silk Road	20 April 2012	30,000	$150,000
May 2012 Bitcoinica Hack	Bitcoinica	12 May 2012	38,527	$91,306.46
Bitcoin Syndicate theft	Mt. Gox	04 July 2012	1852.61	$12,134.61
July 2012 Bitcoinica theft	Bitcoinica	13 July 2012	40,000	$305,200
BTC-E Hack	Btc-e.com: stolen key	31 July 2012	4500	$42,000
Kronos Hack	Kronos.io: hacked	August 2012	4000	$42,859

		2011–2012	700,467	$2,983,473
Bitcoin Savings Trust	—			
Bitfloor Theft	Bitfloor: hacked	04 September 2012	24,086.17	$248,088
Cdecker Theft	Cdecker	28 September 2012	92,22.21	$113,894
2012 50BTC Theft	50BTC mining pool: hack of billing software	13 October 2012	1173.52	$38,000
2012 Trojan	Blockchain, Mt. Gox	18 October–16 November 2012	3457	
Bit LC Theft	Bit LC and miners	13 February 2013	2000	$51,000
BTCGuild Incident	BTCGuild mining pool: related to software bug	10 March 2013	1254	$58,737
2013 Fork	OKPay and mining pools: bug in Bitcoin-Qt clients	11 March 2013	9,60.09	$45,009.02
Bitcoin Rain	Bitcoin Rain, Mercado Bitcoin	03 October 2011–28 March 2013	4000	$258,660
ZigGap	ZigGap	February–April 2013	1708.66	$203,296.37
Ozcoin Theft	Ozcoin mining pool: hacked	19 April 2013	922.99	$94,560.33
Vircurex Theft	Vircurex: hacked	5 October 2013	1454.01	$163,351
James Howells Loss	Hard drive lost	July 2013	7500	$627,659
Just-Dice Incident	Gambling Web site: accounting error	15 July 2013	1300	$121,000
Silk Road Seizure	Underground marketplace	02–25 October 2013	171,955.09	$34,043,668.72
GBL Scam	GBL investors: shut down	May–October 2013	22,000	$3,437,446
Inputs.io Hack (Disputed)	Web wallet service: hacked	26 October 2013	4100	$811,718
Bitcash.cz Hack	Bitcash.cz: hacked	11 November 2013	484.77	$247,422
BIPS Hack	Payment processor BIPS: hacked	11 November 2013	1295	$660,959
PicoStocks Hack	Stock exchange: hacked	29 November 2013	5896	$3,009,397
Sheep Marketplace Incident	Underground market: hacked	2 December 2013	5400	$4,070,923
Silk Road 2 Incident	Underground marketplace: funds stolen	13 February 2014	4400	$3,624,866
2014 Mt. Gox Collapse	Mt. Gox	Ongoing		
Flexcoin Theft	Flexcoin and users: security breach	2 March 2014	896	$738,240
CryptoRush Theft	CryptoRush and users: security breach	11 March 2014	950	$782,641
Total (at $400)			1,399,766	$59,515,695 ($559,906,200)

Source: https://bitcointalk.org/index.php?topic=576337#post_t2014_mtgox.

purchasing items from the black markets. They may have made off with more than $500 million worth of bitcoins since its launch in 2009. Such activities are on the rise as it is easier to trade among existing criminal entities using cryptocurrencies than real money. From the perspective of a Bitcoin exchange, facing a security breach can erase its profits, decrease the cash flow, and lose the confidence of existing and prospective customers. Breached exchanges subsequently close.

With the increase in the value of bitcoins in the recent past, the number of viruses designed to steal bitcoins from wallets also increased. Currently, there are nearly 150 malware for this purpose and more than 100 of them were programmed in the last 1 year. Initially, Internet criminals concentrated on large network of computers affected by malware called botnets to mine bitcoins. As the difficulty of mining increased, it turned out to be less profitable and they focused on stealing bitcoins from wallets and exchanges. Although the Bitcoin protocols are efficient, the vulnerability of the software used in wallets of individuals and exchanges makes them the targets of hackers. Not all standard antivirus software can detect Bitcoin malware because some of them are disguised as bitcoin price trackers. Of all the malware present, only 9% are designed to steal Litecoin in addition to bitcoins, and less than 1% targets the other cryptocurrencies. In order to keep the bitcoins safe from the attacks, one can either use paper to store bitcoins instead of computer or use split wallets. In such split wallets, the keys necessary to make a transaction are stored in a separate computer that is not connected to the Internet. To make a transaction, a user generates a transaction from a computer with Internet access, transfers it into the secure machine with the keys using a USB in order to sign the transaction with the private key, and then broadcasts the transaction to the network from the machine with Internet access. The methods to secure your bitcoin wallet are explained further in http://heavy.com/tech/2014/02/how-to-secure-your-bitcoin-wallet-prevent-malware-theft/ (Heavy, 2014).

28.4.3 Compliance capabilities

Many regulatory bodies are working together to frame consistent rules and regulations in order to curb the criminal activities and provide more security to the network (Nermin, 2014). The risk exposure and vulnerabilities to the operations of the banking sector from virtual currencies are described in the research work of Peters et al. (2014). Digital currency exchanges have to register with FinCEN (Financial Crimes Enforcement Network) as per the current antimoney laundering requirements for recordkeeping and reporting. Approximately 40 exchanges registered by the end of 2013. Bitcoin exchanges face pressure from the regulatory entities that try to restrain certain activities under the antimoney laundering/countering the financing of terrorism (FATF Report, 2014). This may also cause the exchanges operating in countries with greater emphasis on antimoney laundering efforts to shut down.

28.4.4 Backroom and settlement support

Exchanges will have to deal with financial intermediaries, and unless the backroom functions efficiently, the exchanges will face tremendous pressure on dealing with banks and others that are spending more and more time on compliance. If there are any issues on settlement and payments are delayed, the trust in the exchange will be eroded. There is generally an underestimation of the exchanges in dealing with financial transactions given that most of the founders are conversant in technology but have no prior experience in running a financial firm. The learning curve can be steep and some may not understand the concerns of banks and the ability to give comfort to the bank that they will not affect the banks' own reporting and compliance function. Banks are set up under the supervisory regime and operations are geared toward detailed reporting, especially when they are dealing with retail customers. Given that these exchanges are not regulated entities, every transfer of funds is subject to very stringent check and requires a lot more justifications for funds to move in and out from each account.

28.4.5 Financial strength

Unlike regulated exchanges, most exchanges are not subject to the usual capital adequacy requirements as stipulated by financial regulations. Most exchanges are undercapitalized, and when there is a breach of security, these exchanges are neither covered by insurance nor have enough financial strength to deal with mishaps. Those with financial strength will be able to have a full-time compliance officer, a risk manager, and an experienced backroom for settlement but those are far and few. This is one of the greatest hurdles and subjects executive officers of these exchanges to high risk of prosecution and commercial litigation.

28.5 DISCUSSION

What is interesting about bitcoins is that the exchanges are almost all unregulated, even though some are registered. But at the same time, the key difference between Bitcoin and traditional currencies handled by financial institutions is the open nature of Bitcoin: each transaction is publicly announced and captured in the blockchain. It is therefore more transparent than fiat currency transactions and other over-the-counter complex products such as derivatives. Even in the case of regulated stock exchanges, the central scripless depository does not give many clues to the trading patterns as detailed as those of Bitcoin.

Academics are already downloading the blockchain data and analyzing each individual transaction to model the behavior. It is known that basic network characteristics can be identified into two distinct phases in the lifetime of the system. According to Kondor et al. (2014),

(i) When the system was new, no businesses accepted bitcoins as a form of payment, therefore Bitcoin was more of an experiment than a real currency. This initial phase is characterized by large fluctuations in network characteristics, heterogeneous indegree- and homogeneous outdegree distribution. (ii) Later Bitcoin received wider public attention, the increasing number of users attracted services, and the system started to function as a real currency. This trading phase is characterized by stable network measures, disassortative degree correlations and power-law in- and outdegree distributions. We have measured the microscopic link formation statistics, finding that linear preferential attachment drives the growth of the network.

As in other published research his results are consistent with the finding that the ability to attract new connections and to gain wealth is fundamentally related. In others words, the more people use the system, the more valuable it will be. Some network models and processes are discussed in Newman (2003).

Some believe no regulation is needed for Bitcoin or its exchanges, but an underlying governance structure is already emerging for both. Kroll et al. (2013) observed that with version 0.7 Bitcoin, software bug nearly resulted in a Bitcoin fork with two new currencies, Bitcoin A and Bitcoin B. As a result, Bitcoin is no different to any open source software governance that the emerging leaders will make decision on behalf of the community. The mandate given to them, and therefore the power, is constrained by the possibility of a fork. The current issue for exchanges is that while it is possible to regulate, there is no incentive to do so as the number of traders involved is small. There is a strong argument against regulation given that it stifles innovation and the growth of business.

There will be a strong call to regulate if the network effect starts to accelerate. The proof of identity will gain momentum if more scandals surface and in the name of anti-money laundering and combating the financing of terrorism. The government will be able to apply pressure for the Bitcoin community to be regulated and part of community may want to be regulated because of the incentives of gaining access to the mainstream of finance. Those who don't wish to be regulated will be able to fork the rules and carry on under the rule set of its choice.

Another challenge facing the exchanges is the possibility of lower transaction volume as new coins are created at an exponential decreasing rate. The percentage of dormant coins for a 3-month cutoff seems to stabilize around 60% (Ober et al., 2013). Given that the maximum supply is 21 million coins by 2040, the dormant coins will be around 12.6 million. Unless the value of bitcoins continues to rise, the exchanges will have to be trading other cryptocurrencies as Bitcoin exchanges do not seem to be a scalable business on its own.

Ron and Shamir (2012) analyzed the statistical properties of all transactions from the genesis block (Block 0 on 3 January 2009) to the last block ending (Block 180,000 on 13 May 2012). The distribution of addresses per entity is as follows:

Larger or equal to	Smaller than	Number of entities
1	2	2,214,186
2	10	234,015
10	100	12,026
100	500	499
500	1000	35
1000	5000	41
5000	10,000	5
10,000	50,000	5
50,000	100,000	1
100,000		1

Their analysis suggests that there were 7,134,836 single-sender and single-receiver transactions, of which 11% involved a mining pool Deepbit and 7% involved Mt. Gox and 10% self-loops. Consistent with previous studies, they discovered that more than half of the minted coins remained dormant in addresses that had never participated in any outgoing transactions. Reid and Harrigan (2012) had also done similar analysis using earlier data.

Until software that mimic what academicians are doing to identify and uncover suspicious transactions, the financial institutions especially banks will be reluctant to deal with exchanges. Software will be developed over time and many network analysis techniques are already available. Discussions of operation risks of banks to cryptocurrency and virtual currencies are given in Peters et al. (2014). The paper gives the perspective of how banks view cryptocurrencies and one can infer their likely response to exchanges. Barber et al. (2013) had proposed fair exchange protocol to counter the malicious problems caused by "mixers," which mixes up the addresses like a tumble dryer. But such suggestion will only complicate compliance matters and thus harder for Bitcoin to be accepted to the mainstream financial institutions that have to comply with Basel III and other MAL/CTF requirements.

28.6 CONCLUSION

Bitcoin could potentially be recognized as the common medium of exchange in a few years. Once it is accepted as a money commodity in the society, its value would increase greatly as it could be traded for various goods priced in terms of bitcoins itself. On wide acceptance, the demand for Bitcoin exchanges will decrease as the need for trading fiat currency against bitcoin reduces. This demand would reduce much further when Bitcoin replaces the government's fiat monetary system. In such a case when Bitcoin exchanges lose their importance and influence, security breaches and exchange failures would be less devastating for the Bitcoin community as the number of investors and traders in exchanges would also reduce. However, it is likely that cryptoexchanges would still exist for trade among the different cryptocurrencies and an overall positive advancement in the cryptocurrency economy is probable.

REFERENCES

Barber, S., Boyen, X., Shi, E., Uzin, E., 2013. Bitter or Better—How to Make Bitcoin a Better Currency. Palo Alto Research center, University of California, Berkeley.

Financial Action Task Force (FATF) Report, June 2014. Virtual currency key definition and potential AML CFT risks. http://www.scribd.com/doc/231929964/Virtual-Currency-Key-Definitions-and-Potential-Aml-Cft-Risks.

Heavy, 2014. How to secure your bitcoin wallet and prevent malware theft. http://heavy.com/tech/2014/02/how-to-secure-your-bitcoin-wallet-prevent-malware-theft/.

Kondor, D., Pósfai, M., Csabai, I., Vattay, G., 2014. Do the rich get richer? An empirical analysis of the Bitcoin transaction network. PLoS One 9 (2), e86197.

Kroll, J.A., Davey, I.C., Felten, E.W., 2013. The Economics of Bitcoin Mining, or Bitcoin in the Presence of Adversaries. Princeton University, Princeton, New Jersey.

Moore, T., Christin, N., 2013. Beware the middleman: empirical analysis of bitcoin-exchange risk. Finan. Cryptogr. 7859, 25–33.

Nermin, H., 2014. Isle of man clarifies regulation for digital currency businesses. http://www.coindesk.com/isle-man-clarifies-regulation-digital-currency-businesses/.

Newman, M.E.J., 2003. The structure and function of complex networks. SIAM Rev. 45 (2), 167–256.

Ober, M., Katzenbeisser, S., Hamacher, K., 2013. Structure and anonymity of the Bitcoin transaction graph. Fut. Int. 5 (2), 237–250.

Peters, G.W., Chapelle, A., Panayi, E., 2014. Opening discussion on banking sector risk exposure and vulnerabilities from virtual currencies: an operation risk perspective. https://www.researchgate.net/publication/265385603.

Reid, F., Harrigan, M., 2012. An analysis of anonymity in the Bitcoin system. In: Altshuler, Y., Elovici, Y., Cremers, A.B., Aharony, N., Pentland, A. (Eds.), Security and Privacy in Social Networks. Springer Verlag, Berlin, Germany.

Ron, D., Shamir, A., 2012. Quantitative Analysis of Full Bitcoin Transaction Graph. The Weizmann Institute of Science, Israel.

ADDITIONAL READINGS

Anderson, R., Moore, T., 2006. The economics of information security. Science 314 (5799), 610–613.

Brito, J., Castillo, A., 2013. Bitcoin: A Primer for Policymakers. Mercatus Center, George Mason University, Virginia, VA.

Cremonini, M., Nizovtsev, D., 2006. Understanding and influencing attackers' decisions: implications for security investment strategies. In: Proceedings of the Fifth Annual Workshop on Economics and Information Security (WEIS), Cambridge, UK.

Dinesh, et al., 2014. Operational Distributed Regulation for Bitcoin. arXiv preprint arXiv:1406.5440.

Fultz, N., Grossklags, J., 2009. Blue versus red: towards a model of distributed security attacks. In: Proceedings of the 13th International Conference on Financial Cryptography and Data Security (FC), Accra Beach, Barbados, pp. 167–183.

Liu, P., Zang, W., Yu, M., 2005. Incentive-based modeling and inference of attacker intent, objectives, and strategies. ACM Trans. Inf. Syst. Secur. 8 (1), 78–118.

Manshaei, M., Zhu, Q., Alpcan, T., Bacsar, T., Hubaux, J.P., 2013. Game theory meets network security and privacy. ACM Comput. Surv. 45 (3), 1–25, 39.

Schechter, S., Smith, M., 2003. How much security is enough to stop a thief? In: Proceedings of the 7th International Conference on Financial Cryptography and Data Security (FC), Gosier, Guadeloupe, pp. 122–137.

Spyridopoulos, T., Karanikas, G., Tryfonas, T., Oikonomou, G., 2013. A game theoretic defence framework against DoS/DDoS cyber-attacks. Comput. Secur. 38, 39–50.

Varian, H., 2004. System reliability and free riding. In: Camp, L., Lewis, S. (Eds.), Economics of Information Security. Advances in Information Security, vol. 12. Kluwer Academic Publisher, Dordrecht, The Netherlands, pp. 1–15.

Vasek, M., Thornton, M., Moore, T., 2014. Empirical analysis of denial-of-service attacks in the Bitcoin ecosystem. In: 1st Workshop on Bitcoin Research. Lecture Notes in Computer Science, South Methodist University, Dallas, TX.

Wallace, B., 2011. The rise and fall of Bitcoin. Wired Magazine.

INDEX

Note: Page numbers followed by *b* indicate boxes, *f* indicate figures, *np* indicate footnotes and *t* indicate tables.